D1622974

Marketing Channels

A Relationship Management Approach

McGraw-Hill/Irwin Series in Marketing

Alreck & Settle
THE SURVEY RESEARCH HANDBOOK
SECOND EDITION

Anderson, Hair & Bush
PROFESSIONAL SALES MANAGEMENT
SECOND EDITION

Arens
CONTEMPORARY ADVERTISING
EIGHTH EDITION

Arnould, Price & Zinkhan
CONSUMERS
FIRST EDITION

Bearden, Ingram & LaForge
MARKETING: PRINCIPLES & PERSPECTIVES
THIRD EDITION

Belch & Belch
INTRODUCTION TO ADVERTISING & PROMOTION: AN INTEGRATED MARKETING COMMUNICATIONS APPROACH
FIFTH EDITION

Bernhardt & Kinnear
CASES IN MARKETING MANAGEMENT
SEVENTH EDITION

Berkowitz, Kerin, Hartley and Rudelius
MARKETING
SIXTH EDITION

Bowersox and Closs
LOGISTICAL MANAGEMENT
FIRST EDITION

Bowersox and Cooper
STRATEGIC MARKETING CHANNEL MANAGEMENT
FIRST EDITION

Boyd, Walker, Mullins & Larreche
MARKETING MANAGEMENT: A STRATEGIC DECISION MAKING APPROACH
FOURTH EDITION

Cateora & Graham
INTERNATIONAL MARKETING
ELEVENTH EDITION

Churchill, Ford, Walker, Johnston, & Tanner
SALES FORCE MANAGEMENT
SIXTH EDITION

Churchill & Peter
MARKETING
SECOND EDITION

Cole & Mishler
CONSUMER AND BUSINESS CREDIT MANAGEMENT
ELEVENTH EDITION

Cravens
STRATEGIC MARKETING
SEVENTH EDITION

Cravens, Lamb & Crittenden
STRATEGIC MARKETING MANAGEMENT CASES
SIXTH EDITION

Crawford & Di Benedetto
NEW PRODUCTS MANAGEMENT
SIXTH EDITION

Duncan
IMC: BUILDING RELATIONSHIPS THAT BUILD BRANDS
FIRST EDITION

Dwyer & Tanner
BUSINESS MARKETING
SECOND EDITION

Dolan
MARKETING MANAGEMENT: TEXT AND CASES
FIRST EDITION

Eisenmann
INTERNET BUSINESS MODELS: TEXT AND CASES
FIRST EDITION

Etzel, Walker & Stanton
MARKETING
TWELFTH EDITION

Futrell
ABC'S OF RELATIONSHIP SELLING
SIXTH EDITION

Futrell
FUNDAMENTALS OF SELLING
SEVENTH EDITION

Hair, Bush & Ortinau
MARKETING RESEARCH
FIRST EDITION

Hasty and Rearden
RETAIL MANAGEMENT
FIRST EDITION

Hawkins, Best & Coney
CONSUMER BEHAVIOR
EIGHTH EDITION

Hayes, Jenster & Aaby
BUSINESS TO BUSINESS MARKETING
FIRST EDITION

Johansson
GLOBAL MARKETING
SECOND EDITION

Lambert, Stock & Ellram
FUNDAMENTALS OF LOGISTIC MANAGEMENT
FIRST EDITION

Lehmann & Winer
ANALYSIS FOR MARKETING PLANNING
FOURTH EDITION

Lehmann & Winer
PRODUCT MANAGEMENT
SECOND EDITION

Levy & Weitz
RETAILING MANAGEMENT
FOURTH EDITION

Mason & Perreault
THE MARKETING GAME
SECOND EDITION

McDonald
DIRECT MARKETING: AN INTEGRATED APPROACH
FIRST EDITION

Meloan & Graham
INTERNATIONAL AND GLOBAL MARKETING CONCEPTS AND CASES
SECOND EDITION

Mohammed, Fisher, Jaworski, & Cahill
INTERNET MARKETING
FIRST EDITION

Monroe
PRICING
SECOND EDITION

Patton
SALES FORCE: A SALES MANAGEMENT SIMULATION GAME
FIRST EDITION

Pelton, Strutton, Lumpkin
MARKETING CHANNELS: A RELATIONSHIP MANAGEMENT BUILD BRANDS APPROACH
SECOND EDITION

Perreault & McCarthy
BASIC MARKETING: A GLOBAL MANAGERIAL APPROACH
THIRTEENTH EDITION

Perreault & McCarthy
ESSENTIALS OF MARKETING: A GLOBAL MANAGERIAL
EIGHTH EDITION

Peter & Donnelly
A PREFACE TO MARKETING MANAGEMENT
EIGHTH EDITION

Peter & Donnelly
MARKETING MANAGEMENT: KNOWLEDGE AND SKILLS
SIXTH EDITION

Peter & Olson
CONSUMER BEHAVIOR AND MARKETING STRATEGY
SIXTH EDITION

Rangan
BUSINESS MARKETING STRATEGY: CASES, CONCEPTS & APPLICATIONS
FIRST EDITION

Rangan, Shapiro & Moriaty
BUSINESS MARKETING STRATEGY: CONCEPTS AND APPLICATIONS
FIRST EDITION

Rayport, Jaworski & Breakaway Solutions
INTRODUCTION TO E-COMMERCE
FIRST EDITION

Rayport & Jaworski
E-COMMERCE
FIRST EDITION

Rayport & Jaworski
CASES IN E-COMMERCE
FIRST EDITION

Stanton & Spiro
MANAGEMENT OF A SALES FORCE
TENTH EDITION

Stock & Lambert
STRATEGIC LOGISTICS MANAGEMENT
FOURTH EDITION

Sudman & Blair
MARKETING RESEARCH: A PROBLEM SOLVING APPROACH
FIRST EDITION

Ulrich & Eppinger
PRODUCT DESIGN AND DEVELOPMENT
SECOND EDITION

Walker, Boyd and Larreche
MARKETING STRATEGY: PLANNING AND IMPLEMENTATION
THIRD EDITION

Weitz, Castleberry and Tanner
SELLING: BUILDING PARTNERSHIPS
FOURTH EDITION

Zeithaml & Bitner
SERVICES MARKETING
SECOND EDITION

MARKETING CHANNELS

A Relationship Management Approach

SECOND EDITION

Lou E. Pelton
University of North Texas

David Strutton
University of North Texas

James R. Lumpkin
Bradley University

Boston Burr Ridge, IL Dubuque, IA Madison, WI New York
San Francisco St. Louis Bangkok Bogotá Caracas Kuala Lumpur
Lisbon London Madrid Mexico City Milan Montreal New Delhi
Santiago Seoul Singapore Sydney Taipei Toronto

McGraw-Hill Higher Education
*A Division of The **McGraw-Hill** Companies*

MARKETING CHANNELS: A RELATIONSHIP MANAGEMENT APPROACH
Published by McGraw-Hill/Irwin, an imprint of The McGraw-Hill Companies, Inc. 1221 Avenue of the Americas, New York, NY, 10020.
Some ancillaries, including electronic and print components, may not be available to customers outside the United States.

This book is printed on acid-free paper.

domestic 1 2 3 4 5 6 7 8 9 0 DOC/DOC 0 9 8 7 6 5 4 3 2 1
international 1 2 3 4 5 6 7 8 9 0 DOC/DOC 0 9 8 7 6 5 4 3 2 1

ISBN 0-07-289512-8

Publisher: *John E. Biernat*
Executive editor: *Linda Schreiber*
Developmental editor: *Sarah Crago*
Marketing manager: *Kimberly Kanakes Szum*
Associate project manager: *Destiny Rynne*
Production supervisor: *Susanne Riedell*
Producer, media technology: *Todd Labak*
Coordinator of freelance design: *Mary E. Kazak*
Supplement producer: *Matthew Perry*
Photo research coordinator: *Judy Kausal*
Photo researcher: *Michael Hruby*
Cover design: *Mona Grigaliuna*
Cover Images: *©Eyewire, ©PhotoDisc*
Interior design: *Kay Fulton*
Typeface: *10/12 Times Roman*
Compositor: *Techbooks*
Printer: *R. R. Donnelley & Sons Company*

Library of Congress Cataloging-in-Publication Data

Pelton, Lou E.
Marketing channels : a relationship management approach/Lou E. Pelton, David Strutton, James R. Lumpkin.—2nd ed.
p. cm.—(The McGraw-Hill/Irwin series in marketing)
Includes bibliographical references and index.
ISBN 0-07-289512-8 (alk. paper)
1. Marketing channels. 2. Relationship marketing. I. Strutton, David. II. Lumpkin, James R. III. Title. IV. Series.
HF5415.129 .P45 2002
658.8′4—dc21

2001031257

INTERNATIONAL EDITION ISBN 0-07-112100-5

www.mhhe.com

DEDICATION

With love to my wife Evelyn.

Lou E. Pelton

With love to my wife Sandra Stokes Strutton.

David Strutton

With love to my wife Linda, and daughters Kristi and Kelli.

James Lumpkin

PREFACE

"We find our most soothing companionship in trees among which we have lived, some of which we may ourselves have planted. We lean against them and they never betray our trust . . ."

—Oliver Wendell Holmes

With much humility and appreciation, we concede that the serendipitous success of *Marketing Channels: A Relationship Management Approach* has little to do with the authors. While this text has become the most widely read primer in marketing channels worldwide, we recognize that our role in developing this text was likened to a *pruner* rather than a *planter*. At the end of the 20th century, just a stone's throw from Emory University's Center for Relationship Marketing, the seeds for this text were planted. The grandfather of contemporary marketing channels knowledge, Louis W. Stern, delivered a telling address to an assembly of marketing scholars. In his address, he pronounced a fundamental shift in marketing channels theory and practice: an approach that championed long-term, win-win *channel relationships*. This long-term orientation was not confined to business-to-business exchanges. In fact, the pioneer of relationship marketing and consumer behavior, Jagdish N. Sheth, elucidated the universal application of channel relationships in marketing exchange. So, this text is (and always will be) rooted in the seminal contributions of these knowledge seedsmen.

21st Century: Seeds of Change in Marketing Channels Practice

At the onset of the 21st century, this revised edition owes much to another knowledge seedsman: the French novelist Jean Giono. Having grown up in the poorest of tenements in the small town of Manosque, France, Giono became the financial supporter of his family, leaving school at the age of 16 to clerk at a bank. Three years later, Giono was inducted into the French army. He was later held captive by a communist band of Resistance fighters who interpreted his pacifism as collaboration with the Nazis. Giono survived the hardships of imprisonment just as he had endured the burden of poverty. Years later, the self-taught Giono escaped the fallacious Nazi stigma and became a celebrated novelist.

So, what does Giono have to do with our revised text? Though most of his writings were completed in the first half of the previous century, Jean Giono's writings presaged the environmentalist movement of the 21st century. You see, Giono penned the novella, "The Man Who Planted Trees," a story about a shepherd who planted oaks, beeches, and other trees in a dry wasteland. Through some miraculous intervention, water was conserved, dry streams filled, and seeds germinated. In this French parallel to America's Johnny Appleseed, Giono's shepherd developed a relationship with his environment to create prosperous vegetation:

> The old streams fed by the rains and snows that the forest conserves, are flowing again. Their waters have been channeled. On each farm, in groves of maples, fountain, pools overflow on to carpets of fresh mint . . . People from the plains, where land is costly, have settled here, bringing youth, motion, the spirit of adventure.

The landscape of Vergons may be an appropriate descriptor of the 21st-century marketing channels landscape. We hope this new edition instills a sense of newness and a spirit of adventure to both educators and students alike. In this revised edition of *Marketing Channels: A Relationship Management Approach*, we explore how organizations grow channel relationships that create sustainable market value and competitive advantage.

Adapting the Course to a Changing Environment

The door to sustainable competitive market value hinges on channel relationships. Market giants across industries—organizations such as AMR, EDS, General Electric, i2 Technologies, IBM, Microsoft, and Nestlé—forge collaborative channel relationships to improve their global positioning. In this revised edition, we focus on the latest examples of winners and losers in the global channels environment.

Just as the environment changes, so too must marketing channels practice. Today's marketing channels operate in the Network Economy, where the death of distance spawns even greater connectedness in marketing channels. Accordingly, we have enriched the text and pedagogical support package to confront the ever-changing channels terrain. Specifically, we afford special attention to the impact of information technology and globalization on marketing channels practice in the 21st century.

A Model-Driven Approach: The Ecology of Channel Relationships

Marketing channels educators lauded the model-driven innovation in the first edition. The Channels Relationship Model is back (and better than ever). We have improved the graphic representation, and we continue to provide the CRM as an easy-to-understand directional guide for students.

Based on users' feedback, the popular Channel Relationships Model (CRM) introduced in the first edition has been enhanced. There are three notable branches from the original CRM grounded in ecological theory. As an ecological framework, the CRM emphasizes the effect of environmental influences on channel member development. The three major environments entrenched in the CRM are channels exosystems, microsystems, and mesosystems. These three components of the CRM provide a map for guiding students through marketing channels principles and practices.

- Channel exosystems involve the externalities or outer environments in which channel members operate. Channel members are not directly involved in the exosystem, but these settings indirectly impact the channel members' goals, actions, and outcomes. This is Part II of the new edition.
- The channels microsystem consists of the internal channels environment. The internal channels environment encompasses the role perceptions and expectations between channel members. The channels microsystem includes the ensuing relationships that develop from those expectations. This is Part III of the new edition.
- The channels mesosystem involves the resource exchanges between channel members that result in formal organizational linkages. This is the last Part of this revised text.

Again, it is no coincidence that the CRM is the same acronym for Customer Relationship Management, a reigning normative framework in most organizations. In the very first Part of the text, we introduce the role of each component of the CRM and its relationship to managing customer expectations in channels of distribution. From the outset, we emphasize that marketing channels are information-driven and customer-steered.

Back to the Future: New Perspectives Gleaned from Surveys of Students, Researchers, and Educators

To assess how we might enhance the text and pedagogical support materials, we conducted both quantitative and qualitative surveys of educators, researchers, and students from around the globe. Lou Pelton embarked on speaking tours at major universities and businesses in 20 countries throughout Asia, Australia, Europe, North America, and South America. His experiences coupled with key informants' input resulted in several enhancements to this revised edition.

Enhancement One: Streamline the Presentation

You will note that we have reduced the number of chapters to accommodate the traditional semester system. It was clear that many educators were unable to cover every chapter, and many students were overwhelmed by the minutiae in the first edition. As a result, we cover even more material in fewer chapters. How did we accomplish this objective? We focused on providing more real-world marketing channels practices in lieu of long-winded explanations. We have provided greater depth through pedagogical support materials available on both CD-ROM and an interactive website. We also combined several chapters, such as the legal and ethical issues underlying marketing channels practice. We discovered that many educators were already doing this in their course designs.

Second Enhancement: Make Marketing Channels Sexy!

The second enhancement was to build some excitement into marketing channels. As an academic subject matter, marketing channels sometimes lacks some of the surface appeal of advertising or consumer behavior. How do you make marketing channels more exciting? We abandoned conventional minutiae and replaced them with thought-provoking imagery. The McGraw-Hill Irwin "Team" added an inviting layout and design, featuring many unique photographs and exhibits. Finally, we supplemented each chapter with Channel Surfings, which are short, timely vignettes that illustrate important themes in the chapter.

Third Enhancement: Connect Channels Theory and Practice

Our third enhancement is marrying existing marketing channels theory with cutting-edge channels practice. *Marketing Channels: A Relationship Management Approach* introduces students to the political economy model (Chapter 5), transaction cost economics (Chapter 11) and relational exchange theory (Chapter 13). While it would have been easier to avoid these difficult topics, our research indicated that professors would welcome extended coverage of channels theory. We used many practical examples and simplified terms to make these principles relevant and understandable to students.

Fourth Enhancement: Include New, Up-to-Date Cases and Vignettes

Educators and students agreed that the new edition could be improved by including new cases. In this edition, you will find cases written expressly for this text. We have also included more than 50 new company examples throughout the text. We feature companies that are having a major impact on marketing channels practice in the Network Economy. You and your students will encounter companies like eBay, Visteon, and McKesson HBOC. On our interactive website, you will find hyperlinks to many other channel members, ranging from e-retailers to supply-chain management companies.

Our informants also recommended short company vignettes at the start of each chapter. We have moved the critical-thinking metaphors to the website and added a company minicase to each chapter. But we didn't eliminate the critical-thinking exercises at the end of each chapter. Educators told us that these were great platforms for class discussions. We have kept your favorites and supplemented the chapters with several new Channel Challenges. We have also provided many new Channel Surfing real world critical-thinking exercises with our signature Points to Ponder.

You will notice that the timely readings for each part no longer appear in the text. Why? Because we want to have the option of offering more timely readings that can be just-in-time. You will still be able to access all of the previous readings on the interactive website. In addition, we have added new readings on a variety of marketing channels subjects to supplement the text materials. We want to acknowledge the top marketing scholars who contributed readings to the website:

G. Ian Burke
Latrobe University

Brenda Ponsford
Thiel College

Jhinuk Chowdhury
University of North Texas

Wilkie English
Mary Hardin University

O. C. Ferrell
Colorado State University

Faye W. Gilbert
University of Mississippi

Christian Grönroos
Swedish School of Business and Economics

Dawn Iacobucci
University of Arizona

Denise G. Jarrett
Charles Sturt University

John T. Mentzer
The University of Tennessee

Madhav Pappu
University of North Texas

John F. "Jeff" Tanner
Baylor University

Alma Mintu Wimsatt
Texas A&M University—Commerce

Joyce A. Young
Indiana State University

Current marketing channels students demanded that we make the material relevant. We do. Our book offers dozens of real world examples of each channel principle. Moreover, this is the first channels text to feature two marketplace phenomena that epitomize the critical role of channel relationships in strategic decision making. We think that the unprecedented growth of franchising in the United States and abroad warrants attention throughout the text. That is why we provide coverage (Chapter 12) on franchising as an emerging global vertical marketing system. The book also features an entire chapter on strategic partnering agreements (Chapter 14).

In addition to the readings, we have compiled a comprehensive **Instructor's Manual** on a CD-Rom that includes chapter outlines, test questions, answers to review questions, discussion of critical-thinking questions, and sample marketing channels projects. Course preparation has been made especially easy: A full-color, customized Microsoft **PowerPoint** slide presentation is offered that provides a chapter-by-chapter, ready-to-use teaching tool. Professionally produced **videos** also offer insightful case scenarios that reinforce key marketing channels principles.

We sincerely thank the students and educators—too numerous to individually mention—who offered directional insights to improve the text. Their insights and suggestions provided a general direction for our efforts. We also thank Gilbert A. Churchill, Jr., the first reviewer of our efforts, for his encouragement and advice on how to develop this project. As a result of their efforts, this is truly a market-driven channels text.

A host of reviewers made sure that our text preparation adhered precisely to the letter and spirit of the prescriptive insights. We extend our sincere gratitude to them. Without these reviewers, this project could not have been successfully completed.

As Oliver Wendell Holmes advised, we leaned on some very mighty trees in the conception, development, and marketing of this project. Each member of the McGraw-Hill Irwin team is a soothing companion who never betrayed our trust.

Our first edition was stewarded by Stephen Patterson, the savvy savant who ditched the Four "Ps" in search of net present value. He will always be the "editorial grandfather" of this text—which speaks more to his caring guidance and enthusiastic support than to his chronological age. Thankfully, our revision had an equally masterful team of McGraw-Hill Irwin professionals. Margaret Carty once wrote, "The nice thing about teamwork is that you always have others on your side." And, we were blessed with a great editorial and production team on our side. We appreciate the contributions of past executive editor Rick Adams and editorial assistant Mary Shannon.

Most of all, we appreciate the team that brought this project to fruition. Executive editor Linda Schreiber provided thoughtful leadership and editorial wisdom, harnessing our ideas, ideals, and intensity to yield an ever better harvest. The following members of the McGraw-Hill team epitomized the cooperation and coordination that produce long-lasting channel relationships and superior bottom-line performance. Linda was the nucleus of a dedicated team that prepared this final text in record time. Destiny Rynne played the important team role as the affable and meticulous associate project manager. We are very grateful to the other team members who contributed to our project: Sarah Crago, editorial assistant; Michael Hruby, photo researcher; Kurt Strand, marketing manager; Mary Kazak, designer; Michelle Lulos Livingston, copy editor; and Rob Zwettler, publisher.

Like channel relationships, *Marketing Channels: A Relationship Management Approach* is an ongoing process. So we look forward to hearing your suggestions for improvements and your experiences using our book in the classroom.

We agree with Professor Drucker: Marketing channels *will* be the route to sustainable market value. We sincerely hope that *Marketing Channels: A Relationship Management Approach* is a worthy vehicle for providing market value to your students.

Lou E. Pelton
David Strutton
James R. Lumpkin

About the Authors

Lou E. Pelton is an award-winning professor and researcher in the Department of Marketing and Logistics at the University of North Texas. Dr. Pelton's principal research interests include marketing channels, relationship marketing, and international distribution. He is editor of the *Journal of Marketing Channels,* the only journal solely dedicated to marketing channels theory and practice. He has published more than 80 research articles in prominent journals and international conference proceedings. Lou E. Pelton has conducted executive education and professional development seminars in Australia, Asia, Europe, South America, and the United States for governments, universities, and major corporations.

David Strutton is the chairman of the Department of Marketing and Logistics at the University of North Texas. He was previously Associate Dean and MBA Director at the University of Louisiana at Lafayette, where he also served as the Acadiana Bottling Distinguished Professor of Marketing and J. W. Steen Regents Professor of Business Administration. Strutton's academic research has been extensively published in leading marketing and business journals. His latest book, *Lessons Learned: What Cancer and Bone Marrow Transplantation Taught Me (and What You Need to Learn to Win Your War against Cancer)* is available at Amazon.com and other leading book distributors. During the last three years, Strutton has worked in varying capacities with the Leukemia Society of America, Leukemia Society of Louisiana, and National Bone Marrow Donor Program and frequently speaks to cancer support groups. He is married to the former Sandra Stokes, father to Ariadne Strutton, and stepfather to Catherine, Caroline, and Christina Sciarrillo.

Dr. James R. Lumpkin is the Dean of the College of Business Administration, Oklahoma State University. Dr. Lumpkin is a past president of the Academy of Marketing Science and was named "Distinguished Fellow" of the Academy in 1992. He is a past marketing editor of the *Journal of Business Research*. Dr. Lumpkin's primary research interests include retail patronage theory, health care marketing, and research methodology. His recent research has focused on the elderly consumer. He has received a number of research grants to study the marketplace behavior and long-term health care decisions of the elderly consumer. Before entering academe, Dr. Lumpkin worked as a chemist and in marketing research for Phillips Petroleum Company. In addition to his corporate experience, he has directed two consumer research panels.

Brief Table of Contents

PART I:

Marketing Channels Framework

Chapter 1: Marketing Channels: Information-Driven, Customer-Steered 2

Chapter 2: Channel Roles in a Virtual Marketplace 32

Chapter 3: Attaining Competitive Advantage through Channel Design 58

Chapter 4: Marketing Mix and Relationship Marketing 88

PART II:

Channel Exosystems

Chapter 5: Managing Uncertainty in the Channel Environment 156

Chapter 6: Channel Relationships in the Global Village 180

Chapter 7: Legal and Ethical Imperatives in Channel Relationships 208

PART III:

Channel Microsystems

Chapter 8: Conflict Resolution Strategies 262

Chapter 9: Information Systems and Relational Logistics 282

Chapter 10: Developing Positive Channel Relationships 312

PART IV:

Channel Mesosystem

Chapter 11: Transaction Costs and Vertical Marketing Systems 356

Chapter 12: Franchising in the Global Economy 384

Chapter 13: Developing Long-Term Value 414

Chapter 14: Strategic Partnering Agreements 438

Contents

PART I:

Marketing Channels Framework

Chapter 1: Marketing Channels: Information-Driven, Customer-Steered 2

What Is a Marketing Channel? 4
Evolution of Marketing Channels 6
The Production Era and Distributive Practices 6
The Institutional Period and Selling Orientation 7
The Marketing Concept 7
Relationship Marketing Era 8
The Elements of Successful Marketing Channels 10
Pooled Resources 10
Collective Goals 11
Connected System 13
Flexibility 14
Channel Intermediaries: Customer Value Mediators 14
Contactual Efficiency 15
Routinization 17
Sorting 17
Minimizing Uncertainty 18
Channels Relationship Model (CRM) 20
An Ecological Framework 20
Applying the CRM to Channels Strategy 23
Creating Customer Value 24
Products and Services Flows 25
The CRM: Compass Points 26
Key Terms 27
Chapter Summary 28
Channel Challenges 29
Review Questions 29
Endnotes 30

Chapter 2: Channel Roles in a Virtual Marketplace 32

Channel Behaviors in Competitive Environments 35
Competing in a Virtual Marketplace 35
Changing Environments: A Shared Concern 36
Diversity in Complex Environments 38
Disintermediation: Transforming Channel Roles 39
Channel Roles in the Exchange System 40
Channel Roles and Expectations 41

Supplier Relationships 42
Customer Relationships 48
Lateral Relationships 51
Establishing Channel Role Identities 52
Services 52
Innovation 53
Flexibility 53
Timing 54
Key Terms 55
Chapter Summary 55
Channel Challenges 56
Review Questions 56
Endnotes 57

Chapter 3: Attaining Competitive Advantage through Channel Design 58

The Nature of Competitive Advantage 60
Marketing Channels as Organizational Teams 61
Marketing Channels: Issues and Answers 62
What Is Channel Design? 62
Why Are Channel Design Decisions Critical? 62
How Do Marketing Functions Factor into the Channel Design Decision? 64
When Is It Time to Design (or Redesign) a Channel? 65
Channel Design Decisions 67
Channel Design Options 68
Evaluating Channel Design Alternatives 71
Selecting the Best Channel Design 74
Analyzing Desired Channel Output Utilities 75
Analyzing Channel Objectives and Product Characteristics 76
Analyzing Market Behaviors and Segments 77
Evaluating Channel Structure Performance 78
Modifying Existing Channels 78
Product Life Cycle Changes 79
Customer-Driven Refinement of Existing Channels 79
Growth of Multichannel Marketing Systems 80
Designing Channels to Capture Channel Positions 81
Key Terms 83
Chapter Summary 83
Channel Challenges 84
Review Questions 85
Endnotes 85

Chapter 4: Marketing Mix and Relationship Marketing 88

The Marketing Mix 90
The *Product* Ingredient 90
Fusion of Attributes 93
Product-in-Process? 94
Value Satisfaction 94
The *Pricing* Ingredient 96
Algorithmic Pricing Methods 97
Market-Oriented Pricing Methods 99
Relationship-Oriented Pricing Methods 101
The *Promotions* Ingredient 103
Promotional Mix 103
Traditional versus Relational Communication 103
Promotional Objectives 106
Pull versus Push Strategies 107
The *Place* Ingredient 110
Strategy Formulation: Role of the Marketing Concept 111
Key Terms 112
Chapter Summary 112
Channel Challenges 113
Review Questions 114
Endnotes 114

Part I: Cases 116

Case 1.1 Compaq Computer Corporation: The Dell Challenge 116
Adrian Ryans
Mark Vandenbosch
Case 1.2 Sunshine Juice Company 132
Professor Elizabeth M.A. Grosby
Christine A. Veber
Case 1.3 Eggsercizer: "The World's Smallest Exercise Machine" 135
Henry S. Maddux, Stamford University
Marlene M. Reed, Stamford University
Case 1.4 Opus One: A Marriage of Wine-Making Magnates 145

PART II:

CHANNEL EXOSYSTEMS

Chapter 5: Managing Uncertainty in the Channel Environment 156

Channel Entropy and the Exosystem 159
Working Systems 160
Market Intelligence 160
Different Effects 164
Channel Dynamism 164
Decision Support Systems 165
The Channels Exosystem 167
Competitive Environment 168
Economic Environment 169
Technological Environment 171
Sociocultural Environment 172
Legal, Ethical, and Regulatory Environment 174
Internal and External Political Economies: An Environmental Framework 175
Key Terms 176
Chapter Summary 176
Channel Challenges 177
Review Questions 178
Endnotes 178

Chapter 6: Channel Relationships in the Global Village 180

Reasons for International Exchange Relationships 182
Facilitating Market Entry 183
Boosting Market Share 184
Introducing New Products through Existing Channels 184
Improving Service Performance 185
Responding and Adapting to Shifting Market Conditions 185
Typology of International Exchange Relationships 185
Multinational Exchange Relationships 188
Global Exchange Relationships 188
Transnational Exchange Relationships 189
Direct and Indirect International Marketing Channels 190
Interface between International Marketing Channels and the Environment 193
Economic Factors 193
Political/Legal Factors 195
Sociocultural Factors 196
Technological Factors 197
Selecting International Exchange Partners 199
Costs 200
Coordination 200
Coverage 201

Control 201
Cooperation 201
International Exchange Relationships: Successes and Failures 202
Wal-Mart: The All-American Retailer? 202
At Sea in an Ocean of Beer 203
GloboCop 203
International versus Domestic Channel Relationships: Some Perspective 204
Key Terms 204
Chapter Summary 204
Channel Challenges 206
Review Questions 206
Endnotes 207

Chapter 7: Legal and Ethical Imperatives in Channel Relationships 208

A Historical Overview of Federal Legislation Affecting Channel Practices 211
Early Legislation 211
Later Legislation 212
The Per Se Rule versus the Rule of Reason 213
Traditional Legal Issues in Channel Relationships 213
Price Discrimination 215
Resale Price Maintenance 217
Vertical Integration and Mergers 217
Dual Distribution 218
Tying Arrangements 219
Refusals to Deal and Resale Restrictions 220
Emerging Legal Issues in Channel Relationships 221
Slotting Allowances 222
Parallel Import Channels 224
International Business Law 227
Moving beyond Legality: Toward Ethical Channels Management 228
Social Tact and Relationship Ethics 228
The Ethics Continuum 229
Caveat Emptor 230
Caveat Venditor 232
Moral Codes in Channel Relationships 232
Rules-Based Moral Codes 233
Consequence-Based Moral Codes 234
Experience-Based Moral Codes 234
Moral Codes in Combination 235
The Components of an Ethical Exchange Process 235
Equality 235
The Promise Principle 236
Morality of Duty 237
Morality of Aspiration 237
Key Terms 237
Chapter Summary 238
Channel Challenges 238
Review Questions 239
Endnotes 239

Part II: Cases 242

Case 2.1 Wal-Mart Stumbles with Hong Kong Shoppers 242
Neil C. Herndon, Hofstra University
Case 2.2 Partnering for Success: Federal Express and Netscape Join Forces for Information Technology 247
Thomas J. Dixon II
Karen Flanigan
Vanessa Izaguirre
Eddie Jackson
Elizabeth Walden

Case 2.3 Necessity to Luxury: Cool Moves–The Cooling of Two Countries 253
Jenell Galpin
Randy Lippies
Julie Runde
Jennifer Lawhon

PART III: Channel Microsystems

Chapter 8: Conflict Resolution Strategies 262

- Negotiation: The Art of Give and Take 265
  - Evaluating Desired Relationship Outcome 266
  - Choosing a Negotiation Strategy 267
  - Creating versus Claiming Value 270
- Problem-Solving Strategies 273
- Persuasive Mechanisms 275
- Legalistic Strategies 278
- Interdependence Tying It All Together 279
- Key Terms 279
- Chapter Summary 279
- Channel Challenges 280
- Review Questions 281
- Endnotes 281

Chapter 9: Information Systems and Relational Logistics 282

- Logistics 286
  - The Importance of Logistics 287
  - Measuring Logistics Performance 289
- Logistics and Channels Management 290
  - Attaining Market Coverage 290
  - Delivering Customer Service 290
  - Ensuring the Right Product Characteristics 291
  - Achieving Cost Containment 292
- Relational Logistics Model 292
  - Supply Chain Management 294
  - Supply Chain Management and Fluid Performance 295
- Logistics Inputs 295
- Logistics Mediators 296
  - Inventory Management 296
  - Transportation 300
  - Warehousing 302
  - Purchasing 303
  - Packaging 304
- Logistics Outputs 305
- Key Terms 306
- Chapter Summary 306
- Channel Challenges 307
- Review Questions 308
- Endnotes 308

Chapter 10: Developing Positive Channel Relationships 312

- Recruiting and Screening New Prospects 316
  - Recruiting 316
  - Screening 317
- Selecting the Right Channel Partners 319
- Motivating New Channel Members 321
- Securing Recruits for the Long Term 322
  - Recognizing the Channel Relationship Life Cycle 323
  - Improving Service to Channel Partners 324
- Key Terms 328
- Chapter Summary 328
- Channel Challenges 328

Review Questions 329
Endnotes 329

Part III: Cases

Case 3.1 SAP/Microsoft: Dancing with the Bear 331
Case 3.2 AmeriServe 336
Case 3.3 Indiana Wine Grape Council 341
Joyce A. Young, Indiana State University
Faye S. McIntyre, Rockhurst College
Case 3.4 Factory Direct Selling by Cironi's Sewing Center 345
J. B. Wilkinson, Youngstown State University
Gary B. Frank, University of Akron

PART IV:

Channel Mesosystem

Chapter 11: Transaction Costs and Vertical Marketing Systems 356

Transaction Cost Analysis 359
Internal versus External Transactions 361
Information: The Core of Transaction Costs 362
Transaction Cost Analysis: Problems and Limitations 364
Bounded Rationality 365
Opportunism 366
Uncertainty 366
Number of Firms 367
Data Impact 368
Specificity of Assets 368
Economic Exchange Relationships 369
Building Channels 370
Vertical Marketing Systems 371
When Should Organizations Vertically Integrate? 373
Benefits of Vertical Integration 374
Costs of Vertical Integration 375
Improving Relationships through Traditional Vertical Channel Design 376
Key Terms 377
Chapter Summary 378
Channel Challenges 380
Review Questions 380
Endnotes 381

Chapter 12: Franchising in the Global Economy 384

Franchising Systems 387
Benefits of Franchising 388
Types of Franchising 389
Concerns of Franchisees 391
Concerns of Franchisors 391
Relevant Trends in the Franchising Environment 392
Social, Cultural, and Demographic Trends 392
Economic Trends 393
International Trends 394
Industry Trends 395
Technological Trends 395
Internal Environmental Factors 397
Conflicts in Franchising 397
Up-front Fees 398
Tying Agreements 398
Capricious Termination 399
Encroachment 399
Lack of Cooperation 399
Current Legal Standards in Franchising 400
Disclosure 400
Mandatory Purchases from the Franchisor 401

Termination and Renewal 401
Advertising and Promotions 401
Expansion (Encroachment) 402
Making Franchise Relationships Work 403
CARE 404
Intelligent Contracts 404
Strategic Franchising Partnerships 405
What's in Franchising's Future? 408
Diversity 408
Flexibility 408
Conversion Franchising 408
Multiple Unit Franchising 409
Key Terms 410
Chapter Summary 410
Channel Challenges 411
Review Questions 412
Endnotes 412

Chapter 13: Developing Long-Term Value 414

Exchange Relationships: Bridging Transactions 416
Calculative Exchange Relationships 416
Ideational Exchange Relationships 417
Genuine Relationships 418
Exchange Episodes 418
Products and Services 419
Information Exchange 419
Financial Exchange 420
Social Exchange 421
The Discrete/Relational Exchange Continuum 423
Stages of Channel Relationships 427
Awareness 427
Exploration 428
Expansion 428
Commitment 429
Exchange Governance Norms 430
Reciprocity 430
Relational Communication 431
Other Exchange Governance Norms 432
Relationship Selling 434
Key Terms 434
Chapter Summary 435
Channel Challenges 435
Review Questions 436
Endnotes 436

Chapter 14: Strategic Partnering Agreements 438

Strategic Alliances: Definition and Characteristics 440
Coalignment 442
Exchanging Technologies, Products, Skills, and Knowledge 442
Competitive Edge 443
The Nature and Scope of Strategic Alliances 445
Impact of Strategic Alliances 445
Rationale for Strategic Alliance Formation 447
Types of Strategic Alliances 449
Licensing Arrangements 450
Joint Ventures 451
Consortia 452
Developing Strategic Alliances 454
Achieving Strategic Harmony 454
Selecting Alliance Partners 456
Developing Action Plans 458
Assessing Alliance Performance 459
The Downside of Strategic Alliances 459
Key Terms 461
Chapter Summary 461
Channel Challenges 462

Review Questions 463
Endnotes 463

Part IV: Cases

Case 4.1 The Country's Best Yogurt 466
Lisa Hill, Ouachita Baptist University
Carl Stark, Henderson State University
Anita Williams, Henderson State University
S. Darren Hollingsworth, Southwest Arkansas Planning and Development District, Inc.

Case 4.2 Tom, Dick, and Harry Consider a Pretzel Franchise 469
Wilke D. English, University of Mary Hardin—Baylor

Case 4.3 MEMC: The Silicon Wafer Industry 480

Case 4.4 Divorce on the Alliance Highway 485

Case 4.5 EQUILON: A Texaco/Shell Strategic Partnership 490

part

I

Marketing Channels Framework

chapter 1	Marketing Channels: Information-Driven, Customer-Steered 2
chapter 2	Channel Roles in a Virtual Marketplace 32
chapter 3	Attaining Competitive Advantage through Channel Design 58
chapter 4	Marketing Mix and Relationship Marketing 88

chapter

1

Marketing Channels: Information-Driven, Customer-Steered

Learning Objectives

After reading this chapter, you should be able to:

- Identify emerging characteristics of marketing channels in the Net Economy.
- Discuss how pooled resources, collective goals, connected systems, and flexibility relate to successful marketing channels.
- Defend the association between a marketing organization's mission statement and the market(s) that it serves.
- Define a marketing channel, and explain how marketing channels create exchange utility.
- Understand the compelling role of spatial utility in the evolution of marketing channels from a production to a relationship orientation.
- Define channel intermediaries, and explain how they create customer value.
- Describe how the definition of marketing channels relates to the Channels Relationship Model (CRM).

Used by permission of PEZ Candy, Inc. TM & © PEZ 2002

Historian and Pulitzer prize–winning author Daniel J. Boorstin has asserted, "The greatest words ever written on the maps of human knowledge are *terra incognita*—unknown territory." Terra incognita may be an appropriate descriptor for our journey through contemporary marketing channels principles and practices. After all, 21st-century marketing channels represent a marked departure from traditional market settings where physical proximity was the defining characteristic of economic exchange. Electronic technologies, globalization, and new market structures have redefined the nature and scope of economic exchanges between buyers and sellers. Today's marketing channels are cast against a backdrop where millions of buyers and sellers can be connected regardless of their geographical locations.

Indeed, marketing channels have traditionally resided in the "place" setting among the other marketing mix variables: product, price, and promotion. However, the notion of place is ever changing, the Industrial Economy has long been displaced by a Network Economy, and the dusk of distance has given way to a new era: the dawn of information-driven, customer-steered exchange relationships. In this chapter, we explore the emergent role of marketing channels in the Net Economy.

Let's begin our journey in the historic city of Vienna, Austria. Why Vienna? Well, Vienna has been the crown jewel for a multitude of explorers; it has been conquered by the Celts, the Romans, the Babenbergs and the Habsburgs. Like marketing channels, it holds a prominent role in cultural, economic, and political exchange. It is the sole European Union capital with a United Nations headquarters, and it has earned a global reputation as a meeting place. During its Golden Age, Vienna was the nucleus of intellectual and cultural innovation; and innovation is an important property of contemporary marketing channels.

Vienna evokes vivid images of grand Habsburg palaces, lofty Baroque churches, and trotting white horses. Vienna's coffeehouses were meeting places for the likes of Freud, Klimt, and Schoenberg. Vienna has been the showcase for great cultural icons like Beethoven, Mozart, Strauss . . . and Haas.

Haas? Yes, Eduard Haas is the Austrian candy executive who may be credited with initiating one of the most dramatic electronic revolutions in marketing channels history. In 1927, Eduard Haas invented small candy peppermints—PfeffErminZ—that were marketed as PEZ. The first PEZ dispensers appeared in the 1950s. Almost 50 years later, those PEZ dispensers spawned a $50 billion electronic marketing channel: online auction sites. You see, eBay was founded to trade PEZ dispensers. Ebay president and CEO Meg Whitman's passion for PEZ dispensers propagated nearly 19 million buyers and sellers exchanging over $5 billion worth of products annually via the Internet.

From PEZ dispensers to Jacqueline Onassis's BMW, millions of products are listed on eBay's site daily. The growing portfolio of products includes eBay Motors, an automotive marketplace featuring all makes and models of automobiles, financing and insurance services, and automotive collectibles. Ebay's business is an exchange targeted to the small business marketplace, and eBay Premier features fine art and antiques. EBay has become a meeting place for buyers and sellers worldwide. It boasts users from over 150 different countries with specific Internet sites in Australia, Canada, France, Germany, Japan, and the United Kingdom. And it all started with a Viennese candy maker, Eduard Haas.

Today, PEZ candy is manufactured in Connecticut and distributed through a variety of marketing channels, including discount stores like Wal-Mart and Target, supermarkets like Kroger's and Safeway, convenience stores like Circle K and 7-Eleven, toy chains like Toys "R" Us, and electronic channels like www.burlingamepezmuseum.com. The collectible dispensers have become a mainstay of American culture, and PEZ candy and dispensers are distributed in more than 60 countries worldwide. While PEZ candy and dispensers are distributed through both bricks 'n mortar retailers and electronic channels, the same guiding principle underlies the exchanges among PEZ collectors. As Meg Whitman aptly notes, "Sellers want to be where the buyers are, and buyers want to be where the sellers are." Now, let's explore how marketing channels connect buyers and sellers.

* * * *

What Is a Marketing Channel?

For many of you, the word *channel* may conjure up images of a waterway. Our exploration of early 20th-century Austria invokes images of the Danube River. (The Danube, the second-longest river in Europe, has a course that runs through nine countries. It is an important commercial highway connecting Austria, Bulgaria, Croatia, Germany, Hungary, Slovakia, Romania, Ukraine, and Yugoslavia. Historically, the Danube served as a mechanism for economic exchange, but it also provided a political boundary among great empires.) Likewise, you might envision the English Channel—a formidable geographic barrier that has kept England secure from foreign invasion since the year 1066. On the other hand, the term may remind you of the mechanical device that allows you to flip from one football game to another on an autumn weekend.[1]

Regardless of the image, each implies the presence of a passageway, a real or imaginary conduit allowing certain processes to occur. Such imagery offers a surprisingly accurate description. The term *marketing channel* was first used to describe the existence of a trade channel bridging producers and users.[2] Early writers compared marketing channels to paths through which goods or materials could move from producers to users. This description makes it easy to understand how the term *middleman* came into being as a way to explain product flows.[3]

When you bite into a peanut butter and jelly sandwich, you can appreciate the middle. After all, it just doesn't taste the same without the filling between two slices of bread. There are many kinds of peanut butter, ranging from smooth and creamy to chunky styles, and many flavors of jelly to complement that peanut butter. Today, you can even buy a swirled combination of peanut butter and jelly in a single jar. This analogy is intended to whet your appetite for the complexities of the middleman or intermediary in the Net Economy.

Not too long ago, you would have no choice but to purchase that peanut butter, jelly, and bread at a grocery store, convenience store, or other bricks 'n mortar retailer. Indeed, the success or failure of intermediaries was tied to Dillard's department store founder William Dillard's adage, "Location, location, location." The emergence of retailers and wholesalers was largely based on closing the location gaps between buyers and sellers. Your ancestors might recount the days when street peddlers would personally visit their homes with a vast array of products. Today, you can select from a variety of peanut butter, jelly, and bread flavors and brands without ever leaving home. You can simply point and click to have the ingredients delivered to your home via websites like Groceryworks.com or Webvan.com. In many ways, this technologically enabled channel is a remnant of the days of street peddlers: a home delivery channel for groceries, sundries, and other specialty products.

Intermediaries create value by reducing the spatial separation—the physical distance between the point of production and point of consumption—between manufacturers and ultimate users of products and services. In Channel Surfing 1.2 (on page 13), you will get a taste of the complex network of connections that facilitate exchanges between buyers and sellers through Blockbuy.com. In the Net Economy, it is increasingly apparent that marketing channels facilitate the flows of products and services.

By now, you may be flooded with our allusions to water and flows. Their purpose has been to instill a sense of movement in your understanding of marketing channels. This movement of products and services is made possible only through the exchange process. Recall that marketing is an exchange process. In fact, the concept of exchange lies at the core of marketing. Exchange occurs whenever something tangible (e.g., a meal) or intangible (e.g., a political concept) is transferred between two or more social actors. In fact, marketing is generally studied as an exchange process.[4] Marketing is a "social process by which individuals and groups obtain what they need and want through creating and exchanging products and value with others."[5]

Now consider that *marketing channels facilitate the exchange process.* Since marketing focuses on the activities and behaviors necessary for exchange to occur, channels should be thought of as *exchange facilitators.* Thus, any connection between individuals and/or organizations that allows or contributes to the occurrence of an exchange is a marketing channel.

So, a **marketing channel** can be defined as exchange relationships that create customer value in the acquisition, consumption, and disposition of products and services. This definition implies that exchange relationships emerge *from market needs* as a way of *serving market needs.* Channel members must come to the marketplace well equipped to address changing market needs and wants.

On your next trip to the supermarket, consider the variety of prepared foods in and around the deli case. Consumers are increasingly opting for fast, convenient, ready-to-serve meals. With supermarket managers pressured to compete in the emerging prepared foods market, restaurant equipment manufacturers are lending a helping hand by partnering with other suppliers to offer turnkey food preparation programs. These turnkey programs offer grocery retailers a "ready-to-serve" package that includes equipment, training, and in-store promotional support. One such program is Hobart Corporation's Pizza-To-Go, which offers retailers (and their customers) a variety of pizza options. Hobart's "Pizza Planning Guide" covers everything from cheese suppliers to triple cheese pizza recipes. Turnkey programs like Pizza-To-Go offer retail grocers big returns on small space investments, and the programs ultimately help supermarkets create satisfied customers.

By definition, activities or behaviors that contribute to exchange cannot exist without first having markets. In market settings, it is understood that no individual or organization can operate for long in complete isolation from other individuals or organizations. The interaction between Hobart (equipment producers), cheese suppliers (wholesale distributors), supermarkets (retailers), and hungry patrons (consumers) demonstrates how exchange relationships emerge *from market needs* as a way of *serving market needs.* In each case, some interaction must exist for marketing to occur. In the next section, we investigate how, as a result of such interactions, marketing channels have evolved from a distribution to a relationship orientation.

Evolution of Marketing Channels

Marketing channels always emerge out of a demand that marketplace needs be better served. However, markets and their needs never stop changing; therefore, marketing channels operate in a state of continuous change and must constantly adapt to confront those changes. From its inception to its contemporary standing, the evolution of marketing channels thought can be divided into four stages.

The Production Era and Distributive Practices

The origins of marketing as an area of study are inextricably tied to distributive practices. The earliest marketing courses, in fact, were essentially distribution courses. Course titles like "Distributive and Regulative Industries of U.S. Distribution of Agricultural Products" and "Techniques of Trade and Commerce" abounded at Schools of Commerce during the early

1900s. These courses addressed the ways in which marketing channels spawned middlemen who, in turn, facilitated more efficient movements of goods and services from producers to users.[6] As American productivity and urbanization increased with each passing decade of the 20th century, the demand for a variety of production resources to be used as manufacturing inputs naturally followed suit. Rapidly growing urban centers demanded larger and more diverse bundles of goods than had previously been available. By 1929, retailing accounted for nearly $50 billion of U.S. trade.[7] Modern-looking market channels emerged in response to the need for more cost-effective ways of moving goods and raw resources.[8]

One description of marketing channels taken from this era stated, "Transportation and storage are . . . concerned with those activities which are necessary for the movement of goods through space and the carrying of goods through time."[9] Increasingly, *facilitating devices* were needed to transport, assemble, and reship goods. Thus, the origins of the modern marketing channel cannot be separated from purely distributive practices.

The Institutional Period and Selling Orientation

The gross national product of the United States grew at an extraordinary rate during the 1940s, and this industrial expansion contributed to the emergence of sizeable inventory stockpiles. The cost of managing these inventories grew rapidly as well.[10] Production techniques and marketing channel processes each became more sophisticated during this period. Issues pertaining to distribution primarily revolved around cost containment, controlling inventory, and managing assets. Marketers were shifting from a *production* to a *sales* orientation. The attitude that "a good product will sell itself" receded as marketers encountered the need to expand sales and advertising expenditures to convince individual consumers and organizations to buy their specific brands.[11] The classic marketing mix, or *Four Ps,* typology—product, price, promotion, and place—emerged as a guiding marketing principle. Issues relating to distribution were relegated to the place domain.[12] The idea that relationships between buyers and sellers could be managed did not yet exist as a topic of study.

Many new types of channel intermediaries surfaced during this period. For example, industrial distributors emerged in the channel of distribution for most industrial products and consumer durables. And by the late 1950s, sales by merchant wholesalers reached $100 billion.[13] Producers were continuously seeking new ways to expand their market coverage and distributive structures. Several giant retailers had emerged by this time, and small retailers were increasingly formalizing and specializing their operations to meet the needs of a more refined marketplace.[14]

The Marketing Concept

In 1951, vice president of marketing at Pillsbury Robert Keith introduced a seminal marketing principle to the business world: the marketing concept. According to the marketing concept, the customer is the nucleus of all marketing mix decisions. As such, organizations should only make what they can market instead of trying to market what they have made.

The marketing concept is intuitively appealing because its focus is on the customer. In this sense, however, the marketing concept paints a very one-sided approach to reconciling a firm's mission with the markets it serves because it positions marketers as reactive exchange partners—adapting channels of distribution to meet market needs.[15] A few of the ways that Coke is applying the marketing concept through its marketing channels are described in Channel Surfing 1.1, which follows.

Relationship Marketing Era

The marketing concept proved a logical precursor to the total quality management (TQM) philosophy espoused by the late W. Edwards Deming. TQM suggests a highly interactive approach in which customers become active partners with producers, wholesalers, or retailers (channel members) to solve marketplace problems. The TQM philosophy has initiated a mindset among managers that a firm's relationship with its customers fosters market-share gain and customer retention. This mindset parallels an emerging era in marketing theory and practice.

This emerging era, known as the Relationship Marketing Era, is characterized by a fundamental shift from a customer *voice* to a customer *dialogue.* Rather than just reacting to customer-initiated feedback, the channel member proactively initiates and maintains a participative exchange with its customers. The concept of participation implies a high degree of cooperation and coordination between customers and their suppliers. Close relationships between customers and their suppliers have revolutionized marketing channels in many ways:

- Close relationships emphasize a long-term, win-win exchange relationship based on mutual trust between customers and their suppliers.[16]
- They reinforce the relationship dimension of exchange that is at the heart of marketing.

In the Net Economy, information technology enables highly interactive, one-to-one relationships between channel members. One-to-one relationships can be viewed as the dynamic of managing customer information to create intimate relationships between channel members. The dynamic is the give and take between customers, and it is based on information. In one-to-one relationships, the seller is continually querying customers, "How can I best serve your needs?" And the customer is responding. Information technologies empower channel members to engage in a dialogue. In one-to-one relationships, customers are actively investing in the ongoing value that channel members are creating and delivering.

The most important impact of the Internet Age on marketing channels is the creation of long-term, one-to-one customer relationships. Each buyer expects to be recognized and known by the seller. The Internet and related technologies are helping channel members cultivate these close relationships. The overarching challenge for channel members in the 21st-century is **customer relationship management** (CRM)—a business process that delivers personalized goods and services by harnessing and mining customer information. We will discuss CRM throughout this book. CRM reinforces the value creation that underlies each stage in the evolution of marketing channels.

The progression through these four stages—from a production to a relationship approach in marketing channels—has been fostered by the evolving contributions channel intermediaries have made toward the creation of customer value.

Channel Surfing 1.1

Coca-Cola Bottler Ensures Customer Satisfaction through Its Intermediaries

Coca-Cola Bottling Company United, Inc., is the largest independent bottler of Coca-Cola products in the United States. Headquartered in Birmingham, Alabama, United's territory covers part of Alabama, Mississippi, Georgia, South Carolina, and Tennessee. The company supplies Coca-Cola products to many different intermediaries including supermarkets, drugstores, mass merchandisers, convenience/oil stores, restaurants, and vending machines. It is also present at special events such as the Master's Golf Tournament and local events such as county fairs. Its customers' satisfaction depends on quality delivery. United ensures that quality by maintaining regular delivery schedules, prompt and accurate invoicing, and proper maintenance of its customers' inventory.

Points to Ponder

- Often, the flows of seemingly simple products are not simple at all. Why?

Source: Based on author conversation with Tom Smillie, Marketing Analyst, Eastern Region, Coca-Cola Bottling Company United, Inc.

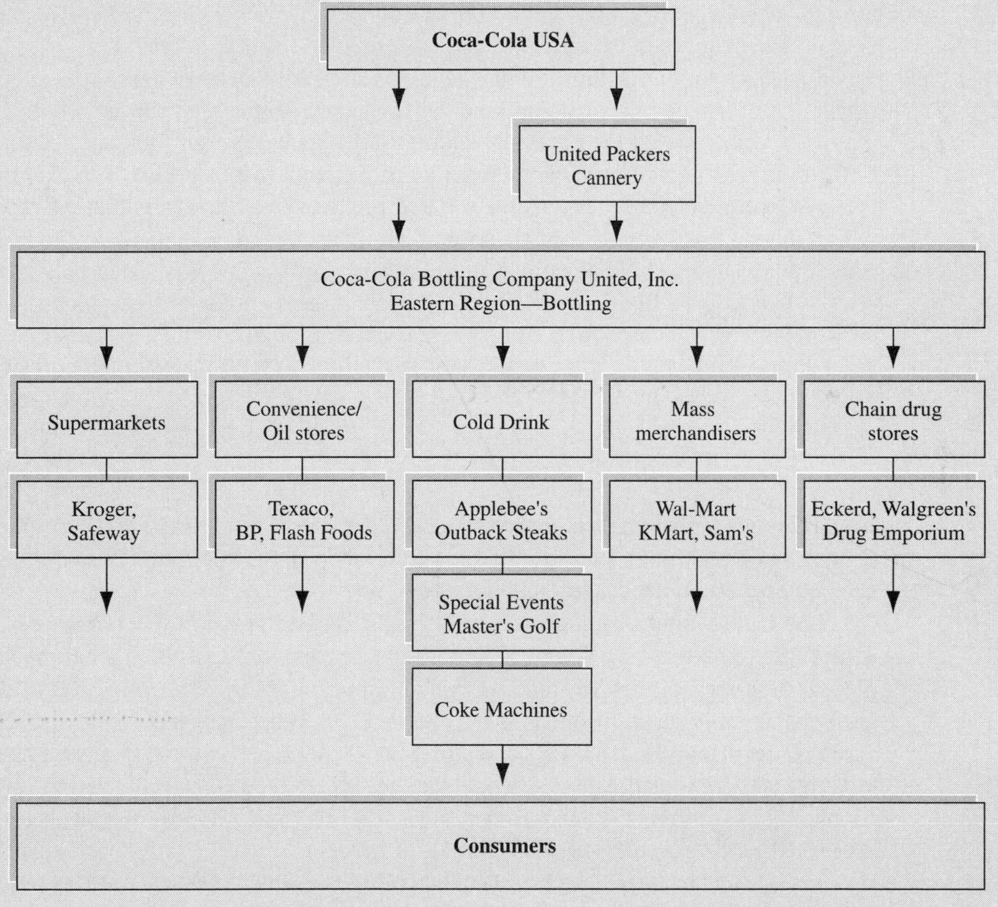

The Elements of Successful Marketing Channels

By now, you can appreciate the consequential role of the customer in steering marketing channels. But how do marketing channel members work together to create satisfied customers? Let's return to the mighty Danube River—site of the 2000 World Cup rowing competition—to fully understand the interdependency between channel members. Rowing competitions can take place on rivers, lakes, bays, oceans, or any other body of water large enough to support the boat commonly referred to as a "shell." Like markets, they must be large enough to support competition and be accessible to various competitors.

Rowing is the ultimate team sport. The various parts of the rowing crew must fit together to operate as a single, cohesive unit. In fact, each rowing crew is a blend of individuals' stroke techniques, strengths, conditioning, and mental preparedness. At the same time, each crew member has to acclimate herself to different water and competitive conditions. At the heart of the shell's speed is teamwork. Without perfect synergy, shell speed is lost. To achieve success in a competitive arena, rowers must *pool individual resources* to achieve *collective goals* through a *connected system.* In addition, this connected system must be *flexible* enough to accommodate changes in the environment, as demonstrated in Exhibit 1.1.

Similarly, for marketing channels to succeed in a competitive marketplace, independent marketing organizations must combine their resources to pursue common goals. Each rower plays a special role on the crew, depending on her positioning in the shell. From the front bow to the rear stern, each crew member has a different responsibility. For example, the cox is the only crew member responsible for steering the shell, and she is the only one watching where the shell is going. All of the other crew members must depend on the cox's navigation and leadership skills. Information truly drives rowing success. The cox signals when to start, when to stop, and how to stroke. Obviously, this entails a great deal of trust among crew members. This high level of dependency and implicit trust is a cornerstone of contemporary marketing channels, as well. Let's take a look at the four key elements of success in channels.

Pooled Resources

A marketing channel operates as a team, sharing resources and risks to move products and resources from their point of origin to their point of final consumption. Consider how the U.S. beer industry operates, for example.

The United States has a three-tier beer distribution system, which consists of brewers, distributors, and retailers. Over 3,000 beer distributors, most of them small businesses employing less then 50 people, manage the multibillion-dollar business of delivering brew to retailers. From Anaheim (California) to Zanesville (Ohio), these wholesale distributors make sure that beer flows from brewers to a variety of retail outlets ranging from neighborhood taverns to local convenience stores. In the United States, brewers are allowed to own beer distributors, but distributors cannot own retail outlets that sell beer. So, for a consumer to quaff a beer, a literal "give and take" has to unfold between breweries, wholesale distributors, and retailers. As one manager of a small Atlantic City inn puts it, "What [brewery] would deliver to me if I only need two kegs a week?" For the channel to function smoothly, there has to be a distributor.

Exhibit 1.1

Rowing: Synergy in the marketing channel

	Characteristics of Marketing Channels	
Rowing Crew	*Similarities*	*Differences*
Pooled Resources Each crew member contributes her overall mastery of rowing strokes to the overall team effort.	**State of Interdependency** Each channel member is dependent on all other members in the marketing channel. For a channel to exist, the behavior of one channel member *must* influence the behavior of other members.	**Uneven Pooled Resources** On a rowing crew, everyone uses essentially the same strokes. However, it is unusual for each channel member to perform the same functions in the same quantity.
Collective Goals The shared desire to win the race bonds crew members.	**A Shared Objective** Channel members must share one or more common goals to ensure a seamless flow of goods and services.	**Duration of Goals** Rowing crews usually are linked by short-term goals: to win the race. The shared objectives of channel members are far more complex, and they are (ideally) linked by long-term objectives.
Connected System A rowing team cannot exist with one player, and a competition cannot exist with only one team. Each team is governed by rules of competition.	**Sets of Norms** Marketing channels feature an established set of behavioral norms which keeps the exchange together. These norms reflect the rules of marketplace competition.	**Nonlinear System** The relationship between team members on a crew is linear. They each perform one function. Channel members engage in a wide variety of interactions in many directions.
Flexibility Rowing crews must adapt to changing conditions. Each water course presents a different challenge.	**An Open System** Organizations can enter or exit channel systems with relative ease. Therefore, channel members are free to accept or reject these norms.	**Parallel System** On a rowing crew, each crew member follows another. However, channel members likely perform functions at the same time.

Beer distributors do more than pool resources for retailers. It is not unusual to see distributors acting as field operatives, talking with customers, straightening up cases of beer on retail floors, and cleaning draft-beer lines. Not only do distributors provide retailers with merchandising and promotional assistance, they also gather market information for the breweries' marketing staffs.[17]

Collective Goals

The challenge of winning helps bond rowing team members. Coordinated rowing strokes build speed and ultimately impact rowing performance. A rowing crew simply cannot exist with only one rower. It takes a team effort, pooling their resources together, to achieve

Terry Eggers/The Stock Market

"swinging": the code for perfect synergy in rowing. The willingness to work together outweighs individuals' sheer power. A similar sense of shared purpose helps unite organizations within market channels, particularly when the organizations sense a chance to win a critical competition for market share. While at times these connections are short in duration, they sometimes last for decades.

The purpose shared by members of an organization is reflected in the organization's mission statement. A **mission statement** is an organization's strategic charter—a public declaration of why it exists. A mission statement proclaims (1) an organization's goals, (2) the procedures to be employed in pursuit of those goals, and (3) how the organization intends to satisfy the needs of its internal and external customers. When U.S. Olympic team members don their red, white, and blue uniforms, they are undoubtedly consumed by a mutual desire to honorably represent their country. Indeed, national pride is likely a strong motivational force for each Olympic team. Members of organizations are similarly linked together by a shared purpose.

The mission statement of Canadian National Railroads (CNR) indicates that its purpose is: "To meet customers' transportation and distribution needs by being the best at moving their goods on time, safely and damage-free."[18] Three critical marketing principles are inherent within CNR's mission. First, CNR's mission describes *whom the firm intends to serve:* anyone having transportation and distribution needs. The mission then explains *how the firm intends to serve its market:* by positioning CNR as the best transportation supplier. Finally, the statement discloses *the criteria that CNR must meet or exceed to establish a competitive advantage:* timely, safe, and uninjured delivery. But if brevity is indeed the soul of wit, FedEx's mission is the wittiest of all. Its entire mission statement is: "To create a satisfied customer at the end of each transaction."[19] Customer needs lie at the heart of both CNR's and FedEx's business purpose. Clearly, these organizations recognize that customers steer marketing channel activities.

Connected System

A rowing competition cannot exist with a single team. Similarly, organizations cannot exist without markets. All business competition emerges within marketing channels, and the success or failure of all individual enterprise is ultimately decided there.[20] Channel members regulate the flows of goods and services in the marketplace. The degree to which channel members regulate these flows has never been more significant than it is today, as illustrated in Channel Surfing 1.2. Blockbuy.com is just one example of the complex linkages that regulate flows of products and services in the Net Economy.

Channel Surfing 1.2

These Blockheads Are No Dummies

They jokingly refer to themselves as "blockheads," but the team members at Blockbuy.com are no dummies. Seattle-based Blockbuy.com is a syndicated commerce site targeting restaurateurs, café owners and greasy-spoon proprietors. What is syndicated commerce? You might call it a business-to-business (B2B) matchmaker because it marries small and mid-size businesses.

You are already familiar with eBay. Online auction sites like eBay popularized the single-seller, single-item, single-buyer marketplace. But suppliers want to sell multiple products to multiple buyers. Syndicated commerce aggregates buyers through a network of Internet sites. Together, these buyers have greater purchasing power, affording them greater price savings. Simply, Blockbuy.com aggregates demand around specialty products.

On Blockbuy.com, the registered seller starts by listing a price schedule, where the order price declines as the total quantity of orders increases. At the same time, buyers list the maximum price that they are willing to pay and the quantities that they are willing to order. When a "match" is made, buyers get the lowest price and suppliers get the promised order quantities: it is a virtual win-win. This is all made possible with an intricate portfolio of supplier, technology, and distribution channel partners.

When you feast on that grilled panini or sip a refreshing smoothie at your neighborhood café, you might consider the restaurant equipment necessary to prepare these delicious foods. Maybe the café used a Sirman panini grill or a Santosafe restaurant blender. Blockbuy.com brings together over 30 supplier partners, ranging from ABC Coffee & Pasta to Wurlitzer Corporation. Yes, Wurlitzer sells juke boxes and other vending products to restaurants, taverns, and small businesses via Blockbuy.com.

Technology partners are a key to Blockbuy.com's channel strategy. Blockbuy.com does not rely on its proprietary website. It places its private-label technology with technology partners like Foodhunter.net and RestaurantOwner.com. Blockbuy.com leverages the market power of its technology partners to provide a group purchasing network. It also partners with Verisign. Verisign payment services allow Blockbuy.com's buyers to use a major credit card, debit card, or electronic check to complete their purchases. Finally, Blockbuy.com partners with distribution service providers like freightquote.com to provide online business freight solutions for shippers and e-commerce companies.

This intricate web of suppliers creates value for small restaurant and greasy-spoon owners by providing a full-service, one-stop, virtual marketplace. In doing so, it requires that each partner meet and exceed customers' expectations. The blockheads are optimistic about Blockbuy.com's growth, forecasting over $110 million in evenues by 2005. One thing is certain: To make Blockbuy.com a blockbuster, it will require a total team effort.

Points to Ponder

- How does success of Blockbuy.com ultimately depend on the success of its team of supplier partnerships?
- Can you imagine any problems that may emerge from these close channel member associations?

Source: Adapted from Callahan, Sean (2000), "An e-Hub for Eateries," *BtoB*, 85 (July 3, no. 9), 3, 35.

The next time you sip a cup of coffee (at your neighborhood Starbuck's), consider the connected forces that impact its distribution. For one, there is a good chance that those brewed coffee beans were grown in Colombia, the world's largest producer of premium-grade coffees. When Mother Nature abuses Colombia's coffee crop with tropical rainfalls or frost, prices skyrocket on New York's Coffee, Sugar & Cocoa Exchange. On the other hand, coffee prices plummet when word of a good crop spreads across the trading floor. In turn, these price fluctuations surely affect the behavior of the companies that purchase green coffee beans to roast and resell to wholesalers. Ultimately, the success or failure of Colombia's coffee crop affects the price you pay for roasted beans at your local grocery store or coffeehouse.[21]

Flexibility

As any rower will tell you, each water course is different. Rowing teams must constantly adapt their body rotations and rowing strokes to the competition site. Team members may even need to switch positions to maximize their team performance. Similarly, marketing channels must be flexible systems in order to be successful. Wroe Alderson, the father of modern marketing thought, described marketing channels as *ecological systems.* Alderson offered this description because of the unique, ecological-like connections that exist among the participants within a marketing channel. As Alderson put it, the organizations and persons involved in channel flows must be "sufficiently connected to permit the system to operate as a whole, but the bond they share must be loose enough to allow for components to be replaced or added."[22]

Whether you prefer cold beer or hot coffee, you probably don't consider how the barley or beans arrive in a consumable form at your favorite watering hole or coffeehouse. Your lack of concern is exactly what this flexible system is striving to create: a seamless flow from farm to mug. In this book, we discuss how independent organizations form marketing relationships to create satisfied customers.

Channel Intermediaries: The Customer Value Mediators

The relationship perspective introduced above is a far cry from the traditional view of markets as physical places where people gathered to engage in trade. A glimpse at ancient Rome's economy will help you understand the progression of marketing channels from a distribution to a relationship orientation:

> At one end of the busy process of exchange were peddlers hawking through the countryside; . . . daily markets and periodical fairs; shopkeepers haggling with customers . . . A little higher in the commercial hierarchy were shops that manufactured their own merchandise . . . At or near ports were wholesalers who sold . . . goods recently brought in from abroad.[23]

This passage shows how a logical channel structure emerged very early in the history of institutionalized markets. An established channel structure is clearly reflected within the organized behavioral system of peddlers, auctioneers, merchant wholesalers, and shopkeepers who directed the flow of goods and services in Rome. Each market player described above performed a role fulfilled by entities now known as *channel intermediaries.*

Channel intermediaries are individuals or organizations who mediate exchange utility in relationships involving two or more partners. Intermediaries generate form, place, time, and/or ownership values by bringing together buyers and sellers. While the names of the players have changed, the functions performed by channel intermediaries remain essentially the same. Intermediaries have always helped channels CRAM it: create utility by contributing to *C*ontactual efficiency, facilitating *R*outinization, simplifying *A*ssortment, and *M*inimizing uncertainty within marketing channels.

Contactual Efficiency

Channels consist of sets of marketing relationships that emerge from the exchange process. An important function performed by intermediaries is their role in optimizing the number of exchange relationships needed to complete transactions. **Contactual efficiency** describes this movement toward a point of equilibrium between the quantity and quality of exchange relationships between channel members. Without channel intermediaries, each buyer would have to interact directly with each seller, making for an extremely inefficient state of affairs.

When only two parties are involved in an exchange, the relationship is said to be a **dyadic relationship.** The process of exchange in a dyadic relationship is fairly simple, but it becomes far more complicated as the number of channel participants increases. Consider the following formula to understand how quickly the exchange process within a given channel can become complicated. The number of exchange relationships that can potentially develop within a channel is equivalent to $(3^n - 2^{n+1} + 1)/2$, where n is the number of organizations in a channel. When n is 2, only one relationship is possible. However, when n increases to 4, up to 25 relationships can unfold. Increase n to 6, and the number of potential relationships leaps to 301.

The number of relationships unfolding within a channel would quickly become too complicated to efficiently manage if each channel member had to deal with all other members. In this context, the value of channel intermediaries as producers of contactual efficiency becomes obvious. Still, having too many intermediaries in a marketing channel likewise leads to inefficiencies. As the number of intermediaries approaches the number of organizations in the channel, the law of diminishing returns kicks in. At that point, additional intermediaries add little to no incremental value within the channel. These relationships are illustrated in Exhibit 1.2.

The pharmaceutical drug industry illustrates how contactual efficiency shapes up in the marketplace. McKesson Drug Company, the nation's largest drug and personal care products wholesaler, acts as an intermediary between drug manufacturers and retail pharmacies. About 600 million transactions would be necessary to satisfy the needs of the some 50,000 pharmacies in the United States if these pharmacies had to order on a monthly basis from the 1,000 U.S. pharmaceutical drug manufacturers. When our example is broadened to the possibility of daily orders from these pharmacies, the total number of monthly transactions required rises to over 13 billion. This number would be nearly impossible to consummate. However, introducing 250 wholesale distributors into the pharmaceutical channel reduces the number of annual transactions to about 26 million. This reduction illustrates the essence of contactual efficiency.[24]

The nexus between technology and customer satisfaction is being achieved by McKesson's HBOC's supply management business every day. Consider the vast array of

Exhibit 1.2

Contactual efficiency

No Intermediary

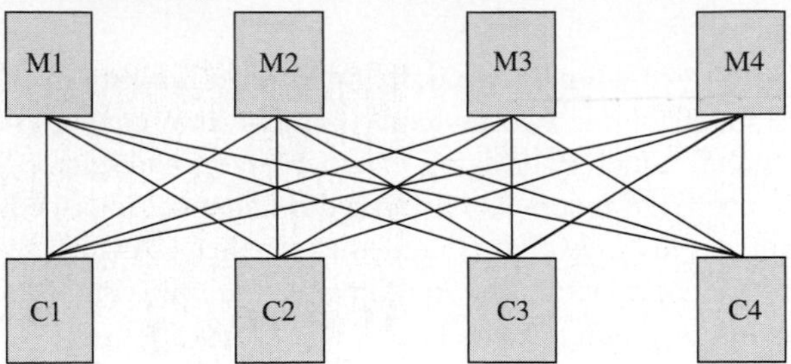

Single Intermediary

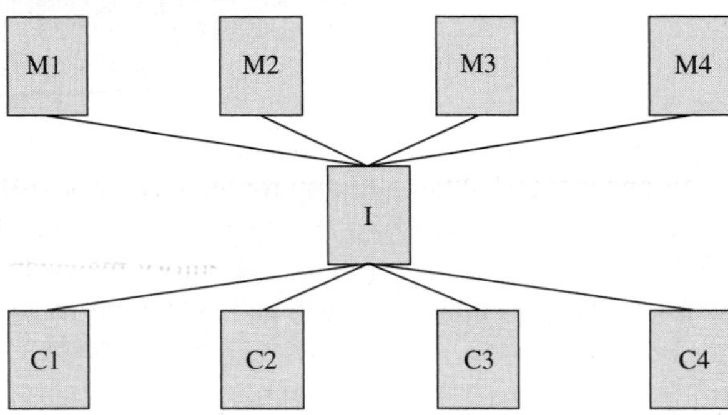

Four Intermediaries
Law of Diminishing Returns

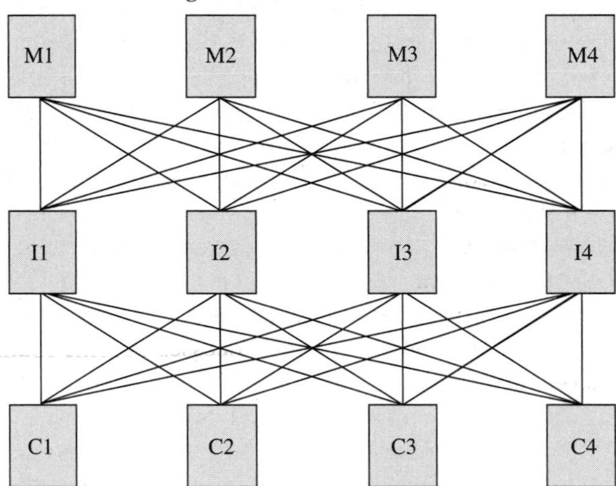

C = Customer
I = Intermediary
M = Manufacturer

McKesson Drug Co., a pharmaceutical wholesaler, provides independent retailers with its proprietary inventory management software. Now, a Web-based system facilitates routinized ordering in the channel of distribution for pharmaceutical products.

Courtesy McKesson Drug Co.

pharmaceuticals and medical-surgical supplies that McKesson distributes to more than 25,000 retail pharmacies and 5,000 hospitals nationwide. Using state-of-the-art Web-based technologies, McKesson complements its proprietary inventory management system with inventory, logistics, and third-party adjudication management systems on the Supply Management Suite. All of these value-added benefits fortify the relationship between McKesson and the customers it serves.

Routinization

The costs associated with generating purchase orders, handling invoices, and maintaining inventory are considerable. Now imagine the amount of order processing that would be necessary to complete millions upon millions of pharmaceutical transactions. McKesson Drug Company offers an interactive computer-networked ordering system for pharmacies that provides fast, reliable transaction management. The system processes each order within one hour and routes the order to the closest distribution system for delivery. It relieves retailers of many of the administrative costs associated with routine orders and, not coincidentally, makes it more likely that McKesson will also get their business as a result of the savings.[25]

This system represents the state of the art in routinization. **Routinization** refers to the means by which transaction processes are standardized to improve the flow of goods and services through marketing channels. Routinization itself delivers several advantages to all channel participants. First, as transaction processes become routine, the expectations of exchange partners become institutionalized. There is then no need to negotiate terms of sale or delivery on a transaction-by-transaction basis. Second, routinization permits channel partners to concentrate more attention on their *own* core business concerns. Furthermore, routinization provides a basis for strengthening the relationship between channel participants.

Sorting

Organizations strive to ensure that all market offerings they produce are eventually converted into goods and services consumed by those in their target market. The process by which this market progression unfolds is called *sorting.* In a channels context, sorting is often described as a *smoothing function.* This function entails the conversion of raw materials to increasingly more refined forms until the goods are acceptable for use by the final consumer. The next time you purchase a soda, consider the role intermediaries played in converting the original syrup (often produced in powdered form) to a conveniently consumed form. Coca-Cola U.S.A. ships syrup and other materials to bottlers throughout the world. Independent bottlers carbonate and add purified water to the syrup. The product is then packaged and distributed to retailers.

Two principal tasks are associated with the sorting function. They are:[26]

- **Categorizing.** At some point in every channel, large amounts of heterogeneous supplies have to be converted into smaller homogeneous subsets. Returning to our pharmaceutical example, the number of drugs or drug combinations available through retail outlets is huge. Over 10,000 drugs or drug combinations currently exist. In performing the categorization task, intermediaries first arrange this vast product portfolio into manageable therapeutic categories. The items within these categories are then categorized further to satisfy the specific needs of individual consumers.
- **Breaking bulk.** Producers try to produce in bulk (i.e., large) quantities. Thus, it is often necessary for intermediaries to break homogeneous lots into smaller units. How does this apply to distribution of drug products? Over 60 percent of the typical retail pharmacy's capital is tied to the purchase and resale of inventory. The opportunity to acquire smaller lots means smaller capital outflows are necessary at a single time. Consequently, pharmaceutical distributors must continuously break bulk to satisfy the retailer's lot size requirements.

The sorting function's contributions to profit are astounding. In a keynote address to inaugurate National Quality Month, Procter & Gamble one-time Chief Executive Edwin L. Ardzt commented, "As an industry, we've estimated annual grocery sales in the U.S. to be about $300 billion. Out of that, there's between $75 billion to $100 billion of inventory, much of it unproductive, caught between the manufacturer, the manufacturer's supplier, and the retailer—up to a third of total sales just trapped in the pipeline."[27]

Minimizing Uncertainty

The role that intermediaries play in reducing uncertainty is perhaps their most overlooked function. Several types of uncertainty develop naturally in all market settings.[28]

Need Uncertainty. Need uncertainty refers to the doubts that sellers often have regarding whether they actually understand the needs of their customers. Most of the time neither sellers nor buyers understand the exact machines, tools, or services required to reach optimal levels of productivity. Since intermediaries function as bridges linking sellers to buyers, they can become much closer to both producers and users than producers and users are to each other. As a result, the intermediary is in the best position to understand each of their needs and reduce sellers' uncertainty by carefully reconciling *what is available* with *what is needed.*

Few members within any channel are able to accurately state and rank their needs. Instead, most channel members have needs they perceive only dimly, while still other firms and persons have needs of which they are not yet aware.[29] In channels where there is a lot of need uncertainty, intermediaries generally evolve into specialists. The ranks of intermediaries must then increase, while the roles they play become more complex. Conversely, the number of intermediaries generally declines as need uncertainty decreases.

Market Uncertainty. Market uncertainty depends on the number of sources available for a product or service. Market uncertainty is generally difficult to manage because it often results from uncontrollable environment factors—i.e., social, economic, and competitive factors. One means by which organizations can reduce their market uncertainty is by broadening their view of what marketing channels can and perhaps should do for them.

Transaction Uncertainty. Transaction uncertainty relates to imperfect channel flows between buyers and sellers. When we consider product flows, we typically think of the delivery or distribution function. Intermediaries play the key role in ensuring that goods flow smoothly through the channel. The delivery of materials frequently must be timed to precisely coincide with the use of those goods in the production processes of other products or services. Problems arising at any point during these channel flows can lead to higher transaction uncertainty. Such difficulties could arise from legal, cultural, or technological sources. When transaction uncertainty is high, buyers attempt to secure parallel suppliers, although this option is not always available.

Consider Merck's pharmaceutical product for Parkinson's disease, L-Dopa. The chemical compound for this drug is actually produced by Searle Pharmaceuticals under the name Levodopa. Levodopa must be converted into a tablet form and, thus, its delivery must coincide with the intermediary's tableting of the Levodopa compound. The production of Levodopa and its tableting process must be precisely synchronized to ensure the flow of L-Dopa to people suffering from Parkinson's disease. When our illustration is extended to the over-the-counter sector of the pharmaceutical market, we can easily see the large number of potential retail outlets that are available to address the consumer's needs. Intermediaries regulate the flow of goods and services to the vast number of pharmaceutical retailers. By performing this function, these intermediaries reduce uncertainty within the pharmaceutical marketing channel.

Uncertainty within marketing channels can be minimized through careful actions taken over a prolonged period of exchange. Naturally, as exchange processes become standardized, need, market, and transaction uncertainty is lessened. Furthermore, as exchange *relationships* develop, uncertainty decreases because exchange partners have gotten to know one another better and are communicating their needs and capabilities.

The functions performed by marketing intermediaries concurrently satisfy the needs of channel members in several ways.[30]

- **Facilitating strategic aims.** The most basic way that the needs of market channels can be assessed and then satisfied centers on the role channel intermediaries can perform in helping channel members reach the goals mapped out in their strategic plans.
- **Fulfilling interaction requirements.** This refers to the degree of coordination and on-site service required by members of a marketing channel. Coordination provides the means by which harmony in ordering systems, delivery timing, and merchandising is achieved between buyers and sellers.

• **Satisfying delivery and handling requirements.** How often do customers need deliveries? What are their order quantities? To what extent will demand fluctuate? These questions typify the processes involved in matching channel functions to the need for efficient resource management within marketing channels. Channel members are often unaware of their precise delivery and handling requirement needs. By minimizing transaction uncertainty, channel intermediaries help clarify these processes.

• **Managing inventory requirements.** The costs of financing and carrying inventory differ across product categories and channel members. The proficiency with which they determine and ultimately satisfy warehousing, stock-out, and product substitutability needs sets intermediaries apart from each other.

To summarize, channel intermediaries, by bridging producers and their customers, are instrumental in aligning an independent organization's mission with the market(s) it serves. Channel intermediaries foster relationship building by providing these fundamental functions in the marketing channel.

Channels Relationship Model (CRM)

Earlier in this chapter, we defined a marketing channel as exchange relationships that create customer value in the acquisition, consumption, and disposition of products and services. Each component of this definition is embedded in the Channels Relationship Model (CRM), shown here in Exhibit 1.3. The acronym CRM concurrently describes customer relationship management as well as the guiding model for this book. This is no mistake. After all, relationship management is the backbone of any channel system.

Earlier in this chapter, we discussed the teamwork that epitomizes rowing crews. The interdependencies between crew members determine the performance outcomes of the rowing team. This interdependency is likewise embedded in the Channels Relationship Model (CRM). The CRM may be described as an ecological framework. As ecological framework, the CRM emphasizes the effect of environmental influences on channel member development. There are three major environments that are entrenched in the CRM: channels exosystems, microsystems, and mesosystems.

An Ecological Framework

Channel exosystems involve the externalities or other environments in which channel members operate. Channel members are not directly involved in the exosystem, but these settings indirectly impact the channel member's goals, actions, and outcomes. There are many externalities in a channel exosystem. We address the multitude of exosystem factors in Part II of this text. However, let's consider one externality: the impact of information technology on channel members in the Net Economy.

The **World Wide Web** is a "virtual, many-to-many hypermedia environment incorporating interactivity with both people and computers." It may seem like the World Wide Web has been around forever. Yet, it has only been part of the U.S. marketplace since 1991. The Internet is at the core of the World Wide Web. The **Internet** is "a global network of networks enabling computers of all kinds to directly and transparently communicate and share services

EXHIBIT 1.3

Channels Relationship Model (CRM)

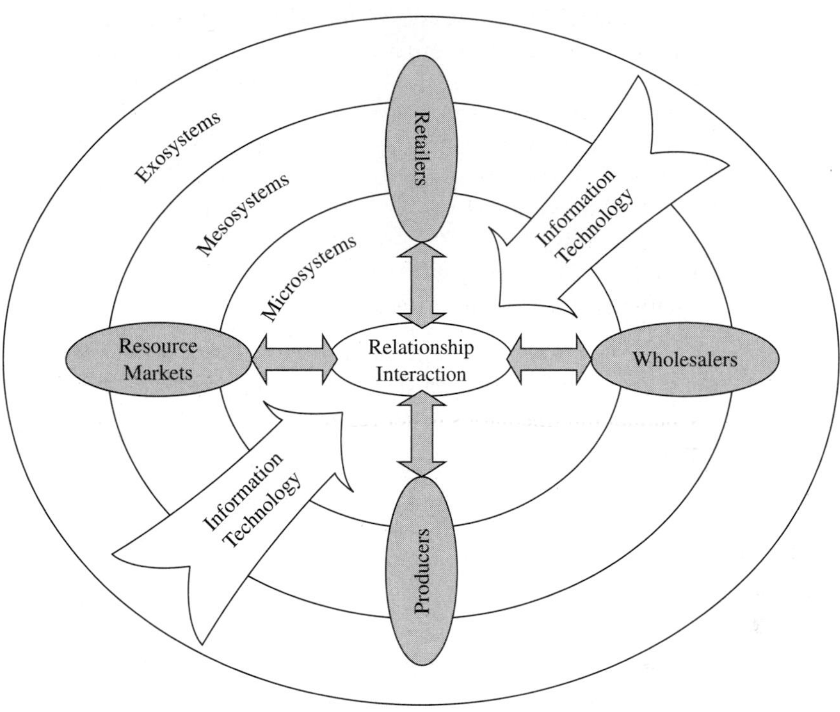

throughout much of the world."[31] There are countless examples of how the Internet has enabled direct and transparent communications between buyers and sellers.

Today, more than 600 million people worldwide account for nearly $1.3 trillion in electronic commerce. The Internet connects buyers and sellers, removing the distance obstacle to create a fluid exchange platform. The Internet is surely a major influence on suppliers, producers, retailers, and consumers. In Channel Surfing 1.3, we discuss how Web-enabled information search is driving built-to-order automobile sales. By 2005, more than 20 percent of all domestic automobile searches in the United States will be influenced by Web-enabled information searches.

The **channel microsystem** consists of the internal channels environment. The internal channels environment encompasses the role perceptions and expectations between channel members and the ensuing relationships that develop from those expectations. In Part III of the text, we discuss how attitudes, behaviors, and learning effectuate channel climates. Role perceptions and expectations can result in either positive or negative channel climates.

In the Net Economy, an ongoing conflict between manufacturers and their customers relates to direct-to-consumer sales. For instance, Sony is embroiled in a conflict with many of its best customers. Why? Sony angered retail customers by requiring them to sell Sony-labeled CDs that include hyperlinks to direct-sel.sony.com and (its partially owned) columbiahouse.com, which are direct-to-consumer sites that bypass leading retailers like Tower

Channel Surfing 1.3

Driving on the 21st-Century Virtual Highway

The next time you're cruising down the highway, you may take notice of the wide array of makes and models of vehicles that meet our transportation and lifestyle needs in the United States. In the 1970s, there were just over 100 models of cars and about three dozen pick-ups to choose from. Today, Americans enjoy nearly 300 vehicle models in more than 1200 different styles. There were about 40 styles of sport utility vehicles (SUVs) introduced in the U.S. market in the last 20 years. What's driving all of these choices? The notion of mass customization, propelled by Internet and other one-to-one information technologies.

We've come a long way from the basic black Model Ts that rolled off the assembly lines during the Production Era in the United States. Consider that Ford Motor alone offers a palette of nearly 50 colors. The one-time American icon now includes a family of brands that span the globe, including Aston-Martin, Jaguar, Mazda, and Volvo. In the Net Economy, buyers can customize the finishing touches on their next Ford by visiting www2.Ford.com. But it goes beyond cosmetic changes to simply color the world of automotive customization. Qualcomm has teamed with Ford to offer customers telephone, entertainment, and Internet services in their vehicles!

The trend toward customization is a newly traveled road in the automobile industry. According to a J. D. Powers study, only 7 percent of new vehicle buyers purchased a built-to-order (BTO) vehicle in 1999. Yet, 70 percent of consumers considered a BTO in that same year. Industry experts expect BTO vehicles to become an important part of the marketplace. By some estimates, BTO vehicles could comprise a significant chunk of the market.

BTO vehicles do not just offer customization to vehicle buyers; they also fuel marketing channel efficiency. Manufacturers and their suppliers can reduce costs associated with excess production, minimize incentive costs, and control inventories. Increased Internet connectivity coupled with consumers' growing confidence in online ordering is expected to have a fundamental impact on future vehicle buyers' behaviors.

Charles Mills, director of e-commerce strategy at J. D. Powers, notes that "Automotive consumers—perhaps all consumers—are showing greater activism in their desire to design, configure and order their products the way they want them . . . they are leveraging the aggregation and searching capabilities of the Net to conveniently take action on how they buy." This has serious implications for channel intermediaries: Dealerships will need to redefine their roles as online sales become a consequential avenue for purchasing automobiles. The future is fast approaching. About 10 percent of GM vehicles are BTO. The race is on to capture market share for the growing segment of BTO vehicle buyers!

Points to Ponder

- While there is a great deal of appeal to customizing a vehicle, what may impact your decision to buy your next car online?
- What value-added benefits do automobile dealerships currently provide? Do you expect that to change?

Source: Adapted from Gallop-Goodman, Gerda (2000), "The Right Fit: Built-to-Order Cars Fuel Consumer Interest," *American Demographics,* 22 (October, no. 10), 15.

Records. Stan Gorman, a Tower Records executive and chairman of the National Association of Recording Merchandisers (NARM) retorts, "I'm angry that after all Tower puts into helping Sony artists, these links are being used to drive sales at Sony stores instead of at our stores."[32]

The **channel mesosystem** involves the resource exchanges between channel members that result in formal organizational linkages. In the Net Economy, formal and informal linkages between channel members are vital to channel flows. You will recount the compound linkages in the distribution of restaurant specialty equipment at Blockbuy.com (see Channel Surfing 1.2). In Part IV of this book, we will explore vertical marketing systems, franchising, strategic alliances, and the economic exchange that underlie these channel systems.

Applying the CRM to Channels Strategy

Have you ever dropped a pebble in a still water creek? If so, you may have noticed the concentric circles that emanate in the water: a pattern of round circles, each enveloping the other. In the CRM (see Exhibit 1.3), you will recognize a similar pattern. These concentric circles, each representing a component of the marketing channels ecology, express the connectedness between a channel member and the environments in which it operates.

To illustrate how the CRM impacts real marketing channels strategy, let's play around in the mammoth worldwide toy industry. Within the $71 billion worldwide toy industry, there are several retail channels, including brick 'n mortar retailers like Wal-Mart and Toys "R" Us, as well as electronic retailers (a.k.a., e-tailers) like eToys.com and SmartKids.com. Despite the overwhelming impact of the Internet, traditional brick 'n mortar retailers are critical to any toy manufacturer. Wal-Mart is the leading retailer of toys in the United States, and Wal-Mart and Toys "R" Us combined account for about one-third of all toy sales in the $30 billion U.S. toy industry. Mergers and acquisitions have reduced the number of manufacturers in the toy industry, but there remains a great deal of disparity across toy manufacturers. Apart from industry giants like Hasbro and Mattel, there are thousands of very small manufacturers.

One such manufacturer is Table Toys, Inc., a small Texas-based toy maker that competes with the likes of Hasbro and Mattel for merchandising space. But it has been an uphill battle for this small toy maker. Its flagship table product was developed as a result of the channels microsystem: a true marriage of channel members. You see, the company's founder Donna Buske asked her husband to build a table to organize the Lego blocks scattered on the floor at the Houston day care center where she worked. Her husband, a furniture maker, returned with a wooden table equipped with a recessed basket for the loose blocks. That table eventually became the prototype for the popular Fun Tables and Play Tables that accommodate Lego blocks at doctors' offices, day care centers, and homes throughout the United States.

In spite of their creativity, however, the Buskes found it difficult to get their product on retail store shelves. For example, Toys "R" Us initially told them, "We don't talk to manufacturers and we don't look at prototypes." So the Buskes connected with a toy industry veteran who introduced the Buskes to a manufacturer's sales representative (intermediary). He, in turn, successfully forged relationships with other organizations, including Target and Toys "R" Us! Upon getting the orders, the Buskes then had to develop relationships with plastic molders to fill market demand.[33]

Indeed, the procurement of shelf space required a great deal of gamesmanship among the Buskes, their toy industry representative, and retailers. The development of formal agreements among retailers regarding order quantities, returns, and profit margins occurs within the channels mesosystem.

Today the Buskes face still another problem: copycats in the competitive environment. Many manufacturers are producing similar tables at lower cost. The Buskes will have to operate in the exosystem to maintain their competitive position in the marketplace just as they had to develop relationships between organizations.

Fundamental changes are currently unfolding in nearly all industries, and these changes are redefining the nature of the marketplace. The needs of industrial users and consumers are becoming increasingly sophisticated, to the point where many now insist on consultative and value-added partnerships rather than impersonal and brief encounters.[34] As Channel Surfing 1.3 illustrates, a variety of exchange relationships is critical to the development of customer value.

Creating Customer Value

Organizations take part in marketing channels because they receive a certain value, known as *exchange utility,* from their participation. **Exchange utility** is the sum of all costs and benefits realized separately or jointly by all the persons or organizations participating in an exchange relationship.

Four Components of Customer Value. For customers, marketing channels create form, place, possession, and time utilities. To illustrate how channels create utility, consider the seemingly routine purchase of a gallon of milk. Because of the value added by marketing channels, milk is available for immediate consumption in the form sought by consumers (e.g., skim, low-fat, or whole; white or chocolate; gallon or half-gallon). This creates *form utility. Place utility* saves buyers from having to go to the farm and find a cow when they need milk. *Possession utility* offers consumers a convenient way to take ownership of the product. Retail outlets usually have clearly established prices, eliminating the need to negotiate terms of sale. The presence of *time utility* implies that goods and services will be available when they are needed. Milk shortages are thankfully rare. Consequently, few of us think about the complicated system of flows that are responsible for bringing milk from farms to kitchens.

In another industry, American Hospital Supply Corporation (AHSC) pioneered a computerized system that routinely orders, tracks, and manages the flow of each item it sells. This system links AHSC directly to thousands of its customers. The value of such a system in an industry that is so concerned with cost control is obvious. In addition, the system enables AHSC to strengthen customer relationships in an extremely competitive market through this technological connection to its customers. Inland Steel and General Foods have adopted similar systems to safeguard their market positions.[35]

Maintaining Customer Relationships. Investing in efforts to maintain existing customers is far more cost efficient than investing in attracting new customers. In fact, businesses spend 10 times more money attracting new customers than they do to keep existing ones. This is one reason why companies like Coca-Cola take customer service so seriously. Coke's Industry and Consumer Affairs Department handles over one-half million customer complaints each year by mail and through its toll-free hotline. Dissatisfied customers receive a letter of apology for the problem and coupons that can be used to replace any unsatisfactory purchase. Follow-up questionnaires are mailed two weeks later to measure customer perceptions of the effectiveness of Coke's response. Coke "strives to exceed customer expectations *every* time."[36]

About 70 percent of complaining customers will continue doing business with an organization if they perceive the problem has been resolved in their favor. Typically, the newly satisfied customer then spreads the good word to about five other people. Given such word-of-mouth communication, it is obvious that the way problems within the customer-supplier relationship are resolved has far-reaching ramifications. And the opportunity to develop long-term customer relations is not limited to product manufacturers or suppliers. For instance, American and United Airlines have each developed their own ticketing and reservation systems. These systems generate information that they subsequently use to fashion unique customer alliances within the highly price-competitive air travel industry.

Products and Services Flows

In the past, channels management almost exclusively focused on the activities necessary to acquire goods and services.[37] However, the activities associated with the other two stages of exchange between producers and consuming organizations in marketing channels—consumption and disposition—should not be overlooked.

Acquisition. **Acquisition** involves the acts by which channel entities obtain products and services. Professional contract-purchasing (PCP) organizations are an emerging force in marketing channels. These organizations provide their customers with increased purchasing power by connecting them to established networks featuring, in some industries, thousands of suppliers. Teams of PCP specialists save clients time and money by eliminating costly details associated with order processing and price shopping. As a result, their clients can often free up capital and labor resources which they can then redirect to more profitable operations.[38] Marketing channels are also changing in response to the increasing number of alliances that have emerged between purchasing firms and their suppliers. These alliances are becoming popular as tools for carving out competitive advantages.[39]

In marketing channels, the act of **consumption** involves the utilization of resource inputs (goods and services) in the production of resource outputs. Consumption in marketing channels is typically evaluated as a function of materials management. That is, consumption activities relate to how materials and information flow from the point of production to the final user. Increasingly in marketing channels, products and services are being consumed in new and different ways.

A growing practice known as **outsourcing** lies behind many of these changes. Outsourcing occurs when companies hire outside providers to assist them in any of a variety of business practices. The use of outsourcing has grown as manufacturers and suppliers face the need to replace outdated technologies while maintaining customer satisfaction. Organizations who use outsourcing gain updated technological links to customers without a significant upfront investment.[40]

The unprecedented adoption of outsourcing has precipitated the development of a new, dominant channel role: extramediaries or outside suppliers. **Extramediaries** are highly specialized organizations that fill value gaps in the channels of distribution. They operate tangentially to existing channel members and have flourished to over $88 billion in sales in the Net Economy. Why use extramediaries? Why not merely fill the value gaps within the channel organization? The answer is twofold:

- Extramediaries bear the cost of infrastructure and processing associated with these value gaps. By providing the same (or similar) services for many channel members, they are able to achieve economies of scale not afforded to any individual organization.

- Extramediaries allow manufacturers, wholesalers, and retailers to focus on their core competencies.

Electronics companies worldwide are selling off factories, outsourcing manufacturing, after-sales services, and even product design. To illustrate, let's navigate south of the border to Guadalajara, Mexico, home of a burgeoning manufacturing campus. At the heart of this massive manufacturing campus is Flextronics—an extramediary that produces components for electronics manufacturers. Flextronics has been the beneficiary of the 21st-century shift toward outsourcing everything from manufacturing to logistics. Chairman Michael E. Marks forecasts that Flextronics will become a $50 billion business by 2005.[41]

What is the downside of the major shift toward extramediaries? Channel members are entrusting valuable intellectual property and customer information with these barons of outsourcing. This is never more evident than in the case of Dallas-based Electronic Data Systems (EDS), the outsource pioneer founded by billionaire Ross Perot. EDS prospered by providing services to the data-processing operations of a broadly diversified client base. But EDS's longstanding market dominance is currently being challenged by competitors offering lower prices. For example, IBM's Integrated Systems Solutions is now poised to capture a share of this market. A new generation of smaller and mid-sized information outsourcers are also currently establishing their own niches within the lucrative banking, health care, and telecommunication industries. Perot's flagship operation may have to shift its emphasis to management consulting to help renew its channel relationships.[42]

Disposition. At some point, all entities who have participated in channels relationships must engage in the act of disposition. **Disposition** refers to all behaviors or activities associated with channel members' efforts to detach themselves from tangible and intangible goods.[43] Many firms have developed relationships with specialists who understand environmental regulations, hazardous waste treatment, and physical plant safety. These responses have been prompted by what is either a genuine concern for the environment or a logical concern for what may happen to firms who appear unconcerned with the environment. Regardless, Resource Management Inc. (RMI) has taken advantage of these concerns. RMI's principal purpose is to assist public and private sector organizations in the removal and treatment of asbestos.[44]

When recycling products, consumers become de facto producers, supplying manufacturers with presorted materials that reenter production systems as inputs in the creation of new products. This process has become known as **reverse logistics.** Have you ever taken aluminum cans to a recycling center? By doing so, you took part in one of the many marketing channels for recycled goods.

The CRM: Compass Points

This textbook takes you on a journey through marketing channels principles and practice from a relationship marketing perspective. Each of the major ideas and themes examined in the rest of this book is grounded either directly or indirectly in the Channels Relationship Model (CRM). The CRM is illustrated at the beginning of this text and again in Exhibit 1.3. The CRM captures many aspects of the interplay among channel members and the environment in which they operate and their leveraging of economic and information resources.

- The relationship between a channel member and its *exosystem* is shown in the CRM and is addressed in Part II of the textbook. Part II investigates how various macroenvironmental forces such as economic, technological, political, legal, ethical, and sociocultural dynamics affect channel members' goal-oriented activities.
- The relationship between a channel member and its *microsystem* is shown in the model and is addressed in Part III. In Part III, we critically assess the setting (atmosphere) in which social and economic interactions between channel members take place. Part III also considers the social issues and problems which beset the relationship process: coordination, conflict, and cooperation.
- In Part IV, the channels *mesosystem* is discussed. Part IV discusses vertical integration in marketing channels, the emerging role of franchising, and strategic partnering agreements.

Before we proceed, however, we need to develop a framework for this discussion by considering the individual channel member and the marketplace in which it operates. We will do this in the remainder of Part I.

In the first half of this chapter, we introduced you to the fiercely competitive setting of rowing crews. Rowing crews rely on speed, endurance, and savvy to compete against other teams in a race where the difference between success and failure is usually measured in only hundredths of a second. Likewise, channel members must be equipped to contend in a fiercely competitive marketplace. In Chapter 2, we will discuss how channel members strive for a competitive advantage in a dynamic marketplace.

Key Terms

acquisition
channel exosystem
channel intermediary
channel mesosystem
channel microsystem
consumption
contactual efficiency
customer relationship management
disposition
dyadic relationship
exchange utility
extramediaries
Internet
marketing channel
mission statement
outsourcing
reverse logistics
routinization
sorting
World Wide Web

Chapter Summary

Historically, marketing channels have been viewed as a bridge between producers and users of goods and services. While these same bridges exist in the Network Economy, information technologies, globalization, and new market structures are reshaping the nature and scope of marketing channels. Accordingly, the "bridge" perspective fails to capture the complex network of relationships that facilitate marketing flows. Consider the impact of the Internet where more than 600 million buyers and sellers transact over $1.3 trillion in marketing exchanges. The Internet and other information technologies are making one-to-one, interactive dialogues a mainstay of buyer-seller exchanges.

Marketing and distribution were inextricably intertwined at the beginning of the 20th century. As the Production Era of marketing emerged, the demand for middlemen increased. In a historical sense, these middlemen contributed substantially to the movement of goods and people from rural areas to new industrialized urban centers. By the 1940s, when the Selling Era in marketing began, a new sort of middlemen—now known as intermediaries—had surfaced in the marketplace. Large retailers expanded further, while smaller retailers generally settled into unserved or underserved market niches. The Selling Era rather quickly gave way to the Marketing Concept Era. The increasingly widespread recognition of the importance of the marketing concept during the latter half of this century has been paralleled by an emerging behavioral thrust in marketing channels.

Since the core of marketing is the exchange process, marketing channels can be viewed as *exchange facilitators.* This allows marketing channels to be defined as an array of exchange relationships that creates customer value in the acquisition, consumption, or disposition of goods and services. Exchange relationships, and thus marketing channels themselves, emerge from market needs as a way of more efficiently serving market needs. Exchange utility is the sum of all costs and benefits recognized by the exchange parties. Utility can feature form, place, possession, and time dimensions.

This broadened definition of marketing channels offers several advantages: (1) it allows marketing channels to be studied as behavioral systems, (2) it extends the scope of the functions performed within marketing channels to include those involved with usage and disposition, and (3) it illustrates the trade-off of costs and benefits that inevitably occur in exchange relationships.

A sense of shared purpose connects organizations and individuals in the marketplace. This is also true of marketing channels. For this reason, the activity known as *channels management* can be viewed as the point at which an organization's mission and the market(s) it serves come together. An organization's mission is its strategic charter that describes the ways the firm will seize market opportunities while satisfying the needs of internal and external customers. A mission statement also describes *whom* the firm intends to serve, *how* it intends to serve them, and *what* means will be used to establish competitive advantages in the market(s) of interest. Toward this end, the overriding mission of channel intermediaries is to serve as middlemen. But this role should be broadly defined—for any organization or individual whose mediate exchange is a middleman. Channel intermediaries serve four key functions: to promote contactual efficiency and routinization, to provide assortment, and to minimize uncertainty.

In the Net Economy, there is a significant shift toward outsourcing nonessential services that were traditionally provided by producers and channel intermediaries. These outside sources are called *extramediaries.* They fill value gaps to enhance channel relationships, and they generally bear the costs of infrastructure and processing associated with the provision of these value-added benefits. Extramediaries allow manufacturers, wholesalers, and retailers to focus on their core competencies.

A contemporary relationship-oriented approach to the study of marketing channels is adopted in this book. A Channels Relationship Model (CRM) serves as a framework for presenting the material addressed throughout the text. The CRM intentionally is also an acronym for *customer relationship management,* the backbone of contemporary marketing channels practice. The CRM is an ecological framework, illuminating the effect of environmental influences on channel member development. There are three major environments that are entrenched in the CRM: channels exosystems, microsystems, and mesosystems. Through the CRM, the role of channel environments, channel climates, and interaction processes in fostering business relationships is investigated. The CRM perspective will ultimately enable you to better understand how exchange partners can achieve their strategic aims through interacting in marketing channels and dynamic marketplaces.

Channel Challenges

1. In 1915, Harvard University Professor Arch Shaw stated that the "most pressing problem in marketing . . . is systematically to study distribution." As the new millennium approaches, how has the broadened perspective of the marketing channel embraced the changing marketplace? Could one now say that the most pressing problem in marketing is the systematic study of *exchange relationships?*
2. The emergence of a Virtual Economy challenges buyers and sellers alike to re-think the notion of marketing exchange. Historically, physical proximity between buyers and sellers adjured an economics of exchange based largely on spatial utility. The physical closeness between buyers and sellers facilitated efficiency by matching market offerings with market needs. How do you see the notion of marketing exchange evolving from the early 1900s to today's Virtual Economy?
3. Many of us are accustomed to using automated teller machines (ATMs) for our banking. ATMs demonstrate how technology can foster *exchange utility*. Several thousand retailers across the United States are expanding the ATM principle. They have "scrip ATMs," which issue receipts that may be redeemed for merchandise. The receipts are drawn against the customer's checking account. Retailers view these machines as a way to build business. In what way(s) may these scrip machines provide exchange utility for customers? Would you characterize the scrip ATMs as a marketing channel?
4. There is a Japanese proverb which states, "The go-between wears a thousand sandals." How does this proverb support or refute the functions of channel intermediaries?
5. IKEA is a multinational group of wholesaling and retailing firms in the home furnishings industry. It was initially established as a mail-order marketer in the 1950s in Sweden. Since then, it has experienced spectacular growth. Today, IKEA represents a multitude of suppliers and distributors stretching from the United States to the Far East. This complex network of distribution channels has been cited as IKEA's competitive advantage. IKEA can be considered an expert on initiating, developing and, if required, settling supplier relationships. How can the IKEA network of exchange relationships be likened to a rowing team? What is the role of each player in IKEA's overall competitive advantage?

Review Questions

1. How do information technologies and globalization impact the nature and scope of marketing channels in the Network Economy?
2. How is the role of an organizational mission critical for marketing channel management?
3. How does a rowing team epitomize the characteristics of successful marketing channels?
4. Describe the exchange processes of acquisition, consumption, and disposition as they relate to a marketing channel.
5. How do the four characteristics of marketing channels relate to the exchange process?
6. What is the compelling role of spatial utility in the evolution of marketing channels?
7. Discuss how marketing channels functionally relate to real-world market settings.
8. How do marketing channels develop?
9. Describe the stages of the historical evolution of marketing channels in the United States.
10. Discuss the CRM model of marketing channel transactions.

Endnotes

1. Pelton, Lou E. (2001), "Navigating the Three Cs: Continuity, Collaboration, and Coordination," *Journal of Marketing Channels,* 8 (112), 1–3.
2. Lewis, Edwin E. (1968), *Marketing Channels: Structure and Strategy,* Perspectives in Marketing Series, Robert D. Buzzell and Frank M. Bass, eds., New York, NY: McGraw-Hill, 2.
3. McCammon, Bert C., and Robert W. Little (1965), "Marketing Channels: Analytical Systems and Approaches," an excerpt in *Marketing Channels & Institutions: Readings on Distribution Concepts & Practices,* Bruce J. Walker and Joel B. Haynes, eds., Columbus, OH: Grid, Inc.
4. Alderson, Wroe (1957), *Marketing Behavior and Executive Action,* Homewood, IL: Richard D. Irwin; Bagozzi, Richard P. (1975), "Marketing as Exchange," *Journal of Marketing,* 50 (April), 81–87; Blau, Peter M. (1967), *Exchange and Power in Social Life,* New York, NY: John Wiley & Sons; and Weber, Max (1974), *The Theory of Social and Economic Organization,* New York, NY: Oxford University Press.
5. Bagozzi, Richard P. (1979), "Toward a Formal Theory of Marketing Exchange," *Conceptual and Theoretical Developments in Marketing,* O. C. Ferrell, Stephen W. Brown, and Charles W. Lamb, Jr., eds., Chicago, IL: American Marketing Association.
6. Bartels, Robert (1988), *The Development of Marketing Thought,* Third Edition, Columbus, OH: Publishing Horizons; and Stock, James R., and Kathleen R. Whitney (1989), "A Historical Assessment of the Development of the Discipline of Logistics: An Appraisal and a Critique," in *Proceedings of the Fourth Conference on Historical Research in Marketing: The Emerging Discipline,* Terence Nevitt, Kathleen R. Whitney, and Stanley C. Hollander, eds., Lansing, MI: Michigan State University, 54–73.
7. Many large retailing establishments emerged prior to the 20th century. R. H. Macy & Company (1858), John Wanamaker (1861), and F. W. Woolworth (1879), to name a few, were a response to the shifts in population to urban centers. The problems of the flows of goods and services (between rural and urban areas) are demonstrated by the formation of two general-mail houses, Montgomery Ward (1872) and Sears Roebuck (1886). For a more in-depth discussion, refer to Brisco, Norris A. (1947), *Retailing,* New York, NY: Prentice Hall.
8. Duddy, Edward A., and David A. Revzan (1947), *Marketing: An Institutional Approach,* New York, NY: McGraw-Hill.
9. Shaw, Arch (1915), "Some Problems in Market Distribution," *Quarterly Journal of Economics* (August), 706–65.
10. Harris, William D., and James R. Stock (1985), "Reintegration of Marketing and Distribution: A Historical and Future Perspective," in *Proceedings of the Second Conference on Historical Research in Marketing* (April), Lansing, MI: Michigan State University, 420–440.
11. Boone, Louis E., and David L. Kurtz (1992), *Contemporary Marketing,* Seventh Edition, Fort Worth, TX: Dryden Press.
12. McCarthy, E. Jerome (1971), *Basic Marketing: A Managerial Approach,* Fourth Edition, Burr Ridge, IL: Richard D. Irwin.
13. Brion, John M. (1965), *Marketing through the Wholesaler-Distributor Channel,* Marketing for Executives Series #10, Chicago, IL: American Marketing Association, 53.
14. For an interesting account of the evolution of the retailing trade industries, see Bucklin, Louis P. (1972), *Competition and Evolution in the Distributive Trades,* Englewood Cliffs, NJ: Prentice Hall; and Dean, James W. Jr., and James R. Evans (1994), *Total Quality: Management, Organization and Strategy,* St. Paul, MN: West Publishing.
15. Iacobucci, Dawn (1994), "Toward Defining Relationship Marketing," in *Relationship Marketing: Theory, Methods and Applications,* Proceedings of the 1994 Relationship Marketing Research Conference, Jagdish N. Sheth and Atul Parvatiyar, eds., Atlanta: Goizueta Business School.
16. Grönroos, Christan (1990), "Relationship Approach to Marketing in Service Contexts: The Marketing and Organizational Behavior Interface," in *Journal of Business Research,* 20 (January), 3–11.
17. Charlier, Marj (1995), "Beer Brouhaha: Existing Distributors Are Being Squeezed by Brewers, Retailers; Biggest Discounters, Chains Seek Ways to Eliminate 'Middlemen' Wholesalers Trend Worries Little Guys," *The Wall Street Journal,* November 22, A1.
18. Tenner, Arthur R., and Irving J. DeToro (1992), *Total Quality Management: Three Steps to Continuous Improvement,* Reading, MA: Addison-Wesley.

19. Oberhaus, Mary Ann, Sharon Ratliffe, and Vernon Stauble (1993), *Professional Selling: A Relationship Process,* Fort Worth, TX: Dryden Press, 47.
20. Bowersox, Donald J. and M. Bixby Cooper (1992), *Strategic Marketing Channel Management,* New York, NY: McGraw-Hill.
21. Adapted from McGee, Suzanne (1995), "Commodities: Coffee Prices Plunge to Lowest Levels Since June," *The Wall Street Journal,* C14.
22. Alderson, Wroe (1957), *Marketing Behavior and Executive Action,* Burr Ridge, IL: Richard D. Irwin.
23. Durant, Will (1944), *The Story of Civilization: Part III, Caesar and Christ,* New York, NY: Simon and Schuster, 328.
24. Smith, Mickey C. (1991), *Pharmaceutical Marketing: Strategy and Cases,* Binghamton, NY: Pharmaceutical Products Press, 252–64.
25. Adapted from Cook, Kathleen, and Glenn L. Habern (1987), "In-Store Systems Improving Profitability," *Retail Control,* 55 (December), 11–13; Gebhart, Fred (1992), "Harder Times Hit California Wholesale/Retail Leaders," *Drug Topics,* 136 (January 20), 58; and Clemons, Eric K., and Michael Row (1988), "A Strategic Information System: McKesson Drug Company's Economost," *Planning Review,* 16 (September/October), 14–19.
26. Adapted from Stern, Louis W., and Adel El-Ansary (1992), *Marketing Channels,* Fourth Edition, Englewood Cliffs, NJ: Prentice Hall.
27. Fuller, Joseph B., James O'Conor, and Richard Rawlinson (1993), "Tailored Logistics: The Next Advantage," *Harvard Business Review,* May/June, 89.
28. Adapted from Häkansson, Hakan, J. Johanson, and B. Wootz (1976), "Influence Tactics in Buyer-Seller Processes," *Industrial Marketing Management,* 4 (September), 319–22.
29. Fuller, O'Conor, and Rawlinson (1993), "Tailored Logistics," 93.
30. Ibid., 92. While the article largely concentrates on logistics, the position is taken that these criteria are generalizable to all marketing channel functions.
31. Hoffman, Donna L., and Thomas P. Novak (1997), "A New Marketing Paradigm for Electronic Commerce," *The Information Society,* 13, 43.
32. See http://www.marketingprofs.com/emarketing/sonyconflict.asp.
33. Johannes, Laura (1993), "Texas Journal: Babes in Toyland: A Tale of a Start-Up," *The Wall Street Journal,* December 22, T3.
34. Anderson, David (1986), "Case Studies and Implementations of LDI Arrangements (Part II)," *Data Communications,* 15 (February), 173–82; and Short, James E., and N. Venkatraman (1992), "Beyond Business Process Redesign: Redefining Baxter's Business Network," *Sloan Management Review,* 34 (Fall), 7–20.
35. Adapted from Dean, James W., Jr., and James R. Evans (1994), *Total Quality: Management, Organization and Strategy,* St Paul, MN: West Publishing.
36. LeBoeuf, Michael (1987), *How to Win Customers and Keep Them for Life,* New York, NY: Putnam's Sons.
37. This conclusion is based on the definitions of marketing channels. One example is the definition proffered by Stern, Louis W., and Adel El-Ansary (1992): "sets of interdependent organizations involved in the process of making a product or service available for use or consumption," in *Marketing Channels,* Englewood Cliffs, NJ: Prentice Hall.
38. Pupis, Patricia M. (1991), "Purchasing Firms Handle Myriad Details of Design," *Hotel & Motel Management,* 206 (November 4), D6.
39. Gentry, Julie J. (1993), "Strategic Alliances in Purchasing: Transportation Is the Vital Link," *International Journal of Purchasing & Materials Management,* 29 (Summer), 11–17.
40. Verity, John W. (1992), "They Make a Killing Minding Other People's Business," *Business Week,* November 30, 96.
41. Engardio, Pete (2000), "The Barons of Outsourcing," *Business Week,* August 28, 177–78.
42. Willey, David (1993), "Who's Outsourcing What," *Journal of Business Strategy,* 15 (May/June), 54–55.
43. Young, Melissa Martin, and Mellanie Wallendorf (1989), "Ashes to Ashes, Dust to Dust: Conceptualizing Consumer Disposition of Possessions," in *Marketing Theory and Practice,* Terry Childers et al., eds., Chicago, IL: American Marketing Association, 33–39.
44. DeLizzio, James T. (1990), "Borrower's Viewpoint . . . What an Environmental Company Needs from Its Lender," *Journal of Commercial Banking,* 72 (January), 23–32.

chapter

2

Channel Roles in a Virtual Marketplace

Learning Objectives

After reading this chapter, you should be able to:

- Discuss the impact of the Internet on channel roles.
- Relate role identity to channel member performance.
- Compare and contrast the wholesaling and retailing channel functions.
- Identify major trends in the wholesaling and retailing sectors.
- Demonstrate how SIFTing can be used to establish differential advantage in the marketplace.
- Explain the perils and promise of disintermediation in marketing channels.

Courtesy Visteon

In Chapter 1, **we** started our journey in Vienna, Austria. Now let's visit another European city to demonstrate how information technology and globalization are impacting marketing channel roles in the Net Economy. Born in September 1997 at the Frankfurt Motor Show, this channel member has grown beyond its years. It is now larger than many Fortune 500 companies. With over 80,000 employees in 23 countries and $19 billion in annual revenues, it rivals global marketing giants like Eastman Kodak, Federal Express, and McDonalds. But you won't find any snapshots, any freight jets, or even burgers in this company's inventory. You see, Visteon is the second-largest automotive supplier in the world—not bad for an adolescent in the competitive automobile supply industry!

A descendent of the Ford Motor Company, Visteon is a full-service supplier of technology solutions to 18 of the 20 largest automotive manufacturers worldwide. Clearly, the development of electronic channels of distribution has fueled Visteon's growth. Through multiple channels—including a prominent Web-based bidding and ordering system—Visteon may be called a "Phat Cat" in the global marketplace. No, there's no spelling oversight. Among Visteon's rich inventory of automotive technology solutions, it is teaming with PhatNoise, an award-winning multimedia platform provider, to introduce an awesome vehicle audio system that can play up to 4,000 high-quality digital audio tracks. The PhatNoise MACH MP3 Jukebox provides drivers access to a massive digital music collection at their fingertips, all without the hassles of replacing their current car stereos.

Visteon's product portfolio includes dynamic seating systems, voice technologies, hands-free entry systems, and air bag deployment systems, as well as thousands of other automotive supplies. It is a virtual one-stop marketplace for anything automotive. Visteon's products are centered around comfort, convenience, safety, and security, and they are changing the driving experience in tomorrow's vehicles. Visteon has even ventured into biometrics, fingerprint identification systems that match drivers' preferences to their vehicles.

Visteon does not boast a go-it-alone strategy. Much of its success can be linked to channel partnerships with technology affiliates like Microsoft, Intel, Nintendo, Texas Instruments, Fujitsu, SAP, Sumitomo, and Motorola. In most channel systems, a lot can be said about the company that you keep. In today's integrated network of marketing channels, channel roles are deep-seated in their relationships with channel partners. The challenge for channel members is developing and maintaining an identity that is focused on their customers' needs.[1]

* * * *

Channel members must evolve to meet the demands of an ever-changing marketplace. As the number of people in U.S. households who go online continues to rise, traditional bricks 'n mortar retailers are adjusting their channel roles. With active Internet users approaching 75 million, it is no wonder that OldNavy.com, ToysRUs.com, Target.com, VictoriasSecret.com, and Walmart.com are popular shopping sites. But would founder Sam Walton have ever imagined Wal-Mart as a virtual retail site with partners like American Greetings and Southwest Airlines?

Channel members need to continually monitor the environment in which they operate, and tailor their identities to changing market needs. This ultimately involves capitalizing on internal strengths and identifying external opportunities. As Visteon founding president Charlie Szuluk summarized, "We always knew we had the energy and the talent. All we needed was a focus and a well-organized structure. Visteon's spirit comes, in part, from a great history and its understanding of the future."[2]

The Channels Relationship Model (CRM) illustrates the complex environments in which channel members operate. The CRM connects each distinctive channel role and recognizes that channel members collectively thrive on both proprietary and shared information. The connectivity between organizations in any channel system is a major part of Visteon's positioning strategy.

In the dog-eat-dog marketplace, bigger is not necessarily better. As a result, small-volume channel members like neighborhood cafés, specialized distributors, and low-volume producers are able to survive in highly competitive markets. As Dwight D. Eisenhower, 34th president of the United States, aptly noted, "What counts is not necessarily the size of the dog in the fight—it's the size of the fight in the dog." In this vein, there are three possible outcomes derived from the CRM:

- **Competitive superiority.** A particular species (or channel member) may emerge as *competitively superior.* This superiority can force rival species into extinction as competitors for limited resources are eliminated. This is the essence of the Darwinian concept called "survival of the fittest." Transportation industry channels are littered with the carcasses of companies, such as Pan American Airlines, who failed to change as their competitive environments changed.

- **Restrictive ranges.** The competitive advantages of any species (or channel member) may differ across distinctive environmental conditions. Thus, another possible outcome is that some species prosper in one place while others flourish in different domains. This process is known as *range restriction.* Ideally, each species recognizes its limitations in any environment, then chooses to compete in the setting most conducive to its well-being. For instance, Sears recently recognized that its expertise (and future) lay in retailing, and pulled out of the financial services industry. Realistically, however, many species fail to recognize the perils of their current environment until after it is too late to act.
- **Character displacement.** The final possible result is that species (or channel members) rapidly evolve in diverse ways, taking on different properties to minimize direct competition. This is called *character displacement.* It suggests that each corporate species must continuously adapt to dynamic channel environments. Harried grocery shoppers are increasingly turning toward businesses like Groceryworks.com, an online virtual supermarket that currently offers grocery and gourmet products.

These outcomes promote role specialization in competitive channel environments. In this chapter, we will discuss the types of roles that develop out of interspecific competition. First, however, we need to look at the behaviors that channel members must develop in response to the strengths and weaknesses of other firms. They must also respond to opportunities and threats in the environment itself. Over time, these adaptive behaviors may become nearly instinctive.

Channel Behaviors in Competitive Environments

Children know lions as kings of the jungle, predators activated by instinct to eat their prey. However, a lion's behavior is neither static nor mindless. For example, circus lions quickly adapt to their environment, recognizing that good performances bring more food. Even apparently disadvantaged animals survive the literal jungles of the animal kingdom. By anyone's standards, giraffes are awkward. Yet evolution has enabled them to obtain food—tree leaves—available only to them. Giraffes' long necks also provide them with an enhanced sensory system that warns them of predators.[3]

Distinguishing features allow animals to survive as long as their environments do not change too drastically. However, it is not always enough just to be equipped with tools for survival. Most higher-order organisms also must rely on other animals to exist. They live together with others of their species because cooperation can prevent extinction.[4]

The advantages of cooperation are embedded in the CRM. In the CRM, the arrow connecting channel members to one another suggests that coexistence, or partnering, is necessary to successfully meet the challenges of channel environments, as are shared concern and diversity.

Competing in a Virtual Marketplace

Bruce Henderson, chairman of the Boston Consulting Group, advises that competition explains how different businesses can exist in the same economic community by occupying different niches. Like any living organism, each business must set itself apart in some meaningful way to endure and prosper in competitive markets. Henderson suggests: "Consider Sears, Kmart, Wal-Mart, and Radio Shack. These stores overlap in the merchandise they sell, the customers they serve, and the areas where they operate. But to survive, each of these retailers has had to differentiate itself in important ways."[5]

Wal-Mart and Kmart have certainly differentiated their operations from other retail competitors. In lieu of traditional promotional sale pricing, both adopted an everyday low price strategy. The character of their businesses also evolved in response to changing environments during the past few years. Wal-Mart and Kmart each extended their product mix to better satisfy new or anticipated customer needs. Kmart, Wal-Mart, and Target, traditional general merchandise discounters, have aggressively added groceries to their shelves. And this repositioning has increased customer traffic and gross sales. Consumers can buy everything from athletic shoes to frozen pizza from these retailers. Today, there are more than 800 Wal-Mart Supercenters generating nearly $40 billion in sales in the United States. Wal-Mart has been successful in achieving the **halo effect**—the transfer of retail patronage from its traditional, general merchandise stores to the retail food sector. Super Target and Big Kmart are enjoying similar success in the retail food business. Even deep discounters that target lower-income shoppers are following these mega-discounters' lead. Family Dollar and Dollar General are increasing their food offerings, as well.

What impact have these nontraditional food retailers had on the marketplace? By some estimates, over $62 billion in food sales now channel through nontraditional food outlets such as warehouse clubs, mass merchandise stores, and drug chain discounters. Over 12 percent of the current food retailing market is expected to shift to nontraditional retailers in the next few years. These dollars will come directly from the market share currently held by conventional grocers.

In the Net Economy, shoppers don't have to leave home to get everything from fresh produce to fully prepared dinners. Instead, they can access newcomer home-delivery retailers with virtual grocery stores online like Groceryworks.com, Peapod.com, YourGrocer.com, and Webvan.com. However, don't discount your traditional supermarkets. Safeway is an equity partner in privately held Groceryworks.com, and it co-brands its Randall's and Tom Thumb stores on the Groceryworks.com site. The Internet is replete with specialty groceries, as well. For example, Kosherfoods.com is the world's largest kosher supermarket, offering everything from gefilte fish to kosher wines.

Traditional grocery chains plan to lower certain prices by as much as 12 percent to combat the mega-discounters' strategies. Some supermarket chains are considering the introduction of their own warehouse club stores. Others are reemphasizing the quality of supermarket services. For example, Dominick's Finer Foods, a major supermarket in the Chicago area, competes head-to-head with Wal-Mart by proclaiming "Not for Members Only" in its advertising.[6] New channel lifeforms are emerging to meet changing marketplace needs and in response to competitive pressures. Below, we explore the ways in which these lifeforms take shape. In Channel Surfing 2.1, feast on new marketing channels for your favorite restaurant foods.

Changing Environments: A Shared Concern

In the global ecosystem, each species has evolved in reaction to changing environmental conditions to achieve its current position. Channel members likewise must adapt to attain or

Channel Surfing 2.1

Austria's Prize Chef in Your Local Grocer's Freezer?

He began his training at the age of 14 as a hotel chef, requiring him to leave Austria to apprentice at L'Ousteau de Baumaniere in Provence, France. Not long after showcasing his culinary creativity at the Hotel de Paris in Monaco and Maxim's in Paris, Wolfgang Puck migrated to the United States. In 1982, Puck established the trendy, chic Sunset Boulevard restaurant, Spago's. At Spago's, chic diners feasted on Wolfgang Puck's gourmet pizzas.

These gourmet pizzas are the signature dishes at Wolfgang Puck Pizza Cafes, located in such diverse settings as select Macy's Department Stores and the University of Southern California campus. No need to travel to Austria, France, or even select U.S. cities to enjoy Puck's premier pizzas. Now you can enjoy these Wolfgang Puck pizzas in your own home. Wolfgang Puck Food Co. is joining a host of other restaurants that are packaging their products for grocers' shelves, refrigerated sections, and freezers. The insurgence of restaurant-brand foods in the grocery segment is an example of channel members adapting to ever-changing market demands.

Not in the mood for pizza? Wolfgang Puck is not alone in pursuing nontraditional channels to increase sales revenues. Fast-food restaurants like Nathan's Famous, Taco Bell, and White Castle are also packaging varied product lines in grocery stores throughout the United States. Old-line operators like Friendly's and TCBY are joining newcomers like Starbucks and The Cheesecake Factory to fight for valuable grocery shelf space. Peter Stack, Taco Bell's vice president of public affairs, acknowledges: "Consumers are now expecting access to their favorite products—the ones they know and love—everywhere, not just in the traditional restaurant locations." The National Restaurant Association confirms that U.S. consumers continue to desire more convenience, less cooking, and greater spontaneity.

Undoubtedly, consumers' changing lifestyles present a monumental opportunity for restaurant-branded foods: "Meals away from home" are approaching 50 percent of total food dollar expenditures in the United States. And restaurants with strong brand identities are cashing in. Friendly Ice Cream stores currently distribute desserts in 5,000 supermarkets, accounting for about 10 percent of its total sales.

What about cannibalization? These restaurants are finding that the nontraditional outlets complement existing marketing channels. TCBY's Stacy Duckett says, "Without question, those sales in grocery outlets, including our own products and private-label sales, have been a big growth area for our company. In many markets where we have put branded items in retail grocery and club store locations, we have actually seen increases in sales at TCBY stores." Wolfgang Puck agrees that the mass merchandising of his pizzas has not hindered consumer patronage at his restaurants like Chinois, Granita, Postrio, and Spago's. The Net Economy offers another marketing channel for Puck. Online groceries feature many restaurant brands, and it looks like this Puck is headed for the Net, as well.

Points to Ponder

- With Wolfgang Puck and Pizzeria Uno in your local grocers' freezers, what recommendations might you offer to home-delivery pizza retailers like Domino's, Pizza Hut, and Pappa John's Pizza?
- Brands that succeed in restaurant sales may be the best crossover opportunities for grocers. How does this merchandising affect grocery stores' private-label products (that traditionally offer higher margins)?

Source: Adapted from Papiernik, Richard L. (1999), "Shopping for Dollars: Chains Expand Brand to Supermarkets," *Nation's Restaurant News,* 33 (April 5, no. 14), 46–48; and www.wolfgangpuck.com.

maintain desirable positions in increasingly competitive markets.[7] In this process of adaptation, each channel member attempts to differentiate itself from other members operating at the same level. Manufacturers attempt to distinguish themselves from other producers, wholesalers from other wholesalers, and retailers from other retailers. Each is pursuing a **differential advantage.** Differential advantages emerge from an organization's distinctive characteristics, if these properties set it apart from competitors in ways that prove enticing to customers. Consider the following:

- Gitman Brothers, a major retailer of private-label shirts in the United States, distinguished itself from other retailers by assuming an unprecedented commitment to quality. Gitman's prompt, reliable delivery permits the retailer to stand out in the crowded clothing industry.
- Timberland differentiated itself by responding directly to increased domestic demand for high-quality, U.S.-made products. The outdoor footwear retailer's success bucks the trend toward imported, low-cost footwear.
- Similarly, Trafalger Limited exploits its "Made in the U.S.A." label as a selling point in a saturated luggage industry. Increased competition in the domestic luggage industry has come from value-priced imports *and* high-end European entries.

At the same time they are pursuing these differential advantages, Gitman, Timberland, and Trafalger strive to develop more cooperative arrangements with selected manufacturers and wholesalers. Manufacturers and wholesalers are interested in attaining precisely the same outcome with these and other retailers. As a result, channel systems are formed. Such channel systems will then compete against other like systems. Channel-level competition is also based on each system's ability to develop and sustain differential advantages in the face of changing environmental circumstances.

Recall that in the preceding chapter, marketing channels were described as organized behavioral systems. The next section discusses how these networks of channel members emerge in the diverse marketplace.

Diversity in Complex Environments

Environmental diversity refers to the variety of environmental forces facing a channel member. Because of environmental diversity, even mundane products often require complex channel systems. For instance, not so long ago women's hosiery was sold exclusively through department stores and specialty retailers. Then L'eggs Products, Inc., came along with a creative channels strategy. Packaged in its trademark egg-shaped package, L'eggs was the first supermarket panty hose success. Today, L'eggs is sold in a variety of outlets ranging from convenience stores to supermarkets. Spontaneous creativity? Not quite. Sara Lee Corporation, parent company of L'eggs and Hanes, and the largest U.S. apparel company, had already developed long-term relationships in these outlets because of its food lines. As a result, Sara Lee was uniquely positioned to develop new market outlets for its hosiery products.

More recently, L'eggs has had to overcome a significant culturally induced problem in the U.S. market. As American women increasingly opted for bare legs, pants with socks, or spandex tights, domestic sales of L'eggs dipped by over 20 percent. L'eggs was forced to seek new markets. One new market was achieved through Marks & Spencer, a dominant retail chain in the United Kingdom. To gain entry into the U.K., L'eggs used the Howard Marlboro Group to bridge a relationship with Marks & Spencer. But problems quickly surfaced. For instance, all Marks & Spencer products were sold under a proprietary brand name, St. Michaels. L'eggs had a policy of selling only under its own brand name. Moreover, cultural differences between the United States and the U.K. required some product redesign. With the help of Howard Marlboro Group, however, the two channel partners forged a compromise. In it, L'eggs agreed to modify the product while Marks & Spencer agreed to carry L'eggs in a slightly modified package featuring the L'eggs logo and a "for St. Michael" inscription.[8]

L'eggs Products' reaction to declining domestic market potential for women's hosiery illustrates how shifting environmental conditions can create the need for new channels. As the CRM shows, environmental changes may emerge from a variety of sources outside of the channel itself. These actions allowed L'eggs to outflank the competition and expand its worldwide market share. Marks & Spencer increased sales as well. In this instance, each channel member needed to perform specific tasks and assume certain responsibilities to ensure the new channel's success. As this example illustrates, the interests of any single channel member are wrapped up with the interests of all other members of the channel. The virtual marketplace holds serious implications for channel members, as discussed below.

Disintermediation: Transforming Channel Roles

In the previous chapter, we explored the paramount role of the middleman or intermediary in marketing channels. You may wonder whether the Internet and other direct-to-customer technology tools will result in the demise or extinction of the intermediary. After all, the marketplace is abound with examples of manufacturers directly interfacing with their customers. You can directly order a customized computer system from Dell.com, procure a prescription drug on Drugstore.com, or send a tropical bouquet of flowers on 1-800-Flowers.com.

This process of eliminating the middleman from a transaction is termed **disintermediation.** Stated another way, disintermediation is the process of direct interaction between producers and consumers that bypasses the intermediary. It is based on an assumption that information technology breeds connectivity and connectivity reduces the need for wholesalers, retailers, and other middlemen in human transactions.

Yet, there are compelling reasons why the intermediary has more than survived direct-to-consumer channels. Intermediaries have actually thrived in the Net Economy. Sure, you can order a cheesecake over the Internet, but you can't have your cake and eat it to! In order to savor the flavor, you cannot bypass the physical distribution of the cheesecake. The Internet can find suppliers and even engage, to some extent, in price and quality negotiations. But no computer can assemble, deliver, and service market offerings. There are several rationale for the aggrandized role of the channel intermediary:

- **Human interaction.** A determinant factor in the future of intermediaries is human interactions. Can a computer replace human interaction? For some products, the answer may be yes; but for many products and services, human interaction is a must. More than $30 million adults receive health and medicine via the Internet. You can receive medical advice and information from WebMD.com, but it cannot take your temperature, feel your glands, or rub a sore muscle. Some customers prefer dealing with a "real" person whose dialogue can extend beyond product-centric queries.

Human experience. Go ahead and navigate through the myriad of automobile websites. No matter how sophisticated the website may be, high-intensity graphics, streaming videos, and digitized audio are no replacement for the test-drive. Test-drives, automobile pick-ups, and after-market services reinforce the importance of automobile dealers as retail intermediaries. You might liken this to many of the driving or pilot video simulations in your local arcade. It may be fun, but it is no substitute for the real thing!

Human relationships. There are many retailers selling replacement parts, tools, tool storage systems, and diagnostic equipment to automobile dealers, service shops, and independent mechanics. So why do so many mechanics rely on the Snap-On "showroom on wheels"—a network of dealers who personally visit as many as 100 businesses each week? Because mechanics develop relationships with Snap-On dealers. Customers report high levels of trust in and commitment to their Snap-On dealers. The dealers develop and maintain long-term customer relationships by providing customized, high-tech business solutions.

Snap-On's success is largely based on knowing and understanding individual customers. While www.SnapOn.com offers more than 15,000 products and replacement parts, it is no replacement for dealers' personal demonstrations and expert knowledge. As the CRM suggests, information stewardship is at the heart of customer relationship management. So, channel members can be viewed as the customer information stewards or guardians. This information stewardship has taken new forms in the paperless market environment.

So, there are many reasons for an emerging phenomenon of hypermediation. **Hypermediation** involves the transformation of traditional channel intermediaries into new highly specialized value providers. In the Net Economy, there are content providers, Web affiliates, search engines, and search engines that effectuate the distribution of information.[9] Surely, the Internet offers many new ways of collecting information, and of using that information to facilitate buyer-seller exchanges. In Exhibit 2.1, you can discern among the myriad of complex online mechanisms for exchange.

Channel Roles in the Exchange System

Chapter 1 described how individual channel members function as a part of a marketing exchange system. How the relationship perspective differs from the conventional view of

EXHIBIT 2.1

Online marketing exchange

Static Call	Online catalogs with fixed prices
Dynamic Call	Online catalogs with dynamic pricing and features
Customer-Tailored	Products and prices are tailored to specific customer characteristics
Retrologistics	Prices posted by buyers for sellers' acceptance: reverse product flow
Auctions	Buyers and sellers determine pricing based on interactive bidding
Negotiations	Bargaining: dialogue between one buyer and one seller
Barter	Buyers and sellers exchange goods rather than hard currencies
Recurrent Fulfillment	Ongoing replenishment of orders based on prespecified terms
Clearance	Limited quantity, discounted goods posted on bulletin board
Partnership	Integration of channel member processes

Source: Adapted from Nunes, Paul, Diane Wilson, and Ajit Kamil (2000), "The All-in-One Market," *Harvard Business Review*, 78 (May/June, no. 3), 20.

marketing channels was also discussed. The relationship perspective, as illustrated in the CRM, suggests that channel members evolve and prosper as a result of their interactions with one another. Channel roles also emerge through this interaction. Three types of channel relationships exist:[10]

- **Supplier relationships.** In supplier relationships, firms provide products or services to other firms. These are then either used in manufacturing processes or resold. For example, as a global supplier of copper, Freeport-McMoRan provides copper for a variety of products and customers, ranging from pennies (for the U.S. government) to plumbing tools (for manufacturers). Supplier relationships always involve a negotiatory role. The *negotiatory role* refers to the ways in which intermediaries arrive at acceptable exchange terms in channel systems.
- **Customer relationships.** Customer relationships involve the sale and service of products to individuals and organizations for final consumption. Customer relationships largely involve retailers selling to consumers. Office Max sells a wide variety of office and school supplies to business and nonbusiness consumers.
- **Lateral relationships.** Not so long ago, firms operating at the same channel level in the same industry barely acknowledged one another's existence. Today such firms are increasingly going into business with one another. Lateral relationships occur between two channel members who occupy a relatively equivalent position in the channel system. These channel members may even perform similar functions in the channel system. Partnerships between channel members often strengthen their mutual competitive position.

Each type of interaction—supplier, customer, and lateral relationships—demands different behaviors of the participating channel members. **Channel roles** are the sets of activities or behaviors assigned to each intermediary in a channel system.

To understand how these roles work, let's return to our L'eggs example. L'eggs Products, Inc., was expected to have the capability to design products appealing to women in the U.K. This was the role it was expected to bring to the channel system. Howard Marlboro Group's role was to negotiate the details of the contract between L'eggs and Marks & Spencer, design the packaging, and provide point-of-purchase displays. The channel role assigned to Marks & Spencer included the provision of personal selling efforts, quicker *entree* to choice U.K. markets, and its merchandising skills. In short, each member was doing what it did best.

Channel Roles and Expectations

Over time, each channel member should attain a special role identity. **Role identity** specifies the traits of an individual or organization that are considered appropriate to and consistent with the performance of a given channel role. A channel member's role identity is basically akin to its reputation. Within established channels, role identity allows suppliers to easily recognize the means by which their products can be distributed. Role identity also allows buyers to routinely seek out sources for products or the information necessary to satisfy their needs. The home improvement sector provides an example. Do-it-yourselfers and building contractors alike are increasingly patronizing large warehouse building supply centers. Home Depot and Lowe's have capitalized on the tremendous growth in the home improvement market. In each case, these giant home centers have established a role identity distinguished by more inventory, wider assortment, better service, and lower prices. Consumers and contractors are confident that they will find what they need at these stores.[11]

Exhibit 2.2

Channel roles in the exchange system

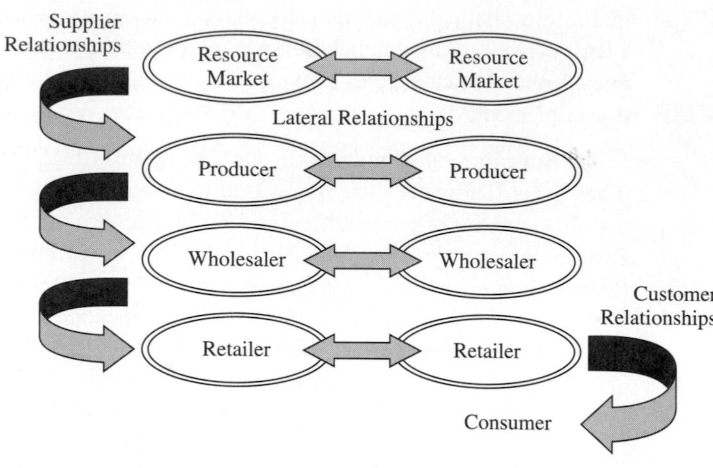

The building supply industry once consisted exclusively of independently owned specialty stores. But new channel role expectations have emerged over time. **Role expectations** encompass the exchange attributes and benefits expected by customers when they interact within a marketing channel. Changing consumer role expectations prompted new marketing approaches—you might call them a new species of retail outlets—within building supply channels.

Changing role expectations have affected suppliers as well as buyers. For example, Armstrong World Industries, a major producer of vinyl flooring, ceiling panels, and other building products, had to reconsider its traditional channel strategy. No longer could Armstrong rely upon specialty flooring retailers to deliver it sufficient market share. Instead, Armstrong had to adapt its operations to the changing expectations of flooring and ceiling end users. In response to its changing customer needs, Armstrong has cultivated relationships with these warehouse home center outlets.[12] As buyers increasingly acquire building supplies from nontraditional outlets, suppliers must modify their channel strategy to satisfy their market's needs. Suppliers must also adapt for purposes of self-preservation. Whether the role expectations of suppliers or buyers are met affects relationships among all channel members, from producers to ultimate users.[13]

Channel members clearly play a variety of roles in the flow of goods and services from producer to ultimate user. Supplier, customer, and lateral relationships provide a framework for discussing the most important roles in marketing channels. This framework, and the principal channel roles performed within it, are illustrated in Exhibit 2.2.

Supplier Relationships

Supplier relationships involve three principal channel roles: source, producer, and wholesaler. **Sources firms** supply raw materials that enter the production process.

Among consumers, the word *denim* generally suggests traditional jean brand names like Levi Strauss and Wrangler. Or, the word may evoke fashion jean marketers, such as Armani, Donna Karan New York, and Versace. But you probably don't think of Group Ashima, one of the fastest-growing sources for denim fabric—a supplier to many of these leading marketers of jeans. Group Ashima, located in India's textile hub Ahmedabad, exports over $280 million of cotton products to 26 countries worldwide.

Born in Europe, denim's resource markets stretch from the United States to the Philippines. In fact, Southeast Asian denim suppliers are fast becoming the principal source firms for high-quality finished denims. As Exhibit 2.2 illustrates, these source markets or resource firms are the starting point in the channel of distribution for many finished goods. In this way, they may be viewed as the anchor for production of consumer and industrial products.

Producers generate component parts, process materials, or finished goods. Producer firms include agricultural, forestry, fishing, mining, construction, and manufacturing entities, as well as a host of service industries. Producers range from cotton farmers to textile mills. Producers can also sell to other producers, meaning producers perform in both *buyer* and *seller roles*. Ultimately, producers' outputs are marketed to final consumers. **Consumers** are individuals who purchase goods and services for their household or personal use.

The third type of supplier is the wholesaler. **Wholesalers** are organizations that market products and services for resale or institutional use. Wholesalers typically sell goods to retail, industrial, governmental, and agricultural concerns. Products distributed by wholesalers are generally obtained from the manufacturing sector, but wholesalers can market products or services to other wholesalers. Wholesalers are particularly important because they connect producers (upstream) with retailers (downstream). The U.S. Bureau of Economic Analysis studies indicate that the wholesaling industry has been a major impetus for growth in the U.S. economy. In fact, it suggests that wholesaling accounted for nearly 18 percent of U.S. economic growth in the 1990s. Because of the importance of this intermediary role, we devote the remainder of this section to an in-depth discussion of wholesalers.

The wholesaling industry has a major impact on the U.S. economy. It employs over 8 million people and accounts for nearly $3.5 trillion in annual sales. Two major trends continue to change the wholesaling industry. First, mergers and acquisitions are decreasing the number of wholesalers, creating large, diversified wholesalers in lieu of the small and regional Mom and Pop wholesalers. In fact, the number of prescription drug wholesalers has been nearly halved in recent years. The proposed merger of Cardinal Health and Bergen and the proposed merger of McKesson and Amerisource—the four largest drug wholesalers in the United States—would result in a combined market share of about 80 percent. While the Federal Trade Commission (FTC) did not approve these proposed mergers, it did acknowledge the merits of efficiencies and savings that could be passed on to consumers through industry aggregation.

The absolute number of wholesalers has and will continue to decline as a result of mergers, acquisitions, and business failures. Drug wholesaler Bergen Brunswig Company's purchase of Durr-Fillauer directly illustrates this contraction.[14] In Channel Surfing 2.2, we examine the role of the Internet in the pharmaceutical marketing channel.

The Changing Role of Wholesalers. The role identity of wholesalers has traditionally been based on the branded products they carried. However, as the wholesale industry changes, the role of wholesalers must change with it. The large numbers of similar-quality branded

Channel Surfing 2.2

The Internet: A Prescription for Pharmaceutical Supply Chain?

The rise in e-commerce is having a wholesale impact on the pharmaceutical supply chain. In fact, the Internet is expected to account for nearly one-third of all U.S. health transactions by 2005. Will the bulk of these transactions be between patients (consumers) and direct-to-consumer resellers like Drugstore.com and PlanetRx.com, or bricks 'n clicks retailers like CVS.com? Will they be between patients and medical content sites like WebMd.com and NetDoctor.com? No, about 90 percent of Internet activity in the channel for pharmaceuticals will be business-to-business transactions, resulting in wholesale changes!

The primary goal of drug wholesalers is to provide economies of scale to ensure a fluid, efficient flow of thousands of pharmaceuticals in the most cost-efficient manner. Think of the thousands of different pharmaceuticals that need to be dispersed in economic quantities and transported to retail pharmacies. Ultimately, drug wholesalers reduce the number of transactions required to serve pharmacies, physicians, and patients.

The Healthcare Distribution Management Association provides data that illustrate the fundamental role of the wholesaler: When wholesalers are used, the total number of transactions are reduced by 98 percent! You will recall from Chapter 1 that these are smoothing and sorting functions, and they are vital to distribution efficiency.

The Internet will drive many costs out of the pharmaceutical supply chain by providing faster and more efficient information exchange. Consider that the average retail pharmacy holds about 45 days' stock, and wholesalers typically carry two or three weeks of stock. More effective inventory management via Web-enabled systems can cut inventory "safety stock," simplify administrative activities, and drive down costs. Drug wholesalers will use the Internet to:

- Reduce paperwork and inaccuracies
- Provide real-time information
- Pioneer and deploy new technologies

Drug wholesaler Bergen Brunswig is teaming with Sentara Healthcare to offer the Intelliorder and DOCxdirect system, an online ordering system that allows physicians to order products and receive instant order confirmation, electronic invoicing, and customized inventory management tools. Competitor and global industry leader McKessonHBOC leverages a variety of Internet-based solutions to automate and streamline the entire claims process, linking third-party payers, physicians, and health care institutions to accelerate accurate reimbursements.

Points to Ponder

- While Steve Kilguss, vice president of the Electronic Commerce Group (ECG) of McKessonHBOCs, maintains that McKesson adheres to the highest standards of privacy and confidentiality, how might Internet-based wholesaling systems affect the rights of the final consumer (the patient)?
- The U.S. health care bill is about $1.2 billion, and the government pays for about 45 percent of every health care dollar. How can systems like Intelliorder and Docxdirect reduce transaction costs for the government?

Source: Compiled from www.nwda.org and www.bergenbrunswig.com/news.

products introduced over recent years have made it difficult to establish a product line wholesaler role identity. When coupled with the extensive geographic expansion of some wholesalers, this has lead to a glut of look-alike competitors in the wholesaling sector. To combat this trend, wholesalers are offering proprietary services as a way to differentiate themselves. Wholesalers are also performing sales and marketing functions that had been previously assigned to producers. These new functions are reshaping the wholesaler's role identity.[15] With the average cost of a sales call now exceeding $260, manufacturers are turning to wholesalers as a means of decreasing their sales and marketing costs.

In the future, wholesalers' role identities will be largely based on the success with which they engage in relationship-building efforts with upstream and downstream channel participants. Building these relationships requires that wholesalers know their customers' needs, anticipate changes in those needs, and be willing to adopt new technologies to better satisfy those specialized needs. Such efforts should generally include the use of electronic data interaction for expediting deliveries, product-lot tracking, and intelligent inventory control systems. As Channel Surfing 2.3 illustrates, Ben E. Keith is a full-service distributor of a portfolio of brands.

In marketing channels, wholesalers create exchange utility by reducing discrepancies in assortments of goods. Essentially, this means that wholesalers allow a supplying firm to produce large, homogeneous product lots. These lots are then broken down by wholesalers into smaller shipments to accommodate consuming firms' need for relatively small quantities of a broad variety of products. This sorting process describes the classic function performed by wholesalers as **intermediaries** between supplying and consuming firms. In their intermediary roles, wholesalers provide a fundamental link between producers and retailers. It is important to realize, however, that either the producing or retailing firm could also perform some or all of this intermediary function for itself. This would effectively eliminate the wholesaler

Channel Surfing 2.3

A Cold Start for Some Hot Brands

The next time you are at your favorite watering hole, you may wonder how an early 20th-century distributor could be responsible for providing you with so many choices of brews. Whether Budweiser, Bud Light, Bud Ice, Kirin, Michelob, or Natural Light is the cold one of choice, chances are that they all originated from one wholesale distributor. However, did you ever consider that your draft started with a head of lettuce?

Gaston Hallam, a pioneer wholesaler, founded his distribution business on one unique attribute: refrigeration. In 1933, chairman of the board and owner of Gaston Hallam began selling Anheuser-Busch products under the trade name Ben E. Keith. Hallam acknowledges, "Refrigeration was the key to becoming a beer distributor when Prohibition ended." But Ben E. Keith did not start as a beer distributor. The company had refrigerated storage coolers and delivery trucks because it was in the produce business.

Nearly one century later, Ben E. Keith is the largest independent Anheuser-Busch wholesaler in the United States. It also distributes Kirin and Redhook brands. But the Ben E. Keith name stands for more than beer. Ben E. Keith Foods, a sister operation to the beer distributor, supplies a full line of produce, frozen goods, meats, dry groceries, and restaurant equipment and supplies. While Ben E. Keith Company's customers include such diverse segments as bars, restaurants, hospitals, and nursing homes, its philosophy is universal: "To earn the loyalty of our customers by handling only products of the highest quality and value, and by providing excellent service and responsiveness to customers' needs."

Points to Ponder

- How does Ben E. Keith Company's philosophy apply to all wholesale distributors? What would you say is Ben E. Keith's differential advantage?
- Ben E. Keith's customer base is fairly diverse. How can Ben E. Keith customize relationships to so many different types of customers?

Source: Compiled from www.benekeith.com.

from the channel, although the *functions* are still performed. This latter issue is discussed in greater detail in the third and fourth parts of this book.

Beyond the sorting function, how do wholesalers add value to channel relationships? Consider the following additional advantages that wholesalers can offer producers:

- Wholesalers enhance customer relationships by providing more frequent and customized attention to customers' needs. Wholesaling agents are conveniently located near buyers. They can be more receptive to customer inquiries.
- By inventorying stocks, wholesalers help producers convert finished inventories into monetary assets. Cash flows are freed up, allowing manufacturers to invest more in research and product development.
- Wholesalers give manufacturers sales and marketing assistance.

The functions performed by wholesalers also benefit retailers. For instance:

- Wholesalers assist retailers by performing merchandising activities. They may provide point-of-purchase displays and cooperative advertising.
- Wholesalers often assist retailers in building and floor plan designs. They offer retailers advice on how to develop *atmospherics*—those physical elements in a store's design that strike a positive chord with buyer's emotions and encourage purchase.
- Wholesalers often help retailers with accounting and inventory management procedures.

Wholesaler Classification. As summarized in Exhibit 2.3, wholesaler roles can be classified into merchant wholesaler, manufacturers' sales organization, agent/broker, and commission merchant categories. **Merchant wholesalers** are independently owned businesses that take ownership or *title* to goods. Accounting for approximately 60 percent (or about $1.9 trillion) of all U.S. wholesale sales each year, merchant wholesalers represent the principal form of wholesaling. In fact, about 90 percent of wholesaling firms are merchant wholesalers. Functions of merchant wholesalers relating to their physical possession of products include receiving, inventorying, and transporting goods. Merchant wholesalers also perform several negotiatory functions. These include acting as unit buyers and sellers, exchanging information, and consummating transactions.

Still other value-added services are provided by merchant wholesalers. For instance, nearly two decades have passed since merchant wholesaler Bergen Brunswig Company

Exhibit 2.3

Wholesaler role classifications

Wholesaler Classification	*Take Physical Possession*	*Take Title to Goods*	*Negotion Function Performed*	*Promotional Function Performed*
Merchant wholesaler	Yes	Yes	Yes	Yes
Manufacturer's sales organization	No	Yes	Yes	Yes
Agents/brokers	No	No	Yes	Yes
Commission merchants	Yes	No	Yes	Yes

(BBC) pioneered the use of computerized ordering and inventory systems in the pharmaceutical industry. These systems tie BBC to its customers to improve efficiency in order flows. BBC also offers its retail pharmacy clients cooperative advertising and promotional programs, one-stop coupon redemptions, and magazine allowance programs. Not surprisingly, BBC has enjoyed considerable increases in market share over this same period.[16] As you read in Channel Surfing 2.2, Bergen Brunswig has taken many of these technologies to the Web.

Similar value-added services are increasingly being offered by other wholesalers in their efforts to build customer relationships. For instance, merchant wholesalers may assort and grade bulk goods. To differentiate themselves in the marketplace, merchant wholesalers often use proprietary packaging and labeling, as well. The channel functions featured in merchant wholesalers' role set is still expanding as alternative channels of distribution emerge. Types of merchant wholesaler roles can range from industrial distributors to wholesale cooperatives, such as those found in the agricultural and petroleum industries.

Manufacturer's sales organizations (MSOs) are producer-owned firms that are physically detached from the manufacturing location. Generally speaking, MSOs distribute their parent manufacturer's goods. For example, Black & Decker has sales offices dispersed throughout the country. Black & Decker has been able to strengthen customer relationships through the use of its manufacturers' sales organizations.[17] MSOs often engage in autonomous negotiatory functions that are entirely separate from the producer role. This is why MSOs are viewed as marketing channel intermediaries.

Agents (also known as **brokers**) represent a variety of manufacturers and product lines. They differ from other wholesaler types in that they do not take title to or physical possession of the goods they market. Also, wholesaling agents are generally compensated on a commission basis. Agents may assume various forms, ranging from auction houses to manufacturer representatives, from export agents to merchandise brokers. Regardless of their form, agents will be actively engaged in negotiating relationships.

Agents prove useful to producers for several reasons. For one thing, agents typically cover their own costs. For another, they generally do not get paid until they have made a sale. Most significantly, agents already have established customer relationships and can provide immediate ties to those customers. Wholesaling agency relationships are most popular in the motor vehicles and parts industries. They are playing an increasingly important role for small- to mid-sized manufacturers.

Commission merchants take physical possession of the goods they market, but they do not assume ownership. Commission merchants are likely to perform promotional, negotiating, financing, and ordering functions for the producers they represent. Commission merchants, who handle a limited range of products, have generally experienced more market success than MSDs.

Each wholesaler type faces its own unique environmental challenges.[18] There are, for example, competitive threats from wholesaling forms like online catalogs and warehouse chains. Wholesalers also face threats from the recent increase in merger activities. Mergers have allowed many producer and retailer firms to achieve more diversification and the economies of scale necessary to perform many traditional wholesaling functions themselves. For example, did you know that Good Neighbor Pharmacy stores are drug wholesaler Bergen Brunswig's network of independently owned stores that compete with Walgreen's, CVS, Rite-Aid, and Eckerd? And traditional bricks 'n mortar drug retailer Rite-Aid is in a strategic alliance with online retailer Drugstore.com. Online pharmacy Soma.com was acquired by pharmacy retailer CVS. These are just some of the examples of the integration between wholesalers and retailers in the Net Economy. Wholesalers' gross margins have generally declined in the face of rising customer service requirements. But the most significant threat to traditional wholesalers lies in the growth of alternative channels of distribution. Without question, direct manufacturer-to-retailer relationships most seriously threaten the growth of wholesaling. In fact, direct manufacturer-to-retailer alliances may eventually lead to a 20 percent decline in wholesaling. Producer alliances with warehouse clubs, discount stores, and home center stores also promise to scramble traditional wholesaling role identities. The availability of consumer direct ordering through electronic media and direct mail poses another potential difficulty for traditional wholesalers.

Despite these environmental threats, wholesalers can look forward to several opportunities. The North American Free Trade Agreement (NAFTA) and other multilateral trade agreements suggest wholesalers will have more opportunity to enter global markets in the future. Furthermore, continuing consolidation within the wholesaling sector suggests that value-added services, new product lines, and new geographic penetration will foster market expansion. Wholesale distributors who transform themselves in response to changes in their CRM environments should be better able to satisfy their customer needs through performing their trademark intermediary functions.

Customer Relationships

The second type of channel role is customer relationships. The principal channel role in customer relationships involves retailers. **Retailers** are individuals or organizations who sell products or services to the ultimate consumer. The roles of retailers are much more complex than those of wholesalers. Retailers must manage supplier relationships, as well. And like wholesalers, retailers are also intermediaries in channel systems. Most importantly, in traditional marketing flows retailers provide the final link in channels of distribution: They obtain goods from producers and/or wholesalers and then resell those same products to final consumers. The retailing role thus performs dual functions within marketing channels. First, retailers act as selling agents for their suppliers—either manufacturers or wholesalers. Retailers provide the buying function for their customers. They also provide the closest link to consumers. Retailers' relationships with wholesalers and producers shape the effectiveness with which each function will be performed.

U.S. retailing sales volume exceeded $2.7 trillion in 1999, with about 25 percent of that volume attributable to general merchandise, apparel, and furniture sales. Consider that total U.S. retail sales in 1995 only edged over the $2.2 trillion mark, and you can appreciate the tremendous strength of this sector in the United States. In fact, U.S. retailing has created over 800,000 new jobs in the 1990s.

The conventional notion of retailing confined to a physical setting is seriously contested as catalog companies (e.g., Eddie Bauer, Fingerhut), websites (e.g., Amazon.com, Dell Computer), and other media (e.g., Comcast and QVC television shopping networks) offer customers a wide assortment of goods and services. The hybridization of retail formats makes it increasingly difficult to classify retailers.

Hybridization refers to the mixed formats that characterize the global retail sector in the Net Economy. Earlier, you read about the striking impact deep discounters like Wal-Mart and Target have had in extending their merchandise lines to include groceries. With its new Neighborhood Market format, super-center growth, and European acquisitions, Wal-Mart could soon become the world's leading food retailer.

Hybridization and the emergence of bricks 'n clicks (integration of both physical and virtual location) decimates traditional classifications of retailing. Alternatively, we identify several traditional retailing formats, emphasizing that each format is increasingly prone toward complementary physical and virtual retail locations.

Department stores are large retail units featuring extensive assortments of products that are categorized into departments. The U.S. government views department stores as stores that carry such lines as apparel, soft goods, furniture, and housewares, where no single category constitutes more than 80 percent of total store sales. Generally, an establishment with total sales of $10 million or more is classified as a department store.

Most department stores are not independents, but are part of large retail conglomerates. For example, Federated Department Stores is one of the leading operators of full-line department stores in the United States, with over 400 department stores in 33 states as of 2000. Federated operates department stores under the names Bloomingdale's, The Bon Marché, Burdines, Goldsmith's, Lazarus, Macy's, Rich's, and Stern's. These department stores sell a wide range of merchandise and are diversified by size of store, merchandise positioning, and target market segments.

Specialty stores are retailers that concentrate on one merchandise or service line. Many specialty stores are parts of large retail conglomerates. For example, The Limited boasts 13 separate retail divisions and operates over 5,600 stores across the United States. From its namesake, The Limited to New York & Co., The Limited has a diversified portfolio of specialty stores. The Limited includes Lane Bryant, Lerner New York, and Structure. In 1995, The Limited completed an initial public offering (IPO) of Intimate Brands, Inc., a company consisting of Victoria's Secret, Bath & Body Works, and White Barn Candle Company.

Convenience stores, like 7-Eleven and Circle K, are fairly small (less than 8,000 square feet) and provide a limited assortment of products and services at a convenient location. Today, even smaller convenience stores at self-service gas stations are gaining market share in this sector and imposing a competitive threat to 7-Eleven and Circle K. Another new market entrant is the supermarket. Albertsons and Kroger are testing convenience stores with gas pumps on the parking lots of their existing supermarkets. Convenience stores generally are open 24 hours.

Discount stores are varied, ranging from full-line discounters such as Wal-Mart and Kmart to off-price retailers like TJ Maxx and Marshalls. They also include **category killers** like Best Buy (home electronics), Office Depot (business and school supplies and equipment), and Lowe's (home building and improvement). Category killers are deep discounters in a defined merchandise category. Sam's and Costco membership clubs are warehouse forms of discount retailers.

• A **supermarket** category also exists. Supermarkets like Kroger or Safeway are self-service stores with groceries, meats, and/or produce departments. To qualify as a supermarket, this type of outlet must exceed a minimum of $2 million in annual sales.

In any language, "Always the Lowest Price, Always" captures Wal-Mart's retail positioning strategy. This sign dons customer value in a Wal-Mart located in a working-class neighborhood in Mexico City. Could this store be in your neighborhood?

Wide World Photo

In the late 1990s, strong consumer confidence, record stock market returns, and low interest rates contributed to strong gains across many formats in the U.S. retail sector. Competition for customers has intensified in both the United States and abroad, with nonstore direct selling accounting for nearly 3 percent of nonautomobile U.S. retail sales.

Nonstore retailers are equally diverse. The rapid emergence of nonstore retailing is due to the growth in information technologies and the typical American consumer's increasingly busy lifestyle. Nonstore retailers include vending machines where one can buy everything from a soft drink to french fries. French fries? Yes, new technologies now offer consumers many nontraditional vending products. Still, vending plays a fairly small role in nonstore retailing.

Nonstore retailing is growing at a tremendous rate, thanks in part to the likes of the Home Shopping Network, Internet, and QVC. In-home retailing allows consumers to shop by television and then phone in orders for a wide assortment of products. Consumers can also connect to retailers through a host of Internet sites. Direct marketing outlets such as mail catalogs and telephone selling are also types of nonstore retailing. Cultivating customer relationships in nonstore retailing is challenging because of the consumer's physical detachment from the shopping experience.

New technologies have created a number of innovative modes and intense competition in the retailing sector. In response to this competition, retailers are using customer-oriented service strategies to build consumer loyalty. Toward this end, in the 1990s many retailers have downsized and restructured. Traditional merchandising mixes have, in many cases, been tossed aside. Moreover, retailers are constantly augmenting their operations with new customer services. Never mind the merchandise category, the location, or the shopping experience. Retailers are collectively interested in delivering customer satisfaction.

The influence of changing demographics and lifestyles in the United States—more older consumers, ethnic diversity, longer work hours—is reflected in the emergence of new channels and the resurgence of some traditional channels. Increasingly, a demand for convenience, rather than lower prices, underlies the growth of nonstore retailing.

- **Increases in the use of electronic shopping.** Electronic shopping opportunities include video kiosks, teleshopping (including interactive), and online computer shopping services such as those available on the Internet.
- **Increases in the use of mail-order catalog/direct mail.** Catalog and direct mail retailers have become more competitive because of technological improvements, more appealing product offerings, less-expensive and more time-efficient delivery systems, and generally improved economies of scale.
- **More manufacturers' outlets.** Especially throughout the Northeast and Midwest, manufacturers' outlets are becoming fashionable. These centers draw bargain hunters by the busload. Names such as Corning Ware, Dansk, American Tourister, and Van Heusen are among the better-known manufacturers' outlets.
- **Hypermarkets.** Truly one-stop shops, this retailing form offers an immense selection of products. Hypermarket retailers must be willing to accept low margins across a wide assortment of products to secure the level of consumer traffic needed to support a high sales volume. Hypermarketers feature low- or self-service display areas and no-frills atmospheres.

Despite substantial differences in the structure of these retail channel members, each must forge relationships with the ultimate consumer. One way to create those relationships is through the use of expert systems and other technological advances.

Lateral Relationships

The third and final type of channel role in channel systems is lateral relationships. Lateral relationships involve partnerships between firms operating at the same channel level—that is, between manufacturers, wholesalers, or retailers. For instance, automobile dealers who engage in cooperative advertising with one another have entered a lateral relationship at the retail level. Lateral relationships must be based on cooperation and trust. Channel partners should have shared goals and must work together to improve the design, quality, delivery, promotional, or manufacturing aspects of their products and operations. Firms involved in lateral relationships will only gain sustainable competitive advantages if this sense of shared goals exists. Lateral relationships are increasingly important in today's global marketplace.

Lateral relationships feature a sort of "co-opetition"—note how the term blends cooperation with competition. The trend toward joint ventures underscores big changes in how American companies view their world and in the business environment itself. Many American firms so dominated their industries in the 1950s and 1960s that they had little need for outside help. But as foreign competitors gained increasingly larger shares of U.S. markets, these firms needed help to obtain new technology quickly and/or hold down the costs of producing and distributing new products. In the early 1980s, Detroit's Big Three automakers led the way, teaming with Japanese partners to produce and distribute the smaller cars customers sought at the time.

Lateral relationships are not successful by accident. Hewlett-Packard Co. has kept its many strategic alliances running smoothly by designating one employee as a "relationship manager" for each. This person ensures that each partner remembers they are in the relationship for good business reasons. Since Hewlett-Packard and its channel partners still compete in other places, the relationship managers have the responsibility of separating areas of cooperation from areas of competition.[19]

Virtually all channel intermediaries will be facing increasingly competitive marketplaces in the years ahead. The formation of lateral relationships is a natural and logical reaction to these competitive circumstances.

Establishing Channel Role Identities

The overriding purpose of channels is to serve consumer and end user needs. For this to happen, each channel member must perform the tasks appropriate to its own particular role. How do channel members establish role identities? Several divergent perspectives on how channel members differentiate themselves are summarized within the term SIFTing: providing value-added *S*ervices, pioneering market *I*nnovation, offering *F*lexibility, and demonstrating *T*imely delivery of products and services. Successful performance of the channel functions embodied within the SIFTing acronym allows channel members to differentiate themselves and establish unique role identities. Let's look at each dimension.

Services

The first component of the SIFTing process involves the provision of value-added services. Such services may include special delivery, credit terms, or a variety of supplemental utilities beyond the basic market offering. For instance, Software Publishing Corporation, producer of Harvard Graphics software, has introduced The Advice Line. Staffed by customer support specialists, The Advice Line is offered at no charge to customers. The Advice Line offers graphic design recommendations, presentation expertise, and output media selection counsel. It also furnishes a quarterly newsletter, *The Advisor,* which offers graphic design and presentation tips. The key to the success of such services is to develop a role identity that allows channel members to provide more need-satisfying features than their competition. Software Publishing Corporation has succeeded with The Advice Line.

Value-added services also lie near the heart of what today's warehouse consumers seek. Atlantic Distribution, a public warehousing affiliate, offers services such as label altering, repackaging, and resealing of goods—benefits which can translate into major savings for producers by reducing costly returns of damaged shipments. In the beverage industry, warehouses frequently provide value-added services such as hydrating and carbonating soft-drink syrups or cutting high-proof imported alcoholic beverages. These services reduce transportation costs by limiting the distance that nonessential ingredients like air and water must be moved between producers and consumers.[20]

Innovation

Innovation is another dimension of role identity. Innovation involves the introduction of new methods or technologies to strengthen exchange relationships within channels. A recent example of channel innovation is the virtual elimination of physical inventory. In many industrial sectors, significant advances in information-transfer technology have led to virtual inventory systems. Virtual inventory systems use telecommunications technology to deliver products and services with precision, eliminating much of the need for a standing physical inventory. Retailers like Egghead Software and Blockbuster Entertainment Corporation now use electronic distribution to deliver a host of information and entertainment products directly to homes and offices.[21] By pioneering virtual shopping, these companies hope to strengthen their customer relationships.

Channel innovations are sometimes evident in the imaginative forms of new retail outlets. Market phenomena like in-home television and computer shopping networks have compelled in-store retailers to move beyond tradition. For example, U.S. sports industry conglomerate Nike has opened several retail sports museums, called Nike Towns, to help products stand out in a cluttered sneaker environment. Consumers are dazzled by each sports pavilion's innovative fixtures, video backdrops, and sound effects customized to regional allegiances—Tar Heels in North Carolina, Ragin' Cajuns in Louisiana, Rebels in Mississippi. In these *showcase stores,* all goods are sold at the full retail price. But regardless of whether or not customers buy at Nike Town, Nike intends to impart a lasting impression.[22] Channel Surfing 2.4 sheds more light on the Nike Town story.

Flexibility

Firms can also differentiate themselves in the marketplace by exhibiting flexibility in their channel relationships. Flexibility reflects an ability to successfully accommodate exchange partners' needs as environmental and process conditions change. Flexibility can assume many forms. It is, for instance, shown in a firm's willingness to adjust delivery schedules, transportation modes, or credit terms. Firms often employ flexible ways of settling payments for goods, particularly in international settings. For example, just a few years ago, Indonesia sorely needed a steelmaking facility but lacked the fiscal capability to support the development of such a facility through traditional financial channels. In response, the Southeast Asian nation engineered a flexible channel arrangement wherein it exchanged oil for access to Germany's engineering technology.

Many producers have adopted flexible assembly processes because they recognize that customers' needs are always changing. These processes can quickly shift product lines and meet market needs. Toshiba is one such company. Its computer factory assembles nearly a dozen different word processors on a single production line; about twenty different models of laptop computers are produced on another. Toshiba's output is thus aligned with customer demand.[23] The concept of flexible production has prompted suppliers to be more flexible, as well. Marketers of mechanical engineering processes have developed programmable process controllers to allow producers to swiftly switch from one line to another. At literally the touch of a button these engineering suppliers can accommodate producers' complex needs![24]

Channel Surfing 2.4

Nike Town: Stores That Don't Sell (Art for Shoe's Sake)

New York City's Museum of Natural Art displays one of its priceless Rodin sculptures by hanging it from the ceiling. At Chicago's Nike Town, a life-size model of a cyclist dangles from the rafters. To make its product stand out in today's cluttered sneaker retailing environment, Nike is opening stores across the country that are half art galleries, half walk-in advertisements.

Every item is displayed at full retail price. The idea is not to attract customers with discounts but with glamour. Nike's intent is to compensate for the lack of time and attention most retailers give to their products and/or customers. In many other shoe stores, sales help is often rude or inattentive, and boxes are stacked high or haphazardly. But in these new gallery stores manufacturers showcase their wares with pride and pizzazz—under the assumption that even if visitors do not buy, they will leave with an impression that persists when they actually go shopping for similar products elsewhere.

The 68,000-square foot Chicago Nike Town store is an ode to athletic footwear and its myriad uses. Nike wants, and usually gets, the customers to ooh and ahh; Nike also wants them to reach for their wallet. Each Nike product line is fully represented—shoes are retrieved from inventory in less than 60 seconds via a computerized shoe tube—and all salespersons work on full commission. These stores are, to put it succinctly, a raging financial success. Which of course means that in the world of business, where imitation is indeed the sincerest form of flattery, the trend away from the traditional and mundane will undoubtedly spill over to other manufacturers. Doc Martens? Just below the Picasso.

Points to Ponder

- Where do you think other opportunities for creative retailing distribution and presentation packages lie?

Source: Adapted from Comte, Elizabeth (1992), "Art for Shoes Sake," *Forbes,* September 28, 128–30; and Fitzgerald, Kate (1992), "Marketers Learn to 'Just Do It,' " *Advertising Age,* January 27, S7–S8.

Timing

Timely delivery, a key component of channel efficiency, is a primary part of role identity. From our discussion of intermediaries in Chapter 1, you will recall the importance of getting the right products and services to the right place at the right time. The apparel and textiles industries are making fast delivery the cornerstone of their reemerging global competitiveness. Technological breakthroughs in sewing machinery are reducing turnaround time, and data processing directly links retail purchases with designers and fabric suppliers. In reaction, many Asian and European apparel producers are actually setting up shops in the higher-cost U.S. labor markets to reduce lead times.[25]

High-technology firms like Motorola are also competing on fast delivery. The Motorola Order Center is a telemarketing hotline, which enables customers to place and receive orders on standard products very quickly.[26] PaperDirect, a Lyndhurst, New Jersey, supplier of preprinted papers and presentation products, offers its customers overnight delivery for just $1. Indeed, support service intermediaries such as Federal Express have made it possible to receive almost anything overnight.

The attributes and benefits featured within the SIFTing function provide channel members an opportunity to carve out distinctive role identities in competitive markets. However, some structure must underlie this process. Channel structure refers to the patterned behaviors and attitudes associated with a set (producer-wholesaler-retailer) of channel members. Channel structure is discussed in the next chapter.

Key Terms

agent
broker
category killers
channel role
consumer
commission merchant
differential advantage
disintermediation
environmental diversity
halo effect
hypermediation
intermediary
manufacturer's sales organization (MSO)
merchant wholesaler
producer
retailer
role expectation
role identity
sources firm
wholesaler

Chapter Summary

No two biological forms can survive for long in the same finite ecosystem when they require the same resources. Each animal species has evolved to reach its current position in the world. Marketing channel members are likewise having to adapt to attain or maintain their positions in increasingly competitive markets. In this process of adaptation, each channel member attempts to differentiate itself from any other members. This process describes the pursuit of a differential advantage. A differential advantage may be viewed as the marketplace's perception of an organization's distinctive characteristics that set it apart from competitors in ways enticing to customers. Like any living organism, each business entity must distinguish itself in some way to persist and/or prosper in a competitive marketplace.

Channels are not formed through an arbitrary process. Instead, an underlying structure shapes members' behaviors. This structure makes it possible to explain and predict how channel members will perform in market settings. The basis for this structure is referred to as *channel roles.* Channel roles are sets of activities or behaviors assigned to each intermediary operating in a channel system. Over time, each channel member will attain a special role identity. Role identity specifies the characteristics of an individual or organization that are considered appropriate to and consistent with the performance of a given channel role. New channel role expectations encompass the exchange attributes and benefits expected by customers. Role expectations capture the potential of alternative channel intermediaries to satisfy the consumption decision criteria.

All intermediaries play a negotiatory function within marketing channels. The negotiatory function can take different forms and extends beyond assembling, grading, and sorting products. Intermediaries may intercede in the distribution, merchandising, and/or service processes associated with marketing flows. Some intermediaries simply provide a means for transportation and logistics management, while others supply merchandising assistance to sellers. Still others offer a variety of intermediary services to the channels they serve, ranging from the warehousing of goods to the provision of consumer services.

Disintermediation is the process of direct interaction between producers and consumers that bypasses the intermediary. It is based on an assumption that information technology breeds connectivity and connectivity reduces the need for wholesalers, retailers, and other middlemen in human transactions. Yet, middlemen continue to thrive in the Net Economy. Why? Because human interactions, experiences, and relationships remain important value-added benefits provided by intermediaries.

It is clear that channel members play a variety of roles in the flows of goods and services from producer to ultimate user. These channel roles emanate from the nature of channel member interactions or relationships and can be categorized into supplier, customer, and lateral relationships. Supplier relationships include source firms, producers, and wholesalers. Each of these channel members sells goods for input into production processes or for resale. Wholesalers market products and services for resale or institutional use. Customer relationships are handled by another type of intermediary: retailers. Retailers sell products or services to the ultimate consumer. Lateral relationships occur between channel members at relatively equivalent positions in the channel system.

Channel Challenges

1. Futurist David Pierce Snyder has suggested, "Just as plants and animals adapt to changes in their physical environment to survive and thrive over the long term, so too must institutions . . . adapt themselves to changes in their economic and technological environments if they are to remain viable from generation to generation." How does Snyder's contention support or refute Gause's principle of *interspecific competition?* Select an industry in which intermediary roles have changed. What was the impetus for these changes?
2. In this chapter, we visited retail conglomerate Federated Department Stores. So, you are already aware of the more than 400 department stores donning brands like Bloomingdale's, The Bon Marché, Burdines, Goldsmith's, Lazarus, Macy's, Rich's, and Stern's. But you may not be aware of their nonstore retailing portfolio: Bloomingdale's by Mail, Bloomingdales.com, Macy's by Mail, and Macys.com. These appear to be natural extensions of existing bricks 'n mortar operations. So, why do you think Federated Department Stores acquired Minnesota-based cataloger Fingerhut? Fingerhut is also a major third-party consumer fulfillment service for Wal-Mart, Pier 1, and eToys. What does Federated Department Stores' acquisition of Fingerhut suggest about lateral relationships among retailers?
3. When you think barbeque, you may not immediately think of Aunt Rita. But Aunt Rita—the Simi, California, originator of the famous recipe and producer of famous Aunt Rita's Barbeque Rub—is grilling the competition. Since its market introduction in February 2000, Aunt Rita has developed a U.S. distribution network, ranging from California to Maine. Why would major grocery retailers like Albertson's be willing to join small, specialty retailers like Bear Valley Ranch Market and Uncle Fred's Foods as distributors of Aunt Rita's? Would you recommend direct distribution instead? Please defend your answer.
4. In the Washington, DC, area, Byerly groceries carry anywhere from 40,000 to 50,000 items in its stores. Byerly stores are widely known for their high-end product mix and lush decors. Each location offers full-service dining, postal and fax services, and other upscale amenities. Byerly also employs home economists in each of its stores to assist customers with special dietary needs. By contrast, competitors like Giant Foods are adopting cost-cutting methods in response to market saturation. Giant Foods and other grocery chains are also increasingly manufacturing their own neogenerics (store brands). Byerly is directly bucking these industry trends. Which chain is pursuing a better strategy? How do these programs help differentiate Byerly in the competitive food retailing industry?
5. Tyco International Ltd. is a diversified global manufacturer and supplier of industrial products and systems—a marked departure from the research laboratory pioneered by Dr. Arthur Rosenburg in 1960. From electrical components to health care products, from specialty products to security services, Tyco has experienced dramatic growth through strategic acquisitions and market expansions. Today, Tyco operates in 80 countries and employs about 160,000 people. Visit Tyco's website. How would you describe Tyco's channel role? Would you say that it has fundamentally changed over the past 40 years? Please defend your answer.

Review Questions

1. Why has disintermediation increased in the Net Economy? Why have intermediaries continued to thrive in the Net Economy?
2. How does role identity relate to channel member performance?
3. What are role expectations? How do changes in role expectations affect channel members?
4. Define and explain the purpose of channel SIFTing.
5. Discuss the two levels of channel roles.
6. Describe the role of intermediaries in the marketing channel.
7. Compare the roles of wholesalers and retailers. What are some of the advantages provided to producers by these intermediaries?
8. Discuss some of the future trends of market channel intermediaries.

Endnotes

1. Compiled from http://www.visteon.com.
2. Ibid.
3. Lipper, Arthur III, and George Ryan (1991), *Thriving Up and Down the Free Market Food Chain,* New York, NY: HarperCollins Publishers.
4. Kevles, Betty Ann (1986), *Females of the Species: Sex and Survival in the Animal Kingdom,* Cambridge, MA: Harvard University Press.
5. Henderson, Bruce D. (1989), "The Origins of Strategy," *Harvard Business Review,* November/December, 140.
6. Adapted from Liesse, Julie (1992), "Food Marketers Get the Big Picture; Store Monopoly Broken," *Advertising Age,* 63 (April 27), S–1, S–8; and Morris, Kathleen (1993), "Beyond Jurassic Park," *Financial World,* 162 (June 22), 28–30.
7. Trachtenberg, Jeffrey (1986), "Marketing: The Not-So-Ugly Americans," *Forbes,* 138 (December 1), 212–14.
8. Adapted from Wahl, Michael (1993), "Pushing Yankee Products in Lord Rayner's Court," *Brandweek,* 34 (July 12), 26–29; and Slutsker, Gary (1993), "The Naked Truth," *Forbes,* 152 (August 16), 94.
9. Morgan, Robert M., and Shelby D. Hunt (1994), "The Commitment–Trust Theory of Relationship Marketing," *Journal of Marketing,* 58 (July), 20–38.
10. Carr, Nicholas G. (2000), "Hypermediation: Commerce as Clickstream," *Harvard Business Review,* January/February, 46–47.
11. David, Gregory E. (1993), "Stomping Elephant," *Financial World,* 162 (September 28), 40–41; and Drummond, James (1989), "Trial by Fire," *Forbes,* 144 (December 11), 148, 152.
12. Henkoff, Ronald (1994), "Floored? You Can Come Back," *Fortune,* 129 (February 21), 53–54.
13. Cronin, J. Joseph Jr., and Michael H. Morris (1989), "Satisfying Customer Expectations: The Effect on Conflict and Repurchase Intentions in Industrial Marketing Channels," *Journal of the Academy of Marketing Science,* 17 (Winter), 41–49.
14. Rosendahl, Iris (1992), "Merger Moves Still Strong in Drug Wholesaling," *Drug Topics,* 135 (November 9), 101–5.
15. Michman, Ronald D. (1990), "Managing Structural Changes in Marketing Channels," *Journal of Consumer Marketing,* 7 (Fall), 33–42.
16. Murphy, Liz (1987), "America's Best Sales Forces: Wholesale Distribution—Bergen Brunswig Locks in Sales with Service," *Sales & Marketing Management,* 138 (June), 48.
17. Kelley, Bill (1987), "America's Best Sales Forces: Industrial & Farm Equipment—Black & Decker Rebuilds," *Sales & Marketing Management,* 138 (June), 49.
18. Narus, James A., and James C. Anderson (1986), "Industrial Distributor Selling: The Roles of Outside and Inside Sales," *Industrial Marketing Management,* 15, 55–62.
19. Templin, Neal (1995), "More and More Firms Enter Joint Ventures with Big Competitors," *The Wall Street Journal,* November 1, A1–A12.24.
20. Ettorre, John J. (1988), "Value In, Value Out," *Transportation & Distribution,* 29 (March), 32–33.
21. "Retail Technology: The Evolution Is Giving Way to Revolution," *Chain Store Age Executive,* 69 (October), 8–13.
22. Adapted from Gold, Jacqueline S. (1993), "The Marathon Man?" *Financial World,* 162 (February 16), 32–33; Comte, Elizabeth (1992), "Art for Shoes' Sake," *Forbes,* 150 (September 28), 128–30; and Fitzgerald, Kate (1992), "Marketers Learn to 'Just Do It,' " *Advertising Age,* 63 (January 27), S7–S8.
23. Stewart, Thomas A. (1992), "Brace for Japan's Hot New Strategy," *Fortune,* September 21, 62–73.
24. Valenti, Michael (1993), "Increasing the Flexibility of Process Control," *Mechanical Engineering,* 115 (October), 62–67.
25. Weiner, Elizabeth, and Dean Foust (1988), "Why Made-in-America Is Back in Style," *Business Week,* November 7, 116–20.
26. Bramson, Laura (1990), "Make Sales a Partner in Lead Generation Process," *Sales & Marketing Management,* 142 (July), 94, 96.

chapter

3

Attaining Competitive Advantage through Channel Design

Learning Objectives

After reading this chapter, you should be able to:

- Discuss how conventional marketing channels are like business teams.
- Explain conventional channel design.
- Discuss why channel design decisions are critical to the success of marketing organizations and marketing channels.
- Discuss the various channel design options.
- Describe how to identify the best channel design.
- Explain how to evaluate the performance of channel structures and how to modify existing channel arrangements.
- Discuss the growth of multichannel marketing systems and how to design channels to capture channel positions.

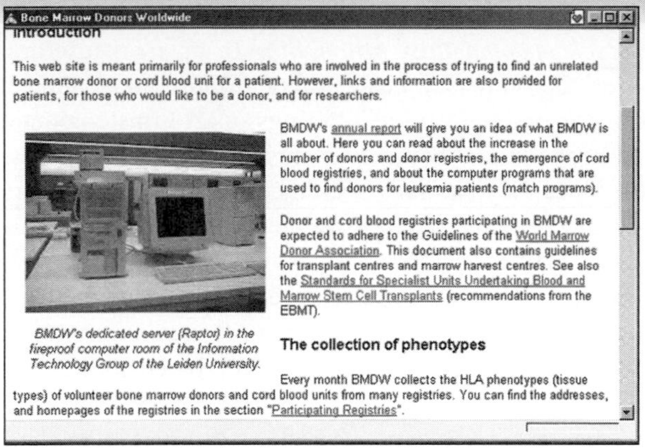

Corbis

In many traditional global business markets, there is an oversupply of products or services. Think personal computers, hotel space, tires, or rental cars. There are more than enough of each to make many choices available to consumers. But to understand the complexity of channel design, we investigate a product in high demand, but in low supply. Although there are nearly 7,000,000 units worldwide, they remain in short supply.

You see, one of the few markets for which there is not an oversupply is the donation of organs for transplantation. Think hearts, livers, lungs, or bone marrow. The needy recipients—the consumers (patients)—who populate this special market usually are lacking many choices or, perhaps, they have none at all. Imagine the awesome task of collecting, coordinating, and distributing Human Leukocyte Antigens (HLA) phenotypes of volunteer bone marrow donors, and you can begin to comprehend the complexities of channel design. The Bone Marrow Donors Worldwide (BMDW) is a channel intermediary predicated on data mining and matching. BMDW connects 48 bone marrow donor registries from 37 countries, and 22 blood registries from 15 countries. At its nerve center is *Raptor*, a dedicated server in a fireproof computer room at Leiden University.

* * * *

In the Net Economy, the importance of information exchange is vital to channel efficiency and effectiveness. In the case of organ transplants, information exchange is a matter of life or death. The efforts of agencies like the BMDW to convince people to increase the supply of organs have usually fallen short of the ideal. Potential donors prefer not to be reminded that they will one day die or simply remain indifferent to the needs of others. (Of course, the fact that one must die to donate—with the exception of bone marrow—may have a dampening effect on the motivation of donors.)

These facts provide us with a useful setting from which we can introduce the concept called *the cycle of competitive rationality*.[1] In any market setting, oversupply leads to one critical outcome: Consumers or business organizations have more choices. Customers are free to choose from among the various offerings of all firms competing in the market, all of whom want to make the sale. When customers have abundant choices, they tend to get really smart, really fast. Since they naturally seek the most value, customers learn to make price comparisons, seek new benefits, and look for the opportunity to play one supplier against another. It's a dog-eat-dog market out there.

The marketing firms themselves, we would like to assume, are already wise to this game. They develop new products or services, introduce different price options, attempt to distribute the offerings in ways not previously seen by customers, and strive to communicate with customers in new and enticing ways. In short, marketing firms attempt to innovate. And all this innovation occurs in—you guessed it—the marketing channel.

This type of innovation sounds good, you may be thinking. And you would be right. The problem is that, in most markets, successful innovation quickly leads to imitation by competitors. That, in turn, leads to equilibrium in the marketplace, with all competitors basically back where they started from. By the way, all the imitation usually leads to even more oversupply.

To keep up with the cycle of competitive rationality, firms need to constantly pursue what is known as a *sustainable competitive advantage*. Two basic sources of competitive advantage are available for any firm to pursue: superior resources and superior skills. Some firms have both, like Cisco Systems or Sun Microsystems. Superior resources is a catchphrase that implies a firm enjoys greater reserves of or access to financial capital, superior production abilities or capacities, better location, or prime access to supplies. Superior skills suggest the firm enjoys more human talent, know-how, competencies, or managerial ability.

Supposedly, either source of competitive advantage can contribute to a situation where the firm can differentiate itself or its offerings or become recognized as the low-cost supplier. Low-cost competitors can presumably produce and distribute the product or service at the lowest price and capture all the market opportunities. Those firms who cannot or do not wish to become low-cost suppliers must do something different. They can make their offering bigger, faster, prettier, higher in quality, more flexible, or just plain better than their competitor's offerings. Or, such firms can undertake promotional or distribution efforts that lead the market to believe that such differences exist. The fact of the matter is that the channel provides the most logical place through which either outcome can be achieved.

What else happens when firms achieve a position of competitive advantage? Two outcomes result, and each is desirable. First, customer satisfaction is likely to be enhanced. All things being equal, the firm that passes on the benefits of a differentiated offering or the gains accorded by lower cost will deliver more satisfaction to its customers. The other is customer loyalty. Satisfied customers tend to remain loyal to the firm that fulfills their expectations. In short, they are unlikely to go out looking for other competitors to make them happy.

The Nature of Competitive Advantage

It is critical to the success of all marketing organizations that they achieve some sort of competitive advantage in the marketplace. A competitive advantage can be achieved only when two distinct conditions are met. First, for an organization to enjoy a competitive advantage in a market, the difference or differences between it and its competitors must be felt in the marketplace: that is, the difference(s) must be reflected in some characteristic of the offering (product or service) that is a *critical buying criterion* for customers or prospects. And the product/service offering must be differentiated enough to win the loyalty of a significant set of buyers; it must leave a footprint in the market.[2]

Few people, for example, would argue about the off-road prowess of Japanese-built four-wheel-drive trucks. They have a reputation for reliability, maneuverability, and economy that is hard to beat.[3] Japanese Sports Utility Vehicle (SUV) manufacturers have earned their footprint in the market over time. In this chapter, we explore how marketing channel design facilitates differentiation to achieve competitive advantage.

Marketing Channels as Organizational Teams

There is a great deal of talk these days about team building. What's new about this concept? Most marketers have always worked in teams. Shoemakers, blacksmiths, and woodworkers worked with their wives as their teammates. While husbands took care of production, wives took care of customers, apprentices, and the books. In fact, until the early part of this century, such teams were the most important marketing dyads and business systems.[4]

Until recently, individual organizations have received more attention than organizational teams. Now, with knowledge- and information-based work groups growing in significance and effectiveness, conventional channel teams are emerging as the most important work units. **Conventional channel teams** are loosely aligned teams of organizations designed to bridge gaps between producers and consumers. They are perhaps the most difficult type of marketing team to assemble and make work effectively. But this is a difficulty that simply has to be faced in today's marketplace. To achieve success, marketing organizations must learn to use different types of channel designs (teams) for different purposes.

Each organization in a conventional channel team is a functional specialist. But for conventional channels to succeed, each member still must perform as part of a system. These systems must be properly designed to achieve the continuity that channel members need to convert their special skills into a successful team performance. For this to happen, channel organizations must agree on what results are being sought through the channel. Channel members must also define their purpose, core competencies, system of rewards and punishments, means of conflict resolution, and behavioral norms. Good channel design often paves the way to market leadership and overall business success. Without the benefits of solid marketing channels, even superior products can fail. Because they require years of continuous attention to develop, sound manufacturer → intermediary → end-user linkages are often barriers to competitive entry. Before we begin discussing the specifics of channel design, we need to address a few general issues and questions concerning conventional marketing channels.

Marketing Channels: Issues and Answers

Producers, wholesalers, other intermediaries such as agents or support servicers, and retailers all face channel design decisions.[6] Retailers look upstream, that is, back up the channel, in their efforts to secure suppliers. Retailers like Toys "R" Us and Home Depot have flourished in large part because of their ability to design and then successfully lead channels. Wholesalers look upstream toward suppliers and downstream toward retailers. McKesson Drug Co. and American Hospital Supply, for example, have emerged as dominant players in their respective industries through effective channel design decisions. Each has achieved its dominance while occupying classic intermediary positions. As you might expect, producers look downstream—toward the market. It might surprise you to learn that they also look upstream toward their own supply sources. Read Channel Surfing 3.1 to unravel a few other myths about how channels of distribution operate.

The perspective employed in this chapter reflects the traditional view that channel flows begin with a producer-manufacturer and end with the user-consumer. Thus, our discussion of channel design and related processes generally will be conducted from the producer's perspective. This perspective is adopted to simplify the discussion that follows; however, the principles discussed here are equally applicable to wholesalers or retailers.

What Is Channel Design?

The concept of *design* can be used descriptively to indicate a pattern, arrangement, or meaningful structure of parts. In this chapter the term *design* pertains to the pattern or arrangement that exists between organizations in marketing systems. Design reflects the rules and regulations that system members use to create and sustain the system. **Channel design** refers to those decisions associated with the formation of new marketing channels or the alteration of existing channels. Channel design should be viewed as a strategic decision. This is because a properly executed design can provide a differential advantage in the marketplace. Differential advantages are also called **sustainable competitive advantages (SCAs).** SCAs allow firms to gain long-term market advantages relative to their competitors.[7] It is no less important for firms to seek SCAs through their channel design decisions than through product, promotional, or pricing decisions. In fact, pursuing SCAs through channel design makes more sense. Why? Because a superior channel design yields long-term, that is, sustainable, advantages that cannot be easily imitated by competitors.

Why Are Channel Design Decisions Critical?

The type of channel a producer chooses directly influences all of its other marketing decisions. For instance, producers' prices vary substantially according to whether they use mass merchandisers or high-quality, high-prestige boutiques to distribute their goods to final users. Promotional decisions depend, in part, on how much training or motivation their intermediaries or retailers need. Channel design decisions typically involve relatively long-term commitments to other organizations and to the particular markets those channel members serve. Once Toyota contracts with an independent dealer in Memphis to sell its vehicles, for example, that dealer cannot easily be replaced with company-owned outlets.

Channel Surfing 3.1

Some Distribution Myths

Oftentimes, manufacturers' decisions about their distribution channel are based on conventional wisdom. Unfortunately, conventional wisdom is often flawed. Witness the timely demise of the following four bits of conventional wisdom (C.W.) as they relate to marketing channels:

- **C.W.** A channel of distribution is the movement of a product from the manufacturer to the ultimate user.
- **Reality.** No product is ever bought strictly as a physical entity. Instead, it is always sold with some added service or value. Even the shady street merchant who pulls up his sleeve to offer you a choice from among a dozen watches on his arm provides you some service along with your selection. After all, you receive immediate delivery and a "killer" price. Return policies, however, are usually a little dicey.
- **C.W.** A firm sells to or buys from another firm.
- **Reality.** Manufacturers never simply sell their products to intermediaries. At that point, the manufacturer's job has just begun. After the sale, the manufacturer should strive to do everything possible for the intermediary so that the inventory will move quickly and the product will be reordered. In consumer markets, the distribution burden of the manufacturer should almost certainly extend to retailers (in the form of cooperative advertising, point-of-purchase displays, demonstrations, missionary sales calls, and the like) and consumers themselves (in the form of product warranties, instructions, information, coupons, and national advertising). In reality, manufacturers do not sell *to* middlemen, they sell *through* middlemen.
- **C.W.** Distribution channels are managed by manufacturers.
- **Reality.** If so, then someone had better tell Sears, Wal-Mart, and Kmart, among numerous other retailing and wholesaling behemoths. They manage their channels by deciding what to buy, whether to make their own products, which manufacturers to purchase from, and so on. Manufacturers are no different. They are involved in planning and managing channels, as well, by addressing such questions as: Should we use exclusive, selective, or intensive distribution? Should we distribute through our own salespeople or through manufacturer's representatives? Should we own our retailers?
- **C.W.** Planning distribution strategy is the responsibility of the distribution manager.
- **Reality.** Most distribution managers deal with distribution purely in a physical context. Distribution strategy is so significant and all encompassing that it has a profound influence on all other areas within the firm (i.e., personnel, finance, and production, not to mention the other areas of the marketing mix). The producer's decision to open its own retail outlets has so many implications that it can only be made at the highest decision-making levels of the firm.

Points to Ponder

- Did you have any other misconceptions about marketing channels prior to taking this course? What were they?

Source: Adapted from Pearson, Daniel M. (1981), "Ten Distribution Myths," *Business Horizons*, 24 (May–June), 17–23; Anonymous (1993), "Expo Educates Shippers," *Transportation & Distribution*, 34 (6), 15–16; and Focht, William L. (1992), "Brokerage Marketing Today," *Broker World*, 12 (10), 18–30.

Channel design discussions are also critical because a channel system is the key external resource of many manufacturers. Successful channels often take years to build and, once established, are not easily changed. Channel design decisions represent a commitment to a set of policies and procedures. Because channels are sometimes easier to get into than they are to get out of, channel managers should design channels with a forward view based on the likely shape of tomorrow's market environment. Avon, beauty aid provider for more than a century, is doing just that.

There was a time when the "Ding-Dong, Avon Calling" promotional campaign had built a universal awareness of the direct-selling-in-home brand. But market environments constantly change. Today, Avon might still ring that doorbell, but it is almost a sure thing that the lady of the house won't be there to answer. In response to these market shifts, Avon has made over itself and its distribution channels. In Great Britain, Avon launched a quarterly women's lifestyles magazine, available only through its sales force. The move followed Avon's decision to sell its products through retail outlets such as Sears and J.C. Penney.[8]

How Do Marketing Functions Factor into the Channel Design Decision?

Marketing channels perform the task of moving goods from producers to consumers. In doing so, the channels close time, place, and possession gaps that separate goods and services from consumers. To achieve these outcomes, channel members must perform several marketing functions. These marketing functions are listed below in the order in which they would normally arise in an automotive distribution channel:

- **Information.** The accumulation and distribution of information about current and potential customers, competitors, and others in the marketing environment.
- **Promotion.** The construction and distribution of persuasive and/or informative communications designed to attract buyers.
- **Negotiation.** The means by which final agreement on price and other terms (financing, features, etc.) is reached so that transfer of ownership and possession can be completed.
- **Ordering.** The communication of an end-user's intention to purchase through the channel members to producers.
- **Financing.** The procurement and allocation of funds required to finance automotive inventories at the channel's differing levels.
- **Risk-taking.** The bearing of the risks associated with carrying out channel-related work.
- **Possession.** The successive stages by which the storage and movement of physical products from the raw materials to final customers occurs.
- **Billing.** The forward movement of a detailed list of goods sold or services provided, together with the charges and terms.
- **Payment.** In response to invoices received, payment involves the means by which buyers pay their bills through financial institutions to sellers.
- **Title.** The actual transfer of automobile ownership from one organization to another, or to the final consumer.

Certain channel functions flow forward (promotion, possession, billing, and title). Other functions flow backward (ordering and payment). Still others flow up and down the channel (information, negotiation, financing, and risk taking). Typically, several different channel members are involved in the performance of these functions. Five of these functions and their flows are shown in Exhibit 3.1.

The 10 functions listed above share three characteristics: (1) They usually can be performed better through specialization, (2) they can be shifted among channel members, and (3) they invariably use someone's resources. If the performance of functions is shifted, some or all of their associated costs are also shifted. To the extent that producers perform these functions themselves, their costs and prices increase. As functions are shifted to intermediaries, producers' costs and prices decrease, but the intermediaries must add a charge to account for their efforts. However, since intermediaries are typically specialized and more proficient in their functional area(s) than producers, end-user prices may actually decrease. Moreover, the final users may perform some of these functions themselves, in which case they should benefit from lower prices. Regardless, the total costs and profit margins demanded by each channel member are reflected in the final buyer's price.

Whether these or similar functions need to be performed in marketing channels is never at issue. The functions cannot be eliminated. They can only be shifted from one channel member to another. Therefore, the key question asked in the channel design process is, Who will perform these functions? The answer to this question turns on two issues: efficiency and effectiveness. The process by which alternative channel designs are evaluated in terms of their ability to perform a function with a minimum expenditure of effort or expense is called a **channel efficiency analysis.** Similarly, a **channel effectiveness analysis** considers the strategic fit of a channel design with the channel member's overall marketing strategy. Effectiveness relates to a channel design's ability to perform competently. The evaluation of channel effectiveness requires a longer time horizon than does efficiency analysis.

Two basic types of intermediaries—those who take title to goods (resellers) and those who do not (agents)—are available to perform channel functions. Promotion and selling activities are one such function. Changes are occurring in the insurance distribution landscape. The traditional means of selling insurance products to customers via an agent in a face-to-face exchange is being challenged by an alternative distribution approach. Alternative distribution is any means of promoting, selling, or delivering financial products to the consumer other than through an agent in a traditional face-to-face setting. Only time and the individual firm's strategic intentions will tell which channel is more effective.

Some intermediaries are specialists who perform one or a limited number of functions. Others are generalists who perform multiple functions. All intermediaries charge either upstream or downstream channel members for all functions performed. The total costs and profit margins demanded by each channel member are reflected in the final buyer's price. Whether the final buyer actually purchases the product or service depends in part on alternative choices available or, possibly, the decision to do without or solve the need without the purchase.

When Is It Time to Design (or Redesign) a Channel?

When a new firm is established, either as a start-up or from a merger or acquisition, the need to design new channel arrangements is clear. When markets change, the need for channel redesign may arise. For instance, the increase in discount megaretailers in the United States over the last 10 years recently prompted high-prestige home furnishing manufacturers such

EXHIBIT 3.1

Five different marketing functions in an automobile channel

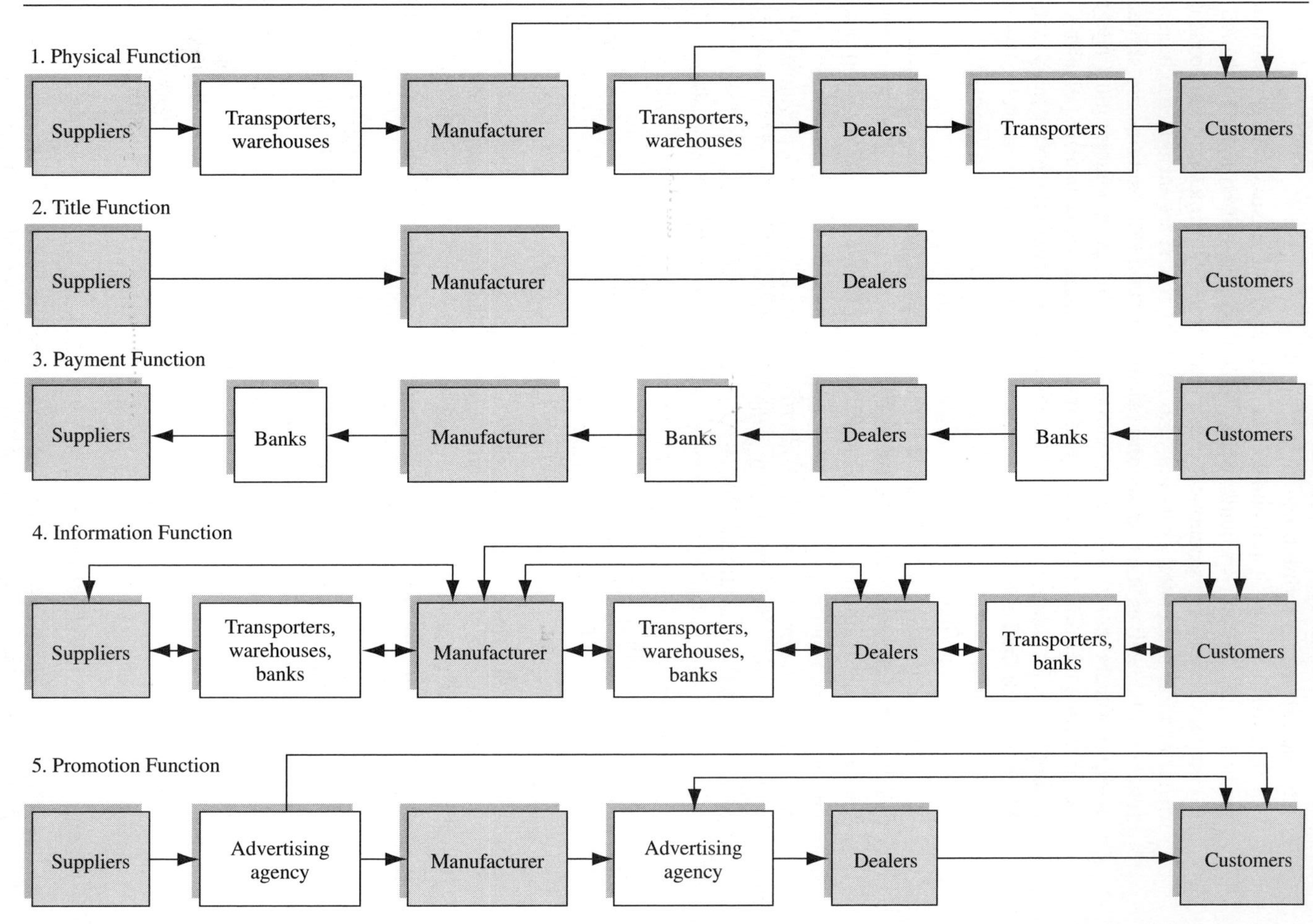

Source: Adapted from Kotler, Phillip (1994), *Marketing Management: Analysis, Planning, Implementation and Control*, Englewood Cliffs, NJ: Prentice Hall.

as Dakota, Inc., to seek out these retail settings.[9] In the past, Dakota had shunned such outlets out of concern for its image as a high-quality supplier.

A variety of other circumstances might indicate the need to design or redesign the channel. Such circumstances include the organization's development of a new product or product line or a decision to target new markets. For example, when General Motors introduced Saturn automobiles in 1990, a radically different distribution system had to be developed to minimize competition with existing General Motors products. Additionally, the need for channel design could be precipitated by existing channel members changing their policies, failing to perform as expected, or engaging in practices that cause conflict. External environmental changes (e.g., economic, competitive, sociocultural, technological, legal) might also trigger the need to design or redesign a channel.

Channel Design Decisions

When designing marketing channels, organizations should pursue a workable compromise among what is ideal, what is adequate, and what is obtainable. To illustrate, consider that new manufacturers often feature small operations within a limited market area. Because smaller firms generally have restricted capital resources, they usually use existing intermediaries. Further, the number of intermediaries available in a given local market is frequently small, possibly consisting of a few manufacturer's sales representatives, a couple of wholesalers, several established retailers, and a trucking company or two. Deciding on the best channel design in such an environment may be no problem at all. Few to none of the potential intermediaries may actually be available. In this case, the small firm's channel design decisions may be easier than they would prefer, that is, they may be forced to perform many channel functions themselves.

Larger firms, on the other hand, tend to use different types of channels in different markets. A producer might market through wholesale distributors in its larger markets, while in smaller markets it might sell directly to retailers. In one part of the country, the firm might sell through all of the retail outlets willing to handle its goods; in another, the firm might grant exclusive arrangements to a few retailers. In rural areas, manufacturers might distribute to consumers through full-line merchandisers; in more heavily populated areas, distributors might be limited-line retailers.

Large or small, an organization's channel designs should evolve in response to a **SWOT analysis,** an evaluation of the firm's *S*trengths and *W*eaknesses and the *O*pportunities and *T*hreats present in the relevant market environment. Information relating to a channel member's profitability, sales volume, brand associations, product portfolio and life cycles, and relative costs should be evaluated in a SWOT analysis. This analysis should likewise consider an organization's employee/managerial attitudes, performance, and capabilities, along with its past and current marketing strategies. In addition, a SWOT analysis should consider key market success factors and the market's attractiveness to new entrants, cost structures, and barriers to entry. Finally, technological issues, key societal/cultural trends and developments, and competitors' strengths and limitations should be evaluated.

Channel Design Options

In making channel design decisions, a number of conventional channel systems are available. These designs vary along three dimensions: (1) number of levels present in the channel, (2) number of intermediaries operating at each level, and (3) types of intermediaries used at each level. Each dimension, along with its consequences for channel design and management, is discussed below.

Number of Levels in the Channel. Each intermediary that performs a function necessary to convey a good or service closer to final users represents a **channel level.** Since the producer and the final user also perform certain functions, they are part of any channel design. A **channel's length** is described by the number of intermediary levels other than the producer and user that it contains.

A zero-level channel or direct marketing channel exists when a producer sells directly to the final user. In consumer channels, door-to-door selling, mail-order catalogues, telemarketing, or manufacturer-owned retail outlets each illustrate zero-level channels. One-level channel designs feature one selling intermediary, such as a retailer who buys directly from the producer. Two-level channels feature two selling intermediaries, such as a wholesaler and a retailer. Three-level channels feature some combination of three intermediaries, such as a wholesaler, agent, and retailer. Consumer channels rarely extend beyond four levels.

Industrial marketing channel designs usually differ only slightly from consumer channels. In zero-level industrial channels, producers use their sales force to market directly to industrial customers. However, that same sales force might also market to industrial distributors who then sell to final industrial users. Or, producers can sell directly to industrial users through manufacturers' representatives or use those reps to market to industrial distributors. Industrial channel levels often prove more extensive than the channel relationships depicted in Exhibit 3.2.[10]

While channels normally describe a forward movement of goods, backward-flowing channels also exist.[11] Solid waste recycling has emerged as both a major ecological goal and an ongoing need in the United States. To accommodate this need, several intermediaries have emerged who play a role in backward-flowing channels. These intermediaries include manufacturers' redemption centers, community recycling groups, and trash-collection specialists. In these reverse channels, goods and materials flow from end users backward to production sectors for use as cost-effective inputs.[12] Reverse channels accommodate backward flows for used goods such as homes, computers, automobiles, and commercial aircraft.

Number of Intermediaries at Each Level. Organizations must next determine the number of intermediaries to be used at each channel level. Three basic choices are available:

- **Intensive distribution.** In this design, producers distribute through as many outlets as possible. The decision whether to use intensive distribution depends on the nature of product and consumer characteristics and the level of control desired by the channel designer. When consumers demand location convenience or when a product is low involvement, producers offer a greater intensity of distribution. Convenience-oriented consumer goods such as snack foods, gasoline, or razors are usually distributed in this fashion.

EXHIBIT 3.2

Number of levels: Consumer and industrial channel design

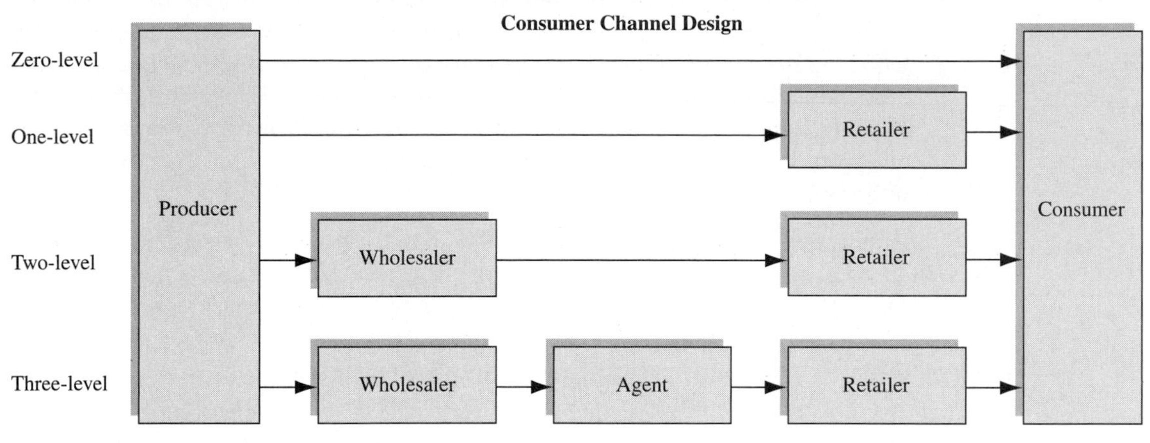

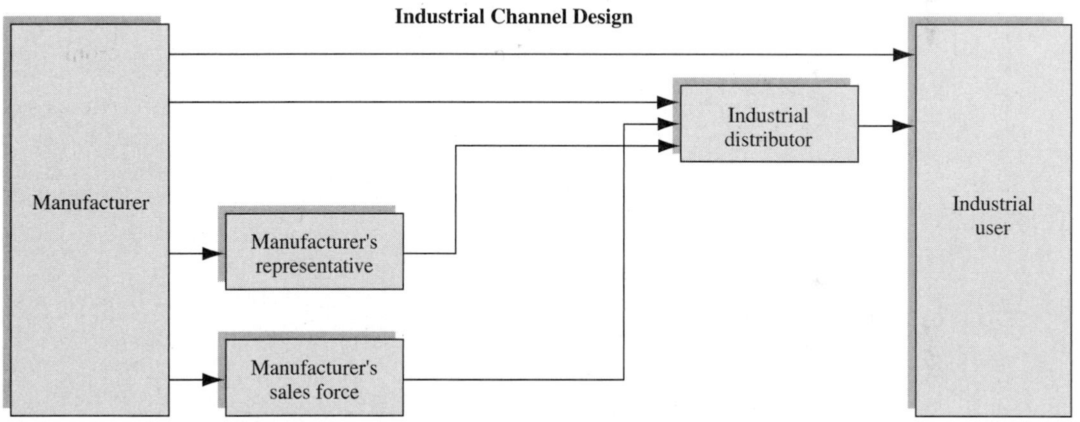

- **Exclusive distribution.** On the other end of this spectrum, exclusive distribution places limits on the number of intermediaries operating at any given channel level. Exclusive distribution is used when producers want to retain control over the quality of service levels provided and involves dealers agreeing to not carry competing brands. Intermediaries who enter exclusive distribution agreements are likely to be relationship-oriented. By entering exclusive arrangements, producers hope to secure more aggressive and knowledgeable sales efforts. The image of products distributed in this manner is typically enhanced. Higher markups follow. Most new automobiles, certain major appliances, and a few clothing lines like Armani or Pucci are distributed through exclusive channels.

- **Selective distribution.** This distribution strategy lies between the two extremes. In this case, more than one but fewer than all available intermediaries are used. Manufacturers do not have to spread their limited resources over too many outlets, including many that are possibly marginal. Better relationships with intermediaries who are selected can be developed and producers can logically expect better-than-average marketing efforts. Manufacturers can also gain sufficient market coverage with more control and less cost than with intensive distribution. Downstream intermediaries benefit from the opportunity to market somewhat more exclusive offerings.

Manufacturers often face a decision whether to move from exclusive or selective distribution to intensive distribution to increase market coverage and sales. Such a move may help short-term performance while actually diminishing long-term prospects. Consider what might happen if a prestigious fashion manufacturer like Georgio Armani moved toward intensive distribution. As the firm expanded from high-end retailers to mid-level merchandisers, it would likely give up control over its display arrangements, service levels, and pricing policies. Further, as its wares entered outlets with lower overheads, retailers might begin undercutting competitors with lower prices. If a price war ensued, buyers would attach less prestige or value to Armani apparel, and the designer's ability to command premium prices would shrink.

Types of Intermediaries at Each Level. In channel design decisions, firms must also identify the types of intermediaries that are available at each channel level. Suppose that a hypothetical test equipment manufacturer called Delta Dog, Inc., perfected a measurement tool that was useful for detecting poor mechanical connections in equipment with moving parts. Delta Dog's marketing managers believe that the product will be well received in all industrial markets where electric or combustion-powered engines are used. Such markets include the automotive, aviation, railroad, and construction industries.

Unfortunately, the company's sales force is small and incapable of making significant inroads into these sectors in the near term. Delta Dog is also undercapitalized. Its problem is how best to effectively reach these diverse industrial markets in a timely and cost-efficient fashion. Delta Dog also needs to exploit its technological advantage while it lasts. In a scenario such as this, several intermediary options are available:

- **Manufacturer's sales force.** Despite Delta Dog's relative undercapitalization, the firm's unique device might be sufficiently attractive to induce outside investment. The company's sales force could then be expanded. At that point, salespeople could be assigned to exclusive territories and charged with the responsibility of contacting all prospects in that geographic area. Or the firm could develop separate sales forces that specialize in calling on different industry sectors. Members of a manufacturer's sales force perform the promotion function. They are employees and are paid a salary/commission plus benefits for performing this function.
- **Manufacturer's representatives.** Delta Dog could enter a contractual agreement with existing manufacturers' representatives who currently do business in the targeted geographic regions or with the targeted industries. These reps would be assigned responsibility and control over the marketing of Delta Dog's measurement tool.

Manufacturer's representatives are intermediaries who primarily perform the promotion function. They act as agents for manufacturers and receive a commission for their services.

- **Industrial distributors.** Lastly, Delta Dog could seek out prominent distributors that operate in the different regions or end-user industries. The distributors would buy the product for resale. In turn, Delta Dog would probably have to grant these industrial distributors exclusive territorial distribution rights and provide them with acceptable margins. It would also be expected to provide these distributors with product training and promotional support. Industrial distributors are intermediaries who take title to product and who typically perform promotional, informational, negotiation, risk-taking, and possession functions. They recover the costs for performing these functions by making profits on whatever price the market will bear and the unit volumes that can be sold to downstream buyers.

Companies often seek out innovative intermediaries. For instance, an in-ground swimming pool manufacturer might consider merchandising its products and services through home improvement stores. At the very least, such an approach would attract more consistent attention than would typical, stand-alone outlets. Sometimes firms pursue unconventional channels because of problems associated with more traditional channels. Avon became master of its own universe that way. Originally unable to break into regular department stores, the cosmetics maker opted for and mastered door-to-door selling. For years, it made more money than most of its in-store competitors.[13] That, of course, has changed, as discussed earlier.

Sometimes, formerly innovative intermediaries transform quickly into the norm. Such has often been the case with eBusiness channels, as described in Channel Surfing 3.2.

Evaluating Channel Design Alternatives

Knowing their options (based on the dimensions discussed above), most organizations can generally identify several intermediary alternatives from which to choose. Before the best channel design can be selected, these alternatives must be evaluated on three criteria: (1) *expected sales and costs,* (2) *control and resources,* and (3) *flexibility.* To illustrate this process, let's examine a hypothetical company called Tar Heels, a North Carolina–based boot manufacturer that wants to begin marketing its women's line on the East Coast. The company is deciding between the following intermediary alternatives:

- Hiring 10 new sales representatives who would operate out of a sales office located in Raleigh. They would receive a base salary plus commission.
- Using a New Jersey–based manufacturer's sales agency by the name of Jersey Girls. Jersey Girls' representatives have far-reaching contacts with shoe and boot retailers up and down the East Coast. Jersey Girls has 30 representatives who would receive a commission based on sales.

Expected Sales and Costs Criteria. Tar Heels' two distribution options will yield differing levels of sales and costs. The first question to be answered is: Which intermediary option will produce more sales? For a number of reasons, most marketers believe corporate sales forces usually sell more. Company salespeople must rely entirely on their own products to succeed.

Channel Surfing 3.2

Meet the New Way, Same as the Old Way

When eBusiness burst onto the scene a few years back, it was deemed a savior. But to the surprise of many, eBusiness was accompanied by several potential reversals of existing channel partnerships. Many firms bought into the underlying logic: Now they could sell direct, with no need to deal with those sometimes messy channel relationships. In turn, such companies began to believe their own press: No longer was there a need, many deduced, for dealers, distributors, agents, and resellers. Customers could buy directly off the Web.

But, by now, many businesses have discovered how wrong they were. Most companies have found out that they cannot profitably sell directly on the Web. As always, they need the help of reliable channel partners. After learning their lessons, companies are beginning to use the Web to strengthen opportunities, not the least of which is instant communication between partnering firms. Where communication between channel partners was once limited to monthly or even quarterly sales updates, the parties now receive data in real time. When channel partners want, say, a price quote, they can now log on to request one, without having to make a phone call and write down the information. Paperwork? What paperwork? "The race," suggests George Mele, sales director for software maker Tivoli Systems, "will be won by the swift, not the big or technologically advanced."

Resellers are no longer being casually tossed aside or largely ignored. The Internet can help—not hurt—the fruitful development of new channel designs. The Web has definitely enhanced the ability of most producers to support their resellers by complementing existing channels, improving responsiveness, servicing inventory agreements, and lowering overall costs. Channel efficiency, as well as its effectiveness, can be improved through Net-based technologies.

Points to Ponder

- What is involved when any channel introduces new types of intermediaries into its channel system?

Source: Adapted from Cioci, Michelle (2000), "Bridging the Gap," *Sales and Sales Management,* 152 (10), 134.

Naturally, they should be better trained to sell those products. Moreover, company sales forces should be more service-oriented because their success ultimately depends on their company's success. Finally, customers may prefer to deal directly with manufacturers.

Still, the sales agency *might* sell more. Jersey Girls has 30 sales reps, 20 more than Tar Heels could afford to hire. Depending on the commission structure involved, Jersey Girls' representatives may well be as aggressive as a company direct sales force. Also, customers may prefer dealing with sales agents who represent several boot makers, rather than corporate salespeople who represent only one. Finally, Jersey Girls' reps presumably have extensive, long-standing relationships with and knowledge of the target market. Tar Heels' salespeople would very likely have to build these relationships from scratch.

There is a third factor to consider, as well: Often, resellers like Jersey Girls have little interest in selling unproved products. Tar Heels may have no logical choice but to use a company-owned sales force.

Once expected sales from each intermediary have been estimated, the next question to be answered is: What are the relative costs of selling different amounts through the two intermediaries? These cost schedules are illustrated by the graph shown in Exhibit 3.3. Notice that

EXHIBIT 3.3

Break-even cost analysis: Company sales force and a manufacturer's sales agency

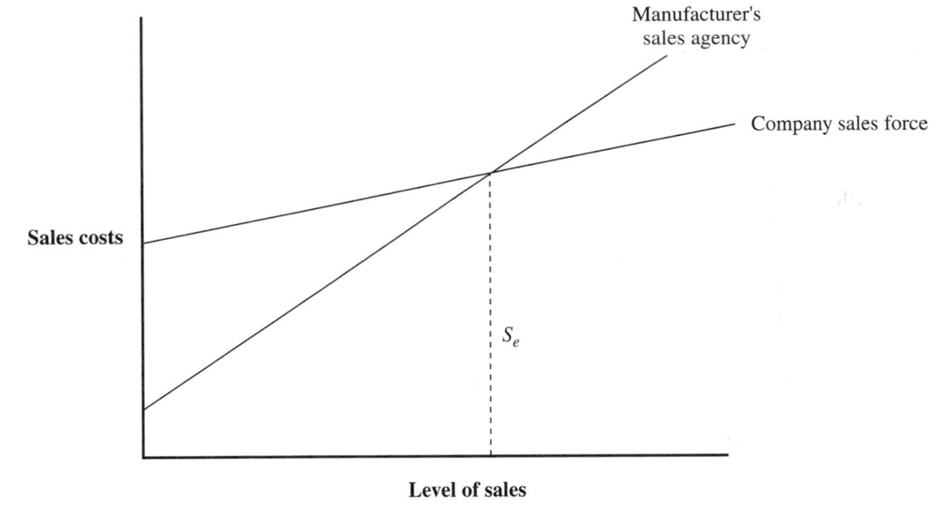

the costs of using a manufacturer's sales agency rise more quickly than do the costs of using a company's sales force. This is because, while the fixed costs of using a sales agency are always lower, costs increase faster because sales agents get higher commissions than corporate reps. At one sales level (S_e), selling costs are the same for each alternative. At that sales level, the manufacturer would be indifferent to using one or the other sales force type if it were acting strictly on an economic basis. Below that sales level, a manufacturer's sales agency like Jersey Girls provides the preferred option. Above it, a company-based sales force is preferable. Not surprisingly, sales agencies tend to be used by smaller firms, by bigger firms when they enter smaller territories, or when sales volume is too small to warrant an internal sales force.

It is important to note that distributors like Jersey Girls sometimes act opportunistically by limiting market development. Sales volume then remains below the level needed to support Tar Heels' use of direct sales channels. That's bad enough, but a distributor might then demand slotting or promotional allowances, exclusive dealing agreements, or inordinately high margins as a "levy" for continuing to carry the product. For this reason alone, other criteria must be weighed when evaluating channel design alternatives.

Control and Resources Criteria. Why might two companies manufacturing similar products that are sold to the same end users use different intermediaries? Two reasons relate to the relative control sought and resources possessed by the two firms.[14] Organizations are generally not self-sufficient. This is certainly true of Tar Heels, which requires resources such as Jersey Girls in order to survive, but wants to retain as much control over its product and resources as possible. As Exhibit 3.4 illustrates, the fewer its intermediaries and the higher its financial resources, the more control Tar Heels retains; conversely, the more Tar Heels depends on resources such as Jersey Girls, the less control it retains.

Exhibit 3.4

Issues of control vs. resources in channel design

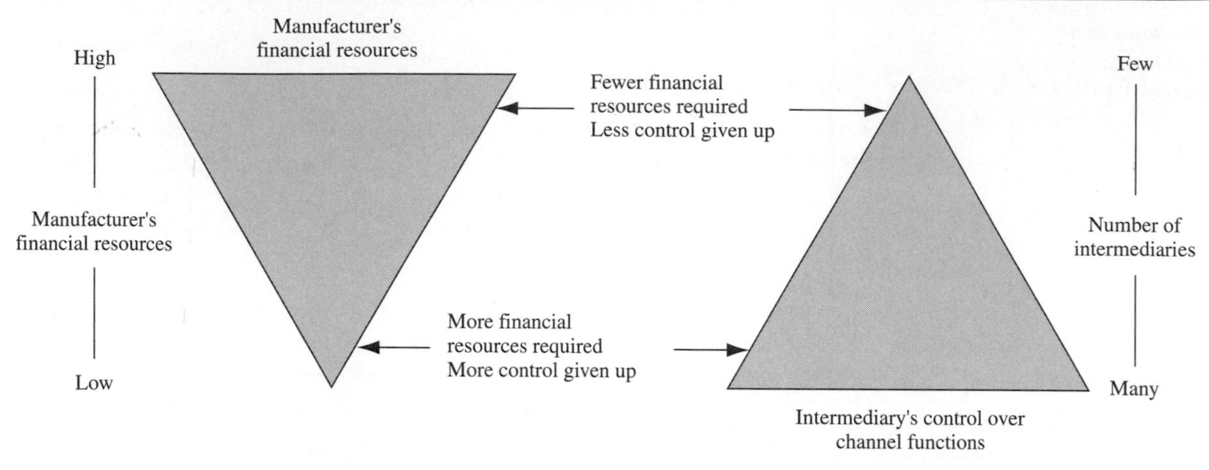

Thus, in Tar Heels' channel design decisions, a need exists to *control* important channel functions directly while leveraging limited *resources*. Intermediary selection often requires a compromise between the desire to control key functions and the need to develop maximum market coverage for a given expenditure level. Control often proves the deciding factor in this intermediary selection decision.

Flexibility Criteria. The final criterion is flexibility. Before an intermediary can be selected, channel members must reach some degree of commitment to the proposed relationship. This commitment inevitably lessens the channel member's ability to respond to changing environmental opportunities or threats. In highly volatile or uncertain markets, manufacturers seek channel structures that allow them to rapidly shift their channel strategy. If the East Coast women's boot market was stable, and maintaining control was important to Tar Heels, the manufacturer would probably opt for a company sales force.

On the other hand, if control were not so important to Tar Heels, the company would likely use Jersey Girls when facing a volatile market. That's because the latter arrangement would give Tar Heels more flexibility to exit if the market declined. Most manufacturer's representative agreements can be terminated in 30 days by either party. Moreover, Tar Heels would not have to absorb the fixed costs associated with having a company sales force.

Selecting the Best Channel Design

The best channel design is one that offers the highest performance effectiveness at the lowest possible cost. To select an optimal structure, the channel manager would have to calculate the expected revenues and costs associated with each channel alternative. However, most managers are incapable of precisely specifying all the possible design alternatives. And even when they are, calculating the exact revenues and costs associated with each alternative would be impossible. Still, several criteria can be used to estimate an optimal allocation of key marketing functions. In Channel Surfing 3.3, we critically investigate Kmart's channel design.

Analyzing Desired Channel Output Utilities

To select the best channel design, the organization first needs to understand why its targeted customers buy. Customers seek certain need-satisfying benefits from whatever goods and services they purchase or use. This makes it easy to categorize the basic utilities that channel members are generally seeking, as shown below. Different marketing channel designs will yield more or less of the following benefits:

- **Convenience (time and spatial) utility.** Waiting time—the time that customers must wait to receive goods—is a direct indicator of *temporal convenience.* Customers normally prefer fast delivery channels. In turn, faster delivery requires higher service levels. *Spatial convenience* reflects the ease with which a product or service may be acquired. Ford Motor Company, for example, offers greater spatial convenience through its marketing channels than does Mercedes Benz. Because of the number of intermediaries it has available at the retail level, Ford's customers can save on search costs when buying and servicing cars.

Channel Surfing 3.3

A Kmart Special: Better Service through Better Channel Design

Just like its slightly more glamorous competitors, Wal-Mart Stores, Inc., and Target Corp., Kmart is a retailing icon. It features a strong lineup of private-label brands like Route 66 casual clothing and Sesame Street children's clothing. Even Martha Stewart is on the team. Yet for virtually all of the 1990s, Kmart has struggled to survive following an ill-conceived foray into specialty stores. As Kmart director James B. Adamson reports, "We were on the precipice of death." What went wrong?

Many things did, including muddled merchandising. But we would argue that structural design problems within Kmart's distribution channels served to undermine its position with customers. Inefficient distribution problems plagued Kmart for years: poor inventory management that led to chronically barren shelves, too little focus on customers' needs, and a muddy marketing strategy that failed to distinguish Kmart from its competitors.

Unlike Wal-Mart's efficient channels, Kmart's are largely outdated and laded with bottlenecks. Such channel inefficiencies resonate throughout the company. What happens? Kmart ends up with too little of what customers want and too much of what they have little interest in. That, in turn, ties up salespeople in backrooms dealing with paperwork rather than waiting on customers. Getting a grip on inventory and its management should free employees to spend more time where they belong—on the sales floor. Ouch! It is obvious that the channel positions earned—for better or for worse—by even retailing giants like Kmart really count.

Points to Ponder

- What are your strategic recommendations regarding how Kmart should reengineer the distribution arm of its marketing mix?

- **Lot size utility.** The number of product units that a typical customer acquires during a transaction is the *lot size.* When securing cars for their rental fleets, companies such as Hertz or Avis demand channels through which they can acquire a large lot size. You, on the other hand, probably prefer automotive channels that allow you to purchase a lot size of one. In response, Ford has established different distribution channels for fleet and household car buyers. The smaller the lot size, the greater the service utility that the channel design must provide.
- **Selection utility.** *Selection* is the product assortment breadth (variety) provided by the marketing channel. Business and household consumers normally prefer greater selection because the chances of their needs being exactly satisfied are then improved. For that reason, car buyers often prefer doing business with dealerships that carry a variety of manufacturer brands.
- **Service utility.** *Service utility* is the value-added dimensions of a market offering (e.g., easy credit, free delivery, installation, repairs) provided by a channel. The greater the service, the higher the number of marketing functions provided by the channel.

Marketing channels can be designed to provide more or less of these four basic channel output utilities. When organizations' channel designs provide more of a value that is especially desired by end users, they will enjoy a competitive advantage. But providing increased levels of any value means increased channel costs and, usually, higher prices for end users. The success of discount stores such as Target or Kmart suggests that many consumers are happy to forgo higher channel output utilities in exchange for lower prices. Remember, though, this means consumers must provide more utilities themselves. When a mother buys her eight-year-old son a bike at Kmart, she receives no promise of additional service. If the bike's chain breaks, Kmart will not repair it and she knows it.

The trade-off between prices charged and channel utilities received is an important competitive weapon. Many consumers place little importance on some channel outputs and, therefore, will not pay for them. That many price discounters are so successful is no surprise. But certain outputs (e.g., the deep product assortments or personalized attention available at specialty clothing stores) are highly valued by consumers, and they will pay for them. When important outputs are delivered at little or no expense through a channel design, customers receive extra value. Competitors then feel pressure to follow suit through their own channel design.

Analyzing Channel Objectives and Product Characteristics

Naturally, channels should be fashioned in ways that help firms achieve their **distribution goals**—outcomes toward which distribution efforts are directed. These goals should be consistent with the firm's overall marketing strategy. To achieve these goals, many marketing functions have to be performed and channels must be designed so that they are capable of performing these necessary functions.

Distribution goals should be expressed in terms of the channel output utilities sought. Organizations should arrange their functional tasks in ways that minimize total costs while achieving the desired channel output utilities.[15] Usually, several segments of end users who seek different levels of output utilities can be identified (recall the Hertz and individual car buyer example). Effective channel design dictates identification of which segments to pursue and the best channel structures for each segment.

Distribution goals change depending on several product characteristics. These include:

- **Unit value.** Generally, the lower the product's unit value, the longer its distribution channel will be. The product's lower value leaves only a small margin to cover each intermediary's costs. High-value products are often sold directly through a company sales force rather than through intermediaries.
- **Standardization.** Nonstandardized products, such as custom-built machinery, are usually sold directly because intermediaries often lack the necessary specialized knowledge. Products requiring installation and/or heavy maintenance service are also sold directly to end users. Standardized products, such as office supplies, are typically sold through channels featuring more than one intermediary.
- **Bulkiness.** Bulky or heavy products often have high handling and shipping costs relative to their value. Such products demand channels that minimize distance and the amount of handling that occurs on the path between producers and consumers. Basic cola drinks are bulky, suggesting that their channels should be as short as possible. Channels for *perishable* products should also be shortened to accommodate the need for timely delivery.
- **Complexity.** Highly complex products are usually distributed to consumer and industrial markets through direct channels. Complex products need salespeople who are capable of conveying the product's technical features to potential users, and service people who provide continuing value after the sale.
- **Stage of product life cycle.** Many new products require extensive and aggressive promotional efforts during their introductory stage to establish primary demand. The longer the channel, the more difficult it is to attain this type of effort from each intermediary. As products progress through their life cycles, their channels are generally lengthened.

Analyzing Market Behaviors and Segments

Current and potential buyer behaviors need to be evaluated. The question, *who* is doing the buying is crucial. For example, if spouses or other life partners each have significant input into a purchasing decision, the product should be distributed through intermediaries that successfully service the needs of both. The distribution channels through which homes are sold illustrate this point. Conversely, certain key employers are likely to influence the outcome of important industrial purchases. This implies that direct distribution is preferable, since it permits greater control over the sales force. The use of a company salesperson can ensure that all parties who have input in buying decisions are contacted.

Other questions pertaining to when, where, and how end users buy also need to be answered. For example, if buying patterns are seasonal, intermediaries that can perform a storage function should be added to the channel. The storage function flattens what are otherwise peaks and valleys in production. Consumers are increasingly shopping for products from their homes. This trend implies that producers should eliminate intermediaries such as wholesalers and retailers and sell direct. By contrast, for environmental products that consumers typically buy in small quantities, long channels involving several intermediaries are usually needed.

Many manufacturers think primarily in terms of geographic coverage before considering the coverage of distinct market segments. Large portions of America's fishery and forest industries operate in the same Pacific Northwest region. Customers in these two industries frequently purchase the same item in the same region from different distributors. Fishery-based customers buy primarily from marine supply distributors while forest-products customers buy the same items from their own distributors.

Finally, customers prefer to deal with intermediaries that know their industry's language. Navistar employs different distributors to serve the agriculture and construction equipment market segments. Caterpillar uses three different channels to serve the construction equipment, light truck, and diesel truck engine markets located in the same geographic region. In short, wise manufacturers design different types of marketing channels to serve specialized market segments.

Evaluating Channel Structure Performance

Once a channel design has been established, firms should periodically review the performance of their intermediaries. Channel systems inevitably require changes to meet new or changing conditions in the marketplace. Channel members should first review the sales growth that the intermediaries allow them to achieve and consider eliminating intermediaries whose sales fall below expectations. Such decisions are not as cut-and-dry as they may appear. Navistar once observed, for example, that several of its dealers were selling fewer than five trucks a year. The cost to Navistar of servicing these particular dealers actually totaled more than their truck sales. Still, after it concluded that dropping the dealers would have negative ramifications for the distribution system as a whole, Navistar elected to retain the dealers. Dropping the dealers would have required that some employees be terminated and that equipment be shut down, and end-user business in the affected markets would have been lost. When it examined the whole picture, Navistar realized that dropping the low-seller dealers would actually incur more long-term costs than would keeping them.[16]

By performing a thorough evaluation, firms occasionally discover that they are paying channel members too much in relation to what they receive in return. Underperforming intermediaries should be counseled, retrained, or remotivated. Channel members should terminate their relationship with intermediaries who do not perform satisfactorily if they do not respond favorably to recommended modifications.

Modifying Existing Channels

Organizations must do more than construct a good channel design, set it in motion, and then sit back and watch. **Channel adjustments**—purposeful modifications to intermediary relationships—become necessary when customer buying patterns change, markets expand, new competition arises, or as innovative distribution channel options become available. Channel members should consider carefully how proposed changes in their channels structure would impact relationships at each level of their distribution systems. Channel adjustments generally involve one of three possible changes:

- Add or drop individual intermediaries.
- Add or drop particular marketing channels.
- Develop new ways of distributing or selling goods within a particular market.

The most difficult adjustments are those whose implementation necessitates revising the overall channel strategy.[17] For instance, a heavy truck manufacturer might elect to replace independent dealers with company-owned dealers, or a cola manufacturer might replace locally operated franchised bottlers with a centralized bottling and marketing system. Such decisions would require changes in at least three of the four marketing mix decision areas; that is, product, promotion, and, of course, distribution. Price will probably change, as well. The consequences associated with each channel adjustment would also be significant.

Three specific types of channels adjustments are those associated with product life cycles, customer-driven refinement, and the need for multichannel systems.

Product Life Cycle Changes

Many companies either fail to recognize or do not act on the fact that the distribution and selling requirements for a product change over its life cycle. No single channel design will prove ideal during the entire product life cycle. Products that are "new to the world" require a specialized channels design that can provide both technical assistance as bugs are worked out and missionary efforts as new users are developed within the marketplace. To justify all these educational efforts, distributors may demand an exclusive arrangement. As a product matures, becoming more standardized and better known, less-specialized knowledge and efforts are needed to sell it. Producers can then expand the number of intermediaries distributing the item, as buyers invariably switch to lower-cost channels.

The matrix shown in Exhibit 3.5 illustrates how the ideal marketing channels for individual pieces of designer apparel change across time and the item's life cycle. The product's market growth rate and value added by channel intermediaries (e.g., type and level) drive preferred channel design. In the introductory stage, new fashions usually enter markets through specialty channels such as boutiques that spot trends, cater to early adopters, and add substantial value to the item. As market interest grows and demand takes off, the fashion item is distributed through better department stores that provide specialized services, but not as many stores as the previous channel. As the product matures and demand flattens, the garment will appear in lower-cost, mass-merchandising venues. Less value is added there. When decline sets in, lower-cost channels like low-end mail-order houses, off-price discounters, or outlet stores dominate designer apparel's distribution.

Customer-Driven Refinement of Existing Channels

The capability of any channel that is not modified decreases as time passes. Gaps inevitably arise between an existing channel and an ideal system. Eventually, customers will switch to those distribution systems that deliver the sought-after benefits and services. To be successful, marketing organizations must be aware of these customer-driven changes and be willing

EXHIBIT 3.5

Changes in life cycle and channels: The case of designer apparel

Utility Added by Channel

Market Growth Rate	High	Low
Low	**Introductory stage** Boutique (e.g., service utility)	**Declining/Death** Off-price outlets (e.g., convenience utility)
High	**Growth stage** Better department stores (e.g., selection utility)	**Mature stage** Merchandisers (e.g., lot size utility)

to switch, as well. You'll have 125 million well-heeled customers perched outside your door. Each wants his favorite department, services, or products, within easy reach; and while you're at it, no waiting at the checkout line please. Sound like the kind of benefits and services that any group of consumers would want.

It is a small wonder, then, that so many channels are being refined through the addition of online commerce. Take the New Iberia, Louisiana–based StokesTropicals.com, one of the world's largest tropical plant nurseries, which now deals almost exclusively with online customers. Many other direct marketers are capitalizing on the Web to enhance their traditional promotional and distribution efforts.

Yet, channels of distribution are difficult to change. Proposed changes often meet resistance and implemented changes sometimes encounter outright subversion.

Growth of Multichannel Marketing Systems

The third type of channels modification relates the recent growth of multichannel marketing systems. In the past, many manufacturers sold through a single channel. Today, with the growth of more precise segmentation, many firms are adopting multichannel marketing. **Multichannel marketing** occurs when a single firm uses two or more marketing channels to reach one or more market segments.[18] This practice is also called **dual distribution.**

By pursuing more segments, firms usually achieve increased market coverage, lower distribution cost, and more specialized marketing efforts. Firms often add a channel to reach customer segments that their current channel cannot reach. On other occasions, organizations add distribution channels to reduce their costs of goods sold. For example, an intermediary may specialize in telemarketing rather than regular field sales calls. Or, channels may be added because the intermediary's marketing strengths (e.g., a technically adroit, up-and-running sales force that can effectively market complex equipment) fit the firms' needs (e.g., a small, start-up manufacturer).

Companies also establish different channels to sell to different-sized customers. Direct sales may be best for handling larger customers. By contrast, a telemarketing company that features a field sales force supplement on an as-needed basis may prove best for dealing with smaller customers and prospects. Such a solution is often attractive because the producing firm can contact and service more customers at a cost and customization level that is appropriate to each.

But the gains from adding new channels may come at a price. New channels typically introduce more conflict and control problems into the distribution system. Conflicts can arise when two or more channels end up vying for the same customers, and control problems can arise when new channels are more independent than older ones.

Designing Channels to Capture Channel Positions

Meeting customer needs is a necessary but insufficient condition for success in the marketplace. Marketers must also battle competitors for each consumer. In marketers' attempts to gain an edge through channel design, the concept of a channel position should not be overlooked. A **channel position** is reflected in the reputation a channel member earns among its current and potential intermediaries for supplying market offerings, financial returns, programs, and systems that are better than those offered by competing channel members.[19] For example, a supplier that provides retailers the most exhaustive, productive, and state-of-the-art merchandising assistance is likely to cultivate and earn a reputation as the industry's promotional leader. On the other hand, a supplier that sometimes delivers products late or sells defective products is likely to be thought of as shoddy or over-priced. To succeed in today's markets, marketers must gain a reputation for providing their customers superior value. A reputation for furnishing such value is reflected in the position firms enjoy in the marketplace.

Intermediaries may easily carry more than a hundred lines, sometimes even those of direct competitors. Therefore, wholesalers should strive to provide intermediaries with superior value relative to outcomes offered by competing channel members. Value may come from the resale of products, from support programs and incentives, or, perhaps, from the channel relationship itself. Intermediaries themselves are more willing to contribute to a partnership/relationship orientation through improved marketing efforts on the producer's behalf. Channel Surfing 3.4 presents several key partner-building practices.

The typical channel manager evaluates alternatives and arrives at decisions in a far narrower context and shorter time frame than most channel theories would allow. Such circumstances, in fact, reinforce the reasons why managers should carefully weigh and continuously evaluate their channel design.

Channel Surfing 3.4

Turning Industrial Channel Intermediaries into Channel Partners

After the channel is designed and working relationships have been established between manufacturers and their distributors, certain attitudes and behavioral practices have been shown to contribute to successful, long-standing relationships. Here are several key partner-building practices:

- **Making multilevel calls.** Timken Corporation, a producer of roller bearings, has its sales representatives make multilevel calls on its distributors, including general managers, purchasing managers, and salespeople.
- **Working the counter.** Square D, a manufacturer of circuit breakers and switchboards, has its sales representatives spend an entire day with each distributor, working behind the counter in order to understand the distributors' concerns, problems, and opportunities.
- **Distributor marketing steering committee.** DuPont has established a *Distributor Marketing Steering Committee*. This group meets on a regular basis to discuss problems, trends, and opportunities.
- **Annual retreats.** Dayco Corporation, which produces engineered plastics and rubber products, conducts an annual retreat. Twenty young or relatively inexperienced distributor managers and a similar group of Dayco salespeople are chosen to attend and interact together in educational seminars and social outings.
- **Annual mail surveys.** Parker Hannifan Corporation sends out an annual mail survey to each of its distributors. In this survey, the distributors are asked to rate the corporation's performance on key dimensions. Feedback is provided to the distributor respondents.
- **Newsletters and videotapes.** Parker Hannifan also informs its distributors about new products and new product applications through newsletters and videotapes. Photocopies of distributor invoices are also collected and analyzed. From this analysis, customized advice on how the various distributors might improve their sales is provided.
- **Formal distributor marketing plans.** Cherry Electrical Products, a maker of electrical switches and electric keyboards, appointed a distributor marketing manager who works with distributors to produce formal distributor marketing plans.

Points to Ponder

- What does a manufacturer gain when it "changes" intermediaries into channel partners? Are there situations or circumstances where a manufacturer would not want to "partner-up" with intermediaries? When? Why?

Source: Adapted from Narus, James A., and James C. Anderson, (1987), "Turn Your Industrial Distributors into Partners," *Harvard Business Review*, March–April, 66–71; and Joseph, W. Benoy, John T. Gardner, and Sharon Francis (1995), "How Partnership Distributors View Distributor-Supplier Partnership Arrangements," *Industrial Marketing Management,* 24 (1), 27–36.

Better-designed channels invariably enjoy advantages. Less-intensive and more harmonious contacts among channels members, fewer duplications of efforts, greater standardization of those activities performed at different market levels, less reliance on fewer product lines, faster and better communications, lower-risk operations, more introductions of advanced technologies, and higher productivity all emerge from effective design. Each advantage leads directly to greater efficiency and profitability for the better-designed and more effectively coordinated channel. As many successful and not-so-successful firms have discovered, channel design issues really do matter. Selecting the right intermediaries, assigning them the proper functions, and formulating the channel design necessary to ensure that everyone fulfills their responsibilities will go a long way toward allowing a firm to capture—and hold onto—its intended channel position.

Key Terms

channel adjustments
channel design
channel effectiveness analysis
channel efficiency analysis
channel length
channel level
channel position
conventional channel team
distribution goals
dual distribution
multichannel marketing
sustainable competitive advantages (SCAs)
SWOT analysis

Chapter Summary

Good channel design is often the key to market leadership and overall business success. Because they generally require years of continuous attention to develop, sound manufacturer-intermediary-end-users linkages are often barriers to competitive entry. Without the benefits that accrue from solid market channels, even marketers with superior products can fail in the marketplace.

Using channel design as a strategic weapon creates sustainable competitive advantages (SCAs). SCAs refer to skills that a firm does exceptionally well which also have strategic importance to that business. SCAs allow firms to gain an advantageous position in the market relative to their competitors on a long-term basis. Channel design decisions are among the most critical facing marketing managers. The type of channel chosen directly influences each of the other marketing decisions.

Marketing channels essentially perform the task of moving goods from producers to consumers. In doing so, they overcome the time, place, and possession gaps that separate goods and services from the consumers. To achieve these critical outcomes, channel members must perform several key marketing functions, including information, promotion, negotiation, risk-taking, and billing, among others.

The process by which various channel design alternatives are evaluated in terms of their performance competencies is known as *channel efficiency analysis.* This assessment centers on the relative performance of alternative channel designs. Channel effectiveness analysis, on the other hand, considers the strategic fit with the overall marketing strategy of potential changes in the channel design. When compared to efficiency analysis, the evaluation of effectiveness factors in a marketing channel requires that the evaluator assume a longer time horizon.

A variety of circumstances can indicate that a marketing organization needs to design or redesign its channel. Such circumstances would include the organization's development of a new product or entire product line, its decision to target existing products or product lines to new consumer/business markets or geographic areas, or an awareness that significant changes have been or are about to be introduced to some other aspect of the organization's marketing mix. Moreover, such circumstances could arise when existing channel members change their policies, consistently fail to perform as expected, or are engaging in practices that cause conflict. When a new firm is established, either from scratch or as the result of merger or acquisition, the need to establish new channel arrangements is clear.

The various channel structural alternatives available to a producer firm can be identified in terms of the following three dimensions: (1) the number of levels in the channel, (2) the number of intermediaries operating at the various levels, and (3) the types of intermediaries used at each level. Each intermediary that performs a function necessary to convey the market offering closer toward the final user represents a channel level. A channel's length is described by the number of its intermediary levels. Second, companies must determine the number of intermediaries to be used at each channel level within a given market area. Three basic designs are available: intensive, exclusive, and selective distribution.

Finally, firms must identify the types of intermediaries that are available at each channel level. The following distribution alternatives are generally available: manufacturer's sales force, manufacturer's representatives, or industrial suppliers. In most instances, producers will be able to identify several intermediary alternatives. The intermediary alternatives need to be evaluated against expected sales and costs, control and resources, and flexibility criteria.

The best channel structure is reflected in the design that offers the desired performance effectiveness, at the lowest possible cost, along each marketing function to be executed. Unfortunately, reality dictates that the selection of the optimal channel design will often prove impossible. Therefore, managers should strive for the best possible design alternative by evaluating the various design options along the following criteria: service output levels desired by customers, channel objectives and product characteristics, and market behaviors and segments.

Once they have entered into a channel arrangement, channel members should periodically review their intermediaries' performance. Channels or intermediaries can be evaluated on the quality of their customer service, competence with which they manage the marketing functions assigned to them, share of the market they have achieved in the assigned area and their potential for additional share gains, and the level of attention they pay to the manufacturer's product(s).

Channel adjustments—purposeful modifications to intermediary relationships—become necessary when conditions in the marketplace change. Three specific types of channels modification are those associated with product life cycles, customer-driven refinement, and the need for multichannel systems. The most difficult adjustments are those whose implementation necessitates revising overall channel strategies.

Meeting customer needs is a necessary but insufficient condition for success in the marketplace. In marketers' attempts to foster every edge possible through channel design, the concept of a channel position should not be overlooked. A channel position is reflected in the status a channel member earns among intermediaries for supplying market offerings, financial returns, programs, and systems that are better than those offered by competing manufacturers. An enticing channel position can be achieved by treating each relationship with one's fellow channel members as partnerships that should provide desired benefits to the partner on a long-term basis. Channel members should strive to provide their intermediaries with superior value from the resale of products, support programs and incentives, or the channel relationship itself, relative to those outcomes offered by other producers. This is known as the pursuit of a sustainable partnership advantage, and, in their channels design efforts, marketers should also be guided by this goal.

Channel Challenges

1. The growth of the home business market is making high-technology product producers rethink their conventional channels of distribution. For instance, companies like Sun Microsystems have been considering alternative channels of distribution as new market opportunities arise. Consider the increasing number of individuals who are working in home offices equipped with high-technology products. How can Sun Microsystems and other technology firms design channels to capitalize on this growing market? What are the possible pitfalls of developing new channel systems?
2. In the grocery distribution system, retailers' evaluation of new products is the cornerstone of the manufacturer → wholesaler → retailer channel's success or failure. A recent study of 200 top U.S. supermarket chains suggests that almost 7 out of 10 new products never make it to store shelves, and nearly half of newly accepted products are removed from the shelf within one year of adoption. How does this study reinforce the integral role of the supplier's sales representative in new product development (in the grocery sector)?
3. In Chapter 2, you read about discounters, warehouse clubs, and other retail formats impinging on the traditional supermarkets' dominance of the food retailing sector. Supermarkets have countered this attack by offering nontraditional offerings such as video rentals, banking services, dry cleaning, and even child care. For example, Wegmans Food Markets opened a New Jersey store with on-site cooking classes, child care services, and a full-line beauty department. How will Wegmans and other supermarkets modify their channel designs to sustain and grow their market position?

4. About 10 years ago more than 80 percent of all goods in China were distributed through the state-run system. Today about 80 percent of all goods in China are expected to run through independent distributors. Clearly, China's distribution systems are unstable, but they continue to evolve. To date, China is still plagued by inefficient distribution processes, and the distribution of goods still endures an antiquated and congested infrastructure. How can new market entrants forge relationships to exploit this lucrative market? What are the likely barriers to developing conventional channels of distribution?
5. The Inernet provides more channels to customers. As you read in the preceding chapters, lateral relationships can often be used to forge competitive advantage. Consider retailing giants Sears, Carrefour, Kroger, and Metro AG, who have jointly formed GlobalNetXchange. GlobalNetXchange enables retailers to reduce procurement costs and improve channel efficiencies by using a common Internet buy, sell, and trade site. Why would these competitors agree to join forces in one site rather than develop individual Internet sites? What potential conflicts may arise on GlobalNetXchange?
6. Banks in the United States are quickly discovering that they are incapable of marketing home-based services directly to consumers. They concede that technology intermediaries—companies like Microsoft Corporation, and EDS Corporation—will provide them with the necessary skills to sell banking services. The problem is that banks are skeptical about becoming dependent on these potential competitors for selling banking services directly into consumers' households. What channel design would you recommend to U.S. bankers to penetrate the home-based banking services market?

Review Questions

1. Discuss some of the reasons behind the development of marketing channels as organizational teams.
2. What is channel design?
3. Why are marketing channel design decisions critical to the success of marketing organizations? How are marketing functions taken into consideration in channel design?
4. Discuss the circumstances which indicate a need for channel design or redesign. What market features should be considered in channel design?
5. Discuss the three dimensions of channel structure.
6. Describe the criteria used to evaluate intermediary alternatives.
7. How does a firm select the best channel structure?
8. What criteria are used to evaluate marketing channel structure? How is a desired channel structure maintained?
9. What is channel position? Why is channel position important in marketing channels?

Endnotes

1. Dickson, Peter (1992), "Toward a General Theory of Competitive Rationality," *Journal of Marketing*, January, 69–83.
2. Coyne, Kevin (1986), "Sustainable Competitive Advantage—What It Is, What It Isn't," *Business Horizons*, 20 (January–February), 54–61.
3. Shandley, Rick (1998), "New Nissan Frontiers," *Off Road*, January, 23–25.
4. Drucker, Peter (1994), "The Age of Social Transformation," *Atlantic Monthly*, November, 53–80.
5. Revesz, Therese R., and Mimi Cauley de La Sierra, (1987), "Competitive Alliances: Forging Ties Abroad," *Management Review*, March, 57.
6. Aspinwall, Leo (1958), "The Characteristics of Goods and Parallel Systems Theories," in *Managerial Marketing*, Eugene Kelley and William Lazer, eds., Homewood, IL: Richard D. Irwin, 434–50.
7. Aaker, David A. (1992), *Strategic Market Management*, New York: John Wiley & Sons, Inc.
8. Singh, Sonoo (2000), "Avon Calling for a Radical Makeover," *Marketing Week*, September 28, 27–28.

9. Ferrell, O. C., George H. Lucas, Jr., and David Luck (1994), *Strategic Marketing Management*, Cincinnati, OH: Southwestern, 221.
10. Jackson, Donald M., Robert F. Krampf, and Leonard J. Konopa (1982), "Factors That Influence the Length of Industrial Channels," *Industrial Marketing Management*, 11, 263–68.
11. McVey, Phillip (1960), "Are Channels of Distribution What the Textbooks Say?" *Journal of Marketing*, January, 61–64.
12. Pelton, Lou E., David Strutton, James H. Barnes, Jr., and Sheb L. True (1993), "The Relationship among Referents, Opportunity, Rewards, and Punishments in Consumer Attitudes toward Recycling: A Structural Equations Approach," *Journal of Macromarketing*, 13 (1), 60–74.
13. Adler, Lee (1966), "Symbiotic Marketing," *Harvard Business Review*, November–December, 59–71.
14. Cespedes, Frank V. (1988), "Control versus Resources in Channel Design: Distribution Differences in One Industry," *Industrial Marketing Management*, 17, 215–27.
15. Bucklin, Louis P. (1966), *A Theory of Distribution Channel Structure*, Berkeley, CA: Institute of Business and Economic Research; and Bucklin, Louis P. (1972), *Competition and Evolution in the Distributive Trades*, Englewood Cliffs, NJ: Prentice Hall.
16. Mele, Jim (1993), "Straight Trucks Take to the Air," *Fleet Owner*, 88 (12), 38–41.
17. McCammon, Bert C. (1963), "Alternative Explanations of Institutional Change and Channel Evolution," in *Toward Scientific Marketing*, Stephen A. Greyser, ed., Chicago: American Marketing Association, 477–90.
18. Moriaty, Rowland T., and Ursula Moran (1990), "Marketing Hybrid Marketing Systems," *Harvard Business Review*, November–December, 150–157.
19. Narus, James A., and James C. Anderson (1988), "Strengthen Distributor Performance through Channel Positioning," *Sloan Management Review*, Winter, 31–40.

chapter

4

Marketing Mix and Relationship Marketing

Learning Objectives

After reading this chapter, you should be able to:

- Describe why the marketing mix variables are key ingredients in successful channel relationships.
- Define the concept of *product* and the connection between product and relationship marketing.
- Relate agile competitive environments to the concept of products-in-process.
- Explain the general approaches to marketing channels pricing, and identify the relative advantage of the relationship pricing approach.
- Distinguish between push and pull promotion strategies and relate these strategies to relationship building.
- Demonstrate an understanding of the relationship between place and marketing channels management.
- Explain how relationship building may ultimately attain the marketing concept.

Corbis

It was the Spirit of St. Louis meets Akron, Ohio. Charles A. Lindbergh, flying the *Spirit of St. Louis,* electrified the world by becoming the first aviator to make a solo, nonstop, transatlantic flight. He departed from Roosevelt Field on Long Island, New York, on May 20, 1927, and landed at Le Bourget Field in Paris 33 hours and 30 minutes later.

Lindbergh never flew over Ohio, but Akron was a historic part of his journey. After all, his plane was equipped with tires from BF Goodrich. In 1870, Benjamin Franklin Goodrich founded the first rubber company west of the Allegheny Mountains. In the 20th century, Akron became the Rubber Capital of the World. As a manufacturer and supplier, this was not BF Goodrich's only signature on world history.

In 1937, BF Goodrich helped the United States win World War II by discovering a method for producing synthetic rubber. This helped the United States deal with an inopportune embargo when the nation's supply of natural rubber was cut off. Nearly a decade later, BF Goodrich researchers revolutionized the tire industry, inventing the first tubeless tire. And in 1961, BF Goodrich designed the first space suits for America's space pioneers.

BF Goodrich's historic achievements were undoubtedly driven by its channel role as an innovator, manufacturer, and distributor of tires, though changes in the global marketplace coupled with new market opportunities paved the way for important changes in BF Goodrich's marketing mix. And one of America's oldest companies has now become one of its newest: BF Goodrich has not manufactured or sold a tire in nearly two decades. Surprised? BF Goodrich, following a 1999 multibillion dollar merger with Coltec Industries, has emerged as a major player in aerospace systems and engineered industrial products. The BF Goodrich brand signature is still imprinted on tires, but BF Goodrich tires are sold by one-time competitor Michelin.

In this chapter, we discuss how channel members adjust their marketing mix to capitalize on opportunities and confront challenges in an ever-changing global marketplace. You might say that the marketing mix is where the "rubber meets the road" for channel members.

* * * *

The Marketing Mix

In the kitchen, a recipe is a catalog of carefully measured ingredients that are to be assembled in a given order to produce a given dish. Recipes for even seemingly mundane dishes like meatloaf can be amazingly diverse. Some recipes are outlandishly complicated, some strikingly simple. Either way, it's okay. There is no one best recipe for any given dish. What counts are the quality, taste, and appeal of the final product that results from putting the recipe into practice.

The concept we know as the marketing mix can be defined in much the same way. The **marketing mix** offers a means by which product, price, promotion, and place variables can be assembled to meet channel needs. But just as the ingredients of a recipe are not thrown together in an arbitrary way, marketing mix variables are not combined haphazardly. Instead, successful marketers must carefully consider how to combine these elements to achieve the desired strategic outcome. Channel Surfing 4.1 illustrates how the marketing mix can be changed to develop a new market position for an old product.

The relationship marketing perspective emphasizes each channel member's need to be sensitive to the other party's needs and wants. One set of tools that can be used to address customers' needs and wants is the marketing mix. These mix elements represent the manageable components by which the terms, norms, behaviors, and outcomes (i.e., sales, profits, market shares) of channel relationships can be developed. As manageable components, the product, price, promotion, and place activities must be aligned to match up with the expectations present in various channel relationships. In this chapter, we discuss each of the marketing mix elements in connection to the Channels Relationship Model.

The *Product* Ingredient

Just like a recipe is a fusion of ingredients, a **product** is a unique bundle of intangible and tangible attributes offered en masse to customers. Marketing channels create value via the acquisition, usage, and disposition of products and services. Products are the vehicles through which exchanges of value concurrently satisfy both buyers' and sellers' needs.[1] The total product concept is illustrated in Exhibit 4.1, which shows how a simple telephone (core product) can be transformed into a computer terminal (potential product). This progression suggests that a continuously evolving blending of intangible and tangible characteristics can

Channel Surfing 4.1

How B2B Advertising Agencies Are Gaining Competitive Advantage

Riding the e-business wave, the business-to-business (B2B) advertising sector has spawned hundreds of firms offering to build websites. In quick order, advertising agencies have transformed their traditional marketing mixes by adding Internet-based service capabilities—often through entering partnerships with or outright acquisitions of Web-based advertising shops.

The current marketplace is featuring a wide mix of e-advertising agencies. All boast interactive capabilities; many operate in an exclusively B2B market. Some agencies specialize in particular channels, like apparel marketing. Others are repositioning themselves as advertising generalists in far broader markets. And while some exclusively work on media strategy and branding efforts—leaving the technical implementation to others—many agencies have modified their marketing mix offerings and repositioned themselves as "full-service" shops. For example, Chicago's MarchFirst, Inc., features strategic advertising consulting, systems integration, and advice on marketing strategies, and even claims an "offline" (read as "old-fashioned") advertising capability. This type of repositioning—based on acquiring and exploiting strategic resources or superior skills—seems certain to continue as advertising agencies pursue new sources of competitive advantage.

Points to Ponder

- Do you think other companies operating in different product or service markets are feeling like a similar e-business gun is being pointed at their heads to jump on board the Web?
- Should most companies be making this jump?
- Through what other means could ad agencies that are competing in a New Economy marketplace gain sustainable competitive advantages?

enhance exchanges of value between buyers and sellers. Our attention now turns to this blending, or *fusion,* of product attributes.

Exhibit 4.1 highlights several important characteristics of the interface between product and channel. These include:

- **Fusion of attributes.** A telephone is not merely a collection of transmitters, speakers, and microprocessors. It is a bundled system that connects signals between senders and receivers. Likewise, products are bundled attributes. Marketing channels provide the conduit that allows these bundles of attributes to be connected between buyers and sellers.
- **Product evolution.** Did Alexander Graham Bell envision speed dialing, caller identification, or voice mail? Not likely! As Exhibit 4.1 shows, the telephone has evolved into a virtual computer. As products evolve to meet marketplace needs, marketing channels must adapt to accommodate the new requirements of emerging products and services.
- **Value satisfaction.** A telephone may satisfy a wide variety of communication needs. For example, the telephone satisfies the need for relatives separated by long distances to share experiences and emotions. (You may recall AT&T's classic promotional message, "Reach Out and Touch Someone.") Products are need-satisfying goods and messages, and marketing channels add value to those goods and services.

Exhibit 4.1

The total product concept

Product Level	*Buyer's View*	*Seller's View*	*From Telephone to Computer Telephone Integration*	*Connecting to Channel Members*
Core product	Customer's generic need which must be met.	Basic benefits which make product of interest.	A simple telephone that connects callers to friends and family.	Producer → Intermediaries → Consumers
Expected product	Customer's minimal set of expectations.	Marketer's product decisions on tangible and intangible components.	A brand-name telephone that offers speed dialing, a speaker function, and a a manufacturer's warranty.	Producer (SONY, PANASONIC) ↕ Intermediaries (Best Buy, CIRCUIT CITY) ↕ Consumers
Augmented product	Seller's offering over and above what customer expects or is accustomed to.	Marketer's other mix decisions on price, distribution, and promotion.	A brand-name speaker telephone that includes an answering machine, caller I.D. function, and intercom. The telephone interfaces with AT&T, GTE, or any type service provider to add voice-mail caller identification or other communications services.	Producer ⟷ (AT&T, GTE, MCI, SPRINT) ↕ Intermediaries ↕ Consumer
Potential product	Everything that potentially can be done with the product that is of utility to the customer.	Marketer's actions to attract and hold customers regarding changed conditions or new applications.	A brand-name virtual computer that provides a direct connection to airlines, banks, and thousands of retail direct marketers. Potentially remote operation of household appliances and office machines.	Producers ⟷ (AT&T, GTE, MCI, SPRINT) ↕ Wholesalers and Retailers ↕ Consumers ↕ Retailers

Source: Adapted from Collin, B. (1989), "Chapter 11: Marketing for Engineers," *Management for Engineers,* D. Sampson, ed., Melbourne, AU: Longman Cheshire, 372.

Fusion of Attributes

Tangibility is the extent to which something is capable of being touched. The concept typically refers to the physical characteristics of a product. Tangible attributes possess substance; they actually exist in some physical form. An automobile, for instance, has a number of tangible components that are bundled together and offered as a package—you can kick a car's tires, ease into the driver's seat, and start the engine. However, any number of nonphysical considerations are also associated with an automobile. A car may evoke a sense of excitement (i.e., a Ford *Mustang*), a feeling of security (i.e., a Ford *Crown Victoria*), or a sense that success has been attained (i.e., the Lincoln *Town Car*). All of these automobiles are branded under the Ford Motor Company family and each has essentially the same tangible components, but each model produces very different sensory outcomes.

When it comes to satisfying customers, a product's *intangible* aspects—those properties that cannot be easily defined or grasped by human hands—are often more important than its tangible characteristics. The value of exchange relationships is gauged on the basis of both tangible and intangible attributes. How can intangible considerations translate into better exchange relationships? Consider these examples:[2]

- General Motors' Saturn has redefined the exchange encounter in automobile purchasing. Many dealers are attempting to emulate Saturn's no-haggle pricing and low-pressure approach.
- Reliability, as reported in the *Consumer Reports* Trouble Index, is often used as an indicator of customers' satisfaction with an automobile. Saturn has consistently earned high marks for reliability.
- General Motors' Chevrolet division has designated several employees as CEOs (Customer Enthusiasm Officers). Their sole purpose is to develop better relationships with current and prospective customers.

Products have traditionally been portrayed along an attribute-based scale, ranging from purely tangible goods to purely intangible services; but it is often difficult to separate intangible and tangible product attributes.

The growing complexity of product offerings has been linked to agile competitive environments.[3] An **agile competitive environment** is a marketplace in which channel members constantly modify and improve their product offerings to better satisfy changing customer needs. In a traditional production-oriented economy, the market environment generally features autonomous manufacturers producing mass quantities of long-lifetime generic products. Naturally, there is a low level of product differentiation. Within these traditional market settings, efficiency is based on the *movement* of goods. By contrast, today's dynamic market environments are characterized by high levels of product customization. Because of this customization, product life cycles are usually shorter.

In agile competitive environments, a combination of physical and nonphysical attributes is aimed at meeting distinctive challenges in the exchange relationship. Differences between goods and services become blurred. As a result, there is a greater reliance on the interaction among channel members. In fact, management guru Peter Drucker contends that this interaction or relationship among channel members is the last frontier of sustainable advantage in the global marketplace.

Product-in-Process

The concept of agile competition requires that products continually evolve. Therefore, each market offering is really a *product-in-process*. In some instances, this evolution is governed by constraints of the exchange relationship itself. A newly launched website, for example, is available that helps consumers create custom-designed toys for their tots. Here's how it works: Visitors to the site answer a few questions concerning the toy desired. Within 24 hours, they receive a quote and must give permission to continue. After that, the toy is generated as a solid model, then, using e-Drawing software that allows solid models to be e-mailed and viewed, the drawing is sent to the client for final approval. The toy is then produced using the technology best suited for the intended user.[4] How's that for a toy in process?

Other more traditional companies like Campbell's now customize products in response to regional preferences. Campbell's hopes their efforts at a product-in-process contribute to stronger relationships, new competitive advantages, and increased brand loyalty. Soup, too, is a product-in-process!

Product evolutions may also result from good relationships gone bad. Consider Coca-Cola's entry into the Gatorade-controlled sports drink market. After failed attempts to form a distribution relationship with Quaker Oats Company, Gatorade's parent, Coke USA, introduced its own product. Coke USA's entry, called PowerAde, offers 33 percent more carbohydrates than Gatorade. But PowerAde also has to battle PepsiCo's All Sport and Dr Pepper's Nautilus for market share in the sports drink category. Pierre Ferrari, Coke USA's senior vice president of marketing, suggests that Coke USA will eventually exploit its access to a wide assortment of outlets and distribution channels to gain market share.[5] Clearly, successful products of the future will have to evolve in response to the needs associated with exchange relationships. Channel Surfing 4.2 describes how, in today's world, products may continue to evolve even after customers have purchased them.

Value Satisfaction

A product's capacity for value satisfaction is perhaps its most difficult characteristic to describe. **Value satisfaction** is a channel member's perception of the benefits derived from owning or consuming the product. Each product should deliver some measure of value satisfaction to both the buyer and seller. Still, different exchange partners will have different assessments of the worth of a product.

The concept of products as value satisfiers suggests channel members should transform themselves from functions delivery to value delivery systems. In a functions delivery system, attention is typically focused inward. For instance, channel partners might attempt to develop superior physical processes for moving products from the factory to the market. While nothing is inherently wrong with such an objective, it is limiting. The view of a functions delivery system is that products begin within the organization.

In a value delivery system, attention first focuses on external concerns. Channels partners look outward to identify customer needs, and products originate from a desire to satisfy these needs. The value delivery sequence involves three stages:[6]

- **Assess customer value.** Channel members identify customer needs and translate those needs into a value-producing product concept. One example of this is Apple's

Channel Surfing 4.2

It Is Already Happening: When What You Buy Changes after It's Yours

Okay. We'll admit it. You already knew the world was changing rapidly. But are you ready for gadgets that may reinvent themselves when you're not looking. You had better be, because such products-in-process are already among us. Most of us are used to software upgrades on our personal computers, and the *hassles*—economists call them *switching costs*—that accompany them. The fact is that more and more of our everyday devices—phones, TVs, even cars—contain software. As marketers increasingly connect such devices to the Internet, they are gaining the ability to "morph" products through remote control. It is a fact that any day now, your new replay TV device may mutiny against you, as a result of uninvited electronic upgrades imported without your awareness. It is a cyber-Darwinian marketplace out there.

Opportunities such as these promise greater convenience and additional value for consumers. But they also introduce tough ethical and strategic questions about consumers' abilities and needs to exercise their free will. Traditionally, when consumers purchased a VCR or stereo, they were able to compare features and price, choosing what they wanted and rejecting what they spurned. What is going to happen when marketers can change products—and those products' features—after they are sold? Are customers going to be happy with changes they don't like or believe they need?

Of course, smart marketers are unlikely to make drastic changes that would scare off new buyers. But when it comes to incremental changes in the capacities or characteristics of products, consumers who have already plunked down their cash may have little recourse. As smart products-in-process proliferate, consumers should expect less of what they don't want and more of what they do. Companies should discuss planned changes and give customers the opportunity to decline upgrades they do not want, or selectively install new features. After all, that's just smart marketing. In the absence of such consideration, marketers will be far less likely to develop lasting relationships with their customers, regardless of how "teched-up" their products become.

Points to Ponder

- What sorts of opportunities do these technological abilities present to the marketers of products-in-process?
- Are there other threats beyond those already mentioned?

Source: Adapted from Weber, Thomas E. (2000), "Morphing via Remote Control," *The Wall Street Journal,* November 6, B1.

Newton, a personal digital assistant (PDA). Newton is a pocket-size computer—essentially an electronic secretary. Apple's chairman, John Scully, describes how PDA technology was developed based on customer value assessments: "You go out and take a problem that is real and you solve it in a compelling way."[7]

- **Provide customer value.** This stage involves converting the value-producing concept into a product offering. Here, product design, service development, pricing, sourcing, and distribution are considered. Each function is evaluated with respect to how it can be used to maximize customer value. To transfer the technology concept into a value-satisfying market offering, Apple formed an alliance with Sharp Corporation to develop the Newton. Sharp Corporation's early product entry into this market segment was its Wizard. The Apple/Sharp alliance was consummated with the intention of improving upon the Wizard through shared technologies.

- **Communicate customer value.** In this stage the channel member communicates the benefits of the product offering in solving customer problems to the intended market audience. In support of their new product, Apple launched a massive electronic and print promotional campaign to broadcast the benefits of Newton to prospective customers.

Value satisfaction is especially important in building channel relationships. Value satisfaction suggests that exchange partners are matching their market offerings to customer needs. By doing this, channel relationships evolve along with the evolution of the product itself. PCs, mobile phones, and digital TVs—all products-in-process themselves—are opening up new channels direct to customers' homes, and the Internet is creating new ways for supply chain managers to work together. The weak link in this value chain is obviously order fulfillment. What home shopping customers want is the right goods delivered in the right place at the right time, and right now they are not always getting what they want. Guess what happens then? The marketer loses. Clearly, firms and channel systems that solve this problem first will be delivering a highly satisfying value to consumers and will have earned a true competitive advantage along the way.

The *Pricing* Ingredient

The concept of *value* satisfaction through exchange lays the foundation for a discussion of the next ingredient in the marketing mix, price. **Price** is the ultimate measure of a good's or service's exchange value as agreed upon by the seller and buyer. Price is important because it directly affects the channel member's profitability.

Any discussion of pricing in marketing channels must begin with the notion of valuation. **Valuation,** or perceived value, is the simultaneous appraisal by buyers and sellers of the economic and psychological worth of a market offering. The valuation of a good or service is implicitly linked to the exchange relationship. In marketing channels, each exchange partner provides some added value to the offering. Channel members expect and must receive some compensation in exchange for their role in enhancing the value of the market offering. Often, intermediaries' willingness to carry a product is based on the margins available to them. The price should allocate compensation among channel members proportionate to each member's contribution to the exchange relationship. Conflicts often arise in how to make this allocation.

Valuation of a product or service is related to the type of buyer. It is now widely understood that the personal computer market has been a commodity market. But while there has been a proliferation of discount, direct marketing channels in the industry, not all buyers are looking for the lowest price. Corporate buyers are most likely to buy personal computers from resellers. Why? Because brand name and value-added services, such as on-site service of computer problems, are highly valued by institutional buyers.[8] Putting a price on such intangible factors is difficult. Yet, intangible attributes like brand names or service commitments significantly impact purchasers' valuation of product offerings.[9] In some cases, channel members are willing to pay a price premium to a preferred exchange partner. A **price premium** is a price level in excess of the normal market or industry value. Channel members may justify price premiums for a number of reasons including:[10]

- **Building a relationship.** A channel member may willingly pay a price premium in order to develop a long-term relationship with a prospective exchange partner.
- **Preserving a relationship.** A channel member may willingly pay a premium because it has a long history of association with an exchange partner. A past shared among true channel partners may contribute to feelings of trust or dependency that outweigh more traditional market-based valuations of the product offering.
- **Reducing risk factors.** In risky situations, channel members may willingly pay a premium to secure the intangible attributes associated with the good reputation of another channel member. Similarly, consumers often pay more for an established brand name product in exchange for a reduction in their perceptions of risk.
- **Obtaining perceived quality.** Channel members can rationalize that the price premium is related to higher-quality exchange performance, such as on-time delivery.
- **Possessing limited information.** Channel members may pay a price premium because they do not have sufficient information with regard to market pricing.

Product valuation is, by its nature, unique to each channel partner. Accordingly, it is difficult to formulate a true price for many market offerings because channel members will derive varying benefits from any exchange relationship. How much is a prescription drug product worth if it merely relieves discomfort? Would the drug's valuation change if it were lifesaving? Of course. These situational considerations affect a product's price elasticity.

Prices have traditionally been established through either algorithmic or market-oriented methods. The *algorithmic pricing method* may be viewed as an inside-out approach, in which price is derived from the channel members' forecasts of their own costs and revenues. *Market-oriented pricing methods* represent an outside-in approach to valuation, in which pricing cues are generated from an evaluation of the threats and opportunities in the marketplace, that is, outside the organization. In addition to these two traditional methods, a third perspective on how to derive prices in marketing channel relationships is now emerging: relationship pricing. *Relationship-oriented pricing* requires a broader, more encompassing orientation. Before a price is established, internal and external cues are simultaneously evaluated in an effort to build and maintain exchange relationships. Each pricing method is summarized in Exhibit 4.2.

Algorithmic Pricing Methods

A firm's long-term survival depends on its profitability. Consequently, unit profits must exceed unit operating costs. **Algorithmic pricing methods** are based on the associations among profits, revenues, and expenses. While by no means exhaustive, the three techniques shown below are often used by sellers as price-setting algorithms:

- **Cost-plus pricing.** In cost-plus pricing, a percentage or fixed markup is added to the cost to establish a price. Cost-plus can lead to poor pricing decisions because of its simplicity: Cost reductions lead to price reductions and cost increases lead to price increases. But in either scenario, cost-plus pricing ignores the effects of market factors such as consumer preferences, brand loyalty, the competition, and the price elasticity of demand.

- **Break-even analysis.** Break-even analysis is based on the convergence between the costs associated with making a product and the revenues realized from selling it. On the surface, a break-even pricing approach appears perfectly rational. But buyers do not always behave rationally in the marketplace. Furthermore, revenues depend on demand, which has proven difficult to estimate in most industries.
- **Modified break-even pricing.** Modified break-even pricing attempts to overcome the difficulties of elasticity by extending the break-even analysis across several estimations of quantity and price. Again, this approach provides little predictive value to channel members because of the opportunity costs associated with uncertain demand.

Each algorithmic method of pricing described above is limited in some ways. Each approach largely ignores the effects of legal or regulatory market conditions as well as the influences of competition and changing market needs.

Exhibit 4.2

Pricing methods

Pricing Method	*Orientation*	*Types*	*Positives, Plusses*	*Negatives, Deficits*
Algorithmic	Inside-out	• Cost-plus • Break-even • Modified Break-even	• Simplicity	• Ignores effects of legal and regulatory conditions, influences of competition and changing market needs

Market-oriented	Outside-in	• Competitive
		• Market-entry
		  • Penetration
		  • Skimming-the-Cream
			• Sensitivity to customer needs
			• Good entry strategy in elastic market
			• Generates quick cash flow; good in inelastic markets
				• Reactive, not proactive
				• Attracts new market entrants

Relationship	Both	• Volume pricing • Functional Allowances • Promotional Allowances	• Cooperative and collaborative • Goal-oriented pricing shared • Consideration for fostering communication through channel	• Cooperation is a must • Requires ongoing and consistent communication between channel members

Market-Oriented Pricing Methods

Prices can also be established by considering market forces. That is, **market-oriented pricing methods** allow prices to be sensitive to customer needs. This sensitivity reinforces the presence of agile competition in the marketplace.

The children's clothing product category illustrates how market-oriented approaches to pricing are implemented. Healthtex, a marketer of children's apparel, has long been recognized for the high-end quality and craftsmanship of its clothing line. However, increased competition has forced Healthtex to launch a new Kid's Addition clothing line aimed at cost-conscious parents. Healthtex is test marketing the line at Wal-Mart—an unusual outlet for high-end market offerings. Oshkosh B'Gosh, Inc., another competitor in the high-end children's apparel category, quickly found it had to follow suit.[11] These decisions to enter the lower-end discount retail market represent a radical shift from each company's traditional mode of distribution. To preserve their own positions in the children's clothing market, Healthtex and Oshkosh B'Gosh have had to adjust their pricing strategies in response to market changes.

While there are several market-oriented pricing methods, the most common is competitive pricing. With **competitive pricing,** channel members match competitors' pricing. The use of competitive pricing strategies often provides a means of market entry for new channel members. But the business environment is changing rapidly, with many of those changes driven by the arrival of e-business. Even traditionally complex products like cars, computers, and health care services are being effectively marketed on the Internet. Most experts are assuming that consumers and businesses will benefit from the new-found ability to search products, compare features, conduct transactions, and negotiate prices while online. Not surprisingly, the changes have forced many channel members to adopt marketing mix strategies that are pushing them away from price competition. And as huge grocery stores chains and supersized retail discounters like Wal-Mart are introducing store brands, even dominant manufacturers like Coke or Pepsi are finding that their traditional pricing strategies can no longer hold.

Competitive pricing is inherently *reactive* rather than *proactive.* Moreover, competitive pricing provides no assurance that "meet or beat" prices will increase market share or sustain profit objectives. A more likely outcome is that competitive pricing leads to price wars that, in turn, hurt the entire channel. Channel members can effectively counter competitive pricing by differentiating their offerings.[12] Price is almost always the worst aspect on which to compete.

Market-entry pricing offers two strategies for pricing goods and services that are new to the marketplace. The first strategy is called *penetration pricing.* **Penetration pricing** features a low entry price aimed at capturing market share. Priced below the existing competition, penetration pricing can be particularly effective as an entry strategy in markets where demand is highly elastic. Pricing at penetration levels can also be used as a preemptive strike against potential market entrants by firms already operating in a market. New firm entry is usually blocked because its costs are generally higher. Also, because firms usually hope to avoid price wars, existing competitors often are disinclined to match penetration strategies.

The other market-entry pricing strategy is known as **skimming-the-cream pricing,** or *price skimming.* Here, high initial prices are established to attract those willing to pay.

Naturally, profit margins for each unit sold are high. Accordingly, price skimming is often employed in an attempt to quickly generate positive cash flows to recoup research and development costs. Price skimming is often used in the pharmaceutical industry due to high research and development costs. However, the practice has also exposed the industry to widespread accusations of price gouging, that is, price levels that are deemed unfairly high and exploitative to consumers.

The escalating debate over drug availability and pricing has made price gouging a hot media issue. Pharmaceutical pricing is a major issue for the AIDS community because new lifesaving drug "cocktails" carry very high price tags. It is wonderful that such treatments are now available. The problem, however, is that AIDS patients in Africa have as much moral right to such treatments as do more affluent, fully covered by American patients. But such drugs are not widely available because of their high prices. The impact on the image of the pharmaceutical industry has generally not been positive.

A price-skimming strategy is more likely to prove successful in relatively inelastic markets. The problem with price skimming is that the high entry price frequently attracts new market entrants, who see opportunities for profits. If you still don't think pricing is an important marketing mix ingredient, read Channel Surfing 4.3, about the surprising impact that prices may be having on the development of an entire continent's economy.

Channel Surfing 4.3

European Net Surfers Can't Wait until the Price Is Right!

Europeans who want to surf the Net must pay dearly for the privilege. Unlike in the United States, where consumers enjoy comparatively low monthly rates for unlimited Internet access, European surfers are charged high telephone charges for every minute spent online. Apparently, the high prices that European consumers must pay to play have proven detrimental. Not only have these skimming-the-cream pricing policies limited the growth of the European Internet, they may have actually hindered the emergence of a U.S.-style New Economy in Europe. Price matters, and pricing levels sometimes have far-reaching and unexpected consequences.

Not surprisingly, several United States-based firms are developing their own market entry pricing strategies in response to what they see as an opportunity. Internet search engine Alta-Vista Co. and communications group NTL, Inc., have introduced a flat rate, unlimited access, penetration pricing scheme in Britain. Almost instantly, a host of competitors followed. The entry prices of the respective companies varied, but the underlying product concept was uniform: all-you-can-use Internet access for a one-time, penetration-level price.

Europe's current population of 3,000 Internet service providers will probably suffer the greatest losses as the cost of access plunges. Their pricing structures, and entire business models, may eventually be rendered obsolete. Yet consumers and the European economy alike should benefit from these new market-oriented prices as well as a double-quick rollout of exciting new Web services. Sometimes, when the price is right, the sky's the limit.

Points to Ponder

- Do you think that new entrants into the European market should price at penetration levels? Why or why not?

Source: Adapted from Capell, Kerry (2000), "Now, Brits Can Surf to Their Heart's Content," *Business Week*, April 17, 186–88.

Relationship-Oriented Pricing Methods

Pricing strategies do not always have to be combative, especially *within* channel settings. The **relationship-oriented pricing** approach is grounded in a cooperative and collaborative orientation. Relationship pricing may assume many forms; however, the practice generally involves volume, functional, and promotional allowances.

- **Volume pricing.** Volume pricing provides quantity discounts to channel members based on purchasing economies, and it rewards buyers for large lot size purchases. Volume pricing is commonly used in industries with little product customization, such as the paper industry. Volume pricing simultaneously helps several exchange partners: Producers gain the opportunity to more fully utilize their production capacity because longer and more cost-efficient production runs are made possible; resellers gain better cash flow; and buyers gain the opportunity to establish consistent and routine procurement procedures. There are downsides, however. Volume pricing can damage buyer-seller relationships when the smaller volumes demanded by smaller customers effectively preclude their opportunity to receive such discounts. This problem can be overcome when cumulative volume discounts are made available to exchange partners for ongoing, consistent orders. Volume pricing levels may also be made available to smaller channel members through negative option contracts. **Negative option contracts** are agreements in which buyers accept an ongoing flow of goods from vendors. Buyers continue to receive those goods until they tell their vendor to halt supply. Negative option contracts are established based on a sense of confidence regarding the continuity of their exchange relationship.[13]
- **Functional allowances.** Functional allowances involve reductions in the list price in exchange for the buyer's agreement to perform specific functions. These allowances involve the performance of logistic functions such as transportation, warehousing, or order processing. Or, they may involve the performance of customer service or personal selling functions. Functional allowances account for the value one channel member receives by shifting various functions to another channel member.
- **Promotional allowance.** Promotional allowances are considerations given to channel partners in exchange for their agreement to provide promotions to current and prospective customers. These considerations may take the form of free goods, cash payments, or support services. For example, Coca-Cola is increasing its promotional allowances to retailers in markets where it is losing market share to private-label soft drinks. Bar soap and laundry detergent maker Unilever provides retailers with cash payments and free goods.[14] Promotional allowances may also assume the form of service provisions. Any number of manufacturers now provide cutting-edge information technologies to their exchange partners. For example, some manufacturers give wholesalers software that helps the exchange of information on pricing changes, inventory positions, and promotions. There is a common misconception that promotional allowances are exchanged exclusively between producers and retailers. This is not necessarily so. Promotional allowances may be provided at any channel level. For instance, consumers often take advantage of trade-in allowances or rebates.

Regardless of the approach used, pricing is a powerful ingredient in relationship building. But price itself is not the only factor in relationship-oriented policy. Each of these relationship pricing forms involves volume or functional discounts, as well as an adjustment to the list price. Also, each relationship pricing form can be either company policy or negotiated. The spirit in which the negotiation unfolds is actually more critical to the relationship-building process.

An underlying factor influencing any channel pricing decision, but in particular relationship-oriented pricing decisions, is the notion of price legitimacy.[15] **Price legitimacy** exists whenever a buyer's and seller's perceptions of a market offering's value converge or come together. Research has found that the single issue making consumers feel most exploited in America today is the idea of a "list price." Consumers simply don't believe the list price is the *real* price. They view a list price as an artificially inflated price.

Customers are increasingly aware of presumed-price/quality relationships for goods and services. For example, customers expect higher prices to result in better service but do not view low prices as a justification for poor service. Moreover, increases in consumer knowledge have lead to increases in their demands for value.[16] Such trends are prompting manufacturers, wholesalers, and retailers to reexamine their pricing policies. Resellers now use several techniques to justify their pricing levels:[17]

- **Price guarantees.** With price guarantees, channel members communicate assurances to buyers or prospects that their posted prices are the lowest available in a given market. If a buyer finds a lower price, a refund or reimbursement for the price difference will be paid.
- **Price posting.** Prices are prominently displayed by retailers. This technique reflects the fact that increased information is now generally available to those customers who seek it. For example, the widespread use of unit pricing within grocery stores makes it easier for consumers to make price comparisons.
- **Cost of service pricing.** Customers need only pay for the level of service(s) they need. For example, cost of service pricing may account for the difference between an "installed" and "pick-up" price of home appliances.

One of the most popular price legitimizing techniques is an *everyday low price* policy. This policy offers buyers consistently lower prices than competitors. Championed by Wal-Mart, Kmart, and Toys "R" Us, everyday low pricing (often denoted by its acronym, EDLP) is becoming a mainstay of channel pricing. Wal-Mart's now decades-long success has largely followed from its EDLP pricing strategy. To this day that strategy remains rooted in an item merchandising tactic. Perhaps the best-known example of this tactic is the company's volume-producing-item (VPI) context. Store associates are encouraged to derive creative ways to merchandise items chosen for inclusion in the program. VPI items usually are products that can be stacked-out, case-cut, and have single point features that are priced to generate large sales volumes. And the items selected could be put "on sale" again and again. By not selecting one-time sale items, Wal-Mart avoids supply-chain problems and angry customers who encounter an out-of-stock situation.

EDLP and the item philosophy remains the primary driving focus on Wal-Mart, some 40 years after Sam Walton first began promoting the "item." The formula is simple: Keep channel costs low, sell more goods, then lower distribution costs and prices further, and sell even more. EDLP worked then and it still works today.[18]

The EDLP movement provides the best examples of how pricing is linked to channel relationships. The use of EDLP requires cost reductions at every channel level. EDLP is a relationship-oriented principle that necessitates a passing on of cost savings from channel member to channel member all the way to the ultimate consumer. EDLP requires a collaborative pricing strategy between channel members.

By their nature, prices usually can only deliver short-term rewards (i.e., lower prices). Moreover, the prospect of illegal price discrimination generally prevents channel members from offering their better customers many discounts or allowances they might otherwise provide. So price alone is unlikely to inspire long-term buyer-seller exchanges in channel settings. When used wisely in combination with the other marketing mix elements, however, fair prices can prove effective in building long-term channel relationships.

The *Promotions* Ingredient

A primary purpose of each of these price legitimizing techniques is to communicate a sense of fair play or equity to customers. In each instance, the seller is attempting to *promote* a sense of value. As such, price legitimacy serves as a suitable lead-in to the next ingredient in the marketing mix, promotion. **Promotion** involves any form of purposeful communication employed by channel members with the intent of informing, reminding, and/or persuading prospects and customers regarding some aspect of their market offering.

Promotional Mix

Several promotional options are available to channel members. For the sake of simplicity, the *promotional mix* can be divided into personal and nonpersonal selling. Personal selling is especially important in marketing channels because the act of selling itself is a major function of virtually all exchange partners. Invariably, some channel members must assume responsibility for the personal selling function. A good definition of personal selling is one that embraces a relationship-building perspective. Accordingly, **personal selling** is defined as an interpersonal communication process by which a seller uncovers and satisfies the needs of a buyer, to the mutual long-term benefit of both parties.[19]

Nonpersonal selling involves all other types of promotions. These include advertising, public relations/publicity, and sales promotions. Advertising is paid nonpersonal communications delivered by an identified organization targeted toward some particular audience. It is generally intended to either inform or persuade the audience. Public relations and publicity include all forms of nonpaid communication of information about a channel member or market offering, generally in some media form. Sales promotions include all those marketing activities, other than personal selling, advertising, and publicity, that stimulate customer demand and channel member effectiveness. These include displays, trade shows, exhibitions, demonstrations, and other selling efforts not in the ordinary sales routine. Sales promotion is enormously important within marketing channels.

Traditional versus Relational Communication

The role of the promotions ingredient in the marketing mix is often misunderstood. Marketers have traditionally viewed promotions from a *tactical* standpoint. As such, promotion has been seen as a portfolio of persuasive *tactics* used with the intention of informing, changing preferences and attitudes, positioning and/or repositioning products, and, ultimately, stimulating sales.[20]

But the contemporary view of promotions suggests they represent yet another way to build relationships. **Relational promotion** involves a communication *process* between channel members. The purpose of this communication is to encourage new or to strengthen existing exchange relationships. Since the foundation of relational promotions is communication, several fundamental concepts associated with communication should be reviewed.[21] The traditional communications model, illustrated in the top half of Exhibit 4.3, depicts a series of sequential message flows between senders and receivers. Note that:

- The *message* is the central idea one party is attempting to deliver to its counterpart.
- The source of the message is the *sender*.
- The *receiver* is the recipient of a message.
- *Feedback* is the means by which receivers acknowledge receipt and understanding of the message.

In the conventional model of the communication process, messages are essentially bilateral. The sender initiates a message, conveys this central idea through some sort of medium and, in turn, the receiver responds to his or her receipt of this message. This two-way communication exchange is greatly influenced by the process of encoding and decoding. The sender of a message must package this central idea in such a way that it can be understood by the receiver in the manner intended. This is known as **encoding** a message. Without

Exhibit 4.3

Traditional versus relational communication models

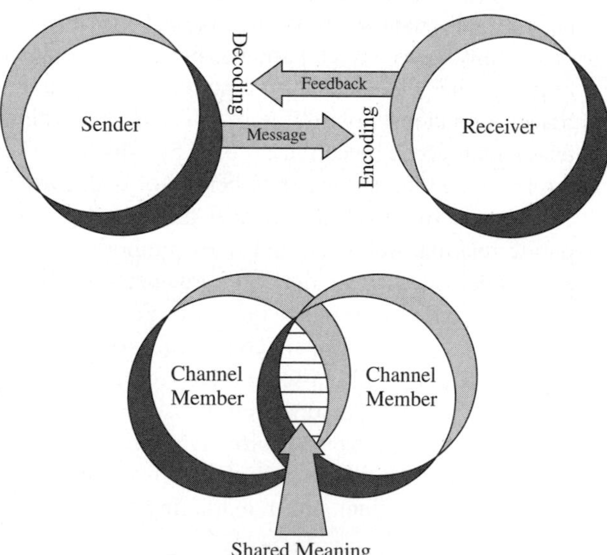

encoding, successful communication has not occurred. Concurrent with his or her receipt of a message, the receiver then decodes it. **Decoding** is the process through which the receiver interprets and assigns meaning to the message. The acts of encoding and decoding often lead to distorted communications. In some cases, the *message* is responsible for the decoding error. For example:

- When a national brand of dish detergent featured a corsage of fresh lemons dangling around its product, it did so with the intention of communicating the lemon-fresh scent. Some consumers were exceptionally receptive to the message. But was it the right message? Not necessarily. Across the nation, numerous consumers were hospitalized because they drank the detergent.
- When Chevrolet marketed its popular Nova model in Spanish-speaking countries, some consumers may have gotten the wrong idea. In Spanish, *va* is a form of the verb *ir* ("to go"). When translated, the Nova model was decoded as "no go"—not a particularly good message for promoting a transportation vehicle!

At other times, the *source* is responsible for decoding problems:

- When the Beef Industry Council promoted leaner cuts in its Real Food/Real People message, it backfired. Soon after the campaign began, actor and Beef Council spokesperson James Garner had heart-bypass surgery, and some consumers naturally linked his health problems to eating too much red meat. This debacle came on the heels of the actions of its previous spokesperson, actress Cybil Shephard, who confessed she didn't eat beef in a national magazine article.[22]
- No Excuses Sportswear, a line of casual clothing, intended to promote the free-spirited woman of the 90s. But spokespersons, like comedienne Joan Rivers, led to decoding errors. River's husband committed suicide during the campaign and consumers instead often perceived her as a callous shrew.

In each case, some unanticipated external factor interfered with the communication process. This interference is known as *noise*—any physical or psychological barrier impeding the proper receipt or decoding of a message. More often than not, *noise* is unintentional and has a detrimental effect on the message. Noise can occur at any stage in the communication process.

In the traditional model, communication involves a succession of discrete exchanges. But in the relational model, communication is represented as a continuous, perpetual process in which the sender and receiver are essentially indistinguishable. The message and feedback are nearly simultaneous. The outcome of relational communication is shared meaning. **Shared meaning** refers to the interwoven communications that occur in the marketing channel. The bottom half of Exhibit 4.3 illustrates the relational communication model. This model accommodates the agile competitive environment that marketers will surely face because it accounts for the possibility of continuous adaptation. As each exchange partner (i.e., each circle) moves closer to the other, shared meaning, or synchronous cognition, increases. This is a striking departure from the traditional view of channel communications processes. Shared meaning encourages the alignment of promotional objectives among exchange partners within marketing channels. When exchange partners achieve high degrees of shared meaning, they are likely to realize similar channel goals.

Shared meaning is vital to building effective and efficient marketing channel relationships. Consider the case of Cannondale Corporation, a Connecticut-based bicycle manufacturer specializing in high-performance mountain and racing cycles. The manufacturer has enjoyed an astounding 3500+ percent growth in export sales in the 1990s, a portion of which can surely be attributed to the spirit of synchronous cognition it creates with final customers in Japan. Toward this end, it has hired Japanese-speaking Americans who live in Japan to engage in highly relational promotional communications with Japanese prospects and customers. In fact, these consultants actually compete in races with potential Cannondale customers. They share technical information, advice, and industry information.[23]

By making customers part of their promotion, firms can strengthen their exchange relationships. For example, Miller Brewing uses customers as the stars of regionally aired commercials. By involving the customer in the advertisement, Miller is bonding with them. In Detroit, local retailers supply Miller Lite testimonials against a backdrop of landmarks and the tag line, "Come on, Detroit, let me show you where it's at." These relationally oriented promotions extend Miller's relationship with a few customers to potentially include all Detroit-area beer drinkers.[24]

Promotional Objectives

For relational promotion to flourish, suppliers and retailers must jointly pursue a promotional strategy. Channel members often form trade marketing departments as a means of achieving promotional cooperation. These departments are designed to learn as much about exchange partners' objectives as possible.[25] Consistent objectives are a prerequisite to relational promotions. In fact, some alliances between previously independent marketers have developed solely as a result of promotional cooperation. For instance, Del Monte, a consumer foods firm, and Lego Systems, a major marketer of toys, allied with one another for a promotion in which free Lego toy samples were attached to more than 77 million packages of Del Monte's line of children's desserts such as Fruit Snack Cups and Pudding Snack Cups. This promotional alliance presented both companies with the opportunity to strengthen relationships with their target market—children.[26]

Five objectives are generally associated with relational promotions in marketing channels:

- **Stimulating sales.** Fuji Photo Film USA is using relational promotions to remind consumers of its information and imaging product lines. Their objective is simple: boost sales! A "Quality Above the Rest" campaign is aimed at arousing interest in Fuji floppy disks, audio and videotapes, and photofinishing equipment.[27] To offset declining sales, Levi Strauss & Company has used promotions to reinforce the lifestyle relationship between consumers and its Levi jeans.[28]
- **Differentiating offerings.** Promotions are also intended to differentiate channel members' offerings. This is especially important in highly competitive markets. Many hotel restaurants are employing regionalized menus to accomplish this goal. Promotion-oriented recipes are attempting to lure diners—from Westin Hotels' Steamed New Zealand Greenshell Mussels to the Seattle Sheraton Hotel's Blueberry Flan.[29]

- **Sharing information.** A primary function of promotion is to provide information to current and prospective exchange partners. This is particularly important within relational promotions. As discussed earlier, synchronous cognition can only be achieved when information is shared. Colleges and universities are all using regularly updated websites as a means of informing present and prospective customers. The promotional information featured on these sites typically includes updated curriculum offerings, enrollment or degree requirements, and other, less academic, "come-ons" that are unique to each academic institution.
- **Accentuating a market offering's value.** Relational promotions can be used to demonstrate the value of a product or service. You might recall the Listerine commercials suggesting that the product not only freshens breath and kills germs, but that it also provides protection against gingivitis. The value added by this attribute provides an extra incentive for customers to purchase Listerine. One caveat is in order: Before one accentuates a product's or service's value by playing up the existence of a previously unconsidered or underconsidered attribute, be sure the offering in question actually has the attribute.
- **Stabilizing seasonal demand.** Because many products are seasonal, relational promotions provide a cooperative, low-pressure mechanism through which customers can be induced to consider purchasing products at out-of-season intervals. Relationship-oriented pricing allowances strategies may be used.

Pull versus Push Strategies

While there are several situation-specific promotional objectives, relational promotion tactics as a whole can be classified into two strategic categories, *pull* and *push* promotions. A **pull strategy** describes persuasive communications aimed directly at the ultimate consumer. The goal of pull promotions is to stimulate the final user's desire for the offering. It is assumed that this demand will subsequently *pull* the market offering through the channel. The manufacturers' coupons that fall out of your Sunday newspaper are examples of a pull strategy. These promotional messages—generally involving price incentives—are conveyed by the manufacturer directly to the consumer through the newspaper medium. Then, consumers presumably encourage their retailers to carry the couponed merchandise to facilitate redemption, if they do not already do so.

As the top half of Exhibit 4.4 demonstrates, pulling strategies presume that the ultimate consumer will take the initiative to create product flows. For example, Hoehcst Marion Nicorette smoking cessation program is advertised directly to the consumer. The hope is that the promotional message will induce consumers to see a physician who will then write a prescription for the product. After this happens, the product will be pulled through the channel. The promotional sequence works like this:

> pharmaceutical manufacturer → consumer → physician → retail pharmacist → pharmaceutical wholesaler → manufacturer.

Pull strategies often are used with new product introductions to entice the consumer into creating early demand for an offering. Pull strategies can also be used to create loyalty in the face of price competition.

Exhibit 4.4

Pull-push promotion strategies

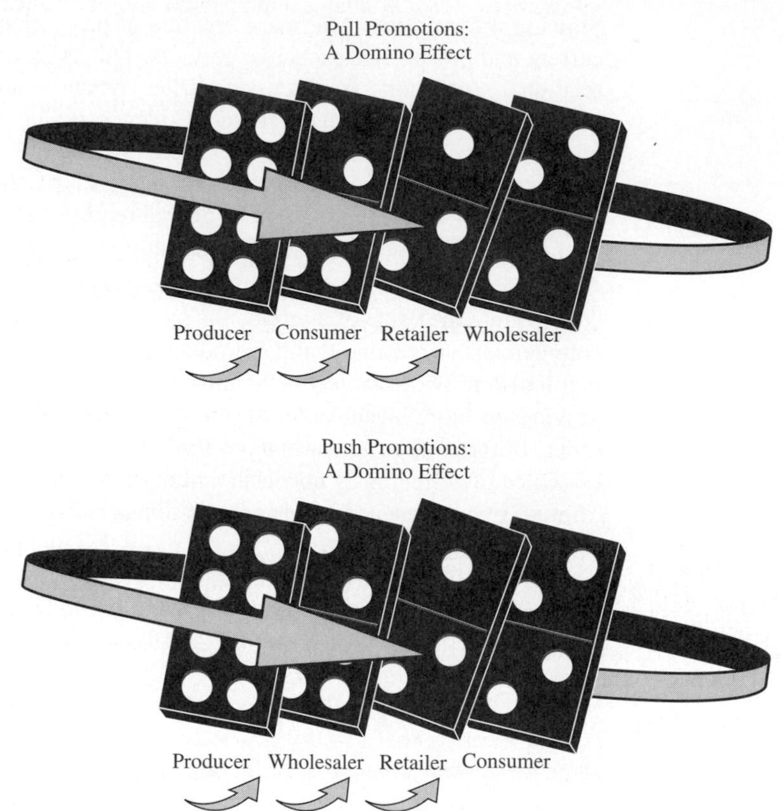

Pull strategies have occasionally been known to resurrect marketing *dinosaurs*—products from another time that have since lost customer interest. A popular pastime for kids in the 1950s and 1960s, yo-yos no longer have the children's toy market on a string. The yo-yo competes for valuable shelf-space near cash registers in discount and specialty toy retailers. Hoping to rejuvenate children's interest in the yo-yo and away from high-tech video games, Duncan marketing director Michael Caffrey went directly to kids. Caffrey offered $25 to kids who could perform yo-yo tricks. He was hopeful that kids' resurgent interest would force retailers to carry inventories and provide prime shelf space.

By contrast **push strategies** target their persuasive communications at intermediaries—pushing against the next link in the distribution chain. As illustrated in the bottom half of Exhibit 4.4, push promotions hopefully create a domino effect through the channel on the way to the ultimate consumer. The typical push promotion is launched by manufacturers and aimed at resellers. The success of push strategies rests with the intermediaries' receptiveness to the promotion. Push promotional strategies allow the channel participants to exercise greater control over the promotional message.

Manufacturers and wholesalers should consider certain elements before they elect to pursue a push promotional strategy. The following factors are likely to exercise a critical influence on the acceptability and ultimate success of push promotions in most marketing channels:

- **Allowances.** Price discounts and promotional allowances are generally considered to be the most important factors influencing the willingness of downstream channel members to participate in manufacturer-sponsored push promotions.
- **Advance notice.** The provision of long lead times for distributors should heighten their interest in participating in manufacturer-sponsored promotions.
- **Training and support.** When manufacturers provide ample training and support materials, retailers and wholesalers are more likely to embrace a push program.

Several issues should be considered by exchange partners when deliberating whether a push or a pull promotional strategy should be pursued. The nature of these issues reinforces the interrelatedness of the marketing mix variables. The issues include:

- **Budgetary constraints.** All firms face limits on the amount of money they can spend on promotions. In channel relationships, it is particularly important to determine the amount of promotion expenditures expected at each channel level. Ideally, this amount should be jointly determined and agreed upon in advance.
- **Nature of the product offering.** Exchange partners should consider which promotional strategy is most appropriate given the tangible and intangible characteristics of the market offering. For example, using a pull strategy for products featuring little to no opportunity for differentiation makes little sense. Are ultimate customers likely to pressure channel members to carry special inventories of commodity products such as milk or eggs? Probably not. Moreover, there should be a high level of agreement among exchange partners regarding the nature of the product offering before either strategy is selected.
- **Product life cycle.** Whether the product is in its introductory, growth, maturity, or decline stage should impact the promotional strategy employed. Different objectives—informing customers, blocking competitive entry, differentiating products through repositioning—are appropriate as a market offering passes from one life cycle stage to another. The challenge, of course, is to determine where a product offering is in its product life cycle at a given point in time—a task far easier to describe than it is to achieve.
- **Product valuation.** The promotional efforts of channel members are constrained by the ceiling on the selling price of a product offering. To preserve the profit objectives at each channel level, promotional budgets must be reasonable. If promotional expenditures are too high, operational costs will have to decrease or the selling price will have to increase.
- **Market conditions.** The prevailing conditions within a target market will invariably affect the magnitude and effectiveness of promotional strategies. Any firm that is weighing which promotional strategy to use should concurrently consider the characteristics, needs, attitudes, preferences, likes and dislikes, and strengths and weaknesses of its customers and competition.

Most channel members will not opt solely for either a pull or push strategy. Instead, exchange partners operating in today's marketplace are much more likely to employ a combination of push and pull promotions in their attempts to build long-term relationships with other channel members.

The *Place* Ingredient

The final ingredient in the marketing mix of any channel participant is place. The place element is given only a brief treatment here because the topic is the primary subject of this book. But the place ingredient is critical. All products/services must be communicated and distributed through a marketing channel regardless of the number and type of intermediaries used.

Place is often described as distribution. However, the term *place* is more inclusive of the relationship functions in marketing channels. Consider the distribution relationship between American Greetings Corp. and PC Flowers & Gifts. The relationship connects consumers with American Greetings's cards via the World Wide Web. Consumers can select a card, personalize it, and address it to the recipient—all on the PC Flowers & Gifts Internet site. The message is immediately processed by American Greetings, and the card is mailed directly to the recipient. By forming the distribution alliance with PC Flowers & Gifts, American Greetings is able to offer consumers a new place to shop for cards on the Information Highway.[30]

It is important to remember that relationship building is an interactive process; it cannot merely be relegated to the place ingredient. Accordingly, **place** may be defined as all those distribution, logistics, and behavioral functions that regulate the flow of market offerings between exchange partners. The goal of *place* is to minimize the costs of these functions while maximizing customer satisfaction and market coverage.

Minimizing distribution costs can damage long-time channel relationships, as well. Procter & Gamble Co. has recently forced retailers to buy in large quantities to cut its distribution costs. The new ordering guidelines require retailers to order more than 500 cases (or full truckloads) at one time. This new policy forces many small to mid-size retailers—long-time, loyal Procter & Gamble customers—to pay a premium by buying through wholesalers. As one drugstore chain executive notes, "For a lot of retailers, [it's] a reason not to favor P&G on how they stock their shelves."[31]

The place element provides the means to tie together marketing management and relationship marketing. After all, relationship marketing is part and parcel of exchange, and the marketing channel provides the place where exchanges occur. There, manufacturers and intermediaries such as wholesalers and retailers work together to add value to the exchange process. Decisions relating to product, promotional, and pricing variables are all made within the context of a marketing channel.

For example, manufacturers often include intermediaries in product development or line extension decisions because retailers have limited shelf space. Likewise, a retailer's private labeling decision usually involves at least one other channel partner. Product-positioning decisions impact channel member choices: Just as there are manufacturers who would not want their products sold by Target stores, other producers would love to be one of Target's suppliers.

Or, consider that many aspects of promotional programs are actually executed within channels. Outsourcing decisions—pertaining, say, to whether a third-party specialty service provider such as an advertising agency should be used—are made and administered there. In effect, a decision to outsource advertising differs little from a manufacturer's decision to use an independent retailer or own the store. Manufacturers often use intermediaries to perform most, if not all, of their sales effort. This is why producers bring most merchant and agent middlemen into the channel in the first place. Finally, consider that a firm's pricing program affects its positioning strategy and vice versa. Target stores are not likely to provide a suitable outlet for a manufacturer pursuing a premium pricing policy, but then again, Target is not likely to partner-up with such a manufacturer in the first place.

The definition of *place* indicates that there is a trade-off between channel costs and the benefits afforded to exchange partners. The relationship perspective advances the point that these trade-offs are linked to the other ingredients in the marketing mix. Because the overriding purpose of place is to satisfy customer needs, we now turn to the concept known as the *marketing concept.*

Strategy Formulation: Role of the Marketing Concept

The marketing mix is a set of marketing programs relating to product (development, positioning), promotion (personal selling, sales promotion, and advertising), pricing (skimming-the-cream, discounting), and distribution (logistics, channel structure, efforts at relationship management) decisions. These programs jointly support a marketing strategy. In turn, the marketing strategy is guided by corporate-level objectives. Ultimately, the marketing mix becomes the channel member's market offering.

Any marketing strategy can be defined along three basic dimensions. Within the framework of a strategic marketing channel decision, these dimensions are:[32]

- **A channel member's markets.** Channel members' strategies are defined by the products they offer, the markets they serve, their competitors, and their degree of vertical integration.
- **A channel member's functional area strategies.** Channel members' strategies can be defined by the functional area strategies emphasized in their chosen markets. These strategies might include a promotion-oriented positioning strategy, pricing strategy, distribution strategy, or product line strategy.
- **A channel member's strategic assets or skills.** Strategic assets or skills are critical to strategy in that they enable channel members to create sustainable competitive advantages in selected markets. *Strategic assets* are earned resources, such as a favorable brand image or customer loyalty, that are strong relative to competitors. *Strategic skills* represent something a channel member does particularly well, such as on-time service delivery, that has strategic relevance to the marketer's success. Marketing strategies should create the assets or skills that lead to sustainable competitive advantages.

The marketing concept is the core of any marketing mix strategy. The **marketing concept** asserts that customer satisfaction is the basis for all marketing mix decisions. But the marketing mix is not a cure-all for ensuring profitable customer relationships. Southwest Airlines boasts low-price leadership in the airline industry and succeeds. So why did other low-price airlines like People Express fail? People Express had low prices, but it also had one of the industry's worst on-time takeoff records.[33] Southwest Airlines offers customers low prices, enthusiastic flight attendants, and an exceptional on-time takeoff record. Southwest Airlines's marketing mix is based on more than customers' desire for low-cost air transportation. The success of Southwest Airlines is based on building relationships with internal customers (employees), external customers (businesses and consumers), and travel intermediaries (travel agencies, airport personnel).

The marketing concept suggests that a channel member's marketing mix strategy flows from the customer. Southwest Airlines's marketing mix strategy goes beyond the marketing concept; it subscribes to the relationship marketing concept. The **relationship marketing concept** delivers exchange value by addressing simultaneously the needs of each link in the marketing channel. In this way, the relationship marketing concept may be viewed as the thread that stitches channel members together. Consider Wal-Mart's marketing mix strategy: "Far and away the price leader in its field, [Wal-Mart] gives the best value for customers, has a tremendous rate of return for shareholders, and has created a place where employees love to work.[34]

The relationship marketing concept is the culmination of all exchange relationships. The marketing concept is a relationship-building tool. The relationship marketing concept suggests that channel members should focus outwardly on satisfying their partners' needs, rather than their own. The marketing concept begins with well-defined markets. The relationship marketing concept begins by focusing on and coordinating those marketing mix activities that affect customer needs, and ends by producing long-term relationships and profits through creating customer satisfaction.

Key Terms

agile competitive environment
algorithmic pricing method
break-even analysis
competitive pricing
cost-plus pricing
decoding
encoding
functional allowance
market-entry pricing
marketing concept
marketing mix
market-oriented pricing method
modified break-even pricing
negative option contract
nonpersonal selling
penetration pricing
personal selling
place
price
price legitimacy
price premium
product
promotion
promotional allowance
pull strategy
push strategy
relational promotion
relationship marketing concept
relationship-oriented pricing method
shared meaning
skimming-the-cream pricing
valuation
value satisfaction
volume pricing

Chapter Summary

The marketing mix offers the means by which the product, pricing, promotion, and place variables present in a channel relationship can be strategically apportioned to meet the channel's needs. Marketers must carefully consider how to combine the marketing mix ingredients to achieve the desired relationship outcomes. These mix elements are the manageable components by which the norms, behaviors, and functional outcomes of marketing relationships can be developed over time.

A product is a unique bundle of intangible and tangible attributes offered *en masse* to customers. Products provide the vehicles through which exchanges of value can simultaneously satisfy buyer and seller needs. Portraying products as value satisfiers in marketing relationships implies channel members should transform their operations from function delivery systems to value delivery systems. In a function delivery system, marketers' attentions are typically focused inward; products begin with the organization and channel partners aim to develop superior physical processes for moving products from the factory to the market. In a value delivery channel system, marketing attentions are first focused upon external concerns. Channel partners look outward to identify customer needs. Products, thus, originate from a desire to satisfy customer needs. The value delivery sequence involves the assessment, provision, and communication of customer value.

Price is the final exchange value of a good or service, as has been agreed upon by the seller and buyer. Any discussion of pricing should begin with the notion of valuation, or the simultaneous appraisal by potential channel partners of an offering's economic and psychological worth. In marketing channels, each exchange partner provides some added value to the offering. Channel members expect and must receive compensation in exchange for their role in enhancing the value of an exchange object. The price should allocate compensation proportionate to each channel member's contribution. Algorithmic (cost-plus, break-even, modified break-even), market-oriented (competitive pricing, market-entry, skimming-the-cream) and relationship-oriented (volume pricing, functional allowances, promotional allowances) methods of setting prices exist and each can be applied within marketing channels. An underlying factor influencing any channel pricing decision, but in particular relationship-oriented pricing decisions, is the notion of establishing price legitimacy, or the convergence of the buyer's and seller's valuation of a market offering.

Price-legitimizing techniques are supposed to communicate a sense of fair play to customers. The seller is attempting to promote a sense of value to customers. Promotion involves any purposeful communications employed by channel members to inform, remind, and/or persuade prospects and customers regarding some aspect of their market offering. In channel relationships, promotion is a portfolio of persuasive tactics that can be wielded with the purpose of informing, changing preferences and attitudes, positioning and/or repositioning products, and, ultimately, stimulating sales. But the contemporary view also posits promotions as a means of relationship building. Relational promotion involves any communications between channel members that is intended to facilitate new or fortify existing exchange relationships. Over time, relational promotions should lead to relational communication. Relational communication is a continuous process in which the sender and receiver of a message become essentially indistinguishable, since the message and feedback become virtually simultaneous events. The outcome of relational communications is shared meaning, or synchronous cognition. Five objectives are usually associated with relational channel promotions: stimulating sales, sharing information, differentiating offerings, accentuating value, or stabilizing seasonal demand. Relational promotions tactics can be classified into two strategic categories, consisting of *pull* and *push* promotions.

The final ingredient in the marketing mix of any channel participant is place, or all those distribution, logistics, and behavioral functions that regulate the flow of market offerings between exchange partners. The goal of place is to minimize the costs of these functions while maximizing customer satisfaction. A trade-off exists between channel costs and the benefits afforded to exchange partners. These trade-offs are linked to the other ingredients in the marketing mix.

The four components of the marketing mix support a channel member's marketing strategy and, ultimately, its market offering. A marketing strategy can be defined along three basic dimensions: the channel member's markets, functional area strategies, and strategic assets or skills.

The marketing concept is the core of any marketing mix strategy. It asserts that customer satisfaction is the basis for all marketing mix decisions. The contemporary view is that this idea needs to be taken one step further, to a relationship marketing concept. The marketing relationship concept is the culmination of all exchange relationships; it delivers exchange value by addressing simultaneously the needs of each link in the marketing channels, and it produces long-term relationships and profits by creating more customer satisfaction.

Channel Challenges

1. The second-largest distribution channel for soft drinks? You guessed it: the soft drink fountain. The soft drink fountain has been the battleground between PepsiCo and Coca-Cola for years. However, growing consumer preferences for nontraditional beverages are forcing a broadened selection of soft drink alternatives. Consumers are increasingly opting for ready-to-drink teas, fruit drinks, and New Age natural sodas. Juice

consumption in the fountain segment, for example, has risen dramatically in recent years. How do Coke's Minute Maid, Fruitopia, and PowerAde products address changing consumer needs? How might these products enhance or diminish Coke's leadership in the fountain segment?

2. Carmike Cinemas was heralded as the "Wal-Mart of theater chains" by *Forbes* magazine. The Columbus, Georgia–based theater chain buys or builds theaters in small and mid-size cities where there is little competition and land/rent prices are comparatively low. This strategy has propelled Carmike to a place among the top four theater chains in the United States. A theater is a key link in the distribution of cinematic entertainment. Carmike is a movie retailing business. What is the role of the product in Carmike's efforts to solidify its relationship with its customers? How might its expansion strategy hamper its ability to procure some distributors' products?
3. Traditionally, hotel room service may have been characterized as pricey. However, hotels and motels are beginning to experiment with outside sources for room and food service. For example, McDonald's delivery services have been tested at Super 8, Howard Johnson, Ramada Inn, Days Inn, and Park Inn motels. Many pizza delivery services are now available in even the most elite of hotel franchises. Why would high-priced hotels build relationships with low-cost food delivery services for its patrons?
4. Consumer product life cycles are often plagued by significant shifts in consumer preferences. Yet some product pioneers seem to challenge this assumption. For instance, the toy industry is often a victim of short-lived product introductions but some classic toy products have defied competitive entrants. Binney & Smith's Crayola Crayons were introduced at the start of the 20th century. Lego Building Blocks and Parker Brother's Monopoly board game hit the market in the 1930s. Mattel's Barbie dolls celebrated its 25th anniversary in 1994. So, how can marketing channels help extend product life cycles?
5. Sears Roebuck & Company has identified a select group of its charge card customers. The "preferred" customer status is based on the frequency of shopping visits and the average amount of their purchases. These customers receive special perks ranging from 60-day deferred payments on large purchases to exclusive storewide coupons. During Christmas, Sears invited these customers to receive a free ornament or box of candy. This gave their retail salespeople an opportunity to thank the customers for their patronage. How does Sears' strategy strengthen its relationship with customers? What is a potential problem with this relationship-building effort?

Review Questions

1. What are the four key ingredients in the marketing mix? How is management of the marketing mix critical to successful marketing channel relationships?
2. Define the product element of the marketing mix. How do the two key attributes of the product component combine in relationship marketing?
3. How do agile competitive environments modify the product offerings in the marketplace?
4. Explain the relationship among products, value satisfaction, and value delivery systems.
5. Define the price ingredient in the marketing mix. How is price important in marketing channel relationships?
6. Describe how promotional strategies impact relationship building in the marketing channel.
7. How do push and pull promotional strategies differ in their effects on relationship building?
8. What is the fourth element of the marketing mix?
9. How do the elements of the marketing mix relate to the marketing concept in relationship marketing strategy?

Endnotes

1. The definition of product is still fairly controversial. The definition used here represents a more popular view, and it coincides with the definition proffered by Berkowitz, Eric N., Roger A. Kerin, Steven W. Hartley, and William Rudelius (1992), *Marketing,* Third Edition, Homewood, IL: Irwin, 254.
2. Adapted from Miller, Krystal (1992), "Saturn's Success Breeds Low-Pressure Copy-Cats," *The Wall*

Street Journal, July 31, B1; and Pyatt, Rudolph A. Jr. (1993), "Doing Away with Dealership Dinosaurs," *The Wall Street Journal,* May 24, 3.
3. Goldman, Steven L. (1994), "Agile Competition and Virtual Corporations: The Next 'American Century,' " *National Forum,* The Phi Kappa Phi Journal, LXXIV(Spring), 43–47.
4. Schmitz, Barbara (2000), "Custom-Designed Toys Rely on RP Technology," *Computer-Aided Technology,* 19, 14–16.
5. Jabbonsky, Larry (1992), "Coke, Gatorade Agree to Disagree, Wait and See Who Sweats Most," *Beverage World,* May 31, 1, 4.
6. Bower, M., and Garda, R. A. (1986), "The Role of Marketing in Management," in *Handbook of Modern Marketing,* Victor P. Buell, ed., New York, NY: McGraw-Hill, 1–10.
7. "Apple Chairman John Scully Has Seen the Future: He Calls It PDA" (1992), in "Technology (A Special Report)," *The Wall Street Journal,* November 16, R27.
8. Evans-Correia, Kate (1993), "PCs Turned Commodity? Well Almost—In a Way!" *Purchasing,* 114 (January 17), 54–56.
9. Conatser, Kelly R. (1993), "Direct Comparisons," *InfoWorld,* 15 (June 28), S80–92.
10. Adapted from Rao, Akshay, and Mark E. Bergen (1992), "Price Premium Variations as a Consequence of Buyers' Lack of Information," *Journal of Consumer Research,* 19 (December), 412–23.
11. Shea, David C. (1993), "Value at Forefront of Children's Wear," *Bobbin,* 34 (June), 85–88.
12. Wills, Gordon, Sherril H. Kennedy, John Cheese, and Angela Rushton (1990), "Maximizing Market Effectiveness," *Management Decision,* 28 (2), 87–101.
13. Phillips, Owen R. (1993), "Negative Option Contracts and Consumer Switching Costs," *Southern Economic Journal,* 60 (October), 304–15.
14. Hynowitz, Carol, and Gabriella Stern (1993), "Taking Flak: At Procter & Gamble, Brands Face Pressure and So Do Executives. . . ," *The Wall Street Journal,* May 10, A1.
15. Stern, Louis W., and Adel I. El-Ansary (1992), *Marketing Channels,* Fourth Edition, Englewood Cliffs, NJ: Prentice Hall, 82.
16. Parasuraman, A., Leonard L. Berry, and Valerie A. Zeithaml (1991), "Understanding Customer Expectations of Service," *Sloan Management Review,* 32 (Spring), 39–48; and Caudron, Shari (1993), "The Unhappy Consumer," *Industry Week,* 242 (November 15), 26–28.
17. Stern and El-Ansary (1992), *Marketing Channels,* Fourth Edition, 403.
18. Wechsler, Jill (1999), "Policy Issues for 1999," *Pharmaceutical Executive,* 19 (1), 20–26; and Anonymous (1999), "Complex System Grounded in EDLP," *Chain Store Age,* 75 (13), 71-72.
19. Weitz, Barton A., Stephen B. Castleberry, and John F. Tanner, Jr. (1992), *Selling: Building Partnerships,* Homewood, IL: Richard D. Irwin, 5.
20. Robinson, Brian J. (1993), "Promotion Is a New Way to Make Brand Contact with Buyers," *Marketing News,* 27 (April 12), 4, 16.
21. Weitz, Castleberry, and Tanner (1992), *Selling: Building Partnerships,* 5.
22. Bird, Laura (1992), "Advertising: Sour Remarks on Milk May Focus Attention on Big Dairy Campaign," *The Wall Street Journal,* October 1, B5.
23. Tanzer, Andrew (1992), "Just Get Out and Sell," *Forbes,* 150 (September 28), 68–72.
24. Khermouch, Gerry (1993), "Miller Taps Bartenders for TV Ads," *Brandweek,* 34 (April 26), 6.
25. "Trade Marketing: A Retail Perspective" (1990), *International Journal of Physical Distribution & Logistics Management,* 20 (3), iii–v.
26. Lefton, Terry (1993), "Lego/Del Monte Double Team Kids," *Brandweek,* 34 (June 14), 1, 6.
27. "Fuji: Products and Promos Lead to Success" (1991), *Dealerscope Merchandise,* 33 (January), 100, 102.
28. Black, Susan S., and Anne Imperato Colgate (1990), "Levi's Sings the Blues," *Bobbin,* 32 (November), 42–48.
29. Lamalle, Cecile (1993), "Profitable Promotions," *Restaurant Hospitality,* 77 (November), 102–13.
30. Adapted from "Technology: American Greetings to Sell Cards using the Internet," (1995), *The Wall Street Journal,* May 2, B6.
31. Stern, Gabriella (1993), "P&G Mulls Plan to Cut Costs of Distribution; Retailers Would Be Forced to Buy in Big Amounts, Burdening Small Outlets," *The Wall Street Journal,* November 8, A3.
32. Aaker, David A. (1995), *Strategic Market Management,* Fourth Edition, New York: John Wiley & Sons, 4.
33. Treacy, Michael (1995), "You Need a Value Discipline—But Which One?" *Fortune,* April 17, 195.
34. Ibid.

part I

Cases

Case 1.1

Compaq Computer Corporation: The Dell Challenge

By Adrian Ryans and Mark Vandenbosch

In early October 1999, Michael Capellas, the recently appointed 45-year-old CEO of Compaq Computer Corporation, was facing some difficult decisions about how to combat the increasing threat posed by Dell Computer Corporation to its leadership position in the PC business. With sales of over $31 billion in 1998, Compaq was the second-largest computer company in the world (see Exhibit 1.1.1 for a five-year summary of Compaq's financial results).

On April 17, 1999, the Compaq board had dismissed Eckhard Pfeiffer, who had served as Compaq's CEO since 1991. The board meeting occurred about a week after Compaq had announced that first quarter profits would be only about half what Wall Street had been expecting. Its U.S. PC sales in the first quarter were up only 10 per cent, while Dell's were up over 50 per cent. In key segments of the PC market Compaq's sales and/or gross profit margins had declined between 1997 and 1998 (see Exhibit 1.1.2).

Between April and July 1999, Compaq was run by Ben Rosen, Compaq's chairman, and two other board members.

Developments at Compaq from 1995 to 1999

By 1995, Compaq was the global leader in PCs with a particularly strong position in the PC server business (accounting for about 25 per cent of revenues and 50 per cent of operating profits). During 1996, Compaq saw an opportunity to move into the enterprise segments of the computing market with servers and powerful workstations. This placed Compaq into direct competition with IBM and

---

IVEY Adrian Ryans and Mark Vandenbosch prepared this case solely to provide material for class discussion. The authors do not intend to illustrate either effective or ineffective handling of a managerial situation. The authors may have disguised certain names and other identifying information to protect confidentiality.

Source: This case has been written on the basis of published sources only. Consequently, the interpretation and perspectives presented in this case are not necessarily those of Compaq Computer Corporation or any of its employees.

EXHIBIT 1.1.1

Selected financial data on Compaq Computer Corporation

Year Ended December 31 (in millions, except for per share amounts)	*1998*	*1997*	*1996*	*1995*	*1994*
STATEMENT OF INCOME					
Revenue:					
Products	$27,372	$24,122	$19,611	$16,308	$12,274
Services	3,797	462	398	367	331
Total revenue	31,169	24,584	20,009	16,675	12,605
Cost of Sales					
Products	21,383	17,500	14,565	12,026	8,671
Services	2,597	333	290	265	214
Total cost of sales	23,980	17,833	14,855	12,291	8,885
Gross margin	7,189	6,751	5,154	4,384	3,720
Selling, general and administrative expenses	4,978	2,947	2,507	2,186	1,859
Research and development costs	1,353	817	695	552	458
Purchased in-process technology[1]	3,196	208	—	241	—
Restructuring and asset impairment charges[2]	393	—	52	—	—
Merger-related costs[3]	—	44	—	—	—
Other income and expense, net	(69)	(23)	17	79	50
	9,851	3,993	3,271	3,058	2,367
Income (loss) before provision for income taxes	(2,662)	2,758	1,883	1,326	1,353
Provision for income taxes	81	903	565	433	365
Net income (loss)	$(2,743)	$ 1,855	$ 1,318	$ 893	$ 988
FINANCIAL POSITION (selected data)					
Cash and short-term investments	4,091	6,762	4,081	745	471
Accounts receivable, net	6,998	2,891	3,718	3,141	2,287
Inventories	2,005	1,570	1,267	2,156	2,005
Other current assets	2,073	794	1,203	485	395
Total current assets	15,167	12,017	10,089	6,527	5,158
Total assets	23,051	14,631	12,331	7,818	6,166
Accounts payable net	4,237	2,837	1,962	1,379	888

[1]Represents non-recurring, non-tax deductible charges associated with purchased in-process technology of $3.2 billion in connection with the Digital acquisition in 1998, and $208 million and $241 million in connection with acquisitions in 1997 and 1995.

[2]Represents a $393 million charge for restructuring and asset impairments in 1998 in connection with the Digital acquisition and the closing of certain Compaq facilities, and a $52 million charge related to restructuring actions taken by Tandem during 1996.

[3]Represents a $44 million non-recurring, non-tax-deductible charge in 1997 related to the Tandem merger.

Source: Compaq 1998 Annual Report and selected SEC 10-K and 10-Q filings.

HP. In October 1996, Compaq entered the workstation market with an Intel-based Windows NT machine.

In order to penetrate the enterprise segment against the strong sales and field service and support organizations of IBM and Hewlett-Packard, Compaq developed alliances with systems integrators, such as Andersen Consulting, and with SAP, the leading enterprise resource-planning software vendor. This allowed Compaq to begin delivering solutions involving servers, networks and associated services. It also continued to use its existing network of value-added resellers

Exhibit 1.1.2

Comparison of Compaq's performance in 1997 and 1998 in PC market

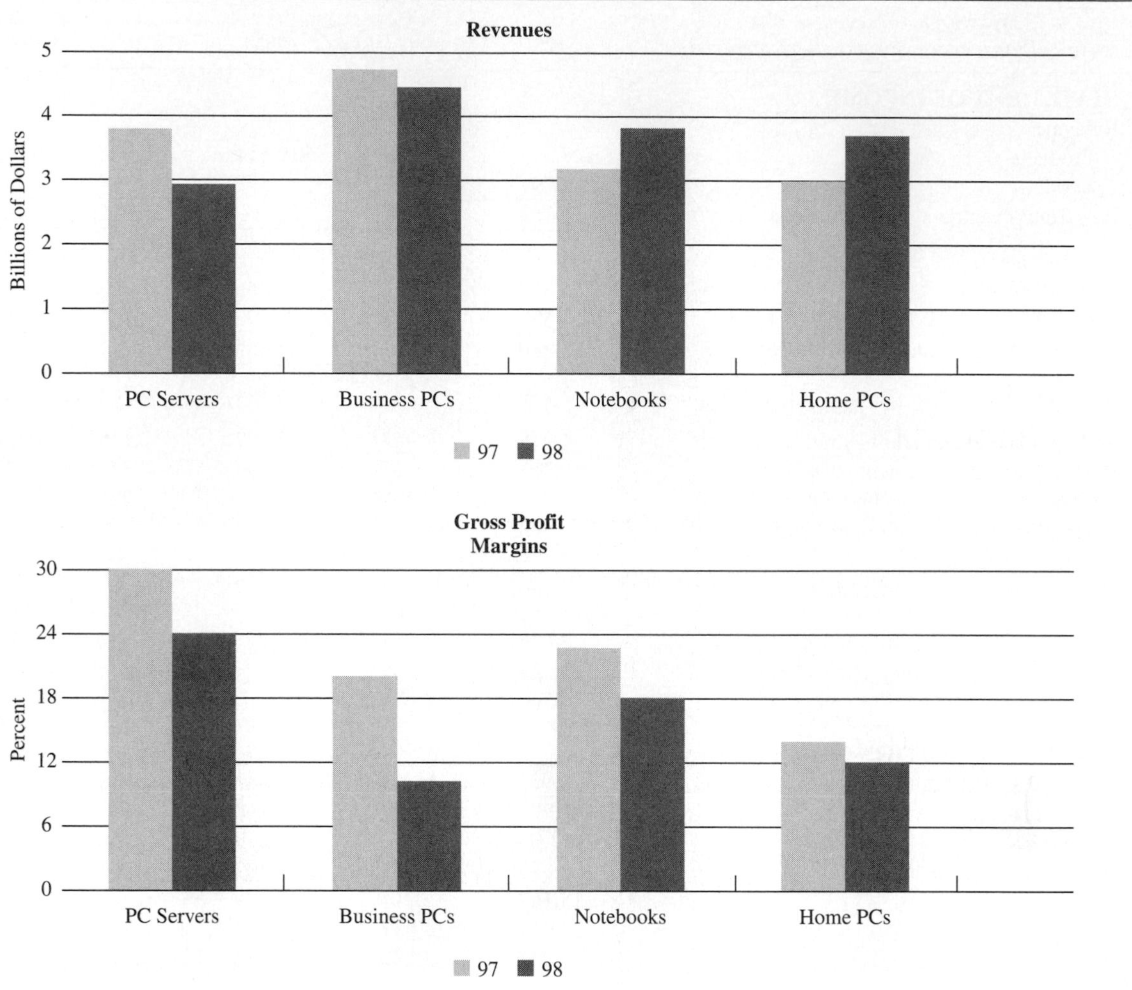

Source: "Where Compaq Is Losing Ground," *Business Week,* April 26, 1998.

(VARs) to provide similar solutions to smaller organizations. Within a year of entering the Intel-based workstation market, it had captured a 16 per cent market share giving it the leadership position in this segment of the workstation market.

In June 1997, Compaq acquired Tandem Computers for $3 billion. Tandem was the world leader in fault-tolerant computer systems, which were used in high-end, mission-critical applications. Compaq believed that the acquisition would strengthen Compaq's position in the enterprise market and would double the field resources deployed against enterprise customers. In a much more controversial move, in January 1998 Compaq announced its acquisition of Digital Equipment Corporation valued at about $9.6 billion. From Compaq's perspective the jewel in Digital was its large services organization, which could further strengthen Compaq's position in the enterprise market. Compaq believed that the acquisition would also give it the largest channel structure in the world with 80 per cent of its products and solutions being delivered through its channel partners. A major challenge that faced Compaq when the acquisition was approved was the merging of Digital's 50,000 employees with Compaq's 33,000 employees. Many observers felt that the two cultures were quite different and the physical distance between the two headquarters in Texas and Massachusetts was expected to add to the integration challenge. The acquisition was completed in June 1998.

Compaq was also increasing its share of the home PC market. By 1997, Compaq held about 30 per cent of the retail home PC market, almost tying Packard-Bell for leadership in this segment of the market. By using low-cost chips, outsourcing assembly, and tightening sales terms and policies, Compaq claimed to earn the same 11 per cent gross margin on an $800 home PC as it did on its more powerful home computers.

In order to reduce inventories, Compaq began to move to just-in-time inventory stocking and building business PCs to fill dealer orders rather than relying on its own forecasts. By the fourth quarter of 1996, it had shrunk its inventories to 30 days from more than double that in late 1995.

However, Compaq was not performing as well among business users. As the decade progressed, more and more business users were moving away from buying PCs through indirect retail channels. This change impacted the sale of Compaq's PC servers and business computers. Despite growing markets, Compaq's sales in these two categories declined in 1998 (see Exhibit 1.1.2). In addition, gross margins were being squeezed.

Among the reasons given for Pfeiffer's dismissal were Compaq's weakening position in the high-end, profitable segments of the PC business against Dell; its failure to effectively respond to increased pressure from sub-$600 home PCs; its failure to resolve the direct distribution challenge; and the poor progress on the Compaq-Digital integration. Many observers felt that the root of many of Compaq's problems was the Dell Direct Model and the way Dell had been able to use this model to erode Compaq's strong position in many of the key PC market segments.

Dell Computer Corporation

Michael Dell entered the computer business in 1983, when he began upgrading and selling IBM PCs from his dorm room at the University of Texas at Austin directly to end users.[1] He incorporated Dell Computer Corporation in May 1984. In 1985, Dell introduced the first PC that it had designed itself. At the Spring Comdex trade show in 1986, Dell introduced a new 286 computer that offered higher performance than either IBM or Compaq and that was priced about 50 per cent below IBM's computer. Dell ran ads in two of the leading PC magazines comparing its computer with IBM's. These events built Dell's visibility in the market. By the end of 1986, Dell had sales of $60 million. Michael Dell decided that if the company was going to achieve sales of $1 billion by 1992, it would have to target larger corporations, which meant that excellent customer support would be a critical success factor. In 1987, Dell became the first personal computer company to offer next-day, on-site service in certain markets. Also in 1987, Dell began its global expansion by establishing a subsidiary in the United Kingdom. It entered 11 additional national markets over the next four years.

In July 1987, Dell published a private placement memorandum. In the memorandum it identified three key strengths that contributed to Dell's competitive advantage: its ability to produce a line of high-quality products that were IBM-compatible; its direct relationship marketing concept (at that time Dell was receiving 1,400 telephone calls per day); and its ability to maintain an efficient and flexible manufacturing operation. In 1988, Dell raised $30 million in its initial public offering.

Dell stumbled for the first time in 1989. Dell had accumulated an excess amount of 256K memory chips just as the market for the chips peaked and a technological transition to one megabyte chips was beginning. The value of the inventory plunged and Dell had to sell it off with a large negative impact on profitability. In the same year, Dell was forced to cancel a very large product development effort, when feedback from customers about the proposed new product line was very negative.

In 1990, in an effort to grow even faster, Dell decided to augment its direct channel with indirect sales through some of the new emerging channels for PCs: computer superstores, such as CompUSA, and club stores, such as Price Club and Sam's. However, by mid-1994, Dell decided to exit the retail channel despite continued rapid growth in the retail channel and focus totally on the direct model. After a detailed financial analysis of the retail channel, Dell's top management convinced itself that Dell's retail business was not profitable due to significantly higher operating expenses and lower gross margins. Dell's management was also convinced that many of their competitors were also losing money in the retail market.

Dell had entered the notebook market in 1988. After some initial successes, Dell ran into some serious problems with its notebook line in 1993, including a major recall of its laptop product. After a thorough review of the product line Dell decided to focus on one new product, the Latitude XP. The Latitude XP was launched in August 1994 and the product was an immediate hit and helped drive notebook revenue from 2 percent of net revenues to 14 percent of net revenues within a year.

At the same time that the notebook business got into serious trouble, Dell was experiencing severe cash flow problems, partly as a result of its very high growth rate. This caused Dell to refocus on liquidity and profitability as well as sales growth. This led to a major effort to understand the financial models underlying Dell's different businesses, so that it could really understand the profitability of the businesses.

By 1995 Dell was on a roll. Sales in the Americas were growing at three times the industry rate and Dell was well established in Europe with offices in 14 countries and a long-established manufacturing centre in Limerick, Ireland. In 1993 Dell had established its first beachheads in Asia-Pacific with subsidiaries in Australia and Japan. By 1995 Dell had direct operations in 11 countries in the region, and distribution alliances in 37 more.

Despite the rapid growth in its core desktop and notebook product line, Dell decided it had to enter the server market. Servers were experiencing very rapid growth as a result of the growth of networking in organizations; Compaq, IBM and Hewlett-Packard were all benefiting from the growth of this very high margin business. In addition, standards were being set for multiprocessor servers and Windows NT was emerging as an industry standard for operating systems. Thus Dell could design its own server systems with the support of Intel and Microsoft without the need for the development of proprietary technologies. Entering the server business successfully meant that Dell would have to develop the capabilities to sell, service and support these higher end products. In September 1996, Dell launched a new line of entry level, mid-range, and high-performance PowerEdge servers at prices significantly below those of its established competitors. By the fall of 1997, Dell was the fourth-largest server supplier in the world and the third-largest supplier in the United States.

In 1998, Dell entered the engineering workstation market with Intel-based systems using the Windows NT operating system. By mid-1999, Dell was the largest (in units, but not revenue) supplier of workstations in the world (combining both Windows NT and Unix workstations). In fiscal 1999, Dell also became a significant player in the storage area with its line of PowerVault storage products. With servers, workstations, and storage products it had a more complete line of products for its enterprise customers. In fiscal 1999 Dell had revenues of $18.2 billion and net income of $1.5 billion. Industry analysts estimated its global market share at 8.6 per cent. See Exhibit 1.1.3 for a five-year summary of Dell's financial results.

By mid-1999, Dell was a global company. Its products were marketed in over 170 countries and it had manufacturing facilities in the United States (Austin, Texas, and Nashville, Tennessee), Ireland, Malaysia, and China with an additional manufacturing site in Brazil scheduled to open in late 1999.

Dell Direct Model

The Dell Direct business model had evolved significantly since the mid-1980s. By 1999, it was a very powerful model that relied heavily on a sophisticated IT infrastructure to deliver a superior customer experience. The infrastructure enabled direct relationships with customers, alliances with key technology partners, and computer solutions tailored to customer needs.

The close relationships that Dell forged with its customers were a key element in the model. Starting in the late 1980s, Dell began to carefully segment its markets and to focus on those segments it could serve profitably as it achieved scale. Over time it segmented its markets more finely (see Exhibit 1.1.4), identified the particular issues facing the different segments, and then developed products and strategies to deal with the identified issues. In 1999, 90 percent of Dell's sales were to institutions and almost two-thirds of its sales were to large corporations, government agencies and educational institutions buying more than $1 million of products and services per year. The balance of Dell's sales went to medium and small businesses and home-PC customers. Unlike PC companies that sold through reseller channels, Dell only shipped product when it had a firm customer order in hand. Since it usually knew exactly who in a customer's organization had bought a particular computer and what software had been preloaded on the PC, it had precise data on each user's exact configuration. This greatly simplified the task of providing technical support over the Internet or by telephone. The intimate knowledge of an enterprise's total global purchases of PCs was valuable information that Dell could feed back to its customers.

Dell had established two broad types of customers: relationship customers and transactional customers. Relationship customers were large corporations, governmental, medical and educational customers and small to medium businesses with which Dell had ongoing relationships. Dell had about 2,000 field salespersons throughout the world to call on these types of accounts and attractive prospects. The company had developed direct sales marketing programs for its relationship customers and prospects. For large customers, Dell had dedicated account teams, with sales, customer service and technical support representatives, which provided these customers with assistance on such issues as technology

EXHIBIT 1.1.3

Selected financial data on Dell Computer Corporation

	Fiscal Year Ended				
	Jan. 29, 1999	*Feb. 1, 1998*	*Feb. 2, 1997*	*Jan. 28, 1996*	*Jan. 29, 1995*
OPERATING RESULTS					
Net revenue	$18,243	$12,327	$7,759	$5,296	$3,475
Gross margin	$4,106	$2,722	$1,666	$1,067	$738
Operating expenses					
Selling, general and administrative	1,788	1,202	826	595	424
Research, development & engineering	272	204	126	95	65
Total operating expenses	2,060	1,406	952	690	489
Financing and other income	—	—	33	6	(36)
Income before extraordinary loss	$1,460	$944	$531	$272	$149
Operating income	$2,046	$1,316	$714	$377	$249
Net income	$1,460	$944	$518	$272	$149
PERCENT OF NET REVENUE					
Operating income	11.2%	10.7%	9.2%	7.1%	7.1%
Net income	8.0%	7.7%	6.7%	5.1%	4.3%
Net revenue, by region					
Americas	68%	69%	68%	66%	69%
Europe	26%	24%	26%	28%	27%
Asia-Pacific and Japan	6%	7%	6%	6%	4%
System net revenue, by product line					
Desktops	64%	71%	78%	81%	87%
Enterprise	13%	9%	4%	3%	5%
Portables	23%	20%	18%	16%	8%
Non-system net revenue, percent of total system net revenue	7%	9%	10%	11%	12%
FINANCIAL POSITION (selected data)					
Cash and marketable securities	$3,181	$1,844	$1,352	$646	$527
Accounts receivable, net	2,094	1,486	903	726	538
Inventories	273	233	251	429	293
Other current assets	791	349	241	156	112
Current assets	6,339	3,912	2,745	1,957	1,470
Total Assets	6,877	4,268	2,933	2,148	1,894
Accounts payable, net	2,397	1,643	1,040	466	403

Source: Dell Computer Corporation 1999 Annual Report.

needs assessment, technology planning, system configuration, lifecycle cost management, installation system and detailed product, service, and financial reporting. For customers with in-house maintenance capability, it could provide a variety of customized support programs, including access to Dell's technical support capabilities. For companies operating globally, Dell could provide global pricing, support, and co-ordination through a single point of contact. For example, one of its service and support options allowed notebook computer users to have access to service and support in any country in

Exhibit 1.1.4

Dell Computer's evolving market segmentation

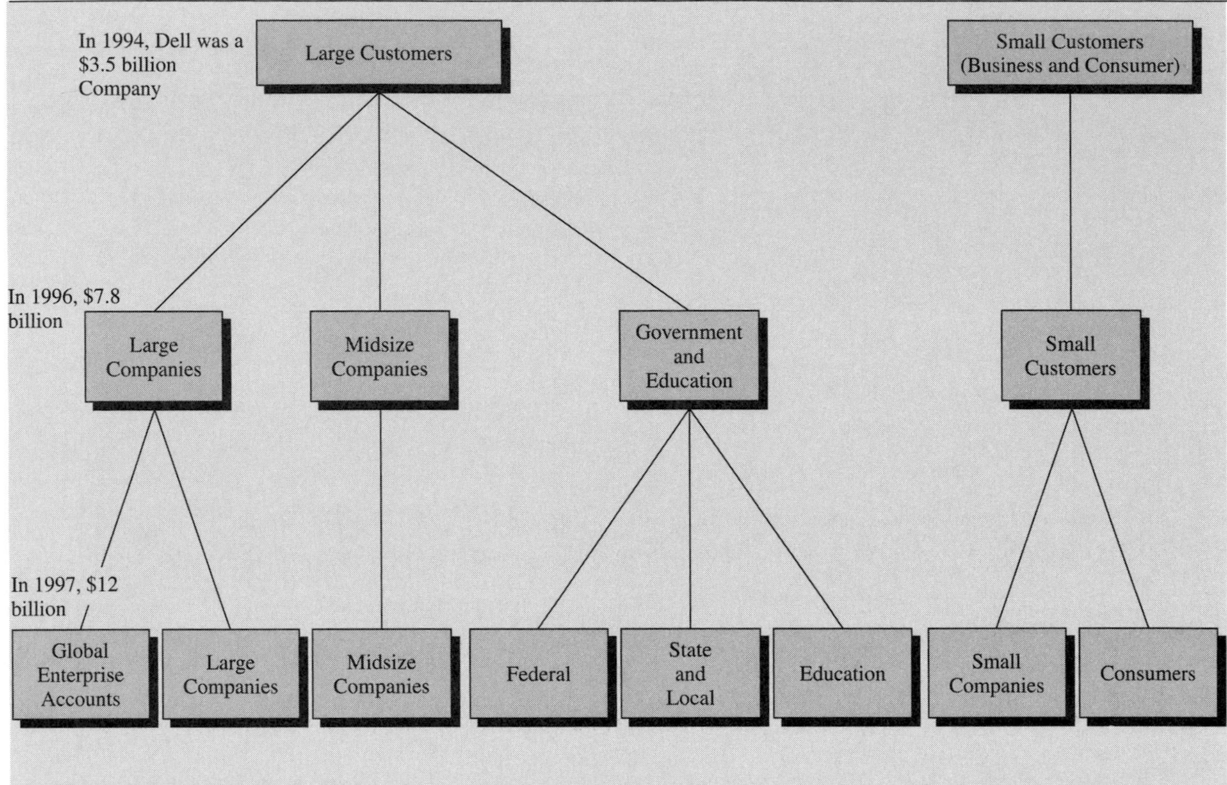

Fast-Cycle Segmentation

Dell's rapid growth in recent years has been accompanied by ever finer cuts at customer segmentation. This is an important element of Dell's virtual integration with customers. The finer the segmentation, the better able Dell is to forecast what its customers are going to need and when. Dell then coordinates the flow of that strategic information all the way back to its suppliers, effectively substituting information for inventory.

Source: Adapted from: Joan Magetra, "The Power of Virtual Integration: An Interview with Dell Computer's Michael Dell," *Harvard Business Review,* March–April 1998, p. 78.

the world in which Dell operated, if the user ran into problems while travelling outside the user's home country.

Dell also did a significant amount of business with small to medium businesses and individuals with which it did not have as strong an ongoing relationship. These were its transactional customers. Dell marketed its products to these customers by advertising in trade and general business publications, and by a variety of direct marketing approaches. Dell provided these customers with sales assistance, custom-built computer systems at competitive prices, and post-sales service and support.

Another key element of the Dell Direct business model was the close working relationships it had with key suppliers. In particular, it had worked very closely with Intel and Microsoft. An important role of Dell's research and development group was the selection of appropriate technology for customer segments. The other important focus of this group was process research and development, where the aim was to improve the efficiency and quality of the assembly process. The close working relationships and sophisticated data exchanges that Dell had built up over the years with its key suppliers allowed it to operate very efficiently. As orders flowed into Dell from customers, it shared these data in real time with its key suppliers so that they knew exactly what Dell's daily requirements for a particular part or assembly would be. In some cases, the components of a PC system might never even be shipped to a Dell factory. For example, when a customer ordered a desktop system with a Sony monitor, the first time the PC and monitor were paired up could be in the back of the United Parcel Service or Federal Express delivery truck. Sony would ship the monitor from its manufacturing plant at precisely the right time to marry with the PC. The Dell organization would never see or touch the monitor. During the 1990s, despite the tremendous growth and global expansion of its operations, Dell Computer had actually reduced the number of suppliers it used and by 1999 about 40 suppliers supplied 90 per cent of its material needs.

Over time, as Dell developed a more and more intimate understanding of its market segments and customers, it began to provide more and more customized solutions to their needs. For its larger customers, it could preload both standard and firm-specific software for a particular type of user in the customer's organization (which would vary between a junior financial analyst and a person working in technical support) and place the customer's asset tags on the computers before shipping. It also provided a variety of different levels of service and support for its customers. Some of its largest customers had dedicated on-site teams and Dell essentially functioned as the customer's in-house PC department. Much of Dell's after-sales service was provided by third parties. An interaction with Dell about a problem might lead to the generation of two electronic messages—one to have parts shipped to the customer and one to the third party maintainer to send a service engineer to the customer site to install the parts. The information about the service problem and the resolution would be captured by Dell's systems and could be used to provide feedback to the Dell parts vendors and for Dell's own internal decision making.

Starting in 1996, Dell began selling its computers over the Internet. Its use of the Internet expanded dramatically over the next three years. Dell developed customized Extranet sites called Premier Pages for its larger customers. These Premier Pages allowed approved employees to configure systems within approved parameters established by the IT department with Dell, pay for them, and track their delivery status in real time over the Internet. Employees could also access sophisticated technical troubleshooting tools over the Internet that often allowed them to solve many of their own technical support issues. Premier Pages could dramatically shorten the time and paperwork involved in ordering and tracking computer purchases and providing technical support for installed systems. This benefited both Dell and its customers. By June 1999, Dell was providing more than 19,000 Premier Pages. By mid-1999, about 40 percent of Dell's orders came in over the Internet, over 70 percent of order status checking was being done online, and almost 40 percent of technical support was online. Dell was continually looking for new opportunities to leverage the capabilities of the Internet to enhance the Dell Direct business model. In 1999, it had over 50,000 pages of technical support data available to all its customers over the Internet. Hardware was increasingly being equipped with self-diagnostic capability that allowed the hardware to notify Dell and the customer when problems were detected.

In 1999, Dell launched www.gigabuys.com, which was an online source for more than 30,000 computer-related products, including peripheral equipment and software.

Dell's management information systems enabled it to track each unit sold from the initial sales contact, through the manufacturing process to post-sale service and support. The information systems allowed Dell to track key information about its customers. Dell was able to use its database to segment its customers, to assess purchasing trends, to monitor advertising effectiveness, and to develop targeted marketing activities for particular customer segments. By using its extensive database Dell was able to quickly identify customer satisfaction issues and to test new value propositions in the marketplace prior to the product or service being introduced.

Dell's Product Line in 1999

Dell sold a range of products and services in 1999, including desktop systems, notebook computers, workstations, network server and storage products, as well as a variety of software, peripherals and service and support programs.

Dell offered two lines of desktop computers. The OptiPlex line was designed for corporate and institutional customers, who required reliable systems for use in networked environments. These customers also valued stability in technology. The Dimension line was designed for small businesses and individuals, who frequently demanded up-to-date technology and fast performance and didn't need remote management. Some systems in the Dimension line contained the latest technology and were targeted at sophisticated users, whereas other systems contained slightly older technology and were targeted at more value-driven users.

Dell also offered two lines of notebook computers. The Latitude line was targeted at a corporate segment similar to the OptiPlex line of desktops that valued durability and reliability with connectivity, so that the computers could be used in networked environments. The Inspiron line was targeted at the home and small business user, who required the latest technology and who valued multimedia performance.

Dell's enterprise systems included workstations, network servers, and storage products. The Dell Precision workstation line was a Windows NT-based workstation intended for professional users who required a high-performance machine to run sophisticated and demanding applications, such as computer animation, computer-aided design, software development, and financial analysis. Dell's PowerEdge line of network servers consisted of systems that could operate as file servers, database servers, application servers, and communication/groupware servers in networked environments. The PowerVault line of storage products was designed to provide high-end storage features for standard computing environments to meet a range of customer storage needs.

Compaq's Other Major PC Competitors

The PC market continued to consolidate in the late 1990s. The U.S. data shown in Exhibit 1.1.5 were characteristic of what was happening globally.[2] Exhibit 1.1.6 shows the logistics and distribution structures of the PC industry in the late 1990s with the names of some of the major companies active in the North American market.

Besides Dell, the two leading direct PC makers were Gateway Computers and Micron Electronics. Gateway had revenues of $7.5 billion and net income of $346 million in 1998. Eighty-six percent of its revenues came from the United States. Relative to Dell, Gateway was much more focused on the home and small business markets. In 1999, Gateway was attempting to offset declining profits on PCs with profits from Internet-related services.[3] Gateway had established almost 200 Gateway Country stores that were designed to allow consumers and small business owners to get their hands on PCs and surf the Internet before placing an order at an online kiosk in the store. Knowledgeable salespersons were available to answer customers' questions and help them to order computers. Part of its services strategy was to help its PC customers get online by bundling a year's worth of free Internet access through its own Internet service provider (ISP) for anybody buying a Gateway PC costing more than $999. Gateway hoped to lock in many of these customers by providing financing, Internet access and a personalized portal that would steer customers to Gateway's e-commerce sites. A second part of Gateway's services strategy was to offer consulting and training to small businesses and consumers.

Micron Electronics was a wholly owned subsidiary of Micron Technology, Inc., a U.S.-based manufacturer of semiconductor memory components and modules with expected fiscal 1999 (year ending September 2, 1999) sales of $3.7 billion. Micron Electronics was formed through the merger of three predecessor companies in 1995 and was expected to have sales of $1.4 billion in fiscal 1999. Micron Electronics provided a range of competitively priced computing solutions.

In addition to manufacturing custom notebooks, desktops, and servers, Micron sold bundled packages of hardware, Web hosting, ISP services and data management, designed to meet the e-commerce needs of small businesses.

Besides Compaq, the other two leading suppliers of Windows/Intel (Wintel) PCs that primarily used indirect channels were IBM and Hewlett-Packard. In 1998, IBM was the fourth-largest manufacturer of PCs in the United States and the second-largest globally. IBM was a strong full-line supplier of computer hardware. In the 1990s it had managed to grow its services business very rapidly and was a leading supplier of e-commerce solutions. In 1998, it reported external revenues of $12.8 billion in its personal systems segment, which provided hardware and some software for individual users, servers and display devices. Many analysts

Exhibit 1.1.5

Consolidation in the U.S. PC industry

	1996	1997	1998	1999
Top 3 Direct PC Makers	18.6%	21.8%	27.5%	34.5%
Top 3 Indirect PC Makers	26.9	30.4	33.0	35.0
Others*	54.6	47.8	39.5	30.5

*Includes Apple and eMachines.

Data: ZD Infobead Insider as reported in "The Big Squeeze in the PC Market," *Business Week,* September 20, 1999.

Exhibit 1.1.6

Personal computer logistics and distribution structure

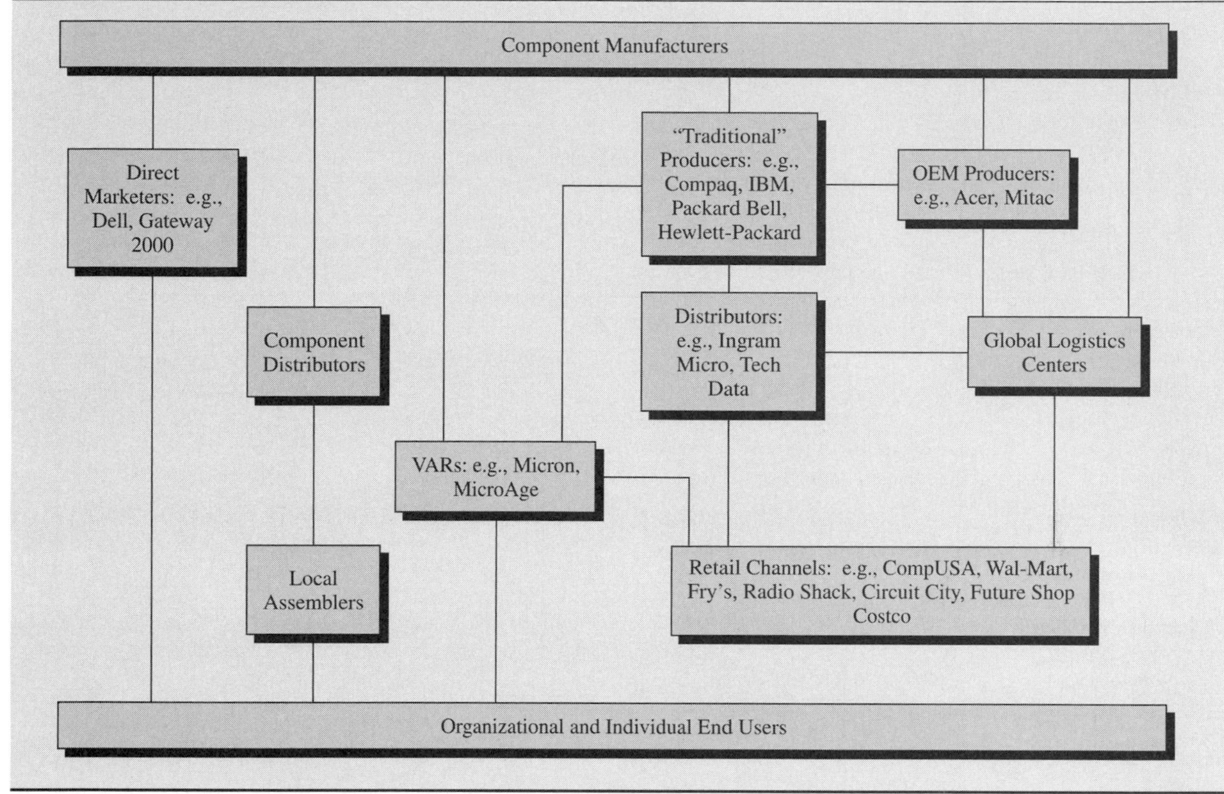

Note: Dotted lines indicate component or sub-assembly flows, solid lines represent complete or semi-complete systems.

Source: Adapted from: Curry and Kenny, "Beating the Clock," *California Management Review,* Fall 1999, p. 21.

viewed IBM's notebook line as the strongest part of its PC product line. IBM reported a pre-tax loss of $1.0 billion on sales to the personal systems segment. However, its server segment reported revenues of $10.6 billion and pre-tax income of $2.8 billion. This segment produced more powerful multi-purpose computer systems that operated many open network-based applications and were used primarily by multiple users at the same time.

Hewlett-Packard (HP) was the fourth-largest PC manufacturer worldwide in 1998, and was a major supplier in most segments of the computer hardware market. It was also the global leader in the printer business, which was believed to account for well over 50 percent of HP's profits. In the late 1990s HP was making a major push into providing a variety of e-services, providing hardware, software and services. In 1998 it had total revenues of $47 billion and net income of $2.9 billion. On June 1, 1999, HP announced a new channel strategy for its PC business. The HP Prime customers were enterprise-class customers for whom HP would take the responsibility of involving channel partners as needed. Its second channel was the Business Store, where HP referred customers to the VAR channel, but allowed customers to purchase directly, if they wished. The Partner Prime channel involved the partners playing the lead role and HP saw this as the ideal solution where third-party integration was required and a multi-vendor solution was required by the customer. HP sold its PCs to home and home office users through both its online store and retailers and other online vendors.

Market Positions in the Late 1990s

As can be seen in Exhibit 1.1.7, the personal computer market, which included both desktops and notebooks,

EXHIBIT 1.1.7

Worldwide PC market (including desktops and notebooks); market sizes and market shares by segment

Global	*1996*	*1997*	*1998*	*1H 1999*
Compaq	10.2%	14.2%	14.8%	14.5%
Dell	4.3%	5.9%	8.5%	10.4%
Packard Bell/NEC	6.1%	5.2%	4.2%	5.9%
IBM	8.9%	9.0%	8.8%	9.0%
Hewlett-Packard	4.3%	5.6%	6.4%	6.6%
Others	66.2%	60.1%	57.3%	53.6%
Total	100.0%	100.0%	100.0%	100.0%
Market size (millions of units)	69.3	80.3	90.0	51.0
United States	*1996*	*1997*	*1998*	*1H 1999*
Compaq	12.9%	16.9%	16.7%	16.3%
Dell	6.8%	9.3%	13.2%	15.7%
Packard Bell/NEC	11.4%	8.8%		
IBM	8.3%	8.6%	8.2%	8.0%
Gateway	6.1%	7.0%	8.4%	8.5%
Hewlett-Packard		6.6%	7.8%	8.2%
Others	54.5%	42.8%	45.7%	43.3%
Total	100.0%	100.0%	100.0%	100.0%
Market size (millions of units)	26.5	31.5	36.3	20.7
Europe, Middle East, and Africa	*1996*	*1997*	*1998*	*1H 1999*
Compaq		15.5%	16.8%	17.2%
IBM		8.4%	8.5%	8.9%
Dell		5.1%	7.5%	8.9%
Hewlett-Packard		6.3%	6.5%	5.9%
Siemens-Nixdorf		4.7%	5.2%	
Fujitsu				6.0%
Others		60.0%	55.5%	53.1%
Total		100.0%	100.0%	100.0%
Market size (millions of units)		24.3	28.5	14.7
Asia-Pacific (excluding Japan)	*1996*	*1997*	*1998*	*1H 1999*
Compaq	6.5%	9.2%	8.5%	7.5%
IBM	7.5%	7.8%	8.1%	8.8%
Legend		3.1%	5.4%	6.2%
Hewlett-Packard	3.5%	4.6%	5.4%	5.3%
Acer	6.2%	5.7%	4.7%	
Samsung	6.5%			5.5%
Others	69.8%	69.6%	67.9%	66.6%
Total	100.0%	100.0%	100.0%	100.0%
Market size (millions of units)	8.9	10.5	10.5	6.6

Source: Various reports of International Data Corporation and casewriter estimates.

continued to grow in the late 1990s, although the growth rates were much lower than those experienced earlier in the decade.[4] Compaq was still the market leader on a global basis, but Dell was closing the gap rapidly, particularly in the United States. Overall personal computer shipments in Japan in 1998 were about 8 million units, but all the top five players in Japan were Japanese companies.

In the enterprise market, the market growth rates varied significantly by market segment. Workstations were used for high-performance computing by engineers, scientists, and analysts. There were two major product segments: Intel-based Windows NT workstations and Unix-based workstations (see Exhibit 1.1.8). The typical Intel-based workstation had a manufacturer's selling price of about $4,000 (this included some powerful desktop PCs that were used as workstations) versus over $13,000 for a Unix-based workstation. Sun dominated the Unix-based workstation market with a market share of about 50 percent in early 1999, followed by Hewlett-Packard and IBM. In the Intel-based Windows NT market, Dell and Hewlett-Packard were virtually tied for leadership with 21 percent market shares in 1998 with Compaq in the third position with a market share in the teens.

The server market was divided into three major sub-segments: entry, mid-range, and high-end. Gross margins in the entry server market were about 10 to 20 percentage points higher than they were for desktop systems. (For an illustrative example of the gross profit margins in different segments of the PC business, see the Compaq data in Exhibit 1.1.2). The lower end of the entry segment was called the PC Server segment. Market sizes and market growth rates for the three major segments and the PC server segment for 1998 are shown in Exhibit 1.1.9. The overall market was expected to grow 5 percent by 2000 with the fastest growth occurring in the entry server market segment where margin pressure was also expected to be the highest. Compaq and Dell were the only significant players in the entry server segment of the market with particular strengths in the PC server sub-segment. In the PC server market Compaq had lost 4 percent market share between 1997 and 1998, but still was the clear market leader with a 29 percent market share. Dell had achieved a 76 percent growth and had a 1998 market share of 13 percent. IBM was the overall market leader in entry, mid-range and high-end servers. Hewlett-Packard was strong in both entry and mid-range and Sun had a growing presence in all three segments. Exhibit 1.1.10 shows worldwide revenues for all the major server vendors in the fourth quarter of 1998 and the change from the same quarter in 1997.

Compaq's Channel Issue

By the fall of 1999, Compaq was organized into three large business units: Enterprise Solutions and Services, Commercial Personal Computing (small and mid-size businesses), and Consumer. Sales and operating income by business for 1998 and the first nine months of 1999 are shown in Exhibit 1.1.11. As this exhibit demonstrates, a significant proportion of the revenues in the Enterprise Solutions and Services segment came from professional and support services, an important result of the Tandem and Digital acquisitions. The business critical server business was largely a legacy of the acquisition of Tandem's fault-tolerant computer business. Compaq had about a 25 percent share of the storage business (excluding mainframe storage), which represented a much bigger market share than that of any of the other major PC competitors.

Compaq used a variety of channels to sell its products. It sold to large and medium-sized business and government customers through dealers, value-added resellers and system integrators. It reached its small business and home customers through dealer and consumer channels. It also had a direct sales force and sold its products on its Internet site and by telephone. By 1999, Compaq had about 44,000 resellers globally with about 11,000 in the United States, including

Exhibit 1.1.8

Worldwide workstation market size (billions) and growth rate by type of operating system

	1997	*1998*	*% Change*
Intel-based Windows NT	$5.76	$6.80	18%
Unix-based	$9.40	$7.90	−16%
Total	$15.17	$14.70	−3%

Source: International Data Corporation.

Exhibit 1.1.9

Worldwide server market—Revenues and market share by segment

Entry Servers	*1998 Revenues (billions)*	*Market Share*
IBM	$5.2	21%
Compaq	$4.5	18%
Hewlett-Packard	$3.1	12%
Sun	$2.7	11%
Dell	$1.7	7%
Market size (billions)	$25	
1997 to 1998 growth	−2%	
PC Servers (sub-segment of Entry Servers)	*1998 Revenues (billions)*	*Market Share*
Compaq	$3.80	29%
Hewlett-Packard	$1.70	13%
Dell	$1.60	13%
IBM	$1.50	12%
Market size (billions)	$13	
1997 to 1998 growth	8%	
Mid-Range Servers		
IBM	$4.90	28%
Hewlett-Packard	$4.10	23%
Sun	$2.30	13%
Market size (billions)	$18	
1997 to 1998 growth	5%	
High-End Servers	*1998 Revenues (billions)*	*Market Share*
IBM	$6.00	37%
Sun	$0.90	6%
Amdahl	$0.70	4%
Hitachi	$1.10	7%
Fujitsu	$1.40	9%
NEC	$1.10	7%
Market size (billions)	$16	
1997 to 1998 growth	−8%	

Source: Various reports of International Data Corporation.

about 2,000 resellers that focused on the important small and mid-size business segment. Reseller margins on name-brand desktop PCs had been shrinking over the years and by early 1999 they were about 4 to 5 percent.[5] Even the white box desktop PCs built by or for the resellers had margins of only 8 to 10 percent.

On November 11, 1998, Compaq had unveiled a "customer choice" model, which actively promoted the direct sale of a new Prosignia line of customizable desktop, portable and server products specifically targeted at small and medium-sized businesses. Compaq argued that the customer choice model allowed customers to do business with Compaq in the way they chose, whether through one of its resellers, through a customer account team, or directly via the Internet or telephone. The Prosignia line was to be available either directly from Compaq or from one of its 11,000 resellers. This represented the most aggressive promotion to date of Compaq's buy direct program, which had been available in a relatively low key way for a couple of years under such names as DirectPlus, Compaq At Home, and Compaq GEM (Government/Education/Medical) Online. Authorized Compaq resellers, who referred customers to Compaq for direct fulfillment, could earn agent commissions of 4 to 6 percent.

Driving the decision to move away from Compaq's traditional indirect distribution model was an internal study of channel economics for traditional indirect, partner direct and customer direct models in the commercial personal computing market (see Exhibit 1.1.12). In the partner direct model, a channel partner or complementary product supplier redirected the customer to the Compaq website for a direct sale. In return, the partner would receive an agent's fee. In the customer direct model, the customer contacted Compaq directly.

By early 1999, it was estimated that 20 percent of Prosignia's sales were the result of reseller referrals. Many of Compaq's resellers were angry at Compaq, feeling that their customers could easily bypass them, buy directly over the Internet and save 8 or 9 percent relative to the reseller price.[6] Compaq executives argued that 70 percent of the Web sales were coming from customers who wouldn't have bought Compaq without the direct option. Some resellers felt that Compaq was obsessed with Dell and was abandoning the very people who had made it the world's largest PC company. A number of resellers began steering their customers to other brand-name manufacturers, such as Hewlett-Packard, or to their own "white label" PCs.

In early 1999, Compaq issued a warning about lower than

EXHIBIT 1.1.10

Top 10 server vendors, worldwide factory revenue, Q4 1998 ($M)

	Q497	*Market Share*	*Q498*	*Market Share*	*Growth Q498/Q497*
IBM	$5,234	31%	$4,553	28%	−13%
Compaq	$1,430	8%	$2,072	13%	45%
Hewlett-Packard	$1,782	11%	$1,886	12%	6%
Sun Microsystems	$1,275	8%	$1,508	9%	18%
Fujitsu	$766	5%	$766	5%	1%
NEC	$630	4%	$638	4%	1%
Dell	$319	2%	$603	4%	89%
Simens	$381	2%	$599	4%	57%
Hitachi Ltd.	$693	4%	$500	3%	−28%
SGI	$392	2%	$271	2%	−31%
Others	$4,038	24%	$2,796	17%	−31%
Total market	$16,940	100%	$16,202	100%	−4%

Source: International Data Corporation, 1999.

expected sales to small and mid-size businesses, because sales to distributors, such as Tech Data Corporation and Ingram Micro, Inc., did not meet expectations. Compaq was forced to significantly increase its agent commissions and introduce new programs to help some of its resellers set up their own online storefronts. In late March Compaq announced a range of enhanced services for Prosignia customers, including online services that would allow small businesses to set up electronic storefronts and a 24-hour toll-free business support service dedicated to Prosignia customers. They could also purchase various service and support packages direct from Compaq. Overall, analysts believed that the Prosignia line had improved Compaq's market share position in the crucial small business market.

In conjunction with this greater emphasis on direct selling and support Compaq began to rebuild its supply chain to support customer choice, including both its customers and channel partners. It began to enhance its configure-to-order capabilities and to use the Internet and database tools to maintain real-time connections with its customers and suppliers. It hoped to be able to better tailor products, services, and solutions to individual customer needs and to reduce the time between order and shipment of an order to five days or less by the end of 1999. Compaq hoped to be able to sell 25 percent of its products online and by phone by the end of 1999.

The Situation in October 1999

Compaq's results for the first nine months of 1999 were not very encouraging. Revenues were $28 billion (the increase from 1998 being largely attributable to the inclusion of Digital results for the full period), but after-tax income was only $237 million (again see Exhibit 1.1.11).

Clearly, one of the major issues facing Michael Capellas in his new role as Compaq CEO was the resolution of the channel issues, particularly in the important Commercial Personal Computing segment. In this segment of the business more than 85 percent of Compaq's sales were still generated by the traditional indirect channel and less than 10 per cent by the customer direct channel. The partner direct channel generated the rest of the business. Some analysts were even calling Compaq's customer choice strategy a "customer confusion" strategy.

Exhibit 1.1.11

Compaq Computer Corporation segment information (unaudited)

(in millions)	*Nine Months ended September 30, 1999*	*Twelve Months ended December 31, 1998*[1]
Enterprise Solutions and Services		
Revenue[2]	$14,810	$14,488
Operating income	1,635	1,724
Commercial Personal Computing		
Revenue	9,052	11,846
Operating income (loss)	(369)	(46)
Consumer		
Revenue	4,028	4,932
Operating income	193	183
Other		
Revenue	157	(97)
Operating loss	(280)	(115)
Consolidated Segment Totals		
Revenue	28,047	31,169
Operating income	1,179	1,746
A reconciliation of the company's consolidated segment operating income to consolidated income (loss) before provision for income taxes follows:		
Consolidated segment operating income	1,179	1,746
Corporate and unallocated shared expenses	(994)	(819)
Purchased in-process technology	—	(3,196)
Restructuring and related charges	(868)	(393)
Gain on sale of business	1,182	—
Income (loss) before provision for income taxes	499	(2,662)
Net income (loss)	237	(2,743)

[1]Digital Equipment results only incorporated for last six months of 1998. This has the biggest impact on Enterprise Solutions and Services segment comparisons.

[2]Approximate percentage breakdown of Enterprise Solutions and Services revenue:

Business critical servers	16%
Industry standard servers	23%
Storage	25% (about 16% of which was sold attached to industry standard servers)
Services	36%

Source: Company data.

Exhibit 1.1.12

Comparison of different go-to-market models for small and mid-sized businesses

A. Typical Costs across Channels			
	Traditional Indirect	*Partner Direct*	*Customer Direct*
Channel mark-up	4–6%	0%	0%
Agent fee	0%	4–6%	0%
Co-op marketing	3%	1.0%	0%
Financing	1%	0.5%	1.0%
Price protection	4%	0%	0%
Obsolescence	1.5%	1.0%	1.0%
B. Typical Gross Margins and Operating Expenses by Channel			
Gross margin %	8–10%	15–17%	20–22%
Operating expense %	10–12%	8–10%	10–12%
C. Industry versus Compaq Mix (Global)			
Industry	70%	10%	20%
Compaq	85%	6%	9%

Source: Compaq presentations to analysts.

Endnotes

1. Parts of this discussion are based on Michael Dell, *Direct from Dell* (New York: HarperCollins, 1999).
2. "The Big Squeeze in the PC Market," *Business Week,* September 20, 1999, p. 40.
3. "A Net Gain for Gateway?" *Business Week,* July 19, 1999, pp. 77–78.
4. Most of the market size and market share data in this case are taken from reports prepared by International Data Corporation.
5. "The Death of the Reseller," *Business Week,* February 4, 1999.
6. "Internet Defense Strategy: Cannibalize Yourself," *Fortune,* June 9, 1999.

Case 1.2

Sunshine Juice Company

By Professor Elizabeth M.A. Grasby and Christine A. Veber

It was early December 1994 and Cynthia Morrison, Sunshine Juice Company's chief financial officer, sat at her desk at the company's production facilities located in Oakville, Ontario. Having experienced encouraging initial success with the introduction of the company's product—orange juice packaged in a bag-in-a-box—details of Sunshine's marketing plan, specifically the pricing strategy, needed to be finalized for the upcoming year. In addition, Morrison wanted to analyze what impact various price levels would have on Sunshine.

Sunshine Juices Limited was founded in April of 1991. At that time, management performed two years of market research to get a clear understanding of potential customers and to develop a product, pricing, and promotional strategy that would best meet their needs. In 1993, Sunshine chose to enter the juice market with a four-litre bag-in-a-box orange juice product. This product package was modelled after the package design which has been successful in the wine industry. At the time, this packaging concept represented 30 percent of wine sales by volume in Canada.

Sunshine's product was sold by retailers such as large chain grocery stores, as well as newly introduced club stores. Initial sales had been concentrated on grocery stores, but Morrison believed that club stores offered an exciting opportunity for Sunshine, and could account for the bulk of sales in the future.

IVEY Christine A. Veber prepared this case under the supervision of Elizabeth M.A. Grasby solely to provide material for class discussion. The authors do not intend to illustrate either effective or ineffective handling of a managerial situation. The authors may have disguised certain names and other identifying information to protect confidentiality.

Club stores represented a new retailing concept where customers were required to be members. Club stores provided shopping in a warehouse atmosphere. Only one brand of each type of product (i.e., corn flakes, or orange juice) was carried by the stores, at a target "unit price" of at least $5. In order to meet this requirement, grocery items were usually sold in either large-size portions, or in multi-packs. This allowed club stores to offer discount prices to their customers for "buying in bulk." Club stores required an 8 to 10 percent margin on the goods they sold, where grocery stores required 25 to 30 percent. Exhibit 1.2.1 lists competitive products found in grocery and club stores. All competitive juice products were 100 percent pure orange juice, in most cases, made from concentrate.

Sunshine's strategy was to be a significant player in the wholesale beverage market by designing and promoting unique new and innovative packaging; by increasing consumption of beverages through club pack formats; and by expanding outside of the Ontario market. Sunshine's goal was to improve profitability through increased sales, strict cost control, and an aggressive pricing strategy.

The Marketing Strategy

Sunshine's orange juice was 100 percent pure Brazilian orange juice from concentrate. In consumer testing, Sunshine juice met or surpassed all of the criteria which consumers used to evaluate juice:

- Shelf life
- Great taste
- All natural ingredients
- Freshness
- Smooth texture
- Delicious flavor
- Naturally sweet
- No after-taste

In addition, 85 percent of consumers who tasted Sunshine's juice said they would buy it.

Exhibit 1.2.1

Competitive orange juice products[1]

	Product	*Price*	*Size*
Grocery Store			
Refrigerated	Tropicana	\$2.49	946 ml
		2.99	1.89 L
		4.39	2.84 L
		1.99	3 × 236 ml
	Minute Maid	3.89	1.89 L
	Old South	2.69	1.89 L
	Everfresh	2.29	1.5 L
		2.59	2.5 L
		3.79	3.78 L
	Sealtest	1.46	1 L
		1.99	2 L
	Beatrice	2.42	2 L
	President's Choice	2.39	1.89 L
	No-name	1.79	2 L
Non-refrigerated	McCain	1.29	3 × 250 ml
	Minute Maid	1.09	3 × 250 ml
	Allen's	1.19	3 × 250 ml
	No-name	0.89	3 × 250 ml
	No-name Drink	0.89	3 × 250 ml
	No-name	1.99	1.36 L
	Fruite Drink	1.79	2 L
	Sunlike	3.99	12 × 300 ml
	No-name	6.99	9 × 3 × 250 ml
	No-name Drink	6.49	9 × 3 × 250 ml
Club Store			
Refrigerated	Old South	\$2.29	1.89 L
	Minute Maid	3.99	2.84 L
Non-refrigerated	Everfresh	1.79	1.89 L
	Minute Maid	7.89	9 × 3 × 250 ml
	Fairlee	8.49	24 × 300 ml

[1]Those products with minimal juice content (less than 25 percent) are referred to as "drinks."

Sunshine's packaging was designed keeping in mind the needs of the end consumer. Sunshine selected the highest quality juices and packaged the product in a convenient four-litre box. The tap allowed the consumer to dispense the desired amount of juice, and then resealed itself maintaining the freshness of the juice for about 40 days after the package had been opened. As the product did require refrigeration, the tap also allowed families the convenience of dispensing the juice right from the refrigerator.

The easy carrying handle allowed each box to be removed easily from the cooler by the consumer and checked out by the cashiers more effectively. All Sunshine universal products codes were located on the bottom of each box. This allowed the product to be scanned much quicker at the checkouts. The

Sunshine label had outstanding graphics that were displayed on all four sides.

Distribution

A very simple, yet effective distribution strategy had been developed. Initial contact was made and a trial order solicited by the sales manager. The product was then either shipped directly to the retailer or to a distributor. The sale was followed by periodic visits to the store to monitor accurate product rotation and shelf facing. All future orders were produced on an order-by-order basis.

Promotion

Sunshine's promotional strategy consisted primarily of extensive in-store demonstrations and point of purchase advertising. In-store sampling was believed to encourage consumers to try Sunshine's orange juice.

Pricing

A detailed analysis of the consumer identified that the price set for Sunshine's orange juice would have a significant impact on sales. At a wholesale price of $4.49, keeping in mind the 10 percent margin required by club stores, and the 25 percent margin required by grocery stores, retail prices would be set at $4.99 and $5.99 for club and grocery stores, respectively.

At a retail price of $4.99, it was expected that over the next year, 30,000 units per month could be sold through club stores. Through extensive discussions with buyers, Morrison felt that a price of $4.49 would modestly increase sales, but a retail price of $3.99 would have a significant impact on sales volumes. Volume figures for grocery stores had not yet been estimated. Sales volumes through this channel were expected to be significantly lower than those for club stores, due to the higher price charged for the product.

Production

To produce a four-litre bag-in-a-box juice product with minimum overhead costs and maximum flexibility, the bag was filled by a juice co-packer. In 1993, a large Canadian packaging company was contracted by Sunshine to perform this juice packing operation. The filled bags were then brought to Sunshine's production facility and stored in a cooler until they entered the packaging process. The process began with the boxes being manually erected and glued with an industrial hot melt glue gun. The bags were then placed into the box and again the box was glued manually. The finished product was organized in either a shipping carton or directly palletized. Finally, the finished product was returned to the cooler before shipping. The time period from when the bags were delivered from the juice packer, to when the finished product was shipped, was typically no longer than three days, due to the perishable nature of the product.

The total variable cost to manufacture the product was $3.81. This amount included the juice, packaging, box, bag, production supplies (i.e., glue), transportation-in, labor, and delivery. Exhibit 1.2.2 contains a schedule of Sunshine's fixed costs.

Sunshine's current manufacturing facility has a maximum capacity of 100,000 units per month. In order for growth to continue, a larger facility would have to be secured. A facility of about 14,000 square feet would be necessary to increase the capacity to approximately 200,000 units per month. A facility this size would double current rent costs.

In addition to larger facilities, additional equipment would be required. The most important acquisition would be a larger cooler, which would allow for better product rotation and decreased handling time. Automated packaging equipment would also assist in reducing labor costs. The cooler and the automated packaging equipment would cost $80,000 and $110,000 respectively.

EXHIBIT 1.2.2

Schedule of fixed costs[1]

Salaries[2]	$ 10,000
Rent and utilities	3,960
Insurance	210
Maintenance and repairs	1,500
Depreciation[3]	2,300
Telecommunications[4]	325
Professional fees	500
Stationery	400
Telephone	700
Travel	500
Miscellaneous[5]	200
Total fixed costs	$ 20,595

[1]Expressed on a monthly basis.

[2]Included all factory, selling, and general and administrative salaries (including benefits).

[3]On production and office equipment.

[4]Includes computer and cellular expenses.

[5] Includes bank service charges.

Sunshine's Facilities

Sunshine's production facilities, cooler, storage, office and shipping area were located in a 5,880-square-foot industrial unit in Oakville, Ontario. In the unit, the two production lines, the raw material storage, the cooler, and the offices occupied about 40 percent, 30 percent, 11 percent, and 19 percent of the floor space respectively. The shipping and receiving was done through a single, ground-level door using an outside loading ramp and a forklift.

Human Resources

Sunshine employed 10 people; three in management and sales, six in production, and one as a truck driver. It was hoped that the close, hands-on approach of the management team and the commitment by the production workers would allow Sunshine's sales to grow while adding proportionately fewer employees. The board of directors has also had significant influence on the growth of the company. Their diverse backgrounds included experience in the food, packaging, and investment banking industries.

The Future

Sunshine planned to continue its growth through new product introductions and new market developments. At the current time, several new product ideas were being explored including three new products—apple juice, fruit punch, and lemonade. In addition, a shelf-stable, bag-in-a-box product, frozen concentrate, and food service dispensers were also being researched. Morrison was unsure of the dilative effect of adding new products to existing accounts.

Since Sunshine had explored, and was currently developing all Canadian markets, introduction to the American market could significantly contribute to the company's growth strategy. The American market was attractive due to its size and geographical proximity, therefore ensuring reasonable transportation costs. An additional $0.70 cost per box would be required for shipping and distribution to the United States.

Sunshine's decision on a pricing strategy would have implications on the probability of U.S. orders. Based on sales presentations made to several large American retailers, it was estimated that at a retail price of US$4.99 in club stores, initial American sales would be approximately 110,000 units per month. Club stores and grocery stores in the United States required the same margins as Canadian stores. Therefore, in order to set the retail price at US$4.99 in club stores, at a 10 percent margin, Sunshine's wholesale price would be US$4.49 (Cdn$6.15). Morrison kept in mind the US$.0725 (Cdn$.0993) cent-per-litre import duty on orange juice that was not produced from Florida oranges.

Case 1.3

Eggsercizer: "The World's Smallest Exercise Machine"

Henry S. Maddux
Stamford University

Marlene M. Reed
Stamford University

Mark Davis, the 41-year-old President and Founder of Eggstra Enterprises, Inc., sat in his office late one Wednesday night in the latter part of June 1994 and pondered the future of his company. His Manager of Marketing, Johnny Laskin, had just resigned that day. Part of the problem, Mark knew, lay in differences in marketing philosophy. Mark had confessed to himself that he utilized a shotgun approach to selling his main product, the Eggsercizer, which was a small hand-held, hand, wrist, and arm exercise device bearing the shape of an egg. For example, he believed it made sense to distribute the product as extensively as possible to maximize exposure. Johnny, on the other hand, supported a more deliberate approach that would include development of a marketing strategy and targeting customer groups based on that strategic plan. Mark did agree that marketing should be based on the firm's overall goal and the anticipated future direction of the company, but the strong growth in sales of the company had preempted his energies, and he had not had enough time to focus on long-range planning. The most promising growth in sales appeared to be with those marketers such as Wal-Mart and Kmart, but he wondered if such sales would cannibalize his high-end sales to retailers like Brookstone.

Background on the Founder

Mark Davis had grown up in Montgomery, Alabama. After graduating from high school and attending a junior college for almost two years, he joined the Navy near the close of the Vietnam War. Upon the urging of a superior, Mark spent a year in the Navy's nondestructive testing (NDT) school and served the remainder of his six and a half years of service inspecting nuclear powered submarines. When he reentered private life in 1979, he worked with power utility companies performing nondestructive testing. From 1985 until 1988, he worked with the Electric Power Research Institute (EPRI). Then in 1988, Mark decided to form his own consulting company, performing NDT testing and training for the nuclear and petrochemical industry. His income from consulting provided a moderate but not lucrative means of support.

The Idea for the Eggsercizer

Mark loved softball, and sought a way to improve his arm strength. In early 1989, he started squeezing a tennis ball as he traveled from nuclear plant to nuclear plant. On Memorial Day weekend of that year Mark was scheduled to meet with General Electric in Atlanta to set up a training and consulting program worldwide. He went to bed around 10:30 P.M. and woke up around midnight with the thought, "What is a new and novel shape which is better than this tennis ball?" Mark went downstairs and started brainstorming ideas and uses for a new hand and arm exercise device. However, he knew that he didn't have the unique shape that would be a breakthrough in the market. Later in the night, Mark got up and went to the refrigerator to get cream for his coffee. As he opened the refrigerator door, his eyes focused on some eggs on a shelf. It occurred to him that the egg shape fit the natural contour of his hand, and Mark realized he had the appropriate shape for his hand exerciser. The rest of the night, Mark's mind raced ahead fashioning marketing and promotional ideas.

He immediately took his idea to a patent attorney. The attorney told him that he did not have a patentable idea. The attorney said, "It would be like trying to patent this ashtray." However, Mark was not satisfied. He had a friend who had patented the idea of a baby seat on a grocery store cart called "The Baby Sitter." That friend led him to another attorney who was excited about the idea and agreed to conduct the patent search and application for about one-half of the amount the first attorney had wanted for his efforts. It was now June of 1989.

Mark now had an idea for a new product, but a serious question was how to produce the egg. He found a rubber company in South Carolina that agreed to build a four cavity prototype mold for $1,400. The eggs were made from neoprene, a hard, durable rubber. Mark also originally wanted the product to bear the soft, fuzzy covering found on tennis balls, so he found a company in Indiana that could apply this coating called "flocking." Mark had obtained $18,000 of initial financing from friendly investors (friends, training students, etc.). This he partially used to finance a production mold which cost $8,000 and also to purchase product packaging inventory. Production started in February of 1990, and 4,000 eggs were made before Mark visited his first trade show in July of 1990. The eggs were green and purple and fuzzy, but they were hard. Mark sold about 600 eggs at that first show—mostly to hospital gift shops. At this time, he was working out of his house to reduce the overhead of the operation. However, there were expenses associated with the shows. It often cost $1,000 for a booth in addition to his travel expenses.

Early in 1989, Mark moved his residence to Alabaster, Alabama, near Birmingham. Later that year he moved the molds from South Carolina to a local rubber company in the same community. After a $2,000 modification of the mold, the rubber company projected it could manufacture and deliver eggs for $0.75 a unit. The flocking cost an additional $0.43. In addition, there were expenses such as shipping and packaging. Mark enlisted the help of his brother who owned Krout Davis Marketing, a local marketing company, to help design the packaging. The first package was a colorful 2″ × 2″ × 3″ gift box which Brookstone, a national gift product retailer and Eggstra's largest customer, continued to use. In November of 1992, the company began using a clear plastic clam shell or two-sided enclosure measuring about 4″ × 8″. It fit snugly around the egg and also contained an attractive full color point-of-purchase display tray. Twelve eggs plus a display tray fit in each box. (See Exhibit 1.3.1 for a picture of the package Brookstone used.)

Mark continued to attend local and regional trade shows,

EXHIBIT 1.3.1

but sales were slow. The product idea seemed right; the packaging was attractive; yet the texture of the egg seemed to be a problem. In order to make the neoprene more pliable, oil had to be added. This made the surface slick, and it became difficult to make the flocking adhere to the surface. Davis was forced to settle for a rubber that was hard to compress, but he began talking to mold manufacturers to ascertain if there was another substance that might be used. One manufacturer suggested that he needed to make his eggs out of Sorbothane. Mark had heard of this unique, flexible rubber but had not been able to locate the manufacturer. After some further investigation, he discovered that Hamilton-Kent Sorbothane of Kent, Ohio, was the only manufacturer, and that the material was patented. He called the company in the summer of 1991, and they agreed to look into making the eggs. A new prototype mold was produced at a cost of $600. Mark sent a sample of his eggs to Hamilton-Kent to be used in designing the product. Once Mark received the new egg made of Sorbothane, he knew his search had ended. Four production molds, each with six mold cavities, were manufactured. Each production mold cost Mark $1,500. The eggs were manufactured using the extrusion technique. Rubber material was placed between the two hinged faces of the mold. A hydraulic press placed the mold under pressure and high temperature, and the rubber was extruded into the mold cavities. Eggs were made in production lots of 600 to 1,000 units. The per unit cost to Mark was $2.74. The flocking process was discontinued.

Growth in Product Sales

In the Fall of 1991, Mark received his first significant order from HealthSouth Rehabilitation Corporation for two cases of 30 units each per month. The price of the eggs was set at $4.75 each. (See Exhibit 1.3.2 for a cost analysis of the Eggsercizer.) Mark started his "guerilla" marketing (a term interchangeable with the "shotgun" approach). He sent an egg

EXHIBIT 1.3.2

Cost analysis—-Original Eggsercizer

WHOLESALE PRICE*		$4.75
Cost of Goods Sold		
MATERIAL COST**	$1.18	
LABOR	0.06	
INBOUND SHIPPING	0.03	
PACKAGING	0.22	
TRAY COST***	0.26	
TOTAL		$1.75
CONTRIBUTION MARGIN		$2.56
ESTIMATED PER UNIT GENERAL AND ADMIN****		$0.46
ESTIMATED COMMISSIONS AND ROYALTIES		$0.52
OUTBOUND SHIPPING		$0.35
ESTIMATED PER UNIT PROFIT		$1.23

*With prepaid shipping; 12 units to a box; one $3.10 display tray per box

**Purchase quantity = 50,000 units per order

***$3.10/12 = $0.26 per egg

****Historically 10% of sales

to a *Wall Street Journal* columnist and heard nothing for six months. In March 1992, the columnist, John Pierson, replied by phone. He wanted to feature the Eggsercizer in his column, "Form and Function." The article ran on March 30 of 1992. Readers started calling Mark, and he began selling directly to the customer.

Mark also used the *Journal* article to create brand awareness. He had been trying unsuccessfully for several months to get the Eggsercizer into the Brookstone chain of 100 high-end, novelty and gift stores. For *The Wall Street Journal* article, Mark conceived the idea of referencing a major competitor, the Grip Gym, currently offered at Brookstone. People started calling Brookstone wanting the Eggsercizer. Of course, Brookstone had no eggs to sell. Just three weeks later, Brookstone tested an order for 2,500 eggs. The price to Brookstone was $3.60 per unit wholesale. Brookstone's retail price was $7.95. That initial order sold within one week. The time was now May of 1992.

The Brookstone account provided the national exposure for which Mark was looking. Other stores began to call. A buyer for a chain of stores would purchase an egg at Brookstone, then they would call the company to inquire about ordering the product.

In order to reach the sporting goods retail business, Mark decided to attend his first national trade show, the National Sporting Goods Association show in August of 1992. After this show, sales began to rise rapidly. The 1992 sales volume was approximately 90,000 units. In 1993, sales had grown to 364,000 eggs. (See Exhibit 1.3.3 for a monthly history of 1993 and 1994 sales revenue and Exhibits 1.3.4 and 1.3.5 for financial statements for 1992 and 1993.) Two-thirds of 1993 sales occurred in the last half of the year. Total sales of eggs by mid-1994 were 650,000 units.

The typical order called for boxes of the standard egg. Each box contained 12 packaged Eggsercizers of varying colors and a display stand if requested. The price of a box was $57.00. (See Exhibit 1.3.6 for the quantity discount schedule.)

Exhibit 1.3.3

Sales activity 1993 and forecast for 1994 (in thousands of dollars)

Month	*1993 Sales*	*1994 Sales*
JAN	$ 38.3	$159.4
FEB	47.8	70.0
MAR	57.8	148.7
APR	74.9	135.6
MAY	67.6	41.6
JUN	46.1	19.6
JUL	75.6	100.0
AUG	85.9	100.0
SEP	174.7	100.0
OCT	247.7	100.0
NOV	132.5	100.0
DEC	61.9	100.0
TOTAL	1,112.9	

Note: Davis projected sales after June 1994 at a flat rate of $100,000.

An Attempt at Forecasting

Davis knew that his forecasting techniques were very simple. His 1994 projections for $100,000 did not seem to reflect the cyclical nature of his business. He wondered how he might adjust the forecast for the remainder of 1994 and what his forecast for 1995 might be.

While no formal marketing research had been done, Davis knew that price was an important issue—especially for the mass market business. He did feel that the demand for his product was price inelastic. That is, if the prices were changed some percentage, there would be a smaller percentage change in the amount demanded. He had no real data to back up his intuition.

Davis found it necessary to purchase an 81-cavity mold to keep up with production requirements. The cost of this mold was $8,500.

During the first two years, Mark did not perform any extensive formal planning or operational analysis. He did obtain advice and planning assistance from the Business Incubator Center at the University of North Carolina at Charlotte before he moved to Alabama. The Service Corps of Retired Executives (SCORE) also assisted Mark in developing a formal business plan and setting goals.

The first business plan developed was for a period of three years. The business plan called for four phases of the business. During the first phase, the product would be brought to market and promoted at trade shows. Phase two would see sales rise to 70,000 units, while in the third phase this number would rise to 700,000 units. In phase four, sales would again rise to 1.5 million units. No time frame for each phase was projected. The plan was based on the initial flocked design of the product. An allowance of $0.25 for general operating and administrative costs and $0.80 for profit was included. No specific allowance was made for salaries or any other expense.

Exhibit 1.3.4

Balance sheet as of December 31, 1993

	As of 12/31/92	*As of 12/31/93*
ASSETS		
CURRENT ASSETS		
Cash - AmSouth	$ 12,548.73	$ 20,161.43
Petty Cash	0	250.00
Inventory	14,397.66	112,687.19
Accounts Receivable	76,534.83	54,048.72
Allowance for Bad Debt	0	(620.00)
TOTAL CURRENT ASSETS	$103,481.22	$186,527.34
FIXED ASSETS		
Furniture & Fixtures	$ 725.00	$ 2,638.76
Accumulated Depreciation	(119.30)	(590.98)
Molds	0	59,899.93
Accumulated Depreciation	0	(40,912.70)
Equipment	34,154,93	11,179.42
Accumulated Depreciation	(13,960.75)	(1,755.43)
Intangible Assets	12,014.99	20,975.39
Accumulated Amortization	(686.18)	(1,856.21)
Deposits	100.000	100.00
TOTAL FIXED ASSETS	$ 32,228.69	$ 49,678.18
TOTAL ASSETS	$135,709.91	$236,205.52
LIABILITIES & EQUITY		
CURRENT LIABILITIES		
Accrued Wages	$ 0	$ 2,230.00
Payroll Taxes Payable	(1,442.50)	1,278.75
AmSouth - Line of Credit	3,800.00	0
Equipment Lease Payable	0	1,926.37
Accounts Payable	38,771.48	124,561.75
Royalties Due Krout/Davis	0	45,047.39
Royalty draws Krout/Davis	0	(8,000.00)
Royalties due P. Netter	0	15,893.70
Royalty draws P. Netter	0	(39,996.00)
Officer Loans	1,872.07	(20,128.95)
TOTAL CURRENT LIABILITIES	$ 43,001.05	$122,813.01
LONG TERM LIABILITIES	0	0
TOTAL LONG TERM LIAB	0	0
TOTAL LIABILITIES	$ 43,001.05	$ 122,813.01
EQUITY		
Common Stock	$100,900.00	$100,900.00
Retained Earnings	(56,366.90)	(8,191.14)
Current Earnings	48,175.76	20,683.65
TOTAL EQUITY	$ 92,708.86	$ 113,392.51
TOTAL LIAB & EQUITY	$135,709.91	$236,205.52

Exhibit 1.3.5

Adjusted statements of revenues and expenses

	Year Ended 12/92	*Year Ended 12/93*
Sales	$265,044.90	$987,065.42
Cost of Goods Sold	(153,709.07)	(540,866.65)
Contract Labor	0	(21,159.42)
Returns and Allowances	0	(15.90)
Bad Debt Expense	0	(620.00)
Interest Income	164.13	0
Other Income	0	12,992.00
Commissions	0	(3,990.31)
Miscellaneous Expense	0	(500.00)
Freight & Shipping	0	(28,051.87)
Total Income Less COGS	$111,499.96	$404,853.27
Officer Salaries	$ 0	60,000.00
Salaries & Wages	0	45,552.49
Accrued Wages	0	2,230.00
Employee Per Diem	0	14,108.57
Bank Charges	0	317.81
Payroll Taxes	0	9,445.39
Taxes & License	106.00	1,441.62
Office Expense	3,883.20	16,094.01
Telephone	5,971.91	16,112.52
Charitable Contributions	300.00	565.95
Travel	2,392.70	12,046.48
Meals & Entertainment	295.73	1,347.71
Dues & Subscriptions	20.00	278.95
Auto Expense	477.99	1,036.80
Supplies	433.18	388.44
Equipment Rental	0	401.28
Advertising & Marketing	5,725.80	53,305.63
Insurance	2,350.75	4,860.74
Legal & Professional Fees	8,593.75	42,069.06
Postage & Shipping	4,864.70	1,645.60
Rent	492.80	9,463.95
Trade Shows	3,427.64	19,210.26
Commissions	62.08	0
Royalties	0	54,354.09
Depreciation	4,544.05	29,179.06
Amortization	350.18	1,170.03
Interest Expense	342.68	706.70
Consulting Expense	7,666.00	0
Utilities	11.88	1,457.14
Janitorial & Maintenance	0	628.57
Equipment Maintenance	0	500.00
Contract Labor	11,011.18	1,460.64
TOTAL EXPENSES	$ 63,324.20	$401,379.49
NET INCOME	$ 48,175.76	$ 3,473.78

Exhibit 1.3.6

Quantity discount schedule

Order Size	*Unit Cost*
2500<Q<10,000	$1.36
10,000<Q<20,000	$1.30
20,000<Q<50,000	$1.25
50,000 OR MORE	$1.18

Davis admitted that the sales projections on the business plan were somewhat optimistic.

Davis' plan projected the following amounts for unit sales, total sales revenue, and contribution to GOA and profit:

Table 1.3.1

Sales and Contribution Projections

Sales in Units	*Sales Revenue*	*Contribution GOA and Profit*
10,000	$ 27,000	$ 10,500
50,000	135,000	52,500
70,000	189,000	73,500
700,000	1,890,000	735,000
1.5 million	4,050,000	1,575,000

No time schedule was associated with these projections.

Accounts receivable were tracked by an in-house bookkeeper. The accounts receivable were larger than accounts payable. A "Picture of the Company" encompassing cash account balances, accounts receivable, and major accounts payable was constructed weekly.

In February of 1993, Eggsercizer was shown at the World's Largest sporting goods show, The Super Show in Atlanta. There were about 9,000 exhibitors at the show which displayed approximately 30,000 sports-related products. Attendance for the show approached 100,000.

Eggsercizer was introduced in the new products section of The Super Show. It was picked by the *New York Times* as one of the ten top products of the show. Television shows wanted to feature the Eggsercizer as a new product. Magazines picked up on the Eggsercizer as well. As a result, product awareness through print and electronic media began to drive the generation of sales to retail customers.

Financing the Company

The company struggled with insufficient working capital from the start. Mark had little capital to invest himself. The first investor provided the company with $1,400 in exchange for a 1.4 percent ownership of the company. Other investors wanted Mark to initiate a stock offering before they invested. Mark decided instead to offer stock at a discount. He discounted a share priced at $25 to $20 per share to investors who agreed to put up the capital in advance of incorporation. By this method, Mark was able to raise $20,000 before Eggstra Enterprises, Inc., was formed as a Subchapter S Corporation in the State of North Carolina. After that, the company raised an additional $50,000 from stock offerings to investors. Ultimately, there were 25 investors in the business.

When the company moved to Alabaster, Davis had to register it as a foreign corporation doing business in the state. The State of Alabama itself restricts new investors in a Subchapter S corporation to 10 per year. The SEC also sets a limit of no more than 35 investors and $250,000 invested before the corporation is required to register with them. The registration fee is $20,000.

The company was able to establish a line of credit with AmSouth Bank for $50,000. As of June 1994, $40,000 of this had been used.

Davis pursued a small business loan through the SBA in 1992. The amount requested was $195,000. However, he was not able to gain approval of the loan from a bank, which is a necessary prerequisite for the SBA to guarantee the loan. Loan officers pointed to the lack of cash flow and earnings history as a primary reason for rejecting the loan. Davis wondered if his cash flow and earnings history in 1994 would overcome these obstacles.

The Evolving Product

The primary distinctive characteristic of the Eggsercizer was its shape. There was already in existence a rubber ball made of Sorbothane which was marketed as a hand exerciser. However, the egg shape had been endorsed by therapists as being ergonomically correct ("eggonomically," according to Davis). It allowed all four fingers and the thumb to be exercised simultaneously. It also strengthened thirteen muscles in the hand and arm.

The Sorbothane material offered both positive and negative resistance, a feature which the sand-filled and putty hand exercise products lacked. The rubber was resilient, durable, inert, and non-toxic. It posed no threat if swallowed and would hold heat well. Sorbothane was used in U.S. Navy

Exhibit 1.3.7

submarines to insulate the engine from the submarine hull in order to achieve maximum quietness during operations. It was also used in jogging shoe soles. The Eggsercizer could easily be cleaned with soap and water. It was heat resistant and easily stored.

There were three versions of the standard-sized Eggsercizer. The red version was the softest and had a durometer reading of 35. The blue version was more dense than the red version (durometer reading of 45). The hardest version was purple. The three different versions of the standard model allowed one to scale up as hand strength developed. A fourth model was the Pro Eggsercizer, which was an oversized version for large hands. The Pro Eggsercizer was red, was the same hardness as the red standard version, and weighed twice as much as the standard egg. (See Exhibit 1.3.7 for a blue egg in use.)

Primary Markets

Mark had identified four primary markets for the Eggsercizer. One market was the medical and rehabilitation market. Due to the unique exercise characteristics which the egg offered, Davis had been able to establish acceptance of the Eggsercizer as a physical and occupational therapy product. Physicians and therapists had endorsed the product as a therapy device for arthritis, carpal tunnel syndrome, cardiac related, and recovery from mastectomy surgery (the egg works on the pectoral muscles). The company had contracted with Hygenics Corporation, an international medical distributor, to promote and distribute the Eggsercizer in the medical field. Hygenics was located in Ohio, close to the manufacturing plant which produced the product and received most orders directly from that facility. The usual product, sold by Hygenics was a three-pack. This was a box which held one of each of the three versions of the standard Eggsercizer. This arrangement allowed a physician or therapist to prescribe and build a regimen of exercise starting with the softer red egg and progressing to the purple eggs.

Another major market was the exercise and fitness market. GNC was one customer which served the fitness submarket. GNC ordered 18,000 eggs in 1993 (5 percent of sales). Davis also focused on sporting goods stores. The Eggsercizer had been accepted by 25 out of the top 100 sporting goods stores. Davis' goal was to be in 40 by the end of 1993.

The Eggsercizer was also promoted as a stress reduction product. Davis had been able to get his egg into President Bush's hands during the Persian Gulf War. He reportedly used it for stress reduction. Other celebrities had also supported this use of the egg. On the whole, however, Davis admitted that this market remained largely untapped.

Another major market was the gift or novelty market. Brookstone's accounted for the lion's share of this market segment (90,000 eggs in 1992 and 165,000 ordered in 1993).

The final major market was that of premium and ad specialty items. Eggstra had printed company logos or slogans on the Eggsercizer, and they served to promote the client's product or company awareness. The eggs could also be scented.

One problem Davis had with the marketing data was that he did not know his sales to the various segments. While Brookstone accounted for a large proportion of his sales, he could not determine if those sales were made for exercise, fitness, or therapy purposes or if they were bought purely as a novelty.

Davis continued to attend several trade shows a year, including sporting goods and gift shows. Many contacts are made at the shows and the company experiences a surge in sales after shows. Most retailers bought sporting and exercise-related products in February for the spring market and bought again in August for the Christmas season. (See Exhibit 1.3.8 for a sample of a sports-theme promotion.)

As a result of the trade shows, Mark received many orders from small retailers. Some of these businesses purchased no more than one or two dozen eggs a year. The Eggsercizer was also sold to individuals directly, although this was not a significant portion of sales. If a sales representative made a sale to a retailer, the commission paid usually fell in the 15 to 20 percent range.

EXHIBIT 1.3.8

The international market for the Eggsercizer was growing. The product had been sold in 24 countries; however, there were problems with this market. Due to the country-specific import taxes, shipping, and other add-on expenses of dealing with a foreign intermediary, gross margins averaged only 8 percent. With this low return, Davis decided not to focus on international sales at that time.

In 1993, Eggstra spent just over $50,000 on marketing efforts. The amounts to be spent on various market segments had not been determined. One specific support system that had been installed on the company's computers was a store identification program. When a customer called in, an Eggstra employee could use the system to locate the retail outlet selling the Eggsercizer which was nearest to the customer's location. This had been a good marketing tool, as Davis had been able to tell retailers that he would not undermine their business with direct sales.

Any opportunity for a sale was immediately pursued by Mark. In addition to the traditional channels of distribution, Mark had used such media as the Home Shopping Network and Examples. One question that Davis faced was projecting the life of the product. Originally, he thought that sales over the life cycle would be 3.5 million eggs. One marketing company had projected sales of 20 million during the product's life.

The Competition

There were over 100 different hand exercisers on the market. The initial patent search uncovered a hand exerciser patented in 1926. Putties and mechanical spring-loaded devices were the primary competitive products. However, spring-loaded devices often failed to exercise the spectrum of muscles which the Eggsercizer exercised. Also, these devices were potentially unsafe due to their moving components.

During the 1993 Christmas season, the Eggsercizer was accepted by one store of a major mass marketing chain. It outsold its two major competitors by a 4 to 1 margin during that period. (See Exhibit 1.3.9 for a description of major competitors' products.)

Organization of the Company

Mark Davis was the majority owner and President of Eggstra Enterprises, Inc. He assumed most marketing duties. (See Exhibit 1.3.10 for an organizational chart.) The Operations Manager had been with Eggstra for four years. The Warehouse Manager (currently vacant) ensured that all products were received, processed, checked for quality, packaged, and distributed efficiently and on time. Part-time packaging workers were contracted when larger orders were to be processed or a sufficient number of eggs needed to be packaged.

The Mass Market Question

The most pressing decision that Davis faced was whether or not to enter the mass market business. Davis knew that Kmart and Wal-Mart combined had 51,000 stores. He also knew that a significant price reduction on his sales price would be

EXHIBIT 1.3.9

Major competitive product information

Product	*Company*	*Location*	*1993 Sales ($1,000)*	*Price*
Sorbothane Ball	Spectrum Sports	Ohio	385.0	$ 6.99
Grip Master	Inter'l Metal Components	New York	1,350.0	$10.99
Exerflex(Silicon Putty)	Bollinger Industries	Texas	500.0	$ 5.87
Flex-O-Grip	Everlast Fitness	Missouri	1,200.0	$ 4.99

Exhibit 1.3.10

Organizational structure

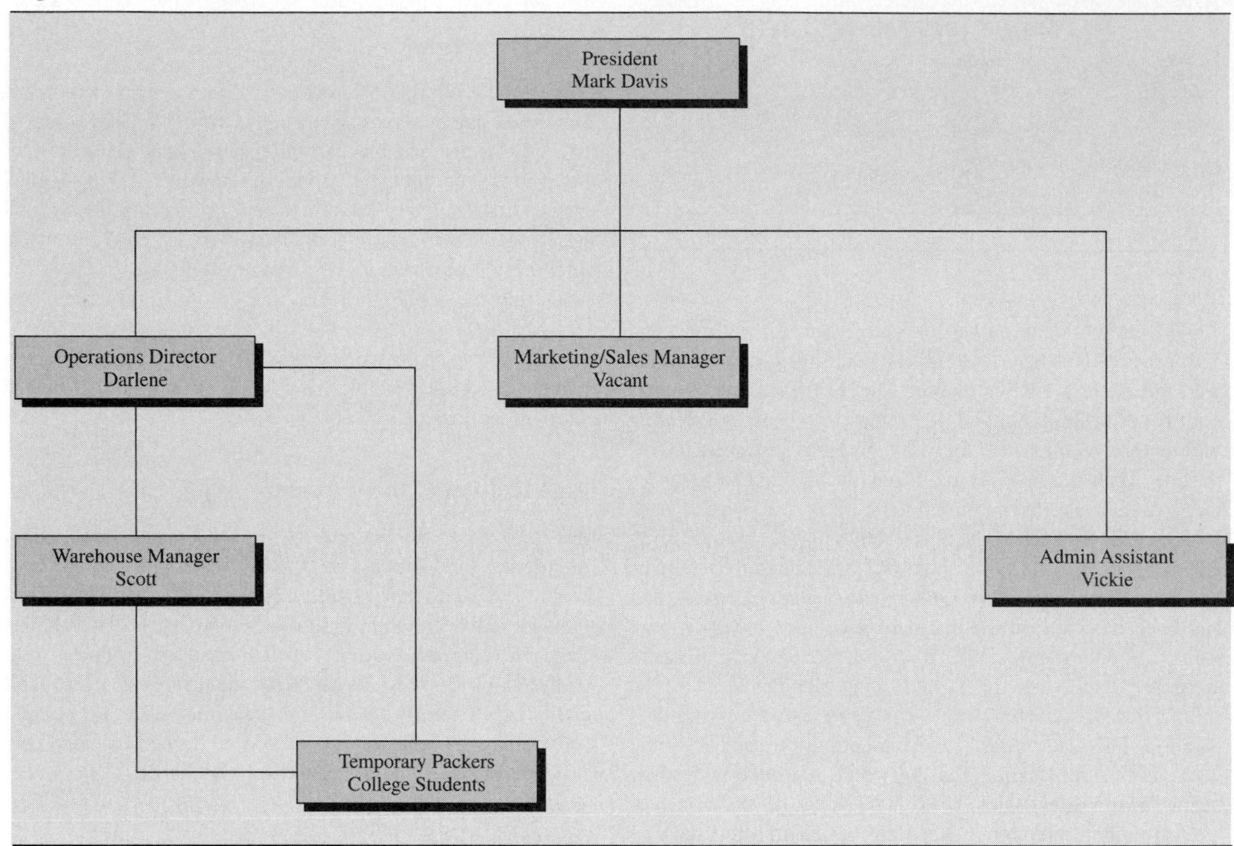

necessary in order to allow those stores a 40 percent mark-up and still sell the Eggsercizer for under $5.00. From discussions with mass market buying agents and managers, Mark determined that was the price the product would have to sell for when offered alongside its competition. He made a tentative cost analysis of a knock-off egg designed just for this market which showed a possible $1.30 per unit margin (see Exhibit 1.3.11).

To complicate the decision, an additional expenditure of $180,000 in equipment would have to be incurred in order to increase production capacity to the levels projected. Davis had projected that 12 cases per store would be sold annually. For Wal-Mart's 2,300 stores alone, that would mean over 330,000 units of production.

Exhibit 1.3.11

Cost analysis—-Eggsergrip

Wholesale Price	$3.00
COGS	
Material Cost	$1.00
Inbound Shipping	0.00
Packaging	
Total	$1.00
Contribution Margin	$2.00
Estimated per Unit General and Admin	$0.20
Estimated Commissions and Royalties	$0.50
Estimated per Unit Profit	$1.30

Of course, additional packaging design, production, and procurement would be necessary to enter the mass market arena. Davis also knew that his current human resources infrastructure would not support the added burden of managing this extra business segment. He had not determined what changes would be necessary.

Some Possible Options

Davis had several options with which he was wrestling. The first option was to enter the mass market. He knew this would mandate many changes for his organization and would increase the risk of failure. He could even lose money on this end of the business. He also ran the high risk of losing Brookstone as a customer since they had promised to drop the Eggsercizer if it appeared at Wal-mart or Kmart. Davis wondered what the net impact might be on the bottom line.

Davis also wondered what changes in the organization might be justified. Did he need to replace the Marketing Manager with another marketing officer? Or should he handle the marketing himself? He wondered what operations he should personally handle and which he should delegate to others.

While the company was funding current operations with its current cash flow, Davis knew that for the company to grow, additional capital would be needed. But how much? And when? Should he sell stock? Or should he actively seek debt financing? He even wondered if he might sell the company. When should a person sell his company? HealthSouth Rehabilitation, Inc., had been interested in buying the company.

Davis admitted that these decisions were affected by his own personal goals which were to "make money; fund new inventions with a portion of this money; and retire by the time I am 45."

Case 1.4

Opus One: A Marriage of Wine-Making Magnates

The sun's rays kiss the blossoming fruit, while the rich valley soil nourishes the burgeoning vines. As the day comes to a close, the sun yields to twilight. Fog will settle upon the valley to cool the grapes, while the evening breeze caresses them to sleep. Ultimately, the hot summer will concede to the temperate moodiness of autumn, and the rains will come. The harvest is near, and emotions are high. At last, the opulent bounty of Mother Nature is gathered, and a transformation will soon begin. There is a momentary pause to bless the grapes and give thanks. The fruit is crushed and the nectar flows into the vessels where the metamorphosis will take place. Man will nurture and taste until it is time to lay the young wine to rest in oak where it will complete its transformation. Thousands will enjoy the harvest for years to come. The final product is a symbol of the collaborative relationship that exists between man and nature. Opus One was born from the passion that Robert Mondavi and the Baron Philippe de Rothschild felt for the art of winemaking. These two premier wine authorities have teamed together to create an ultra premium wine unlike any other.

Focal Firm: The Robert Mondavi Corporation

The Robert Mondavi Corporation is the parent company of ten separate brands of wine, each of which produces yearly vintages of several wine varieties. Established in 1966 by Robert Mondavi and his eldest son Michael, the Mondavi Corporation is currently the most famous winemaker in America (Barrett, 1995). Arguably America's most successful wine producer, Mondavi has reached new heights in innovation and promotion of his company and the wine industry as a whole. The Mondavi Corporation has grown rapidly over its 33 years, having gone public in 1993 and engaging in three joint ventures that cross national boundaries (Marcus, 1997). Its most successful partnership, the Opus One venture with one of France's leading winemakers Baron Philippe de Rothschild, is examined in this case.

Source: This case was prepared in August 1999 by Ellen Carpenter, Alper Cinar, Pamela Duffy, and Mike Kidd under the Supervision of Dr. Lou E. Pelton, University of North Texas.

Mission

The philosophy of the Robert Mondavi Corporation has remained unchanged since the company's conception over 30 years ago. The mission states, "to produce world-class, fine wines, to educate the public about wine and its importance as a mealtime beverage of moderation, and to promote wine with the arts as an integral part of a balanced lifestyle" (Mondavi company website, 1999). The Mondavi Corporation has lived up to its mission and continues to strive toward greater fulfillment of its aspirations.

Principal Decision-Makers

The Robert Mondavi Corporation is a family run company, with each family member playing a role within the company. Robert Mondavi, his wife, and his three children are the principal decision-makers within the firm, each residing on the Board of Directors, In 1990, Robert Mondavi passed the majority of the executive powers to his eldest son Michael. Michael holds the highest position in the corporation, having cofounded the Mondavi enterprise. Son Timothy Mondavi also has significant authority within the winery, with most of his efforts focused on managing the grape and wine production. Daughter Marcia is a director, and she is in charge of most of the company's public relations and special promotional events across the country. Margrit Bevier, Robert Mondavi's wife, is the Vice-President of Cultural Affairs and directs most public relations and promotional events outside the U.S. A few other high-ranking employees are on the Board of Directors along with the Mondavi family members. However, the majority of the governing power still lies with the family members (Mondavi company website, 1999). An advantage to this corporate structure is that trust, support, and loyalty preexist the business relationships between the members and need not be developed over time in the workplace like non-familial entities. This aspect of the Mondavi Corporation makes it a good match for the family-operated Rothschild Winery, given that they have similar structures and a personal interest in the well-being of their wineries. Both being family-operated businesses, the partnership between the two is conducive to a healthy alliance since friendships are meshed among many of the family members. The partnership between the two families is highly relational, with exchanges being based on personal affiliations rather than just financial ties. The common threads between the Mondavi Corporation and the Rothschild Winery make them ideal partners for a genuine exchange relationship.

Organizational Design

Robert Mondavi and his son Michael founded the Mondavi Corporation in 1966 and ran it as a family business until 1993 when the corporation went public (Mondavi, 1998). Although Mondavi is no longer family owned, it is still family operated. The corporation consists of five general departments including sales and marketing, finance, general administration, retail and hospitality, and information systems (DeLoach, 1999). The corporation has a relatively flat structure, which encourages a free flow of communication and cooperation among the different levels of management. Please refer to Exhibit 1.4.1 for an organizational diagram.

Market Position

The Mondavi Corporation is a leader in the U.S. wine industry and is gradually gaining international attention. Mondavi has captured a significant market share, which will be further discussed under Nature and Scope. Currently, Mondavi sells most of its wine in the U.S., but marketers intend to expand its exporting operations in the future. Opus One, despite its niche market share in the domestic marketplace, has given the Mondavi name worldwide recognition. The prominent status of Opus One has enhanced demand for California wines around the globe (Marcus, 1997).

Mondavi produces a wide variety of wines ranging from its ultra premium Opus One to several moderately priced wines. Marketers have positioned the Mondavi Corporation as a maker of only top quality wines, regardless of price. Mondavi wines can be found on restaurant wine lists across the nation, and it is gradually attempting to repeat this trend in other countries around the world. Michael Mondavi has proclaimed that his company sells two things: a quality image and quality wines. Wine critics and connoisseurs alike have dubbed Mondavi the American standard-bearer of fine quality wines (Marcus, 1997).

Nature and Scope of Operations

The Robert Mondavi Corporation is the largest exporter of premium wine in the U.S., with sales in more than 90 countries (Mondavi company website, 1999). It produces under ten separate labels, four of which are the products of international relationships. Mondavi wineries produce between seven and ten million cases of wine per year, with Opus One accounting for only 30,000 cases of its total production (Workman, 1999). The firm focuses on producing high quality wines in all classes and price categories, allowing it to reach a broad market. Mondavi presently enjoys a 2.7

Exhibit 1.4.1

Organizational chart

Robert Mondavi
Chairman of the Board

Michael Mondavi
President
Chief Executive Officer

Timothy Mondavi
Managing Director
Wine Grower

Gregory Evans
Chief Operating Officer
Executive VP

Stephen McCarthy
Chief Financial Officer
Senior VP

Margrit Bevier
Senior VP
Secretary

Mitchell Clark
Senior VP

Martin Johnson
Senior VP

Alan Schunur
Senior VP

Peter Mattel
Senior VP

Steven Soderberg
Senior VP

Marcia Mondavi
Director

Frank Farella
Director

Philip Greer
Director

Bartlet Rhoades
Director

James Barksdale
Director

Sales & Marketing

Finance

Hospitality & Retail

General Administration

Information Systems

General Management

Public Relations

Human Resources

Logistics

Winemaking & Production

Vineyard Management

General Staff

percent market share in the U.S. It has also captured a 0.0006 percent worldwide market share. While this may seem insignificant, the global market for wine exceeds $300 billion annually (*Wine Business Monthly Online,* 1999). Ninety percent of Mondavi wine is distributed in the U.S., while the remaining 10 percent is exported. The Mondavi Corporation grosses nearly $325 million in revenue annually from all of its operations (DeLoach, 1999). Please refer to Exhibit 1.4.2 for Mondavi Corporation annual financial statements.

Motivation for Engagement in Partnering

There were several motivations for Mondavi and Rothschild to engage in the Opus One partnership. As with any business, there were certainly financial incentives to establish a new venture. Although profit was not their primary motive, the pair intended to capitalize on the combination of their company reputations and extraordinary winemaking capabilities. Opus One was not a "get rich quick" scheme, but a plan for reaping the benefits of their talents over the long haul (Barrett, 1995).

A second reason for engaging in the partnership was to facilitate entry into international markets with Opus One. Licensing and many strict distribution laws make it difficult to export to many foreign nations. For example, the European Union has imposed strict regulations on beverage imports as an entry barrier. The EU's motive for doing so is to give local beverage makers the upper hand in their domestic market. Canadian ice wine producers faced the EU's barriers when it prohibited their product's import due to strict standards on beverage preparation (*CBC News Online,* 1999). Mondavi could have easily faced the same problems, but its strategic alliance with a company operating in the EU facilitated entry into the European markets.

The foremost motive for Mondavi and Rothschild to initiate the Opus One partnership was quite simply "to make a great wine" (Workman, 1999). Personal accomplishment was the primary initiative behind establishing their joint venture. Both Mondavi and Rothschild had already realized numerous successes in their respective wine businesses, Personal gain, not financial gain, inspired this partnership that was established to make a wine unlike any other. Both partners wanted to celebrate and collaborate on their winemaking abilities and leave behind a legacy that reflected their personal accomplishments and love of wine (Workman, 1999). One might also argue that this venture was intended to provide a sense of immortality to its original partners. The $27 million Opus One winery was built with extreme attention to detail and was purposely structured to last several centuries (Marcus, 1997). Filled with portraits and memorabilia of their lifelong achievements, the winery reflects the genuine exchange relationship between the partners. Mondavi and Rothschild intended the Opus One organization to manifest their friendship, their love for fine wines, and their personal feats.

Organizational Culture

Most winemakers can be characterized as having a relatively informal, relaxed atmosphere. The Mondavi Corporation and its subsidiaries (including Opus One) do not adhere to this industry norm (Workman, 1999). Surprisingly, the small staffs of some of the Mondavi wineries have not adopted informal workplace environments. The Mondavi organizations recruit highly skilled, proactive professionals with strong leadership qualities (Marcus, 1997).

Expertise and continuous questioning of the actions of the firm are likely to be driving forces behind the punctilious workplace environments in the Mondavi wineries. In addition, the staff is described as being cooperative and respectful. Compromise among staff members also plays a role in resolving minor conflicts that arise daily (Workman, 1999). Many Mondavi wineries have partnerships with winemakers of foreign nations. Compromise and flexibility are a necessity since winemaking and administrative methodologies vary across cultures. The leaders' abilities to compromise are imperative because both partners must strive to achieve common goals. Given the varying methodologies amidst international partnerships, the compromising nature of its corporate culture appears to be suitable for the Mondavi Corporation.

The Decision Environment

Economy

Economic conditions have a greater effect on the sales of premium wines than other grades of wines. Current economic conditions are favorable for the premium wine industry in the U.S. and abroad. For instance, while the Asian crisis caused an overall decrease in the exports of alcoholic beverages, premium wine exports actually grew by about 35 percent due to a high global demand for varietal grape wines (*Investor Relations,* 1999). Today, U.S. wine consumption is up due to a thriving economy and high consumer confidence, which support trade-ups by consumers to more expensive wines such as Opus One (*Investor Relations,* 1999). While there will always be a niche demand for ultra-premium wines, an economic recession would significantly reduce demand for Opus One since it is a luxury good. Most consumers will typically purchase luxury goods only when their disposable

Exhibit 1.4.2

Financial statements

Balance Sheet

Annual Assets ($000)

FISCAL YEAR ENDING	06/30/1998	06/30/1997	06/30/1996	06/30/1995
CASH	2,683	150	NA	900
MRKTABLE SECURITIES	NA	NA	NA	NA
RECEIVABLES	68,656	59,222	39,495	32,601
INVENTORIES	226,141	167,695	142,565	113,375
RAW MATERIALS	NA	NA	NA	NA
WORK IN PROGRESS	NA	NA	NA	NA
FINISHED GOODS	NA	NA	NA	NA
NOTES RECEIVABLE	NA	NA	NA	NA
OTHER CURRENT ASSETS	10,366	7,270	3,780	886
TOTAL CURRENT ASSETS	307,846	234,337	185,840	147,762
PROP, PLANT & EQUIP	215,301	186,990	156,754	120,934
ACCUMULATED DEP	NA	NA	NA	NA
NET PROP & EQUIP	215,301	186,990	156,754	120,934
INVEST & ADV TO SUBS	19,349	19,212	17,100	11,792
OTHER NON-CUR ASSETS	NA	NA	NA	NA
DEFERRED CHARGES	NA	NA	NA	NA
INTANGIBLES	NA	NA	NA	NA
DEPOSITS & OTH ASSET	5,512	4,386	1,501	1,826
TOTAL ASSETS	548,008	444,925	361,195	282,314

Annual Liabilities ($000)

FISCAL YEAR ENDING	06/30/1998	06/30/1997	06/30/1996	06/30/1995
NOTES PAYABLE	NA	8,750	403	NA
ACCOUNTS PAYABLE	18,888	14,769	13,733	9,411
CUR LONG TERM DEBT	10,984	6,790	4,115	6,071
CUR PORT CAP LEASES	NA	NA	NA	NA
ACCRUED EXPENSES	7,800	5,446	13,150	11,233
INCOME TAXES	NA	NA	NA	2,655
OTHER CURRENT LIAB	12,499	12,672	1,682	1,493
TOTAL CURRENT LIAB	50,171	48,427	33,083	30,863
MORTGAGES	NA	NA	NA	NA
DEFERRED CHARGES/INC	20,958	16,243	15,042	13,207
CONVERTIBLE DEBT	NA	NA	NA	NA
LONG TERM DEBT	222,557	158,067	123,713	113,017
NON-CUR CAP LEASES	NA	NA	NA	NA
OTHER LONG TERM LIAB	339	1,017	1,102	665
TOTAL LIABILITIES	294,025	223,754	172,940	157,752
MINORITY INT (LIAB)	NA	NA	NA	NA
PREFERRED STOCK	NA	NA	NA	NA
COMMON STOCK NET	90,772	88,462	85,726	47,805
CAPITAL SURPLUS	4,776	3,289	1,334	NA
RETAINED EARNINGS	158,435	129,420	101,195	76,757
TREASURY STOCK	NA	NA	NA	NA
OTHER EQUITIES	NA	NA	NA	NA
SHAREHOLDER EQUITY	253,983	221,171	188,255	124,562
TOT LIAB & NET WORTH	548,008	444,925	361,195	282,314

(continued)

Exhibit 1.4.2

Financial statements (continued)

Annual Income ($000)				
FISCAL YEAR ENDING	06/30/1998	06/30/1997	06/30/1996	06/30/1995
NET SALES	325,159	300,774	240,830	199,469
COST OF GOODS	175,690	165,988	122,385	97,254
GROSS PROFIT	149,469	134,786	118,445	102,215
R & D EXPENDITURES	NA	NA	NA	NA
SELL GEN & ADMIN EXP	90,043	79,831	70,707	64,160
INC BEF DEP & AMORT	59,426	54,955	47,738	38,055
DEPRECIATION & AMORT	NA	NA	NA	NA
NON-OPERATING INC	441	1,880	1,543	215
INTEREST EXPENSE	12,298	10,562	8,814	8,675
INCOME BEFORE TAX	47,569	46,273	40,467	29,595
PROV FOR INC TAXES	18,554	18,048	16,029	11,775
MINORITY INT (INC)	NA	NA	NA	NA
INVEST GAINS/LOSSES	NA	NA	NA	NA
OTHER INCOME	NA	NA	NA	NA
NET INC BEF EX ITEMS	29,015	28,225	24,438	17,820
EX ITEMS & DISC OPS	NA	NA	NA	NA
NET INCOME	29,015	28,225	24,438	17,820
OUTSTANDING SHARES	15,356	15,175	14,957	12,774

incomes are high. Any significant decrease in disposable incomes resulting from weaker economies would have a detrimental effect on the demand for ultra premium wines. With respect to supply and demand, the production of fine wines is a unique industry in which producers do not strive to reach demand. Opus One produces at capacity and has no plans to expand. Fine wine producers actually sustain demand by supplying less than demand. Pricing strategies also affect demand for fine wines. The hefty prices of the ultra premium wines serve to communicate its quality to consumers. When priced too moderately, the perception of high quality is lost and demand tends to fall. Thus, lowering the price of an ultra premium wine such as Opus One is never a viable option. The static retail price and fluctuations in consumers' disposable incomes make the demand for Opus One sensitive to changes in the economy (*Investor Relations,* 1999).

Industry Regulation

The alcoholic beverage industry is heavily governed. Regulation in the wine industry is constantly changing as new laws are imposed in the U.S. and abroad. Violating regulations can be costly to wine producers. There are strict regulations dealing with labeling requirements. Labels must accurately detail Surgeon General health warnings, alcohol content, origin, and wine type. Distribution is also heavily regulated, and U.S. winemakers are required to outsource all distribution (Workman, 1999). Environmental regulations, while sometimes negotiable, tend to also be costly if not followed by wineries.

Falling trade barriers support globalization of the wine industry, but there are numerous foreign labeling and technical requirements that wine producers must keep track of and follow. Because the European Union accounts for about half of all U.S. premium wine exports, it is necessary for American wine producers to follow them. As discussed earlier, Mondavi's alliance with a French winery gives it an advantage in following the regulations in the EU (*Investor Relations,* 1999).

Technology

In the past, the wine industry was relatively unaffected by technology due to its traditional roots and the time involved in aging wine. Today, technology combined with traditional winemaking methods not only contributes to improvements in wine quality, but also supports closer relationships in channels.

Mondavi relies heavily on the use of technology to produce high-quality grapes for its premium wines, and it is presently engaged in a contract with NASA for satellite and aerial photos showing leaf color, leaf density, and diseased areas (Deck, 1999). This is just one example of how Mondavi applies data-collecting technology in crop and vineyard management (Deck, 1999). Other technologies help read and track sugar and tannin levels of grapes, which are essential for consistent quality of premium wines.

Mondavi uses software to track wine and crop production and help to reduce lead times to market. Mondavi also uses computer software to ensure that proper labeling procedures are followed (Deck, 1999). The size of the Mondavi operation makes it financially possible to use technology such as EDI and MRP to gain an advantage over its smaller competitors. Small producers must carefully consider the cost to value ratio of using high dollar data-collecting technology. It is important to remember that technology cannot dictate weather conditions, which can ultimately make or break a vintage of wine.

Competition

Opus One directly competes for a small niche of the total U.S. market. However, as mentioned previously, it will compete more closely with other wine classes when the economy is thriving. Although California wines compete directly with each other, the industry itself has cooperated to build a reputation as a quality wine region (*Investor Relations,* 1999). Robert Mondavi is just one of the winemakers who promotes the California wine industry as a whole, rather than just his own products. Strategies such as cooperative advertising have helped promote California wines, and sales of premium wines have increased significantly in recent years. By bettering the region's reputation, California wines are now able to compete globally (*Investor Relations,* 1999). Opus One's second largest geographical market is the European Union (*Wine Business Monthly Online,* 1999). The EU accounts for about five percent of Mondavi's sales, which is half of all of its exports (*Investor Relations,* 1999). International competition is fierce, but an international strategic alliance gives Opus One a significant marketing advantage. Advantages are realized in areas such as distribution, regulation, and brand recognition.

Socioculture

Sociocultural factors influence pricing decisions as well as production decisions in the premium wine industry. Opus One uses a prestige pricing method. High-priced wines of limited quantities are frequently associated with high social status. In fact, many consumers measure the quality of a wine by its price and availability. The deliberate limited-production of ultra-premium wines also tends to affect demand in a positive manner. Scarce goods are typically highly demanded, which is certainly the case with Opus One. Increased domestic demand also stems from positive health messages put forth by the media and the industry itself (Mondavi, 1998). The alcoholic beverage industry as a whole has traditionally received bad press from politicians and religious organizations over the years, but demand for wines have increased presumably due to the promotion of wine-related health benefits. The social status, price perceptions, scarcity, and health benefits gained from wine consumption are all sociocultural forces that greatly affect the wine industry.

The Marriage of Magnates

Opus One is a self-operating joint venture that was formed in 1979 by Robert Mondavi and Baron Philippe de Rothschild. The primary objective of the alliance was to produce one of the first American ultra-premium wines. The partners equally share all profits, capital, and costs (*Investor Relations,* 1999). Along with sharing the financial responsibilities, both partners equally participate in managerial efforts. One representative from both the Mondavi Corporation and the Rothschild Company work in top management positions of the joint venture, and the remaining managerial staff were hired from outside the parent companies (Workman, 1999).

The terms and conditions of the alliance were specified in a very detailed contract to protect each partner (Workman, 1999). David Workman, Director of Finance Administration at Opus One, characterized the contract as a typical partnership agreement. He added that although friendship was the backbone of the alliance, their partnership does not depend only on a handshake. The contract enumerates issues such as equally divided profits and expenses, wine processing practices, and dissolution procedures. In addition, the contract only specifies guidelines for managerial decisionmaking. In other words, the contract structures the decision making process, but the daily decisions are the responsibility of Opus One's management team (Workman, 1999). The contract clarifies that the partner who owns the majority of the resources will have the first right to the customers (Workman, 1999). Given this and the agreement that each partner will have equal stake in the company, it is assumed that the contract sets procedures for one partner to buy out the other.

The contract further states that each partner has equal

authority to exert influence over Opus One. However, because Opus One targets the U.S. market and the Mondavi Corporation has greater experience in serving this market, it has a distinct advantage over its French partner. Because the Mondavi Corporation headquarters is located less than a quarter mile from the Opus One winery while the Rothschild Company is 6,000 miles away, it is to be expected that Mondavi has greater influence on Opus One (Workman, 1999). Also, at the beginning of the partnership, Opus One was produced at the Mondavi vineyard, which surely initiated this norm. Thus, there is an unwritten norm that Mondavi exerts slightly more influence than its French counterparts.

Critical Issues

The Opus One partnership is currently a genuine exchange relationship between the Mondavi and Rothschild wineries. This is evident because the relationship was based on friendship and many other non-financial incentives such as the personal goal of simply making a great wine. This venture has also fulfilled Mondavi and Rothschild's dream for a certain sense of immortality. The $27 million facility is filled with representations of their lives and feats and serves to portray their legacies. Despite the numerous personal and financial accomplishments that the Opus One partnership has facilitated, there are three key issues that may jeopardize the alliance's health in the future.

The first critical issue that the Opus One winery faces is the enormous amount of risk that surrounds the entire joint venture, along with the absence of strategies to manage probable difficulties. If these risks are not minimized and courses of action to handle these potential problems are not established, Opus One could suffer catastrophic losses. One of the largest risks is Opus One's reliance on the grapes of a single vineyard. The phylloxera disease and vine arrangement problems have plagued the vineyard in the past and have caused enormous replanting expenses. Despite the risk of future vineyard difficulties, Opus One continues to depend on the harvest of a single crop. Wine management consultant, Tom Eddy, proposed another risk affecting the joint venture. He warned California winemakers that partnerships with international wineries will hurt the good reputation that they have worked hard to establish. He claims that bringing another nation's name to a California winery might cause a consumer perception that their wines cannot stand alone in the market as high-quality wines. Eddy says that this is not the case since California has made some excellent wines, but this false perception may hurt their reputation (*Investor Relations,* 1999). Another serious risk to the Opus One venture is that the demand for their wine relies on the consumers' ability to purchase the wine. At about $140 per bottle, Opus One is a luxury good that will only be in demand if the disposable incomes of consumers are high. Changes in the economy can greatly affect the amount of money that consumers will spend on luxury goods. With a single product line that bears a very high price tag, the sales of Opus One will decline drastically along with any significant decreases in disposable incomes. These risks must be addressed to avoid potentially serious difficulties in the future.

Opus One and other Mondavi wineries have expressed an interest in expanding their international distribution efforts. Herein lies the second critical issue that the winery faces. Heightening exportation may pose some significant opportunities for Opus One, but marketers should closely examine several issues before pursuing them. First and foremost, the economies of the contemplated countries of import must be analyzed. Consumer ability and willingness to purchase an ultra premium wine will be the deciding factor as to whether or not to market Opus One to a particular nation. Another issue in distributing abroad is the demand structure of each potential importer. Some regions may not have developed an appreciation for American wines, and some regions may have strong brand loyalty to local wineries. Finally, beverage laws must also be evaluated to avoid violating regulations set by the U.S. or the foreign nations. These issues must be addressed by systematically examining numerous aspects of a potential host country before Opus One expends costly efforts to distribute to them.

The third and final critical issue deals with the leadership of Opus One. Troubles for the winery may lie ahead for two reasons, First, cultural differences between the Mondavi and Rothschild families may threaten their relational exchange. Again, the Mondavi family is American, and the Rothchild's are French. Cultural differences have caused conflict in the past, and Opus One is regularly faced with internal turmoil according to contact David Workman. One previous conflict involved the arrangement of the vines. The Mondavi family preferred an arrangement that gave each vine a very large area to grow. The Rothschild's have a strong preference for the French methodology of planting vines very close together, which supposedly creates competitive growth among plants in the vineyard (Barrett, 1995). Initially, Mondavi's philosophy was practiced in the Opus One vineyard, but later it adopted the Rothschild's preferred arrangement. Replanting efforts resulting from this conflict cost Opus One $3 million (Marcus, 1997). Conflict, as a result of cultural differences, may arise in many aspects of the venture ranging from vine planting through marketing strategies. A great deal of compromising will be necessary to maintain a viable partnership; however, resolving these conflicts may cost Opus One a great deal of time, money, and energy.

The second issue that has a potential for causing serious internal problems at Opus One is succession. Robert Mondavi and Baron Philippe de Rothschild created the partnership, and the headship of the winery has since been passed down to their children Michael Mondavi and the Baroness Rothschild. The venture was originally based on the friendship between their fathers who considered finances a minor concern. Now that their successors head the partnership, there is growing concern that the primary mission may take on a more financial nature. As time passes and the leadership of Opus One is passed down to new generations, the winemakers may lose sight of the personal motives that inspired the venture. With the initial partnership being structured around such roots, one question lingers: Can the Opus One partnership continue to succeed if there is a shift to more financially driven objectives? If not, how can the legacy of their fathers' personal aspirations for Opus One be maintained over the succession of future generations?

References

Articles

Barrett, Jean. "The Opus One Venture." *Wine Spectator,* 20(13): 90–103, November 15, 1995.

Marcus, Kim. "New Era for Opus One." *Wine Spectator,* 16(14): 9, November 15, 1991.

———. "The Rising Son." *Wine Spectator,* 22(11): 68–85, October 31,1997.

Mondavi, Robert. "Robert Mondavi, In His Own Words." *Wine Spectator,* 23(9): 72–89, September 30, 1998.

Morgan, Jeff. "Cultural Breakthrough." *Wine Spectator,* 24(7): 108–9, August 31, 1999.

Personal Interview

Workman, David, Director of Finance Administration, Opus One Winery. Personal interview, July 27, 1999.

Online Databases

Deck, Stewart. "IT-Savvy Wineries Take a Grape Leap Forward." *ABI Inform,* July 18, 1999. (http://www.texshare.edu/ovidweb/ov ... talCit=47&d=infoz&S= PHMKBKJPEBJFCP

DeLoach, Claude. "The Robert Mondavi Corporation." *Compact Disclosure Database by Digital Library Systems,* version 3.0.3w, July 28, 1999.

Online Publications

CBC News Online: "Canadian Winemakers Angry at EU Restrictions." August 6, 1999. (http://www.cbcnews.cbc.ca/c ... lates/view.cgi?/news/1999/07/26/ice990726)

Centre Internet des Vins Bordeaux: "Label Regulations." August 7, 1999. (http://members.aol.com.CIVBassoc/ecivbl70.m)

Wine Business Monthly Online: July 27, 1999. (http://:smartwine.com/wbm/1998/ November/bmk98ndx.htm)

Wine Business Monthly Online: July, 27, 1999. (http://smartwine. com/wbm/ 1999/0899/bmh9928.htm)

Company Websites

Investor Relations, Robert Mondavi company website link: July 17, 1999. (http://media.corporater.net/mediafiles/ NSD/mond/mond_990330_51100/sld003.htm)

Opus One company website: July 17, 1999. (http://www.opusonewinery.com).

Robert Mondavi company website: July 17 1999. (http://www.robertmondavi.com)

Rothschild Wineries company website: July 18, 1999. (http://www.bprothchild-usa.com/preamble.html)

part

II

Channel Exosystems

chapter 5	Managing Uncertainty in the Channel Environment 156
chapter 6	Channel Relationships in the Global Village 180
chapter 7	Legal and Ethical Imperatives in Channel Relationships 208

chapter

5

Managing Uncertainty in the Channel Environment

Learning Objectives

After reading this chapter, you should be able to:

- Understand how channel members affect and are affected by the channel exosystem.
- Discuss the importance of dynamism in marketing channel flows.
- Explain the role of information technology in the channel exosystem.
- Describe the impact of internationalization on environmental scanning.
- Relate the political economy model to contemporary marketing channels.

Perito Moreno/The Stock Market

Ronald Stamp, a former fish wholesaler in Newfoundland, is capitalizing on the natural exosystem. He is melting and bottling the hundreds of icebergs that break off from glaciers, drift south from Greenland, and amass freshwater ice. What could be more pristine than these glaciers formed in 3000 B.C.? It is no easy task harvesting the ice. It takes a floating factory equipped with crane and grapple to harness the iceberg. Then, 250,000 gallons of melted iceberg head for a filtration plant. The harvesting of icebergs can be perilous: Thunderstorms, high winds, and winters daunt the harvest.

* * * *

From glaciers to grocery aisles, Iceberg Corporation of America has an upstream challenge! But these glaciers provide a meaningful backdrop for our discussion of channel exosystems.[1]

It may be time to play "Taps" for that clear, seemingly wholesome beverage from your kitchen faucet. The human body contains over 75 percent water. And consumers are increasingly opting to replenish their bodies with bottled water in lieu of tap water. The bottled water category has been growing by double digits for many years. The International Bottled Water Association estimates that the average American consumer gulps nearly 14 gallons of bottled water each year. Why are consumers willing to pay more for a product that is readily available in household fountains and public water fountains? Water quality concerns, personal fitness, and health awareness are all contributing to the veritable tidal wave of bottled water brands in grocery aisles worldwide.

The bottled water category has swelled to more than $35 billion a year worldwide. It is no wonder that soft-drink giants Pepsi and Coca-Cola are diving into the bottled water market. Pepsi's Aquafina and Coke's Dasani are floating to the top of an increasingly competitive category. Because Pepsi and Coke have an established stream of distribution for soft drinks, they have been able to garner formidable market share and shelf space in a relatively short time. To fully understand how environmental (water quality) concerns, social (health and fitness) trends, and the competitive environment impact this category, we focus on Iceberg Corporation of America.

Because of their constant flux, glaciers can be compared to the nature of channel environments. Just as a glacier's movement and shape are subject to the influences of its surrounding environment, so too are a marketing channel's. A channel must continually adjust to its exosystem—economic, technological, political, legal, ethical, and sociocultural factors. Look back at the Channels Relationship Model and notice that the channel microsystem—the relationship process within a marketing channel—is encased in this exosystem. The forces within the exosystem that change the movement and shape of a marketing channel are the topic of Part II.

Like glaciers, channels are always changing—even when they don't appear to be—because their environments are never static. Moreover, current conditions in the channel environment can influence the strength of the channel relationship. The environment can either enhance or lessen a channel member's control over its counterparts. Changing environmental conditions can also affect channel participants in different ways. As such, channel partners must be concerned with more than just how changes affect their own operations; they must be aware of how the exosystem influences all channel members.

In addition to continual change, three other properties associated with glaciers have relevance to the channel exosystem: variability, potency, and distinctiveness.

- **Variability.** Glaciers are always changing because their environments are never static. The development and subsequent performance of marketing channels likewise depend on the ever-changing environment. Likewise, channel relationships are actually moving even when they appear static. Whether and how channel members remain connected to one another is related to environmental influences.
- **Potency.** Heavy snows add pressure to the bottom-level ice of glaciers, causing them to move faster than they would otherwise. Similarly, current conditions in the channel environment influence the strength of the channel relationship. The environment may either enhance or lessen a channel member's control over its counterparts.
- **Distinctiveness.** Changes in surrounding air and water temperatures trigger different glacial movements. Why? Because the weight and density of each glacier is unique. Each channel member is unique as well. Changing environmental conditions affect channel participants in different ways.

A glacier's relationship with its environment is a two-way street. For one, it influences a region's climate as the temperature decreases. Its movement also transforms the surrounding terrain. A channel member also engages in practices which transform its surrounding environment. For instance, environment changes caused by the reunification of Germany persuaded many producers to opt for the cheaper but still highly skilled labor in formerly Soviet-dominated Eastern Europe. German clothing manufacturer Hugo Boss AG cut its German manufacturing operations by over 70 percent, shifting production to countries such as Romania and Slovenia. These actions had a detrimental effect on the German economy, leaving many Germans under- or unemployed. As a result, the purchasing power of the entire German marketplace was lessened.[2]

Two other properties of glaciers are important to us. First, glacial processes are *irreversible*. Once heat has altered the state of the glacier, the glacier will never be the same again. The same thing can be said of a marketing channel. The impact that any environmental variable has on channel relationships is not reversible. This is not to say that channel members cannot successfully adapt to their changing environment; they can. However, the influence of environmental forces on channel relationships is nonetheless permanent and has a lasting effect on the performance of the marketing channel.

The second relevant glacier property is the fact that the glacier's energy diminishes whenever heat transforms it. Similarly, channels inevitably must expend energy to preserve relationships in the wake of environmental change. This consumption of energy is known as entropy.  **Entropy** accounts for the disorder, uncertainty, and wasted effort present in any physical environment. Unless preventative measures are taken, entropy always increases through a naturally occurring process. As a result, channel managers must continually struggle against entropy's negative effects. This is particularly difficult because of the constant yet unpredictable forces of the external environment that impact marketing channels.

Channel Entropy and the Exosystem

Although channel members do not usually operate in a state of disorder, they do operate under conditions of uncertainty. This uncertainty makes environmental scanning a necessity. **Environmental scanning** involves the appraisal, prediction, and monitoring of channel exosystems. The exosystem contributes to the uncertainty in which marketing channels operate.

Environmental scanning is necessary for other reasons as well. Channels of distribution are usually defined by contractual relationships and use assets that are not easy to adjust or redeploy. Routines are typically well established and decision-making authority is often spread throughout the system. Despite these rather immobile constraints, channel members must work together to provide products and services for consumers whose needs are always changing. The relevant channel environment is equally likely to exist in a state of flux. Under such circumstances, information gained from environmental scanning is more than just useful; it is a strategic resource.

An example from the hospitality industry illustrates the relationship between environmental scanning and channel performance. A restaurant manager once found himself faced with a $2 per pound hike in the wholesale cost of shrimp. The price increase was due to a poor shrimp harvest, so all suppliers were forced to increase their shrimp prices. The restaurant manager failed to change menu prices, though. He would have had to spend over $500 to modify the existing menus. But because he failed to make this investment, his business lost thousands of dollars by selling his shrimp at a loss. He failed to react to a change in the environment.

To fully appreciate the relationship between entropy and the channel exosystem, we need to first consider four important characteristics: working systems, market intelligence, different effects, and channel dynamism.

Working Systems

Entropy arises in all working systems, including marketing channels. *Working systems* are composed of mutually dependent parts (channel members) that support various processes. Working systems feature four stages—input, transformation, output, and adjustment—that are linked together in a continuous loop. As Exhibit 5.1 shows, in marketing channels inputs are the raw materials that are transformed into final outputs as they pass through the various stages of the channel system. The nature of the inputs, outputs, and transformation processes involved are adjusted over time in response to the influence of the changing environment.

The environments in which channels operate are also continuously changing. This points to the need for proactive rather than reactive environmental scanning. Channel members cannot just wait for something to happen; they should proactively participate in their working system.[3] Performance problems emerge when the working system—reflected in the channel members' behaviors—remains static while channel environments change.[4]

Proactive environmental scanning improves channel performance. For example, long before the North American Free Trade Agreement (NAFTA) was signed, proactive U.S. marketers had already scanned their economic environment. They observed declining inflation and external debt trends in Mexico. Coupled with an increasing gross domestic product, these trends indicated that Mexico could be a feasible exchange partner. Some companies sensed the opportunity for a borderless logistical network. By the time NAFTA was signed, these companies were primed to develop new channel relationships because they were prepared before their competition. Distribution is the key to successfully linking U.S., Canadian, and Mexican trade, and these logistic firms were among the front-runners in developing borderless connections.[5]

Market Intelligence

Channel entropy is based on information exchange or lack thereof. To achieve equilibrium, working systems must receive and respond appropriately to information from their

Exhibit 5.1

Working systems

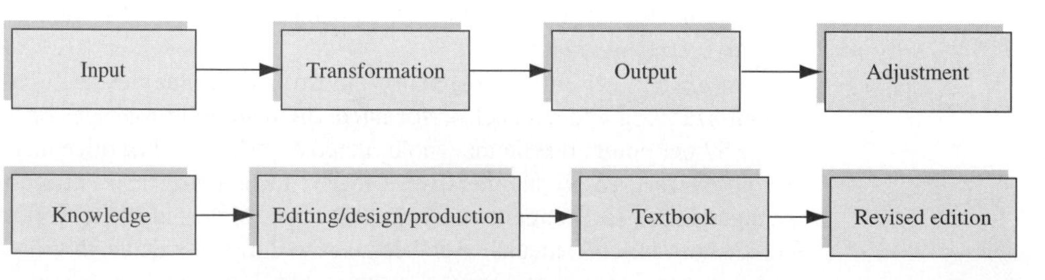

environment. Similarly, if channel members are to accurately assess their position in the system, they must obtain useful and usable environmental information, known as **market intelligence**. The channel member can then adjust in response to this market intelligence received from and about the environment.

One biotechnology company can attest to the value of environmental scanning. Biostat Diagnostics, Inc., develops technologies that provide fast and accurate medical diagnostic testing. Their first product, called Triage, tests urine samples for the presence of up to seven different illegal drugs, such as cocaine and heroin, and provides the diagnostic results in just 10 minutes. Despite the product's obvious strong points, Biostat initially had a difficult time attracting venture capitalists. However, the company conducted an extensive market intelligence program which quickly brought in the capital they needed. Kim Bickenstaff, coowner and chief executive, concluded that this market intelligence defined who its target market was and what channels it needed to use to reach them. Knowledge about its environment also enabled Biostat to attract exchange partners to help in the international distribution of its diagnostic technologies.[6]

In the last several years, technology has dramatically increased the amount of information to which marketers have access. While this access has generally proven useful, channel members have also encountered several challenges as a result. These challenges include information overload, information accuracy, and information rivalry.

Information Overload. Information overload refers to those situations where the capacity of channel members to manage data is strained because excessive amounts of information are available. To avoid information overload, channel members must first decide which information will be most useful for making channel decisions. This is why top management demands executive reports—shorter versions which selectively sift through the information that is available on a given topic. The problem of information overload has been exacerbated by the unprecedented repositories of information available on the World Wide Web. In the Net Economy, channel members' new challenge involves sifting through capacious information.

Information overload can create market opportunities, as well. Teltech Resource Network Corporation is capitalizing on the information overload that modern scientists often encounter. In effect, too much is being written about too many topics for anyone to keep up with. Teltech helps scientists pluck useful needles of data from the virtual haystacks of information that are available on particular scientific topics. The company consolidates intelligence taken from both databases and people, integrating quantitative and qualitative sources.[7]

Information Accuracy. Channel members are also concerned about the quality of market information available to them. Conflicting accounts of changes in the environment are not uncommon. As an example, you are probably aware of the battles that economists wage over the true state of our economy. Each economist cites different sets of data to arrive at her forecast and each is certain that her information is correct. Similarly, channel members must not only decide which marketing intelligence to use, they must also assess the *certitude* of the information. Information accuracy addresses the correctness and precision of market intelligence—the degree to which one can use it with confidence and certainty. In the Net Economy, virtually anyone can post anything. So, channel members need to assess the credibility of the vast amount of information available on the Internet.

Many research companies have prospered from selling huge databases to channel members. For example, multinational corporations like Procter & Gamble, Unilever, and Kraft

General Foods typically rely on shopping data purchased from researchers to make product development, distribution, and other marketing decisions. Many companies also rely on credit reports to assess the attractiveness of a potential exchange partner. An accurate credit history will provide information that is useful in the selection of exchange partners. But the results could be disastrous when this information is based on unreliable data.

Channel members can evaluate the accuracy of information in several ways, including:

- **Source reliability.** Is the source of information credible? Does the information provider have a good reputation for reliability, truthfulness, and accuracy in reporting?
- **Data collection methods.** What methods were used to collect the information? How much confidence can one place in the information-gathering methods employed?
- **Sampling design.** Who were the respondents or participants in the research? Is the information representative of the population of interest?
- **Information context.** For what purpose was the information collected? Does the context for which the information was collected correspond meaningfully with the channel setting at hand?

Accurate information is critical in channel relationships. A relationship orientation to marketing channels requires a customer satisfaction approach. This first requires that customer needs be accurately identified. But as Channel Surfing 5.1 illustrates, sometimes the process by which accurate market intelligence is obtained can be taken to extremes.

Information Rivalry. Because information is so valuable to channel members, it is also a competitive resource which channel members may wish to keep to themselves. For example, when department stores like JC Penney or Target share point-of-sale information regarding which toddler dresses are hot and which are not, Buster Brown Apparel, Inc., can improve its manufacturing and distribution efficiency. All parties in this channel system gain an edge over other channel systems that do not have access to such information.[8]

To a large extent, information rivalry really boils down to information hoarding. The decision to hoard information from a competitive marketing channel system may not be wrong in a legal sense; however, it may raise an ethical dilemma. It also raises the potential for problems and misuse. Environmental information is especially valuable because it assists channel members in planning. The position advocated in this text supports an open exchange of information among channel members, with consideration given to the protection of proprietary information. Given the entropic nature of closed channel systems, open exchange of information will foster better relationships and improve overall performance.

Along with the ethical concerns presented by information hoarding, there are other concerns about the security and inappropriate procurement and use of market intelligence. In 1993, British Airways admitted it had engaged in dirty tricks against rival Virgin Airways. These dirty tricks ranged from tapping into Virgin's computer systems to actual break-ins of Virgin employees' homes.[9] General Electric Co.'s (GE) information security measures were also recently breached by unidentified computer hackers who accessed proprietary information pertaining to GE's channel system relations.[10]

In spite of the concerns, it is clear that market intelligence helps channel members manage their exchange relationships better. Environmental information is often available through

Channel Surfing 5.1

Supermarkets? No, Supersnoops: James Bond Hits the Grocery Aisles

More supermarkets than ever are spying on their customers. But this time, instead of trying to identify shoplifters, they're looking for ways to increase sales. No longer content with rudimentary surveys to obtain information at the checkout, hundreds of retailers nationwide are turning to electronic and infrared surveillance equipment with names like VideOcart and ShopperTrak. Some stores even carry out old-fashioned stakeouts, complete with walkie-talkies, from catwalks above the aisles. The goal is to provide retailers with up-to-date information about shoppers' traffic patterns which can then be used to trace their buying habits.

Take Basha's Markets, Inc., located in Arizona. Studies showed that only 18 percent of the grocery store's customers ever went down the aisle featuring greeting cards. This was disturbing, because greeting cards are high-profit items. So the store layout manager moved the section, sandwiching it between the floral department and an aisle with peanut butter, jelly, and health foods—an aisle that regularly drew 62 percent of the store's traffic. In their new home, greeting card sales showed a quarterly increase of 40 percent.

Literally tracking consumers' every move has turned up some surprises. For example:

- By looking down from catwalks at shoppers, researchers working for Marsh Supermarkets found customers heavily shopped the periphery of the store—the produce, dairy and meat sections—but frequently bypassed the dry goods section that occupies the bulk of store space.The Indiana store chain's inner aisles drew only about 13 percent to 30 percent of customer traffic, while the outside perimeter accounted for as much as 80 percent.
- Traffic does not necessarily translate into sales, according to a study conducted by the Food Marketing Institute. By retracing the steps of 2400 shoppers and inspecting what ended up in the grocery carts, the institute learned that while 77 percent of people walked through the bakery department, only 33 percent actually bought anything there.

With knowledge about shopper behavior and traffic patterns, stores may begin assigning dollar values to particular sections and aisles. Armed with that market information, retailers may soon try to charge producer and distributor firms more to display their wares in better locations.

Points to Ponder

- Does this spying business currently emerging in marketing channels bother you? Why or why not? Can you think of any other nontraditional approaches to environmental scanning beyond those discussed in this example?

Source: Adapted from McCarthy, Michael J. (1993), "Retailing: James Bond Hits the Supermarket: Stores Snoop on Shopper's Habits to Boost Sales," *The Wall Street Journal,* August 25, B1; Galloway, Kenneth W. (1993), "Technodesign: Technology Is Changing the Way Stores Are Designed," *Discount Merchandiser,* 33 (5), 118–23; and Bennett, Stephen (1992), "Store of the Month: Big Bear Sharpens Its Claws," *Progressive Grocer,* 71 (12), 34–43.

open, direct means such as the mass media, trade publications, and salespeople. Other, less-direct means are also available. These include consulting firms, surveillance of clients, surveys, economic reports, and trade shows and conventions.[11]

The uncertainty of channel environments is compounded by an inherent difficulty in predicting the effects of changes in the environment. No matter how much market intelligence a channel member has gathered regarding its environment, entropy tells us that disorder is a natural occurrence. While this circumstance does not diminish the need for information, it does suggest that environmental forecasting is an imperfect science.

Different Effects

We have already noted that different external stimuli affect channel members in different ways. Since a prediction of future events is a major objective of most environmental scanning efforts, it would be helpful to understand the magnitude and intensity of entropic processes. Yet, by definition, the consequences of entropy are not generalizable from one situation to the next. This is because the same environmental trends often have different effects on different channel members.

To illustrate this characteristic we call *different effects*, consider coffee. Health trends indicate that the demand for decaffeinated coffee should be growing. In fact, when the rising demand for healthier foods is coupled with medical studies announcing the harmful effects of caffeine, caffeinated coffee's future appears bleak. But this is actually far from the case because other factors influence the relationship between the environment and coffee demand.

For one thing, most coffee drinkers apparently do not care for the taste of decaffeinated coffee. Therefore, it is not surprising that supermarket sales of decaf have dropped by more than 10 percent annually over the past few years. From Folgers to Maxwell House, this trend extends across brand names. And how can the success of Starbucks Coffee Company's nearly 3,800 coffee bars be explained? Each week, more than 1,000,000 people sip cappuccino or special blends at these coffee bars in North America, Asia, Europe, and the Middle East, contributing to a success story that would appear to buck the general environmental trends. Obviously, the trends present in the external environment have affected different channel members in different ways.[12] Starbucks coffee epitomizes how important it is to purposefully adapt in the face of seemingly negative environmental forces. Starbucks coffee bar customers are not just buying caffeinated coffee, they are consuming a *treat.*

Channel Dynamism

Channel environments are also characterized by a property known as *dynamism.* The notion of **channel dynamism** suggests that the environmental forces concurrently flowing from and directed toward marketing channels are constantly changing. Because channel environments are dynamic, channel members should be:

- **Flexible.** Channel members must be willing and capable of adapting in response to marketplace changes. They must also recognize that changing environmental stimuli do not just affect a single member within a marketing channel. Each channel member will likely be affected, albeit in different ways, by environmental conditions.
- **Prepared.** Since market intelligence is imperfect, exchange partners should use it judiciously. The judicious application of market intelligence can contribute to a state of channel foresight. In channel relationships, foresight relates to a channel member's ability to accurately predict the future of its relevant environment. As we have said, by openly sharing information exchange partners can minimize the uncertainty of their market intelligence and make better decisions. Exchange partners will then be better able to anticipate and prepare for changes in their environments.
- **Attuned.** For channel members to perform effectively in spite of uncertain conditions, they should work together. This requires that channel members be attuned to the cues present in their channel environments. Channel members should also monitor their exchange partners' needs and the ways that changing environmental conditions impact those needs.

Channel Surfing 5.2

The Beer-Mouth Bass Has Gone Fishing . . .

The "beer-mouth" Bass Ale has long been noted for the wide-mouth opening on each bottle. But that Bass has gone fishing . . . and you may be surprised by the catch.

Long ago, Bass PLC reeled in the British Vitamin Product Company, the one-time Clemsford, England, pharmacy famous for its zesty, flavored mineral waters, and in 1949, Britvic juices were born.

Today, Britvic is among Europe's leading soft-drink manufacturers. Bass PLC's Britvic supplies over 250,000 retailers with more than 400 flavors, shapes, and sizes of beverages, capturing nearly 25 percent market share in the ready-to-drink category.

Once the United Kingdom's No. 2 brewer featuring "big catches" like Bass Ale, Caffrey's, and Carling, Bass PLC has sold its breweries to rival Interbrew to concentrate on distribution of some American "breeds." For example, Bass PLC distributes Pepsi and 7-Up, along with a host of other soft drinks, including its anchor label Britvic. While its stock includes a variety of U.S. and long-standing British brands, Britain's biggest-selling brand of beer, Carling, is now a Belgium brand.

Bass PLC's transformation from an institution in European brewing to a major distributor of global soft-drink brands illustrates how channel members must continually adapt to market dynamics.

Besides Pepsi and 7-Up, Bass PLC's Britvic distributes Tango, Britain's best-selling carbonated fruit drink, Ruby's Cranberry and Blueberry sodas, and a variety of other carbonated and noncarbonated beverages.

But Bass PLC does not merely have a penchant for American soft drinks. Bass boasts a couple of other classic American brands: Holiday Inn and Inter-Continental hotels. Bass Hotels & Resorts operates and franchises more than 2,800 Holiday Inn, Crowne Plaza, and Inter-Continental hotels in 90 countries around the globe. Forget your Boston Tea Party, Bass PLC is capitalizing on a profitable marriage between American and British brands.

Points to Ponder

- What environmental factors in the channel exosystem may be responsible for Bass PLC dumping its namesake ales in lieu of soft-drink and hospitality brands?
- Do you think there is any distribution synergy for Bass PLC? Why or why not?

The level of dynamism in a channel's external environment affects channel relationships. For example, as a relationship becomes closer, each party increases its knowledge of the other. This enhances the forecasting capabilities of each channel member. But the opportunity costs of relying on a single or small number of relationships can be high in a dynamic environment. Even channel environments traditionally not thought to be dynamic are changing. An example is presented in Channel Surfing 5.2.

Decision Support Systems

Potentially large payoffs are available for channel members who can detect current environmental trends. Even larger gains will accrue to those who are able to accurately forecast future trends. The first, critical step in this process of forecasting involves identifying the proper strategic considerations (or, issues). Generally speaking, these considerations are:

- Current or future trends that will influence market size.
- Customer preferences that affect their wants and perceived needs.
- Broad industry directions. The success or failure of current channel strategies.

Some trends have a high potential impact but a low probability of actually occurring. Such issues are usually not worth the expenditure of resources that would be necessary to resolve them.

For larger channel members, market intelligence (i.e., the answers to these questions) is best gathered through a **decision support system (DSS).**[13] A DSS features a coordinated set of data systems, tools, and techniques, along with supporting software and hardware for environmental scanning. It provides the means by which a channel organization can gather and interpret intelligence from the relevant environment, then convert this intelligence into a basis for marketing action (see Channel Surfing 5.3).

The data system in a DSS includes the processes used to obtain and the methods used to store market intelligence from inside and outside of the firm. It should contain data sectors on customer (market), economic and demographic, competitive, technological, and industry trends. The customer intelligence sector typically contains information on who buys and uses the product, where the product is bought and used, in what situations and quantities the product is bought, and so on. The module containing general economic and demographic information categorizes relevant factors about what is happening in these external environmental

Channel Surfing 5.3

Using Decision Support Systems to Provide Just What the Market Ordered

Wisconsin-based Amity Leather Products prides itself on being able to use environmental scanning to keep up with what customers want, both in terms of product selection and in the area of electronic data interchange (EDI). In a recent example, Amity noticed that the pressures of complying with quick-response requests were beginning to mount. With the help of a decision support system, Amity took a hard look at its relevant market environment and found its distribution system wanting.

As more of Amity's retail customers came on line with EDI, the environment for ordering products was changing radically. Large, electronically requested orders now had to be sent either to distribution centers or directly to retail stores. Another factor complicating ordering was customers' requests for shipment on particular days. In an online environment, retailers booked orders later, giving Amity shorter lead times and smaller shipping windows.

The antidote for these distribution woes was—not surprisingly—automation in the form of bar code technology. Bar code technology was nothing new to this manufacturer of personal leather goods. It had long been providing universal product code (UPC) labels on products for merchandisers to use in retail scanning operations. Amity's previous experiences with bar coding provided the in-house expertise for much of the software production needed to scan its environment.

Order numbers and the number of pieces in the carton are now entered into computers to generate a side label for the carton. Overhead scanners scan labels inside cartons for order verification. Shipping labels are then produced that tell Amity where items should be placed on shelves, and where and when they should be shipped. This decision support system has allowed Amity to stay in constant touch with its environment and to integrate the resulting information directly into its distribution practices.

Source: Adapted from Anonymous (1994), "Bar Codes: Not Just For the Big Guy Anymore," *Automatic I.D. News*, 10 (12), 30–31; and Witt, Clyde E. (1994), "Smart Scanners Verify Just What the Customer Ordered," *Materials Handling Engineering*, January, 44–46.

components. The competitor module should make available information on current and potential competitors, answering such questions as: Who are they? What are their relative strengths, unique capabilities, and market shares? In which market niches do they operate?

Only the information that is likely to prove useful in marketing or channel decision making should be entered into a DSS. The DSS's basic purpose is to capture relevant market intelligence and to convert that data to useful forms.

The number of online databases that provide information on potential customers, competitors, industries, and general economic trends has expanded rapidly in recent years. This explosion of information has exercised a critical influence on the development of decision support systems. Over 21,500 databases are currently available, and one can only expect this number to increase in the years ahead. Companies are increasingly having to set up separate systems to periodically track and capture this information. Many firms are also establishing the position of chief information officer (CIO). The CIO serves as the liaison between the firm's top decision makers (including those responsible for channels decisions) and its DSS function. He or she is responsible for planning, coordinating, and controlling the firm's intelligence resources. The CIO is more concerned with the firm's big picture than functional area managers' daily activities.

The emergence of online databases and DSSs has not eliminated the need for traditional marketing research aimed at gathering specific pieces of market intelligence. Indeed, the two approaches to gathering and managing market intelligence are complementary rather than competitive. DSSs provide valuable input to strategic channels planning. They allow channel managers to stay in touch with their relevant external environments and serve as valuable early warning devices.

The Channel Exosystem

Channel relationships evolve in a dynamic environment. But merely recognizing the existence of a changing environment is not enough to ensure success. For that, exchange partners must continuously *scan*, or examine, the environment. On the surface, it may appear futile to scan conditions that are always changing. After all, what's the value in spending energy to study an environment if the conditions are likely to change anyway? When viewed as a whole, the environment may prove too difficult to deal with efficiently or comfortably. This is precisely why successful environmental scanning requires channel members to assume a disaggregate perspective. In other words, successful environmental scanning involves studying each component of the external environment individually.

Five key components of the external environment illustrated in the CRM are the:

- Competitive environment
- Economic environment
- Technological environment
- Sociocultural environment
- Legal, ethical, and regulatory environment

The impact of these components is complicated by the global scope of the external environment. Furthermore, each of these environmental components is essentially borderless as depicted in the CRM—the environment never affects only one partner in isolation; it also influences the relationship between channel partners. Because most environmental conditions are beyond the control of individual channel members, pooling resources to anticipate and react more swiftly to environmental changes is one advantage of developing a relationship.

Competitive Environment

Competition is an uncontrollable component of the channel environment. Competition can occur at any level of a marketing channel. The rapidity with which market circumstances can shift makes the environment's competitive component quite difficult to manage. To illustrate, consider that not so long ago Sears clearly led the way in American retailing. Today, however, Wal-Mart is in a commanding position, and its expansion continues from Asia to South America. Wal-Mart's dominance has forced other channel members to adapt to the changes in retail structure. Wal-Mart's success and strength have also inspired many of its exchange partners to introduce changes in their manufacturing and distribution processes.

Channel members often go to great lengths to gain market share. The battle for market share is heating up on fast-food grills throughout the United States. You may know that global fast-food titan McDonald's is facing off against competitors like Wendy's and Jack-in-the-Box. Meanwhile, Burger King, Hardee's, and Taco Bell are trying to recapture the market share that has recently been eaten away by their competition. But market share leader McDonald's is not just flipping burgers. McDonald's menu of offerings is changing the competitive landscape. McDonald's now brings a portfolio of dining options to its menu of market offerings, including Boston Market's rotisserie chicken, Donato's Italian fare, and Chipotle's south-of-the-border burritos. McDonald's recent acquisitions of these restaurant brands may present new opportunities. But they will likely pose new challenges: McDonald's will need to work with a portfolio of suppliers to ensure accurate quality and timely deliveries of diverse ingredients, dry goods, and drinks to each restaurant unit.

There are four types of competitive channel environments: horizontal, vertical, system, and network.[14] **Horizontal competition** occurs between channel members operating at the same level and generally within the same market. For example, stores such as Sears, Kmart, and Wal-Mart usually compete for the same discount-oriented customers, even though exceptions do exist with respect to certain product lines of Sears. While retailers follow different paths to attract their customers, their product width and depth are similar. For certain other product categories, off-price specialty retailers like T.J. Maxx, Ross Dress for Less, and Burlington Coat Factory also compete against Sears, Kmart, and Wal-Mart.

Vertical competition occurs when channel members operating at different channel levels compete for a share of the same market. In other words, vertical competition arises whenever manufacturers and resellers struggle over their share of the system's profits. Retailers may compete against wholesalers. Resellers may also compete against other resellers in the same channel system. Manufacturers may even compete against retailers. For example, on occasion IBM's direct sales force has called on accounts of independent computer retailers who also carry IBM's line of computers. This type of vertical competition, known as *dual distribution,* can be disruptive to the channel system's harmony.

Naturally, dissension can arise between a manufacturer and its dealers who are in competition with each other. A few years ago, Compaq Computer Corporation elected to extend its distribution channels through the use of mail-order and mega-discounter firms. This decision infuriated independent computer retailers who found it more difficult to be price-competitive. Independent retailers also experienced difficulties maintaining sufficient inventories of hot products. One dealer insists that Compaq intentionally diverted inventories to its new sales channels, at the expense of more traditional outlets. Matt Hirzsimmons, a New York ComputerLand dealer, complained: "It's not just that we lose an order. We lose a long-term relationship with a customer."[15]

System competition occurs among complete channel units. The airline industry is a prime example of system competition, where companies like United Airlines, Delta Airlines, and American Airlines all vie for air travelers. These competitors dominate the distribution of airline tickets through their company-owned computerized ticketing systems, travel agencies, and company-vested travel wholesalers. As a result, these companies compete as members of a complete system rather than at any specific channel level.

A new type of competition, driven by the connectivity between channel members, has emerged in the Net Economy. **Network competition** occurs among networks of channel members competing across industries and markets. A *network* is a cluster of channel relationships that are constructed for the purpose of maximizing exchange utility among the partners. These clusters of relationships can exist either at horizontal (i.e., between sets of producers) or vertical channel levels (i.e., between producers and suppliers), or at both levels simultaneously. Several firms may be involved with one another at each level.

An example of network competition is embodied in a Mountain View, California, software concern. General Magic, Inc., is a software consortium that includes more than 10 companies, including Motorola, Fujitsu Ltd., Sony Corp., Apple Computer, Phillips Electronics, and Toshiba Corp., on its roster. While most of these firms compete directly with one another, the General Magic network allows these industry giants to develop and share technologies across a number of video and telecommunications applications. Network competition is a complex and unsettled market factor because it is still in its early stages of development. However, some observers believe network competition will emerge as a dominant environmental issue.[16]

Economic Environment

Predicting and responding to the economy's anticipated impact is a particularly important aspect of channels management. Yet, no single environmental issue is more difficult to forecast. Economic conditions are constantly being measured through a variety of indicators. These indicators range from measures of gross domestic production (GDP) to consumer confidence. Different economic indicators often send mixed signals. At other times, economists themselves cannot agree on the meanings of economic signals.

Economic indicators sometimes provide misleading cues for marketers, as well. Doubts about the timeliness and consistency of many economic measures certainly exist. Moreover, economic indicators are only themselves generalizations, providing an aggregate index of the economic outlook or performance at a particular point in time. For instance, many channel members may flourish despite a drop in the Dow Jones Industrial Average. This should surprise no one since the Dow Jones average is simply a daily compilation of the stock prices for 30 publicly traded U.S. corporations.

Still, economic conditions have a reverberating effect on every level of channel systems. For example, when domestic demand grows, commodities are more likely to be pulled through the distribution system. In response, manufacturers and distributors send larger shipments. This, in turn, signals more economic growth. These secondary effects are magnified by the dual influence of derived demand and joint demand. Because channel members—especially producers—buy goods that will be used directly or indirectly to satisfy consumers' requirements, the demand for all products flowing through channel systems comes from consumer demand. This is known as **derived demand.** For example, the demand for computer chips is derived from consumer demands for faster and smaller personal computers. On the other hand, the channel flows of many other products—especially raw materials and unfinished components—are subject to joint demand. **Joint demand** exists when two or more items are used together to produce a product. For instance, a company that produces axes needs the same number of ax handles as it does ax heads. This is because the two items are jointly demanded.

Additionally, sometimes larger shipments through the channels are merely inventory stockpiles that are being dumped into the marketplace.[17] Such practices occur frequently in the apparel industry. There, unpopular or dated fashions are filtered through off-price retailers to eliminate excess inventories. Consider the early 1990s reintroduction of the mini-skirts and dresses targeted at older, professional women. The targeted audience largely shunned the above-the-knee look, and clothing manufacturers were forced to dump inventories in the marketplace at markedly lower prices. In other words, the movement of some goods is not necessarily based on consumer spending. For this reason, consumer confidence indices can prove to be false indicators of future channel profitability.

In the face of all of this uncertainty, how can channel members effectively scan their economic environments? Literally hundreds of indicators are available from which to choose. The nature of these cues about the economic environment is shaped by the conditions prevailing within four general economic factors:

- Economic infrastructure
- Consumer buying power
- Currency stability
- National trade policies

The *economic infrastructure* is a composite of the communication, education, financial, and distribution support systems in any market sector. For example, the former Soviet bloc countries generally have proven attractive to global marketers because of the size of the consumer population there and their desire for Western goods. However, the problems with developing and sustaining channel relationships in this infrastructure-poor region are astounding. As hard as it is to believe, nearly three-quarters of the potatoes shipped within the former Soviet Union never reach retail markets. The poor local infrastructure contributes to a massive spoilage. Potatoes simply cannot be shipped in time.

Consumer buying power indices generally provide useful insights into future channel performance. When consumers are not buying, there is no force to drive goods through the marketing channel. Because of the effects of joint and derived demand, lower consumer spending can have magnified effects on a channel's overall performance. When consumers have less buying power, retailers make fewer sales and require fewer replacement goods. In turn, a lower GDP results in fewer employment opportunities, decreasing consumers' buyer power. As a result, consumer demand decreases again.

Currency stability often exercises a pivotal influence on channel performance. Small and medium-size U.S. channel members often find that they have to protect themselves against the falling value of foreign currencies. In the 21st century, most U.S. apparel manufacturers are increasingly turning to Asia and Latin America for production, and these U.S. apparel makers are taking no chances. These production outsourcing agreements are written in greenbacks. They no longer have to hedge in futures or forwards markets to compensate for possible losses with foreign currency fluctuations. That's a big advantage when you consider the currency instability in 1998! U.S. apparel manufacturers no longer rely on fluctuations of currencies like the Thai baht, the Indonesian rupiah, the Mexican peso, and the Malaysian ringgit!

A country's *trade policy* can also prove to be a significant economic indicator. United States trade policy with Vietnam received a good deal of attention in the early to mid-1990s. Most U.S. exporters, sensing a market opportunity, cheered when trade sanctions against Vietnam were lifted. Yet many Americans balked at the prospect of open trade with Vietnam. Likewise, during apartheid's final years, many U.S. channel members were forced to abandon exchange relationships in South Africa. Many of these relationships had been extremely lucrative.

These four general economic factors are hardly exhaustive. Other macroeconomic factors such as inflation levels, employment rates, or interest rates can also exercise substantial effects on channel structure and performance. Other environmental cues such as the size of the federal deficit and fluctuations in the stock market can also help channel members manage uncertainty. Still, when taken as a set, these four factors illustrate how complicated exchange relationships can become when economic conditions are uncertain.

Technological Environment

The technological environment primarily confronts those processes by which information- and knowledge-based products are introduced into channel systems. When technology is based on information sharing, channel relationships often develop for the sole purpose of research and development. In Chapter 1, you were introduced to the unprecedented impact of information technology on marketing channels. The channel relationship between Federated Department Stores—the retail conglomerate with more than 400 retail bands (see Chapter 2)—and Manhattan Associates illuminates the role of information technology in the global marketplace. Manhattan is helping Federated build a Web-based integrated solution that enables real-time communication between retailers and their suppliers. Infolink will improve overall supply-chain operations to reduce inventories and stock-outs and to increase profit margins. Infolink is an example of how an "infomediary" connects buyers and sellers in the B2B marketplace.

Technology is making the world of marketing channels smaller and faster, as well. As a result, the balance of power in many channel systems has shifted away from manufacturers and toward retailers. Retailers are now able to quickly gain accurate information regarding items which are or are not popular with their customers. Over the past decade or so, retailers have used this information to leverage their positions with manufacturers and wholesalers. During the same period, however, the information technology revolution has triggered strong growth in nonstore retailers such as Lands' End, Hammacher Schlemmer, and Warner Brothers Studio Stores. The positions of some traditional retailers have been eroded as a result. In any number of industrial and service sectors, old-line channel structures have been weakened by the introduction and rapid growth of the Internet and other third-party information service providers such as CompuServe, Prodigy, and America Online. Late 20th-century technology is making change the only constant in channel relationships.

A *technological imperative* is emerging wherein the channel structure or design stems from the prevailing technology operating within the channel. Two general, technology-based channel structures currently exist. One, called **pooled interdependence,** describes two channel members who operate independently but whose pooled resources simultaneously contribute to each partner's overall success. The other technology-based channel structure is known as **sequential interdependence.** In sequential interdependence, technology and the changes that generally accompany it are *pushed* through a channel system from one member to the next. The flows of information and technology are one way. Two-way exchange of technology requires an integration of channel members' technology-based knowledge. This results in **reciprocal interdependence,** in which knowledge-based products can be jointly developed and marketed. Once reciprocal interdependence emerges, the channel inputs and outputs of exchange partners become essentially indistinguishable.[18]

Sociocultural Environment

Changes in channel structures are frequently due to changes in the sociocultural environment. This is because whenever consumer values, attitudes, or lifestyles change, the way in which consumers express needs and buying motivations also change. For example, consumers have always needed to get from point A to point B. But over the years, the way consumers have chosen to satisfy this transportation need has changed drastically.

When such a sociocultural change occurs, channel members must respond by adapting their need-satisfying marketing mix strategies. This process changes the products and services all of us acquire, use, and dispose of in our roles as consumers. To illustrate how this works, consider that today's households increasingly feature single parents or two parents who work outside the home. Such households often have little discretionary time to spend shopping. Retailers have responded to this change by offering extended store hours, broader product assortments in a single location, and in-home shopping capabilities. Such changes in the retail mix are inevitably accompanied by changes in supply systems within the channel.

The sociocultural environment exists as the point of connection among channel members, society, and its culture. Several sociocultural characteristics influence channel behaviors, including:

- **Cultural diversity.** The ethnic composition of the United States is changing rapidly. In this decade, nonwhite residents will be a majority in some U.S. states like California and Texas. As a result, product packaging, promotional materials, and alternative distribution outlets are being adjusted to rising populations of Asians and Hispanics. For example, most banks are providing bilingual text on automated teller machines (ATMs) throughout the United States.
- **Social issues.** Social concerns also affect the way goods flow through marketing channels. One example is the proliferation of green marketing claims by manufacturers. These product claims are specifically intended to appeal to the

environmental consciousness of consumers. As we noted in Chapter 2, recycling is a channel function that requires consumers to become de facto producers. Recycled materials, then, generally reenter the manufacturing process as raw materials. But, how much do U.S. consumers really care about the environment? Exhibit 5.2 suggests that few Americans viewed themselves as environmentalists at the start of the 21st century!

- **New product channels.** Will ATMs eventually replace the channels traditionally available for banking services? Will consumers buy food and clothing from the Internet? Will consumers opt for home shopping over the shopping mall? These questions address how issues such as convenience, driven by family- or work-related pressures, impact the distribution of goods and services in traditional channel systems.

The sociocultural environment reflects the combined effects of all other environmental factors. Franchisees must adapt to regional preferences. Manufacturers must adapt their products and promotional patterns to changing society-based demands. And, inevitably,

EXHIBIT 5.2

Growing green: Environmentalism and the channels exosystem

REBELS FOR THE CAUSE

The number of people who say they are environmentalists has dropped in recent years.

Question: Do you consider yourself to be an environmentalist or not?

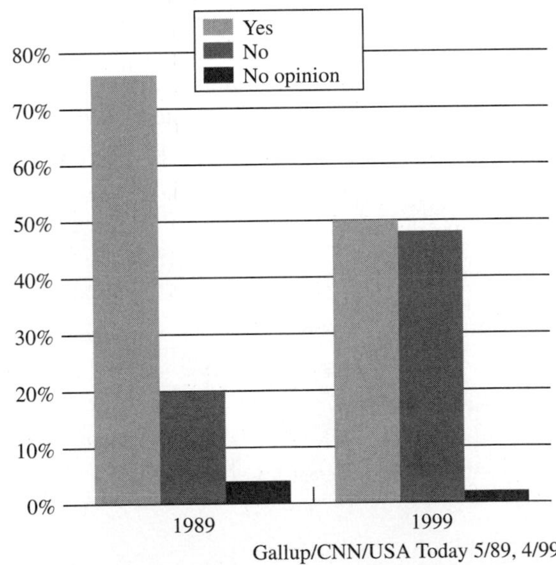

Gallup/CNN/USA Today 5/89, 4/99

ENVIRONMENT VS. ECONOMY

Most Americans say there doesn't have to be a choice between sacrificing environmental or economic health.

Question: Do you believe that economic growth should be sacrificed for environmental quality? Should environmental quality be sacrificed for economic growth? Or does there necessarily have to be a choice between the two?

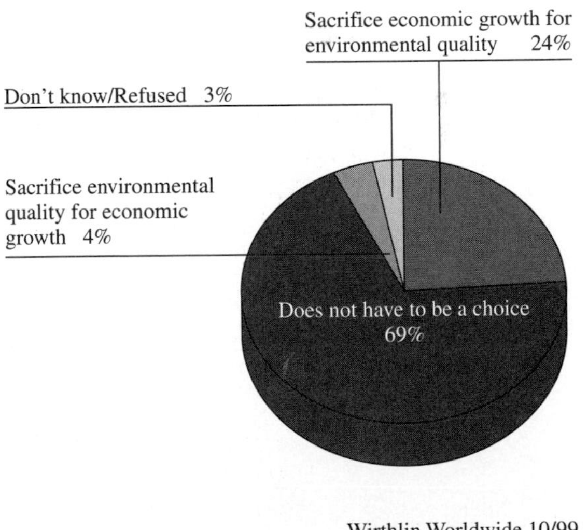

Wirthlin Worldwide 10/99

Source: http://www.publicagenda.com reported in "Earth in the Balance: Public Attitudes on the Issue of Environmentalism," *American Demographics*, January 2001, 24.

intermediaries are obliged to provide new modes of distribution for these altered goods and services. For instance, cultural trends compelled General Mills to reorient its entire approach to distribution. The huge Midwestern food processor had observed how Americans were increasingly consuming food based on their concerns about food quality, diet, physical fitness, and natural ingredients. At the same time, America's eating habits shifted dramatically toward "away-from-home" and "on-the-run" dining. General Mills responded in two ways. First, the firm developed a chain of Good Earth restaurants that featured natural foods. Then, operating within its long-standing distribution channels, General Mills introduced healthy, eat-on-the-run products, such as Yoplait and Nature Valley Granola bars to the grocery sector.[19]

Since all human interactions unfolding within sociocultural settings are motivated at various times by economic and/or political concerns, eco-political interests cannot be easily separated from sociocultural issues. Nor, most likely, should one even try to achieve such a separation. The pressing question that remains, then, is how does the channel environment affect the relationships among exchange partners? One model has proven useful for integrating the effects of these environmental externalities into the channel system. The *political economy framework* describes how interacting sets of *internal and external* environments affect the behavior and performance of channels systems.[20] In the CRM, the external environment envelops the internal environment. The political economy framework provides a more complete picture of the junction between the internal and external channel environments, and it is illustrated in Exhibit 5.3.

Legal, Ethical, and Regulatory Environment

Unlike the economic environment, the nature of the legal and regulatory environment is relatively clear. **Laws and regulations** are an administered body of principles and rules applied more or less uniformly in the face of disputes or problems.[21] Channel members' behaviors are restricted by a series of laws that regulate and govern their actions.

The elimination or introduction of legal and regulatory constraints can pose both major threats and opportunities to channel members and to entire channel systems. For instance, deregulation in the banking, air travel, and railroad industries had enormous implications for

EXHIBIT 5.3

The political economy framework

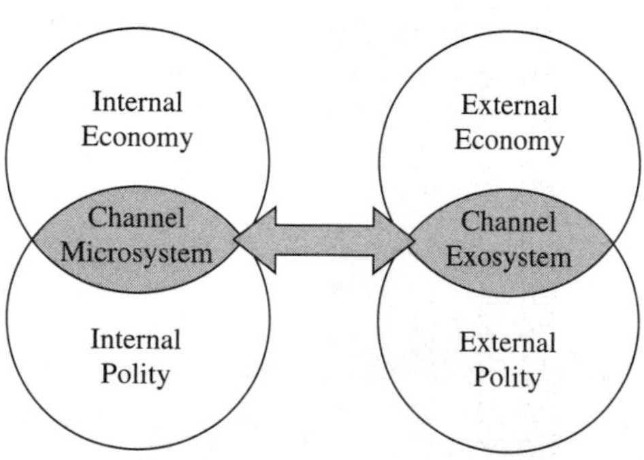

Source: Adapted from Reve, Torger, and Louis W. Stern (1979), "Interorganizational Relations in Marketing Channels," *Academy of Management Review*, 4 (July), 405–16.

the structure of the channel systems that had previously prevailed within each sector. On the other hand, the introduction of legislation aimed at curbing piracy of software, compact discs, and videos significantly impacted the means by which those items were internationally distributed. An extensive discussion of the legal and regulatory environment and how it impacts marketing channels is offered in the next chapter.

Internal and External Political Economies: An Environmental Framework

The act of cooperating through the exchange of goods and services is based on the premise that two or more channel members engage in economic behaviors for their mutual gain. As such, one hopefully enters an exchange relationship to further his or her own interest, and with the intent of benefiting other channel members.[22] In this way, channels are *collectivities* of organizations and their human representatives. It is actually these human representatives who jointly pursue their own self-interests and the channels' common objectives.[23] The interaction process that emerges from such trade-offs could be characterized as a social system. The *social system orientation* is based on the assumption that environmental conditions regulate both organizational and individual behaviors. The political economy framework recognizes and accounts for both the external and internal environment. By now, it should be evident that channel members are *catalysts for* and *victims of* their dynamic external environments. The interaction between channel members operating within any channel system (internal environment) is invariably influenced by the socioeconomic and political forces in the marketplace (external environment).

The *channel microsystem* encompasses the channel structure and processes that are derived from exchange processes. The internal political economy consists of two components: the internal economy and the internal polity. The **internal economy** captures the economic structure and processes of the channel. It would describe, for example, the process by which resources are allocated or terms of exchange are derived. The **internal polity** accounts for the behavioral aspects of the exchange partners. It addresses, for example, the level of cooperation and conflict that exists in an exchange relationship.

The *channel exosystem* is dichotomized into an **external economy** and **external polity.** The external economy accounts for the economic environment in which marketing channels develop and function. The external polity captures the sociopolitical environment. As Exhibit 5.2 illustrates, the political economy framework suggests that channel members not only adapt to their environment, they also help shape it.[24]

Members of channel systems face multiple environments and environmental trends. However, there are important clusters of environmental forces—summarized within the channel micro- and exosystems—that have substantial and predictable effects on channel systems. The political economy framework accounts for these effects.

The political economy (P-E) perspective advances our understanding in a couple of ways. The global automotive sector offers a useful illustration. The P-E framework suggests that channel members are active participants in a dynamic environment. Accordingly, General Motors introduced and positioned its Saturn Division in response to the changing preferences of the consumer market. Furthermore, the environment provides opportunities and presents limitations to all channel relationships. DaimlerChrysler and Mitsubishi would certainly agree with such an assessment and, in response, they entered into a strategic partnership with one another. The framework also suggests that channel performance is ultimately a pursuit of some equilibrium between internal and external environments. The difficulty in attaining such a state of equilibrium is compounded by the complex nature of the environment. A daunting challenge, to be sure, but one that the entire U.S. and Japanese automotives industries have attempted to manage over the last decade through just-in-time supplier agreements and increased vertical integration. The P-E environment in which car producers operate is sure to become even more complex as channel relationships increasingly extend across international boundaries. The need for these producers to scan their relevant environments to lessen uncertainty and prevent entropy can only increase with the passage of time.

Key Terms

channel dynamism
decision support system (DSS)
derived demand
entropy
environmental scanning
external economy
external polity
horizontal competition
internal economy
internal polity
joint demand
laws and regulations
market intelligence
network competition
pooled interdependence
reciprocal interdependence
sequential interdependence
system competition
vertical competition

Chapter Summary

Entropy accounts for the disorder, uncertainty, and wasted effort present in any physical environment. Entropy always increases in any naturally occurring process including working systems such as marketing channels. Channel members always operate under conditions of uncertainty and entropy. Together, these characteristics make environmental scanning a necessity. Environmental scanning involves the appraisal, prediction, and monitoring of all external factors that may substantially impact a channel system. A great many performance problems may be linked to circumstances where the behaviors of channel members remained static while their channel environments changed.

To achieve the state of equilibrium they naturally seek, organisms must receive and respond to information cues from their channel exosystem. Similarly, if channel members are to accurately assess their position in the system, they must obtain useful market intelligence for decision making. Here, market intelligence refers to data that is useful as an input into managerial decision making. In this way, all channel members are, or at least ought to be, information seekers.

Information overload refers to those situations where the capacity of channel members to comfortably manage data is strained because of excessive amounts of information. To avoid such overload, channel members must first decide which information will be most useful for making channel decisions. Information overload can open up market opportunities, as well. Channel members sometimes receive conflicting accounts of changes in the exosystem. Thus, they must address the accuracy and precision of this market intelligence—the degree to which they can use it with confidence or certainty. Because information is so valuable to channel members, it is also a competitive resource. When properly used, environmental information can also help fortify the trust between exchange partners. But there is still potential for problems and misuse.

Channel exosystems are entropic because they are characterized by a property known as *dynamism*. The notion of channel dynamism is that energetic forces concurrently emanating from and directed toward marketing channels are constantly changing. As a result, channel managers need to be flexible, prepared, and attuned to their surroundings. However, merely recognizing the existence of a changing environment is insufficient to safeguard success. For that, exchange partners must continuously scan the environment.

Five key components of the environment must be monitored: competitive, economic, technological, sociocultural, and legal, ethical, and regulatory. Four types of competitive channel environments exist. Horizontal competition occurs between channel members operating at the same level. Vertical competition occurs when channel members operating at different channel levels compete for a share of the same market. System competition occurs among complete channel units. Network competition occurs among a labyrinthine network of channel members contending across industries and markets.

No single environmental issue is more difficult to forecast than the economy. The state of the economy is constantly being measured through a variety of indicators, ranging from gross domestic production to consumer confidence indices. The nature of any cues about the state of the economic environment is always tempered by the conditions prevailing within the following four economic indicators: economic infrastructure, consumer buying power, currency stability, and national trade policies.

The first, critical step in environmental scanning is identifying what questions to ask. These questions might pertain to: current or future trends, customer preferences, industry directions, success or failure of current channel strategies, and competitors' strategies. The answers to these questions can be gathered and interpreted through a decision support system. Only the information that is likely to prove useful should be entered into a DSS.

The technological environment encompasses those processes by which knowledge-based products and information itself are introduced into channel systems. Because technology is predicated on information sharing, one can easily see how channel relationships might develop for the sole purpose of research and development. A sense of a technological imperative is now emerging in many channels settings. The technological imperative suggests that most channel structure is derived from the prevailing technology operating within the channel. Two general, technology-based channel structures currently exist that influence channel relationships. One, called *pooled interdependence,* describes two channel members who operate independently, but whose pooled resources contribute to each member's overall success. The other technology-based channel structure is known as *sequential interdependence.* In sequential interdependence, technology, and the changes that generally accompany it, is *pushed* through channel members. Information and technological flows are essentially one way. For a two-way exchange to occur requires an integration of channel members' technology-based knowledge. This results in a reciprocal imperative.

When the values, attitudes, and lifestyles of consumers change, channel members must adapt their need-satisfying marketing mix strategies in response to these consumers' changing needs. This process changes the products and services all of us acquire, use, and dispose of in our roles as consumers. The sociocultural environment exists as the point of connection among channel members, society, and its culture. In fact, the sociocultural environment is truly an aggregation of all other factors in the channel exosystem.

Channel Challenges

1. In *Panchatantra*, an ancient book of Indian fables, it is asserted, "A frog that lives in a well thinks of the sky as a disc." What is the implication of this statement? How might *environment scanning* keep channel members from being the frog in the well?
2. In *Wholesaling in Marketing Organizations*, David Revzan asserts that the marketing channel "is the managerial battleground in which marketing strategy and marketing tactic activities of each business either succeed or fail." In light of Revzan's assertion, how can exchange relationships prevent onslaughts of competitors?
3. Futurist and business philosopher Peter Drucker asserted that "fools rush in where wise men fear to trade." Given the uncertainty that characterizes the channel exosystem, would you agree or disagree with Drucker's assertion? What advice might you offer channel members competing in the global marketplace?
4. Sumner Redstone grew up on silent films and later ran a chain of movie theaters. The 70-year-old chairman of

Viacom, Inc., is now poised to invade the interactive entertainment market. Viacom will market diversified offerings of interactive games, video-on-demand, home shopping, and sophisticated pocket telephones. Its partners include AT&T and ICOM Simulations. How can exchange partnerships foster proactive channels strategies?

5. The Kiplingers, noted market analysts, have said: "The credibility of a forecast requires a high degree of agreement on where things stand right now . . . current conditions. Those of us in the forecasting business know that a prediction that diverges too far from your perceptions of a present situation just won't be plausible." What is the implication of this statement on the channels environment? If forecasting is an imperfect science, what is the value of environmental scanning?

Review Questions

1. Describe the channel exosystem in terms of three properties that impact channel members.
2. What is environmental scanning? How does it relate to channel entropy?
3. What is marketing intelligence? Describe some methods that channel members can use to obtain market intelligence.
4. Define *dynamism* in terms of marketing channels. Describe three concepts key to channel management resulting from the dynamism concept and their impact on channel relationships.
5. What are five components of the channel exosystem? What is the relationship between these components?
6. Discuss the effect of the competitive environment on channel members.
7. How does the political and economic environment affect marketing channels?
8. How does the legal and ethical environment impact marketing channel members?
9. What is the technological imperative regarding channel structure? What are the three forms of interdependence used to describe channel relationships?
10. How does the sociocultural environment affect the marketing channel?
11. Differentiate between internal and external political economic environments. How has internationalization impacted channel members' abilities to monitor their changing environments?

Endnotes

1. Adapted from Vardi, Nathan (2000), "It's the Tap of the Iceberg," *Forbes*, September 4, 114–15.
2. Rohwedder, Cecile (1994), "It's Time to Leave Home: Menswear Maker Moves Production to Eastern Europe," *The Wall Street Journal*, April 15, B1.
3. Flatow, Peter (1993), "Why Some Companies Just Can't Reinvent Themselves," *Making News*, 27 (October 25), 4.
4. Byrne, Patrick (1993), "Logistics Will Need Borderless Networks," *Transportation & Distribution*, 34 (June), 37–39.
5. Gupta, Udayan (1993), "Enterprise: Costly Research Pays Off for Bio-tech Start-Up," *The Wall Street Journal*, August 2, B2.
6. Kirkpatrick, David (1993), "Groupware Goes Boom," *Fortune*, 128 (December 27), 99–106.
7. "Information Overload," *Economist*, 327 (June 26), 90–91.
8. Sprout, Alison L. (1995), "The Rise of Netscape," *Fortune*, July 19, 140–42.
9. Dwyer, Paula (1993), "British Air: Not Cricket," *Business Week*, January 25, 50–51.
10. Wilder, Clinton (1994), "How Safe Is the Internet?" *Informationweek*, December 12, 12–14.
11. This is compiled from Gelb, Betsy D., Mary Jane Saxton, George M. Zinkhan, and Nancy D. Albers (1991), "Competitive Intelligence: Insights from Executives," *Business Horizons*, 34 (January/

February), 43–47; and Motwani, Jaideep, Gillian Rice, and Essam Mahmoud (1992), "Promoting Exports through International Trade Shows: A Dual Perspective," *Review of Business*, 13 (Spring), 38–42.

12. Deveny, Kathleen (1993), "Marketscan: Decaf Loses Favor with Seekers of Flavor," *The Wall Street Journal*, February 25, B1.
13. Churchill, Gilbert A. Jr. (1990), *Marketing Research: Methodological Foundations*, Fifth Edition, Chicago: The Dryden Press.
14. These categories of competition are loosely based on those presented in Palamountain, Joseph C. (1955), *The Politics of Distribution*, Cambridge, MA: Harvard University Press; and Thorelli, Hans B. (1986), "Networks: Between Markets and Hierarchies," *Strategic Management Journal,* 7, 37–51.
15. Pope, Kyle (1993), "Computes: Dealers Accuse Compaq of Jilting Team," *The Wall Street Journal*, April 27, B1.
16. For an excellent discussion of the impact of network in channel relationships, see Hakansson, II, and L. Snehota (1989), "No Business Is an Island," *Scandanavian Journal of Management*, 4 (3), 187–200.
17. See Arendes, Michael J. (1994), "Traffic & Revenues Abound," *Fleet Owner*, 89 (January 24), 30–31; and Evans, Michael K. (1993), "Trends to Watch For in '94," *Transportation & Distribution*, 34 (November), 13.
18. Thompson, J. D. (1967), *Organizations in Action*, New York, NY: McGraw-Hill, 47.
19. Adapted from Stern, Louis W., and Torger Reve (1980), "Distribution Channels as Political Economics: A Framework for Comparative Analysis," *Journal of Marketing*, 44 (Summer), 52–64.
20. Kresch, Sandra D. (1983), "The Impact of Consumer Trends on Corporate Strategy," *Journal of Business Strategy*, 3 (Winter), 21–28.
21. Paraphrased from the writings of Dean Roscoe Pound of the Harvard Law School in his comments on justice. See also Corley, Robert N., O. Lee Reed, and Peter J. Shedd (1993), *The Legal and Regulatory Environment of Business*, New York, NY: McGraw-Hill.
22. For a detailed discussion of the politics of exchange, refer to Buchanan, James M., and Gordon Tullock (1971), The *Calculus of Consent: Logical Foundations of Constitutional Democracy*, Ann Arbor, MI: University of Michigan Press.
23. Reve, Torger, and Louis W. Stern (1979), "Interorganizational Relations in Marketing Channels," *Academy of Management Review*, 4 (July), 405–16.
24. Pfeffer, J., and G. R. Salaick (1978), *The External Control of Organizations*, New York, NY: Harper & Row, 23.

chapter

6

Channel Relationships in the Global Village

Learning Objectives

After reading this chapter, you should be able to:

- Discuss how environmental uncertainty impacts global channel strategies.
- Discuss the major factors that underlie the selection of international exchange partners.
- Distinguish among multinational, global, and transnational channel relationships.
- Recall the *indirect* methods of developing international exchange relationships.
- Recall the *direct* methods of developing international exchange relationships.
- Explain the connection between the macroenvironment and international channel strategy.
- Describe the process of initiating international channel relationships.

Courtesy Nestle S.A.

Confectioners (candy makers), be they large or small, domestic or international, are finding it increasingly necessary to develop global e-business channels to remain competitive in both on- and offline settings. The world of candy is a surprisingly tough place to play catch-up in because it changes so quickly. Unless confectioners have the right people or technology in place to move globally when the opportunity arises, opportunities can be lost forever.

Swiss-based Nestlé's products have been available online for several years, but it was not until the end of 1999 that the firm opted to form an international team to lead its e-business efforts. The firm developed a four-part international distribution strategy. First, Nestlé, in its own words, sought to "make [its] products available wherever, whenever, and however."[1] Second, Nestlé plans to use the Net to build the relationship between itself and its customers. In doing so, the firm is purposefully seeking "more of a two-way conversation (with its customers), and less of a one-way conversation." The final two components of Nestlé global distribution strategy are to achieve greater efficiencies in its international distribution channels and to develop new global opportunities. Challenges remain, but the future of e-business as a means of entering international markets appears bright.

Nestlé, of course, is best known for the quality and taste of its chocolates. While just about everyone views chocolate as one of life's most reliable pleasures, our individual tastes and preferences for chocolate remain just that—highly individual. This is one reason why it would be virtually impossible for a single chocolatier to satisfy all consumer tastes. Designing an international channel strategy that takes into account the richness of diversity of the global marketplace is, at times, likely to be equally challenging.

* * * *

Several analogies regarding how best to develop and maintain channel relationships in the global village can be derived from our insights about chocolate. The essential nature of chocolate itself offers several useful lessons, among them the facts that:

- **The global village involves more than meets the eye.** A chocolate's shape and design give little insight into the exact nature of its filling. Delightful external appearances by no means guarantee a satisfying taste experience. International exchange relationships are the same way. Developing relationships with exchange partners in other countries can often lead to a bittersweet journey, as well.
- **The global environment is tempting.** Different channel members are likely to be tempted by different, but all apparently attractive, international marketing opportunities. Unfortunately, many such opportunities prove more bitter than sweet.
- **The global environment is full of uncertainty.** When one samples a new bonbon for the first time, one is taking a risk. The unknown filling can be compared to the risky market that firms enter when they first develop international channel relationships.

Perhaps the one thing chocolate aficionados agree on is that tastes and preferences for chocolates are open to personal interpretation. In this chapter, we examine how channel members in all industries confront different tastes and preferences in the global marketplace. First, we consider the reasons for entering into international exchange relationships at all. Next, we explain the various types of international exchange relationships and the various methods of entry. Then, we explore the interface between international marketing channels and their macroenvironment. After all the factors are in place, we answer the question, How does one select an international exchange partner?

Reasons for International Exchange Relationships

The chocolate confectionery industry features four major international competitors: Nestlé, Hershey's, M&M Mars, and Jacobs and Suchard. Each firm follows a distinctive strategy in its development of international exchange relationships. For instance, M&M Mars and Jacobs and Suchard each have just a few production facilities around the world. Both companies remain highly centralized. Nestlé, on the other hand, is famous for its ability to strike a balance between the need for central coordination and subsidiaries' desires for local autonomy. Considerations of the nature of market and competitive factors clearly are driving forces behind each chocolatier's international channel strategy. Other factors are also critical to global success. Several of these factors are discussed in Channel Surfing 6.1.

The chocolate confectionery industry has frequently provided a setting for the development of international marketing channels. International marketing channels are developed for many reasons, including facilitating market entry, boosting market share, introducing new products, improving service performance, and responding to shifting market conditions. Let's look at each of these reasons in detail.

Channel Surfing 6.1

What Winning Takes in a Global Marketplace

Just a few years back, manufacturing executives were preoccupied with eliminating direct labor costs, integrating channels systems with other business functions, and pursuing sustainable competitive advantages. Quality was important, but nevertheless eclipsed by other bases of competition. The global landscape also differed radically. The Toyota production system, for example, dominated world-class manufacturing. Japanese business practices were the envy of the world. The overseas fate of U.S. manufacturers seemed uncertain.

Times have changed. Globalization and rapid technological change have rewritten the rules of global competition. In contrast to the recent past, technology is now affordable and abundant, while skilled technical workers are in short supply. The widespread availability of information and Internet technology is enabling niche channel players to "leap" traditionally cost-prohibitive infrastructure barriers and assert themselves globally. Advances in information technology and telecommunications are accelerating productivity and supply chain integration—distribution bottlenecks are as feared today as bottlenecks in production were during the 1980s. The rising sophistication and expectations of consumers around the world have elevated the importance of coordinating marketing, promotional, distribution, and production efforts.

What are the implications of these for international marketers? It means the game has changed. Since 1900, the production sector has passed through two distinct phases. The first phrase—the "Mass Assembly Era"—was based on the need to develop economies of scale. This led to the "Quality Era" in the 1980s, which reoriented businesses toward continuous process improvements and the elimination of waste.

The Quality Era is clearly evolving into what we are calling the "Era of the Virtual Global Consumer." Customers around the world are deciding what, when, where, and how they will acquire and use goods and services. Customers have virtual access through cyberspace markets to more goods and services then ever before. They are now using "Smart" systems to help them make informed, personalized choices. Customers are now exercising the bargaining leverage to influence price—think Priceline.com. And with instant telecommunications and overnight delivery systems that transcend traditional borders, typical global constraints, like time and distance, are rapidly evaporating. As a result, customers are demanding their products in "zero time."

And you know what? The most successful global competitors will be the ones who provide it.

Points to Ponder

- What key success factors do you think will emerge in the global marketplace during the next few years?

Facilitating Market Entry

Many companies develop international exchange relationships to accelerate and/or ease entry into new markets. On a per-capita basis, Americans consume less candy now than ever before. As health-conscious baby boomers limit their children's candy consumption, the confectionery industry is being forced to explore new markets. Consider the recent actions of Nestlé. The reasoning behind the name change of Nestlé's Quick chocolate flavoring (which we all grew up with) to internationally familiar "NesQuick" became clearer after the planned launch in the United States of NesQuick cereal, long popular in Europe. Nestlé granted cereal maker General Mills licensing rights for U.S. distribution, and thus instantly gained broader market entry. The Nestlé name, by the way, continues to be prominently flagged on package fronts.[2]

"I'm still waiting for my shipment," the African tribesman might report. The diffusion of technology spans the globe, enabling real-time monitoring of transactions between channel members.

The Stock Market

Boosting Market Share

United Kingdom food giant Cadbury Schweppes PLC—its U.S. confectionery operations are now a Hershey's subsidiary—acquired the Spanish firm, Industrias Dulciora SA. Cadbury immediately became the second-largest manufacturer in the Spanish confectionery market. Around the same time, Cadbury also purchased Bouquet D'Or, a French specialty chocolates company. Cadbury's existing distribution arms in Spain and France were further strengthened through this pair of brand acquisitions. Because of their close relationships with Cadbury, these transactions also provided an inroad for Hershey's to improve its own distribution of chocolate goods in the European market.[3] As a result, both Cadbury and Hershey's were able to grab market share while gaining synergistic advantage.

Introducing New Products through Existing Channels

M&M Mars, maker of Mars Bars and Snickers, has entered an international channel arrangement with an Austrian firm, Master Foods. Despite its annual sales volumes of over $11 billion, M&M Mars had never competed in the specialty chocolates business. But in combination with Master Foods, Mars has developed a super-premium line of chocolates called Maogany. Mars's existing distribution channels will eventually permit Maogany to be marketed across Europe.

Improving Service Performance

Although they continued to eat them, stale Turkish chocolates were not really satisfying Russian customers' palates. In response, Mars developed distributor relationships in Russia to bring fresh chocolates to that lucrative market. Their Snickers bar has since become a Russian favorite. Mars took a chance to build for the future and it paid off. In a huge country with a limited infrastructure, Mars has managed to keep retailers stocked with what has emerged as a Western status symbol.[4]

Responding and Adapting to Shifting Market Conditions

Significant worldwide sugar shortages during World War II might have literally blown Hershey's right out of business. But Hershey's overcame the ill effects of these shifting market conditions by securing new suppliers in Cuba. Entering the Cuban market was itself a risky venture. Fortunately, Hershey was able to sell its plantation holdings in the late 1950s—at a profit—on the eve of Fidel Castro's nationalization of U.S.-held assets.

There are other reasons for pursuing international channel relationships. For instance, channel members can also seek new technologies, more stable currencies, or greater sales volume through their entry into international exchange relationships. Other companies enter international relationships to block the entry of foreign competitors into their own markets. For example, Armstrong World Industries, Inc., controls about 9 percent of the U.S. flooring industry. Faced with increased competition from flooring imports, Armstrong is partnering with Austria-based F. Eggert Company to introduce lower-priced synthetic flooring. The Armstrong-Eggert alliance hopes to fend off increasing competition for flooring products in the U.S. market.[5] As U.S. domestic markets become increasingly competitive and saturated, many American channel members will have to seek out new market opportunities overseas.

Typology of International Exchange Relationships

Regardless of how they are classified, the economic impact of international relationships is indisputable. As shown in Exhibit 6.1, billions of dollars are involved. The sheer size of U.S. international transactions has increased by nearly 300 percent in the last 20 years. These international economic activities are certainly not limited to U.S.-based channel members. Unprecedented numbers of firms throughout the world are engaged in the export or import of goods. The ways in which exchange relationships develop across the world are numerous and diverse. Attempts to categorize this vast array of international channel activity are therefore difficult. For the purposes of our discussion, however, we will divide international exchange relationships into three general categories: multinational, global, and transnational. These are summarized in Exhibit 6.2.

Before we discuss each of these exchange relationship types, we need to clarify a few terms.

The term *international* merely suggests something is occurring between nations. Thus, as a term, international fails to fully capture the diversity actually present within international exchange relationships.

Exhibit 6.1

Top 50 purchasers of U.S. exports in 1999 (Last updated July 27, 2000. In millions of dollars.)

Country	1991	1992	1993	1994	1995	1996	1997	1998	1999
Canada	85,150	90,594	100,444	114,439	127,226	134,210	151,767	156,603	166,600
Mexico	33,277	40,592	41,581	50,844	46,292	56,792	71,388	78,773	86,909
Japan	48,125	47,813	47,891	53,488	64,343	67,607	65,549	57,831	57,466
U.K.	22,046	22,800	26,438	26,900	28,857	30,963	36,425	39,058	38,407
Germany	21,302	21,249	18,932	19,229	22,394	23,495	24,458	26,657	26,800
Korea	15,505	14,639	14,782	18,025	25,380	26,621	25,046	16,486	22,958
The Netherlands	13,511	13,752	12,839	13,582	16,558	16,663	19,827	18,978	19,437
Taiwan	13,182	15,250	16,168	17,109	19,290	18,460	20,366	18,165	19,131
France	15,345	14,593	13,267	13,619	14,245	14,456	15,965	17,729	18,877
Singapore	8,804	9,626	11,678	13,020	15,333	16,720	17,696	15,694	16,247
Belgium/Luxemb.	10,789	10,047	9,439	11,168	12,840	12,774	14,132	14,524	13,365
Brazil	6,148	5,751	6,058	8,102	11,439	12,718	15,915	15,142	13,203
China	6,278	7,418	8,763	9,282	11,754	11,993	12,862	14,241	13,111
Hong Kong	8,137	9,077	9,874	11,441	14,231	13,966	15,117	12,925	12,652
Australia	8,404	8,876	8,276	9,781	10,789	12,008	12,063	11,918	11,818
Italy	8,570	8,721	6,464	7,183	8,862	8,797	8,995	8,991	10,091
Malaysia	3,900	4,363	6,064	6,969	8,816	8,546	10,780	8,957	9,060
Switzerland	5,557	4,540	6,806	5,624	6,227	8,373	8,307	7,247	8,371
Saudi Arabia	6,557	7,167	6,661	6,013	6,155	7,311	8,438	10,520	7,912
Israel	3,911	4,077	4,429	4,994	5,621	6,012	5,995	6,983	7,691
Philippines	2,265	2,759	3,529	3,886	5,295	6,142	7,417	6,737	7,222
Ireland	2,681	2,862	2,728	3,419	4,109	3,669	4,642	5,647	6,384
Spain	5,474	5,537	4,168	4,622	5,526	5,500	5,539	5,454	6,133
Venezuela	4,656	5,444	4,590	4,039	4,640	4,749	6,602	6,516	5,354
Thailand	3,753	3,989	3,766	4,865	6,665	7,198	7,349	5,239	4,985
Argentina	2,045	3,223	3,776	4,462	4,189	4,517	5,810	5,886	4,950
Sweden	3,287	2,845	2,354	2,518	3,080	3,431	3,314	3,822	4,251
Domin. Rep.	1,743	2,100	2,350	2,799	3,015	3,191	3,924	3,944	4,100
India	1,999	1,917	2,778	2,294	3,296	3,328	3,608	3,564	3,688
Colombia	1,952	3,286	3,235	4,064	4,624	4,714	5,197	4,816	3,560
Turkey	2,467	2,735	3,429	2,752	2,768	2,847	3,540	3,506	3,217
Chile	1,839	2,466	2,599	2,774	3,615	4,140	4,368	3,979	3,078
Egypt	2,720	3,088	2,768	2,855	2,985	3,153	3,835	3,059	3,001
United Arab Emirates	1,455	1,553	1,811	1,599	2,006	2,533	2,607	2,366	2,708
Austria	1,056	1,256	1,326	1,372	2,017	2,010	2,075	2,143	2,588
Rep. of S. Africa	2,113	2,434	2,188	2,172	2,751	3,112	2,997	3,628	2,586
Costa Rica	1,034	1,357	1,542	1,870	1,736	1,816	2,024	2,297	2,381
Honduras	625	811	899	1,012	1,279	1,643	2,019	2,318	2,370
Russia NA	2,112	2,970	2,578	2,823	3,346	3,365	3,553	2,060	
Indonesia	1,891	2,779	2,770	2,809	3,360	3,977	4,522	2,299	2,038
New Zealand	1,007	1,307	1,249	1,508	1,691	1,729	1,962	1,887	1,923

EXHIBIT 6.1
(continued)

Country	*1991*	*1992*	*1993*	*1994*	*1995*	*1996*	*1997*	*1998*	*1999*
Guatemala	945	1,205	1,312	1,352	1,647	1,566	1,730	1,938	1,812
Panama	978	1,103	1,187	1,277	1,390	1,381	1,536	1,753	1,742
Denmark	1,574	1,473	1,092	1,215	1,518	1,731	1,757	1,874	1,726
Peru	840	1,005	1,072	1,408	1,775	1,774	1,953	2,063	1,697
Finland	952	785	848	1,068	1,250	2,439	1,741	1,915	1,669
El Salvador	534	742	873	931	1,111	1,075	1,400	1,514	1,519
Norway	1,489	1,279	1,212	1,267	1,293	1,559	1,721	1,709	1,439
Jamaica	961	938	1,116	1,066	1,420	1,491	1,417	1,304	1,293
Portugal	792	1,025	727	1,054	898	961	954	888	1,092

EXHIBIT 6.2
Typology of global exchange relationships

	Market Orientation	*Channel Domain*	*Relationship Orientation*
Multinational	International	Prespecified national boundaries	Firm-to-firm partnership: based on market segments
Transnational	Regional	Flexible transcends national boundaries	Nodal partnership: based on regionalization
Global	Global	Unlimited transcends regional boundaries	Channel network: based on a boundaryless market

The term *multinational corporation (MNC)* is usually used to describe firms operating in different countries, yet there is no agreement as to what a multinational corporation really is. Three criteria have been proposed in the identification and characterization of MNCs. Under the first, known as the Structural Criterion, a multinational corporation is described as any firm conducting business in more than one country. This criterion is based on the firm's channel structure. A firm owned and operated by people from many countries can also be labeled as an MNC.

The second criterion, known as the Performance Criterion, is based on the consequences of a firm's international practices. The Performance Criterion defines an MNC on the basis of its asset holdings, employment base, net sales, and/or profitability in a foreign country. According to the Performance Criterion, once a company devotes a substantial percentage of available resources to overseas operations, it becomes an MNC.

Finally, under the Behavioral Criterion, any firm administered by top managers who think and behave internationally is an MNC. This criterion is the most difficult to apply in practice. The larger and more difficult question to answer, of course, is, How does a firm *think* and *act* globally?

Multinational Exchange Relationships

The first category of international channel activity may be referred to as multinational exchange relationships. In **multinational exchange relationships (MERs),** channel members view the global market as segments and employ distinctive marketing mix strategies for each segment. MERs occur between trading partners who operate in foreign markets as if they were local concerns. Such exchange partners can be identified by the extensive development of their assets in two or more countries. In MERs, the exchange partner based in the domestic country essentially acts as the local representative of its foreign partner.

MERs offer international marketers the opportunity to engage in domesticlike strategies executed in foreign markets. As exchange relationships, MERs are based on the ability of the exchange partner located in the target market (country) to effectively adapt and then respond to the environmental circumstances and opportunities prevailing in that market. The local exchange partner in an MER also provides the foreign partner with market experience and knowledge germane to that country or countries. The home-based partner is likely to be an exporting manufacturer. For instance, Cadbury Schweppes operates MERs in many of its markets.

Each MER is customized to satisfy the needs or special environmental circumstances in a single foreign country or market. To achieve such customization, MERs tend to be decentralized, with substantial autonomy given to the exchange partners operating in the local country. This means the foreign partner has less control over the local partner's operational activities. High levels of autonomy sometimes contribute to conflict in channel relationships. At other times, however, autonomy can alleviate conflict.

Regardless of the effects autonomy actually has on conflict, the degree of dependence among exchange partners in multinational exchange relationships is usually low. When dependence is low, dissatisfied partners find it easier to seek alternative channel relationships. Because MER channel strategies are typically based on small territories, it is normally easy to recruit new trading partners from nearby markets.

Cadbury Schweppes employs different strategies that are appropriate to the market being pursued. Naturally, Cadbury's product lines and promotions are adjusted to better meet the demands of particular markets—this is nothing more than a classic strategy involving market segmentation and product positioning, put into place in various foreign settings. But Cadbury also develops different types of exchange relationships in reaction to the demands of particular nations or regions. Depending on the nature of the particular foreign market, Cadbury will employ either a cooperative or competitive arrangement with companies such as Hershey's or Nestlé.

Conversely, in global exchange relationships, channel members see the world as one giant marketplace. Our attention now turns to global exchange relationships.

Global Exchange Relationships

GERs are responsible for a great deal of controversy. **Global exchange relationships (GERs)** are, by far, the most integrated of the international exchange relationships. Whereas MER channel members view the world market as segments, GER channel members view the world as one giant boundaryless marketplace. A GER is based on two or more channel members' mutual pursuit of a worldwide channel strategy that transcends national or regional boundaries. The perspective shared by GER channel members is something like this: One world, one market, one distribution mix.

GERs are the source of much controversy centering on their plausibility. Is it really possible to construct channel strategies that will prove workable throughout the world? This question is not easily resolved. Taken at face value, the notion of a global marketing strategy contradicts the cornerstone principle of market segmentation. However, by definition, GERs are not market-based, nor do they develop on the basis of markets. Instead, they involve strategic alliances and develop from the pursuit of these strategic alignments between channel partners. **Strategic alignments** exist when there is an agreement or shared consensus between the organizational visions and goals of exchange partners. Thus, entry into a GER ideally should result in a single vision shared among exchange partners.

GERs require the highest levels of integration—involving a pursuit of consolidation and synthesis—among exchange partners. By definition, synthesized channel strategies do not come from any individual member. Channel strategies are instead borne from the collective goals associated with the exchange relationship itself. Issues of centralization and control are immaterial.

Obviously, GERs are complex. They are likely to involve several exchange partners. Each exchange partner is expected to make a specialized contribution to the alliance. Therefore, a high level of autonomy usually exists across functional areas within the GER channel. In other words, one partner may perform the distribution function—with no outside interference or assistance. As a result, it is difficult to replace any exchange partner in a GER. Each exchange partner's contribution is highly valued because of that contribution's unique nature. The inclusion of each exchange partner in the strategic alliance is selective from the start. The story of Corning presented in Channel Surfing 6.2 illustrates this point.

Transnational Exchange Relationships

Transnational exchange relationships (TERs) fall between the MERs and GERs. Rather than engaging in country-by-country adaptation, TERs approach international relationships from a regional perspective. TERs employ channel strategies that have been tailored to the requirements of entire market regions. In comparison to MERs, TERs are characterized by greater centralization and fewer exchange partners. TERs should only be used when each regional market of interest constitutes a *reasonably* homogeneous market segment. Channel relationships can then be adjusted to conform to needs and requirements of that particular segment. For example, M&M Mars's launch of Maogany was not designed with any single country in mind. The Maogany line was aimed at the entire European market.

TERs are becoming increasingly important as new regional markets emerge. The European Union, for instance, comprises many diverse nations. The European Union aims to unify distribution practices throughout Europe. Similarly, the North American Free Trade Agreement (NAFTA) has established unencumbered distribution flows among the United States, Canada, and Mexico.

TERs are unique in several ways. While TERs involve fewer exchange partners than MERs, these partners are larger in scope. TER exchange relationships tend to be fairly consistent within a region. For example, Ford Motor Company has a host of distribution and

Channel Surfing 6.2

Corning: Reaching Out around the Globe

With the cost of developing new technologies and entering new markets so high, most companies simply cannot do it all by themselves. Joint ventures and alliances are now a matter of survival. Corning provides an example of this philosophy.

Since its first alliance—manufacturing corrugated boxes with Charles Rohm Co. in 1924—Corning has been involved in more than 48 joint ventures. These ventures have related to everything from the development of new television tubes to the manufacturing of fiber-optic cable and silicon breast implants. Corning has created well-known domestic alliances with companies such as Dow Chemical and Owens-Illinois, as well as overseas ventures in Japan, Germany, China, Korea, and India. While many of these international alliances have been horizontal rather than vertical in nature, the success of each turns in part on how relationships are initially planned and subsequently managed.

Corning currently has a 50-50 share or minority holding in more than 30 ventures in 15 countries. Earning contributions from these equity alliances accounted for more than 30 percent of Corning's net income in the last decade. Perhaps more importantly, Corning's alliances have expanded the company's reach and grasp, enabling Corning to leverage its research skills, develop new products, and enter new markets more quickly and with greater cost efficiency than if it had tried alone.

Corning understands that effective partnerships never develop simply from two sets of executives imposing their wills from the top down. Instead, success in partnering requires that the respective sets of counterpart middle managers get together and discuss what problems are likely to arise in the years ahead. Over the years, this carefully cultivated process has allowed Corning to consistently sidestep the kind of surprises that upset so many joint ventures.

Points to Ponder

- Why has Corning been so successful in its foreign ventures? Can you envision any emerging problems likely to be encountered by those firms, including Corning, that enter foreign joint ventures in the future? What are these problems? How would you recommend that firms attempt to overcome or avoid these problems?

Source: Adapted from Bonsignore, Michael R., James R. Houghton, and Charles F. Knight (1994), "Border Crossings," *Across the Board,* 31 (10), 41–46; and Anonymous (2000), "Corning Adds to Its Fibre Holdings," *Communications International,* 27 (3), 63–67.

supplier relationships in Australia. However, Ford treats the entire continent as a single region. No separate strategies have been developed for the Melbourne, Sydney, or Queensland metroplexes. TERs also tend to develop in highly integrated operations. Consequently, a high degree of dependency quickly emerges between firms engaged in TERs.

Our typology is not intended to capture the universe of exchange relationships that can develop in international marketing channels. The value of the typology is its illustration of how an international channel's macroenvironment impacts different types of international exchange relationships in different ways.

Direct and Indirect International Marketing Channels

Entry-level international exchange relationships can assume many forms. In broad terms, we can classify these entry modes into direct and indirect methods. A **direct marketing channel** is one in which the exchange partner takes a membership position in the home country or region. A *membership position* implies that the exchange partner actually becomes a player in the domestic economy. For example, Ford Motor Company's operations in Australia manage local production, distribution, and dealerships. Ford automobiles are manufactured and marketed locally, while Australia is also used as a distribution base for shipments to other regional markets, like New Zealand. There are several types of direct entry modes:

- **Local facility.** The local facility method involves the development of a company-based management team operating in the host country. The level of corporate involvement tends to vary greatly based on the industry, channel function, and market. This involvement may range from having a local manufacturing facility to simply having a domestic sales force. The host-country facility is usually controlled from a home-country location.
- **Marketing subsidiary.** In this mode, the channel member establishes a subsidiary company in the host country or region. The subsidiary then behaves as an essentially autonomous unit and tries to develop a strong local presence. Subsidiary operations in international channels often operate under a different name or different set of rules. The subsidiary's management is typically based in the host country.

  Subsidiaries offer a popular means of international market entry. VerticalNet spent 1998 and 1999 preaching its gospel across the United States, promising profits and efficiencies to all who would listen. More recently, the firm and many other B2B players have taken their messages to the streets of the world's second-largest economy: Japan. VerticalNet now boasts a new subsidiary, VerticalNet Kabushiki Kaisha, in Japan. VNKK is managed and run by Japanese technology experts.[6]
- **Foreign sales agents (FSAs).** Foreign sales agents are company designates that, for the most part, function as a sales and support staff for goods produced in home-country locations. FSAs do not take title to goods; instead, they operate fairly autonomously, arranging for the consummation of orders. In many cases, FSAs also are responsible for managing return goods and customer satisfaction. FSAs generally represent an entire portfolio of related products produced by several competing firms, and they alone shape the degree of representation afforded to each channel member's offering. Accordingly, FSAs have a great deal of power because they become local industry referents to customers.

The other major international entry mode involves **indirect marketing channels.** When indirect entry is used, the domestic channel member manages the distribution of products and/or services in a foreign target country or region through foreign designates. A *foreign designate* is any intermediary that contributes to the distribution of domestically produced goods through some foreign target market. Foreign designates are also responsible for ensuring local customer satisfaction. The most prevalent types of indirect entry modes are:

- **Export management companies (EMC).** Export management companies offer the services of a manufacturer's representative who specializes in cultivating international exchange relationships in particular locales. The manufacturer's representative is generally based in the country or region and has expertise and experience critical to the market of interest. A manufacturer's representative functions as a front person for the channel member. This individual essentially controls the company's position in the marketplace. As its designate, the EMC is charged with providing a domestic presence for the foreign channel member.

- **Piggybacks.** Piggybacks involve a joint effort at international market entry generally shared among several channel members. Piggybacking is a coordinated effort in which different exchange partners perform their own specialized channel functions in a foreign market. One channel member may provide logistics management and another inventory control, while still another provides customer service. The challenge lies in determining how best to coordinate the piggybacked functions in an international domain. The goal is to synchronize each function to ensure smooth channel flows. While they do not currently account for a large percentage of new foreign market entrants, piggybacks are increasing because of the growing influence of global alliances.
- **Foreign distributors.** Foreign distributors provide the most common way by which firms indirectly enter a foreign market. Here, an established domestically based distributor operating at the wholesale or retail level is contracted to develop and cultivate exchange relationships within the entry market. These distributors take title to goods, usually stock inventories, and provide local marketing activities. These marketing activities vary depending on the nature of the exchange relationship, but may include sales, sales support, and customer service. Foreign distributors are valuable because they provide an immediate market presence. Foreign distributors generally also have pre-existing customer contacts. The disadvantage is that distributors have control over the channel member's marketing efforts in the foreign country.
- **Trading companies.** Trading companies are large, international channel members that have a worldwide presence. Companies like Japan's Mitsubishi trade a wide variety of products across the world. What separates trading companies from other types of indirect marketing channels is the expanse of their market coverage. Trading companies engage in global distribution. They possess a great deal of international marketing expertise and can provide rapid entry into selected international markets.

Although we categorized international market entry modes into direct and indirect methods, do not assume that all channel members seeking foreign expansion are limited to one or the other broad entry option. Channel members may actually use several direct and indirect entry modes simultaneously in a single international market, depending on the level of market presence they wish to establish. Other methods for entering foreign markets such as licensing also exist, but lie beyond the scope of the present chapter. Exhibit 6.3 summarizes the direct and indirect international channel options.

Which entry mode is best? For any given firm the answer still lies in the extent to which that channel member is willing to delegate control and responsibility to its international

EXHIBIT 6.3
Indirect and direct market entry strategies

Activities Performed in Host Country	*Company's Involvement in Activities*	
	Indirect/Low	**Direct/High**
Marketing only	Indirect exporting	Direct exporting
Marketing and production	Contractual methods	Foreign direct investment

exchange partners. In international markets, there is also a need to adapt in the face of changing environmental circumstances.

Interface between International Marketing Channels and the Environment

The influence of the macroenvironment is especially strong in international channel settings. Why is this so? For one thing, the international environmental domain is much larger and more complex. For another, channel members face a far more heterogeneous set of environmental influences in international settings.

As we know, forecasts of the future are usually imperfect. For this reason, those involved in international channel relationships inevitably encounter unexpected changes in their environment. Kryptonite Corporation, an MNC that makes locks for bicycles, cars, and motorcycles, has established relationships with several foreign distributors. Kryptonite has managed these relationships successfully even in risky markets such as Venezuela and China. Peter Zane, Kryptonite's president, suggests the successful management of international exchange relationships depends on a "combination of analysis and gut feeling."[7]

No precise formula exists for dealing with the complexity of international channel relationships. However, it is still important to evaluate each category of environmental conditions before international channels management strategies are formulated. International environmental conditions can be classified into five categories: economic, political/legal, sociocultural, technological, and physical/geographical factors.

Economic Factors

The overall economic condition of the host country exercises a major influence on international channel relationships. Unforeseen changes in inflation, employment levels, monetary policy, or interest rates will each affect channel performance. Unfavorable economic trends can often lead to the termination of international relationships.

Conditions prevailing within a developing nation's economy influence its attractiveness as an international trading partner. Several emerging market economies in Southeast Asia have recently experienced massive exchange rate depreciations as a result of global trends. This, in turn, is reinforcing the absolute cost advantages of companies operating within such nations. These changes in exchange rates have proven especially important for U.S.-based TERs who employ regional-oriented channel strategies in Southeast Asia.

A variety of economic indicators impact channel relationships. In the international arena, some of the most important indicators are recessionary conditions, Gross Domestic Product (GDP), inflation levels, government spending and taxation, and currency availability.

Recessionary conditions usually uncover any underlying structural problems in an economy, such as overregulation. This was the case in Spain, where channel partners had to contend with overregulated service sectors, rigid labor markets, and powerful professional unions. General Motors' plant in Figueruelas, Spain, experienced a loss of competitiveness during much of the 1980s as its labor costs more than tripled. But once the Spanish economy's structural inefficiencies were uncovered by a recession, Spain's socialist government was able to enact several labor reform laws. MNCs were allowed more flexibility, and GM's Spanish operations soon turned a profit.[8]

A falling Gross Domestic Product (GDP) often serves as an indicator of the level of political risk. For example, a severe economic contraction in Russia proved disconcerting to MNC veteran Daimler-Benz AG, Germany's largest manufacturing group. Daimler-Benz then backed away from plans to expand into Russia. While there are opportunities for high returns on infrastructure contracts, the risks of social unrest, a military coup, or even war continue to make Russia a risky market in which to develop channel relationships.

In many developing countries, inflation often runs more than 100 percent annually. The world's ninth-largest economy, Brazil, is struggling against inflation—again. The International Monetary Fund (IMF) is trying to do something about it. The problem is that the economies of the bailout are shaky and, as a result, so are many aspects of Brazil's economy. Brazil's currency is overvalued by some 20 percent, and everyone knows it. The profits of many U.S. multinationals, which make more money in Brazil than in any other developing economy, may end up taking a hit.

But if you look hard enough, you can usually find an opportunity in every dark cloud. To stay ahead of such profit-eating trends, Ford Motor Company raises the prices on its vehicles throughout the year, as the currency is continually devalued. Apparently, however, consumer demand remains strong. Brazilian consumers increasingly view tangible assets like cars, whose real value rises with inflation, as worthy investments. So sales remain strong despite Ford's action.[9]

To bring inflation under control, governments sometimes resort to drastic measures such as wage and price controls. Such was the case with the Cruzado Plan implemented by the Brazilian government in the 1980s, or the wage and price freezes enacted in the United States by the Nixon administration in the early 1970s. History suggests that high inflation is often associated with political unrest in developing nations. Unfortunately, such trends frequently inhibit the types of channel investments that would partially relieve the inflation.

The level of government spending and taxation in the local country of interest should also be contemplated by those firms involved in or considering involvement in international channel relationships. Governments have been known to run large budget deficits. These deficits are basically financed by printing money on a need-to-have basis. Over time, such fiscal mismanagement promotes inflation that, as noted previously, further complicates exchange relations.

Even the largest corporations or strategic alliances will have little control over a nation's fiscal policies. Therefore, channel members should pursue any of several methods available for hedging against unfavorable fiscal policies in target nations. Richard Hall, a senior vice president in corporate risk management at MTB Bank, offers several recommendations for overcoming the negative consequences otherwise associated with unfavorable fiscal policies:[10]

- **Research currency histories.** Channel members should be aware of historical fluctuations in the currency of any country or region. American firms should not be swayed by U.S. dollar-only transaction terms. A currency exchange actually takes place in all international trade regardless of the type of currency used.
- **Establish a "walk-away" rationale.** Because profit margins are allocated among channel members, some prespecified criteria should be in place for deciding when to maintain or forsake an international exchange relationship. If profit margins fall

below a prespecified standard, the channel member should withdraw from the channel relationship. The impact of negative fiscal policies can often even be detrimental to channel relationships transpiring in other countries.

- **Develop flexible transaction structures.** Currencies are not the only options available for consummating transactions. For example, Osbon Medical Systems, a manufacturer of vacuum therapy devices for male impotency, cannot always rely on the value of a country's currency. Osbon willingly uses barter or merchandise exchanges to compensate distributors for returned goods in such situations.
- **Select experienced exchange partners.** Prospective exchange partners should demonstrate knowledge of or experience with the relevant economic environment. Why would anyone initiate a relationship with an exchange partner that possessed no specialized knowledge of the market area?

Finally, whether the host country is experiencing a trade surplus or deficit directly influences the amount of currency available for the exchange partners. In the course of conducting international business, each party to the exchange must possess some confidence in the flow of currencies or other transaction assets. If a country is running a trade deficit, its government is more likely to impose restrictions on foreign channel members. These restrictions will probably involve the repatriation of some profits. In effect, such restrictions impose higher tariffs on goods.

Political/Legal Factors

The extent to which a host nation's political/legal system promotes or represses direct foreign investment or ownership in its local economy dramatically influences international channel environments. Gus Tyler, a Senior Fellow at the Aspen Institute, maintains that economic globalization is leading to an imbalance of power between international and domestic marketing channels.[11] MERs, TERs, and GERs are gaining power at the expense of national governments as countries pit themselves against one another. Furthermore, nations have been known to compete against one another to obtain a particularly desirable MNC. These bidding wars often become so fierce that the economic welfare of the "winning" nation is diminished. At other times, international exchange relationships undermine domestic labor unions by moving operations to low-wage countries.

When the regulatory environment becomes uncomfortable for exchange partners, they can usually relocate to more favorable markets or select alternative channels of distribution. The U.S. mining industry provides an illustration. Jim Hill of Newmont Mining, contends that Peru, even with the threat of Shining Path guerrillas, is politically less risky than the United States. Why? Because environmental regulations and red tape have, on many occasions, delayed American mining activity for years. While domestic court proceedings grind on, U.S. mining companies are increasingly pursuing alternative venues and international exchange partners abroad.

The Crown Jewel Mine, a joint venture involving Battle Mountain, Inc., and Crown Resources Corporation, illustrates the effect of this red tape. The Crown Jewel Mine had to obtain 56 different permits from 32 agencies to begin its operations. The mine's cost of complying with U.S. regulatory requirements was a staggering $5 million—literally before the first spade was turned. An increasing number of U.S. mining companies are moving into Latin America in order to stay in business. Ironically, the big U.S. mining operations follow strict Environmental Protection Agency standards in all of their overseas operations.[12]

Many countries view foreign investment as a necessity for their economic advancement. These nations encourage foreign investment through tax incentives or by providing breaks on infrastructure investment costs. The view that foreign investment is good for most host countries' economies was substantiated by a study commissioned by Coca-Cola, Inc., which has had more than its share of bad press in China. In response to such skepticism, Coca-Cola, like many other high-visibility foreign brands in China, worked hard to persuade the government and marketplace alike that their presence is good for China. This effort culminated in a study researching the impact of Coke and its Chinese bottling partners on China. The numbers were eye-catchingly positive. Channel members who operate under such receptive conditions usually find it easier to coordinate their local exchange relationships.[13]

The view that foreign investment is usually good for the host country is widely held. What is less widely recognized is that the United States is viewed as an attractive foreign investment market by many foreign channel members. But one need only travel along major interstates (I-85) and (I-20) winding through South Carolina and Alabama, respectively, and see the huge, sparkling new Mercedes and BMW factories located along each to witness these views in play. Channel members operating in such nations usually find it easier to coordinate their exchange relationships.

In nations that have a historical basis for distrusting foreign corporations, attempts to restrict or curtail their involvement through regulations, punitive taxes, or outright expropriation are often initiated. Such was the case in India in the late 1970s, when Coca-Cola was required to share its secret formula with the local subsidiary if it wanted to continue doing business there. Coca-Cola refused and halted operations in India for almost 16 years.[14] With some 1 billion potential Indian Coke consumers, you know that decision had to hurt! But no matter how powerful the channel member is, it cannot always control the effects of punitive national policies.

Sociocultural Factors

The beliefs, values, and lifestyles that prevail within a target nation should be evaluated before an international marketing channel is developed. All exchange activity occurs within the boundaries of a social system. That social system reflects the norms and values native to the marketplace. Thus, all marketing channels are affected by the social system in which they do business.

Too often, channel members treat an international market as a single monolithic entity to be conquered. Doing so is usually a mistake. The fact is that virtually all countries' populations are made up of several different homogeneous consumer segments that jointly define the social system of that country. These consumer segments often differ from one another. International marketers must, therefore, deal with the norms and values associated with the different market segments within the countries they pursue. Because of the varying desires of these often different segments, international exchange relationships become rather complex.

To illustrate the effect of social systems, consider that Coca-Cola's Diet Coke product bears a different name in various parts of Europe. For example, in France, it is called *Coca-Cola Light.* While the term *diet* appeals to the health-conscious consumer movement in the United States, a diet evokes different images in Europe. There, *diet* has medicinal connotations. Any misinterpretation of the meaning associated with this simple concept could jeopardize the relationship between Coca-Cola and its consumers in France. This surprising inconsistency among U.S. and French consumers leads us to consider culture.

Culture is the overall shared meaning of individuals' beliefs, values, and customs and of individuals' interactions with their social system. This shared meaning allows members of the social system to feel unified as part of a larger whole. Culture helps members of any society define the appropriateness of their behaviors. It also simplifies behaviors by telling people what they can and cannot do. Remember, however, that individual consumers do not have to follow the behavioral instructions imposed by their culture. Culture has four basic functions:

- Culture provides a way to classify exchange partners' behaviors and events.
- It provides appropriate standards of behavior among exchange partners.
- It prioritizes standards of conduct in exchange relationships.
- Lastly, culture legitimizes the use of certain exchange behaviors, while condemning the use of other exchange behaviors.

Culture can be viewed as both the *lens* and the *blueprint.* The lens analogy implies that culture is a viewfinder through which all phenomena are seen. Culture influences how various symbols will be interpreted and understood by its members. In turn, the blueprint analogy points toward the connection that exists between culturally approved social activity and productivity. To successfully develop international relationships, prospective exchange partners must adapt to the culture of their new channel.

By being sensitive to these socially and culturally based differences in international marketplaces, exchange partners have a better chance to cultivate long-term relationships. Moreover, exchange partners enhance the efficiency with which they utilize the local workforce by eliminating the ill will that would otherwise result if local customs and norms were disregarded. Foreign markets can then be more easily penetrated.

For instance, despite NAFTA's presence, the clash between U.S. and Mexican cultures continues. FedEx found out the hard way about cultural differences when it opened operations in Mexico. In a culture where punctuality is not emphasized and *mañana* reigns supreme, FedEx was delivering over 20 percent of its packages late. Mexican attitudes toward time and the delivery of guaranteed services were quite different from those north of the border. FedEx had to adapt its management style to fit the local environment. The nature of the culture in which Mexican workers are raised essentially requires that managers first develop personal relationships with them in order for things to run smoothly. By pursuing this seemingly simple tack, and using tact, FedEx reduced the number of late deliveries to less than 1 percent.

International exchange partners who fail to adapt to local sociocultural environments also will experience higher rates of turnover and burnout among international employees.[15] Even the largest domestic corporations sometimes underestimate the potential cultural problems of globalization.

Technological Factors

Technological advances can lead to a more efficient use of raw materials, improved manufacturing productivity, and improved product quality. That's not to mention the critically important benefit of improved communications among channel members. Such advances force international exchange partners to monitor competitive technologies. Naturally, the rate at which new technology is introduced and adopted will differ across markets. Innovations diffuse more rapidly through the relevant social system in some nations and regions than in others.

For example, the acceptance of innovations in the emerging economies of Eastern Europe has been much slower than was the case in the many emerging economies in Southeast Asia. The difference is partially due to the absence of a sophisticated infrastructure to support the spread of new technologies throughout the Eastern European region. The slower adoptions may also be linked to the peculiarities of Eastern Europe's sociocultural environment, which was dominated by the Soviet Union for nearly 50 years.

The adoption of new technologies is not stagnant. As Channel Surfing 6.3 illustrates, technological innovations impact channel strategy. It wasn't too long ago that China produced nearly no televisions, while the United States produced many brands of televisions. Today, the opposite is true: the United States does not have a single television manufacturer, and China

Channel Surfing 6.3

Technology's Impact on the New Economy: It's Elementary, My Dear Watson

In the 1940s Thomas Watson, then chairman of IBM, infamously predicted that the world market for computers should top out at around five. That is, 5 computers! Beyond that, he simply did not see any further commercial possibilities. Today, there are more than 300 million active computers in the world, so Mr. Watson's conjecture was a little off. But by how much?

In the developed world, global consumers take it for granted that they will grow richer year by year. Yet for most of human history, world output grew at an indecipherably small rate. It was not until the late 18th century that growth became measurable, thanks largely to a spurt in technological innovation. Since then, the world has experienced four waves of innovation. First, there was the Industrial Revolution, fueled by steam power, followed by the Railroad Age. The third revolution was powered by electric power and the automobile. The fourth—well, you're living in the midst of it. Experts have labeled it the Information Age—powered by you-know-what.

People are often scared of technological change. Yet the world of global distribution would be a much scarier place without it. All economies and all organizations have limited resources of capital and labor. Without improving ways to use those resources, growth always soon runs out of steam.

In the new economy, just how quickly is technology changing? One way to gauge this change is the rate of decline in the cost of the new technology, which continues to accelerate. In addition to this cost decline, four other noteworthy characteristics of technology and its effects on global channels management are apparent. They are: (1) Technology is pervasive. (2) By increasing the accessibility of critical information, technology helps global channels work more efficiently. (3) Technology itself speeds up other channels innovations, reducing the time it takes to develop and introduce new products and managerial practices. (4) Technology truly is global.

Points to Ponder

- What forms do you think the next wave of paradigm-shifting technologies will take?
- Describe the nature of 2010's economy.

is among the world's biggest television producers. China is similarly competing in the computer circuitry industry—a market that was long dominated by neighboring Taiwan. How did China catapult into the computer electronics global market? With a little help from its friends, that's how. Companies in China have partnered with U.S. and other Western firms to learn new technologies.

Indeed, China is now among the world's fastest-growing consumer markets. India and China—two of the oldest civilizations on earth—are embracing market reforms, and both countries are becoming major manufacturing competitors in the global market. Each country's growth is fueled by technology-sharing with such U.S. giants as Cisco and i2 technologies.[16] Motorola, for instance, is among the market leaders in China's growing pagers and cellular telephones market. It has strengthened its relationship with Chinese customers by forming a joint venture with Panda Electronics Group Co., one of China's largest electronics concerns. Together, Motorola and Panda will produce over 100,000 units for distribution in the fast-growing computer market. Motorola provided the expertise (and its jointly developed PowerPC chip) to the venture. Panda is responsible for the distribution of the personal computers into China's retail channels.[17]

Technological advancements may also be adopted in different *ways* by different cultures. While Japan openly embraced the advent of automated teller machines (ATMs), it wasn't at all receptive to the Western idea of more convenient banking. Japanese ATMs do not offer 24-hour banking. In fact, Japanese ATMs close at 7:00 P.M. because the Ministry of Finance fears that 24-hour banking would contribute to unhealthy spending habits.

This region's seaports often compete directly with America's West Coast ports. For example, the Port of Nadhodka has emerged as a bulk cargo powerhouse operating in the Russian Far East. This otherwise desolate area is exploiting its geographic proximity to the Pacific Rim nations to build a differential advantage through its channel of distribution.

In some ways, however, natural physical and geographic advantages are diminishing with the emergence of new distribution technologies.[18] A country or region's size is no longer so critical, either. For instance, the small Benelux region (Belgium, The Netherlands, and Luxembourg) dominates European transportation. Two-thirds of all goods shipped transnationally inside European borders during recent years have passed through the Benelux region. The differential distribution advantage enjoyed by Benelux is based on its central location, excellent roads and ports, and transportation savvy. But, above all, Benelux's advantage is predicated on its ability to develop friendly relationships.

Selecting International Exchange Partners

The process by which international partners are chosen warrants special attention. International relationships are particularly difficult to manage successfully because of the macroenvironments's complex nature. This makes channel member selection even more important. The overriding goal in selecting international exchange partners should be to identify opportunities to develop and secure mutually strategic alignments. If prospective partners are pursuing goals that conflict with one another, there will be little opportunity for the relationship to flourish. Indeed, the quality of the channel relationship is the most important factor affecting the success with which new foreign markets can be entered.[19]

Selecting the wrong channel partner invariably proves costly. In many instances, the local exchange partner is held accountable for performance in the target marketplace. Each firm taking part in an exchange relationship wields substantial power because of the need for someone to have local market expertise. So even the less powerful partner—usually operating in the target country—is still influential. To illustrate, in recent years PepsiCo discontinued its relationship with Perrier, which had been charged with handling the distribution of PepsiCo products in France. When PepsiCo's market share declined, they laid much of the blame at the feet of Perrier.[20] Although this relationship had spanned more than two decades, it was summarily terminated. Perrier is now part of Nestlé, which is counting on Perrier to help improve its market position in France and other European nations. And, yes, Perrier now competes directly with PepsiCo.

Regardless of the care taken, the extraordinarily dynamic nature of international channel environments guarantees that there is no way to ensure that firms will successfully select their partners in international marketing channels. In most instances, significant environmental circumstances lie beyond the control of either partner. The process of selection, then, may be best approached as a refinement process with multiple decisions.

Several basic criteria need to be evaluated when international partnerships are being initiated. We call these factors the *Five Cs:* Costs, Coordination, Coverage, Control, and Cooperation. The Five Cs are useful for several reasons. First, they are easily identifiable—most exchange partners have access to this information in some form. Second, these factors are applicable across all countries or regions. Finally, firms can make quantitative assessments of each "C" prior to entering any international exchange relationship.

Costs

What costs are associated with the selection of a particular exchange partner? Three types are germane. The first is **initial costs,** which involve those outlays needed to set up the marketing channel. These outlays include the expenses of identifying and initiating communications and negotiation with prospective exchange partners.

Preservation costs are the expenses of maintaining an exchange relationship. They include the disbursements necessary to provide salespeople, promotional materials, and accounting systems, as well as to cover travel expenses. Preservation costs also include the allocation of profit margins between the exchange partners. Preservation costs are often difficult to estimate. For example, new regulations, technological changes, or the entry of new competitors would significantly influence preservation costs.

The third major consideration is **logistics costs.** Logistics costs reflect the expenses related to transporting goods and managing inventories. Several questions must be answered to calculate logistics costs. These include: Who will be responsible for stocking inventories? Who receives returned goods? Who is responsible for making transportation arrangements?

Coordination

This factor requires that prospective partners estimate how each of the necessary marketing functions (i.e., pricing, promoting, distributing, negotiating, etc.) will be allocated among the channel participants. A preliminary description of which partner will perform what channel function(s) should be derived for each potential exchange partner. This preliminary description draws heavily on the expected competencies that each firm brings to the international marketing channel. While a firm's distinctive competencies are usually easily identifiable, each partner's competencies *relative* to the other partners can prove difficult to assess without prior experience. It would not be unusual for a prospective exchange partner to provide hard evidence of his or her past or current competencies.

Considerations of coordination also involve projecting how well the new exchange partner will fit within an existing channel system. International exchange relationships often involve *networks* of exchange partners. It is imperative that members of these networks be able to work well with one another.

Coverage

The territorial coverage that a prospective exchange partner can comfortably handle should be determined and agreed upon. Will a single exchange partner provide sufficient coverage for the targeted market? Or, are several exchange partners required? This criterion is not as easily evaluated as it might seem. Too many international exchange relationships are based on inappropriately loose assumptions about the actual size of the target market. Realistic assessments of how much effort will be required by each exchange partner to facilitate customer satisfaction, while achieving reasonable profits, should be made.

The existence of special environmental circumstances that may inhibit a new exchange partner's ability to successfully service a trading area is another coverage issue that merits attention. For example, channel ownership is regulated in many parts of Southeast Asia. In Malaysia, a local distributor must have partial Malay ownership in order to operate. The Malaysian constitution has designated Malays as the chosen people, and they are given preferred status. On the other hand, neighboring Singapore requires no Malay ownership in its businesses. Thus, one might expect to find less-restrictive distributors available from countries contiguous to Malaysia than in Malaysia itself.

Control

Exchange partners must negotiate with one another to determine who will control key channel resources. When an exchange partner demands an inappropriately high level of control in certain areas, the chances for cultivating a long-term relationship are dampened. The exchange partner targeted by such control efforts is likely to feel less secure and optimistic. Feelings of vulnerability frequently exist within international exchange relationships anyway because the exporting partner likely already feels a sense of dependency.

It is difficult to forecast precisely how power will be exercised in international channels. Exchange partners may review their prospect's history to assess the prospective firm's tendency to pursue control over channel relations. But questions such as, What is the average length of this prospect's current and past exchange relationships? or Why did its previous relationships fail? should be answered. This research should provide valuable insight into how the prospect is likely to exercise power in future exchange relationships.

Cooperation

Finally, issues of cooperation are an important concern in the selection process, although they may likewise prove difficult to assess. From the early stages of negotiation, potential exchange partners receive cues from one another. These cues can help indicate the degree to which a prospect will be flexible and cooperative in the pursuit of mutually satisfying transaction terms. One such cue may be reflected in a sixth "C," namely, the level of commitment the prospective channel partner has toward the proposed relationship. A U.S. multinational corporation may ultimately select Firm A rather than Firm B as an international partner because Firm A is more committed to the internationalization process. Such commitment also suggests Firm A is more likely to be cooperative. Cooperation is essential because its presence suggests an opportunity to attain strategic alignment in the prospective relationship.

International Exchange Relationships: Successes and Failures

By now, you understand the complexity of successfully developing and maintaining international exchange relationships. International exchange can occur at any channel level and in a wide variety of modes. Still, there is one overriding concern at all channel levels: the ability of the channel member to manage dynamic environmental factors. Failures in international relationships usually result from one or more of the following factors:

- Differing expectations among exchange partners
- Slow reactions to changing market conditions
- Clashes in exchange partners' corporate cultures
- Prematurely developed international exchange relationships

The only thing known for sure about international exchange relationships is that their numbers are increasing rapidly. While international exchange relationships are risky and often difficult to administer, they also provide opportunities or advantages to those firms that elect to participate in them. Among other attributes, international exchange relationships can help channel partners:

- Address shortfalls in how a market's needs and wants are being satisfied by current entrants
- Optimize their manufacturing and distribution capabilities
- Share the risks associated with entering new markets
- Facilitate new product innovation
- Gain and then exploit economies of scale
- Extend the market scope of their existing operations

We close this chapter with brief discussions of several successful and less successful international exchange features.

Wal-Mart: The All-American Retailer?

Guess again. Wal-Mart's nearly $25 billion international division has entered a new phase of development that includes a new and restructured senior management team intent on changing how decisions are made, how information is shared, and how merchandise is bought. The retailer plans to stay the course with everyday low prices and "rollback" promotions.

Wal-Mart's international focus is fundamentally similar to that used so successfully in the United States. They want to continue to work with local suppliers, form partnerships, and cooperatively work out all the supply chain and cost issues. In other words, they are seeking the same competitive advantages originally sought in Bentonville, Arkansas. And why not?

What is different is Wal-Mart's new management structure, which focuses on country-specific leadership. Most important decisions relating to customer service are being made in-country rather than waiting for corporate approval back in the states. Wal-Mart, for one, has bought into the idea of using local management talent and insights.[21]

At Sea in an Ocean of Beer

The Carlsberg Group is the world's seventh-largest brewer. It features some of beer's best brands, not only Carlsberg and Tuborg but others widely recognized outside the U.S. market. But the brands aren't growing, and the company has fallen below 3.5 percent world market share. Meanwhile, other global players like Heineken, Interbrew, and Anheuser have been rapidly expanding their market slices.

What has gone wrong? Experts are suggesting that it is Carlsberg's decision to focus domestically while the world's other big brewers have gone unabashedly global. Several years ago, for example, Belgium's Interbrew expanded into the key North American market by purchasing Canada's Labatt (which had handled Carlsberg's modest distribution in the United States). Heineken, too, invested heavily in a U.S. distribution beachhead.

Of course, these and other events have made the Carlsberg beer operation a tasty target for a global merger or purchase. That would be ironic. You see, the company has long seen itself not just as a moneymaker for its shareholders but also as a standard-bearer for Danish culture. A mission statement carved in stone over the famous Carlsberg elephant reads: *Laboremus pro partria* (we work for our country). These days, though, the beer trade is unsentimentally global.[22]

Anheuser-Busch (AB) has, by contrast, been aggressively global. It strengthened its position in Mexico by entering an international exchange agreement with Grupo Modelo SA, Mexico's largest brewer and bottler of Corona beer. The companies have exchanged representatives on each other's boards. AB didn't stop there. Because the U.S. beer market is saturated, it is pursuing similar arrangements in other countries, such as Japan. Its international alliance with Kirin Brewery allowed Budweiser to reposition itself as one of the kings of beer in Japan. AB has focused less on the traditional adversarial marketing wars in the United States and more on global distribution strategies and the pursuit of amicable relationships with leading brewers in other countries.[23]

GloboCop

Most U.S. companies say they want to do business globally, regardless of what troubles may arise. But Armor Holdings Co. is one of the few that *look* for trouble abroad, pursuing markets wherever there's unrest. Almost one-third of its sales come from protecting oil companies operating in Wild West–like drilling markets such as Russia, Uganda, and Colombia, where Armor Holdings provides on-site and local security. When oil workers go into difficult places, Armor Holdings goes with them, in a power-packed example of direct entry into global marketplaces. Armor does not depend exclusively on international sales; they sell armor and riot gear to state and local police forces throughout the United States.[24]

International versus Domestic Channel Relationships: Some Perspective

Whether they are performed/made for an international or domestic market, marketing channel tasks and management decisions remain the same. Product positioning, pricing, and promotional and distribution programs must be developed in either setting. The same knowledge- and experience-based expertise is required for success in both market settings. The only real difference lies in the context in which they occur.

When undertaking any marketing and/or channels planning effort, the primary task is to learn how various markets *differ* in terms of consumer-organizational choice/patronage behavior, market potential, infrastructure, institutions available to perform marketing functions, and the receptivity of markets to a firm's domestic or nonnational marketing efforts. From this perspective, marketing to diverse cultures in the United States can prove just as challenging as marketing to foreign markets. You can, for example, market to Hasidic Jews, Hopi Indians, Vietnamese, and Lebanese-born consumers—all living in the United States. You may also take into consideration the fact that Hispanics living in Florida, New York, or California differ substantially from one another in their tastes and preferences because of their predominately Cuban, Puerto Rican, or Mexican origins. A unique marketing mix package needs to be designed for each culturally diverse micromarket segment. Nothing more, or less, is necessary in international markets.

In the years ahead, the U.S. population and the demand for goods and services will not grow at sufficient levels to support rapid growth in the domestic economy. Therefore, the future growth and success of American business will depend on its ability to compete vigorously in the international marketplace. From an economic perspective, then, no topic should be viewed as more important than is global village marketing.

Key Terms

culture
direct marketing channel
global exchange relationships (GERs)
indirect marketing channel
initial costs
logistics costs
multinational exchange relationships (MERs)
preservation costs
strategic alignments
transnational exchange relationships (TERs)

Chapter Summary

Channels firms enter risky waters when they develop international exchange relationships. Still, more firms than ever before are engaging in international trade. The primary reasons for seeking membership in international exchange relationships are to facilitate market entry, boost market share while gaining synergistic advantages, introduce new products through existing channels, improve service performance, or respond and adapt to changing local market conditions.

International channel arrangements can be characterized in many ways. The term *international* merely suggests something is occurring between nations. Those firms operating in different countries are generally called *multinational corporations.*

Several categories of international exchange relationships exist. The first is multinational exchange relationships (MERs). MERs occur between trading partners that operate in foreign markets as if they were local concerns. MERs offer international marketers an opportunity to engage in what might be described as a series of domestic strategies executed in foreign markets or countries. MERs are based on one exchange partner's ability to effectively adapt to the environmental circumstances and opportunities prevailing in a market of interest. Each MER is customized to satisfy the needs or master special environmental conditions associated with a foreign market. Transnational exchange relationships (TERs) also exist. Rather than engaging in a country-by-country adaptation, TERs approach international relationships from a regional perspective. TERs follow channel strategies tailored to the requirements of entire market regions. While TERs generally involve fewer exchange partners than do MERs, these partners are usually much larger in scope. Global exchange relationships (GERs) are a third category. GERs involve essentially boundaryless relationships among exchange partners. GERs do not develop on the basis of markets; instead they result from the pursuit of strategic alignments. Strategic alignments exist when there is an agreement or shared consensus between the organizational visions of two or more exchange partners. GERs require the highest levels of integration among international partners.

Entry-level international exchange relationships can assume many forms. For simplicity, we classify these entry modes into two opposing categories: direct and indirect methods. The direct method is one in which the exchange partner takes a membership position in the home country or region. A membership position implies that the exchange partner actually becomes a player in the foreign economy. When indirect entry is used, the channel member manages the distribution of products in a target country through foreign designates. A foreign designate is any intermediary that facilitates the distribution of domestically produced goods through some foreign target market.

The repercussions of the macroenvironment are acute in international channel relationships. No formula exists for dealing with the complexity of international exchange relationships. It is nevertheless important to evaluate environmental conditions before an international channels relationship is consummated. These environm[illegible] tions fit into five basic categories: economic, pc[illegible] sociocultural, technological, and physical/geogr[illegible] tors. Unforeseen changes in economic cycles, monetary policy, and interest rates always influence channel performance. Unfavorable economic factors often lead to the termination of international relationships. The extent to which the political or legal systems of a host nation promote or repress foreign investment in its local economy dramatically influences international channel environments.

The beliefs, values, and lifestyles that prevail in a target nation should be evaluated when international marketing channels are developed and executed. To develop successful international relationships, prospective partners must adapt to any cultural idiosyncrasies present in their new channel role expectations. By being sensitive to these socially and culturally based differences in international marketplaces, exchange partners can better cultivate long-term relationships.

Technological advances are leading to more efficient use of raw materials, improved manufacturing productivity, and superior product quality in all marketing channels. Changes in technology also influence how channel transactions are conducted. The topographic layout, natural resources, regional climates, and weather patterns of a target country also affect the exchange relationships consummated there.

The process by which international partners are chosen warrants special attention. The overriding goal in selecting international partners should be to identify opportunities to develop and secure strategic alignments. When prospective partners pursue conflicting goals, the relationship is unlikely to flourish. International channel environments are dynamic, and in many instances significant environment circumstances lie beyond the control of either partner. The process of selection, then, may be best approached as a refinement process. Several rudimentary factors should be evaluated in this process. We call these factors the Five Cs: costs, coordination, coverage, control, and cooperation.

Three types of costs are germane. The first is initial costs, involving outlays associated with setting up a marketing channel. Preservation costs address the forecasted expenses of maintaining an exchange relationship. Finally, logistics costs reflect the expenses related to transporting goods and managing inventories. The coordination factor requires that prospective partners estimate how the necessary functional operations will be allocated among the channel participants. The territorial coverage that a prospective exchange partner is able to comfortably handle needs to be determined and agreed upon, as well. A realistic assessment of how much effort will be required by each partner to ensure customer satisfaction should also be launched. Exchange partners likewise need to negotiate who will have control over key channel resources. Issues of cooperation remain an important consideration in this selection process. Cooperation is essential to attain strategic alignment in the prospective relationship.

Failures in international relationships usually result from a breakdown in how one or more of the following issues are handled: differing expectations among exchange partners, slow reactions to changing market conditions, clashes in exchange partners' corporate cultures, or prematurely developed international exchange relationships.

While international relationships are risky and difficult to administer, they still offer great promise. International relationships help channels partners to address current gaps in a market's needs or wants, optimize their manufacturing and distribution capabilities, share the risks associated with entering new markets, facilitate new product innovation, gain and then exploit economies of scale, or extend the market scope of their existing operations.

Channel Challenges

1. Philips Electronics, a major player in the digital music technology, has experienced major setbacks in its global marketing battle in the dynamic music system industry. A number of emerging technologies make the battleground very complex. Consumers, even within the same international regions, are demonstrating different preferences across the music formats. How might Philips Electronics react to the many-sided technology? Would you recommend a global, multinational, or transnational channels study?
2. You think you've memorized the McDonald's menu? Well don't be so sure. Around the world, McDonald's has altered its menu to appeal to consumer preferences. From McPizza to McRib, McDonald's strives to satisfy cultural preferences. For example, in Malaysia, you are likely to find fried chicken, McRendang (a "sloppy joe"–like sandwich), and McEgg (not to be confused with an Egg McMuffin) on the menu. How about some fresh sugar cane juice to wash it down? One of McDonald's recent market entries is particularly challenging. McDonald's introduction into India may seem contrary to its cultural norms. Many Indians don't eat meat, and they believe that cows are sacred. Should McDonald's offer hamburgers in India? How will its decision affect its multinational positioning?
3. United Parcel Service (UPS) is thinking global. It has installed a satellite earth station in New Jersey to provide a direct data link between the United States and Germany. It envisions future links to include Africa, South America, and other parts of Europe. How might these global data linkages improve UPS's international channels strategy? How does this strategy provide exchange utility across national boundaries?
4. A Lebanese saying is, "To change customs is a difficult thing." Should international channel members always adapt to a country's customs? Should they ever try to change customs? When addressing this question, keep in mind that PepsiCo's Pizza Hut restaurants were only introduced to the Commonwealth of Independent States since the dissolution of the Soviet Union. Also, keep in mind that the Pizza Hut in Russia is among the most profitable worldwide.
5. General Electric (GE), the U.S.-based electronics giant, has formed an alliance with Japan's Sanyo. It will market Sanyo batteries using joint branding. Why would GE elect to market a Japanese battery when it is fully equipped to produce and market its own batteries? What does joint branding suggest about global channels strategies?

Review Questions

1. How does environmental uncertainty affect global channel strategies?
2. Discuss the five primary reasons for developing international marketing relationships.
3. How do multinational, transnational, and global channel relationships develop?
4. Describe the relationship between the macroenvironment and the international strategy.

5. Describe the influence of economic environmental factors on international marketing exchange relationships.
6. Discuss the impact of social systems and cultural environments on multinational marketing channels.
7. How are international exchange relationships initiated? What are five key factors that must be evaluated when entering into international exchange relationships?

Endnotes

1. Amire, Roula (2000), "Confectioners Harness E-Commerce," *Candy Industry*, May, 6–8.
2. Thompson, Stephanie (1999), "NesQuick Redux: Next Comes the Cereal," *Brandweek,* March 29, 49–53.
3. "International: Cadbury Buys Spanish Concern," *The Wall Street Journal*, April 22, A6; "International: Cadbury to Buy French Firm," *The Wall Street Journal*, January 20, A10.
4. Banerjee, Neela (1993), "Russia Snickers after Mars Invades," *The Wall Street Journal*, July 13, B1.
5. Welsh, Jonathan (1995), "Armstrong Forms Alliance to Sell a Product in U.S.," *The Wall Street Journal*, December 7, B6A.
6. Clark Phillip B. (2000), "U.S. Firms See Asia's Promise," *B to B*, 13, 1–36.
7. From "An Interview with Peter Zane: A Booming Market for Security Locks" (1993/1994) in *Trade & Culture: How to Make It in the World Market*, 1 (Winter), 101–02.
8. Choi, Audrey, and Carlta Vitzhum (1994), "GM's Success in Figueruelas Shows How Spain May Make Itself a Better Home for Auto Makers," *The Wall Street Journal*, April 29.
9. Cooper, James C., and Kathleen Madigan (1999), "Looks Like a Recovery Coming," *Business Week,* November 22, 36–39.
10. Hall, Robert (1993/1994), "Finance," in *Trade & Culture*, 1 (Winter), 11.
11. Tyler, Gus (1993), "The Nation-State vs. the Global Economy," *Challenge*, March–April, 26–32.
12. Charlier, Marj (1993), "Going South: U.S. Mining Firms, Unwelcome at Home, Flock to Latin America; Citing Environmental Woes, They Step Up Spending in Newly Friendly Lands; Richer Ores Also Play a Role," *The Wall Street Journal*, June 18, A1.
13. Lawrence, Susan V. (2000), "From Hero to Villain," *Far Eastern Economic Review*, October 5, 50–52.
14. Dubey, Suman (1993), "Coca-Cola Resumes Presence in India, Expects Profits in Two or Three Years," *The Wall Street Journal*, October 25, A15.
15. Moffett, Matt (1992), "World Business: Moving to Mexico: Culture Shock; High Growth Lures Business to Mexico, but Staying There Requires Determination," *The Wall Street Journal*, September 24, R13.
16. Brauchli, Marcus W. (1995), "Outlook: India and China Take Far-Different Paths, *The Wall Street Journal,* A1.
17. "Joint Venture Established to Produce PCs in China," (1994), *The Wall Street Journal*, December 5, A12.
18. Sheppard, Matthew (1993), "The Changing Face of Intermodalism," *Global Trade & Transportation*, 113 (July), 14.
19. Jeannet, Jean-Pierre, and Hubert D. Hennessey (1992), *Global Marketing Strategies*, Second Edition, Boston, MA: Houghton-Mifflin, 385–416.
20. Dawkins, William (1990), "PepsiCo Gets Go-Ahead to End Perrier Contracts," *Financial Times*, November 28, 32.
21. Troy, Mike (2000), "Global Group Ready for New Growth Phase," *DSN Retailing Today,* June 5, 135–39.
22. Heller, Richard (2000), "At Sea in an Ocean of Beer," *Forbes,* October 30, 135–36.
23. Heckler, Mark (1996), "Anheuser-Busch Buys Stake in Mexican Brewer: Underscores New Trend in U.S. Expansion Abroad," *The Wall Street Journal,* March 23, B4.
24. Glanton, Eileen (2000), "Eleven to Watch," *Forbes,* October 20, 194–218.

chapter

7

Legal and Ethical Imperatives in Channel Relationships

Learning Objectives

After reading this chapter, you should be able to:

- Provide an overview of the U.S. antitrust legislation that relates to marketing channels.
- Discuss the differences between per se- and rule of reason-based court decisions.
- Discuss how existing legislation influences channel practices such as tying arrangements, resale price maintenance, and dual distribution.
- Discuss evolving legal issues such as slotting allowances and parallel import channels.
- Understand the importance of ethics in building and sustaining channel relationships.
- Describe the ethics continuum and the balance of interest between buyers and sellers.
- Identify and discuss the basic ethical dilemmas that can arise in marketing channels.
- Distinguish between rules-based, consequence-based, and experience-based moral codes.
- Describe individual, organizational, and environmental factors that affect a channel member's ethical or unethical behaviors.
- Assess why *codes of ethics* offer no panacea for resolving ethical conflicts in channel relationships.
- Describe the four components which must be in place for an ethical exchange to occur in a channel relationship.

Wide World Photo

What do companies as apparently diverse as Unilever, Coca-Cola, Volvo, and Levi's have in common? In the past two years, each firm has been embroiled in legal battles over its use of vertical integration and exclusive distribution practices in the United Kingdom (U.K.) marketplace. Coca-Cola has come under legal assault over the shelf stocking and price deals it has established with certain European retailers. The U.K. antitrust system is threatening to dismember Unilever's stranglehold over ice cream distribution in England. Both the U.K. and European antitrust regulators are putting Volvo's "block exemption" links with dealers (and the consequent influence on pricing) under a legal microscope. And Levi's is wrangling to maintain its selective distribution strategy to stop U.K.-based retailers like Tesco from selling its jeans at discounted prices.[1]

Of course, the details vary from case to case. There is a big difference between the actions of Unilever, which built its dominant position in the ice cream marketplace through decades of intensive investment, and Volvo, whose control over distribution may derive more from effective lobbying than promotional proficiency. But either way it is clear that the regulatory pendulum in the U.K. has swung against practices which potentially stifle competition and push up prices.

Who knows? The U.K. authorities may be right. Coke has been ordered to revise its practices before. Volvo was once convicted as a price fixer. But there are other elements which will not only affect the future of some "too cozy" business relationships and price-fixing strategies, but bring sweeping changes to channels as a whole. Marketing channels are already experiencing tectonic shifts as technological changes break down formerly logical separations between producers and retailers.

One need look no further than Black Crowe's lead singer Chris Robinson, who claims that music distributors like Napster "are ripping him off," to see evidence of the changes. "Most [record buyers] are just starting to figure it out," says rock music producer Ron Stone. "[Musicians] see all their work being given away for free, and are horrified. [Producers'] rights are never discussed in the arrangement between Internet firms and the record companies."[2] Napster, of course, was effectively put out of business through legal proceedings that culminated during late 2000.

* * * *

Although one might assume that clear guidelines are in place that permit an easy assessment of the legal risk associated with various channel behaviors, this is not entirely the case. The U.S. justice system colors most legal issues in shades of gray, rather than in black and white. It is obvious that Old Economy and New Economy firms alike that want to manage their channel relationships with efficiency must understand the laws that apply to their particular marketing activities.

Regardless of how they arise, legal problems in competitive markets can be neither avoided nor resolved without a general understanding of the relevant laws. The laws defining the nature of legal channel behaviors must be understood as a complete body, even though that is not how they evolved. Otherwise, a course of action intended to avoid or escape one legal transgression may only result in a firm being entangled in the web of another law.

When developing channel strategies, managers must understand the laws affecting those strategies, as well the legal defenses available under those laws. Perhaps most importantly, channel managers must also understand how the courts interpret these statutes. These interpretations establish precedents regarding what is and what is not acceptable channel practice. Finally, effective managers should be sensitive to signals that suggest these legal roadmarks are likely to be redefined in the future. In this chapter, we present an overview of the U.S. laws affecting channels practices and discuss their judicial interpretations. We also look briefly at what the future holds in the way of emerging legal issues. We then discuss the best method for steering clear of possible legal difficulties—by grounding channel strategies in ethical criteria. The chapter next offers an in-depth deliberation of the nature of moral and ethical behavior in marketing channels and the delicate balance between the interests of buyers and sellers. We close the chapter by discussing a variety of approaches to moral decision making that are available to help channel members act in legal and ethical ways.

A Historical Overview of Federal Legislation Affecting Channel Practices

The U.S. government seeks to reconcile profit-seeking behaviors with the interests of various channel members, competitors, and consumers. Federal antitrust laws are the most important tools in this effort. **Antitrust laws** seek to inhibit or prohibit certain undesirable channel member behaviors. Antitrust laws also attempt to shape channel structure along what the government views as more competitive lines. The broad purpose of antitrust legislation is to introduce sound economic analysis and rationality into the legal decision-making process. Still, this body of antitrust legislation remains open to differing interpretation depending on political or judicial thought and opinion.

Early Legislation

Antitrust law in the United States generally rests upon three early statutes: the Sherman Act of 1890, the Clayton Act of 1914, and the Federal Trade Commission (FTC) Act of 1914. Section 1 of the **Sherman Act** prohibited contracts, combinations, and conspiracies in restraint of trade—all activities that would tend to lessen free market competition. Section 2 outlawed monopolization, attempts to monopolize, and combinations or conspiracies to monopolize "any part of the trade or commerce among the several states, or with foreign nations."[3]

Enforcement of the Sherman Act during its first two decades of existence was unspectacular. However, two other landmark sets of legislation were passed in 1914 to give the paper tiger some teeth. The **Clayton Act**'s first section outlawed practices not covered by the Sherman Act and sought to restrain the growth of monopoly before Sherman Act violations could develop. Section 2 prohibited price discrimination that substantially lessened competition or tended to create a monopoly. Section 3 outlawed any tying clauses and exclusive dealing arrangements tending to adversely affect competition. Section 7 forbade mergers which would lessen competition. Section 8 prohibited interlocking boards of directors among competing firms. As you can see, Sections 1, 2, and 3 each feature ambiguous wording, leaving room for future subjective interpretations. The prevailing law of the land was essentially in place by 1914, but the element of chance remains to this day.

Proponents of antitrust efforts also saw the need for an organization that would perform both investigatory and judicial functions and possess special competence in matters of business. Such an agency was created with the 1914 passage of the **Federal Trade Commission (FTC) Act.** Section 5 of the FTC Act also outlawed "unfair methods of competition," leaving the commission and ultimately the U.S. Supreme Court the task of determining what practices were subject to this catch-all prohibition.[4] Section 5's vague wording contributed a few more touches of gray to some already subjective business activities.

Does this body of legislation seem a bit old to you? Perhaps a little out of touch with what is really happening in today's world? Don't assume that at all. This is the same legislation that the U.S. Federal courts just used to reach their verdict in the landmark Microsoft case that examined whether the software giant engaged in anticompetitive business practices.[5]

Later Legislation

By 1936, it was apparent that stronger measures were necessary to protect smaller and/or independent enterprises from larger firms' predatory pricing. The **Robinson-Patman Act** attempted to do exactly that. As Wright Patman, the bill's cosponsor, said, the legislation was designed to "give the little fellows a square deal."[6] In short, the Robinson-Patman Act heavily amended Section 2 of the Clayton Act. It prohibited practices in which sellers charge different prices to different purchasers of "goods of like quality," where the effect "may substantially lessen competition or tend to create a monopoly in any line of commerce, or to injure, destroy, or prevent competition with any person who either grants or knowingly receives the benefit of such discrimination."[7]

In spite of its strong wording, three potential escape routes were then specified for firms accused of price discrimination. The Robinson-Patman Act stated that price discrimination *may* be justified if: (1) it is carried out to dispose of perishable or obsolescent goods; (2) it merely makes due allowance for differences in the "cost of manufacture, sale or delivery resulting from differing methods or quantities" in which the offering is sold or delivered; or (3) it is effected "in good faith" to meet a competitor's equally low price.[8]

The act also prohibited the payment of brokerage commissions or any allowance or discount except to middlemen actually performing services as independent middlemen. No defenses were permitted for this offense.

In 1948, the FTC released a report suggesting that if nothing were done in response to a recent flurry of merger activities, "the giant corporations will ultimately take over the country."[9] In response, Congress passed the **Celler-Kefauver Act** in 1950, which closed some loopholes in the Clayton Act's seventh section. Mergers between firms at different channel levels were also brought within the law's reach by the Act. It stated that any merger, either horizontal or vertical, that inhibited free market competition was illegal.

Since 1950, several lesser statutes have been passed that also affect marketing channel behaviors. These include the Lanham Act (concerned with trademarks and promotions); the Food, Drug, and Cosmetic Act (extending the Pure Food and Drug Act, which created the Food and Drug Administration); the Consumer Product Safety Act (which established the Consumer Product Safety Commission); and various other statutes aimed at safeguarding the rights of consumers. Basically, however, the legal playing field on which channel members perform today had already been ploughed by 1950. But how the laws themselves are interpreted by the courts continues to evolve as markets and marketing practices each change.

The Per Se Rule versus the Rule of Reason

The Sherman Act forbade "every contract, combination or conspiracy in restraint of trade or commerce among the several states."[10] Court decisions have interpreted this language as making all activities aimed at fixing prices, restricting or pooling output, or sharing markets on a predetermined basis, *per se* illegal, or illegal as such. To win judgment under a **per se rule,** the U.S. Justice Department only needs to prove the existence of a certain prohibited practice and that this conduct falls within a class of "plainly anticompetitive practices."[11] In other words, these three practices are subject to prohibition and punishment each time they are detected. Their per se status means that no inquiry into the organization's economic rationale for the practice is required, nor is any examination of the consequences of the practice in the marketplace necessary.

The notion of per se illegality was introduced to provide more efficiency in the courts. Rather than having to listen to every suit, courts can use the per se rule to dispose of "clones"—legal disputes involving circumstances similar to those of previous cases—coming before them. Those per se rulings must be based on preceding case rulings. When a channel practice is per se prohibited, issues of legality can be framed starkly in black and white.

Unfortunately, such clear-cut rulings are rare. This is because the Sherman Act was also accompanied by a concept known as the rule of reason. When the **rule of reason** is introduced, the courts undertake a broader inquiry into the facts associated with the dispute. The history leading up to the dispute, the reasons why the practices were implemented, and the effect the practices had on competition in and outside of the channel are also considered. The rule of reason was introduced because during the early 20th century many business leaders felt a verdict of monopoly was inevitable if more flexible interpretations of the Sherman Act were not employed by the courts. The suppression of competition is automatically presumed for practices falling clearly within the bounds of per se rules. By contrast, when the rule of reason is invoked, the courts embark upon a careful factual inquiry to determine whether, on balance, competition has actually been suppressed.

The first risk an organization assumes when it acts illegally in a channel is whether someone will detect the act. There are times, particularly in the short run, when no one does—or at least no one files a complaint. The Russian roulette really begins when the rule of reason is used to resolve legal disputes in marketing channels. Some emerging legal issues are discussed in Channel Surfing 7.1.

Traditional Legal Issues in Channel Relationships

How does federal legislation affect business practices? In many ways, that's how. Because it was designed to bring a wide range of business behaviors under its dominion, U.S. antitrust legislation is written in general terms and thus affects a wide range of business practices. Moreover, the FTC's and Department of Justice's enforcement policies have proven more permissive than the law would otherwise suggest, and the courts have tended to rule in the favor of business over the interests of consumers or competition.

Questionable pricing activities, however, have been subjected to particular scrutiny, with the practice known as *resale price maintenance* singled out for special attention in recent

Channel Surfing 7.1

What Sorts of Legal Issues Are Likely to Arise in E-Channels?

E-commerce is hot. Clearly, it is not going to go away. No one would deny those two facts. Today consumers can buy—well, you name it: banking services, books, entertainment, computers, and lodging, just to list a few offerings—on the Net. The Internet brings together buyers and sellers in types of transactions that were never before possible. E-commerce provides a cost-effective channel for distributing products such as software and music and services such as travel.

The Internet has placed many old legal issues in an entirely unfamiliar context. Business organizations need to understand the consequences of these changes to minimize their legal jeopardies. Traditional contracts, for example, usually involve negotiation of terms and a written signature on a permanent document. In the e-marketplace, however, many agreements are consummated solely in a "cyberspace." This makes it more difficult to determine precisely when an agreement was reached or the exact nature of the terms of the agreement. In many jurisdictions, the legal eagles, not to mention the courts, have yet to even decide whether this type of transaction represents an enforceable contract.

The Internet has no geographic or political boundaries. While this boundlessness presents virtually unlimited opportunity to many marketers, e-commerce transactions are frequently subject to multistate or even international business and legal concerns. Conflicts among legal systems, business climates, and ethical cultures are likely to arise. Traditional marketing channels operating in traditional business contexts typically exercise great control over their target markets. But when the Internet is involved, firms often end up doing business with customers from countries that they would have never anticipated reaching in the past. What happens when a Louisiana-produced product is sold directly to someone in France? Whose product liability or consumer protection laws apply? When disputes arise, which courts have jurisdiction to hear the issues? These, and many other issues, have to be resolved.

Companies should not assume that they are protected if they are doing business as usual over the Net. CyberBusinessLaw, as it is being titled, is an area of law that is rapidly evolving. Channel members throughout the world will need to monitor those changes closely.

Points to Ponder

- What does this story tell us about the risks associated with e-commerce?
- Is e-commerce worth all the apparent hassles?

Source: Adapted from Bingi, Prasad, Ali Mir, and Joseph Khamalah (2000), "The Challenges Facing Global E-Commerce," *Information Systems Management,* 17 (4), 26–34.

years. Since 1950, mergers also have received special attention. Still, a given merger's legal status has remained subject to the comings and goings of Democratic- and Republican-dominated administrations, with Democratic administrations generally favoring consumer interests over the interests of business. Additionally, in recent years, the U.S. government has increasingly encouraged America's foreign trading partners to strengthen their own free competition laws and to open their markets. American business can only view this as a positive development.

How does federal legislation specifically affect channel relationships? Six practices are of particular interest to us. These are price discrimination, resale price maintenance, vertical integration and mergers, dual distribution, tying arrangements, and refusals to deal and resale relationships. Each of these channel practices and the legislative acts that affect them are discussed below. They are also summarized in Exhibit 7.1.

Exhibit 7.1

Summary of legislation affecting marketing channels

Year Enacted	*Legislative Act*	*Channel Practices Potentially Affected*
1890	Sherman Act	Resale price maintenance, illegal vertical integration and mergers, exclusive dealings, refusals to deal, resale restrictions
1914	Clayton Act	Tying contracts, exclusive dealings arrangements, dual distribution
1914	Federal Trade Commission	Price discrimination, dual distribution
1930	Tariff Act (Amended)	Parallel import channels
1936	Robinson-Patman	Price discrimination, promotional allowances
1950	Celler-Kefauver	Horizontal mergers, vertical mergers
1975	Consumer Goods Pricing Law	Resale price maintenance
1985	Vertical Restraints Guidelines	Exclusive dealing arrangements

Price Discrimination

Price discrimination involves the sale or purchase of a good or service at differing price levels, when the differing prices are not directly related to differences in the seller's cost. Buying and selling firms can each engage in price discrimination.

When a seller charges competing channel members different prices, the behavior might be viewed as a reward to one channel member. However, if the channel member receiving the lower price used its channel position to force lower prices, such an action may be considered coercive. The Robinson-Patman Act makes it unlawful for an organization to knowingly induce or receive a discriminatory price. Recent interpretations suggest the act functions to equalize buying power so that larger channel members do not receive better deals than smaller channel members. Robinson-Patman also governs the fairness of promotional allowances granted to customers.

In addition, the FTC Act interprets all coercive activity by larger or more powerful channel members as an "unfair method of competition."[12] Powerful buyers are likewise prohibited from forcing special promotional allowances or other special services from weaker suppliers.

Despite these legal positions, buyer-induced price discrimination is difficult to prove and is widely practiced.[13] Sellers frequently offer one buyer a lower price than another on the same product or by awarding one of them a cash reward. Is this price discrimination or good marketing? Marketing principles teach us to segment based on shared characteristics. Some segments may be more prone to buying on the basis of price than others. Segmentation strategies argue that marketers should design a different marketing mix, including price, to each segment. Still, many channel recruiters and managers currently suggest that too many new managers fail to understand or realize that they cannot offer different discounts to competing purchasings without considering certain issues.

There are times when the use of reward power is considered discriminatory. The Robinson-Patman Act states that price discrimination must injure competition in some manner to be declared illegal.[14] Injury to competition may be shown at either the primary, secondary, or tertiary level. Primary level injuries involve competition among firms that are direct rivals. Secondary level injuries involve firms competing with buyers to whom a discriminatory price has been charged. Tertiary level injury involves firms competing with customers of a buyer to whom favorable discriminatory prices have been offered.[15]

On the other hand, the history of court rulings suggests that injury to competition will not be inferred when the price differentials are too small to have any significant effect on sales or market shares. Nor will injury be inferred when the discriminatory prices were in place for too short a time to meaningfully affect channel member positions. For decades, experts have argued that the criteria used to enforce Robinson-Patman conflict with the broader procompetitive thrusts of other antitrust legislation. At this point, price discrimination in vertical channel relationships is per se illegal only if there is an expressed or implied agreement to fix distributors' or dealers' prices. Otherwise, the issue of what is or is not an illegal pricing behavior remains up in the air.

For instance, in recent years health maintenance organizations have been able to force deep pricing reductions by telling manufacturers that they would eliminate certain drugs from prescription lists used by member doctors. Meanwhile, drug retailers having a broader customer base, such as Kroger grocery stores, must carry a wider range of pharmaceuticals. Their ability to negotiate for lower prices is limited because Kroger is unlikely to remove drugs from their shelves that customers might request. Kroger's drug prices are thus higher than many of its competitors.

In-store pharmacies have long been central to Kroger's profit strategies. In response to these negative trends, Kroger and three other grocery store chains recently brought suit against the Pharmaceutical Manufacturer's Association (PMA).[16] The suit claims that the grocery chain's pharmacy business has eroded in recent years due to price discrimination and alleges that a violation of the Robinson-Patman Act has occurred. Unlike under the Sherman Antitrust Act, Kroger and its fellow plaintiffs do not have to prove a conspiracy existed. Instead, they need only show that the PMA acted unfairly in pricing similar products for different customers. This early 1990s legal battle continues to this very day; a class action lawsuit was recently filed by community pharmacists who are charging drug manufacturers and wholesalers with price discrimination.[17]

Other pricing topics that fall into a legislative gray area are quantity and functional discounts. The provision of quantity discounts is a traditional channel practice. Such discounts are offered based on the number of units purchased, size of load received, or dollars spent by buyers. Quantity is an element of pricing that legally justifies a seller's use of different prices for different customers. Thus, price differentials based on quantities are permissible if they represent true allowances for differences in manufacturing, selling, or delivery costs. The FTC has, however, denied larger discounts on orders placed by chains or cooperative buying agencies where no savings were present in the cost of delivery, production, or promotional efforts.

Suppliers routinely offer different prices to different types of distributors depending on the functions these channel members perform. Traditional trade or functional discounts are straightforward in nature and are granted to wholesalers but not retailers. However, difficulties arise when the performance of channel functions is mixed or integrated across various channel levels. In today's marketplace, this is increasingly the case. When retailers perform the functions normally provided by wholesalers, price discrimination problems may arise. In 1990, the Supreme Court ruled that all functional discounts not justified by the value of services rendered by wholesalers or retailers *may* be illegal.[18]

Resale Price Maintenance

Resale price maintenance (RPM) occurs when a manufacturer sets the price at which its product can be sold by independent wholesalers and retailers. *Minimum RPM* occurs when the producers set only minimum resale prices, allowing distributors to charge higher prices. Conversely, *maximum RPM* occurs when producers set only maximum resale prices, allowing resellers to charge lower prices. Supporters of the practice argue that RPM protects the margin between retail and wholesale prices from being eroded by potentially cutthroat competition. Advocates also suggest that manufacturers benefit because retailers have more funds to spend on advertising and service, which in turn, supports the manufacturer's brand.

All forms of RPM are now per se illegal under current interpretations of the Sherman Act.[19] The prosecution need not prove that the RPM incident had anticompetitive effects. Nor can a manufacturer defend itself by demonstrating, for example, how the RPM provided procompetitive efficiencies that benefited consumers. Such competitive effects could be balanced against other consequences of the RPM if it were evaluated under the same rule of reason that applies to other vertical agreements.[20]

Despite RPM's current legal status, manufacturer efforts to influence the prices charged by their channel partners have not disappeared. Manufacturers are concerned about their product's image and find it in their best interest to provide channel members with substantial profit margins. Higher margins allow intermediaries and retailers to provide better pre- and postsale service.[21] Tactics used to ensure higher resell prices include manufacturer's suggested retail prices, promotional prices advertised on national, regional, or local television, or goods price-marked prior to delivery.

Resale price maintenance is an international issue. The United Kingdom's Office of Fair Trading (OFT) has launched legal proceedings to end RPM on branded over-the-counter pharmaceuticals. Supermarkets such as Asda prompted the move when they challenged current RPM regulations by offering huge discounts on OTCs. The British pharmaceutical industry came up against an opponent as powerful as itself as it argued that stopping RPM would put community pharmacists out of business. In the U.K. supermarkets are able to exert huge pressure on their suppliers (moreso than in the United States). The British Parliament is currently debating the issue.[22]

Vertical Integration and Mergers

Vertical integration occurs when a firm owns and manages organizations at more than one channel level. It emerges through the forward integration of manufacturers, through the backward integration of retailers, or through an intermediary's up- or downstream expansion. Vertical integration is generally motivated by the pursuit of more control over channel member behavior and prices and/or economies of scale.

Vertical integration can result from a firm's natural growth and expansion. For instance, a manufacturer might elect to develop its own warehousing or retailing facilities or outlets. Integration is often pursued to guarantee that downstream distribution outlets have timely and consistent access to products. This sort of *internal expansion* falls under the authority of the Sherman Act, which prohibits monopoly or attempts to monopolize "any part of the trade or commerce among the several states, or with foreign nations." But internal expansion is not

prohibited by Sherman unless the expansionary actions have the intent or effect of injuring competition. The Sherman Act, like most other antitrust legislation, highlights the interrelatedness between the legal and the competitive environments.

Integration can also be achieved when one firm acquires the stock or assets of another company operating at a different (vertical) or the same (horizontal) channel level. This is known as a **merger.** Such *external expansion* is governed by the Celler-Kefauver Act. Celler-Kefauver prohibits one firm's purchase of another's stock or assets if the acquisition or merger tends to substantially inhibit competition or promote monopoly.

The courts have overturned many mergers and acquisitions since 1950. During the same period, vertical integration via internal expansion has received favorable consideration from the courts. The courts have operated under the assumption that internal expansion expands investment and production and, thus, can promote competition. By contrast, the courts have often ruled that vertical expansion through merger removes another competitor from the market. A merger between Brown Shoe, a major shoe producer, and Kinney Shoe Stores, at the time the country's largest chain of independent shoe stores, was voided for this reason. The government ruled that the opportunity for other shoe manufacturers to reach the end-user market would have been significantly reduced by the merger.[23]

The Federal Trade Commission also gets involved in matters pertaining to mergers and vertical integration. For example, Coca-Cola now has to obtain the FTC's approval before acquiring any major brand-name competitors during the next 10 years. This is because in the late 1980s Pepsi moved to acquire Seven-Up. In response, Coke made an offer to buy Dr Pepper. The FTC raised antitrust objections to both mergers which, had they gone through, would have given Coke and Pepsi about 80 percent of the U.S. soft drink market. Coke's efforts were eventually judged in violation of antitrust laws.

The anticompetitive effects of channel mergers sometimes pop up in unusual ways. In the mid-1990s, concert ticket retailer Ticketmaster absorbed its major competitor, Ticketron. Rock concert prices appeared to rise significantly as a result. In response, grunge rockers Pearl Jam brought suit against Ticketmaster, asserting that a near-monopoly position allowed Ticketmaster to charge exorbitant fees for its services. The case was settled out of court, but not before Eddie Vedder's Seattle-based group reaped a whirlwind of goodwill from America's rock fans.

Dual Distribution

Dual distribution occurs when the manufacturer of a branded good sells that brand—or essentially the same product under a different brand name—to the same market through two or more competing channels. Dual distribution is routine in industries such as automotive tires, personal computers, and paint. Suppliers of soft drinks and snack foods also regularly engage in this activity. Dual distribution usually reflects suppliers' efforts to reach a new market or to adapt their products or distribution practices to perceived differences among potential buyer groups.

Dual distribution is not per se illegal under federal antitrust laws. But critics allege that dual distribution negatively affects independent distributors. When a producer distributes through its own vertically integrated channel in competition with independent channel members at wholesale or retail levels, the manufacturer may use the company-owned outlets to undercut the independent intermediary's prices. If this activity tended to drive distributors out of business, it would violate the antitrust provisions of the Sherman and Clayton acts.

Tying Arrangements

The Clayton Act prohibits any contract for the sale or lease of goods that imposes a condition that the purchaser "shall not use or deal in the goods, . . . supplies, or other commodities of a competitor . . . of the lessor or seller, where the effect may be to substantially lessen competition or to create a monopoly." This portion of the Clayton Act has relevance to three types of tying practices: tying contracts, full-line forcing, and exclusive dealing arrangements.

Under a **tying contract,** the purchaser of some good—say, a machine—agrees, as a condition of purchase, to buy the seller's supplies of some other commodity, such as raw materials processed by the machine. This type of agreement shuts out competing materials suppliers from the opportunity to sell the tied commodity to the buyer. Again, competing sellers are edged out of the picture for the contract's duration. **Full-line forcing** is a related issue. This practice, also known as full-line pricing, occurs when dealers must carry a supplier's entire line in order to obtain distribution rights to an especially desirable item.

Finally, in an **exclusive dealing agreement** an intermediary agrees to devote its efforts exclusively toward distributing the product line of a particular manufacturer. Handling competing manufacturers' products is explicitly or implicitly disallowed. For a distributor's willingness to deal exclusively, manufacturers may grant their dealers exclusive franchises. The legality of exclusive dealing agreements is governed by the Sherman Act. Dealers given an exclusive franchise presumably derive benefit from having to face less competition from other dealers handling the same product. The development of exclusive dealing agreements also appeals to manufacturers because such arrangements help attract dealers and ensure that the manufacturers' products will be merchandised with substantial attention and enthusiasm.

The three tying practices described above involve attempts to restrict competition that span different (usually adjacent) vertical stages in the distribution chain between producers and users of a product. As such, the set of practices are jointly known as **vertical restrictions.** The law on these vertical restrictions has evolved along divergent lines.

The Clayton Act's wording appears to offer a flat, per se prohibition of practices involving vertical restriction. However, the presumption against tying arrangements is not nearly as strong as the per se rule against price discrimination. For tying arrangements, antitrust violations will not be found unless a substantial volume—near monopoly-level—of sales is foreclosed by the vertical restriction. For relatively small marketers of unpatented goods, these conditions will likely never be satisfied. Marketers of all sizes attempting to enter new markets through tying contracts are usually safe from legal censure, as well. Furthermore, the courts have also been willing to consider extenuating circumstances under a rule of reason. Extenuating circumstances might include issues such as a seller's need to exercise control over complementary goods or services to ensure the tying product's satisfactory operation. Moreover, the courts will not punish purely voluntary or informal tying arrangements. For instance, buyers may habitually purchase a machine manufacturer's products under the assumption that the product will work better or because doing so makes production more convenient.

Franchise agreements that restrict competition among a manufacturer's outlets are not covered by the Clayton Act. At present, manufacturers are fully within the law in limiting the number and location of outlets to which franchises are granted. But when dealers agree among themselves not to pursue each other's markets or solicit the same customers, the law is violated. These horizontal agreements between channel members represent conspiracies in restraint of trade.[24]

Purely vertical restraints—those imposed unilaterally by a manufacturer (or retailer) on its dealers (suppliers)—have historically been viewed sympathetically by the courts. Essentially, the courts concede that vertical agreements often promote interbrand competition by allowing manufacturers (retailers) to achieve distribution efficiencies. While some forms of vertical integration may well prove anticompetitive, vertical restrictions and exclusive territories are judged under a rule of reason.

The legality of exclusive dealing agreements remains unresolved. The Department of Justice did recognize the potential dampening effects exclusive dealings may have on competition in its 1985 **vertical restraints guidelines.** It also indicated that instances where the practice is likely to substantially harm competition may prove unusual.[25] In short, the courts are unlikely to react harshly to exclusive dealing agreements unless the practice significantly raises rivals' costs of gaining access to input or distribution facilities and raises costs to the point where the firm must raise its own prices.

Assertions of antitrust injury relating to tying arrangements continue to center on the harm done to the competitive marketplace rather than the injury incurred by any particular competitor. For instance, a threat to withhold software service if customers did not also contract for hardware service was not viewed as an unlawful tie under a recent rule of reason judgment. The plaintiff, Datagate Corp., is a supplier of computer services and parts. Datagate sued Hewlett-Packard, Inc. (H-P), accusing H-P of restricting its access to parts, service, and information. Datagate also charged that H-P illegally tied the sale of its software and hardware services together. No injury was found because "Datagate failed to show that H-P service prices or profits had increased during the period in question."[26]

Nor can a tying claim be upheld by the courts unless there is evidence of a conspiracy. In the early 1990s, Wang Laboratories, Inc., offered purchasers of personal computers and hardware a maintenance service known as a *WSS contract.* Once customers were under WSS contracts, to purchase software they also had to subscribe to Wang's hardware maintenance program. Systemcare accused Wang of unlawful tying, asserting that Wang had used its substantial market power in software support channels to eliminate competition in hardware maintenance channels. Current interpretations of the Sherman Act require proof of a "concerted activity" (i.e., a conspiracy) among "two or more separate parties" to sustain an illegal tying claim. Since a company cannot conspire with itself, the district court granted judgment to Wang.[27] In this ruling, the right to compete vigorously was sustained.

Refusals to Deal and Resale Restrictions

In the 1919 case now known as the Colgate Doctrine, the Sherman Act was interpreted as not restricting organizations' rights to:

> exercise [their] own independent discretion to the parties with whom [they] will deal. And, of course, [these organizations] may announce in advance the circumstances under which [they] will refuse to deal.[28]

In other words, marketers can usually choose to do business with whatever channel member they want, and, prior to actually entering into a contract, can also refuse to deal with whomever they want. In the case of existing contractual channel arrangements, however, a channel member's use of a refusal to deal is legally restricted. In particular, refusals to deal cannot be used punitively to eliminate channel members who refuse to accommodate policies stipulated by a seller who may be acting in restraint of trade. In a suit recently filed in Connecticut, Bristol Technology Inc. charged Microsoft Corporation with illegally cutting off access to key Windows NT source-code and application programming interfaces. The suit alleges that Microsoft's motivation is that it wants to interfere with competition in the operating systems market. In its complaint, Bristol cited the doctrine of unlawful refusals to deal in the Sherman Antitrust Act.[29] The matter has yet to be resolved by the courts.

Resale restrictions refer to manufacturers' attempts to designate to whom and in what geographic areas their products may be sold. For over 50 years the courts used the rule of reason to judge whether particular incidents of resale restrictions represent illegal restraints of trade. In 1967, the *U.S. v. Arnold Schwinn and Co.* case argued against the rule of reason approach. For years, Schwinn had informed distributors that some retailers were not to receive its bicycles. But in this landmark ruling, the Court asserted that the Sherman Act made it unreasonable

> for a manufacturer to restrict and confine areas or persons within which an article may be traded after the manufacturer has parted with dominion over it. Once the manufacturer has departed with title and risk, he has parted with dominion over it, and his effort thereafter to restrict territory or persons to whom the product may be transferred is *per se* a violation of Section 1 of the Sherman Act.[30]

For 10 years, the legal use of resale restrictions by manufacturers was essentially eliminated by this decision. But then in 1977, in a decision involving Sylvania, a manufacturer of television sets, the court ruled that disputes involving resale restrictions should again be judged based on the rule of reason. This ruling stipulated that such judgments were to proceed on a case-by-case basis and that resale restraints were no longer viewed as per se illegal if they did not have a dampening "effect on competition without redeeming value."[31] While that seemed acceptable, the notion of what constitutes sufficient redeeming value has remained subject to further legal debate. Once again, we see that the legality of particular channel practices often involves something of a matter of chance.

Emerging Legal Issues in Channel Relationships

New legally controversial channel practices falling outside the province of established U.S. antitrust regulation have been emerging in recent years. Slotting allowances and parallel import channels are clearly the most significant legally controversial practices that have arisen recently. Changing international business law is also affecting channel relationships. In addition, home shopping channels face an effective ban in Europe if proposed legal action taken by the European Commission is successful.[32] Meanwhile, the U.S. Congress has taken an active role in designing regulations aimed at protecting consumer rights against the possibility of unethical telemarketer practices. To that end, the FTC is developing and defining standards for deceptive and abusive practices for a proposed Telemarketing and Consumer Fraud and Prevention Act.[33] The acquisition and use of mailing lists in direct marketing channels is also increasingly subject to legal deliberation at the federal level.[34]

Slotting Allowances

Retail shelf space has become increasingly scarce over the last 15 years. While the number of products stocked by the typical grocery store climbed from 11,800 in 1980 to over 20,000 in 1989, the number of new grocery products introduced grew by over 500 percent during the same period.[35] Similar trends have continued during the 1990s. In all consumer sectors, retailers now confront more product categories and brands than ever before. This product proliferation has contributed to a shift of channel power away from manufacturers and toward retailers. Naturally, competition among manufacturers and wholesalers for this limited shelf space is fierce. The shift in channel power structure and increased competition is evidenced by the growth of slotting allowances paid by producers in recent years. The marketplace is replete with slotting allowances. In Channel Surfing 7.2, you can read about a "fresh" approach to slotting allowances.

Channel Surfing 7.2

A Fresh Way to Impose Slotting Allowances

Fresh perishables (e.g., fruits and vegetables) are now considered such a critical part of modern supermarkets' product mix that they appear to have earned a rather dubious mark of distinction. You can tell that perishables departments have hit the big time in the grocery world because in recent years they developed their very own sets of slotting allowances and up-front fees.

In what could be described as an unofficial right of passage, supermarket fresh perishables departments, led by produce, have finally gained the maturity in terms of the strength of information and brand equity to declare their status as full-fledged members of the grocery buying community: If you are the supplier and have got a boutique brand of bananas or luscious allotment of lettuce, we have just the shelf slot for you, today's perishables departments appear to be saying. It is available, of course, only if the supplier can prove it has the proper commitment to the relationship. And that means ponying up the slotting allowances before you can bring your goods through the back door. In our view, that's not marketing, but it is, in fact, the practice currently prevailing within many supermarket channels—especially the ones involving the larger and more successful retail grocers.

What sorts of change have prompted this transformation? First, this transformation is a function of the development of nationally recognized brands within the produce department. Think iceberg lettuce or Chiquita bananas. The second factor follows from the increased reliance of retail grocers on the perishables side of the store to generate profits. Says Chris Hoyt, president of produce supplier Hoyt & Co. (Stamford, Connecticut), "Their objective is to increase profits and the best way to increase margins is to extract it from manufacturers on the allowance side. That's what slotting allowances are intended to do." Hoyt goes on: "We've had some horrific stories. There's a perception that the money is what it takes to get into supermarkets. It's hard to get there. It's pretty risky—what the supermarkets are asking for is a lot of money up front."

Same old same old, but now the lineup of players is changing. That's marketing channels, and the only thing that remains constant across time is change.

Points to Ponder

- What's your take on this practice? Does it strike you as legal or illegal?

Source: Adapted from Litwak, David (1998), "Money for Nothing," *Supermarket Business,* 53 (6), 105–10.

Slotting allowances are shelf space rental fees paid by manufacturers to retailers. These allowances frequently involve cash gifts or payments in kind, such as cases of free goods, to secure space on a shelf, for end-of-aisle displays, or for special merchandising consideration. Slotting allowances are charged for two reasons. First, they offset retailers' expenses for handling product failures, including the removal of unsold stock. The costs of initial shelf stocking and of updating inventory and information systems are also offset. Second, slotting allowances help balance the supply and demand of scarce shelf space. While the payment of stocking fees to retailers has existed since at least the 1930s-era A&P milk case (the incident most directly responsible for the Robinson-Patman Act), the practice has increased in recent years.

In part, slotting allowance controversies arise because manufacturers and retailers quibble over how to divide the economic gains resulting from their channel transactions. Manufacturers had their own way for a long time. But now, armed with improved information scanning capabilities, retailers are trying to better their position. At another level, slotting allowances could have potential anticompetitive effects similar to those of resale price maintenance (RPM) because both practices involve contractual provisions that can raise retailer prices and profits. When slotting allowances are incurred, manufacturers must raise the wholesale price to their retailers. In turn, this action effectively commits retailers to higher prices. However, certain sellers, such as Kraft or Procter & Gamble, enjoy enviable reputations for successfully bringing new products to market and therefore often refuse (or are not asked) to pay slotting allowances. This strikes some as unfair favoritism and has contributed to a situation in which slotting allowances may soon be viewed through the same lens as is RPM. If this occurs, slotting allowances would be a violation of the Robinson-Patman Act.[36] But for now, they remain legal.

Naturally, producers complain about having to bear the extra costs associated with slotting fees. About 55 percent of all food manufacturers' promotional expenditures—including expenditures at the retailer and consumer level—currently go to slotting fees.[37] Retailers defend their actions, claiming that producers frequently fail to act in retailers' best interest. Retailers charge that producers too often try to sell them products that their customers either don't want or don't need. Retailers may be right.[38]

Major producers compete nationally, but virtually all retailers compete locally. While the producer may be spending $10 million on a national ad campaign, what local retailers are really interested in is how much will be spent on advertising in their local paper. A fresh source of slotting allowances is discussed in Channel Surfing 7.3

The day may come when manufacturers decide to pass on the cost of slotting allowances in the form of increased consumer prices. This is not likely to happen, however, unless their competitors do the same. As long as manufacturers can gain channel advantages by not raising prices, they will probably continue to absorb slotting allowances. So slotting allowances are anticompetitive only if manufacturers collude to raise prices.

On the other hand, slotting allowances increase entry barriers for new grocery products. Whether this is anticompetitive depends on other circumstances. For example, if there are only one or two major producers of a particular product and each pays slotting allowances to keep smaller competitors off supermarket shelves, they might be guilty of anticompetitive behavior.

The practice remains highly subject to debate. The U.S. Senate (Small Business Committee) recently began hearings on slotting allowance practices in the grocery industry. Even

Channel Surfing 7.3

Goats, Rugs, or Pornography?

Strange days indeed. As the sun rises over Oman's Musandem Mountains, some curious scenes often play out in the tiny gulf port called Khasab. Lengthy parades of 12- to 15-foot-long dinghies, usually equipped with powerful outboard engines, stream into the harbor. After having spent hours dodging the Iranian coastguard, the smugglers (creative marketers?) have reached their destination. As they draw toward the shore, an otherworldly cacophony of thuds, moans, yelps, and whines swirls across the quiet water: 25–30 seasick sheep or goats, fated for the dining tables of oil-rich Arabs, have just made land.

Similar spectacles could be observed across the Middle East: Iraqi drivers taping cigarettes to their legs or jerry-rigging cars to stow away extra gas on their way to Jordan; Libyans stuffing hubcaps with subsidized sugar for resale in Tunisia; mules slogging across the mountains between Turkey and Iran packed down with booze, pornography, and playing cards. The area is a paradise for smugglers—not just for illicit imports but for everyday household goods subject to high tariffs and stifling legal barriers.

Of course these activities are illegal, and obviously governments are trying to crack down on smuggling. But regional politics and economic realities impede their efforts. Even legal trade in Iran is so regulated in Iran that many still need to dodge official channels. Iranian carpet exporters complain they face bankruptcy if they do not smuggle out their wares. In Lebanon, a thriving market in smuggled artifacts has sprung up, apparently because legal sales are so difficult.

After reading the legal side of this chapter, you may think that the U.S. legal system tamps down too tightly on many seemingly routine marketing channel practices. But after reading this, you may want to think again. And as you read through its ethical content, you may well want to reevaluate your view regarding what constitutes an ethical distribution practice. At the very least, you should more fully understand that most ethical behavior has a cultural content.

Points to Ponder

- What is your opinion of these practices?
- If you and your company were planning on doing business in the Middle East, how would you adjust to these circumstances?

if nothing comes of it—and based on past results there is little reason to believe otherwise—critic Ken Partch suggests the hearings "may embarrass the FTC and Department of Justice into some kind of action."[39]

Parallel Import Channels

A few years back it was possible for American consumers to buy a new Mercedes-Benz in Europe, pay to ship it home, and still save money—simply by bypassing U.S. Mercedes dealers. **Parallel import channels,** also known as *gray markets,* arise when an authentic, branded product comes into the domestic market of a foreign country through unauthorized channels that rival the product's authorized distribution system. Parallel import also occurs when branded products are exported but returned to the home market, arriving to compete with merchandise moving through the manufacturer's authorized channels. These are known as **reimports.** Some reimports are commercially motivated. For instance, merchants may purchase goods overseas because they are less expensive and/or more easily available, and then return the items to their country of origin. Other reimports are personally motivated. Business or vacation travelers may bring branded merchandise back to the United States because it was cheaper in, say, Hong Kong or Amsterdam.

Gray market problems reached a critical point in 1988 when the Supreme Court handed Kmart a victory.[40] This landmark ruling decreed that American trademark owners such as Cartier watches, Duracell batteries, and Seiko watches could not prevent the unauthorized reimportation of products bearing their marks or names. Legally speaking, an owner's rights to control a trademark ends once ownership changes hands—in this case, in either Europe or Asia. The Court's decision was consistent with long-standing U.S. Customs Bureau practices. The letter of this law, written in 1932, remains unchanged to this day. Exhibit 7.2 illustrates parallel import channels using the Kmart case as an example.

Unauthorized marketing channels in the United States have a surprisingly long history. In the 1880s, a European company granted Appolinaris of New York the exclusive right to

Exhibit 7.2

Illustration of parallel import channels

The most common form of parallel import channels involves products made overseas by American firms. The foreign producer may be a subsidiary, joint venture, or some other business form which has a commonality of interests with the American marketer. Typically, these foreign divisions of U.S. firms then sell to authorized dealers in their own country. But somewhere in the authorized channel, marketing control is lost. As a result, the product gets into an unauthorized channel, with some of it being exported to the United States. Once in the United States, these goods compete with similar domestically produced products.

The way in which the Kmart v. Cartier dispute was resolved made it clear that the Tariff Act of 1930 does not protect the U.S. firm in such situations. Although Cartier was the authorized trademark owner, the ruling disavowed its right to stop unauthorized imports of its watches because the two producing entities were deemed independent of each other.

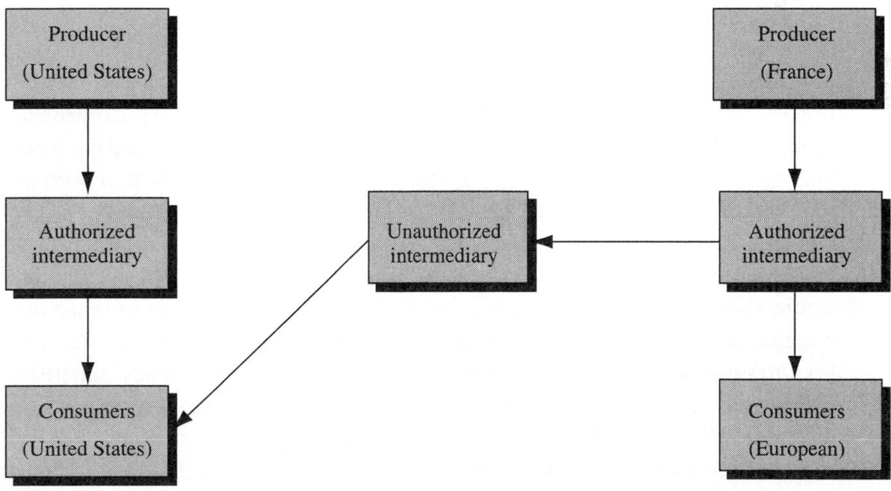

Adapted from Weigand, Robert E. (1991), "Parallel Import Channels—Options for Preserving Traits in Integrity," *Columbia Journal of World Business,* 26 (1), 53–60.

import Janos spring water from Hungary. At about the same time, an astute trader named Scherer learned Janos water could be bought in Germany and transported to America at a cost that would permit him to undercut Appolinaris. Legal remedy was sought by Appolinaris, based on the grounds that Scherer's channel was not the one intended by Janos or Appolinaris. The New York District Court agreed that Scherer's parallel channel practices disrupted some well-laid plans. Still, the goods were genuine. On that basis, it was decided that the practice could not be legally halted.[41] Some 35 years later in a Supreme Court case, an American licensee of a French cosmetics manufacturer was unable to prevent the unauthorized import of certain cosmetics, even though it believed it held exclusive rights to U.S. distribution.[42]

Responding to these two cases, Congress inserted a new paragraph in the Tariff Act of 1930. This insert declared that imports bearing trademarks owned and registered by a U.S. citizen, corporation, or association cannot be admitted unless "written consent of the owner is produced at the time of making entry."[43] Later Supreme Court judgments rejected this position, in effect implying that Congress did not mean what it appeared to say. Finally, in the Kmart case, the Supreme Court held that Congress's intent was to protect only those American licensees' marketing products whose trademarks were owned by European or other foreign countries. What does this interpretation really mean? It works like this: Foreign manufacturers sometimes license an American firm to be the exclusive importer of products bearing a foreign name or trademark. These firms register the foreigner's name, agree to pay royalties and, thus, become legal trademark owners in the United States. Operating under the assumption that it alone will benefit, the American firm then sets forth to develop a domestic market for the product.

Now suppose that a third party distributor in Hong Kong buys several lots of the product, which had been intended for the Australian market. The third party then ships these lots to Los Angeles for sale in America. However, the U.S. Bureau of Customs now interprets the 1930 Tariff Act in a way that effectively prevents goods brought to the United States by a third party distributor from entering the country. These goods can enter the United States only if the American licensee or trademark owner agrees to their importation in writing. Since such agreement is unlikely, their entry is effectively denied. Still, U.S. companies that were taking advantage of parallel import channels were able to claim a victory because only a small portion of their merchandise falls into the foreign licensor-American licensee category.[44]

What should American manufacturers who are being victimized by parallel import channels do? Perhaps the most powerful reactive strategy available is to terminate the opportunistic intermediary. As noted earlier, the Supreme Court has consistently affirmed the Colgate Doctrine's legitimacy. This precedent permits sellers to announce conditions of sales in advance and to terminate buyers/dealers who fail to abide by those conditions. Sharp Electronic's decision to eliminate a retailer who was able to cut prices because of its reimport connection was upheld on these grounds. Although issues of RPM were also at stake, Sharp had not attempted to fix a particular price.[45] Apple Computer's policy statement for resellers is clear: "Any Apple dealer or value added dealer found to be in violation of [gray market] prohibitions will be stripped of its authorized status."[46]

Despite these legal restrictions, build-your-own VARs (also called "box vendors") have been dipping into the gray market for years in their efforts to grab hardware components, such as processors and memory chips. Microsoft Corp., Novell Inc., and others have publicly denounced this practice. One major issue is unbundling software that is supposed to be sold with a PC. In an as-yet-unsettled dispute, Ansell Communications Inc. recently sued Novell for antitrust violations, illegal gray marketing practices, and breach of contract.[47]

International Business Law

When Trinity Motors, the General Motors dealership in Moscow, opened its doors, imported cars were exempt from Russian tariffs. Since then, duties and other value-added taxes have climbed over 300 percent. Such are the perils and paradoxes of doing business in Russia; nothing comes easy. Commercial laws are few and those on the books are poorly enforced or subject to frequent change. But a market economy is taking shape[48] and brave entrepreneurs are plugging ahead—at their own risk. And so it goes in much of the developing and non-Western world where, often, change is the only constant.

It is important to point out, however, that legal differences and higher risk should not necessarily be considered obstacles to international commercial dealings. What are problems for some often represent international opportunities for other, more venturesome channel members. For instance, Saudi Arabian regulations limit direct marketing activities in their kingdom to Saudi nationals or Saudi-owned firms. As a result, then, foreign companies generally must use local agents as distributors. But Saudi law also requires that all import distributor agreements be registered with the Ministry of Commerce (MOC). MOC policy concerns change over time, with or without formal announcements. Currently, MOC's major concerns are that the distribution channel be direct and not eliminate Saudi agents/distributors, and that any transition from an old to new agent be fair.[49] This red tape and relative uncertainty certainly represent a "hassle" for U.S. firms used to operating in a lower risk domestic environment, but the possibility of earning higher returns in the Saudi market often makes such ventures worthwhile. That's just the beginning of the types of hassles that can arise while managing marketing channels in certain Middle Eastern markets, as described in Channel Surfing 7.3

The Sherman, Clayton, and FTC acts are all likely to significantly impact the legality of transactions in international channels. The precise wording of the Sherman Act suggests that it prohibits "contracts . . . in restraint of trade or commerce among the several states, *or with foreign nations.*" The Clayton and FTC acts also define commerce to include foreign nations. In addition, two other acts impact predominately on international channel relationships. The *Webb-Pomerene Act of 1918* provides a limited antitrust exemption for mergers of competing businesses that intend to engage in collective export sales. This exemption does not apply to channel behaviors that harm domestic competitors of either of the merging firms. The *Export Trading Company Act of 1982* was enacted specifically to increase American exports. The act reduced restrictions on trade financing and uncertainty regarding when U.S. antitrust laws apply to international channel transactions. This legislation increased the export efficiency of U.S. manufacturers and suppliers.

When these international antitrust provisions are enforced, the Department of Justice focuses on protecting U.S. consumers from anticompetitive effects. The major distinction between domestic and international antitrust enforcements lies in the regard that the U.S. Department of Justice must have for international comity. *International comity* pertains to the courtesy and respect accorded to other countries' laws in international disputes. Before an activity is challenged as illegal, the Department of Justice must consider the interest of other nations that also have jurisdiction over the transaction in question.[50]

Moving beyond Legality: Toward Ethical Channels Management

We hope it is clear to you by now that U.S. business law—antitrust law in particular—is a murky body. The ways in which current U.S. business law influences the legality of many channel practices are hardly predetermined. No one really knows in advance when injury to competition will be claimed or how a rule of reason judgment in a channel legal dispute will turn out. Because of this lack of clarity, the safest policy for channel members is not to test their judicial fates by engaging in legally risky business practices. How can an organization accomplish this? To answer this question, we first need to understand what the concept of law itself represents. The **law** consists of principles and regulations established by a government that are deemed applicable to a people. The law should be viewed only as a minimum standard of ethical behavior—a baseline for the marketing concept-oriented organization. Thus, the *moral organization* attempts to operate well above the minimum ethical standards prescribed by the law itself, in turn keeping its practices well beyond the murky waters of U.S. antitrust laws.

Most marketers agree that marketing decisions should be made in accordance with accepted ethical principles. Ethics, after all, lay out the differences between right and wrong. But just what is meant by the term *ethics?* A variety of definitions have been offered:

- "Ethics refers to standards of right conduct."[51]
- "Ethics is an inquiry into the nature and grounds of morality where the term morality is taken to mean moral judgments, standards and rules of conduct."[52]
- "Ethics comprise moral principles and standards that guide behavior."[53]
- "Ethics is the art and discipline of applying ethical principles to examine and solve complex moral dilemmas."[54]

Each definition is clearly concerned with the relationship between morality and decision behavior. We provide a definition of marketing ethics that summarizes the descriptions offered above: **Marketing ethics** refers to the moral standards that underlie exchange processes. This definition is applicable to marketing channels because it advances the position that ethics is predicated on interactive decision behaviors.

Critics often charge that marketing is the functional area most likely to be the source of unethical behavior in a business.[55] As evidence, these critics point toward instances of deceptive advertising, unscrupulous sales tactics, misrepresented product capabilities, and unfair pricing tactics. For more than a century, marketers have been singled out as the perpetrators of unethical actions against consumers and other businesses.[56] This is because marketing is the business function most responsible for communicating with prospects and customers and satisfying their needs. As such, the actions of marketers are clearly in the public view and susceptible to close scrutiny.

Social Tact and Relationship Ethics

Since the focus of this book is exchange relationships, it is crucial to acknowledge that morality is a two-way street. Although each exchange partner possesses its own value system, ethical behavior in channel systems depends largely on a shared morality between channel members. The study of business ethics has generally adopted a one-sided, or monadic, perspective. A *monadic perspective* examines moral issues at the level of an individual or single organization and ignores the interaction of individuals or organizations. This perspective leads to false assumptions. For instance, a monadic view implies that individuals' ethical dispositions are formed in isolation from their role in the social system. But this is clearly not the case. The ethical disposition of individuals is affected by their memberships in an industry and society. The ethical attitudes and behaviors of family, friends, co-workers, and various publics also influence these ethical dispositions.

Similarly, a person's workplace ethics cannot be separated from the social system in which the individual operates. This condition is reflected in the concept known as *social tact.* **Social tact** describes individuals' ways of dealing with others in their environment. Social tact evolves over time. As a result of social tact, the relative social status of the persons involved in an exchange dictates, in part, what constitutes appropriate behavior.[57] For relationships to flourish, exchange partners must modify their ethical behaviors to correspond with the behaviors of other exchange partners. This leads us to a concept known as *relationship ethics.* **Relationship ethics** describes the process by which organizational ethics are adapted to suit the needs of particular exchange relationships. Each channel member's representatives—individual employees who interact on behalf of their respective firms—are responsible for preserving the moral footing of a relationship. The preservation of any exchange is based on maintaining a balance among organizational, environmental, and individual employee concerns. Whether at the individual or environmental level, the interaction process itself supplies the basis for ethical or unethical (un/ethical for short) decision making. Thus, a decision to act ethically or unethically should not be viewed as an aggregate of two unit-level (individual) dispositions. To do so ignores the interactive nature of morality in marketing channels.

The Ethics Continuum

In marketing channels, one firm's actions can affect another firm's actions in many ways. But the most ethically relevant transactions are those in which the channels partner's personal or economic well-being is likely to be affected. These are most apparent in their negative forms—for instance, when one person coerces another. A delicate balance exists between exchange partners. Breaches of ethics will reduce the level of cooperation present in any exchange.

To illustrate, consider the buyer-seller relationship. Generally, buyers are aware of seller's persuasive tactics. No problem there, as such tactics are to be expected. But other questions follow from this awareness: Is the seller accurately representing their product's or service's qualities? Is the seller an honest person? Is the seller truly interested in the buyer's welfare? Collectively, such questions and others like them are used to evaluate the seller.

On the other side of the relationship, sellers must pay careful attention to a customer's behavior and body language. Is the customer's interest genuine? Is the customer providing a true account of his or her financial standing? Is the customer going to follow through on his or her commitments? These questions and others like them may be used to evaluate the intentions of the customer.

This balance between the essentially opposing views held by buying and selling channel members is reflected in an **ethics continuum**.[58] The ethics continuum can be viewed as if it

Exhibit 7.3

The ethics continuum as an exchange scale

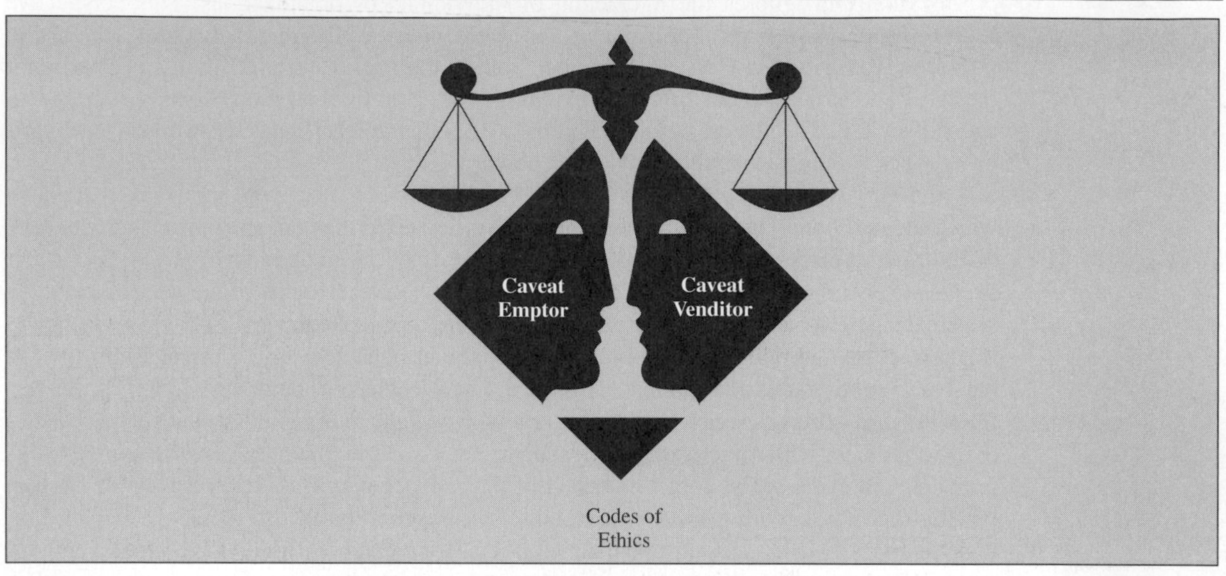

were an exchange scale, as illustrated in Exhibit 7.3. One end of the scale is weighted by the self-interests of the seller. The nature of this weight is reflected in the well-known expression *caveat emptor*—buyer beware. On the other end of the scale is the conflicting stakeholder interest of the buyer. This interest is reflected in the expression *caveat venditor*—seller beware. Let's look at each of these conflicting interests in relation to the scale's fulcrum: the code of ethics.

Caveat Emptor

The caveat emptor ideology is based on the belief that the pursuit of profit maximization is the overriding organizational ethic. This view dictates that the moral baseline provided by the law represents the only constraint on ethical business practice. The goal is to maximize profits within the constraints of laws and regulations.

When **caveat emptor** genuinely applies within a channel relationship, the seller need only ask whether the buyer can legitimately expect ethical marketing behaviors based on some *legal* or *contractual right.* For example, borrowers have a legal right to ethical disclosure of the facts concerning a loan's effective rate of interest that is based on federal truth-in-leading statutes. Likewise, when individuals contract with real estate agents with the intent of selling property, they have a contractual right to a full and truthful disclosure of what their agent knows about the transaction. In many channel relationships, however, there is no regulatory basis that prescribes what level of information should be exchanged among channel

Channel Surfing 7.4

Want to Have Ethical Marketing Channels? That's Easy: Everyone Has to Tell the Truth!

The deceptively simple matter of truth-telling presents an ongoing problem for all business practitioners. No matter what business scandal you consider, it usually involved some aspect of a failure to tell the truth. Whether the misrepresentations have been targeted toward customers, stockholders, or regulators, truth is apparently not always highly valued by many in business.

A fundamental problem associated with the issue of honesty in business, then, is how to motivate people to do what they already know is right: to avoid violating culturally accepted standards of honesty. A related issue involves whether absolute truth-telling standards (e.g., fully disclosing all information) apply in a given situation. This makes ethical decision making harder than many would otherwise assume it to be.

The issue of full disclosure extends to all manner of transactional dilemmas in which businesspeople do not know whether, or to what degree, full disclosure of information is required. Should suppliers ever promise delivery on a date they know cannot be met if similar representations are common within their particular industry? Are negotiators in channel relationships ethically obligated to fully disclose the truth about their full offers? The issue of how much information the ethical marketer is obligated to disclose in such situations is difficult to resolve. Marketers facing such decisions are torn between absolute moral standards requiring truth-telling and a need for realistic and effective marketing practices in a world that is extremely competitive.

Points to Ponder

- Is it really reasonable to expect business people to tell the truth to one another in marketing channels? Can marketers ever tell the truth without fully disclosing all the facts that are relevant to a particular exchange interaction or exchange relationship?

Source: Adapted from Hamilton, Brooke, and David Strutton (1994), "Two Practical Guidelines for Resolving Truth-Telling Problems in Business Transactions," *Journal of Business Ethics*, 13, 899–912; and Smith, C. Jr. (1992), "Economics & Ethics: The Case of Salomon Brothers," *Financial Management Collection*, 7, 3–8.

members. This often creates an ethical dilemma. One means of resolving such predicaments is described in Channel Surfing 7.4.

Caveat emptor usually applies when one or more of the following conditions exist in a channel setting:

- **Nonsubscription to the marketing concept.** Channel members do not always adhere to the principles of the marketing concept. In so doing, the channel member fails to accept the argument that customers and their satisfaction exist as the focus of all marketing mix decisions. Instead, they have a production- or sales-oriented view of exchange.
- **Ignorance of customer needs.** Through an error of omission or commission, channel members are sometimes unaware of customers' needs. Channel members may also misinterpret customer needs in situations involving ethical uncertainty. By default, the channel member is forced to resort to the law as a minimum baseline for providing ethical guidance.

- **Short-term profit goals.** Channel members under pressure to demonstrate profitability in the short run are more likely to engage in opportunistic or exploitative behaviors. The drive for bottom-line performance can often supersede any consideration of the methods or tactics employed.

Caveat Venditor

The concept of **caveat venditor** anchors the other end of our ethics continuum. The school of caveat venditor—seller beware—draws on the pursuit of customer satisfaction as its organizational ethic. Caveat venditor, however, is customer satisfaction taken to its extreme.

Lest we think sellers are the only potentially unethical channel members, buyers themselves sometimes engage in norm-violating behaviors that damage exchange relationships. The opportunity for buyers to engage in unethical practices basically exists as a counterweight to the opportunity that sellers have to engage in exploitative behavior without regard for ethical or moral principles. Such unethical customer practices could include price tag switching (misrepresenting an exchange value), purposely delaying payments or deliveries to fellow channel members, reporting false shortfalls in shipments, and/or intentionally damaging merchandise. This list is far from complete, but it should give you an idea of the many opportunities that buyers have to exploit sellers in channel relationships. These practices are cumulatively known as *buyer backlash.*

Buyer backlash may occur at any level of a marketing channel. However, this inversion of how marketing ethics is conventionally viewed holds particular concern to retailers. Consumer-initiated shoplifting and other forms of fraud cost retailers and wholesalers billions of dollars annually because of increased personnel and security system requirements and actual spoilage.[59] Buyers may rationalize away guilt associated with such misbehavior. If these attempts at self-justifying one's misactions are successful, unethical customer actions become more likely.

Our ethics continuum suggests that channel members on either side of the exchange relationship may be modifying the norms, rules, and standards governing their exchange behaviors over time and across circumstances. Such changes are, in many instances, based on the varying needs of the stakeholders who influence the exchange relationship.

Moral Codes in Channel Relationships

Attaining or sustaining social tact becomes increasingly difficult as exchange processes become more complex. So how can social tact best be achieved in marketing channel relationships? The answer lies within the marketing channel itself: Each channel firm conducts all of its channel affairs based on individual moral codes.

Moral codes deal with how channel members use rules and standards to tell right from wrong. Issues of right and wrong in channel relationships are not always cast in black and white. Consider the case of BMJ, Inc., a former dealership for Chrysler's Jeep and Eagle brands. BMJ brought legal action against the car maker, charging that Chrysler did not treat all dealers fairly. BMJ alleges that Chrysler gave larger allocations and longer credit terms on the financing of new car inventories to selected franchises. Each party agrees that in order to

EXHIBIT 7.4
Alternative moral philosophies

RULES-BASED	CONSEQUENCE-BASED	EXPERIENCE-BASED
Universal moral precepts reconcile ethical dilemma(s).	Consequences of un/ethical decision: • Egoism • Utilitarianism	Subjective evaluation of others' behaviors governs.

consolidate its dealerships, Chrysler terminated some dealership franchises and added the Plymouth line to other existing dealers. But BMJ suggests that Chrysler wanted to reduce financial risk by *weeding out* marginal dealerships.[60]

A sound business decision or an unfair practice? The answer depends on whom you ask. Issues like this often lie in the gray area between right and wrong that must often times be resolved among exchange partners. Moral issues featuring shades of gray are made even more difficult to resolve because perceptions of what constitutes an ethical decision vary across individuals and their respective cultures. Each employee serves as a personal emissary or representative for the channel organization. The problem, of course, is that there is likely no consensus among these employees regarding what is the right set of ethics to use.[61] As a result, contradictory moral positions can come into play when firms interact in channel settings. Three genres of moral codes exist: rules-based moral codes, consequence-based moral codes, and experience-based moral codes. These categories are summarized in Exhibit 7.4.

Rules-Based Moral Codes

A **rules-based moral code** refers to a set of universal principles that people use to resolve ethical conflicts. The Ten Commandments are a well-known set of universal moral rules. The "*Thou Shalt Not . . .*" precursor clearly lays out right and wrong behaviors. Those who believe in using rules-based moral codes argue that outcomes change over time. For this reason, advocates of rules-based moral codes believe that no two behavioral outcomes can ever be exactly alike. Not surprisingly, then, rules-based theory posits that individual evaluations of right and wrong should not be based on behavioral outcomes. Instead, such decisions should be based on universal moral principles.

But as you might expect, universal laws are hard to come by. To illustrate just how hard, let's go back to the Ten Commandments example. Think about the commandment "Thou Shalt Not Kill." The suitability of this universal law would likely evoke some disagreement among members of the U.S. armed services. In a time of war, is it acceptable to kill an enemy? Or, is it right to kill to protect one's family in the name of self-defense?

Similar difficulties arise when moral conflicts must be resolved in traditional marketing channels. Buyers and sellers, suppliers and producers, or wholesalers and retailers are each likely to interpret the same event in different ways. The presumption that moral rules can be established which are universally applicable to the behaviors of each party across all circumstances is, therefore, troubling. Rules-based moral codes are flawed because they ignore the unique needs, interests, and concerns of the employees acting on behalf of the channel firm.

Consequence-Based Moral Codes

Those who subscribe to a **consequence-based moral code** suggest that decision makers can evaluate a behavior's morality based on the behavior's consequences. As such, a morally questionable act can be deemed acceptable if the behavior produces a desirable outcome. The consequence-based approach appeals to channel members because they are concerned with exchange performance and outcomes. Still, problems concerned with how decision makers determine *whom* the consequences benefit can emerge. Here are two separate approaches to consequence-based codes to help resolve this issue.

- **Egoism.** Egoism determines whether an act is right or wrong based solely on whether the outcome optimizes the decision maker's self-interests. An egoistic approach to ethical decision making within channels will injure social tact. Channel members employing an egoistic perspective will act with little regard for their exchange partner's concerns. Therefore, egoism violates a fundamental principle in relationship marketing: a concern for the other channel member's needs. So, an egoistic perspective will almost always lead to poor outcomes in channel relations. Marketers will not be successful in the long run if their ethical actions are motivated primarily by their own self-interests.
- **Utilitarianism.** People who subscribe to utilitarianism believe the proper decision in a moral dilemma is the one that produces the greatest good for the greatest number of people. On the surface, at least, this suggests utilitarians will embrace the need to preserve channel relationships.

Consequence-based approaches to ethical decision making within marketing channels are not foolproof. To illustrate, consider that franchisors invariably recruit new franchisees by promoting their franchising system's profitable *outcomes.* One could argue, therefore, that franchisors have an ethical responsibility to promote each franchisee's profitability. But again, problems can arise in the execution of a moral code. For example, a fast-food franchisor may decide to eliminate a menu item because it has low national appeal. The item may actually be injuring profits throughout most of the franchise system. In response, the franchisor informs franchisees that the item will be discontinued. However, the item happens to be the biggest seller for a particular franchisee operating in a unique market—such as Cajun fries in the heavily French-influenced Acadian region of Louisiana. While the results of the franchisor's action will benefit the greatest number of franchisees, it will harm a particular franchisee.

Experience-Based Moral Codes

Experience-based moral codes suggest that the ethicality of an issue can be evaluated based on the decision maker's previous exchange encounters. Experience-based decision makers subjectively assess cues available from the individuals and organizations involved in the dilemma. Then, based on this assessment, they determine the morality of some action. When one is striving to develop long-term relationships guided by social tact, examining how each member behaved in prior, related situations is logical. The subjective nature of experience-based moral codes is also attractive because they account for the unique character of the exchange relationship itself. Unfortunately, several imperfections are associated with experience-based moral codes. These include:

- **Situational differences.** When individuals use past interactions with channel members as a guide to current ethical behaviors, they assume the prior and current situations are comparable. This assumption may be wrong.
- **Multiple cues.** The experience-based approach is based on moral decision makers' *subjective* interpretations of prior events. But individual channel members are likely to selectively retain different elements from their experiences. Individual channel members are also likely to recall exchange situations in ways that reinforce egoistic interpretations of events. Different exchange partners are not going to behave uniformly. Taken together, these characteristics make it difficult for moral decision makers to decide which individuals, organizations, or situations should be used as cues.
- **A presumption of rightness.** The experience-based approach assumes that prior moral decision scenarios yielded ethical choices. When earlier decision scenarios yield unethical outcomes, channel members using experiential measures tend to repeat the unethical behavior. Over time, unethical behaviors may begin to dominate and become the norm for the relationship.

Experience-based moral codes have appeal because they recognize the multifaceted nature of exchange relationships.[62] When formulating business strategies, channel members ascribing to this situational approach try to predict the conflicts that will arise between their organizations and their suppliers, customers, and the community at large.[63] This is good. But when individual employees look to prior interactions with channel members, there is no guarantee that conflicting moral positions or perceptions can be reconciled.

Moral Codes in Combination

No single moral code offers a foolproof guideline for deciding what is ethical or unethical across all possible situations. In fact, most people use a combination of these moral codes, depending on the types of decisions and the settings in which they confront an ethical dilemma. It is clear, however, that some moral codes are better than others. Selected portions of what we believe is a highly serviceable code of ethics are shown in Exhibit 7.5

In relationship ethics, individuals can be depicted as bundles of moral positions that cumulatively act in channel roles according to some decision rule. Moral codes only partially account for the channel firm's un/ethical behaviors. There are many other factors—including individual, organizational, environmental, and relationship-oriented elements—that influence un/ethical behavior in marketing channels.

The Components of an Ethical Exchange Process

Much of the law governing business exchange is drawn from and formalizes moral principles. Equality in exchange, the Promise Principle, and a sense of morality of duty and morality of aspiration are required for ethical exchanges to occur in channel relationships.[64]

Equality

Ancient Greek philosopher Aristotle's view of exchange was: "[t]here would be no association without exchange, no exchange without equality, [and] no equality without commensu-

Exhibit 7.5

Dow Corning Corporation Code of Ethics

Dow Corning Values

- INTEGRITY Our integrity is demonstrated in our ethical conduct and in our respect for the values cherished by the society of which we are part.
- EMPLOYEES Our employees are the source from which our ideas, actions and performance flow. The full potential of our people is best realized in an environment that breeds fairness, self-fulfillment, teamwork and dedication to excellence.
- CUSTOMERS Our relationship with each customer is entered in the spirit of a long-term partnership and is predicated on making the customer's interests *our* interests.
- PROFIT Our long-term profit growth is essential to our long-term existence. How our profits are derived, and the purposes for which they are used, are influenced by our Values and our shareholders.

Fair, legal and ethical business practice is key to maintaining our corporate integrity. Our code addresses many diverse business situations. Those not explicitly covered can generally be resolved through your own thoughtful judgment or discussion with management or, as needed, a review with the Business Conduct Committee.

Relations with Customers, Distributors, Suppliers

- We are committed to providing products and services that meet the requirements of our customers. We will provide information and support necessary to effectively use our products.
- Business integrity is a criterion for selecting and retaining those who represent Dow Corning. Dow Corning will regularly encourage its distributors, agents, and other representatives to conduct their business on our behalf in a legal and ethical manner.
- The purchase of goods and services will be based on quality, price, service, ability to supply and the supplier's adherence to legal and ethical business practices.

We are committed . . . to the letter and spirit of this code. Our reputation is defined by the individual decisions and actions of each Dow Corning employee. You strengthen Dow Corning's reputation for integrity by knowing and living those standards of business conduct and encouraging the same of your colleagues.

Source: Dow Corning Corporation, 1990, Dow Corning Center, Midland, MI 48640. Reprinted with permission. Only selected portions of Dow Corning Corporation's Code of Ethics appear here.

rability."[65] Such a view emphasizes how important equality is to moral exchanges. Contemporary views of fair exchange suggest that the parties to a fair exchange should be equal in terms of need. Channel partners do not have to be equal in terms of power, knowledge, or moral goodness, but if each is genuinely interested in obtaining something the other has, mutually ethical behaviors will usually develop.[66]

The Promise Principle

The *Promise Principle* suggests that individual channel members can voluntarily impose obligations on themselves under which they can choose to join together for mutual advantage. Trust allows people to cooperate with others to actively serve one another's purposes. Promise keeping is probably the best way to generate trust. Ethical exchange in channel settings is therefore deeply rooted in promise keeping. It follows that channel members are morally obligated to deliver on their promises to one another regardless of whether those promises are legally binding.

Morality of Duty

The concept known as *morality of duty* is characterized by "thou shalt nots" similar to those featured in the Ten Commandments. The morality of duty condemns those who fail to respect the basic moral rules governing individuals and society. Individuals coexisting within channel settings thus operate under the burden of not knowingly doing harm to one another.

Morality of Aspiration

By contrast, the *morality of aspiration* is characterized by "thou shalts"—admonishments for channel members to be *all they can be* in terms of their ethicality. Examples of the morality of aspiration in channel settings include recognition awards for suppliers who achieved planned outcomes, forgiving errors made by an exchange partner, and the accommodating (as opposed to grudging) resolution of conflict.

Imagine, if you will, a circus performer who is struggling to maintain her balance while performing on a tightrope some 60 feet up in the air. Channel members often face an analogous predicament as they stride along, bound together by thin connections that may fray if ethical improprieties arise. Sometimes channel members may feel as though they walk a tightrope between doing the right thing for their channel relationships or doing what appears to be best for their organization. This is a false, and unnecessary, distinction. Over the long run, what is best for channel relationships is always also what is best for the marketing organizations.

Key Terms

antitrust law
caveat emptor
caveat venditor
Celler-Kefauver Act
Clayton Act
consequence-based moral codes
dual distribution
egoism
ethics continuum
exclusive dealing agreement
experience-based moral codes
Federal Trade Commission Act
full-line forcing
law
marketing ethics
merger
moral codes
parallel import channels
per se rule
price discrimination
reimports
relationship ethics
resale price maintenance (RPM)
resale restrictions
Robinson-Patman Act
rule of reason
rules-based moral codes
Sherman Act
slotting allowance
social tact
tying contract
utilitarianism
vertical integration
vertical restraints guidelines
vertical restrictions

Chapter Summary

In the IBM Employee guidelines, it states "First, there is the law. It must be obeyed. But the law is the minimum. You must act ethically." In this chapter, we explore the moral codes and legal imperatives in marketing channel relationships.

Channel members must be aware of a wide array of laws that govern exchange processes. In the channels exosystem, there is a challenge to harmonize the profit-seeking behaviors of sellers with the interests of buyers and the public at-large. Federal antitrust and pricing laws are the most important tools wielded by the U.S. government to address this challenge.

U.S. antitrust law generally rests upon three statutes: the Sherman Act (1890), the Clayton Act (1914), and the Federal Trade Commission Act (1914). Jointly, antitrust laws inhibit or prohibit business activities that lessen free-market competition. Pricing behaviors are governed principally by the Robinson-Patman Act of 1936.

Two important concepts in antitrust legislation are *per se* and *rule of reason* judgments. To win judgment under a *per se* rule, a complainant need only prove the existence of a certain prohibited practice and that this conduct falls within a class of "plainly anti-competitive practices." *Rule of reason* judgments involve a broader inquiry into the facts associated with any dispute, including the evolution and context of the channel members' dispute.

Several channel behaviors have traditionally been subject to evaluation under antitrust and pricing legislation. The practices include price discrimination, resale price maintenance, vertical integration and mergers, dual distribution, tying agreements, refusals to deal, and resale restrictions. More recently, the legality of slotting allowances and parallel import channels have been called into question. The moral organization operates well above the ethical standards prescribed by the law itself.

Marketing ethics refer to the moral codes that underlie exchange processes. Moral codes address how channel members employ rules and standards to help decide what is right or wrong in any exchange process. In marketing channels, one firm's ethical actions can affect another firm's actions in many ways. Marketing ethics is increasingly important as channel members engage in long-term, win-win relationships that require high levels of trust and commitment. Three basic moral codes—rules-based, consequences-based, and experience-based—enable hannel members to make decisions that foster trust and commitment in channel relationships. Still, no single moral code can guide what is ethical or unethical in all possible situations.

Channel Challenges

1. In Chapter 2, we discussed the advent of retail superstores across product categories. From hardware to home electronics, superstores are becoming a popular channel format in the United States and abroad. One product category which has seen an explosion of superstores is bookstores. From Kmart's Waldenbooks to Barnes & Noble, giant chains are at war with the nation's independent book retailers. And the confrontation is escalating. In fact, the American Booksellers Association has filed an antitrust suit against five major publishers, charging that these publishers routinely give secret and promotional discounts to large chains that are not available to small independent stores. Based on your understanding of the channel legislative initiatives in Chapter 7, is this practice legal? Do the small independent bookstores have any legal grounds for combating the special allowances to bookstore giants? How will this battle between intermediaries affect the final consumer?
2. In this chapter, we discussed the impact of *slotting allowances* on channels of distribution. Some manufacturers are shocked by grocers' demands for shelf space. For example, Illinois-based Melting Pot Foods was stunned to discover that some grocers expected as much as $10,000 to stock its Marrakesh Express couscous (a Middle Eastern grain). To avoid slotting allowances, another producer, California Sun Dry Foods, convinced retail grocers to stock its sun-dried tomato products in the produce section—where slotting allowances are uncommon. How does merchandising creativity afford some companies an opportunity to avert slotting allowances? Is this practice fair to all manufacturers?
3. Some of the largest grocery stores in the United States—Kroger Albertson's, Safeway, Inc., and Vons Companies—have filed suit against drugmakers. These grocery giants allege that drugmakers participate in a *two-tier* pricing system: one for grocery chains and

another (more favorable pricing scheme) for institutional pharmacies, health maintenance organizations, and mail-order companies. How does this allegation relate to the Robinson-Patman Act? Should drug manufacturers be forced to sell to all retail formats at the same price? Why or why not?

4. Judge Louis Brandeis once wrote, "Let Americans be under no illusion as to the value of price cutting. It is the most potent weapon of monopoly. Those who succumb to its wiles are thoughtless or weak, but they are selling their birthright for a mess of pottage." How does Brandeis's opinion relate to predatory pricing? How do the successes of mega-discounters like Kmart and Wal-Mart refute Brandeis's argument?
5. A wide variety of branded products are sold through gray market channels. From IBM computers to Mercedes-Benz automobiles, unauthorized channel intermediaries are distributing popular products. In some cases, these products would not otherwise be available to consumers. Does this justify the occurrence of gray marketing? How does gray marketing affect the value of a brand name?
6. *The Satanic Verses,* the Salmon Rushdie novel, was fraught with controversy upon its publication. Many Muslims charged that the novel was an affront to the Islamic religion. The late Ayatollah Khomeini instructed devout Muslims to kill Rushdie, and Muslims worldwide demonstrated their disapproval of the novel. Booksellers like Waldenbooks were faced with the decision whether to stock the controversial novel. How might channel members address this decision using rules-based, consequence-based, and experience-based moral codes? Should retailers distribute a book that offends so many people?

Review Questions

1. Why are U.S. antitrust laws important in harmonizing profit-seeking behaviors among various channel members?
2. Describe the difference between per se- and rule of reason-based court decisions.
3. Which three statutes in U.S. antitrust law are the foundation for preserving free market competition?
4. What is price discrimination? Why is it important to reducing channel conflict?
5. How does existing legislation influence channel practices such as tying agreements, retail price maintenance, and dual distribution?
6. Describe how slotting allowances may be viewed as an impediment to free market competition.
7. How does moral management in organizations foster legal compliance? Does it always ensure legal compliance among channel members?
8. What is generally meant by the term *ethics?* Define marketing ethics and describe the effect of ethics on channel relationships.
9. Describe the ethical continuum that exists between buyer and seller.
10. What are the differences among rules-based, consequence-based, and experience-based moral codes?
11. What is the goal of establishing a code of ethics? Discuss two key features. Why do ethical codes fail?

Endnotes

1. Mitchell, Alan (1999), "Marketers Intensify Push to Control Supply Chains," *Marketing Week* 22 (27), 22–23.
2. Vickers, Graham (2000), "The New Music Men," *Management Today,* June, 6–11.
3. Thorelli, Hans B. (1954), *The U.S. Federal Antitrust Policy,* Stockholm: Stockholms Hogskola, 223.
4. A series of Supreme Court decisions expanding Section 5's scope culminated in *FTC v. Sperry & Hutchinson Co.,* 405 U.S. 233, 244–45 (1972). By this time Section 5's reach included practices that, without having necessarily been previously considered unlawful, offend public policy or cause substantial injury to consumers.

5. Trott, Bob (2000), "Microsoft Disputes Judge's 'Monopoly' Label," *Infoworld,* 22 (4), 8–10.
6. *Business Week* (1966), "Robinson-Patman: Dodo or Golden?" *Business Week,* November, 66.
7. Edwards, Corwin D. (1959), *The Price Discrimination Law,* Washington, DC: Brookings Institute, 6.
8. Shelanski, Howard (1992), "Robinson-Patman Act Regulation of Intraenterprise Pricing," *California Law Review,* 80 (1), 247–87.
9. U.S. Federal Trade Commission (1948), *The Merger Movement: A Summary Report,* Washington, DC: Federal Trade Commission, 68. Time and distance from the events have revealed that the supposed merger-mania triggering the Celler-Kefauver Act was actually of quite modest proportions.
10. Thorelli, *U.S. Federal Antitrust Policy,* 223.
11. For comprehensive but somewhat dated critical analyses of the per se rule in action, see Green, Mark J. (1972), *The Closed Enterprise System,* New York NY: Grossman, 442.
12. See, for example, *Great Atlantic & Pacific Tea Co., Inc., et al. v. F.T.C.,* 87 F.T.C. 99, S.Ct. 925 (1979).
13. *Federal Trade Commission v. Borden Co.,* 383 U.S. 637 (1966).
14. The following cases set precedents in this area: *Samuel H. Moss v. Federal Trade Commission,* 148 F. 2d 378 (1945) and *Federal Trade Commission v. Standard Brands, Inc.,* 189 F. 2d 510 (1951).
15. *Federal Trade Commission v. Anheuser-Busch, Inc.,* 363 U.S. 536 (1960), 289 F. 2d 835 (1961).
16. Kansas, Dave (1994), "Technology and Health: Four Grocery Store Chains Sue 16 Drug Firms in Pricing Debate," *The Wall Street Journal,* March 7, B6.
17. Gebhart, Fred (1999), "Backfire?" *Drug Topics,* 142 (22), 42–45.
18. Hemminger, David G. (1991), "Cost Justification—A Defense with New Applications," *Antitrust Law Journal,* 827–54.
19. The Department of Justice can obtain injunctions and criminal penalties, the FTC can obtain injunctions, and a State Attorney General can obtain damages for its residents. Private plaintiffs generally seek damages but can also seek injunctions. If RPM arises from a manufacturer or retailer cartel, it would be per se illegal as a horizontal conspiracy to set prices. The *Colgate Doctrine* provides a minor exception to this rule in that a manufacturer may set resale prices as long as it unilaterally and immediately terminates retailers for charging different prices. *U.S. v. Colgate,* 250 U.S. S.Ct. 300 (1919).
20. In *Continental T.V. v. GTE* [1977], the Supreme Court held that the rule of reason would apply to vertical agreements that restrict the territories in which retailers can distribute a manufacturer's product.
21. Fabricant, Ross A. (1990), "Special Retail Services and Resale Price Maintenance: The California Wine Industry," *Journal of Retailing,* XX (Spring), 101–8; Sheffet, Mary Jane, and Debra L. Scammon (1985), "Resale Price Maintenance: Is It Safe to Suggest Retail Prices?" *Journal of Marketing,* XX (Fall), 82–91.
22. Anonymous (1998), "Asda Slashes Savlon Price to Prove a Point," *Marketing Week,* 21 (12), 8–9.
23. *Brown Shoe v. U.S.,* 370 U.S. 294, 325 (1962).
24. The precedent for this per se ruling was established by *U.S. v. General Motors Corp., et al.* 384 U.S. 127 (1966) and reaffirmed by *U.S. v. Sealy, Inc., et al.* 388 U.S. 350 (1967).
25. U.S. Department of Justice (1985), *Vertical Restraints Guidelines,* Washington, DC: U.S. Department of Justice, January 23, 18–20.
26. *Datagate, Inc., v. Hewlett-Packard Co.,* CCH 69,523 (CA 9, Aug. 1991), BNA ATRR No. 1529, 205.
27. *Systemcare, Inc. v. Wang Laboratories, Inc., et al.,* CCH 69,829 (DC CO Mar. 1992), 1547, 15.
28. *U.S. v. Colgate,* 250 U.S. S.Ct. 300 (1919).
29. Chen, Zhiqi, and Thomas Ross (1999), "Refusals to Deal in Competitive Markets," *International Journal of Industrial Organization,* 17 (3), 19–26.
30. *United States v. Arnold Schwinn and Co. et al.,* 388 U.S. 365 (1967)
31. *Continental T.V., Inc. v. GTE Sylvania, Inc.,* 433 U.S. 36 (1977).
32. Martin, Michele (1995), "BC Scrutinizes Home Shopping Nets," *Adweek (Eastern Edition),* 38 (18), 14.
33. Wallace, Wade (1995), "Bills Aimed at Rights Protection," *Advertising Age's Business Marketing,* 80 (2), 20–22.
34. McDonald, Bruce A. (1994), "Protecting Your List from Wrongful Use," *Catalog Age,* 11 (8), 97.
35. Shaffer, Greg (1991), "Slotting Allowances and Resale Price Maintenance: A Comparison of Facilitating Practices," *RAND Journal of Economics,* 22 (1), 120–25.
36. Partch, Ken (1990), "Trophies of the Trade Wars," *Supermarket News,* May 11, 25–33.
37. Anonymous (1994), "IRS May Spread Deduction for Slotting Fees for Five Years," *Frozen Food Age,* 42 (10), 67.
38. Chu, Wujin (1992), "Demand Signaling and Screening

in Channels of Distribution," *Marketing Science,* 11 (4), 327–47.

39. Partch, Kenneth (1999), "O' Payola! The U.S. Senate Tackles Slotting Fees," *Supermarket Business,* 54 (10), 122–24.
40. *K-Mart v. Cartier, Inc., et al.,* 486 US 176 (1988).
41. *Appolinaris Co., v. Scherer,* 27 F. 18, SDNY (1886).
42. *A. Bourjois and Company, Inc., v. Katzel.* 692 U.S. SC, 689 (1923).
43. Tariff Act quote.
44. Weigand, Robert E. (1991), "Parallel Import Channels—Options for Preserving Territorial Integrity," *Columbia Journal of World Business,* 26 (Spring), 53–60.
45. *Business Electronics v. Sharp Electronics Corporation,* 486 U.S. SC 1005, *Certiorari* denied (1988).
46. Apple Computer, Inc. (1988), *Transshipping and Mail-Order Policy Statement,* Apple Computer Inc., January, unpaged company document.
47. Copeland, Lee, and Scott Campbell (1999), "Licensed Software Enters Gray Market," *Computer Reseller News,* September 13, 1–8.
48. Ignatius, Adi (1993), "GM Dealer Hits Rough Road in Russia," *The Wall Street Journal,* June 28, A15.
49. Anonymous (1994), "Saudi Arabia: Commercial Agency in the Kingdom," *Middle East Executive Reports,* 14 (12).
50. Department of Justice Guidelines (1988), "International Operations and Enforcement Policy," *CCH,* TRR, 24 November 10.
51. White, Thomas (1993), *Business Ethics: A Philosophical Reader,* New York, NY: Macmillan, 1.
52. Hartley, Robert (1993), *Business Ethics: Violations of Public Trust,* New York, NY: John Wiley & Sons, 117.
53. Taylor, Paul W. (1975), *Principles of Ethics: An Introduction,* Encino, CA: Dickerson, 1.
54. Ferrell, O. C., and John Fraedrich (1994), *Business Ethics: Ethical Decision-Making and Cases,* Boston, MA: Houghton-Mifflin, 6.
55. Weiss, Joseph W. (1994), *Business Ethics: A Managerial, Stakeholder Approach,* Belmont, CA: Wadsworth, 6.
56. Strutton, David, Scott J. Vitell, Jr., and Lou E. Pelton (1994), "How Consumers May Justify Inappropriate Behavior in Market Settings: An Application of the Techniques of Neutralization," *Journal of Business Research,* 30 (July), 253–60.
57. Houston, Franklin S., and Jule B. Gassenheimer (1987), "Marketing and Exchange," *Journal of Marketing,* 51 (October), 11.
58. This section of the ethics continuum is constructed from an excellent and thorough explanation from Smith, N. Craig (1993), *Ethics in Marketing,* N. Craig Smith and John A. Quelch, eds., Burr Ridge, IL: Richard D. Irwin, 21–27.
59. Strutton, Vitell, Jr., and Pelton (1994), "How Consumers May Justify Inappropriate Behavior," 253–60.
60. Tannebaum, Jeffrey A. (1992), "Focus on Franchising: Franchisees Weigh Joint Actions to Gain Protections," *The Wall Street Journal,* September 28, B2.
61. Lewis, Philip V., and Henry B. Speck, III (1990), "Ethical Orientations for Understanding Business Ethics," *Journal of Business Communication,* 27 (Spring), 213–32.
62. Hosmer, Larue Tone (1991), *The Ethics of Management,* Second Edition, Homewood, IL: Richard D. Irwin.
63. Ferrell and Fraedrich (1994), *Business Ethics: Ethical Decision-Making and Cases,* 60.
64. Gundlach, Gregory T., and Patrick Murphy (1993), "Ethical and Legal Foundations of Relational Marketing Exchanges," *Journal of Marketing,* 57 (October), 35–46.
65. Irwin, Terence, trans. (1985), Aristotle's *Nicomachean Ethics,* Indianapolis, IN: Hackett.
66. Cordero, Ronald A. (1988), "Aristotle and Fair Deals," *Journal of Business Ethics,* 7 (September), 681–90.

part II

Cases

Case 2.1

Wal-Mart Stumbles with Hong Kong Shoppers

Neil C. Herndon

Hong Kong retailers didn't seem to notice that one of the world's largest retailers was coming to the Territory in the form of Value Clubs that resembled small Sam's Clubs. Stories appeared in some Hong Kong newspapers following Wal-Mart's announcement in the Fall that three or four of these stores would be opening before Christmas 1994, but otherwise the news barely made a ripple among local retailers.

These merchants just didn't seem to see this retail/wholesale, cash and carry, membership warehouse operation as a credible sales threat. Perhaps they possessed some local insights Wal-Mart executives had missed: the joint venture would dissolve in January 1996 and Ek Chor, now operating Value Club under CP Group ownership, would close all of the Value Club stores by the Fall of 1997.

Source: This case was researched and written by Dr. Neil Herndon, Department of Marketing and International Business at Hofstra University, for classroom discussion rather than to illustrate either effective or ineffective handling of an administrative situation.

The Joint Venture

Ek Chor Distribution System, the parent of Value Club, was a joint venture of Wal-Mart and Charoen Pokphand (CP) Group. They planned to open three or four small warehouse club stores in Hong Kong under the Value Club name and a full-sized Sam's Club and a Wal-Mart Supercenter in different locations just across the Chinese border from Hong Kong in Shenzhen.

The CP Group is a family-owned Thai conglomerate with combined revenues in excess of 4 billion U.S. dollars from over 200 businesses as diverse as chickens and telecommunications, including a supermarket chain and more than 400 7-Eleven convenience stores. Dutch retailer Makro is also a CP Group partner. While little known outside of Asia, it is the largest foreign investor in China with investments estimated to be about 1.3 billion U.S. dollars. The Group started doing business in China almost immediately after then Chinese Vice Premier Xiaoping Deng launched the Open Door economic policy in 1979. Some Asian stock analysts say that the CP Group has more experience with joint ventures and a better track record than anyone else doing business in China.

Doors in high places in China are reported to open to CP Group senior executives. These relationships, called *guanxi* by the Chinese, would likely be helpful to Wal-Mart as it seeks to develop distribution and supplier networks in China. The knowledge that CP Group executives have about the needs of the Chinese customer and why they select particular stores and store locations would also be especially valuable to Wal-Mart. The CP Group appears to prefer low risk ventures and entering a venture with an organization having the retailing expertise of a Wal-Mart would certainly reduce the risk of failure.

U.S. based Wal-Mart is one of the world's largest retailers with over 2,000 stores and 400 Sam's Clubs in the U.S. The financial clout it brings to a new market is immense. But since much of its organizational experience is in the U.S., it had little internal Asian retailing expertise. Despite this limitation, Wal-Mart does have a history of rapid adaptation to change. While it is centrally led, the company is managed at a local level, which means that it can learn and adapt much faster than its size would suggest. It has been able to implement changes in its marketing mix while pleasing customers and making operational changes, especially in its distribution systems, that cut operating costs below that of its U.S. competition.

Wal-Mart has built its U.S. business on providing middle-of-the-market products at the best price with the least inconvenience. Given Wal-Mart's fierce determination to be the low price leader in its U.S. markets, it would be reasonable to assume that they would attract the favorable attention of price-sensitive Chinese customers.

Warehouse Clubs

Warehouse clubs—also called wholesale clubs—are usually thought of as large-scale, members-only, selling operations that combine features of cash-and-carry wholesaling and discount retailing. Their target market is typically both individual customers and small business customers. Despite the image of warehouse clubs as places where people with big families and those who are overly price-sensitive shop, about 70 percent of sales at Sam's Clubs in the U.S. are from business customers. The key operating strategy is to maintain low costs and high turnover so that goods can be sold at prices lower than those in competing outlets.

To follow the low costs and high turnover strategy, warehouse clubs generally offer the biggest-selling brands of consumer goods, usually in bulk packaging. Variety within a product category is usually lacking. Most of the retail store amenities are not offered, providing a "no-frills" feel; goods are often displayed on metal shelving in their original cardboard packing containers. Services are minimal: warehouse clubs usually do not accept credit cards and they usually do not deliver purchases for customers. Advertising typically is also kept to a minimum; promotional tools such as leaflets are sometimes used, leaving the warehouse club to rely heavily on word-of-mouth.

The main way in which the warehouse club retail technology creates value for the customer is probably through the offering of a lower price for goods than that which can be found at competing retail forms such as supermarkets. However, considering only a lower price for goods tends to disguise the true cost of choosing a retail form. The opportunity cost of time, the cost of gathering purchase information not provided by the store, and the transfer of all or part of the costs of providing certain services (such as delivery) to the customer using the store are examples of hidden costs associated with using a given retail form.

Many customers want to shop in an environment that is "comfortable" from their perspective. The low-cost, bare nature of warehouse clubs produces a unique set of atmospherics and store image that may influence store patronage, quality perceptions, value perceptions, and willingness to buy.

It appears that generally warehouse clubs would be attractive to price-sensitive customers who are willing to sacrifice some conveninence, some comforts in the shopping environment, some services, brand loyalty, merchandise consistency, and individual packaging for lower prices. However, not all customers are so price sensitive: some are willing to pay higher price in return for what they perceive to be a higher-quality shopping experience. In short, customers tend to want more of the things they value. This suggests that customers will determine for themselves the value they place on the benefits received from a new retail technology such as warehouse clubs and patronize them accordingly.

The Hong Kong Environment

Hong Kong was a British colony for more than 150 years. Its 415 square miles are located on a peninsula jutting into the South China Sea from mainland China and on about 235 islands, only about four of which contain a significant population. Much of Hong Kong is steep, low-lying hills, leaving only about 15 percent of its area suitable for development. This contributes to astronomical land prices.

Despite its British heritage, the main written language is Chinese, with Cantonese the most commonly spoken Chinese dialect. English is a second language here, but many residents have limited English-language skills. Government and legal documents are available in both Chinese and English. About 98 percent of its 6.2 million residents are Chinese, and there are about 60,000 Americans, Europeans, and Filipinos and 30,000 Indian and Pakistani residents.

Hong Kong is a major center for Asian business. Many companies have corporate offices here because of the high quality of life available and its excellent legal and regulatory environment for business. Government investment in infrastructure has been high, giving Hong Kong some of the largest and most modern port facilities in Asia. It serves as a major trading center providing access to mainland Chinese markets, a role expected to increase once the People's Republic of China (PRC) resumed sovereignty over Hong Kong.

In the fall of 1994 in Hong Kong, retail sales were generally down, but retail rents for prime locations remained among the highest in the world, some 130 percent higher than comparable locations in New York and Tokyo. The stock market was in something of a slump and unemployment was up. Uncertainty about Hong Kong's future after July 1, 1997, when it would cease to be a British colony and would be returned to the PRC, had consumers holding tightly to their dollars.

Hong Kong shoppers are very price-sensitive; they treat shopping as a competitive sport where the lowest price wins. However, they also value convenience, partly because of the difficulty of transporting purchases home.

Most people travel by subway system, bus, or taxi. Only about 4 percent of Hong Kong's 6.2 million inhabitants own private automobiles in this crowded environment due, in part, to a lack of parking space and an excellent public transportation system. Large or heavy bulk purchases must be taken home by taxi, which is more expensive than taking the subway or bus.

Residents of this geographically small Territory seem to perceive even relatively short distances of a few kilometers as "long." They often shop close to home because of the difficulty associated with transporting some bulky purchases and because almost every apartment complex is designed to include some retail shops such as a small grocery store, pharmacy, laundry, and restaurant. Chinese housewives also traditionally shop daily for fresh food to prepare for their family, preferably buying fresh vegetables and fresh meat close to home.

Most residents are apartment dwellers. Their apartments are often as tiny as 400 square feet for five adults. Kitchens may be as small as a closet in a U.S. apartment, the result of very high apartment rents on a per square meter basis in Hong Kong. With small refrigerators and very limited storage space, residents must shop almost daily.

There may be nowhere to store a gallon of cooking oil in an apartment except on the floor. A gallon of orange juice, while a favorite drink for the Chinese, requires refrigeration in Hong Kong's subtropical heat: it may not fit in the small refrigerators common here. Consequently, it is difficult for most Hong Kong consumers to buy in bulk and store unused product even at bargain prices. Most don't want to live with five or six packages of shampoo stored on the bathroom windowsill in order to save a few dollars.

As one petite housewife pointed out, Asian women are not able to accurately pour a small amount from a large bottle of cooking oil or soy sauce into meals they are cooking. The housewife said she needed to buy a smaller container that she could handle easier, pour some of the oil into it, then store the remainder somewhere near her kitchen. She said it's easier to just buy a smaller bottle in the first place.

While attracting many U.S. retail customers, Sam's Club focuses on the small-business owner in its U.S. home market as the wholesale purchasers who give Sam's the majority of its sales. However, the small-business owner in Hong Kong is influenced by many of the same factors, such as transportation and storage, affecting consumers who might buy for personal or household use. In some cases the Hong Kong retail store space becomes the family living room, dining room, and bedroom by night, further limiting the opportunity to store additional goods that might be available even at a reduced price.

The Value Club Stores

The first Value Club store opened in Tuen Mun's Town Plaza October 22, 1994, soon to be followed by stores in the Waterside Plaza in Tsuen Wan and in a basement opening onto Waterloo Road in Homantin. These are secondary locations a taxi ride or bus ride away from the public transportation "backbone," selected in part because of the high cost of primary retail locations. However, while Value Club did not provide parking lots as would be expected at warehouse clubs in the U.S., in a departure from the service levels usually provided at wholesale clubs, free delivery in a limited area with purchases of HK$700 (about US$90) was available in Hong Kong. Parking spaces are also usually easier for drivers to find in these secondary retail locations.

Warehouse clubs in the U.S. typically occupy around 100,000 square feet, so these 20,000 square foot stores were tiny by Wal-Mart standards, but would likely provide training centers for the company's eventual expansion into the Chinese mainland. The interior design was typical for a wholesale club: tile or concrete floors, metal racks, high ceilings, and goods displayed in original cardboard packing containers.

Each Value Club store stocked about 1,000 different items, many directly imported from the U.S., representing the best sellers in categories including groceries, candy and snacks, frozen foods, health and beauty aids, sporting goods, household and janitorial goods, pet supplies, paper goods, and furniture. The smaller size of these stores compared to their U.S. parents suggested a more limited product assortment: a Sam's Club in the U.S. stocks about 4,500 different items.

The Value Club product assortment was about 70 percent U.S. merchandise and 30 percent local products. Many of the products in bulk sizes or multipacks were not available in the grocery stores where Hong Kong women usually shop and were not very familiar to them. Some shoppers appeared to be confounded by curiosities such as a four-pound jar of peanut butter, another food that the Chinese enjoy. One man indicated that the price for the peanut butter was right, but that he didn't know where he would put it.

Customers confronted with products new to them are sometimes willing to try the innovation if the risk is low. If the products came in smaller sizes, shoppers might be willing to try them. But they would not want to risk wasting money and losing "face" by throwing out a large amount of a new product they did not like. The Wal-Mart policy of accepting returned goods without argument and with a smile reduces this risk. Such an approach both surprised and delighted Hong Kong customers; it is simply not done in Hong Kong by other retailers, even if the merchandise is defective. This policy could have been a key to building the long-term reciprocal relationships that the Chinese greatly value.

People wishing to become Value Club members paid an annual membership fee of HK$150 (about US$19). Non-members were also free to shop at the stores, but they paid 5 percent above the posted price.

Overall, Wal-Mart wanted to convince Chinese shoppers that they wouldn't have to pay extra to shop in clean, well-lit stores with wide aisles and smiling salespeople. But a part of the problem was how to adjust the Wal-Mart strategy to accommodate customers who take the bus to the store rather than the family car as they do in the U.S. Value Club tried to attract more customers with its offer of reserved bus service to their stores for a fee. Delivery trucks then would follow the bus to the shoppers' homes with their purchases. Scheduling shopping in advance is a relatively unusual idea for Hong Kong residents, and it did not meet with much success because of the inconvenience involved. A mass catalog mailing that offered ordering by fax, followed by home delivery within two days, also had limited success.

One study found that most Value Club shoppers were women, a situation similar to that of the U.S. where, in over two-thirds of the households, women do the primary grocery shopping. However, in the U.S., the customers of mass merchandising operations such as warehouse clubs tend to be less affluent while the majority of shoppers in this study appeared to have monthly incomes over HK$20,000 (about US$2,580) which is more than twice the 1993 mean monthly Hong Kong income of HK$7,395 (about US$954). About 32 percent of the Value Club shoppers owned automobiles; the norm in Hong Kong is about 4 percent. Warehouse clubs in Hong Kong may appeal to a different market segment than do U.S. stores of this type.

The Warehouse Club Competitors

Value Club had at least two competitors in Hong Kong that operated warehouse clubs. GrandMart with seven stores, first opened in 1993, set its annual membership fee at HK$150 (about US$19) for individuals and at HK$200 (about US$26) for businesses. It stocked about 1,000 products, some of which were the U.S. Price Club's store brands through a special arrangement and some of which were staple items such as rice and instant noodles from local suppliers.

GrandMart generated considerably higher traffic than Value Club by offering bulk packages of products that are often used quickly and are familiar to consumers, such as snacks that families eat while watching TV. Fresh produce, attractive to many Chinese housewives, was available at some GrandMarts, but not at Value Club. GrandMart may have taken a page from Price Club's playbook: offer products that appeal to the greatest number of people. GrandMart locations also appeared to be better suited for daily visits; many were close to large public apartment complexes which are home to many thousands of people.

Like the competition, GrandMart offered free delivery service on orders over HK$750 (about US$97). Smaller orders incurred a HK$60 (about US$8) delivery fee.

Then there was the U-Save Warehouse, which looked like a Value Club right down to the item pricing on the shelf. Shoppers may have needed to check the sign out front to be certain they had not wandered into a Value Club by mistake. Owned by Kitty and Kettie Supermarket Ltd., U-Save opened their first store in the summer of 1995. U-Save had two locations, one among a group of lower-income high-rise public apartment buildings near Kowloon Tong, the other in a more upscale Sunshine City Plaza mall in the New Territories city of Ma On Shan. They offered free delivery on orders over HK$500 (about US$64). As with Value Club, shoppers were passing up U-Save for grocery stores with more familiar products in more convenient sizes.

The Joint Venture Ends

The 50-50 joint venture was dissolved in January 1996, about 18 months after it began. Both the CP Group and Wal-Mart intend to continue their retailing expansion efforts in China. The split appeared to be the result of disagreements between Wal-Mart and the CP Group about the amount of influence CP Group should have on store location and merchandising decisions. Despite CP Group's considerable expertise in the China market, Wal-Mart appeared to find it difficult to deviate greatly from its business model that worked so well in the U.S. The difficulties that the partners have had convincing customers to shop at their three Value Club outlets in Hong Kong probably contributed to the breakup.

Under the terms of the divorce, Ek Chor kept the three Hong Kong Value Club stores and developments in Shenyang and Shanghai in the PRC. Wal-Mart got the 14,000 square-meter Sam's Wholesale Club and the 18,000 square-meter Wal-Mart Supercenter in Shenzhen.

Ek Chor, now operating under CP Group ownership, would open a fourth Value Club store in Hong Kong, also in a secondary retail location. It changed the product assortment in all of the stores to include more products familiar to local shoppers, and it offered more products in smaller sizes. Sales did increase, but not enough to sustain the interest of CP Group. All of the Value Club stores closed by the fall of 1997.

Questions for Discussion

1. How was the environment that Wal-Mart faced in Hong Kong different from the one it faced in its U.S. market?
2. What are the key success factors for warehouse club retailing operations?
3. In retrospect, how might Wal-Mart have approached entry into the unfamiliar Hong Kong environment so that its chances of success would have been enhanced?

References

William Barnes, "Success Built on Friends in High Places," *South China Morning Post,* July 7, 1996, Money Section, 4; Joan Bergmann, "China Reassessed," *Discount Merchandiser,* May 1995, 94, 96, 97, 105; Bloomberg, "Wal-Mart Speeds Up Entry Plan for Mainland Market," *South China Morning Post,* October 21, 1994, Business Section, 2; Christine Chan, "Pokphand and Wal-Mart Split," *South China Morning Post,* June 27, 1996, Business Section, 2; Debra Chanil, "Wholesale Clubs: A New Era," *Discount Merchandiser,* November 1994, 38, 40, 42–46, 48, 50–51; Carl Goldstein, "Full Speed Ahead," *Far Eastern Economic Review,* October 21, 1993, 66–68; Bob Hagerty and Peter Wonacott, "Wal-Mart Expands Cautiously in Asia," *The Asian Wall Street Journal,* August 12, 1996, 28; Neil Herndon, "Wal-Mart Goes to Hong Kong, Looks at China," *Marketing News,* November 21, 1994, 2; Neil Herndon, "Hong Kong Shoppers Cool to Wal-Mart's Value Club," *Marketing News,* November 20, 1995, 11; Neil Herndon, Jr., "HK Shoppers Tell Value Club: Wrong Place, Wrong Product," *Asian Retailer,* May 1996, 30, 32; Neil C. Herndon, Jr. and Cecilia Chi-Yin Yu, "A New Retail Technology in Asia: Warehouse Clubs," *Management Research News,* 19 (no. 9, 1996), 5–27; Journal of Commerce, "Wal-Mart Signs Pact in Orient," *The Kansas City Star,* August 23, 1994, D-4; Louise Lee, Nopporn Wong-Anan, and Bob Hagerty, "Wal-Mart Ends China Venture with CP Group," *The Asian Wall Street Journal,* January 11, 1996, 1, 8; Simon Pritchard and Reuter, "US Retail Giant Wal-Mart to Open Stores in Hong Kong," *South China Morning Post,* August 21, 1994, Money Section, 1; Carla Rapoport and Justin Martin, "Retailers Go Global," *Fortune,* February 20, 1995, 102–4, 106, 108; Tim Wilson, "Wal-Mart Threat to Shenzhen," *Window,* August 16, 1996, 51; Wendy Zellner, "Why Sam's Wants Businesses to Join the Club," *Business Week,* June 27, 1994, 48, 53.

Case 2.2

Partnering for Success: Federal Express and Netscape Join Forces for Information Technology

Federal Express and Netscape: The Strategic Alliance

> It's nearly 10:50 PM. Almost curtain time. The first lights—a series of fuzzy orbs—appear in the distance against the starry Memphis, Tennessee, sky. Down on the ground, the glowing complex of buildings that is the FedEx SuperHub gears for action, like an orchestra warming up. Crews gather in the tarmac. Tug transports rev. Handheld radios crackle with instructions.
>
> In the air, the first lights grow larger and more distinct, followed closely by another set, and behind them still another and another. The sky glows with a string of lights like some floating celestial garland as air freighters from points around the globe bear down like a carrier pigeon on a 294-acre patch of Southern soil, center stage in a nocturnal pageant. Engines whine down as the first plane lands, and the 8,000 employees on duty know what that means: It's show time (Ralston 1998).

Only a few hours later, there is a knock at Billy Murray's door. His eyes widen as he tears down the stairwell anticipating the best birthday present imaginable. Just as he expected, nine-year-old Billy finds a FedEx deliveryman towering over him, holding the very box that could contain the Beast Wars Transformer. This is the present he has been waiting for. With an enormous grin on his face, Billy snatches the FedEx box from the grasp of the deliveryman, as his father signs for the package. In a matter of seconds, Billy rips open the package revealing the vivid colors of the animated box.

If Billy only knew about the panic that overcame his father yesterday, when he realized all of the stores were out of the ultimate present for his nine-year-old child. In a frantic effort to ensure the happiness of his son, Billy's father turned to his personal computer. He linked onto http://home.netscape.com and ordered his gift through the NetCenter General Store. The present was shipped via Netscape's pre-selected carrier, FedEx. Throughout the night Billy's father tracked the package with FedEx's Delivery Center accessed through http://home.netscape.com. He was assured that the package would arrive on time.

Just like Billy's father, businesses and consumers rely on the last minute shipping capabilities of FedEx. There is no doubt that Netscape can benefit from the resourcefulness and dependability of one of the leading express transportation companies. By forming an alliance with FedEx, Netscape is gaining an edge in electronic commerce by getting its foot in the door of the express transportation industry. Together, the two companies can expect a boost in their businesses by focusing on their competitors' weaknesses and expanding electronic commerce.

Federal Express—Corporate Mission Statement: *From the FedEx Web Site (http://www.fedex.com)*

> Federal Express is committed to our People-Service-Profit philosophy. We will produce outstanding financial returns by providing totally reliable, competitively superior, global air-ground transportation of high priority goods and documents that require rapid, time-certain delivery. Equally important, positive control of each package will be maintained using real time electronic tracking systems. A complete record of each shipment and delivery will be presented with our request for payment. We will be helpful, courteous, and professional to each other and the public. We will strive to have a completely satisfied customer at the end of each transaction.

The FedEx mission statement describes the company's commitment to information technology as well as to customer satisfaction. By embracing information technology, FedEx is able to consistently provide superior customer service. Information technology is critical to FedEx's operations, but equally important are the thousands of employees that make the operation work each day.

Source: Prepared by Thomas J. Dixon II, Karen Flanigan, Vanessa Izaguirre, Eddie Jackson, and Elizabeth Walden, under the supervision of Dr. Lou E. Pelton, University of North Texas, November 23, 1999.

Key Decision Makers: ***As taken from the FDX Corporation website (http://www.fdxcorp.com).***

Frederick W. Smith Chairman, President & Chief Executive Officer—FDX Corporation	Smith is responsible for providing strategic direction for all FDX Corporation business units. Smith founded Federal Express in 1971 and the company began operations on April 17, 1973.
T. Michael Glenn Executive Vice President Market Development & Corporate Communications—FDX Corporation	T. Michael Glenn's specific responsibilities include all marketing, sales, strategic analysis, customer service and communications activities for FDX Corporation. He also oversees operations of Roberts Express.
Alan B. Graf, Jr. Executive Vice President & Chief Financial Officer—FDX Corporation	Graf is a member of the five-person executive committee, which is responsible for planning and executing all service functions for the corporation. His specific responsibilities include all aspects of FDX Corporation's global financial functions, including financial planning, treasury, tax, accounting and controls, internal audit and strategic sourcing.
Dennis H. Jones Executive Vice President Information & Logistics Services Chief Information Officer—FDX Corporation	Specific responsibilities for Jones include all aspects of FDX Corporation's logistics and electronic commerce initiatives, as well as strategic information systems processing, systems engineering, software development and design. He also manages information and telecommunications activity for the corporation's five business units: Federal Express, RPS, Viking Freight, Roberts Express and FDX Logistics.
Kenneth R. Masterson Executive Vice President General Counsel & Secretary—FDX Corporation	A member of the five-person executive committee which is responsible for planning and executing all service functions for the corporation, Masterson's specific responsibilities include ensuring that FDX Corporation's global activities are in compliance with international, federal, state and local government regulations.

Corporate Culture

The corporate culture at FedEx is best described as a "can-do" atmosphere. This may stem largely from its founder, Fred W. Smith. In 1965, a Yale undergraduate wrote a term paper encompassing his vision of a time-sensitive air cargo delivery service. His professor thought the idea was unrealistic and deemed the paper average. Ironically, Fred W. Smith, Yale graduate, rose above the professor's expectations and became founder and CEO of FedEx, a multibillion-dollar company recognized as the world's largest express transportation company.

FedEx employees take great pride in their occupations. The company Smith founded has created a cultural phenomenon that evokes high amounts of pride from employees. During end-of-year peak times, even senior level managers volunteer to load boxes at the hub. Some employees claim to "bleed purple and orange" (Ralston 1998, 18).

FedEx spends over $155 million a year to train employees (Ralston 1998). According to FedEx, "An employee can do an outstanding job if he or she is given thorough information on what the job requires and how to perform it" (Ralston 1998, 23).

Couriers are encouraged to share ideas with management. Many of the best improvements to FedEx delivery vans are due to carrier input. However, employee relations do not always go as smoothly as management may desire. In reference to FedEx pilots' attempts to earn better wages and benefits last year, union representative Byron L. Cobb states, "Federal Express is a good company to work for, but we are tired of saying 'please' and getting no response from management" (Field 1998, 3). The average salary for pilots at Federal Express in 1998 was $124,000 yearly. This reflected the lowest wages in the industry. FedEx pilots had not received a wage or benefits increase in several years (Field 1998). This friction caused the pilots to form the first collective bargaining agreement in the twenty-five year history of FedEx. Although Smith reiterated that FedEx did have a contingency plan in case of a strike, he also admitted, "The threat of a pilot strike has seriously jeopardized our outstanding reputation for reliability and customer service, helped our competitors, and resulted in additional, and unnecessary, operational costs" (Field 1999, 3).

Not only is on the job training offered, but many

employees at all levels go on to get bachelor's degrees and MBAs from local universities and colleges. The company is dedicated to promotion from within. For instance, Dave Rebholz started with FedEx as a part-time clerk in Milwaukee, Wisconsin. Today, he manages over 60,000 people as the Senior Vice-President of U.S. Ground Operations (Ralston 1998).

Annually, every FedEx employee scores the company on leadership, pay, job conditions, and general satisfaction. After the results are tabulated, managers receive scorecards. Management then goes a step further and sits down with employees to discuss what changes need to be made and for further clarification. Management takes a vested interest in this because their scores are directly tied to their bonuses.

The Bravo Zulu awards are another way management can recognize superior achievement. Bravo Zulu, the Navy term for "well done," allows management to distribute theater tickets, dinner certificates, or up to $100 cash on the spot. In 1997, FedEx management distributed 111,736 Bravo Zulus to the tune of $7.5 million (Ralston 1998).

There are many other aspects that help define the corporate culture at FedEx. For example, new planes are named after employees' children. Also, grievances are handled by a "Superior Court" of FedEx that can appeal decisions made at lower levels. Fred Smith often attends these appeal hearings (Ralston 1998).

FedEx has had successes in employee relations, such as winning the Malcolm Baldrige Quality Award in 1990. However, they have also encountered defeats such as labor disputes in recent years. Through FedEx's dedication to a strategically designed human resources department, the company has the potential for continued successes in this arena.

Nature and Scope

FedEx is the preeminent express delivery corporation in the industry. Starting business in April 1973, annual revenues now exceed $14 billion. FedEx employs more than 148,000 people worldwide. A fleet of 643 aircraft service 210 countries at 366 airports each day. FedEx utilizes more than 43,500 vehicles driving more than 2.7 million miles daily. Average daily volume is 3.1 million packages, amounting to 54 million pounds monthly (FedEx Information Packet 1999).

The Decision Environment

Competition between express package delivery companies is fierce. Nowhere is this more evident than between Federal Express (FedEx) and United Parcel Service (UPS). These industry giants are ever engaged in a war of one-ups; waging battle in delivery options, information services, and third-party logistics services.

E-commerce has experienced frenetic growth in recent years due to the migration, or at the least integration, from "bricks-and-mortar" retailing to online shopping. While highly capitalized, many online retailers are not turning a profit and are still in the beginning stages of developing their supply chain. Supply chain efficiency is the basis for reducing costs and differentiating a business from the competition. Companies like FedEx and UPS are scrambling to be the preferred link between the retailer's warehouse and the final customer.

To meet the quickly escalating needs of electronic retailers (e-tailers), FedEx and UPS are making immense technological investments that focus on lightning-fast, seamless transfers of information and inventory from the manufacturer to the final customer. The alliance with Netscape has allowed FedEx to expand its third-party logistics services. These services include FedEx-manned call centers and the ability for customers to place orders via the Netscape Internet portal. Orders are picked, packed, and loaded on FedEx aircraft. The customer is notified of the shipment by e-mail and the supplier is notified that there is one less item in inventory (Krause 1999). The crux of e-commerce competition between FedEx and UPS is getting e-tailers to commit to FedEx or UPS as their sole product distributor. So far, UPS asserts to have commitments from around 10,000 e-tailers, while FedEx declares closer to 15,000 (Krause 1999).

FedEx and UPS are competing to expand their customer bases by offering different delivery services and options. While this may make the process more confusing to the occasional customer, it is an all-out effort by the two companies to respond to a customer base that has very specific demands when it comes to package delivery.

FedEx also competes with smaller competitors that have developed strong niche positions within the market. Airborne Express, which focuses on business-to-business documents and small package delivery, now has Internet offerings similar to FedEx and UPS (Bradley et al. 1999). FedEx's concentration on the long-haul has left the door open for many short-haul less-than-truckload (LTL) carriers. Long considered disorganized and inefficient, LTL carriers are now streamlining operations, developing more sophisticated information systems, and capitalizing on their individual strengths (Schulz 1999). LTL strengths include regionalized saturation, high reliability, very competitive short-haul prices, and a variety of value-added services. For example, Overnite Transportation Corporation has personalized its service by ensuring that all phone calls are answered by a human versus a machine (Schulz 1999). This means that CEO Leo Suggs has omitted usage of voice mail. "Provide the best value and you will be rewarded," Suggs said (Schulz 1999, 1).

The biggest threat to FedEx may be the United States Post Office (USPS), which holds a monopoly on first-class shipments (Feulner 1997). USPS is a government entity and as a result is able to offer prices that are considered unfair by many express executives. The USPS is also developing package-tracking systems that will allow the guarantee of two- and three-day deliveries at much lower prices than FedEx or UPS. The USPS has also teamed with private air carriers to offer four-to-five business day service from Hawaii to most Pacific-Rim countries and Canada, at a price 27 percent less than FedEx and UPS services (Gomes 1997).

The Strategic Alliance

The alliance between FedEx and Netscape consists of FedEx using Netscape software as the primary technology for its intranet and Internet sites. FedEx will use Netscape technology in three different areas:

- to publish internal technology reports, personnel guidelines, tax forms, employee evaluations, and project-management documentation.
- to provide a common interface (Netscape) that can be accessed by computers using multiple operating systems.
- to provide easily accessible information to FedEx's technical support personnel, enabling them to answer customer inquiries without delay. (home.netscape.com 1999)

FedEx and Netscape enjoy several benefits with the alliance. Netscape's software has allowed FedEx to move toward a paper-free environment through the intranet. FedEx saves money and time, and employees are empowered with

FDX Corporation Acquisitions and Structure:
As taken from the FDX Corporation website (http://www.fdxcorp.com)

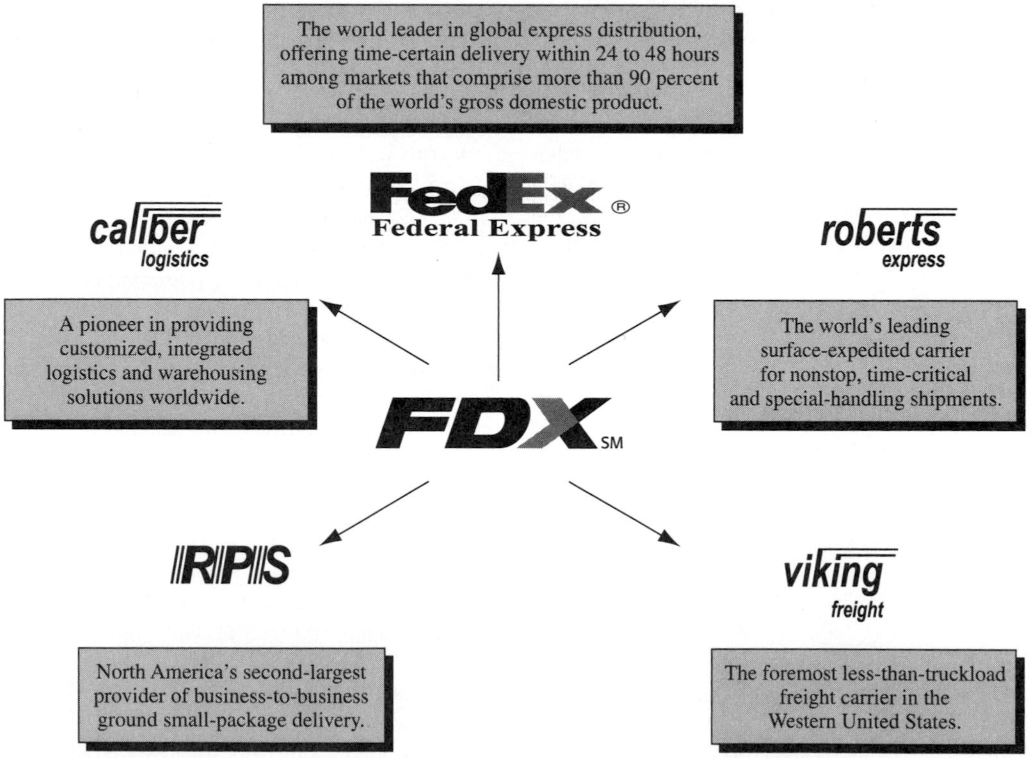

The world leader in global express distribution, offering time-certain delivery within 24 to 48 hours among markets that comprise more than 90 percent of the world's gross domestic product.

FedEx® Federal Express

caliber logistics

A pioneer in providing customized, integrated logistics and warehousing solutions worldwide.

roberts express

The world's leading surface-expedited carrier for nonstop, time-critical and special-handling shipments.

FDX SM

RPS

North America's second-largest provider of business-to-business ground small-package delivery.

viking freight

The foremost less-than-truckload freight carrier in the Western United States.

instant access to corporate information. Intranets flatten organizations, improving structure, communication, and teamwork (www.netscape.com/columns). Technical documents will be readily available to all service personnel on the intranet. FedEx gains a strong internal distribution system; prior to the alliance FedEx depended on faxes, paper documents, electronic mail and file sharing (home.netscape.com).

The alliance offers FedEx a better tracking and customer service system. "It is impossible for our technical help desk personnel to be an expert in every situation. Using the intranet allows us to deliver information to our technical support personnel quickly so they can effectively trouble shoot problems with minimum delays," says Robert Carter, Vice President of Corporate Systems Development with FedEx (home.netscape.com).

The unprecedented increase in e-commerce growth has necessitated that Netscape create innovative offerings that go beyond basic capabilities to include integration tools and services (Halper 1999). Netscape is differentiating itself by aligning with FedEx, an industry leader in express transportation.

An inherent bond exists between FedEx and Netscape. Jim Barksdale spent 12 years at FedEx prior to going to Netscape in 1994. He has greatly enhanced the fit between the two partners and strengthened the strategic alliance. From 1979 to 1983, Barksdale fulfilled the position of Chief Information Officer at FedEx. He then advanced to Executive Vice President and Chief Operating Officer. The success of Barksdale's efforts became well known when FedEx became the first company to receive the Malcolm Baldrige National Quality Award (*Asian Business* 1997).

Barksdale is the link that will sustain the relationship between FedEx and Netscape. He provides relationship solidarity and acts as the "glue" that bonds the partners. During his 12 year tenure at FedEx, Barksdale acquired first-hand knowledge of FedEx operations. His expertise assists in Netscape's overall understanding of their strategic partner. Barksdale's drive to succeed is apparent in the phrase, "God-given 95 percent market share," which he coined while at Federal Express (Copeland 1998, 2). Barksdale believes and understands the necessity to form strategic alliances in today's competitive market place. He states "And the vast majority of the smart people in this world do not work at Netscape, that's why we need partners" (*Asian Business* 1997, 3). FedEx and Netscape believe that the outcomes of the partnership exceed the value that would occur as a result of individual efforts, thereby establishing synergy.

Aside from Barksdale, FedEx's past experience using Netscape products (servers, clients, development tools, and commercial applications that supported their Internet site) greatly influenced their selection of Netscape as a partner (home.netscape.com). FedEx also realizes Netscape's technology leadership. Dennis H. Jones, FedEx Chief Information Officer, sums it up by stating, "We are using Netscape software across the board for accessing our intranet sites because of Netscape's ability to keep in front of the fastest moving technology wave in history" (www.netscape.com/newsref). Obviously, FedEx realizes that Netscape has the expertise and resources to support their efforts.

Critical Issues

Currently, strategic alliances are growing at a rapid rate. While strategic alliances have always existed, advances in technology and increased global competition have driven companies to seek synergy. Synergy is the idea that by working with another party or parties, the outcomes surpass the individual efforts. FedEx and Netscape formed a strategic alliance in order to achieve synergy (Pelton et al. 1997).

Technology in the package delivery industry is extremely important for both the company and its customers. As part of the alliance, FedEx is using Netscape technology for its intranet and Internet sites. With the many benefits Netscape technology brings, will it be enough to help FedEx in the race for global expansion?

In the 1990s, FedEx rushed to "go global" and beat one of its major competitors, UPS. In FedEx's efforts to increase market share globally, it acquired Flying Tigers, an international air-freight operation. The purchase of Flying Tigers added 6,500 employees to FedEx's payroll. The 39 cargo jets purchased in the acquisition needed major repairs to meet government regulations, further cutting into FedEx profit. With the acquisition, FedEx earned unrestricted cargo landing rights at three Japanese airports. FedEx believed the acquisition was the best and fastest way into the global market. FedEx did not, however, foresee the problems Flying Tigers would bring (Calonius 1990). Have experiences such as this helped FedEx to look more carefully before they leap?

Since FedEx began to acquire companies in the early 1980s its international revenues have more than doubled, but losses are beginning to increase. Losses are said to come from FedEx's many acquisitions, particularly the purchase of Flying Tigers, according to market analysts (Calonius 1990). With increasing aggregation of the express package delivery industry, will FDX be able to move forward as one corporation and compete in the world marketplace?

Additionally, with fewer competitors in the marketplace, will the industry become a two or three man race?

FedEx's acquisitions have left the company in debt. UPS, a major competitor of FedEx, announced an initial public stock offering (IPO). UPS, one of the largest privately held companies in the U.S., has $3.4 billion in cash on hand. The IPO will generate several billion dollars to help the company fund future acquisitions and expansion. "There are a lot of new competitors and we're entering new markets," says James Kelly, UPS Chairman and Chief Executive Officer. UPS has seen its competitors, mainly FedEx, acquire other companies and are now ready to do the same. FedEx formed an alliance with Netscape in order to have a competitive advantage in technology, but with UPS's recent announcement of its IPO and intentions of acquiring other companies, will FedEx hold its advantage in the race for dominant share in the package delivery industry?

References

Bradley, Peter, Jim Thomas, Toby Gooley and James A. Cooke. "Airborne, Postal Service Target Business-to-Residence Market." *Logistics Management & Distribution Report.* July 1999. Online. Ovid. 21 September 1999.

Calonius, Erik. "Corporate Performance: Federal Express's Battle Overseas." *Fortune.* 3 December 1990.

Copeland, Lee. "James Barksdale: Netscape." *Computer Reseller News.* 9 November 1998. Online. Ovid. 14 September 1999.

"Experienced Hand Steers Silicon Valley Success Story." *Asian Business.* January 1997. Online. Ovid. 9 September 1999.

Feulner, Edwin. "Postal Service Blues." (1997). Online. Internet. 21 September 1999. Available: http://www.heritage.org/commentary/97/op-ef42.html.

"Federal Express Student Information Packet." *Fast Facts.* (1999). Memphis: Federal Express Corporate Publication.

"Federal Express Intranet Delivers Information Enterprisewide." 1999. Online. Internet. 22 September 1999. Available: http://home.netscape.com/comprod/at_work/customer_profile/fedex.html

"FedEx Standardizes on Netscape Software for Internet and Intranet." (1996). Online. Internet. 23 September 1999. Available: http://www.netscape.com/newsref/pr/newsrelease159.html.

Field, David. "FedEx CEO Warns Pilots of Strike Plan." *USA Today.* 20 November 1998. Online. Electric Library. 1 November 1999.

Gomes, Andrew. "Post Office Targets Mail to Asia-Pacific Region." (1997). Online. Internet. 21 September 1999. Available: http://www.amcity.com/pacific/stories/1997/05/05/story7.html.

Halper, Mark. "The Adolescence of the Upstarts: It's a Pivotal Year for the Commerce Software Pioneers." *Computerworld.* 9 March 1998. Online. Ovid. 21 September 1999.

Krause, Kristin. "And the Winner Is. . ." *Traffic World.* 12 July 1999. Online. Ovid. 21 September 1999.

Pelton, Lou, David Strutton and James Lumpkin. (1997) *Marketing Channels: A Relationship Management Approach.* Chicago: Times Mirror Books.

Ralston, Jeannie, Jack El-Hai, and Vince Giorgi. *How Time Flies: Fedex Delivers the 21st Century.* Memphis: Federal Express Corporation, 1998.

Schulz, John. "Change Is Constant." *Traffic World.* 19 April 1999. Online. Ovid. 21 September 1999.

Case 2.3

Necessity to Luxury: Cool Moves—The Cooling of Two Countries

In 1902, the temperatures in the Northeast were so hot that enjoying a Brooklyn Dodgers baseball game was almost impossible. Ice cream melted off the cone faster than it could be licked and die-hard baseball fans could not even be coerced by free beer promotions to come and sweat out a ballgame. The invention of the air conditioner had little to do with muggy summer nights or the masses of sweat-stained shirts in Brooklyn, New York, and was not aimed to cool down one sweaty Brooklyn resident.

Instead, the birth of the air conditioner was something to *dye* for. This invention was not intended for food preservation or for human comfort, but instead for a custom printer in Brooklyn, N.Y. This company constantly faced printing issues because, it "couldn't print a decent color image due to the changes in heat and humidity which kept changing the paper's dimensions and misaligning the colored inks" (www.carrier.com 1999). So, Carrier's invention that allowed for both temperature and humidity control of the indoor environment was meant for the proper functioning of a printing press and industrial processes rather than for the comfort of people.

Willis Carrier patented this air conditioning device in 1906. This turn of the century invention was labeled, "An Apparatus for Treating Air." As an employee of Buffalo Forge Company, Willis Carrier probably never dreamed that his family name would brand a leading air conditioning system for over 90 years. Some of the first users of Willis Carrier's new system were Southern U.S. textile mills and silk mills in Yokohama, Japan (www.carrier.com 1999). Now as we embark on the 21st century, Carrier's business reappears in Japan as a strategic alliance with the Toshiba Corporation, which is driven by its desire to gain market entry and access to distribution channels.

Carrier Corporation: The Focal Firm

Mission of the Focal Firm

The Carrier Corporation is focused on being a world leader in custom-made indoor weather systems designed for providing personal comfort, while at the same time protecting the environment. Carrier strives to provide customers with state of the art products by continually improving the performance and design of future products and by simultaneously controlling costs. Carrier is a good community neighbor which not only adheres to environmental requirements, but sets higher standards for itself by applying stringent pollution standards to each new product design.

Principal Decision Makers

- John Lord is the President of Carrier Corporation.
- Ed Dabrowski is Chief Operating Officer.
- Larry Sweet is Vice President of Operations, Carrier Corporation, based in Farmington, Connecticut. He provides leadership and global integration of technology, manufacturing, purchasing and quality functions for Carrier Corporation. He has leadership responsibility for the Carrier Electronics and Carlyle Compressor divisions. He joined Carrier in 1995 (Babyak 1998).
- Frank Hartman is the President of Residential/Light Commercial Systems.
- John Malloy is President of Commercial Systems and Services.
- George Saunders is the President of Carrier Enterprises.

All of these people report to John Lord, the president of The Carrier Corporation (www.carrier.com 1999).

Organizational Design

The Carrier Corporation is a decentralized business structure that consists of multiple manufacturing facilities around the world. The manufacturing and selling facilities are regionally linked allowing each to act independently and enabling significant control over brand and product management (Barnes 1999). Research and design centers are located near and work in conjunction with manufacturing facilities allowing them to provide products and services needed by the local markets.

Source: Prepared by Janell Galpin, Jennifer Lawhon, Randy Lippies, and Julie Runde under the Supervision of Dr. Lou E. Pelton, University of North Texas, November 23, 1999.

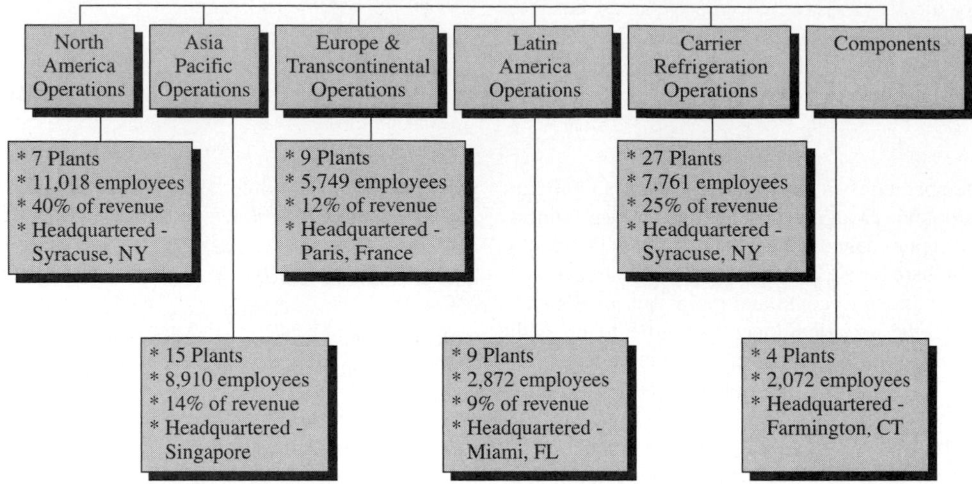

Carrier's Manufacturing and Design Centers

In its North American Opertions, Carrier Corporation is motivated to restructure Carlyle Compressor Division, Carrier Refrigeration Operations, Carrier Electronics, as well as Carrier World Headquarters to better serve its Heating, Ventilation, and Air-Conditioning (HVAC) market. These changes will contribute to the expansion of its customer focus and reduce operating costs. The three business units that make up the North American HVAC Operations are: Residential and Light Commercial Systems, Commercial Systems and Services, and Carrier Enterprises. All three operations

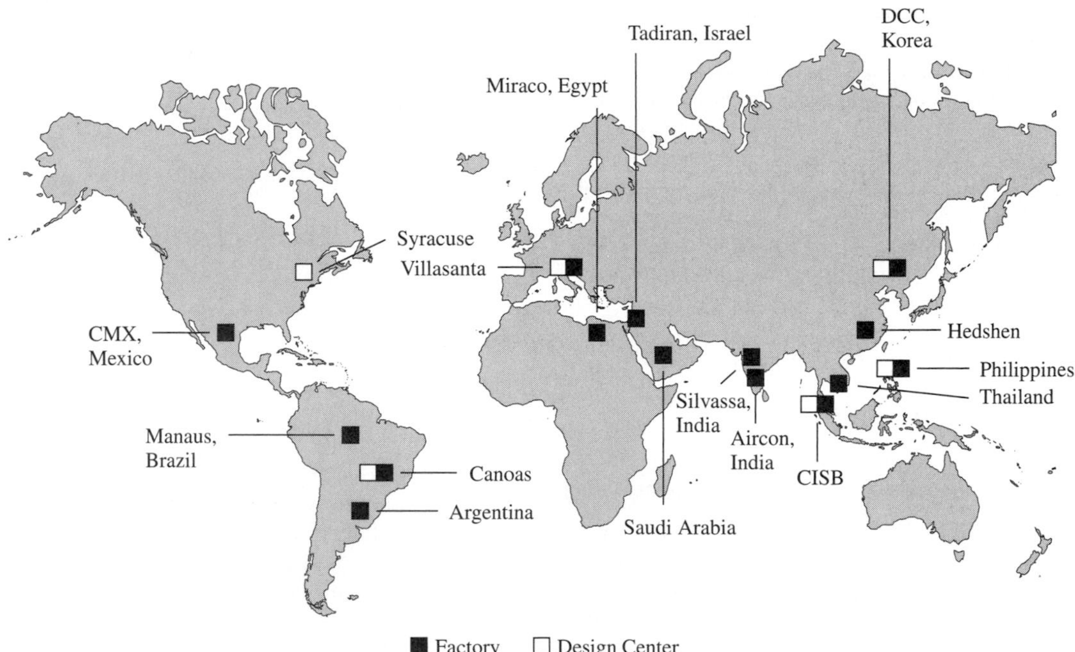

function independently and report directly to the president of Carrier Corporation, and staff functions will be integrated into the World Headquarters in Farmington, Connecticut. The restructuring will take place during the third quarter of fiscal year 1999 and affect 6 percent of Carrier's U.S. salaried work force (www.carrier.com 1999).

Market Position

Carrier, a subsidiary of United Technologies Corporation, is involved in manufacturing of hi-tech products and providing support services. It is the world's largest manufacturer of heating, air conditioning and refrigeration systems and equipment. It has accomplished a 13.7 percent market share in the global market, shipping around 6.2 million units a year. Its regional market share in 1998 consisted of: Latin America up 10.4 percent, North America up 9.7 percent, and Europe Transcontinental up 3.5 percent, However, Carrier's market share in the Asian Pacific market was down 13.6 percent in 1998 (Remich 1998). Carrier accomplished $6.9 billion in worldwide sales during 1998 (www.carrier.com 1999) and $6.1 billion in 1997 (www.theautochannel.com 1999). As a member of a $20 billion North American market, Carrier has grown significantly since its inception in 1915. Due to intense competition and numerous consolidations, Carrier has been forced to increase efficiency to maintain its leading market position. This strong market presence and power has given it the ability to expand globally (Mader 1998). Economic progress and a booming population have generated a need for additional air-conditioning units. With increasing demand for air control systems, partially due to a strong economy, the HVAC market continues to grow and Carrier is in the forefront of the market. "Carrier is the only one of the six largest competitors that is not owned by the Japanese" (Swenson 1998). The presence of Toshiba in Asia will help establish Carrier in this newly expanding market.

Nature and Scope

"As the industry leader, Carrier strives to maintain its dominant position through innovative product design, high-quality, low-cost manufacturing, and time-based competition" (Swenson 1998). Carrier has embarked on a cost complexity reduction process, which has evolved into a formal systematic program with corporate-wide visibility. These programs are called cost of complexity (COC) and are administered at the plant level by COC teams. Carrier forms these teams by recruiting mid-level managers from each functional area. The COC teams receive top management support by means of a steering committee that oversee[s] and monitor[s] the teams' success. Carrier considers the COC program to be one of its critical success factors (Swenson 1998).

The term complexity encompasses variety as well as standardization of parts. A company's complexity grows in proportion to the breadth of products it offers. To accomplish this, Carrier's manufacturing facilities have engaged in activity-based costing, just-in-time inventory control, product and process standardization, strategic outsourcing, supply chain management, target costing, and performance measurement. Activity-based cost management (ABCM) provides the necessary financial and activity information to quantify the benefits of redesigning plant layouts, using common parts, outsourcing, strengthening supplier and customer relationships, and developing alternative product designs. Activity-based cost management helps Carrier make better decisions by considering the entire cost of an activity and not just the out-of-pocket costs such as the cost of raw materials (Swenson 1998).

Each of the manufacturing plants acts as an individual profit center within the Carrier Corporation. An example of a Carrier profit center is the McMinville's facility near Nashville, TN, where Carrier uses ABCM to support its product mix decisions. The product mix at each site is based on a product profitability analysis. Products that are unprofitable at one plant are either dropped or moved to another site location where the product can be produced while achieving maximum profitability. Profitable products are emphasized at each plant; thus each plant focuses on its core competencies. Essentially, this system encourages healthy competition among the plants. With this system, the most efficient plant wins bids for new products and gets to take over production contracts from less efficient plants (Swenson 1998).

Carrier is adopting a Product Delivery System (PDS) which defines how they integrate the supply chain from its suppliers all the way to its customers. The process is based on demand-flow principles rather than batch manufacturing. Demand flow means that a company lets customer orders set production quantities rather than forecasting requirements. This system is difficult to implement in a company with such a full range of products. But by becoming more interdependent with its suppliers and distributors, Carrier actually creates fertile ground for innovation. According to Larry Sweet, Carrier's best ideas come from everywhere, its customers and suppliers worldwide (Babyak 1998).

Motivation to Engage in Strategic Partnering

Almost a century after they entered Japan by way of treating the air of silk mills, Carrier is returning to Japan through its strategic alliance with Toshiba. Carrier's core motivation for engaging in a strategic partnership with Toshiba is to regain access into the Japanese market and improve its competitiveness throughout the world (www.theautochannel.com, 1999).

This new global alliance will focus their complementary capabilities on designing, manufacturing, sales and marketing of air-conditioning equipment/systems to cultivate an ever-growing HVAC global market with both the Carrier and Toshiba trademarks worldwide. This alliance will highlight the successful technological leadership and manufacturing experience of both companies and combine their sales and marketing networks (www.toshiba.com 1999).

The Asian market is one of the largest markets outside of the United States for air conditioning equipment, due to the enormous growth potential of this region since the majority of countries are still in the early stages of their economic development (Babyak 1998). This alliance will allow Carrier to use the established distribution network of Toshiba to distribute and market throughout Asia. It will be capitalizing on Toshiba's technological abilities to help move forward with innovative products. Carrier also will gain access to industrial advances in the areas of power electronics, variable speed systems, alternative refrigerants, and compression. It will help Carrier improve its manufacturing quality and service reliability (www.carrier.com 1999). The companies are hoping for a technologically advanced product that they can market together to expand their market presence. With the two companies combined, Carrier looks forward to the power of the Toshiba Carrier brand name that will evolve from this alliance.

Organization Culture

Carrier tries to balance its customers' needs for comfort with the need for environmental friendliness. Its employees strive to provide customers the most environmentally friendly equipment. They achieved better product standards by exceeding the environmental standards set forth in previous products. The employees are able to accomplish better product design and performance, because Carrier promotes an entrepreneurial spirit. Employees are encouraged to explore and share new ideas though not all ideas are feasible. "This operating philosophy is your assurance that, while Carrier equipment creates unmatched comfort today, our company is hard at work protecting the outdoor environment for enjoyment tomorrow" (www.carrier.com 1999).

The Decision Environment

The decision environment is cost-driven in the HVAC industry and thus causes this industry to be intensely competitive. Carrier mainly competes with Trane, Matsushita, MELCO, Goodman, York, Daikin, Sanyo, Hitachi, and Lennox respectively. Carrier holds the largest market share, which is 13.7 percent. HVAC products must follow a strict production schedule in order to meet demand during seasonal sales windows. Losing two months of sales is like losing a whole year of revenue (Babyak 1998).

Carrier's global market presence is highly visible in the Asian market. Hurried businessmen and world travelers rushing through the recently opened Hong Kong airport will keep their cool thanks to air conditioning provided by Carrier.

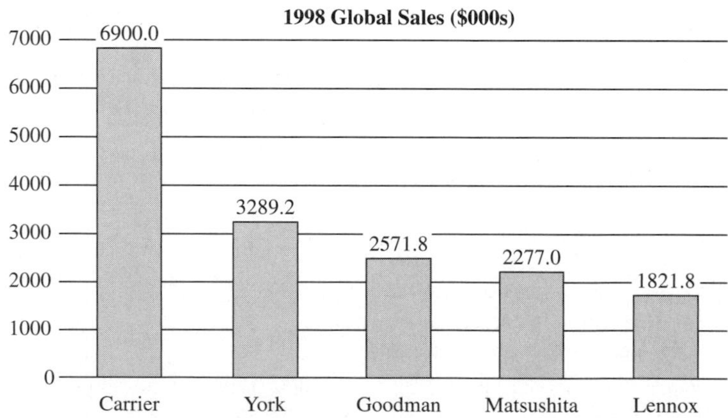

In fact, Carrier cools 15 out of the 16 major airports in Asia, and it uses that as ammunition in its ad campaigns across various product lines (Babyak 1998). Its ability to handle such large cooling projects adds enormous presence in a region where the stifling heat and humidity is a major concern. Its closet competitor in the non-Japan Australasia market is Matsushita, which is one-third the size of Carrier's operations. However, Carrier is not a market leader in Japan due to formidable competition (Babyak 1998). Carrier's Asia Pacific Operations covers 23 countries, including: China, Korea, Japan, Southeast Asia, India, Guam, New Zealand, Australia and the Philippines. Carrier has sales and distribution in each of those countries, and 15 manufacturing plants. The company has design centers in Japan, Korea, Malaysia, and India. Sales from this region reached $1.3 billion and is about 20 percent of Carrier's total revenue. Unlike other regional operations, Carrier's Asian group derives 22 percent of its business from service. This could be due to the fact that it owns their distribution channels in Asia. Carrier sells directly to its retailers and contractors, which positions it closer to the market and allows greater opportunities for direct customer service (Babyak 1998).

The Strategic Partnership

Profile of Toshiba Carrier Corporation

Established	April 1, 1999
Headquarters:	Toshiba Building, 1-1-1 Shibaura, Minato-Ku, Tokyo 105-8001
Factories:	336 Tadehara, Fuji-shi, Shizuoka (current Toshiba Fuji Works) 70 Yanagi-cho, Saiwai-Ku, Kawasaki (within Toshba Yanagi-Cho Works)
Capital:	11.51 billion in Yens
Stockholders:	Toshiba Corporation 60%, Carrier Corporation 40%
Employees:	2100

The Carrier Corporation and Toshiba Corporation announced the formation of a global strategic alliance in the HVAC industry. The alliance combines the companies' complementary product offerings and the capabilities in technological innovation, manufacturing, quality assurance, sales and marketing. Toshiba hopes to leverage its current high-end retail position by creating a network of retail dealers with the highest level of service in the HVAC industry. It's capable of offering such an elevated level of service due to its centralized research and development resources and manufacturing economies of scale. Carrier is planning on leveraging their local market presence and entrepreneurial spirit. It hopes to make a positive impact on the air conditioning industry by preserving and expanding the Toshiba Carrier brand, minimizing market channel conflicts and by planning for future brand equity appreciation (Barnes 1999).

The benefit to Carrier is that it's gaining market entry into Japan, the single largest market outside the United States for air conditioning equipment. The Toshiba brand image is known for excellent quality and the product association is mainly with consumer electronics, laptop PCs, radios and cellular phones. Carrier is attempting to associate their products with the Toshiba brand name, which is widely known throughout the United States and Japan. Toshiba wants to enter the North American HVAC market with a well-known industry leader, which will provide it with an accepted and established air-conditioning brand in the United States (Barnes 1999). Through this union, Carrier and Toshiba feel that they can improve their competitiveness throughout the global market with world-class technology utilizing the Carrier and Toshiba trademarks (www.carrier.com 1999).

Nature and Scope of the Alliance

Under the terms of this alliance, Toshiba's air conditioning equipment division was separated from the parent company to form, with Carrier, a Japan-based joint venture called Toshiba Carrier Corporation. The corporation will be headquartered in Fuji City, Japan. The ownership will be divided with Carrier owning 40 percent of the joint venture and Toshiba owning the remaining 60 percent. Carrier's current Japanese subsidiary, Toyo Carrier, also will become part of the new company.

Toshiba Carrier Corporation Headquarters and Manufacturing Joint Ventures

Toshiba Carrier Corporation is also forming manufacturing joint ventures in the United Kingdom, with Carrier holding a majority interest. The same will take place in Thailand, with both companies owning equal interests. Toshiba is transferring its air conditioner manufacturing operations in both countries to these new joint ventures. Carrier will integrate Toshiba's HVAC sales organizations, which include locations in Singapore, Hong Kong, France, and Germany and combine its current line of products by offering Toshiba-brand HVAC products globally.

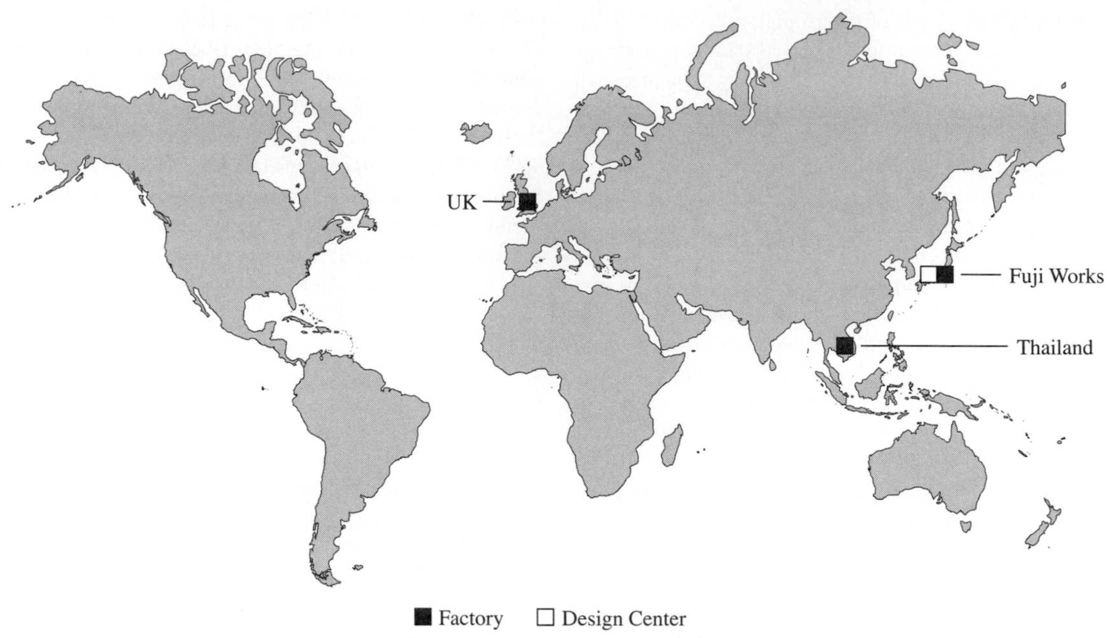

Terms of the Alliance

Due to the recent inception of the Carrier/Toshiba alliance, both parties are still in the process of negotiating the terms of the alliance.

Critical Issues

> "This is an awesome partnership that will allow Carrier to expand its presence in Japan and improve its competitiveness throughout the world with both Carrier and Toshiba technology and trademarks." This is according to John Lord's perception, Carrier's President (www.theautochannel 1999).

Most alliances have been marked by failure. Companies still accept the risk of forming strategic alliances despite the gloomy statistics on survival rates. There are various strengths found with the newly formed Toshiba Carrier Corporation, but it also faces many critical issues. One of the critical issues of this alliance is its organizational design. Carrier is a decentralized organization with many manufacturing facilities. Selling entities have significant control over brands and products produced by the manufacturing plants. On the other hand, Toshiba has a centralized design with few manufacturing facilities independent from selling entities, and selling entities have no control over brands and products. This issue needs to be addressed between the two companies in an effort to compromise what organizational design the Toshiba Carrier Corporation will use.

Another critical issue is the geographical differences between [the] United States and Japan. Such geographical differences influence cultural norms, personal values, and perception of time. The acculturation of both companies is sure to have an impact on the success of this alliance. For instance, in the United States, companies like to have on-time meetings and get directly to business because time is money. In Japan, it is common to establish relationships over a few months before sitting down to close a business deal.

Supplier selection is another critical difference between both companies. American-based companies choose their suppliers globally and are based on the best possible business circumstances for both companies. American companies usually choose their suppliers based on established distribution infrastructure and market access. Japanese-based companies develop keiretsu, which is a pyramid of supplier networks. These supplier relationships consist exclusively of Japanese-based companies and usually last a lifetime.

Final Thoughts

With the developing global economies and advanced technology, the HVAC industry's primary focus has shifted from necessity to luxury. In comparison to the intemperate baseball games of the early 20th century, today's fans are accustomed to valet concessions, air-conditioned box seats and private suites. Since 1902, the Brooklyn Dodgers have repositioned their club to Los Angeles in an effort to boost their ability to win in Major League Baseball. Carrier has also repositioned itself by *teaming up* with Toshiba to facilitate their market entry into Japan. American-based Carrier and Japan-based Toshiba share a common business interest. These diverse companies, although half a world apart, are stepping up to the plate as major league players in the global HVAC marketplace. This *team* will certainly face curve balls and numerous strikes yet hope to hit many grand slams together.

References

Anonymous. (1999, April). "Carrier and Toshiba Make Their Global Alliance Official." *Air Conditioning, Heating & Refrigeration News*, 4.

Babyak, Richard J. (1998, August). "Breaking the Barriers." *Appliance Manufacturer*. Pp. 23–25.

Barnes, Laura, Toshiba Brand Manager for North America, Carrier Corporation [provided corporate literature]. (Personal communication, October and November, 1999).

"Carrier and Toshiba Make It Official" [On-line]. September 21, 1999. Available: www.carrier.com.

"Carrier Announces Air Conditioning Alliance with Toshiba" [On-line]. September 19, 1999. Available: www.theautochannel.com.

"Carrier Announces North American Restructuring" [On-line]. September 21, 1999. Available: www.carrier.com.

"Carrier History" [On-line]. September 21, 1999. Available: www.carrier.com.

"Carrier to Purchase International Comfort Products" [On-line]. September 21, 1999. Available: www.carrier.com.

"Environmental Awareness" [On-line]. September 21, 1999. Available: www.carrier.com.

"Japan" [On-line]. September 21, 1999. Available: www.carrier.com.

Mader, Robert P. (1998, June). "U.S. HVAC Market Worth Nearly $20 Billion: Study." *Contractor*, 7, 44.

"President Appointed to Toshiba Carrier Corporation" [On-line]. September 21, 1999. Available: www.toshiba.co.jp.

Remich, Norman C., Jr. (1999, April). "1998: The Growth Year." *Appliance Manufacturer*, 58.

Swenson, Dan W. (1998, April). "Managing Costs through Complexity Reduction at Carrier." *Management Accounting*, 20–28.

"Toshiba, Carrier Take On the World Together" [On-line]. April 5, 1999. Available: www.esmagazine.com.

"Toshiba Corporation and Carrier Corporation Announce Heating, Ventilation, and Air Conditioning Global Alliance" [On-line]. September 21, 1999. Available: www.toshiba.co.jp.

part III

Channel Microsystems

chapter 8 Conflict Resolution Strategies 262

chapter 9 Information Systems and Relational Logistics 282

chapter 10 Developing Positive Channel Climates 312

chapter

8

Conflict Resolution Strategies

Learning Objectives

After reading this chapter, you should be able to:

- Define negotiation and describe how it can be used to turn conflict into positive channel outcomes.
- Describe several negotiation strategies, and when and how they should be used to resolve channel conflict.
- Discuss how problem-solving strategies can be used in channel settings.
- Understand how persuasive mechanisms operate in channel relationships.
- Understand when legalistic strategies should be used to resolve channel conflicts.

Dennis Scott/The Stock Market

How can a trio of very close friends lead to conflict? Fashion-conscious women around the world consider Estee, Jane, and Bobbi dependable allies. Whether women are looking for upscale Estee, trendy Jane, or professionally styled Bobbi Brown, they collectively trust these fashion companions. As women (and many men) shoppers can attest to, high-profile Estee Lauder cosmetics, fragrances, and skin care products are distributed in more than 100 countries worldwide.

But Estee Lauder Cos., the $5 billion-per-year marketer of female hopes and dreams, now sells one of its flagship brands directly over the Internet. The cosmetics manufacturer chose this strategy despite the almost certain conflict it would create with the retailers who made its Clinique line the top seller in the so-called prestige skin care and cosmetics market. At the same time, Estee Lauder is expanding its chain of freestanding stores and catalogs.[1]

* * * *

The technological revolution is more than a cosmetic change in the channels microsystem. It has created a new source of conflict between manufacturers and their wholesalers, distributors, dealers, resellers, and retailers—as if any more were needed. Now, more than ever, the question of who "owns" the customer tends to arise. This conflict saps the energy and resources of marketing managers around the world, and it has emerged as a barrier to creating a seamlessly integrated buying experience through the marketing channel.

Traditionally, products and information flowed sequentially through the distribution pipeline from a manufacturer to distributors to retailers to final (end-user) customers. The accepted rule was that the manufacturer's customer was the channel; the channel's customer was the end user. Today, as you well understand, products and information no longer flow sequentially. End users can purchase products and download information at any time from multiple sources, including the manufacturer. Trends toward a direct marketing relationship between the manufacturer and end user lie near the heart of most current channel conflict.

The dictionary offers many synonyms for *war. Conflict* is one of them. The word is right there along with *hostilities* or *confrontations*. One source of channel conflict is *disintermediation*. The perceived or actual possibility that one's firm might end up being disintermediated—removed—from the distribution system threatens the continued existence of any channel. On the other hand, the traditional view of the channel as the sole interface with end users can no longer hold. Traditional channel systems made it extremely difficult for manufacturers to increase their market footprint and establish meaningful relationships with end-user customers. No longer. Hence, there is conflict between the old and new ways of doing business.

As you read about in the first two modules of this text, the Net Economy demands a transformation from more conflict to more cooperation between manufacturers and their channel partners. Neither side can prosper when facing prolonged conflict. If the channel partners don't eliminate conflict, it may eliminate them.

With more cooperative channel relationships, both parties "own" the customer and can work together to develop mutually beneficial business strategies, share information freely, gain mutual access to customers, and assume joint responsibility for the total customer experience. Cooperation opens up a genuine opportunity to deliver more value to customers.

Attempts to unilaterally apply power usually fail in today's marketing channels. In today's competitive, information-driven, and globally accessible marketing channels, coercion is no longer a viable management alternative. Successful channel leaders are changing the nature and meaning of power and how it is employed to settle conflicts. Channel Surfing 8.1 discusses several things required for success—and for successfully resolving conflicts—in today's channel relationships. In this chapter, we expand on our earlier discussion about conflict resolution by examining various ways channel partners can resolve their conflicts. Conflict resolution strategies can be divided into five broad types, each of which will be discussed in detail: negotiation, problem-solving strategies, persuasive mechanisms, legalistic strategies, and climate management. To complete the discussion, we will introduce the concept of interdependence, the dimension of conflict resolution that ties all of these strategies together.

Let's enter this chapter armed with the following common thought: Conflict is not necessarily a bad thing. Once managers accept this fact, they will be prepared to develop a climate that will facilitate creativity, innovation, and change. When listening—that's right, just listening—is used as a means of guiding conflict from positional disagreement to an exchange of thoughts and ideas, channel managers will create the right climate to maintain energetic participation and enhance decision making. As channel members adopt a more collaborative mind-set, they will learn to seek resolutions that satisfy themselves while simultaneously satisfying other channel members. Conflict will then become a chance to learn, innovate, and grow.

Channel Surfing 8.1

Key Ingredients for Resolving Conflict in Channels

Like newlyweds, channel members are sometimes shocked by how quickly once cozy relationships can seemingly go awry. Problems arise not only with respect to issues like managing who does what in the channel but also in fuzzy areas such as the personal relationships between managers reared in different corporate cultures. Perhaps the biggest stumbling block to the success of new channels is a lack of trust—a condition to be avoided at all costs. When trust is missing, the relationship is far less likely to succeed.

In the absence of trust, things can get very personal very quick. In times of conflict, most people gravitate naturally to one of two positions: digging in their heels and believing they are right, or having the desire to learn and attempting to understand what is motivating their "opponent's" behavior. How would you think that the presence or absence of trust would affect the position you would be most likely to assume?

Think back to the last argument you had. What if you had trusted the other party so much that you took the position of trying to understand his or her position? There most likely would not have been any conflict at all or, at the least, things would have been resolved more quickly. You may be thinking, "Well, why should I be the one who always has to make it work? Why can't I be the other guy—the one who is not reasonable—every now and then?" The authors of this book would argue that you would simply be the one who figured out how best to manage the conflict first. We assure you that, under such circumstances, you usually end up better off.

Listed below are some more tips for dealing with conflict as it arises in channels:

- Evaluate your—and your channel partner's—conflict resolution styles. Understanding each other offers you a great start.
- Give positive responses and feedback as often as possible to avoid a negative tone.
- Review the value of the channel relationship. Ask yourself whether winning this battle will move you closer to an optimal relationship or further away from one.
- Check your ego at the door. Understand, always, the difference between high self-esteem and high ego. Which one do you think better serves your purpose?
- Keep the consequences of your decisions in mind?

Points to Ponder

- How do you achieve trust in channels relationships? What are the best ways to maintain it?
- Why do you think trust is such a critical ingredient when it comes to resolving channels relationships successfully?

Negotiation: The Art of Give and Take

Today, the powerful and less powerful alike are more apt to ask their channel partners, "How do *you* want to do this, and how can I profitably help you achieve what you want?" The success with which the potential dead-ends that result from conflict can be converted into new avenues to success often depends on the art of negotiation.

Anne Mulcahy claims she actually enjoys the tension that arises from channel conflict. As president of Xerox General Markets Operations, she has steered Xerox away from its tradition of field salespeople and advocated a distribution model that uses retailers, resellers, dealers, the Internet, and inside sales reps. "It's the way to do business," claims Mulcahy. "Firms that don't aggressively embrace multiple channels for multiple products will get left behind." The inherent conflict in this approach to channels management, she admits, is not only a reality of business; it's a sign of a healthy, forward-thinking company.[2]

Negotiation involves discussions aimed at resolving conflict. The thought of active negotiation frightens many people. Tortured images of smoky rooms, raised voices, sweaty armpits, and dirty tricks no doubt come to mind. People often doubt their negotiating skills relative to those of their counterpart. Add to these considerations the fact that negotiation is usually associated with only the most important conflicts and it should not be surprising that many fear it.

But negotiation is a fact of life in marketing channels. For that reason alone it should be mastered rather than feared. Effective negotiation techniques are useful, first and foremost, for self-defense and for improving one's own position. In addition, skilled negotiators will take advantage of you if they sense your fear or incompetence. Once the art is mastered, your prospects of sustaining productive relationships when conflict arises will improve. Many an opponent has been converted to a lasting channel partner after a successful negotiation. Finally, putting the proper negotiating techniques into practice increases the probability that each party to the conflict will ultimately achieve more rewards than would otherwise be the case.

Despite its importance, the negotiation process is often misunderstood and poorly executed. It need not be. Negotiation uses the same steps commonly used for systematic problem solving and joint decision making. These procedural steps are outlined and briefly described in Exhibit 8.1. If these steps are not followed, inferior agreements may result. Worse still, deadlocks may ensue. At that point, conflict is likely to spin out of control.

Evaluating Desired Relationship Outcome

People and organizations usually enter negotiations driven by self-centered desires. However, negotiation should also be influenced by the relationship outcome the person or organization desires after the negotiation process is over. In other words, the type of negotiation strategy one chooses will directly affect the relationship they currently share or hope to develop.

Exhibit 8.1

Procedural steps for a typical negotiation process

Identify and Define the Problem—Remember that a problem well defined is a problem half-solved.
Get the Facts—Be sure to distinguish between facts and assumptions.
Generate Possible Solutions—Suspend all evaluation during the generation session; no criticism, either implied or spoken, should be allowed.
Evaluate Possible Solutions—When and where possible, use logic and mature judgment rather than personal values.
Select Solution(s)—Remember, a combination of alternatives may be preferable.
Implement the Solution(s)—Spell out who will do what to carry out the solution.
Evaluate the Results—If things are not working out, it may be necessary to reactivate the problem-solving process.

Source: Adapted from Shea, Gordon F. (1983), *Creative Negotiating,* Boston: CBI.

One way to evaluate relationship outcomes is to look at relative power. The **relative power** of each channel member is roughly equivalent to that member's dependence on the other. Boundary personnel instinctively evaluate the relative levels of power among channel members. Decisions to compete, retreat, accommodate, or collaborate when conflict arises are in large part based on this understanding of the existing relative power relationships. Conflict may arise from manifest power in the channel relationship. Manifest power is in evidence whenever channel members collectively vie for the "upper hand" in the interaction process.

The frequency and intensity of conflict that emerges between two partners in marketing channels largely follow from whether the members perceive that the relationship supports or undermines their interests. Supportive relationships can act as incentives for continuing negotiation, even at the cost of short-term gains, particularly when the relationship is more highly valued than the stakes under dispute. Channel members should not select negotiating strategies until after they have evaluated what they and other channel members seek regarding the future of their relationship.

Choosing a Negotiation Strategy

Once an evaluation of the desired relationship outcome has been completed, a negotiation strategy can be chosen. Negotiation strategies can be divided into two broad types: predatory and symbiotic. These are discussed below.

Predatory Negotiation. Channel members who use predatory negotiation generally consider as weak or unsophisticated the idea of relationship-sustaining bargaining sessions featuring information sharing, give and take, open communication, creativity, and an attitude of cultivating the common good. They view the economic pie as fixed, which means that any gains must be taken from another channel member. The predatory strategy follows from the view that conflict resolution is a hard and tough process in which neither participant is concerned with the other's needs. This view is consistent with the concept of discrete (transactional) exchange, which will be introduced in Chapter 11. As you might imagine, any possibility of a future relationship is considered less important than the gains that may be realized through winning this particular struggle.

Even in an increasingly cooperative business era, predatory channel partners are still alive and kicking. Why placate partners over e-business channel conflicts when you can boss them around instead? Consider that Tupperware Corporation, after barring its 85,000 sales reps from building order-taking websites, announced that during 2000 it would be marketing its party-hopping plastic ware over the Net. Or that Levi Strauss & Company, despite its declining market share, recently announced it will keep its online marketing efforts to itself, barring retailing heavyweight Federated Department Stores from selling Levi's via Macys.com.[3] Who knows? Perhaps Tupperware and Levi's will end up getting kicked back themselves.

The name of the game in a predatory negotiation is hardball, wherein each negotiator tries to gain as much as possible by giving the other as little as possible. The object is to persuade the other channel member that they need what you have while you are only marginally interested in their offer. The nature of the solution eventually derived through hardball depends on who (1) concedes slowest, (2) exaggerates the value of its concession the most while understating the value of the other's allowances, and (3) argues most forcefully. The channel member who is willing to lose, conceal information, or accept only favorable settlements generally prevails. The most aggressive hardballers—usually those possessing substantial channel power—often make inflexible demands, while threatening to walk away or retaliate if their demands are not met.

Bill Gates, CEO of Microsoft Corporation, once suggested that it is increasingly important to "compete and cooperate at the same time."[4] Yet in its channel relationships, Microsoft has occasionally acted in what negotiation experts label the "jungle fighter" style.[5] That fierceness with which it competed, of course, was part of the reason why Microsoft was sued in 2000 by the U.S. government for violating antitrust statutes. Jungle fighters view channels as "dog-eat-dog" places. They tend to be bold, innovative, entrepreneurial, and willing to take negotiating risks if they think the payoff is more success. Their view is that other channel members are working *for* them rather than *with* them. Such attitudes can occasionally show up in predatory negotiation styles.

There is nothing wrong with negotiating tough and trying to gain an edge when one acts fairly and ethically.[6] Toughness at the bargaining table means sticking to your position, letting your counterpart know you mean business, and being unafraid to ask for concessions when doing so does not violate the sanctity of the relationship. However, there are limits to just how tough one should negotiate. At the height of his career, former UCLA basketball coach John Wooden, an extraordinarily competitive and successful person, was known for telling his players to "be nice to the people you pass on your way up. You may meet those same people on the way down." Good advice, both in the basketball arena and in marketing channels. In most channel settings, also there are limits to how hard you should push your own interests.

Symbiotic Negotiation. Sometimes in nature, two dissimilar organisms live together because doing so is mutually beneficial. This is called symbiosis. Symbiotic negotiation features attempts to create mutual value through trade-offs and bargaining. Symbiotic negotiators believe that conflict resolution is best achieved by being cooperative, imaginative, and persistent in the pursuit of mutual gains relative to the possibility of no agreement. Symbiotic negotiators stress the value of sharing information and open lines of communication.

Under a climate of trust and concern for the relationship's future, symbiotic organizations sometimes pursue a negotiation strategy known as *open submission.* An **open submission** strategy involves one channel member's concessions to another on all but the barest material aspects of the issue in conflict. This is done in an attempt to build a more productive relationship. The judgment that relationship building is the most desirable outcome possible from negotiation yields the joint-gains orientation necessary for a mutually agreeable resolution. One channel member receives gains relating to the issue in conflict; the other receives the benefits of a significantly strengthened channel relationship that should produce rewards in the future. The beneficiary is likely to respond in kind at some point in the future.

I Can't Believe It's Yogurt (ICBIY) used an open submission strategy to settle a dispute that had been heating up for several years with its frozen yogurt franchisees. Many of the chain's franchisees had been pressing for substantial concessions on royalty and marketing promotion payments. Franchisees claimed such allowances were necessary for their financial survival. In a gutsy move, the beleaguered franchisor totally eliminated royalties (5% of sales) and marketing fees (an extra 2% of sales) from current and future franchise agreements. Did ICBIY give up too much through this open submission? Not likely. The company believes it can remain profitable by merely acting as its franchisees' primary supplier. Furthermore, eliminating these fees will likely persuade more people to buy ICBIY franchises.[7]

Another symbiotic negotiation strategy is the well-known **win-win strategy** wherein both sides emerge victorious from a conflict or, in the worst case, no one loses. Joint gains are achieved through a win-win orientation by avoiding behaviors that could worsen the relationship while actively seeking behaviors that could increase the substantive elements of the issue under negotiation. This is accomplished through mutual efforts to increase the size of the pie, thus invalidating much of the natural incentive to fight, or by uncovering elements within the current pie that satisfy the needs of each party.

After decades of battling its suppliers, Harley-Davidson saw the light, put on the brakes, and learned how to use suppliers to pluck itself out of a downward spiral. Harley was once a firm that took a less considerate approach in its supply chain management and suffered steady channel conflict as a result. It was once a company that kept suppliers at a distance. Now it brings them on production sites to develop new products and resolve old problems. The company now purposefully sports a win-win philosophy in resolving conflicts in its supplier channels. The win-win solution has worked wonders and has helped Harley turn around daunting production problems.[8]

Four points that are crucial to the successful application of symbiotic conflict resolution strategies are described in the popular book, *Getting to Yes.*[9] Together, these points comprise the foundation of a channel negotiation based on substance. Channel negotiations can be based on substance when each channel member:

1. **Separates the people from the problem.** The first step to a mutually agreeable solution is to separate the substantive elements of the issue under conflict from the personal relationships between the boundary personnel. The problem and the people can then be dealt with separately. Negotiators should work side by side, not across from one another. They should assault problems, not each other.
2. **Focuses on needs rather than positions.** Boundary personnel's egos often become too closely identified with their respective negotiating positions. Too much concern for positions tends to obscure what the participants actually need or want. A more effective approach is to focus on the underlying human or organizational needs that caused boundary personnel to adopt their positions in the first place.
3. **Develops options for mutual gain.** Having to design optimal solutions under pressure or in the presence of adversaries tends to narrow our vision. Searching for the one perfect solution also inhibits creativity, particularly when the stakes are high. Each side's independent generation of alternative solutions prior to meeting and deciding which actions to pursue overcomes these limitations.
4. **Uses only objective criteria.** When the issue in conflict is discussed in terms of impartial standards such as market value, expert opinion, custom, or the law, the conversation involuntarily moves away from a discussion of what the parties are or are not willing to do. When objective criteria are used, neither party has to give in illogically or under false pretenses to the other; instead both parties can look forward to a fair solution.

Symbiotic negotiation behaviors emphasize open channels of communication and separate the substantive aspects of the issue under conflict from the personalities of the boundary personnel involved in the negotiation. As such, the transactional costs associated with parties entrenching themselves within fortified positions and then having to dig their way out are avoided. By focusing on basic interests, mutual satisfactions, and objective standards, symbiotic negotiation strategies offer legitimate means of resolving conflict. Symbiotic negotiation tends to produce agreements that meet the legitimate needs of each side to the extent possible.

It should be noted, however, that symbiotic strategies will not always lead to best possible outcomes for each party. For instance, what would happen if a symbiotic type of person and a predatory type of person square off in a head-to-head negotiation? It might not be pretty.

Creating versus Claiming Value

Channel members are faced with a predicament when they attempt to resolve conflicts. First, symbiotic strategies designed to create mutual value through cooperation and collaboration are diametrically opposed to predatory strategies intended to claim value. Moreover, the use of negotiating strategies for claiming value generally obstructs its creation and makes one susceptible to predatory negotiation strategies. However, no matter how successful negotiators are in creating value through cooperative actions, each must, at some point, grab some pie in a predatory fashion.

Hardball by either party impairs efforts to satisfy both parties' interests through symbiotic, value-creating strategies. Exaggerating the value of concessions or minimizing the benefits one receives through the other channel member's concessions is highly unlikely to promote open and truthful communication. Threats or demands undermine effective listening and an understanding of another party's interests. But revealing information about one's preferences in a negotiation is also risky, since doing so opens one up to the other party's predatory strikes. The willingness to make new, creative offers is a sign that a channel member is willing to make additional concessions.[10]

The business world is often a harsh place, inhabited by ambitious and/or difficult-to-deal-with people. Some illustrations of just how ambitious or difficult to deal with some of these people can be are provided in Channel Surfing 8.2. So what should organizations do when they are trying to resolve conflicts in their channel settings? While an optimal solution normally results when both parties openly discuss the problem, respect each other's substantive and relationship needs, and creatively seek to satisfy each other's human needs, reality dictates that such behavior cannot be expected to automatically occur. One channel member's genuine attempts to use open submission or a win-win strategy exposes that organization to the predatory strategies of its channel counterpart. Once revealed in the process of one-sided symbiotic disclosure, even shared interests can be held hostage in exchange for concessions on other issues.

In a negotiation between a symbiotic and a predatory channel member, the symbiotic negotiator is susceptible to exploitation at the hands of the predator. For this reason, many channel members develop an aversion toward using symbiotic strategies when they expect their counterparts to act in a predatory fashion. This suspicion—which, in the absence of a relational exchange, is logical—causes many channel members to forgo potential gains. But if both channel members employ predatory strategies, there is a lower likelihood of any new value emerg-

Channel Surfing 8.2

Channel Jerks: Advice on Surviving All the Impossible Folks in Your Channel

In their book, *How to Handle Difficult People with Tact and Skill,* Rick Brinkman and Rick Kirshner offer a list of personality traits that represent people at their worst. Four of these personality traits, and what you should do when you come across them in a channel relationship, are discussed below.

The Tank. Tanks are confrontational, pointed, and angry. Some apparently strive to achieve the ultimate in pushy and aggressive behavior.

Solution: Command respect. Stand your ground, blunt their attack, quickly backtrack from their issues, and state your point in a nonthreatening way.

The Think-They-Know-It-All. These people don't know much. But they are big enough to not let their ignorance get in the way of their opinions. Exaggerating, bragging, misleading, and distancing, "know-it-alls" can pull you off track.

Solution: Give their bad ideas and suggestions the hook. Give them a little attention and ask them to clarify, then you can give an account of the real situation.

The Yes Person. "Yes people" are quick to agree, but slow to deliver. They leave a trail of unkept commitments and broken promises in an attempt to please.

Solution: Make it safe for them to talk honestly, help them plan, and ensure your commitment to them. Try to strengthen your relationship with them.

The No Person. Deadly to morale, "no people" are able to defeat big ideas with a single syllable. Doleful and discouraging, they drive others to despair.

Solution: "No people" should be used as a resource by leaving the door open and acknowledging their good intentions when you can.

Points to Ponder

- What other discouraging personality types are likely to crop up in channel relationships? How would you deal with these types when conflicts arise?

Source: Adapted from Brinkman, Rick, and Rick Kirshner (1994), *How to Handle Difficult People with Tact and Skill,* New York: McGraw-Hill; and Genasci, Lisa (1994) "Office Jerks: You Can Survive the Impossible People in Your Office. Really," *The Advocate,* December 3, 1C–2C.

ing from the resolution process. In the best-case scenario, the use of predatory strategies will result in each party receiving only mediocre outcomes. When the extreme negotiating strategies are aligned along vertical and horizontal axes, a matrix of the probable consequences emerging from the conflict resolution processes can be constructed, as is shown in Exhibit 8.2.

Regardless of either channel member's broad strategic preference, there are five practical tactical behaviors that increase the probability of achieving a mutually acceptable conflict resolution, while at the same time accounting for the needs of their relationship. These tactics borrow notions from both the predatory and symbiotic ideologies. When attempting to resolve conflicts through negotiation, parties should:

- **Do their homework.** This is the most important aspect of any negotiation process. Preparation endows negotiators with confidence in their ability and a stronger, factually based belief in the correctness of their positions. Good negotiators understand the implications of each item on the table, the consequences associated with various concessions, and where the absolute bottom line of the negotiation lies.

- **Deal only from the top of the deck.** Your negotiating success depends on another person's ability to communicate, in minutes, what might have been haggled over for hours or days, unless you deal directly with those individuals having the authority to accept the changes you propose.
- **Remember that quitters never win, and winners never quit.** A point may be reached when you do not like the proposed resolution, but no other alternatives are available. Learn that what looks like a dead-end may actually be a corner. Turn that corner.
- **Remember that attitude is everything.** People often will lose their tempers during negotiations. When this happens, maintain your composure while discerning the other party's true needs. A positive response can be more easily extracted when negative issues are framed positively. Raising controversial or troubling issues between positive points increases the chances of getting the other side to listen and agree to your requests.
- **Build bridges (relationships) rather than walls.** Even if you decide to pursue a predatory strategy, it is easier to communicate with a friend than with a stranger or an enemy. Gains or losses to the relationship should be viewed as a part of the negotiated resolution as much as are more substantive outcomes.

EXHIBIT 8.2

A matrix of likely consequences to channel negotiations

Strategy of Channel Member B \ Strategy of Channel Member A	Symbiotic	Predatory
Symbiotic	*Consequences* Good for Member A Good for Member B	*Consequences* Excellent (in Short Run) for Member A Devastating for Member B
Predatory	*Consequences* Excellent (in Short Run) for Member B Devastating for Member A	*Consequences* Substandard for Member A Substandard for Member B

EXHIBIT 8.3

Potential benefits of conflicts within channel settings

When properly approached, conflict can:

- Bring problems out into the open where they can be effectively dealt with.
- Lead to the development of new perspectives on old problems or situations.
- Lead to new ideas and new approaches to dealing with problems, if creativity and the right negotiating strategies are brought to the table.
- Allow channel members to ventilate feelings that needed to be aired.
- Lead to harmony and more productive, growing relationships.
- Lead to a greater awareness of and appreciation for the needs of other channel members.
- Cause channel members to better understand themselves, their motivations, their goals, and their behaviors.

The party that engages in these five behaviors better then their counterpart generally claims more value from the negotiation. More importantly, this party should also be able to capture the higher ground in a way that enhances and never diminishes the future quality of their channel relationship.

The stockbroker firm Charles Schwab exemplified these negotiation behaviors in the online stock-trading channel, while building a high-growth business that was anything but enthusiastically supported by the group's retail brokerages. But the company effectively managed the conflict, largely by putting these five principles into practice in their negotiation efforts, and in the process established a new channel that provided them a long-term competitive advantage. The e-business stock transactions are flowing while Schwab's retailers are still out there moving shares—often while online themselves. Everyone involved has benefited.

At one extreme, the process of conflict resolution involves a cooperative pursuit of joint gains and a coordinated effort to create more value than previously existed. At the other, it can devolve into a streetfight. The channel member's true dilemma is determining where cooperation should end and the fight should begin. The process of negotiation is never as simple as any book's discussion would have you believe. In such matters, experience (tempered with wisdom) ultimately proves the best teacher. When dealt with effectively and wisely, conflict can lead to a wealth of benefits. Exhibit 8.3 describes several of these benefits.

Every channel arrangement produces conflict. It is impossible for organizations to participate in improving the quality of the products and services, or the quality of their processes, without experiencing it. The only question, the only logical choice, is how best to resolve conflict in the most optimal manner.

Problem-Solving Strategies

Problems that create conflicts routinely arise in channel relationships. When considering the source of the problems, three trouble areas consistently stand out: organizational issues such as timeliness of delivery, employee issues such as failure to follow policy, and channel member issues such as conflicting policies and procedures, poor communication, or ill intent. We are concerned with the latter source of problems. Problems in marketing channels often arise over ignorance of or disagreement with the policies and procedures used to achieve a given channel member's goals, incompatible goals, and simply poor communication.

Disintermediation has caused myriad opportunities and problems as the Internet has reshuffled traditional channel value chains. But offering more options and cutting costs internally and to customers through direct online sales is an opportunity few channel members would want to pass up. Companies that swore they would never sell their products directly online now realize they don't have a choice—unless they want to ignore their customers' demands. It's a tough question, and one that leads to tough problems.

Managers should ask themselves: Are your field salespeople feeling threatened by resellers? Are your resellers complaining that the Web may kill their business? If the answers are yes, those managers are probably doing their job—they are adequately covering their market turf. The resulting channel conflict is just a new cost of trying to extend coverage in the market. When problems like this arise between channel members, several strategies are available to rectify them.

Problem-solving strategies are the actions taken to resolve the disputes, disagreements, or confrontations between the members of marketing channels. Problem-solving strategies involve the pursuit of alternative solutions to the conflict in question.

One problem-solving strategy is **logrolling,** wherein each channel participant identifies its priorities and offers concessions on those issues it views as less significant.[11] For a manufacturer and a retailer to exchange concessions with one another on price and delivery, for example, each would need to know the priority assigned by the other to both price and delivery. Under such circumstances, logrolling can only occur if the manufacturer assigns a higher priority to price, while the retailer attaches greater importance to delivery. The order of priorities could have been reversed among the channel members, of course, and logrolling could still occur.

A central fact underlying all business relationships, whether they exist inside or outside traditional channel boundaries, is the question of power. But when power does not work, or will not work optimally because it will injure the relationship, the parties involved should move to compromise. A **compromise strategy** involves the resolution of conflicts by establishing a middle ground based on the initial positions of both parties.[12] Several issues or concerns may be related to a given conflict. A compromise strategy need not necessarily involve an exchange of information about either party's needs, goals, or priorities. Instead, it is based on appropriate or reciprocal concessions by both parties from their initial positions. For instance, following the death of their bachelor uncle, the only two heirs might wage war with one another over how the uncle's estate should be divided. A compromise strategy yields a solution: One heir could draw the dividing line, while the other receives first pick.

Now when you're the manager who is attempting to mollify an angry channel partner through a compromise strategy, you can gain solace by knowing your conciliatory efforts continue traditions begun by famous peacemakers like Mahatma Gandhi and Nelson Mandela. Each man was known for seeking "the third side" when disputes arose. When there are two conflicting channel members, the third side can come from within the conflict itself when the contending managers honestly seek a compromise solution—something that each can agree upon. Easier said than done, no doubt, but still within the realm of reasonable probability.

A third problem-solving strategy commonly used within marketing channels involves an

aggressive strategy to work out problems by using threats, persuasive arguments, or punishments. In this case, the objective is to extract, through whatever means available, one-sided concessions from the other channel member. For instance, a given intermediary may possess sole access to a key customer at the next channel level. That access provides the intermediary with reward, legitimate, and coercive power. As a result, the intermediary may simply refuse to accept a less-powerful manufacturer's pricing demands—and be able to get away with it. An example of some rather aggressive attempts to resolve conflict in franchising channels is discussed in Channel Surfing 8.3.

Each party's short- or long-term orientation toward the relationship has the most influence on its problem-solving behavior. Channel members with long-term relationship orientations focus on achieving future goals and are concerned with future exchange outcomes. They seek to develop or support relational exchanges to maximize their profits over a series of problem-solving episodes. Channel members with short-term views, on the other hand, are concerned only with the options and outcomes of the current negotiation, relying on the efficiencies of discrete exchanges to optimize their returns.

Channel members seeking relational exchanges benefit from joint synergies. Such firms are likely to use logrolling or compromise strategies to iron out conflicts. Their preferences for relationally oriented problem-solving strategies are based on the objective of maximizing their individual outcomes. Exchange of priority information is possible in relational exchange because the participants believe any short-term inequities will be corrected in the long run.

The problem-solving attempts of members with markedly greater power are often coercive, involving aggressive tactics such as threats, punishments, or argumentative behavior. Nevertheless, the more powerful party's desire to exploit its power through coercive means is generally stifled in negotiations between channel members having prior relationships and the expectation of future relationships. This *dampening effect* results because coercive actions can spark future retaliation. Boundary personnel generally recognize this fact and understand that relative distributions of power can shift over time. Logrolling and compromise are more likely to be used in such contexts. Even when power is inequitably distributed, high levels of mutual dependence or preexisting interfirm cooperation and coordination usually lead to noncoercive problem-solving strategies.[13]

Persuasive Mechanisms

Once negotiation and problem-solving efforts establish open lines of communication, help match up channel member expectations, and educate each party about the preferences of the other, the real work of conflict resolution can begin. Much of that work involves persuasion. The act of **persuasion** implies that one channel member influences another member's behavior. However, persuasion should not be viewed as something one boundary member does to other boundary members. It should instead be viewed as something that is done *with* others. This implies a cooperative effort, a process of give and take. Naturally, this process takes time to develop and requires a willingness to learn what the other channel member has to give and what they are willing to take. The process of persuasion occurs in three steps: gaining personal acceptance, confirming motivation, and dispensing rewards.

The first step in persuasion is gaining **personal acceptance** among the boundary personnel. The channel partners must believe in the rules of negotiation—the explicit or implicit

Channel Surfing 8.3

Why Can't We All Just Get Along?

At 50, you're a successful and still energetic manager who has had her fill of being a corporate warrior. You're not a technical wizard, but you would like to retire early and pursue other business interests. So you buy a franchise. You'll be your own boss, make a decent living, maybe bring the kids into the business, and build it into something significant. Sounds great!

But business life rarely follows the ideal. Real life as a franchisee is rife with potential and genuine sources of conflict. Long John Silver's franchisee Frank Cain, for example, doesn't expect magic from his corporate offices, but he does expect respect. Specifically, the owner of 39 units wants to have a say in the ailing chain's future. Many of his fellow franchisers do as well and are joining the Association of Long John Silver's Franchisees Inc. Cain laments, "Our voices are not being heard loud enough."

Increasingly, franchisees in other chains feel the same. Many are forming independent associations that talk and think purely in franchisee-speak. Like an organized union, these groups believe there is power in numbers to compel changes at headquarters. Franchisees across the country, it seems, truly want more participation in day-to-day activities.

But too often, franchisee-franchiser relationships turn acrimonious, fracturing even the tightest franchise operations. At McDonald's, for example, some franchisees who publicly aligned themselves with the Consortium, an independent group of franchisees dissatisfied with corporate strategy, claim they were pulled off key fax and e-mail lists. At Little Caesars, two organizations are pursuing similar issues. Top among them is that the franchisees believe they can cut costs by purchasing food and other supplies from sources outside the company-owned distributor. But to franchisers, that's a no-no. Both franchisee organizations are simply seeking an open, cooperative, and constructive dialogue with their franchiser.

On the other hand, if you were to ask any franchise CEO if he or she would like the same from franchisees, there would be unanimous agreement. Why, then, do franchisees feel a need to organize? The reasons why are as varied as the franchise concepts themselves, but they each tie back into a single concept: channel conflict. Mostly, franchisees want to protect their investments and promote the brand. Franchisees often believe they have a better feel for what will work across their counter than do executives who may be thousands of miles away. And they may be right.

Clearly, franchising is an imperfect distribution channel. Most experts agree that there are few channel relationships as complex as those contained within the franchise system. The tie is long-term, mutually dependent, and financially connected—not unlike a marriage. And it is ripe territory for conflict to arise—like a marriage. Managing the relationship is more complicated than it looks.

Is a successful relationship possible? Of course it is. When franchisers, who usually possess more channel power, act openly and cooperatively, a mutually respectful, balanced relationship can arise. Relationships and morale will improve, and franchisees should be willing to invest even more in the franchised brand.

Points to Ponder

- Why can so many things go so wrong so fast in franchising relationships?
- Is there anything a little less threatening that franchisees could do to avoid the kinds of problems described here?

Source: Adapted from Higley, Jeff (1999), "New Organization Splits Franchising World," *Hotel and Motel Management,* January 11, 9, 98; and Watkins, Ed (1999), "Why Can't We All Just Get Along?" *Lodging Hospitality,* April, 6, 55.

guidelines that govern acceptable behavior during the bargaining process. Without personal acceptance, persuasion will not occur because the members will not believe in any settlement that is subsequently achieved. Moreover, the costs of surveillance or the need for future incentives to ensure compliance to the solution will increase.

The personal acceptance of key boundary personnel can be achieved more easily if the firm attempting to persuade another channel member acts in ways that are consistent with relational exchange. For instance, when McDonald's enters a foreign market, they now do so by offering 50-50 relationships. This arrangement presumably motivates McDonald's new foreign partners to be more aggressive and innovative in their marketing practices. It also ensures acceptance of McDonald's rules of negotiation among their new alliance partners. McDonald's should then experience less trouble persuading these partners to resolve conflicts their way.

In the second step, the boundary personnel of firms using persuasion to resolve conflict must carefully search out the motivations of their counterparts. Here, assumptions about partner concerns should be avoided because they are likely to be wrong and potentially harmful. Consider, for instance, a channel setting involving an American retailer and a Korean manufacturer. In such a situation, American negotiators who present Korean counterparts with contractual documents burdened with Western legalese can cause offense. In the eyes of Korean businesspeople, the American firm's motives will be suspect from the start. A better approach is to use Korean-style documents composed in a language, style, and form that are likely to be clearer to foreign signatories. Such insights will be easily available to the American retailer who takes the time to gather information on the values and interests of Korean businesspeople.

The best form of persuasion is self-persuasion. *Self-persuasion* is more likely to occur when boundary personnel become thoroughly involved with the issues in conflict and in the process of problem solving.[14] Attribution theory holds that when people observe themselves doing well (i.e., participating in desirable behaviors), they generally accept the reasons for their doing well as flowing from within themselves. It is one thing for a channel member to induce its partner's personnel to change their behaviors through a promise (threat) of positive (negative) sanctions; it is quite another to persuade those individuals to feel at home with the change—in effect, to persuade them that these changes were their own doing. When boundary personnel experience the success associated with adapting in particular ways to settle a conflict, they observe themselves succeeding and are motivated to continue such desirable behavior. These individuals will have persuaded themselves that this solution is the right thing to do.

The third step in the process of persuasion involves the dispensation of rewards. Rewards are likely to favorably affect the recipient negotiator's present behavior, while also influencing the channel member to act in a similar, positive fashion when similar conflicts arise in the future. Rewards should flow only after gaining the target boundary personnel's personal buy-in and self-motivated participation in the process of conflict resolution. In channel conflicts, rewards might involve cost concessions, long-term contractual agreements, or favorable territorial considerations, but they need not automatically assume this form. Verbal appeals, encouragement, and praise are often acceptable substitutes for more tangible appeals.[15]

Most of us perform best when we see visible signs of our progress. As such, channel organizations should identify the most appropriate means of rewarding those firms that cooperate with them in the long-term pursuit of solutions to channel conflicts. Consequently, reward structures that reinforce joint problem solving, communication, and relationship building should be emphasized. Profits alone are rarely sufficient to sustain channel relationships or ensure cooperation throughout a channel.

Legalistic Strategies

There is no question that relationships are tough. All relationships. Ask anybody. We have all got our stories to tell, tales of personal frustration flowing from a failure to achieve open, honest communication between us and our partners—business or otherwise. It seems that similar troubles define the nature of relationships. Sometimes circumstances degrade to the point where legal action seems to present the only and therefore best option. After all, when all else fails, the American way is to file a lawsuit.

Legalistic strategies such as arbitration and settlements are used when one channel member contends that a formal legal contract or agreement requires another member to perform a given action. Don't go there, if you can avoid it, but you don't have to take our word for it. Just consider what happened when two long-time channel partners pursued a legalistic resolution to a pricing conflict. The price was $20.67 per case, far higher than the $14.00 David's Supermarket had paid for the same bags directly from the manufacturer. A closer look by the Texas-based grocery chain revealed it had been paying excessively high wholesale prices on many other goods. Rather than pursuing another strategy to resolving the conflict, David's decided to sue to settle the dispute. It won. The distributor in question, Fleming Foods Inc., is now appealing the verdict, claiming that no wrong was committed. But in a food industry already strained by intense competition, the case has ripped a possibly permanent hole between the Oklahoma City wholesaler and many of its 3,500 customers. At this point, both sides to the dispute probably wish they had pursued a nonlegalistic solution. For instance, when an action urged by a retailer has a clear legal basis in what both channel parties initially endorsed as a fair agreement, legalistic strategies generally will yield a prompt resolution and compliance. However, if a member views the contract or agreement as vague or not applicable to the issue in conflict, further resistance is likely.

A current illustration of legal action can be seen in the issue of franchise encroachment. For years, franchisees have complained about geographic encroachment. Encroachment issues arise whenever franchisees conclude that their franchisors are attempting to develop new franchise locations too close to their own existing locations. Sometimes, they merely watch angrily as franchisors permit new outlets to be opened near theirs. At other times, they file lawsuits. The issue of franchising encroachment is becoming even more complex with the advent of marketing through the Internet. Franchisees of one gourmet coffee chain are already fighting their franchisor's plans to sell coffee on the Internet. Legal action is being pondered.[16]

Legal action should be used only as a final option. This is because when a legal action is threatened or taken, the targeted firm may overtly comply but will likely harbor ill-will toward the channel member bringing the action. As a result, conflict may actually increase rather than decrease. Furthermore, the target firm will likely dissolve its relationship with the firm bringing the suit, regardless of who wins the settlement. At best, highly impersonal, guarded, and generally unfavorable relations can be expected in the future between firms involved in legal actions against one another.

Interdependence: Tying It All Together

In this chapter, we have discussed several negotiation, problem-solving, and persuasive strategies that can be used to resolve conflicts. But a critical dimension of conflict resolution in channel settings, the one that ties each strategy together, still needs to be addressed. This dimension is *interdependence*—the degree to which each channel member needs the other.

It is true that each firm engaged in conflict resolution processes with another channel member is, first and foremost, interested in achieving its goals and meeting its needs. Consequently, many firms think of themselves as autonomously pursuing a goal, and view the other party to the dispute as somehow standing in the way of achieving the goal. This is often the wrong attitude.

Because firms involved in channel relationships are interdependent, over the long run one party cannot get all that it desires without taking others into account. For instance, Levi Strauss cannot possibly deliver sufficient quantities of blue jeans to its end-user market without the good efforts of Sears, the Gap, and other retailers. In channels, firms are partially dependent on others for achieving their distribution or supply goals, either because those goals or the means for achieving them are linked to other firms. Interdependence is what gives conflict resolution in channel settings its complexity, creates much of its inherent tension, and provides the opportunity for achieving mutually satisfactory outcomes.

Key Terms

aggressive strategy
compromise strategy
legalistic strategies
logrolling
negotiation
open submission
personal acceptance
persuasion
problem-solving strategy
relative power
win-win strategy

Chapter Summary

Conflict resolution strategies can be divided into five broad types: negotiation, problem-solving strategies, persuasive mechanisms, legalistic strategies, and climate management.

The success with which channel conflicts are resolved often depends upon negotiation. Negotiation involves mutual discussions aimed at resolving conflict. It is a fact of marketing life that should be mastered rather than feared. Boundary personnel should continuously consider the impact that their negotiating strategies will have on channel relationships. Negotiating strategies should not be selected until after channel members have evaluated what they seek for their relationship's future.

Channel members that use predatory negotiation strategies would consider the idea of relationship-sustaining bargaining sessions unsophisticated or weak. Predatory negotiators try to grab as much as possible by giving the other as little as possible. Channel members who are willing to lose, conceal information, or stand by commitments to accept only favorable settlements generally prevail. By contrast, symbiotic negotiation strategies feature attempts to create mutual value through a process of trade-offs and bargaining. The prevailing atmosphere is, "I will help you if you help me." Open submission strategies involve one channel member's concessions to another on all but the barest aspects of the issue in conflict. Such actions might be taken to build a more productive relationship. Joint gains can be achieved through win-win strategies. Here, participants seek to avoid behaviors that would worsen their relationship.

Behaviors that would increase the substantive elements of the issue under negotiation are actively sought out.

Channel parties should base their negotiations on substance. This involves (1) separating people from problems, (2) focusing on needs rather than positions, (3) developing options for mutual gains, and (4) using objective criteria. Symbiotic strategies designed to create mutual value through cooperation and collaboration are diametrically opposed to predatory strategies intended to claim value. Using negotiating strategies for claiming value generally blocks its creation and makes one susceptible to predatory negotiation strategies. When attempting to resolve conflicts through negotiation, each party should do its homework, deal from the top of the deck, remember that quitters never win and the importance of a positive attitude, and strive to build bridges rather than walls.

Problems routinely arise in channels. A problem-solving strategy is a plan of action based on a channel member's goals or objectives and its analysis of the situation. One problem-solving strategy is logrolling, in which each party identifies its priorities and offers concessions on those issues they view as less significant. Another involves compromise, wherein conflicts are resolved by establishing a middle ground based on the initial positions of each party. A third problem-solving strategy involves aggressive, one-sided attempts to solve problems by threats, persuasive arguments, or punishments.

Once negotiation and problem-solving efforts establish open lines of communication, the real process of conflict resolution can begin. Much of that work involves persuasion. The act of persuasion implies that one channel member has influenced another member's behavior, with those behaviors relating to a course of action sought by the persuader. But persuasion is not something one channel member does to other channel members. Persuasion is done with others. It involves a cooperative effort, and a process of give and take.

Arbitration and settlements are legalistic strategies aimed at gaining compliance or a solution to an otherwise unresolvable problem. Either method should be used only as a final option. Their use suggests that a solution to the problem could not be worked out through other, more harmonious procedures administered through normal marketing channels.

Serious disputes in channel relationships usually do not pop up overnight. Mindful of this, marketers should try to adopt long-run views of how best to handle conflict in channel settings. Perhaps the best way to achieve this is by shaping the channel climate in ways that contribute to the development of trust between the channel members. The use of positive problem-solving and persuasion behaviors is then much more likely.

Channel Challenges

1. The English journalist G. K. Chesterton once wrote, "It isn't that they can't see the solution. It is that they can't see the problem." You will recall that channel conflict refers to a channel member's perception that another channel member (or system) is preventing it from attaining its goals. How does Chesterton's assertion highlight the importance of *problem identification* in resolving channel conflict? If channel members cannot agree on the problem, is it possible to address a system solution?

2. Recently, over 450 owners of Taco Bell restaurants franchised by PepsiCo, Inc., bought their supplies from an independent Louisville, Kentucky, co-op. However, the authorized distributor is PFS, a PepsiCo distribution division that services Taco Bell, Pizza Hut, and KFC restaurants. Why would the Taco Bell franchisees buy through unauthorized suppliers? Is saving money a valid reason for breaking a franchise system's supplier agreement?

3. "Cross each bridge when we get to it?
   That's one outdated goal.
   Today, those who delayed admit
   They can't afford the toll."

   —Bern Sharfman

   How does Sharfman's verse relate to channel conflict resolution? Why might it be more costly to cross the bridge when conflict arises?

4. Pepper Patch, Inc., is a small Tennessee bakery. The bakery's Tennessee Tipsy cakes and whiskey-laced Tennessee Truffles called for Jack Daniels in their recipes. Dot Smith, Pepper Patch's owner, took on powerful liquor distributors to force them to sell her Jack Daniels whiskey directly from the distillery in lieu of higher-priced retailers. Smith is a fighter, and she asserts, "If you fold on a problem it only makes matters worse. You have to have a constitution of iron." How does Smith's assertion support or refute the principles of relationship building?

5. The new International Franchising Association's (IFA) Code of Ethics vows to expel violators. If franchisors behave legally, is it fair to expel them from IFA membership for disregarding one or more ethical codes? Who should police the behaviors of franchisors? Why would the IFA take such a tough stance on its members?
6. Suppose you receive a lower grade than expected on a group project. To make things worse, your section of the project received accolades from the professor. However, the group project grade was the same for all group members. How might you confront this issue with the professor? How might this conflict have been averted before the final project was completed?

Review Questions

1. Why do attempts to unilaterally apply power usually fail in today's marketing channels?
2. Briefly describe the role that the quality of their relationship plays in moderating the frequency and intensity of conflict that emerges between channel members.
3. Under what conditions should a firm consider using an open-submission negotiation strategy to resolve a conflict with another channel member?
4. How can channel members "create" value for themselves and for their channel out of conflict?
5. How does a *logrolling* problem-solving strategy differ from a *compromise* problem-solving strategy?
6. Why should legal approaches to resolving channel conflicts be used only as a last resort?
7. Describe how the dimension that we called *interdependence* ties together all of the conflict resolution strategies described earlier in the chapter.

Endnotes

1. Machlis, Sharon (1998), "Estee Lauder Tackles Web," *Computerworld,* July 6, 79–82.
2. Cohen, Andy (2000), "When Channel Conflict Is a Good Thing," *Sales & Marketing Management,* April, 13–15.
3. Garner, Rochele (1999), "Partners or Patsies?" *Sales and Marketing Management,* July, 98.
4. Gates, William H., III (1995), *The Road Ahead,* New York: Viking Penguin.
5. This discussion is based on the work of Burton, John (1995), "Composite Strategy: The Combination of Collaboration and Competition," *Journal of General Management,* 21 (1), 1–23.; Lewicki, Roy J., and Joseph A. Litterer (1985), *Negotiation,* Burr Ridge, IL: Richard D. Irwin; and Webb, William (1995), "Microsoft to Enter the News Business," *Editor and Publisher,* 128 (14), 26–34.
6. Poslums, Ronald J. (1987), *Negotiate Your Way to Financial Success,* New York: Putman.
7. Tannenbaum, Jeffrey A. (1994), "Brice Offers Its Frozen-Yogurt Franchisees a Sweet Deal," *The Wall Street Journal,* November 9, B2.
8. Milligan, Brian, and James Carbone (2000), "Harley-Davidson Wins by Getting Suppliers on Board," *Purchasing,* September 21, 52–65.
9. Fisher, Roger, and William Ury (1982), *Getting to Yes,* Boston: Houghton-Mifflin.
10. Anderson, Terry (1992), "Step into My Parlor: A Survey of Strategies and Techniques for Effective Negotiation," *Business Horizons,* 35 (May/June), 71–76.
11. Pruitt, Dean G. (1981), *Negotiation Behavior,* New York: Academic Press.
12. Froman, Lewis A. Jr., and Michael D. Cohen (1970), "Compromise and Logroll: Comparing the Efficiency of Two Bargaining Processes," *Behavioral Science,* 15, 180–183.
13. Ganesan, Shankar (1993), "Negotiation Strategies and the Nature of Channel Relationships," *Journal of Marketing Research,* 30 (May), 183–203.
14. Reardon, Kathleen Kelley, and Robert E. Spekman (1994), "Starting Out Right: Negotiations Lessons for Domestic and Cross-Cultural Business Alliances," *Business Horizons,* XX (January–February), 71–79.
15. Lewicki, Roy J., and Joseph A. Litterer (1985), *Negotiation,* Homewood, IL: Irwin.
16. Tannenbaum, Jeffrey A. (1995), "Via Software, Kiosks, Internet," *The Wall Street Journal,* October 30, B1.

chapter

9

Information Systems and Relational Logistics

Learning Objectives

After reading this chapter, you should be able to:

- Explain how systematizing information can enhance channel performance.
- Define logistics and apply the flexible enterprise model to channels management.
- Describe how information and logistics interface with channels management.
- Explain how tailored logistics and supply chain management can foster relationship building.
- Identify the principal inputs and outputs in the logistics system.
- Relate the five logistics mediators to customer satisfaction.
- Discuss major trends in transportation and inventory management.
- List the logistics challenges which accompany global distribution.

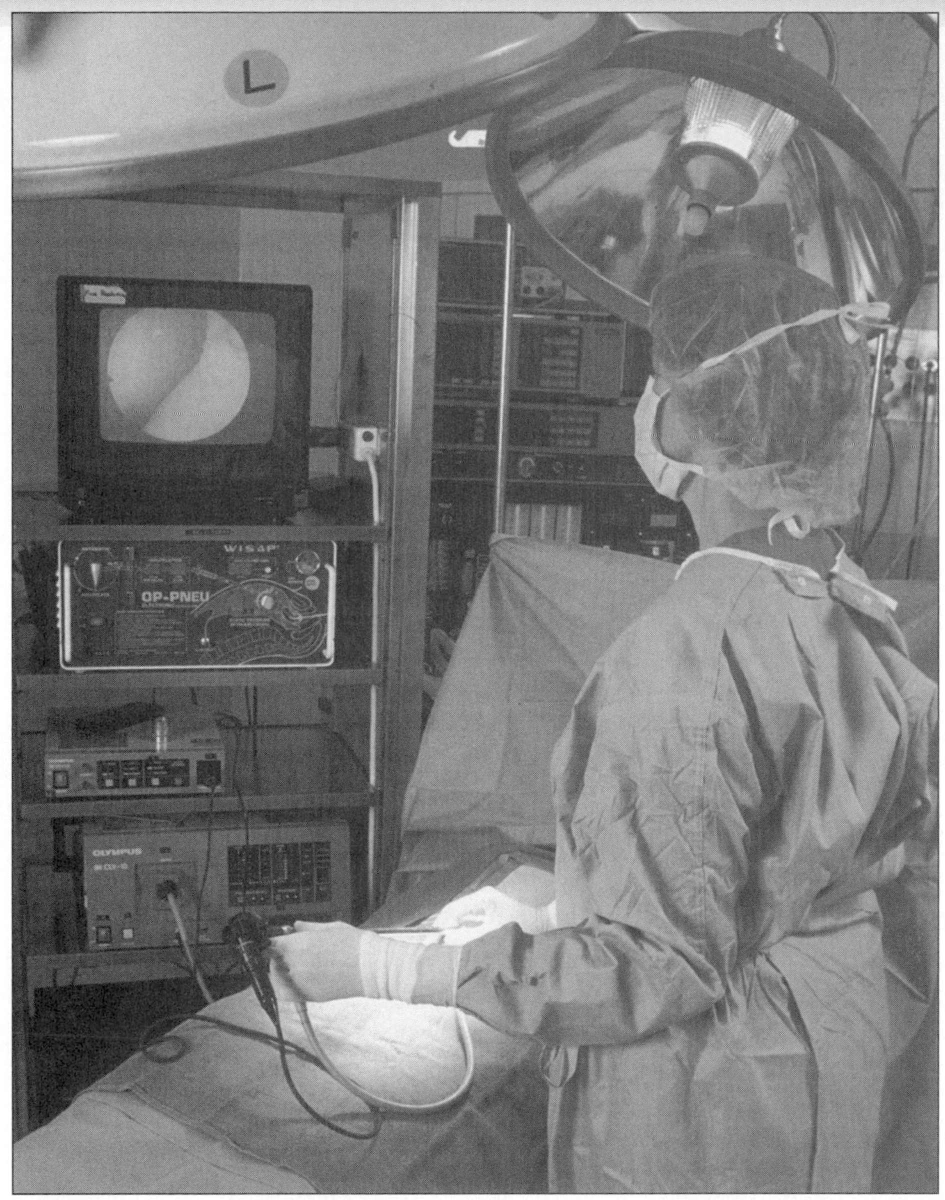

Custom Medical Stock Photography

You won't find these video systems at Best Buy, Circuit City, or your favorite home electronics retail outlet. These highly specialized video systems don't brandish brand icons like Panasonic, Sony, or JVC. Instead, these cameras are produced by Circon Corporation, and they are more likely to be situated in operating rooms rather than in living rooms! U.S.-based Circon Corporation is the nation's largest manufacturer of the optical-video chain of instruments and products used for minimally invasive surgery. A classic American entrepreneurial growth company, this century-old company remains on the cutting edge of medical high technology.

Circon's optical-video chain of equipment affords surgeons an up-front and personal view of the surgical area, and it facilitates surgery performance and recording. This optical-video system consists of high-intensity light sources, light guides, endoscopes, miniature video cameras, high resolution monitors, video recorders, and printers. And this "chain" is analogous to the value chain at the heart of the channel microsystem.

To illustrate, consider a surgical procedure called *laparoscopy*. Each year, more than one-half million gallbladders are removed in U.S. hospitals and surgical clinics. And laparoscopy is the common, minimally invasive procedure used for these removals. Its success is predicated on a fiber-optic device that has a tiny camera inserted. The images of the surgical area are illustrated in full-color on a high-resolution monitor.

Circon's newest optical-video chain not only affords a three-dimensional image of the surgical area, it allows information to be collected, transmitted, and shared among all members of the surgical team. The entire process is video-recorded, and vital patient data is saved on microchips. This computer-enhanced value chain is a conduit for information exchange among the surgeon, surgical nurses, and robots. Yes, robots.

The latest medical technologies allow surgeons to use a remote-controlled robotic arm to perform the actual operation. As the surgeon "operates" on the surgical image, the surgeon's motions are translated into the parallel movements of a robot that is manipulating surgical tools inside the patient. What may be likened to a high-stakes video game is actually a coordinated and collaborative activity—a virtual value chain—across health care practitioners.

In this chapter, we discuss how information exchange creates and sustains value in marketing channels. As Dr. Rick Satava wisely noted, "You can think of medicine as just another aspect of the information age, and what we used to think of as blood and guts are just bits and bytes. That's all it is—transferring information back and forth."

* * * *

The medical technology described above offers a parallel illustration to the emerging role that information and logistics are playing in marketing channels. Like virtual surgery, in logistics each exchange partner's actions are characterized by:

- **Information flows.** Information *drives* channel systems. Just like the parallel transmission of information between the surgeon and the computer-controlled robot, information flows between channel members must be effectively coordinated.
- **Control from a distance.** Computer-controlled robotics allow surgeons to reach hard-to-access areas with great precision. Responsibility for the actual surgical

procedures is assigned to robots and their high-tech dexterity. But control never leaves the surgeon's hands. Likewise, channel members usually cannot personally deliver goods to each of their customers. Channel members often delegate the responsibility for physical distribution to other organizations. Still, ideally, channel members maintain some control over product quality and service.

- **Integrated system.** Telepresence surgery results from the interaction of computer technology, robotics, fiber-optic communications, virtual reality, high-tech medical diagnostics, and surgical skills. Logistics also involves an integrated process. Logistics merges technological, transportation, communication, and information management tools to foster the efficient flows of goods through marketing channels.

Information is an essential element in the exchange process. In this chapter, we will study how information is moved through channel systems and how it relates to logistics management. This process of moving information is known as **systematizing information.** Systematized information involves any rule-based method used to arrange, coordinate, or share data between members of a distribution channel. Systematized information is a cornerstone of logistics.

To appreciate the role of systematizing information, consider how a clothing manufacturer knows what types and sizes of blue jeans to supply to a particular retail store. The answer? It receives systematized information about consumer clothing preferences from the retailer. For example, Vanity Fair Corporation (VF) is a major supplier of apparel to the Federated Stores Group. Federated Department Stores has over 400 stores in 33 U.S. states, including Bloomingdale's, Burdines, Goldsmith's, Lazarus, Macy's, Rich's, and The Bon Marche. VF automatically refills stock to these stores as it is sold. No restocking orders, no approvals, and no guesswork are required in this replenishing process. The need to purchase new stock is transmitted directly to the manufacturers from the retailers' computerized cash registers.

The interchange among Federated's customers, retailers, and a myriad of suppliers is even more convoluted than it may seem. As we discussed in Part I, Federated Department Stores is focusing on direct retailing in the Net Economy. In addition to its Fingerhut, Macy's by Mail, and Bloomingdale's by Mail catalogs, Federated is selling through the Internet. Another Federated website interest—Weddingchannel.com—must ensure that the right wedding gown and wedding apparel accessories arrive on time to adorn the bride and the wedding party. This requires tremendous coordination and collaboration.

Manufacturers, suppliers, and retailers are increasingly sharing information to create competitive advantages in the marketplace. The relationship between VF Corporation and Federated Stores Group shows how such advantages might arise in vertical channel systems. Systematized information can also occur horizontally—that is, at the same channel level. For example, DaimlerChrysler, Ford, and General Motors—all manufacturers—are sharing information. Normally fierce competitors, they are conducting joint teardowns of other global carmakers' vehicles to study their technologies. As a result of this cooperative effort, the Big Three plan to adapt Renault's right-hand drive technology to sell more cars in right-hand drive markets like Japan.[1] The CRM shows how and why information is a key interchange in any channel relationship. Firms simply cannot successfully meet the challenges of a dynamic external environment without continued flows of accurate information.

Earlier, we discussed how major automobile manufacturers are sharing information to forge a competitive advantage in the global marketplace. In the Net Economy, automobile dealers must also rethink their own competitive positioning strategies. After all, you may imagine new car showrooms with just a few cars to test-drive, but no inventory of cars in every style and color. Instead, customers may use the Internet to order a car to exacting specifications and have it delivered right to their own home.

The seamless exchange of information that extends from the customer's home computer all the way back to multifarious suppliers, through dealerships, wholesalers, and manufacturers illustrates a connection between the manufacturing and service arenas. This connection creates the *flexible enterprise:* channel members who are virtually connected with their customers and markets. Flexible enterprises minimize response times and maximize customer satisfaction.

Logistics

In both vertical and horizontal marketing systems, systematized information contributes to the efficient flow of goods and services from the point of origin to the point of consumption. This process of regulation begins with customer service and extends to the procurement, handling, and processing of resources aimed at delivering customer satisfaction. All ways in which resources are procured, handled, and processed fall within a set of activities known as logistics. **Logistics** is a process of systematizing information to facilitate the efficient and cost-effective flows of goods and services to produce customer satisfaction. Each member in the supply chain must be involved in logistics activities. Logistics flows may begin with the supplier/manufacturer relationship, but efficient logistics activities are needed throughout the marketing channel. Relationship marketing epitomizes the interactive process necessary to achieve customer satisfaction by maintaining a participative exchange of information with all of a firm's channel partners.

The *Council of Logistics Management* defines logistics management as: "that part of the supply chain process that plans, implements, and controls the efficient, effective flow and storage of goods, services, and related information from the point of origin to the point of consumption in order to meet customers' requirements."[2] This definition reinforces three universal themes in logistics management. These bear repeating:

- Information *drives* the flow of goods and services.
- Control over marketing channels can be achieved (from a distance) on the basis of efficiency and cost containment in resource flows.
- In marketing channels, resources are recast through an integrated system of technology, information, and communication.

The computer-games giant Sega once faced extreme market pressure from its retailers. Retail chains complained of sluggish product deliveries, frequent stock-outs, excessive shipping errors, and forced bulk purchases. Recognizing the importance of retailer satisfaction, Sega launched a customer-driven logistics system to replace an outdated warehouse system. Sega express was no video game—it was a state-of-the-art logistics system that managed information flows among retailers, other intermediaries, and Sega.

This integrated system of technology and information allows Sega to achieve more efficiency and control over distribution costs. Sega uses sophisticated radio frequency technology to instantaneously collect data from retailers. Radio frequency terminals transmit inventory counts at remote locations between Sega and its retailers. Sega can immediately track product sales and react accordingly. By using bar-coded tracking labels to control the location and timing of its physical distribution, Sega was able to align production schedules with retail sales performance. As a result, Sega attained 24-hour retail delivery with more than 99 percent shipping accuracy. Amazingly, Sega was able to ship 1,000 times more orders each week than in its previous system![3]

Effective logistics management can help a firm create strategic competitive advantages. For example, FedEx recently noted that over 75 percent of its direct marketing clients, such as L.L. Bean and Lands' End, reported that their customers ordered more frequently based on their confidence in fast, reliable delivery of merchandise. The average order size among these direct marketers was 13 percent higher when orders were shipped through FedEx.[4] Calyx & Corolla, a floral arrangement supplier, has used effective logistical management to build several differential advantages.[5] The company guarantees exact-date or next-day delivery of flower arrangements, provides fresher-than-average flowers because they are shipped directly from growers, and includes FedEx delivery in all its catalog and Internet orders.

The foundation of Calyx & Corolla's success is a logistics strategy that relies on strong relationships with suppliers (growers), customers, and channel facilitators. One should not underestimate the importance of logistics management when attempting to develop competitive advantages. Channel Surfing 9.1 discusses how a flexible enterprise model helps Master Lock gain a marketing edge.

The Importance of Logistics

As some strategists note, "Logistics have become central to product strategy because, it is increasingly clear, products are not just things-with-features. They are things-with-features *bundled with services*."[6] This is why properly managed logistical processes can add value for consumers. Manufacturers, wholesalers, and retailers often distinguish themselves by the effectiveness with which they provide bundles of services. These service bundles include billing, forecasting demand, handling returns, inventory management, special packaging, transportation, and warehousing and storage functions.

Many environmental trends have contributed to the growing importance of logistics management. For instance, the globalization of new products and technologies force firms to expand market coverage using the most cost-effective means of distribution. Many consumer goods today are not produced for local or regional consumption but are created for global consumption. One need not cross U.S. boundaries to witness logistics' growing importance, however. According to some estimates, logistics expenditures account for over 12 percent of U.S. Gross Domestic Product (GDP). Over $800 billion per year is spent by domestic firms on logistics, including freight transportation, warehousing, and inventory management. Logistics investment also includes land, labor, and capital expenditures totaling hundreds of billions of dollars.[7] Nearly 50 cents of each dollar spent on goods in the United States is allocated toward marketing activities occuring after production. Given the money spent on logistics, channel members must be keenly aware of measuring logistical performance.

Channel Surfing 9.1

Dodging Bullets, Master Lock Fires Back

At the start of the 2001 National Football League season, few expected that Super Bowl XXXV would feature the Baltimore Ravens romping over the New York Giants. Perhaps the most memorable remnant of Super Bowl XXXV was an Associated Press photo of defenseman Duane Starks holding up the "Key to the City" of Baltimore. Another vestige of this unpredictable Super Bowl was not the key, but the padlock. You see, the Master Lock "Marksman" was recognized as one of the greatest Super Bowl ads of all times. It is only fitting that one of the NFL's best defenses in history would coincide with an indelible advertising image of a Master Lock padlock defraying a stream of bullets.

Despite the doughty defense of a Master Lock padlock, the best defense against its declining business was a good offense. Costly automation and price cuts just didn't shut down the competition. So, Master Lock embarked on a deliberate strategy of replacing a rigid vertically integrated organization with a *flexible enterprise* model. The **flexible enterprise model** was centered on agile distribution processes and increased outsourcing. Its fundamental challenge was to provide products faster and more economically to their retail customers.

The new outsourcing initiative enabled Master Lock to take innovative ideas, like its steering wheel/airbag lock technology, and work with vendors to bring those innovations to market quickly and economically. Further flexibility was achieved by outsourcing its distribution at a new Louisville, Kentucky, facility operated by third-party logistics provider GENCO. At this facility, orders are turned out within one to two days 98 percent of the time, compared with a previous four- or five-day turnaround.

These logistics improvements have given Master Lock a powerful weapon against its competitors. After all, the Asian knock-offs were eroding market share, and Master Lock was a prime target given its stagnant product line and high fixed cost base. What value was delivered to its customers? The sales cycle for major hardware retailers is over the weekend, so the reengineered supply chain allows major customers to determine their sales volume and replenish inventories before the following Thursday. Rather than defending its market share with a commoditized line to mass merchant retailers, Master Lock was able to beat the Asian vendors with quicker turnaround and new product development. But none of this would be possible without unlocking a flexible enterprise model.

Points to Ponder

- As part of Master Lock's flexible enterprise system, it developed an assembly operation in Nogales, Mexico. The Mexico-based plant allows it to get new products to the United States with greater efficiency than its Asian competitors. What other advantages may be afforded by locating an assembly plant in Mexico?
- Do you think Master Lock's new strategy is in accordance with the Council of Logistics Management's definition of logistics? Why or why not?

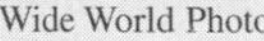

Wide World Photo

Measuring Logistics Performance

Logistics performance is a critical part of an organization's overall performance. Unfortunately, no single measure is available to assess the effectiveness of a firm's logistics program.[8] One common performance measure is profitability. But isolating the costs and returns associated with the flow of goods and services from point of origin to point of consumption is extremely difficult. Different channel members bear different costs depending on the functions they perform and the services they provide.

Another performance measure is the service quality index (SQI), a composite measure of a firm's service capabilities, consisting of on-time performance, transit time, rates, costs of loss or damaged goods, and the like. The SQI offers a way to account for the cost/revenue trade-off when logistics performance is measured. As an example, Unisys recently wanted to reduce its transportation suppliers. In response, the firm used the SQI to assess the quality performance of its suppliers. The results allowed Unisys to reduce its transportation suppliers from nearly 1,500 to just 400. Unisys believes a smaller supplier pool will eventually allow it to develop stronger relationships with the best transportation suppliers in the industry.[9]

Other measures are emerging as tools for evaluating logistics performance. Each shares a common theme: customer responsiveness.[10] **Customer responsiveness** reflects a channel member's ability to adapt to its partners' changing needs. Customer responsiveness captures customers' perception of the logistics quality provided by a supplying firm. As the Malcolm Baldrige National Quality Award states in its guidelines, "Quality is judged by the customer."[11] This premise implies that any logistical strategy should begin with an understanding of customers' service requirements. Four procedures help firms identify customers' service needs:[12]

- **External audits.** An **external audit** identifies the service variables that the firm's customers value most. External audits can involve surveys or personal interviews with the firm's current customers. Customers must be allowed to provide information freely. This provides greater assurance that no critical service attribute is left out. Customers should then evaluate how well the major vendors in the market address each service variable.
- **Internal audits.** Conversely, an **internal audit** is a comprehensive evaluation of how well firms believe their current logistics practices satisfy important service variables. Internal audits identify gaps between a firm's current logistics practices and its customers' service quality expectations.
- **Customer perceptions evaluations.** Once the internal audit is completed, a firm should ask customers how well it performs on each of the key service quality dimensions. This provides specific customer feedback on service quality.
- **Competitive advantage evaluations.** Here a firm evaluates itself in light of its competitors. By identifying weaknesses in competing vendors' logistics practices (as perceived by customers), the firm can concentrate on filling those logistics gaps.

Betz Laboratories, a Pennsylvania-based provider of specialty water treatment chemicals, illustrates the idea that customer value can be effectively delivered through logistics management. Betz's distribution department developed a Custom Distribution Service (CDS). CDS eliminated the cumbersome 55-gallon storage drums that had traditionally stored the water treatment chemicals. In their place, a point-of-feed system was developed that deposits chemicals into the production line or other processes when they are needed. Betz Laboratories delivers other value-added benefits to customers, as well, such as installing a proprietary monitoring system to measure its customers' chemical usage. This value-added feature allows Betz to provide customers with a reliable measure of their chemical usage. Betz also employs experienced delivery specialists trained in regulatory compliance, product safety, and basic chemistry. Armstrong World Industries, a key Betz customer, was delighted to learn that costs were about equal to what they were in the conventional system. But the added convenience and guaranteed delivery system provided substantial extra value.[13]

Computer and communication technologies are making it possible for managers at all channel levels to have a vast amount of logistics-related information at their fingertips. As logistics scholar Tom Mentzer asserts, the diffusion of information technology throughout channels has profoundly affected how "managers look at the problem of managing the channel and the resultant channel relations."[14]

Logistics and Channels Management

In Chapter 1, the ways in which marketing channels provide form, time, place, and possession utilities were discussed. Logistics is uniquely responsible for providing time and place utility to channel members. This is probably why logistics systems are frequently described in terms of delivering the right product to the right place at the right time in the right condition (form) for the right cost. These "rights" of passage in logistics are shown in Exhibit 9.1, with the right product at the core of the process.

Four logistical rights exist within marketing channels. Each right represents a channel function that must be delivered through logistical activities. The focus of strategic logistics is shifting from customer service to customer satisfaction. Logistical strategies are now adopting a longer-term orientation. Their goal? To secure greater market coverage (right place), deliver customer service (right time), ensure the right product characteristics (right condition), and achieve cost containment (right price).

Attaining Market Coverage

The *right place* is where the product needs to be to satisfy customer expectations. Logistics provides firms with an opportunity to capture market share by matching product availability with market demand. For example, as Russia's economy has shown an increasing taste for fast food, PepsiCo's Pizza Hut has developed a multibillion ruble operation in Moscow. Pizza Hut's success in Russia is largely due to having the right product in the right place. Pizza Hut sells more than 15,000 meals each week in Russia. Despite several new market entrants, Pizza Hut continues to control a huge piece of the (pizza) pie![15]

Delivering Customer Service

Earlier, we discussed the connection between high-quality customer service and outstanding logistical performance. In this regard, firms can earn a strategic advantage by developing strong personal relationships with other channel members. Such firms will then be better positioned to

Exhibit 9.1

The "rights" of passage in logistics

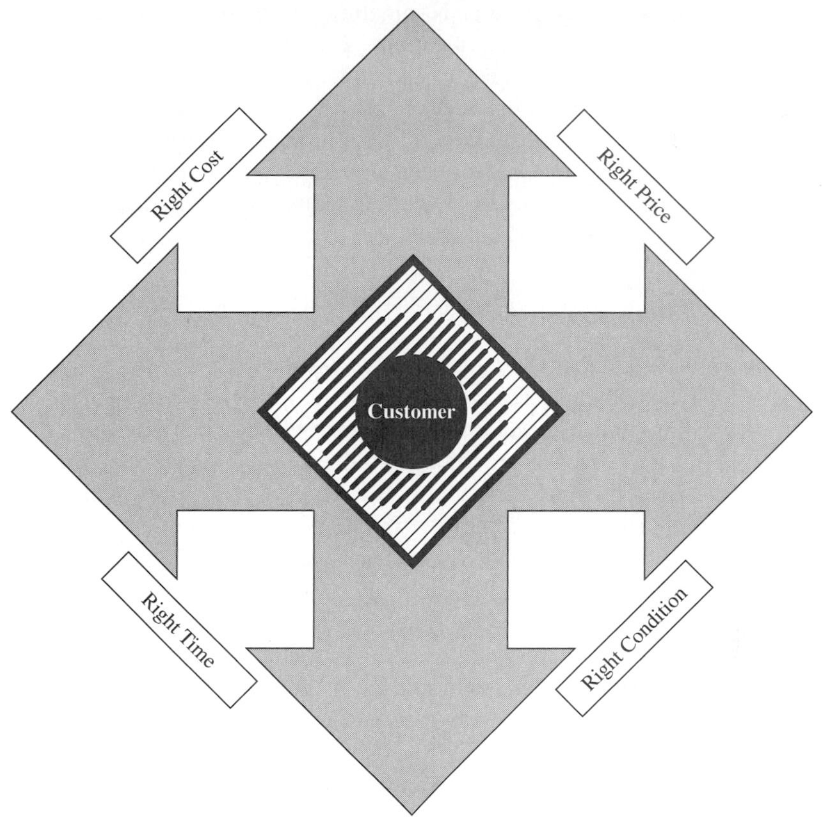

deliver the right product at the *right time*. For example, PepsiCo's relationship with the movers and shakers of Moscow developed long before the first Pizza Hut actually opened. Pizza Hut did not pioneer Western-style pizzas in Russia. However, PepsiCo nurtured a relationship with the state-run Moscow City Council's food service arm long before the first Pizza Hut was opened. It was this relationship that allowed PepsiCo to deliver the pizza at the right time, so to speak.

A combination of place and time utility has contributed to another new market opportunity in Russia: Mexican fast food! Tricon's Taco Bell, in a joint venture with the Moscow Metropolitan Subway System, is bringing burritos to the Park Kultury subway station in Moscow. Moscow's metro is a fast-paced and spotlessly clean setting—ideal for fast foods. These Mexican-style fast-food kiosks give Tricon access to literally millions of passengers each month. Because the Russian government was already comfortable with PepsiCo, it allowed Tricon exclusive food service rights. Tricon will reach 22,000 passengers each hour at its Pizza Hut, Taco Bell, and Kentucky Fried Chicken metro kiosks.[16]

Ensuring the Right Product Characteristics

Bringing products to customers in the *right condition* and in the right amount are critical logistical functions. Today's products are increasingly customized to meet exchange partners' needs. Customization is sometimes accomplished through modifying protective packaging or actual product specifications. Let's briefly return to the Park Kultury subway station in Moscow to demonstrate the importance of product characteristics. While your neighborhood Taco Bell uses shredded cheese bits on burritos, Russian palates prefer premelted cheese. Tricon responded by developing a premelted cheese sauce in lieu of shredded cheese bits for Russian burritos. However, given the subway station's spotless setting, Taco Bell had to be sure that the cheese sauce didn't squirt out of the flour tortilla. So the subway station burritos are designed to be tidier.

Achieving Cost Containment

Cost containment—the *right cost*—is the fourth logistical function performed within marketing channels. The *right cost* is a market-derived assessment. Customers ultimately determine how much they are willing to pay to have a channel function performed. Yet costs are not equally distributed throughout the supply chain. The notion of *who* will bear the costs of performing logistics functions is a major consideration in channels management. This notion, of course, is also a source of frequent channel conflict.

Consider the logistical inefficiencies that frequently afflict food distribution chains.[17] A principal challenge faced by Pizza Hut's Moscow locations was how to secure quality ingredients. Many of Pizza Hut's supplies were traditionally imported into Russia to ensure stable sources of high-quality ingredients. But imported ingredients dramatically increased the cost of pizza to Russian consumers. In an effort to lower the high cost of importing, Tricon is now developing a network of state-run and free-market suppliers in Russia. Tricon is also developing a vertically integrated processing center to stabilize ingredient supplies. Ultimately, these logistical changes should allow Pizza Hut to offer its product at the right cost to Russian consumers.[18]

Relational Logistics Model

How do systematized information and logistics relate? You now know that systematized information facilitates the efficient flow of goods and services through marketing channels. Without these information flows, logistical functions cannot be performed. Our Relational Logistics Model (RLM), illustrated in Exhibit 9.2, shows how this process works. The RLM has five components:

- **Systematized information.** Within the larger framework of the logistics goals, systematized information surrounds the Relational Logistics Model. It involves the communication of firm, market, and industry data between exchange partners. As we have said, this information promotes the efficient flow of products from origin to destination. Relational logistics requires that channel members attain high levels of coordination with each other. This coordination is achieved through information exchange.
- **Logistics inputs.** Logistics inputs are human and capital investments in the flows of goods and services through the marketing channel. Depending on the logistics

EXHIBIT 9.2

Relational logistics model

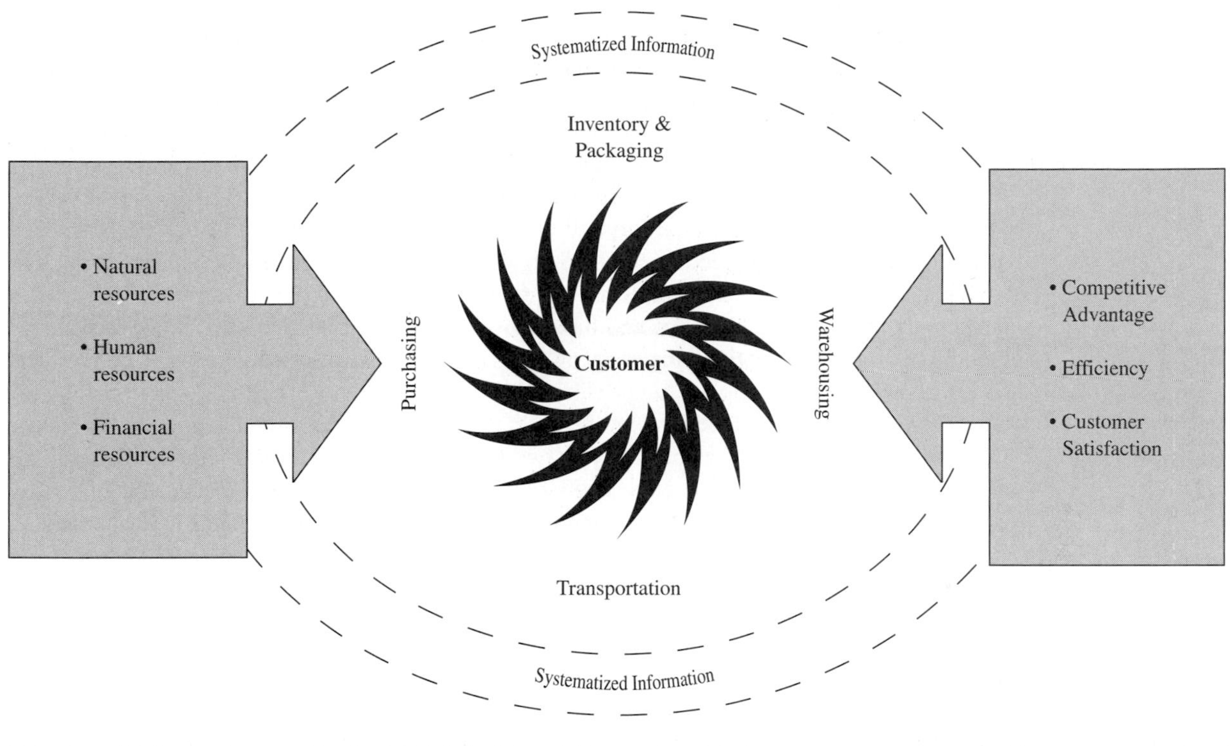

activities performed, these inputs differ among channel members. Relational logistics requires that each channel member commits to the resources agreed upon at the beginning of the exchange relationship.

- **Logistics mediators.** Logistics mediators are the activities that channel members must perform to ensure the smooth, efficient, and cost-effective flow of goods and services through marketing channels. Logistics mediators are necessary to transform raw materials into finished goods. These activities directly shape the nature of exchange relationships between channel members.
- **Logistics outputs.** Logistics outputs are outcomes—competitive advantages, efficiencies, and customer satisfaction—that result directly from channel members' performance in logistics systems. In relationship logistics, outcomes should be fair for each channel member.

We have already discussed logistics goals and systematized information. Shortly, we will describe in detail the three remaining components of the RLM and their positions in the model. First, however, we need to take a closer look at the Relational Logistics Model as a whole by focusing on two topics: supply chain management and fluid performance.

Supply Chain Management

The components of the RLM do not operate in isolation from each other. Rather, they are systematically organized to produce value at each level of the logistics system, with the end goal of simultaneously maximizing logistics outputs and minimizing logistics inputs. In this system, known as **supply chain management,** each logistics mediator is performed by the channel member most likely to minimize costs while delivering customer satisfaction. The overriding goal of supply chain management is to foster cooperative exchange relationships to create the greatest net value for customers.[19]

Kmart's relationship with Lee Apparel illustrates how supply chain management works. Kmart shares sales transaction information with Lee. This data informs Lee of the exact Lee products sold—including color, size, and style—in each Kmart store. With this information in hand, Lee knows which products need to be restocked at each Kmart location, and is thus able to coordinate its production and distribution plans to accommodate a major customer's needs. Lee can also identify early warning signs of merchandising problems for Lee products at particular Kmart locations.[20]

How are logistics outputs maximized as a result of supply chain management? Consider National Semiconductor's success. In just two years, National Semiconductor cut its standard delivery time by 47 percent, reduced distribution costs by nearly 3 percent, and increased sales by about 35 percent. National Semiconductor also used supply chain management to achieve greater customer satisfaction.[21]

The notion of supply chain management rests on channel integration. Channel integration involves systematizing information to reduce suppliers' *and* retailers' inventory needs. All channel members benefit from channel integration. Manufacturers are usually more certain about the resource inputs they need because their production schedules can operate in *real time,* the actual time at which a sale occurs within a channel. Wholesalers can reduce their handling and transportation costs. Finally, retailers only have to replace goods as they are sold, thereby reducing the need for retail-level inventories. At the same time, supply chain management can reduce *stock-outs*—running out of merchandise for which there is customer demand—ultimately increasing customer satisfaction.

Supply chain management focuses attention on the need to develop relational (i.e., ongoing) rather than transactional (i.e., one time) exchange in logistics systems. Effective supply chain management tends to forge cooperative efforts outside the traditional boundaries of channel settings. These cooperative efforts might include market research, product engineering, and total system designs.[22] For supply chain management to foster better retailer-vendor and retail-manufacturer relationships, partnerships must address matters extending beyond the distribution and handling of inventories.

Despite the intuitive appeal of supply chain management, many channel members have not fully embraced this management orientation as a logistics strategy. Perhaps this is because of the high initial investment associated with implementing supply chain management. Or, their hesitation may result from a lack of training aids for channel members.[23] Another problem curbing the adoption of supply-chain integration lies in many channel members' relative inattention to planning and to problem-and-decision support systems.[24]

Supply Chain Management and Fluid Performance

Distribution fluidity describes the extent to which a product offering passes through the logistics system without encountering obstacles. One implication of the Relational Logistics Model concept is that each logistics function mediates (impacts) the *fluidity* with which logistical systems operate. Accordingly, each logistics mediator is critical to the extent that it may impede the flow of goods or services. Unfortunately, channel members often have little control over conditions affecting distribution fluidity.

For example, in 1995, earthquakes in southern California derailed 16 Southern Pacific Lines freight cars. Interstate 5, a major traffic artery between northern and southern California, was also closed. Consolidated Freight was forced to reroute trucks as much as 200 miles to reach their destinations. This resulted in supply shortages and higher prices for those consumer goods that were available.[25]

Barring such natural disasters, distribution fluidity can be best achieved through a comprehensive integration of channels functions. Japanese electronics giant Sony pioneered a distribution fluidity program it calls Sell-One-Make-One (SOMO). SOMO programs rely on established relationships between distributors and retailers. The success of SOMO is attributed to:

- Inventory visibility
- Management of all product flows
- Flexible distribution
- Just-in-time manufacturing
- Interfunctional cohesion

Sony has been able to establish an enviable reputation for supporting retailers through effective planning, implementation, and control. The effectiveness of SOMO or any other supply chain integration system depends on how well each component of the Relational Logistics Model is planned, executed, and controlled at each link in the distribution channel.

Three sections remain to be discussed in this chapter. As you read them, note how the topic of each is taken from the RLM.

Logistics Inputs

Logistical functions cannot be separated from the channel members who carry out those functions. For example, J.C. Penney is not only a major retailer, but is also a huge logistics management company. Penney's customers want more value, better quality, and lower prices. Logically, then, J.C. Penney demands similar outputs from its service providers. J.C. Penney's ability to deliver greater customer value rests in large part on the logistics inputs it receives from its suppliers and channel facilitators.[26]

Logistics inputs—the human and capital investments in the flows of good and services through the marketing channel—involve three major categories of resources: natural, human, and financial. Natural resources include land, facilities, equipment, and raw materials used in the initial processing or subassembly of parts or products. Natural resources represent a major investment in the inbound logistics for the producer.

The second category of logistics inputs is human resources. Human resources are labor units involved in the production, distribution, and/or marketing of raw materials, in-process inventory, or finished goods. The concept of human resources inputs captures the skills, knowledge, and physical energy that individual channel designates who interact in logistics systems bring to the channel.

Finally, financial resources are a critical logistics input. Undercapitalized firms are prone to logistical failures because they are unable to invest in new technologies that yield long-term savings. Sony had to invest millions of dollars in new hardware and software technology to operationalize its SOMO distribution fluidity plan. Financial resources sometimes provide an incentive for strategic partnering agreements in logistical functions.

Logistics Mediators

There are a wide variety of logistics mediators—the activities that impact the flow of goods and services through distribution channels. Our purpose here is not to deal in detail with each activity, but rather to discuss the major categories of logistics functions that encourage smooth, efficient, cost-effective distribution flows. These activities can be grouped into inventory management, transportation, warehousing, purchasing, and packaging categories.

Inventory Management

Inventory is one of the largest investments in any logistics system. **Inventory,** often called *stock,* is a tangible asset capable of being mined, converted, or created. Inventory may take different forms, depending on its location in the distribution system. In the resource market, inventory may be *stockpiles* in mines or extraction sites. For manufacturers, inventory may assume the form of raw, in-process, or finished materials. At the wholesale level, it is the parts and/or products stored in a warehouse or currently in transit. To retailers, merchandise on racks or shelves is called inventory. Finally, to consumers, retail stock represents an opportunity for product choice or to build domestic inventories. Intense competition at each channel level has heightened the importance of making products available when and where customers want them. The costs of providing customer choice are high; however, the costs of failing to provide such service, resulting in a stock-out, can be much higher.

Inventory carrying costs are the expenses associated with holding an inventory. These costs, which are capital investments, may include interest on the investment, insurance, product loss or damage, and storage. Every dollar invested in inventory represents opportunity costs to the firm. Inventory carrying costs compete with other investment opportunities available to firms, such as equipment, land, or research and development. Inventory carrying costs can be substantial. In fact, they account for over 20 percent of manufacturers' total costs, and over 50 percent of wholesalers' and retailers' total costs.[27] That manufacturers, wholesalers, and retailers attempt to lower their inventory carrying costs should surprise no one. Still, as described in Channel Surfing 9.2, it is interesting to note that not every company in today's channels is interested in reducing inventory.

Inventory management involves minimizing inventory-carrying costs while maintaining sufficient stock to satisfy all anticipated customer needs. This is a difficult balancing act.

Tradewell creates exchange value by providing an "after-market" distribution outlet for its clients. Tradewell's principal goal is to complement, rather than compete with, established marketing channels.

Courtesy Tradewell

Excessive inventory can lead to high investment costs. Insufficient stock levels, on the other hand, can incur high opportunity costs in the form of lost customers. Because demand is uncertain, channel members must estimate customer demand to arrive at optimal inventory levels. Channel managers often use industry benchmarks or estimates based on historical sales data to establish inventory levels. These estimates are often flawed.

Inventory managers have traditionally relied upon a basic tenet of cost containment: the *economic order quantity* (EOQ). The EOQ is the order size that minimizes the investment in inventory storage and order processing costs. Inventory carrying costs rise proportionately with inventory levels. At the same time, as order size increases, average ordering costs decrease proportionately. Inventory managers seek a trade-off point—the point at which the sum of inventory-carrying and order-processing costs is lowest. Unfortunately, though, simple EOQ formulas cannot account for uncertain customer demand and delivery times. Several new inventory management tools are allowing channel members a more accurate picture. These tools include electronic data interchange, just-in-time manufacturing, and quick-response logistics.

Electronic Data Interchange (EDI). Throughout the chapter, we have emphasized the importance of information exchange among all levels in the logistics system. **Electronic data interchange (EDI)** is a technology for facilitating information exchange between channel members. EDI involves the paperless transmission of information among manufacturers,

Channel Surfing 9.2

Smaller Inventories? Lands' End Likes Them Big and Loose

Around the world retailers are reducing their inventories in keeping with the trend toward leaner organizations. Not so with Lands' End, the direct marketer of upscale casual clothing. Lands' End is bucking global trends by flaunting one of modern marketing's cardinal rules: It is building rather than cutting inventory. Having a complete inventory is crucial to gaining and cementing customer loyalty, says William T. End, leader of a new management team at the 30-year-old company. According to End, "If [Lands' End doesn't] keep the customer several years, we don't make any money. We need a long-term payback for the expense of coming up with a buyer."

While department store shoppers may easily resign themselves to an occasional missing size or color, mail-order customers are not so forgiving. Lands' End has to make good on back orders at its own mailing expense. Too many of these "make-ups" have shaved Lands' End profit margin to less than 5 percent in recent years. Inventory pullbacks that saved many retailers' necks in recent years don't come off so well at Lands' End. Apparently, Lands' End's decision to go against the grain is a good one.

Points to Ponder

- How is it that traditional marketing rules of thumb are inappropriate in direct marketing channels? What are the trade-offs between lowering distribution costs and increasing customer service levels?

Source: Adapted from Ferguson, Tim W. (1994), "Business World: Shrink Inventory, Lands' End Likes It Loose," *The Wall Street Journal,* January 18, A17; and Marcial, Gene G. (1994), "A Catalog of Mail-Order Buys," *Business Week,* December 26, 128.

suppliers, and retailers. These paperless transmissions include sales data, purchase orders, invoices, shipment tracking data, and product return information.

The use of EDI shifts inventory management goals away from an individual firm perspective and toward a supply chain perspective. When inventory systems fail to work properly, trading partners suffer up and down the supply chain.[28] Because goods become available just as needed, potential conflicts between channel members over inventory carrying costs can be essentially eliminated through EDI.

EDI is profoundly influencing marketing practice. Consider the effects EDI is having on how health services are distributed. Four major hospital suppliers are working together to develop a standardized EDI system to reduce the paperwork involved in buying supplies for hospitals. Hospitals typically spend \$30–\$40 per order on processing costs. EDI has reduced these costs by half. These changes should translate into major savings for all health care system publics.[29] Some other effects of EDI-type technologies are discussed in Channel Surfing 9.3.

Just-in-Time (JIT) Manufacturing. Technologies that assist and expedite information exchange between channel members are also contributing to a revolution in manufacturing processes. Production schedules are increasingly aligned with actual point-of-transaction activities, usually at the retail level. This technology is called *just-in-time manufacturing.* By operating on real-time transmissions of sales and other logistics data between the channel parties operating at different levels in distribution systems, JIT eliminates the need for excess

Channel Surfing 9.3

What Middlemen May Be Called in the Future

The National–American Wholesale Grocers' Association recently discussed some of the names middlemen may be going by in the near future. In this discussion, the group also took a look at the new roles grocery retailers may soon find themselves playing as they try to "break out of the box" and prosper in the 21st century. Here are a few of the names and roles considered:

Automatic Replenishment Coordinator (ARC): This wholesaler will create an information highway for all transactions between retailers and brokers/manufacturers. In effect, ARCs will manage all inventory in the wholesale supplied system—ensuring perpetual inventory at store, stock at the warehouse, and between-warehouse shipments.

Supply Side Optimizer (SSO): This wholesaler will supply refined order management and distribution coordination services, all aimed at optimizing the flow of product. SSOs will combine replenishment orders with promotional orders, while deciding how to cost effectively fill and deliver the order to retailers.

Strategic Marketer (SM): This wholesaler will participate in joint ventures with local brokers to develop and supply marketing services to retailers. SMs will provide data highways for daily point-of-sale information, while using sophisticated product category management skills to develop strategic marketing programs for wholesale-sponsored merchandising groups.

The future for middlemen looks quite interesting, wouldn't you say?

Points to Ponder

- Do you really think these are the roles that intermediaries will be playing during the next century? Why or why not? Do you see any other middleman roles on the horizon?

Source: Adapted from Anonymous (1994), "What Your 'Middleman' May Be Called in the Future," *Distribution*, January, 31; and Weinstein, Steve (1994), "A New Ballgame," *Progressive Grocer*, 73 (12), 9.

inventory. JIT also reduces the size of **safety stocks,** the reserve stock on hand to meet unanticipated demand. Safety stock is an unused capital investment. For this reason, it incurs high opportunity costs.

JIT manufacturing requires openness and trust among producers, suppliers, and retailers. The successful channel relationship enjoyed by Procter & Gamble and Wal-Mart has been mentioned earlier in the text. This relationship is fueled by Wal-Mart's willingness to share ongoing product category and item sales data with Procter & Gamble. Manufacturers like Kodak, Levi Strauss, GE, and Nike have also entered JIT relationships with retailers like Kmart, Wal-Mart, Target, and Foot Locker.

Quick-Response (QR) Logistics. **Quick-response inventory systems** use EDI applications to automatically replenish stock as it is sold. These technologies track each SKU (stock-keeping unit) sold and instantaneously transmit this information to suppliers and manufacturers. QR systems also build customer satisfaction by reducing stock-outs. A high level of commitment between channel members must exist throughout a logistics pipeline for QR to operate. Manufacturers and their suppliers must share the responsibility for incorporating EDI at the retail level. Maidenform, the intimate apparel producer, bar codes all of its branded merchandise. These bar codes electronically link Maidenform with 80 of its leading retail customers. Over half of Maidenform's retailers now place orders through EDI.[30]

Transportation

The physical movement of goods from one location to any other destination is **transportation.** Transportation is a critical element in any logistics system. It accounts for a substantial portion of logistics cost for most firms. Since nearly all materials and finished goods spend time in transit or in warehouses, effective transportation management reduces costs associated with idle inventories.

Several uncontrollable factors affect the transportation function's on-time performance. Weather, government regulation, and fuel availability and cost affect channel members' choice of transportation modes. Nevertheless, a number of factors can be managed to improve the physical distribution of goods through logistics systems. In that regard, several questions need to be addressed when planning the physical movement of products. These include: Should a channel member use its own carriers or outsource the transportation function? What mode of transportation is most suited to the product(s)? How does the choice of transportation mode affect the reliability of the delivery?

The transportation field has become increasingly complex, and these questions are difficult to answer. Many channel members now employ full-time transportation and traffic managers to manage the shipment of goods and services through logistics systems. The types of decisions they make when selecting a mode of transportation include:[31]

- **Product decisions.** A product's physical attributes determine its transportability. When Coors transports Arctic Ice beer, refrigeration is a crucial consideration. A product's perishability creates new challenges. Just how does Pizza Hut ship cheese in equatorial countries such as Malaysia? This issue is critically important because cheese represents a major cost component in each pizza!
- **Location decisions.** Where products are to be sold affects how they are transported. Certain modes of transport are more appropriate than others, depending on the target market's location, climate, and political and cultural environment. In many parts of the world, road systems are not fully developed. There, perhaps, the use of bicycles or other less-sophisticated transportation modes may become necessary. For instance, bicycles are now being used in China to deliver Wrigley's Gum to retailers!
- **Purchasing decisions.** Order quantities, delivery frequency, and availability impact the when, where, and how of transportation. Consider, for example, how many companies now use Airborne Express, FedEx, and other overnight carriers to resolve emergency stock-outs. Some products are extremely costly to ship overnight, however, especially when distribution routes cross international borders.
- **Pricing decisions.** Transportation costs affect the selling price of a product. How much will the customer be willing to bear with respect to transportation? If transportation increases the cost of goods sold too much, the product may not be able to compete with market pricing. For example, will customers pay an overnight charge for a product with a normal selling price of $3.00? Not likely, but the answer still ultimately depends on how important the product is to a customer.

The Asian Princess *illustrates how multiple transportation modes give shipments the "royal treatment" in Hong Kong, a major distribution center for the Pacific Rim.*

Neal Herndon

Many trends are influencing how goods and services are transported. From a relational logistics perspective, the most important trend is the increase in *working transportation partnerships.* In the past, truckers, rail shippers, ship and barge transporters, and other transportation mode operators tended to operate as adversaries. They saw themselves as competing for the same customer. But transportation services have evolved to the point where the services they offer are highly specialized. This specialization has afforded many transportation firms the opportunity to develop long-term relationships to better service the customer. The focus is less on transportation modes and more on cost-effective delivery.

For example, alliances between railroad and truck carriers have resulted in intermodal transportation agreements. **Intermodal transportation** (shown above) occurs when more than one transportation mode is used to haul a shipment. As the photo illustrates, intermodal transportation may combine truck and rail, ship and rail, or any other combination of transportation modes.

Amtrak and the United States Postal Service (USPS) enjoy an interesting transportation relationship. The RoadRailer, a key piece of equipment in Amtrak's express delivery service, zips down the Sante Fe railway track system at more than 100 mph. These vehicles also have highway tires that allow them to be used for highway travel at the end of the (rail) line. As a result, you could have a train conductor delivering your overnight letters and packages mailed through the USPS!

Another trend in transportation is the use of *third-party logistics firms.* Because of the increased complexity of transportation options, the transportation function is now a highly specialized skill that frequently can be handled more proficiently outside the firm. Companies can then focus more attention on improving manufacturing processes, product development, or other marketing functions. DuPont has traditionally been loathe to surrender any operational control. No longer. DuPont now uses a third-party logistics company, Yellow Logistics Services, Inc., to handle all its inbound transportation and international distribution.[32] DuPont invested substantial time and energy into choosing a logistics partner. The nature of DuPont's products demanded a high degree of knowledge about chemical materials handling and transport regulation. Transportation regulations and requirements are constantly changing. With Yellow Logistics now handling these issues, Dupont can concentrate on its core competencies: innovation and production.

Warehousing

Warehousing involves the physical storage or stock keeping of raw materials, product components, and/or finished goods. Channel members' efforts to minimize physical inventories have not lessened the importance of warehousing. Warehousing has three basic functions: movement, storage, and information transfer.

Movement. The first function is **movement,** which facilitates the flows of goods and services through receiving, transferring, and assorting activities aimed at fulfilling customers' orders. The movement function starts with receipt of the customer order. It involves the physical unloading of raw materials or products and the transfer of those materials to storage or transportation areas. During this process, goods are regrouped into assortments, or lots, that meet customers' specific needs. Finally, the goods are packed and prepared for shipping to customers' designated locations.

The movement function is the initial stage in the **materials handling** process. Materials handling involves the physical management of raw materials, component products, and finished goods in warehouses or manufacturing plants. Materials handling represents transaction costs to the firm. Each time materials or goods are moved, the channel member incurs a cost. These costs may be in the form of lost or damaged goods, production delays, and customer dissatisfaction. At the same time, materials handling does not provide any tangible value to the product itself. Therefore, the goal in the movement function is to minimize materials handling, travel distances, and goods in process.

Storage. The second warehousing function is **storage,** the stock keeping of raw materials or products. Storage is classified into *temporary* and *semipermanent* categories. *Temporary storage* accounts for the vast majority of stock keeping in warehouses or distribution centers. Temporary storage includes just enough material or product to ensure inventory replenishment as needed. Temporary storage is the inventory cost-reduction goal for just-in-time manufacturing and quick-response retailing.

However, some materials or products may require extra lead times. In these cases, *semipermanent storage* is necessary. Semipermanent storage provides a buffer or safety stock to ensure that ample materials or products are available to meet customer demand. There are many reasons that semipermanent storage may be used. First, there may be seasonal or erratic demand for the materials or products. Also, some materials or products may have long conditioning processes—this is especially true of many agricultural products that are harvested once or twice each year. Finally, semipermanent storage may be used for forward buying. **Forward buying,** or hedging, denotes the advance purchase of materials or products before they are actually needed to take advantage of the lowest market costs. Forward buying may be risky because of market price fluctuations. In forward buying, channel members must weigh the costs of carrying inventory against the potential costs of market price increases.

Information Transfer. The third function of warehousing is **information transfer.** Just like the overall logistics system, timely and accurate information facilitates smooth materials handling. There are many types of information that impact materials handling, including inventory levels and locations, customer requirements, shipment costs, and facility space utilization.

These three warehousing functions present many challenges to logistics managers. First, logistics managers must decide the location and number of warehousing facilities that are required to meet customer needs. In the early 1990s, there was a general shift toward consolidation of warehouse and distribution facilities. The consolidation trend was largely fueled by transportation deregulation and enhanced information technologies.[33] Now, however, there appears to be a return to market-based warehousing, increasing the number of stock-keeping locations to offer more frequent shipments, smaller lot sizes, and continuous replenishment of goods. The shift back to market-based warehousing is driven by customer service demands. The warehousing function has shifted from its traditional focus on storing products to a facilitating focus. Warehousing now emphasizes the smooth flow of goods and services. In this way, warehousing may be viewed as a link between inventory management and transportation.

Purchasing

Purchasing is an ongoing logistical activity that links every channel member in the system. Exchange is not possible without purchasing. After all, the purchase order begins the logistics process. The increased use of centralized purchasing organizations is forcing supplier and buyers to form closer working relationships—completely supporting the relationship principles framed in the CRM. **Purchasing** involves forecasting materials or product demand, selecting suppliers (sourcing), and processing orders. Parties from both sides of the exchange relationship are involved in these tasks.

Forecasting demand is the first step in purchasing. Forecasting of product demand is a complex process of evaluating macro- and micromarket cues to determine what materials or goods will be needed at which times. In a logistics environment marked by automatic replenishment, forecasting demand means production schedules, materials handling, inventory levels, and transportation mediators must be synchronized. The process of synchronizing these mediators to optimize purchasing levels is called **materials requirements planning (MRP).** MRP mandates that the purchasing decision maker manage more than materials, parts, and services. MRP forces purchasing decision makers to manage the entire supply chain.

The *selection of suppliers,* also known as *sourcing,* has undergone the most dramatic change in the purchasing environment. Traditionally, many suppliers were used to reduce resource scarcity and the possibility of stock-outs. However, you may recall that the emerging trend is to choose a few key suppliers that can best meet a channel member's needs. The trend toward fewer suppliers increases the importance of the purchasing decision maker's role in the logistics system.

The tendency to build fewer, stronger relationships with suppliers influences the means by which products and services are procured. Medco Containment Services, Inc., is a managed-care provider for major corporations. In 1993, 80 percent of Medco purchases were from 25 different suppliers. By the year 2000, Medco's CEO expects 80 percent of its purchases to come from five or fewer suppliers. By reducing its number of suppliers, Medco can reduce transaction costs and develop long-term stability in its sourcing.[34] As another example, Black & Decker's Kwikset is a major user of brass for its lock manufacturing process. Traditionally, Kwikset relied on as many as 20 brass suppliers. Today, Kwikset has "locked in" to a single-source supplier.[35]

Purchasing links buyers and sellers at each channel level. As a logistics mediator, purchasing has two simultaneous goals: minimizing transaction (i.e., administrative) and product costs while maximizing transaction and product quality. Although these goals may initially appear contradictory, they are not. Each outcome can be achieved through better relationship management with a channel.

Packaging

The importance of packaging to the logistics process is manifold. Packaging refers to the materials used to encase materials or products while in storage or transit. In logistics, packaging is concerned with protecting the product. Packaging can optimize logistics efficiency and effectiveness by (1) reducing the weight and space requirements for materials handling and transit, (2) ensuring product quality enroute through the logistics system, and (3) selling the product. In marketing, packaging is also concerned with promotion. In fact, packaging has been called the silent salesperson. Packaging influences a buyer's perceptions of the product through brand identification, colors, texture, and other material visual cues.[36]

The significance of packaging should not be underestimated. Some products have built a reputation on packaging: Recall that L'eggs redefined the shape of women's hosiery with its egg-shaped packaging. Today, after a packaging change from the namesake plastic egg, L'eggs is struggling to maintain its market share leadership in the hosiery category.[37] Packaging offers a final opportunity to sell an image to buyers.

Packaging can initiate changes in buyer behavior, as well. "Who squeezed the tube from the middle?" is a familiar question in many households. Today, toothpaste packaging has changed dramatically. Procter & Gamble's Crest, Cheesebrough-Ponds's Close-Up, and Colgate-Palmolive's lines of toothpastes all come in stand-up pumps or squeeze tubes. The pump did more than quell family conflicts. It provided a more efficient use of shelf space for retailers.

Packaging has other roles to perform in logistics systems:[38]

- **Containment.** Products must be contained before they can be transported from one location to another. Containment can be crucial. Many Coca-Cola beverages are delivered to bottlers in powdered form. Then they are hydrated or reconstituted. Weight and space requirements are lowered, as are transportation and storage costs.
- **Protection.** Packaging has to be customized to minimize product damage or loss. Packaging becomes particularly important when goods are fragile or when goods require special temperature and handling. Consider the delicate properties of an egg. The carton is designed to protect the transport and storage of the eggs while providing for stackability. Each cracked egg is an unrecoverable cost.
- **Apportionment.** Channel members need products and materials delivered in convenient lot sizes. Many consumers would not choose to purchase goods in

excessive bulk because of storage limitations. Many materials are perishable, and lot sizes are very important to preserving product quality.

- **Unitization.** Unitization allows packaging to be broken down into secondary and tertiary packages. Consider your next purchase of dry cereal. The cereal is encased in plastic packaging to protect the food. Then, the plastic packaging is encased in the cereal box. The boxes are delivered by the case. Unitization makes it possible for consumers to buy a box rather than a case of cereal.
- **Communication.** Packaging is replete with information. Packaging symbols and other data inform buyers of the contents, product attributes, weights, storage sizes, perishability, and handling instructions. Other information is aimed at inventory management. Machine-readable bar codes are becoming a norm in packaging. Using bar code scanners, channel members can quickly record inbound shipments, fulfill order requirements, and prepare outbound shipments.

Packaging is also becoming an important consideration in light of growing environmental responsibility. As we discussed earlier in this book, Western European producers are increasingly pressured to make sure their packaging is environmentally friendly. Europe's eco-labeling system introduced a standard for reducing packaging to the minimum encasement needed to protect materials and products. European packaging standards mandate high percentages of recyclable packaging and require that each channel level join in waste reduction and recovery activities.

Logistics Outputs

Earlier, we said that logistics outputs denote the performance (outcomes) of the logistics system. There are three primary outputs in the logistics system. The first is *competitive advantage*. A channel member's logistic performance can differentiate it in the marketplace, providing an advantage over other competitors. Companies like Whirlpool have discovered that customer service standards can be increased while lowering total logistics costs.

When Whirlpool CEO David Whitwam announced Whirlpool's increased profits and market share gains in 1993, he cited logistics as the key to the company's success. Whirlpool's Quality Express system has differentiated the company in the marketplace. By forging partnerships with logistics specialty companies, Whirlpool was able to provide market-based distribution centers and deliver goods within 24 hours of order receipt. Whirlpool's retail customers have lauded Whirlpool's service logistics as a market advantage.[39]

The second logistics output is *efficiency in providing products* when and where they are needed. We said earlier in the chapter that information and logistics uniquely provide time and place utility. There are several components of logistics which foster time and place utility:

- Reducing the time between order receipt and shipment
- Limiting lot sizes and assortments of orders
- Reducing stock-outs
- Ensuring exact materials and product fulfillment through accurate information flows

- Increasing the percentage of goods filled correctly and arriving in good condition
- Reducing order cycle times—the time between order placement and receipt of materials or products
- Providing an efficient and effective mechanism for buyers to place orders

Just as the ultimate goal of any surgical procedure is a healthy patient, the third and definitive outcome of any logistics system is *a satisfied customer.* A patient's well-being is a joint effort between the surgeon and the patient. In logistics systems, suppliers and customers are shifting away from a competitive marketplace orientation and toward a relationship or partnership orientation.[40] In logistics systems, customer satisfaction rests on the success with which each channel member responds to another channel member's needs. Responsiveness builds customer trust, repeat business, and higher profits. So, the key to a healthy logistics system lies in prescribing the right information to foster the smooth flow of goods and services through the marketing channel.

Key Terms

customer responsiveness
distribution fluidity
electronic data interchange (EDI)
external audit
flexible enterprise model
forward buying
information transfer
intermodal transportation
internal audit
inventory
inventory carrying costs
inventory management
logistics
materials handling
materials requirements planning (MRP)
movement
purchasing
quick response inventory system
safety stocks
storage
supply chain management
systematized information
transportation
warehousing

Chapter Summary

Imagining distribution channels without considering the critical role of information is difficult. Systematizing information involves any rule-based method used to arrange, coordinate, or share data between members of a distribution channel. Systematized information is a cornerstone of logistics. Firms cannot successfully meet the challenges of a dynamic external environment without continued flows of accurate information.

Logistics management involves the process of planning, implementing, and controlling the efficient, cost-effective flow and storage of raw materials, in-process inventory, finished goods, and related information from point of origin to point of consumption. These actions are performed so that channel members can transform their market offerings in ways that match customer requirements. Information drives the flow of goods and services through channels; it allows channel members to maintain or achieve control from a distance. Logistics help a firm tailor its efforts to satisfy continually changing customer needs. Logistics also help a firm create competitive advantage.

No single measure can efficiently assess the effectiveness of a firm's logistics program. Isolating the costs and returns associated with the flows of goods through channels is quite difficult. Profitability is a common performance measure. Many yardsticks are emerging as tools for evaluating logistics performance. One such measure is customer responsiveness, or a channel member's ability to adapt to its partners' changing needs and service requirements. A four-step process—consisting of external and internal audits, evaluating customer perceptions, and identifying opportunities to establish competitive advantages—is available for identifying customers' service needs.

Logistics systems are frequently described in terms of delivering the *right product* to the *right place* at the *right time* in the *right condition* for the *right cost.* This sense of *rights* connects customer responsiveness to each level of the marketing channel for any product or service offering.

Logistics strategies are now adopting a longer-run orientation in their efforts to secure greater market coverage, customer satisfaction, product customization, and cost containment. A variety of logistics activities promotes customer satisfaction as goods move toward their point of consumption. These activities range from resource procurement to the management of returned goods. Supply chain management (SCM) is a cooperative approach aimed at maximizing logistical outputs while simultaneously minimizing logistical inputs. Properly executed supply chain management produces value at each logistics system level. The notion of supply chain management rests on channel integration. Channel integration involves systematizing information to reduce suppliers' *and* retailers' inventory needs. Manufacturers are usually more certain about the resource inputs they need because their production schedules operate on real time. SCM can also reduce stock-outs (that is, running out of merchandise for which demand exists).

Supply chain management focuses attention on the need to develop relational rather than transactional exchange in logistics systems. Effective supply chain management tends to forge cooperative efforts outside the traditional boundaries of channel settings. These cooperative efforts might include market research, product engineering, and total system designs. For supply chain management to foster better retailer-vendor and retailer-manufacturer relationships, partnerships must address matters extending beyond the distribution and handling of inventories.

The Relational Logistics Model (RLM) shows how systematized information and logistics relate. The RLM has five components: logistics goals, systematized information, logistics inputs, logistics mediators, and logistics outputs. Logistics goals and systematized information have already been discussed. Logistics inputs are the human and capital investments in the flows of goods and services through the marketing channel. These include natural resources, human resources, and financial resources.

A wide variety of logistic mediators impact the flows of goods and services in a distribution channel. The major categories of logistics functions that contribute to efficient, cost-effective flows through distribution channels are discussed in the chapter. These activities can be grouped into inventory management, transportation, warehousing, purchasing, and packaging categories. Inventory management is aimed at minimizing inventory carrying costs while ensuring that sufficient stock is maintained to satisfy customer needs. Electronic data interchange (EDI) facilitates information exchange between channel members. EDI involves the paperless transmission of information—including sales data, purchase orders, invoices, shipment tracking data, and product return information—among manufacturers, suppliers, and retailers. EDI's use signals a shared commitment toward the efficient management of inventory throughout a channel.

The physical movement of goods from one location to any other destination is called *transportation.* Transportation accounts for a substantial portion of logistics cost for most firms. There is a saying that, "If you aren't managing your transportation, you aren't managing your supply chain." Warehousing is another important influence on logistics costs. Warehousing involves the physical storage or stock keeping of raw materials, product components, and/or finished goods. Warehouses perform three functions: movement of goods, component parts, or raw materials; materials handling; and storage. Purchasing links buyers and sellers at each channel. Purchasing involves forecasting demand, selecting suppliers (also known as sourcing), and processing orders. Packaging refers to the materials used to encase materials or products while in transit. Packaging can optimize logistics efficiency and effectiveness by reducing weight and space requirements, ensuring product quality, and selling the product.

Three primary outputs are associated with logistics systems. The first is a competitive advantage. The second output is efficiency. Finally, logistics systems are responsible for the most important output of all: a satisfied customer.

Channel Challenges

1. Edwin L. Artzt, one-time Procter & Gamble executive, has stated that his company's success is partly attributable to looking beyond the internal value chain. How does the logistics system transcend a firm's internal value chain? How does systematizing information foster an extended vision of customer

satisfaction (e.g., Procter & Gamble's relationship with retailers like Wal-Mart)?

2. "Getting the facts is the key to good decision making," asserted Charles F. Knight, chairman of Emerson Electric. How does Knight's assertion support or refute the use of electronic data interchange? Is EDI a tool to get the facts or a tool to make decisions?
3. Deal buying has been a mainstay of the food and drug retailing industries. Likewise, diversion has been a mechanism for controlling inventories and building competitive advantage. These inventory management techniques have essentially capitalized on the uncertainty in the marketplace. With the emerging adoption of quick response, many retailers (like Kash 'n Karry Food Store's Jack Bullara) think automatic replenishment is a threat to deal buying and diversion tactics. Do you agree with Bullara? Why or why not?
4. Several logistics consultants suggested that in the 1980s logistics strategies could best be thought of in terms of independent boxes (storage centers) linked together by transportation services. In the 1990s, the model is shifting to that of a pipeline, with emphasis placed on integration. By the late 1990s, the more appropriate model will be the hose. Do you believe a hose is an appropriate descriptor of the logistics system in the 1990s? Why or why not?
5. "Everyone with a wheelbarrow or truck has reclassified themselves as a logistics company," according to Joseph McCabe, president of Intral Corporation, a Boston-based logistics firm. What differentiates a logistics company from a transportation company? Considering that most logistics companies were once viewed as transportation companies (i.e., Roadway Services, Yellow Logistics, CSX Logistics), does McCabe's comment have merit?
6. To create demand for recycled corrugated cardboard, McDonald's ordered its suppliers to use boxes with a minimum of 35 percent recycled content. How does this example push environmental packaging through the logistics system? Is it appropriate for McDonald's to dictate logistics practices to its suppliers? Why or why not?

Review Questions

1. How does systemizing information enhance channel performance?
2. Define logistics with respect to marketing channel management. What are three key aspects of logistics management?
3. Why are logistics important in today's marketplace? What measures are used to assess logistics performance?
4. Why is customer service important in logistics management? What are the four steps used to identify a customer's service requirements?
5. How does the logistics function relate to overall marketing channel management?
6. Identify and discuss the five components of the relational logistics model.
7. What is supply chain management?
8. Define the principal inputs and outputs of a logistics system.
9. What is a logistics mediator? Describe the five major functions of logistics mediators that contribute to customer satisfaction.
10. What are some of the major trends in logistics?

Endnotes

1. "U.S. Car Makers May Join to Tear Down Rival Autos" (1993), *The Wall Street Journal,* January 13, A4.
2. This is quoted from the Council of Logistics Management (1986) in Lambert, Douglas M., and James R. Stock (1993), *Strategic Logistics Management,* Third Edition, Burr Ridge, IL: Richard D. Irwin, 4.
3. Feare, Tom (1994), "Sega Racks Up a 99.9% + Shipping Accuracy Score," *Modern Materials Handling,* 49 (October), 46–47.

4. Roman, Margie (1994), "The Art of Effective Corporate Fulfillment," *Adweek,* Infomercial Special Sourcebook Issue, 29–32.
5. Adapted from Cravens, David W., Shannon C. Shipp, and Karen S. Cravens (1994), "Reforming the Traditional Organization: The Mandate for Developing Networks," *Business Horizons,* 37 (July/August), 19–28; Panepinto, Joe (1994), "Special Delivery," *Computerworld,* 28 (March 7), 79–81; and Willis, Clint (1993), "Growing New Markets: Ruth Owades," *Working Woman,* 18 (December), 50–51.
6. Fuller, Joseph B., James O'Conor, and Richard Rawlinson (1993), "Tailored Logistics: The Next Advantage," *Harvard Business Review,* May/June, 87.
7. Lambert, Douglas M., and James R. Stock (1993), *Strategic Logistics Management,* Third Edition, Burr Ridge, IL: Richard D. Irwin, 5, 11.
8. Chow, Garland, Trevor D. Heaver, and Lennart E. Henriksson (1994), "Logistics Performance: Definition and Measurement," *International Journal of Physical Distribution & Logistics,* 24 (1), 17–28.
9. Thomas, Jim (1994), "Magic in the Air," *Distribution,* 93 (August), 62–66.
10. For an excellent overview, please see Mentzer, John T., and Brenda Ponsford Konrad (1991), "An Efficiency/Effectiveness Approach to Logistics Performance Analysis," *Journal of Business Logistics,* 12 (1), 33–62.
11. "1993 Award Criteria," *Malcolm Baldrige National Quality Award,* Gaithersburg, MD: National Institute of Standards and Technology, U.S. Department of Commerce.
12. Lambert, Douglas M. (1992), "Developing a Customer-Focused Logistics Strategy," *International Journal of Physical Distribution & Logistics,* 22 (6), 12–19.
13. Gordon, Jay (1989), "And Then There Was One," *Distribution,* 88 (August), 103–5.
14. Mentzer, John T. (1993), "Managing Channel Relations in the 21st Century," *Journal of Business Logistics,* 14 (1), 33.
15. Adapted from Essig, Bill (1993), "Russia's Economy Shows an Appetite for U.S. Fast Food; McDonald's, Pizza Hut Do Well with Moscow Outlets, See Long-Term Growth," *The Wall Street Journal,* February 26, B5; and Harding, Andrew (1992), "Birth of a New Adland," *Marketing,* February 27, 20.
16. Rubinfein, Elizabeth (1993), "Pepsico's Taco Bell Pulls into Moscow aboard the Metro; Fast-Food Company Expects to Turn Subway Platforms into Showcases for Wares," *The Wall Street Journal,* June 11, B3.
17. Strutton, David, Sheb L. True, and Raymond C. Rody (1995), "Russian Consumer Perceptions of Foreign and Domestic Consumer Goods: An Analysis of Country-of-Origin Stereotypes with Implications for Positioning and Promotion," *Journal of Marketing Theory & Practice,* 3 (3), 76–88.
18. Adapted from Ostrow, Joel (1992), "Fast-Food Prices Jump in Russia," *Advertising Age,* 63 (January 6), 1, 22; and Essig, Bill (1993), "Russia's Economy Shows an Appetite for U.S. Fast Food; McDonald's, Pizza Hut Do Well with Moscow Outlets, See Long-Term Growth," *The Wall Street Journal,* February 26, B5.
19. Langley, C. John Jr., and Mary C. Holcomb (1992), "Creating Logistics Customer Value," *Journal of Business Logistics,* 13 (2), 1–28.
20. Cooke, James Aaron (1992), "Supply-Chain Management '90s Style," *Traffic Management,* 31 (May), 57–59.
21. Henkoff, Ronald (1994), "Delivering the Goods," *Fortune,* 130 (November), 34–47.
22. Adapted from Anscombe, Jonathan (1994), "The Fourth Wave of Logistics Improvement: Maximizing Value in the Supply-Chain," *Logistics Focus,* 36–40; and Mentzer, John T. (1993), "Managing Channel Relations in the 21st Century," *Journal of Business Logistics,* 14 (1), 27–42.
23. A simulation program is now available to assist in SCM training. See Wilson, Mike (1994), "Simulating the Supply-Chain," *Logistics Focus,* 2 (May), 5–8.
24. Goddard, Walter E. (1994), "MRP II: The Evolution Continues," *Modern Materials Handling,* 49 (April), 40.
25. "Southern California Earthquake: Many Businesses Are Disrupted, but Most Damage Is Near Epicenter," (1995) *The Wall Street Journal,* January 18, A6.
26. Richardson, Helen L. (1994), "Get Ready for Change," *Transportation & Distribution,* January, 49.
27. Lambert, Douglas M., and James R. Stock (1993), *Strategic Logistics Management,* Third Edition, Burr Ridge, IL: Richard D. Irwin, 11.
28. Andel, Tom (1994), "Inventory Horror Stories," *Transportation & Distribution,* 35 (May), 77–78; and Biby, Daniel J. (1992), "Who Really Needs EDI?" *Industry Week,* November 2, 45.
29. Winslow, Ron (1994), "Technology & Health: Four

Hospital Suppliers Will Launch Common Electronic Ordering System," *The Wall Street Journal,* April 12, B6.

30. Reda, Susan (1993), "Quick Response: Major Players Report Accomplishments, List Goals," *Stores,* May, 60–61.
31. Lambert, Douglas M., and James R. Stock (1993), *Strategic Logistics Management,* Third Edition, Burr Ridge, IL: Richard D. Irwin, 15–18, 163–65.
32. Bradley, Peter (1993), "Third Party Logistics: DuPont Takes the Plunge," *Purchasing,* June 3, 33–35.
33. Copacino, William C. (1993), "Back to Market-Based Warehousing," *Traffic Management,* 32 (October), 29; and Bruce, Robert (1993), "Industrial Goes Upscale," *Journal of Property Management,* 59 (May/June), 14–17.
34. Tanouye, Elyse, and George Anders (1993), "Merck Weighs Buying Medco Containment; Talks on Purchase Are Said to Have Taken Place, but Difficulties Exist," *The Wall Street Journal,* July 13, A3.
35. Personal interview with Stanley E. Dunsford, Plant Manager, Denison, TX: Kwikset Titan.
36. Sara, Rod (1990), "Packaging as a Retail Marketing Tool," *International Journal of Physical Distribution,* 20 (8), 30.
37. Loro, Laura (1994), "L'eggs: Trend Troubles Category and Creates Snag for Leader," *Advertising Age,* 65 (October 3), S–14.
38. Robertson, Gordon L. (1990), "Good and Bad Packaging: Who Decides?" *International Journal of Physical Distribution and Logistics Management,* 20 (8), 38–39.
39. Byrnes, Nanette (1993), "Whirlpool," *Financial World,* 162 (September 8), 61.
40. Manrodt, Karl B., and Frank W. Davis, Jr. (1993), "The Evolution to Service Logistics," *International Journal of Physical Distribution & Logistics Management,* 23 (5), 59.

chapter

10

Developing Positive Channel Relationships

Learning Objectives

After reading this chapter, you should be able to:

- Understand the recruiting process within the channel microsystem and identify the market, product, and firm factors considered.
- Describe the screening process and the selection criteria considered in the selection of channel members.
- Discuss the special measures that are often necessary to motivate independent intermediaries to support the best interests of their suppliers.
- Describe how recruiters can secure the success of new channel memberships.

Corbis

EMC Corporation is looking for a few good men (and women). More specifically, the Massachusetts-based data-storage hardware producer is seeking a few good data-storage specialists to resell its Clariion line of midrange data storage hardware. "EMC plans on recruiting about 200 domestic partners to sell Clariion in the U.S. market," reported spokesperson Tom Heiser. EMC is looking to recruit, select, and partner with "one or two partners in a specific vertical market, the best one or two in a horizontal market, and the best one or two in a geographic market," he said. EMC is especially anxious to recruit channel members already working with its high-end Symmetrix product line. However, the company is not planning to distribute through two-level distribution channels. According to Heiser, in its role of de facto channel leaders, EMC is "seeking partners that bring unique solutions for product set and our targeted customers. We are not looking for generalists."

Training regarding the professional services EMC has to offer will be provided to its new channel partners. Once the sale is closed, EMC will handle the hardware installation and configuration. The performance of all other value-adding channel functions will be the responsibility of the partner. EMC has committed to providing its newly recruited resellers whatever support they reasonably need.

The response of the data-storage specialists that have been targeted has been mixed. One storage specialist who worked previously with Clariion through the original equipment manufacturing sector decided to take on the new line. The firm's spokesperson said, "Normally, it's a long cycle to get up to speed on a new product. But we've been dealing with EMC for a long time, and this is the first such offer it has extended. We felt we couldn't pass it up." Another storage specialist currently selling Symmetrix was approached by EMC and concluded that the Clariion line complemented its business strategy. But the firm took a pass, anyway, after it decided that the new offering conflicted with other midrange storage products it currently carried. Many other firms that EMC recruited have followed suit and declined its offer.

Phillips Medical Systems, on the other hand, now bundles Clariion as part of its medical radiology offerings. Said spokesperson Milan dePiero, "One of the reasons why we wanted to partner with EMC and they with us is that we don't address the same customers."

In highly competitive and technologically driven markets, these sorts of mixed responses must be expected. In any competitive Microsystem, you must learn to take the good with the bad. After all, no college basketball or football team ever lands all the players it recruits, either.[1]

****

The marketplace circumstances described above are representative of the ups and downs that must transpire before a positive channel setting can be developed. In general, successful marketing channels are characterized by the same type of supportive environments that legendary coaches like Dean Smith (former basketball coach at the University of North Carolina) or Joe Paterno (football coach at Penn State University) provided their prime recruits. Like this pair of extraordinarily successful athletic programs, successful marketing channels are characterized by a suitable match between what each channel member needs and what each is capable of providing to the entire channel system. Highly talented players (corporations) sometimes must sublimate a portion of their skills to the good of the team (channel system). Team members should let a Michael Jordan–type player take the last, potentially game-winning shot if he is the best pressure shooter, just like organizations like UPS or Roadway Logistics should ship components or finished goods if they perform such functions better. All successful college basketball or football teams must begin the coach's successful screening and recruiting of the best possible players—find the best players for the job (as long as they fit into the system). Once a Coach Smith or Paterno successfully recruits the players they want, those individuals must be motivated to blend their particular talents into the overall team effort.

The development of positive, successfully functioning marketing channels and channel relationships follows the same process. In this chapter, we will discuss the five steps that are involved in the cultivation of a positive channel setting: recruiting, screening, selecting, motivating, and securing the recruit's commitment. These steps are shown in Exhibit 10.1. In addition, Channel Surfing 10.1 illustrates just how important the development of a channel of distribution can be in real-world settings.

Exhibit 10.1

Developing positive channel relationships

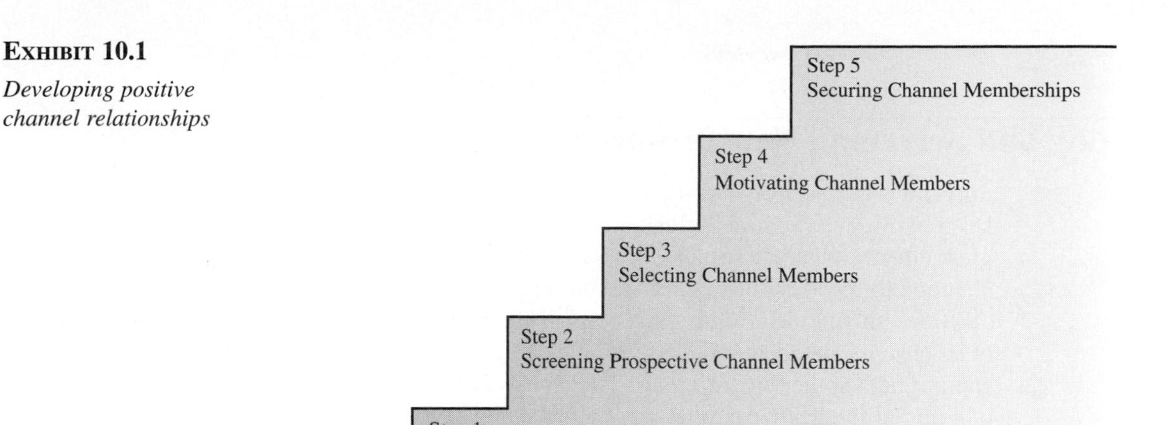

Channel Surfing 10.1

Bridging that Last Mile

The end of 1999 turned out to be something of a celebratory fizzle as high prices, fears about congestion and safety, and the Y2K bug tamped down the party fever. Not so with online consumer sales. The year ended with a phenomenal upsurge—more than tenfold over the previous year—in online purchasing. Dot.coms benefited, at least until the air went out of the Nasdaq bubble in April 2000, and brick-and-mortar businesses that had online channels did even better.

While the outlook for consumer direct channels purchasing remains promising, the shopping experiences of many customers in the last few weeks before Christmas 1999 were frustrating. Too many kids were on the receiving end of late deliveries and mismatched orders. In many ways the final mile of order fulfillment and delivery fell well short of reasonable consumer expectations. Many of these hiccups could be corrected with improved channel member selection, more disciplined distribution management, and more efficient use of technology. However, designing channels to bridge that final mile entails far more than just getting the right goods delivered at the right time.

The reality of the final mile as it currently exists is that it is costly and inefficient. Consumer direct delivery formats are not particularly customer friendly and result in high cost per parcel delivered. A less costly final mile channels model must be developed for the online shopping market to sustain its growth and fulfill its potential. The challenge of developing cost-effective, flexible materials-handling channels to provide such functions is significant. But the opportunity to achieve a sustainable first-mover advantage is tremendous.

For instance, if 20 percent of consumer goods purchases shift to direct consumer markets, more than 1 million new, highly motivated distribution workers will be needed to staff end-user fulfillment centers. The practicality of recruiting and training such vast numbers is debatable. But the opportunity emerges from the financial picture: 1 million workers at $30,000 annually equals $30 billion. Multiply $30 billion by a 2.5 year payback, and the numbers suggest that e-business companies may have to spend huge amounts to bridge that last mile effectively. But the payoff for those firms that do the best job of developing these critically important channels of distribution will be substantial.

Points to Ponder

- What final channel structure form do you believe will develop to bridge the final mile? Is there ever a final channel structure form?

Source: Adapted from Anonymous (2000), "Brainstorm Your e-Business," *Marketing Management,* 9 (1), 55–57; and McIntyre, Nina (2000), "Motivating Sales Channels in an e-Business Environment," *Journal of Compensation and Benefits,* 16 (4), 44–46.

Recruiting and Screening New Prospects

Successful business organizations are almost always built around a few *core competencies*—key activities such as quality manufacturing or low-cost distribution that they perform with great effectiveness. To sustain success, organizations must increase their investments in and attention to the areas that contribute most to their core competencies. This means that organizations should never assign the responsibility for performing these key competencies to other channel members. Conversely, all other functions performed within the business may be sourced out to other organizations. Take Topsy Tail Co. as an example. This business has sales of over $100 million per year—and a few employees. The company has built more than 20 carefully constructed channels with firms that perform tasks ranging from producing Topsy's signature hair care products to servicing retail accounts. By sourcing out these functions, Topsy Tail's core competency is *promotion.*[2]

Like any other chain, channels are no stronger than their weakest link. At best, having to rely on mediocre channel members can create a competitive disadvantage. At worst, dependence on lackluster partners can ruin an entire marketing strategy.[3] Creating strong channel relationships begins with the process of recruiting and screening potential channel partners. In this stage, marketers must select from the alternatives available in their market those intermediaries that are best suited to serve their products, customers, and prospects. Marketers must plan to provide sufficient inducements to recruit from these capable channel partners, then screen them to ensure that the prospective partners will act in the firm's best interests if they are chosen.

Good working relationships among producers, intermediaries, retailers, and end users are not developed overnight. To the contrary, building relationships in new channel settings requires a great deal of time, effort, and financial expenditure. Moreover, once contracts have been signed it is virtually impossible to easily escape from one channel relationship to another, particularly in international settings. Therefore, conscientious recruiting and screening procedures are necessary to help avoid costly selection errors that might prove difficult to remedy. The development of a positive marketing channel should be done right the first time and that means starting with the right pool of recruited and screened prospects.

Recruiting

Recruiting involves those plans and actions aimed at actively soliciting participation by a new channel member. Before active recruiting can begin, key personnel from the recruiting organization must consider and reach agreement on several important issues, including:

- The precise role of the prospective channel members.
- The specific qualifications necessary for success in this channel role.
- The precise products or channel assignments for which the prospective channel member will be responsible.
- The bounds of authority of the prospective channel member.
- The way in which the role might be expected to change over time.

Recruiting as a Continuous Process. For several reasons, the recruitment of new channel members should be viewed as a continuous process. One reason is that an organization's intermediaries sometimes withdraw from the channel relationship of their own accord, and the organization needs to be prepared to respond quickly. At other times, an organization's interests are best served by replacing a current intermediary who, for whatever reason, is performing at less than its potential. Companies as powerful as Wal-Mart or IBM have had to develop new channel relationships because their existing channel arrangements failed to meet their expectations.[4]

Another reason for viewing recruiting as a continuous process is that marketers may need to contract with new intermediaries to help launch new products. In the Michigan headquarters of Johnson Controls, Inc., a major supplier of automotive seats, a team of engineers is devising seats for Chrysler Corporation's next generation of midsized cars. Down the hall, other teams are doing the same for Ford Motor Co., General Motors Corp., Toyota Motor Corp., and the Mercedes-Benz unit of DaimlerChrysler. These manufacturers have each turned to Johnson as an upstream supplier that can help them engineer their new products.[5]

Everdream Corporation found it had to actively recruit partners to sell its Dreammachine service, which includes a PC powered by Intel's Pentium III processor, unlimited Internet access, daily data backup, popular business software, training, and full-time support that includes remote management, all for $150 a month. The company hopes to recruit 450 partners by the end of 2001. Everdream's resellers are distribution agents, who manage installation, network integration, and most service after the sell.[6]

Organizations, particularly producers, also may have to change intermediaries as their products pass through stages in their product life cycle, when buyer behavior changes, or in response to changes in the distribution strategies of competitors. Sometimes channel members also need to seek new intermediaries as a way of penetrating new markets. Like any other process that unfolds in the internal channel environment, recruiting can never be isolated from the marketplace.

Recruiting Manufacturers. Recruiting no longer necessarily involves producer seeking retailer or intermediary. Indeed, because of their power position in the channel, retailers and intermediaries often have more control over the manufacturer's selection process than the manufacturer. For example, Sears aggressively recruits suppliers (manufacturers and intermediaries) that can provide the merchandise Sears' customers want at the prices they seek. To be sure, suppliers do choose retailers—e.g., Levi's chooses to sell its clothes through Sears—but sister retailers like the Banana Republic, The Gap, and Old Navy also select their suppliers.[7]

At the wholesale level, intermediaries like Roadway Logistics are now actively seeking and obtaining channel agreements with manufacturers such as Hewlett-Packard (H-P). After H-P was recruited by Roadway, it handed over complete responsibility for inbound raw materials warehousing at its Vancouver, Washington, facility to Roadway. When an order comes from H-P's nearby printer manufacturing plant, Roadway fills a container, loads it on a truck, and delivers just in time for assembly.[8]

Screening

The Business Imaging Systems Division of Kodak has turned to agency selling as a means of developing its channels of distribution. Clyde Cawley, manager of broker and distribution sales at Kodak's world headquarters, says that everyone at Kodak Business Imaging Systems appreciates the value of the agency method of distribution as a supplemental marketing channel. Within the division's overall team, three levels of managers work very closely with these agents. Paul Artlip, national manager of Kodak's indirect marketing distribution operation, says that his task of building an agency channels network began with recruiting from a pool of people who had retired from Kodak, and then screening other established agencies who already called on and had relationships with accounts Kodak sought as end customers.[9]

Screening involves the systematic consideration, evaluation, and, ultimately, rejection of most of a set of people, things, or ideas. Screening is inherently a negatively oriented process. This is especially true during the early stages of the screening process, when recruiters look for reasons to reject rather than accept prospective intermediaries. When screening potential channel partners, recruiter organizations should keep four guidelines in mind.

First, the organization should think about market segments.[10] Too many marketers think primarily in terms of geographic coverage when screening intermediaries, rather than considering market or customer segments. To illustrate why this is important, consider that John Deere uses different distributors to serve the agriculture and construction equipment market segments. Similarly, Caterpillar uses different distributors to serve construction equipment, lift truck, and diesel truck engine markets even in the same geographic areas.[11]

Second, the selling and distribution requirements for a product change during its life cycle, yet marketers frequently fail to account for these changes in their distribution strategies. For instance, manufacturers that are screening intermediaries to market a new technical product need specialized distributors that can provide technical knowledge to customers or other channel members as bugs are worked out. As the product matures, however, the market needs less-specialized knowledge because the technical know-how has become more widely available. At maturity, off-the-shelf delivery time and price usually become more important than the need for specialized knowledge. Therefore, as a product matures, marketers may need to screen out intermediaries who are unable to satisfy special product life cycle–based needs.

Third, manufacturers and retailers tend to recruit distributors that are already overloaded with products, while shying away from smaller, newer, or temporarily underfinanced intermediaries. This is an understandable reaction, but consider the following issues: Successful intermediaries are likely to be solicited by numerous producers and retailers. Consequently, these intermediaries may already be carrying as many product lines as they can effectively handle. Distributors that are handling fewer product lines, on the other hand, may best supply the attention and assistance to upstream customers that are needed in today's service- and value-oriented markets. Still, distributors may have fewer product lines because they are undercapitalized, incompetent, or undermotivated. Whatever the case, the decision of which intermediary to choose should be weighed carefully by recruiting channel members. In particular, those firms marketing products bought mainly on the basis of price or service should value intermediaries that can provide aggressive distribution.

The fourth criterion that should be weighed by channel members engaged in this screening process pertains to the level of support required by the various prospects. Clearly, this support may be financial in nature. It may involve the exchange of technical or marketing expertise between the recruiting firm and its prospective channel partner. Or, the support might merely involve some "hand-holding" or positive-reinforcement during an extended start-up period. Obviously, if the level of support required by an otherwise "qualified" prospect strikes the recruiting firm as too costly in light of the benefits expected from the partnership, it has a logical basis for eliminating that prospective channel member from further consideration.

Selecting the Right Channel Partners

By now, potential channel partners should have been narrowed to a select few. Macola Software recently did just that. Donna Wehner, the manager in charge of recruiting value-added software resellers, is administering a new program to restock the company's marketing channels. Macola's Associate Business Partner program is targeted toward selecting smaller resellers that do not command the resources to become full-scale business partners, but that can nevertheless add value to the software manufacturer's software reseller channels through their special market expertise.[12]

The goal in channels development, as always, should be to find the best channel partner available from among this smaller pool. So the selection process continues and is now

Exhibit 10.2

Final selection criteria

Criteria	*Definition*
Sales factors	The ultimate justification for using intermediaries is to improve market share, sales, and profitability. Thus, sales and market factors head the list of evaluative criteria. Sales factors to be considered include the intermediary's knowledge and coverage of the market, the number and quality of its sales personnel and management, and the frequency of its sales calls.
Product factors	Product factors include the intermediary's knowledge of the product and of its service or stocking requirements. The quality of the prospect's service staff should also be considered. Each factor is of particular, although not exclusive, interest to firms selecting intermediaries to distribute technological products. An intermediary's product knowledge will influence its performance with respect to product applications, customer requirements, before and after sales service needs, and special end-customer concerns (i.e., packaging or delivery arrangements).
Experience factors	Indicators of intermediary experience and expertise can be obtained by evaluating the prospect's previous customers' satisfaction, whether the prospect has worked successfully with similar products in the past, the prestige of its prior or current channel partners, and the prospect's current technology.
Administrative factors	The administrative and contractual conformance of prospects can be evaluated by examining the prospect's workload and determining whether it is overworked. The competitiveness of a prospect's cost structures and the issue of whether it can meet a distribution schedule should also be assessed.
Risk factors	Considerations of risk include evaluations of a prospect's commitment to the relationship and of how much the proposed channel arrangement will cost the recruiting organization. The prospect's enthusiasm for the product should also be considered. Costs, the extent of a prospect's dealing with competitors, and the career histories of its key personnel should likewise be evaluated.

conducted at a more refined level. Several **selection criteria** should be considered during this final evaluation of channel members. A list of criteria that demonstrates the complexity and depth of the final selection decision is given in Exhibit 10.2 (on page 319).[13] For ease of recall, note how the first letters of each of these criteria can be combined to form the acronym SPEAR. Recruiting channel members therefore might be described as seeking to *spear* the best channel partner from among the remaining pool of prospects.

In addition, unless they elect to perform various distribution functions themselves, producers and retailers need intermediaries that can perform the various distribution functions. Distribution functions include the provision of suitable products, appropriate prices, easy availability, and convenience to upstream or downstream customers. The effectiveness with which prospective intermediaries can perform sales, storage, credit provision, product and customer servicing, and intelligence-gathering functions are also basic concerns that should be evaluated. Finally, the quality of relationships the prospective intermediary enjoys with adjacent up- or downstream channel levels should be carefully weighed.

Channel Surfing 10.2

AT&T Hitting a New Resale Trail

Get out of the way, all you Cisco resellers, IBM integrators, and Novell VARs. And say "howdy" to a channel system in data-networking sales and service: the AT&T value-added reseller. Marking a sea change in its marketing philosophy, in 1999 AT&T begin quietly recruiting a nationwide legion of local network integrators. The resellers were trained on AT&T's data services so they can bundle them along with routers, switchers, and hubs.

The new channels strategy means users will be able to obtain core AT&T services from local VARs and network integrators that also offer LAN/WAN management services. AT&T never before used VARs or resellers except to provide service to a handful of extremely large accounts. Once the quintessential vertically integrated in-house channel system, AT&T has given its managers marching orders to develop new channels for the firm's four principal data services: frame relay, private lines, the WorldNet Managed Internet Service dedicated Internet access offering, and the new WorldNet Virtual Private Network Service.

Ironically, AT&T traditionally has not only operated using a direct sales force but has been particularly hostile to resellers of its services via other channels. AT&T has frequently gone to court with telecom resellers that buy AT&T services in bulk, mark them up, and sell them to small businesses and consumers. But AT&T officials emphasize that their new channel recruitment strategy is aimed at a new breed of reseller—network integrators experienced in installing local area networks and desktops as well as routers and switches. And AT&T is up front about their motivation for taking this approach—the firm needs to increase its revenues. "Certain user organizations are more inclined to purchase from these alternative channels," says an anonymous AT&T partner. "The telecom industry is trying to build off of the channels model long used in the computer industry."

Points to Ponder

- Assume you were an AT&T marketing manager. In such a situation, what, if anything, would be wrong with an outside third party to help you select your new reseller partners?
- On the other hand, what would be right about using outside consultants in such a situation?

Source: Adapted from Laberis, Bill (2000), "Flip the Switch," *MC Technology Marketing Intelligence* 20 (April), 32; and Sampey, Kathleen (2000), "Changes at AT&T Could Lead to Agency Shakeup," *Adweek*, May 29, 6.

Independent intermediaries are not owned by other organizations operating in the channel. This is why recruiting organizations have only limited control over their independent intermediaries' activities after they come on board. Because many intermediaries have needs, operating philosophies, and goals that differ from those of selecting organizations, these differences should have a bearing on selection decision. Intermediaries generally act in their customers' interests and only secondarily on behalf of their suppliers' needs.

Recruiting organizations can exert only limited influence over the business conduct of their intermediaries. This is true even when recruiters enjoy dominant channel positions and are willing to exercise power in pursuit of their interests. But when recruiters fail to acquire their intermediaries' loyalty and commitment, the performance of the entire channel can suffer. Naturally, appropriate selection criteria can help in this regard.

Lastly, it should be noted that some organizations enlist third-party assistance in the selection of new channel members. Channel Surfing 10.2 (on page 320) describes how an old economy workhorse is now recruiting new economy channel partners.

Motivating New Channel Members

There is an ancient business saying that goes something like this: "If someone is going to eat your lunch, it might as well be you." One other thing is clear in new economy marketing channels: The nature of channels is going to continue to change, and rapidly. Channel members who are used to getting paid just because they are there are in for a rude awakening. Motivating channel members to do what they need to do—namely, deploying a business model that delivers more value to customers than the competition—is an increasingly critical consideration.

In marketing channels, success or failure usually depends on how well channel members tailor their products or services to meet customer requirements.[14] This is more likely to occur if new channel members are motivated to perform effectively as part of a team. But motivating channel intermediaries is quite unlike motivating one's own employees. In fact, when compared to what would motivate an internal customer, special measures are required to motivate new channel intermediaries. First, the needs and problems of the new intermediary should be determined. Then, in response to this new understanding, recruiting firms should provide the type and level of support that is appropriate to those needs and problems. Finally, recruiting firms should exercise the leadership necessary to maintain motivated teams of intermediaries.[15]

Distributor advisory councils (DACs) are useful for identifying the needs and problems of intermediaries. Distributor advisory councils facilitate the exchange of information regarding the plans, ideas, and attitudes of channel members by bringing together boundary personnel from producers and intermediaries. All parties can then be informed regarding what is expected of them. Each party can then more easily understand the roles they should play. DACs also provide intermediaries with recognition and the opportunity to contribute to planning within the channel. This raises the sense of security enjoyed by intermediaries, thereby inducing them to feel greater loyalty to their channel partners. The intermediary's motivation to pursue its suppliers' interests should be enhanced by displays of the suppliers' regard for the intermediary's ideas and opinions.[16]

While DACs are useful, any other avenue through which new channel partners can communicate their needs, problems, opinions, and ideas can serve the same end. Personal contact affords the most assurance that reliable communication will take place. Thus, personal visits between producers or retailers and their intermediaries at conferences or on-site meetings is a good idea. Planned contacts by phone, fax, or e-mail can substitute for personal visits. Joseph McKenna, CEO of Allen-Bradley (A-B) Corporation, suggests that successful motivation of his channel partners is largely a matter of focusing A-B's attention on their shops.[17] McKenna contends that if his channel partners don't do well, then he and his company will not be successful either.

A problem that consistently plagues all participants in packaged goods grocery channels pertains to the issue of unsalable merchandise. Recent efforts by manufacturers have yielded some dramatic results,with General Mills, Kellogg, and Tropicana establishing leadership positions in working with their grocery store customers to rectify the problem. Their efforts have motivated grocers to identify the root causes of problems and tackle those parts caused by their own policies, procedures, and activities. The profits of all channel members have since grown.[18]

Intermediaries are likewise motivated by their partner's willingness to provide them with adequate support. Support generally involves the provision of some combination of personal selling, advertising, or promotional assistance or training for selected intermediary personnel. Profit making is a principal requirement of business. Profits are a prime motivator, as well. The assurance of a future business relationship and an ongoing stream of income are also prime motivators for intermediaries. On the other side of the coin, threats to discontinue dealings with intermediaries whose performances are unsatisfactory have at times proven motivational, too. However, the quality of the relationships themselves generally suffers from the recurrent use of such tactics.

Connecticut-based Loctite Corporation, a maker of adhesives and sealants, has managed to avoid making price the major issue in its dealings with distributors and customers. This result has been achieved through a "Loctite Partnership program," which was established through its Distributor Advisory Council. These programs help distributors more effectively sell products to the end user, aid in the construction of individual marketing programs, and channel cooperative promotional funds to the appropriate parties. Loctite is known for having highly motivated distributors.[19]

Securing Recruits for the Long Term

Once the recruiting and recruited firms join together, a marriage of sorts begins. Naturally, a brief honeymoon period follows. But when the honeymoon is over, the firms must start working at converting their fledgling relationship into an ongoing success. With this in mind, we consider how new channel memberships may be secured by recruiting firms.

The notion of a partnership remains essential throughout these early stages of the relationship. When producers or retailers turn to intermediaries for distribution help, they do so out of a perceived necessity. However, recruiting organizations should not give up their responsibilities for effective marketing, nor can they reasonably expect their new intermediaries to react favorably to all suggestions. As a case in point, domestic manufacturers and wholesalers are both feeling the effects of a consolidation that is under way in retailing.[20] Giant retailers such as Target, Office Depot, Barnes and Noble, and others are using sophisticated inventory management, finely tuned merchandise selection practices, and competitive prices to crowd out weaker players in numerous product categories. Consumers flock to these powerful retailing outlets, but manufacturers and wholesalers often complain about these retailers' demands—from seeking discounts to allowances for new store openings to penalty payments for shipping errors. These giant retailers must keep in mind that they are engaged in a relationship with their suppliers and assume part of the responsibility for making their intermediaries more effective.

Such outcomes can sometimes be achieved through joint product development, careful pricing and ordering policies, or shared training programs. However, some semblance of equity is still required for these new channel exchanges to be successful beyond a honeymoon period. In channel settings, **equity** relates to the fair and impartial distribution of exchange outcomes.

The behavior of professional, relationship-oriented boundary personnel should be similar to the behaviors of physicians, engineers, or academic advisors. Note how members from each profession bear the responsibility of identifying and responding to a unique problem of a patient, student, or channel partner. The sets of needs that exist among channel partners are never going to be identical. But that's OK, because recruiting channel members have substantial leeway to adapt and then creatively respond to their new partners' needs. Like all marketers, channel professionals should view themselves as need satisfiers and problem solvers, and respond accordingly. One key to solving or preventing problems between producers or retailers and their intermediaries may lie in the well-known biological life cycle model. This possibility is discussed below.

Recognizing the Channel Relationship Life Cycle

Given enough time, products inevitably pass through distinct stages involving the processes of birth, growth and maturation, and death. The same is true of every living thing on this earth. It is no surprise, then, that the relationship emerging between channel members after one has recruited the other passes through a channel relationship life cycle.

After legally contracting with one another, the relationship usually begins with a *birth stage.* During this stage, the recruiting firm more fully explains to recruits its operating philosophy, goals, and growth objectives. In turn, recruits generally describe what they seek in their relationship, as well as the positive attributes they can bring to a channel setting. During the birth stage, both parties tend to be very excited about their new opportunity. One or the other partner often looks the other way when its counterpart does something it does not support. Unfortunately, when these concerns are not communicated, hairline cracks sometimes arise that can potentially splinter the entire relationship. These problems could take the form of a supplier not shipping correctly or not offering technical support that was originally promised or a retailer not meeting its commitments by adhering to supplier terms. If these initial problems are addressed by both partners, the pair can usually form an efficient channel team. Such a team can become opportunity driven, rather than internally focused. If the two parties feel confident about their match, their relationship passes into a toddler stage. If either feels extremely uncomfortable at this stage, the relationship can be dissolved without too much difficulty.

Channel relationships that reach the *maturity stage* should operate with great efficiency. As partners, the channel members can grow profitably. If all is working well, each partner benefits from the synergies they both share. Neither has to rely exclusively on its own unique strengths, because it is part of a channel. In spite of this great potential, maturity is also the most dangerous stage of a channel relationship. Unless both channel members take constant measures to strengthen their relationship, the only direction from here is down. Cracks in the relationship can result from late service, processing errors, one party's decision to curtail its investment in the relationship, or from a unilateral decision to introduce an unnecessary third party into the relationship.

The key to sustaining maturity is continual communication. Wants, goals, problems, objectives, perceived difficulties, and issues should be exchanged between partners. Producers have the right to expect and demand the best marketing efforts from their distributors, and intermediaries have the right to expect the best support services from their suppliers. But a firm operating on either side of a channel relationship would be foolish to expect its business partner to automatically see complex issues or concerns the same way it does. So each partner must communicate effectively and constantly with the other. A summary of the desired channel member behaviors during each stage of the relationship life cycle is provided in Exhibit 10.3.

George Harrison's first solo album after the breakup of the Beatles was entitled *All Things Must Pass,* a title which presumably indicated his acceptance of the fact that nothing lasts forever. So it is with channel relationships; they too cannot reasonably be expected to last forever. When a mature channel relationship is plagued by truly irreconcilable differences that have destroyed whatever efficiencies once existed between the channel partners, it is time for each to pull the ripcord and bail out of its relationship—fast.

Apple Computer recently did just that, and the initial results suggest it made the right move. Apple recently dissolved its relationships with national consumer electronics retailers Best Buy and Circuit City. An exclusive "store-in-a-store" program with CompUSA replaced each long-standing channel. In 1998, Apple had about 3,000 outlets around the nation; today it has about 600 at CompUSA and regional resellers.[21] Companies like Apple are recognizing and responding to the value of superstores and office supply stores as places where people frequently buy computer products.

Improving Service to Channel Partners

As Forrest Gump might put it, ultimately a relationship is what a relationship does. But what exactly makes up that relationship? First, a relationship is no better or worse than the total

Exhibit 10.3

How to secure channel memberships

Relationship Life Cycle	*Desired Channel Member Behaviors*
Birth	Explain its operating philosophies, goals, and objectives
Growth	Address initial problems; don't let issues linger unresolved
	Honestly and sincerely strive to be opportunity driven
	Seek efficiency within and through the relationship
Maturity	Communicate, communicate, communicate
	Continuously strive to strengthen relationship
Death	Get out—fast

package of benefits channel partners achieve from it. In the language of modern marketing, such a benefit package is called a **bundle.**[22] This package of benefits includes, first and foremost, the functional utility received as a result of the exchange object. The package may also include any technical or economic assistance either partner receives from the relationship, assurances and the actual receipt of timely delivery through the channel system, and brand-name or reputation benefits. An automotive reseller, for instance, might make a bundled relationship option available to an automotive manufacturer. The cost will be far less than the producer would pay had it acquired each benefit separately. Benefits can also result from the relationship itself. Interpersonal exchanges among persons involved in buying and selling relationships can have intangible but genuine value. Conversely, in some situations the package of benefits might not include personal contact. In many business sectors, reordering or conducting other aspects of the transaction through automated, online systems is more efficient.

Efforts aimed at securing relationships by providing better service should feature more than product-related functions or camaraderie among boundary personnel, however. Instead, an entire range of possibilities by which a producer (retailer) can contribute to its customers' (suppliers') operations should be considered. Many companies struggle with customer service because they treat service as a constant event between channel partners—a uniform set of characteristics channel partners seek. This is inappropriate. Different channel partners will seek different benefits. Indeed, the same channel partner will seek different benefits at different times. The type and level of service desired typically varies by type of channel partner, phase of the order cycle, stage of product life cycle, and the sort of relationship currently engaged in with the channel partner. For example, applications engineering or other technical services may loom important for companies that have few R&D and in-house service capabilities. However, these same perquisites would be valued less by companies that have their own R&D and in-house service personnel. Instead, they might place a higher valuation on ease of ordering or prompt delivery. Sometimes marketers as big, experienced, and successful as Sony or Monsanto don't get it right, as illustrated in Channel Surfing 10.3

Approaching the issue of service provision from a broader perspective allows producers or wholesalers to develop value-based pricing. *Value-based prices* reflect the costs and benefits associated with the entire relationship, not just the product. When properly executed, these incentives shift the purchase decision of intermediaries away from simple price considerations and toward other value elements. These value elements allow channel members to differentiate themselves. Truly excellent service allows producers and wholesalers to differentiate products or services traditionally viewed as commodities.

To illustrate, L. E. Muran sells stationery, pencils, and other supplies in a tough market made tougher by the entry of high-volume, low-priced office superstores such as Office Warehouse.[23] In response to this heightened competition, Muran with individual corporate clients entered into a series of value-added relationships to jointly produce a catalog of regularly ordered items. This catalog is distributed to each of the corporate clients' secretaries, who then check off the supplies they need. Muran's sales representatives pick up the orders daily, then deliver individual orders to each customer location within two days and ship regular reports of usage by departments to their customers' headquarters. Muran's unique answer to the low-priced competition has secured its relationships with these customers, who recognize the value of Muran's service quality.

Channel Surfing 10.3

Reasons Why Good Products Go Bad

Statistics can be discouraging. Today, new product failures are estimated to be between 80 and 95 percent, depending on how success is defined. This fact is widely recognized. That means managers face the chillingly real possibility of failure, even as they are constantly ordered to "lead or get out of the way."

Why are new product launches so difficult? Is it because new ideas are a dime a dozen, or is something else underlying the problem? Clearly, some new products fail because they come from bad ideas. But others offer unique, compelling benefits and still fail. And the curse seems to afflict everyone, including highly innovative companies like Sony or Monsanto.

The rest of the story is that "it is getting harder to distinguish new products in the marketplace," say 3M's Steve Webster. The playing field is far more crowded, and getting "true differentiation has become even more challenging."

Sounds like a channels challenge to us. Seemingly superior products have been known to fail because a company's channel partners had too little incentive to market or support them appropriately. Customers always buy an experience with a desired result, and the manufacturer and channel partner must work in concert to create a superior experience. One key to new product success is to convince channel partners that their best choice is not just to carry your product, but to motivate them to market in a way that is consistent with your strategy. This is not ever an easy task, as Monsanto learned in the early 1990s with its line of Salflex glass products. Salflex offered many benefits over competing products, but Monsanto still had a tough time convincing resellers to carry it. Salflex, you see, was priced at a 30 percent premium over traditional glass, and the various stages after Monsanto in the value chain didn't think there would be a demand for such an expensive product.

In 1998, Salflex was relaunched as KeepSafe. This time, however, Monsanto worked to coordinate the value propositions in the product's channels. It analyzed each member in the channel with the goal of gaining an understanding of their experiences and costs, and then created specific marketing programs that would help each partner build its business by selling KeepSafe. This time things worked out just fine. The lesson, apparently, is that a key to motivating channel partners to work hard for you is to understand how your new product will affect operations and profitability at each stage of the channel. Vendors like Monsanto need to understand their channel partners' hidden costs when launching a new product so they can adapt their expectations and requests to the constraints of their distributors.

Points to Ponder

- What are some other reasons why new products fail?
- What are some other tactics that could be followed to alleviate these reasons?

Source: Adapted from Berggren, Eric, and Thomas Nacher (2000), "Why Good Ideas Go Bust," 89 (2), 32–36; and Willow, Jack (2000), "Offerings in the Offings: Here We Go Again," *Barrons,* October 16, 40.

The provision of good service can be likened to an ongoing, continuously adaptive performance. In the movie-making business, one crew member has the job of maintaining continuity. This person makes sure that scenery layout, time on clocks, or the sun's position is consistent from day to day in order to achieve consistency in filming. Someone should be similarly responsible for maintaining the continuity and consistency of service in channels relationships. Boundary personnel need to become action-oriented devotees of their customers, uninhibited by plans or budgets that force them into short-run frames of reference.

In response to these and similar needs, many wholesalers have reevaluated their basic channel missions and have devised ways to get closer to their customers. Many have rid themselves of marginal operations, thus allowing them to concentrate on strengthening core operations. In the food and drug industry, for example, SuperValu elected to focus on food operations. It spun off its ShopKo general merchandise store division. SuperValu then acquired Wetterau and has since become the largest food wholesaler in the United States. Similarly, Owens and Minor, a drug wholesaler, decided to concentrate on the distribution of medical and surgical supplies. In response, it sold its pharmaceutical distribution operations to Bergen Brunswig. In turn, Bergen Brunswig sold its home entertainment subsidiary and strengthened its drug distribution operations by acquiring Durr-Fillauer Medical Co.[24]

As recently as early 1999, new B2B channel members still thought that they could build a website in a particular market niche, and business would immediately come streaming in. Reality set in when the Internet bubble burst, and many such companies begin rethinking their strategies. Their first revelation was that bricks and mortar can be a good thing. Holding and delivering inventory was an asset rather than a liability. B2B intermediaries also realized the role that the provision of quality service had to play in developing durable customer relationships. Need2Buy is using the Web to make buying and selling inventory more efficient. By recently adding Unimate Electronics to its channels lineup, Need2Buy obtained a strong operations infrastructure, region-specific expertise, and numerous customer relationships to drive its expansion into European markets. The company plans to merge its Web-based purchasing model with Unimate's infrastructure to create a full-service "clicks and mortar" company.

The theme of this discussion is hardly new. Sales and marketing managers have chanted the mantra, "Get and keep close to customers," for years. One reason channel relationship problems continue to persist is that individuals active in different functional areas within a given organization often have different incentives. Thus, they view customers and the need for service differently. Marketers usually welcome—and indeed argue for—customized product solutions to cover the different needs of different customers. However, what may appear to be only a minor modification to a salesperson may actually require new processes, employee training, different production equipment, or disruptions of established operating procedures.

In a marketing channel, external responsiveness to customer needs requires internal coordination among the channel members. The paradox is present in all internal channel settings. External channel members rarely consider or explicitly care about this paradox, but how it is resolved can secure relationships. If it is resolved poorly, perhaps there will be no relationship at all.

In the end, long-standing relationship principles override most other considerations when it comes to developing positive channel settings. Old-time mottos such as J.C. Penney's "The golden rule store," Sears's "Satisfaction guaranteed," or the unattributed haberdasher's jewel, "Find out what they want, give it to them, and keep on doing it," still say it best. The need to offer as much added value as possible—in the form of reciprocity, peace of mind, and need satisfaction—to firms that choose to buy functions and utilities from the channel rather than making them themselves should never be forgotten.

Key Terms

bundle
equity
recruiting
screening
selection criteria

Chapter Summary

Cultivating positive channel relationships is a matter of serious concern. The five steps that are involved in developing long-term channel relationships are recruiting, screening, selecting, motivating, and securing.

Recruitment involves those plans and actions aimed at actively soliciting participation of a new channel member. When recruiting prospective channel partners, the recruiting organization should consider how its needs relate to the prospects' qualifications and needs, and vice versa; communicate honestly about the constraints and realities of the channel role; and learn all it can about the prospects' expectations and be prepared to fulfill them.

Not every firm that is recruited is eventually selected for channel membership. In fact, most firms are screened out as inappropriate candidates. Screening is an inherently negative process in that recruiting organizations are seeking reasons to reject rather than accept prospective partners. When screening prospective channel members, recruiters should consider their market segments and products, fit the prospects' strengths and competencies into their products' life cycle, remember that bigger is not always better, and consider the support that is likely to be required by the various prospects.

Once prospects have been recruited and screened, the right partner is selected from among this smaller pool. Various criteria should be considered during this final evaluation of channel member prospects, including sales factors, product factors, experience factors, administrative factors, and risk factors. Distribution functions, service functions, intelligence-gathering functions, and quality of relationships should also be considered as new channel partners are selected.

Recruiting organizations usually have only limited control over their independent intermediaries after they come on board the channel. Special measures—including Distributor Advisory Councils, personal contact, assurances of future relationships, threats, and/or the provision of adequate support—are often required to motivate partners to act in the recruiting organization's best interests.

Finally, securing recruits for a positive, long-term relationship requires developing a partnership between the channel partners. Boundary personnel must be able to identify and respond to their new partner's unique needs and problems. One way to do this is to recognize that, just as any other living thing, relationships pass through a life cycle of birth, growth and maturity, and death. Each stage has different needs and effects on the relationship. In the end, a relationship is what the two parties make of it. The two primary factors are the total package of benefits the partners achieve from it and the level of customer service involved.

Channel Challenges

1. The Chemical Manufacturers' Association has a Responsible Care Program. The program is designed to emphasize safety fitness and regulatory compliance among its membership. One such issue in the distribution of chemical products is the selection of distributors that meet these tough safety standards. Why? Because the Chemical Manufacturers' Association suggests that many chemical distributors are not ascribing to high safety standards. Why should manufacturers be concerned about selecting safety-conscious distributors? Isn't it the responsibility of the distributors to conform to regulations?
2. Aridi Graphics, a Dallas-based software company, uses trade shows to recruit potential sales distributors for its high-quality line of proprietary software for graphic designers. At one MacWorld exposition, President Marwan Aridi met an individual based in France who showed great interest in Aridi's products. The man

agreed to promote the software and serve as a Western European distributor. While he was a small operation, Aridi recognized that individuals who are well networked in the computer industry often account for major distribution of software packages. What are the pros and cons of choosing this distributor? Are trade shows good venues for selecting distributors?

3. An old German saying is, "Marrying is easy, but housekeeping is hard." How does this statement apply to the channel member selection process? The chapter advised that it is important to match channel personalities. If channel personalities change over time, will the exchange relationship change as well?
4. The Seagram Co. pulled off an Absolut coup. Seagram snatched the global distribution rights for the popular Swedish vodka from Grand Metropolitan PLC. Grand Met was said to be taken by surprise over the new distribution agreement. Grand Met also distributes Smirnoff in some markets. Seagram was willing to accept a smaller percentage of profits to get global distribution rights. What does this say about the importance of monitoring exchange relationships? What is the implication for continually exploring new relationship opportunities?

Review Questions

1. Discuss the importance of the recruiting process in marketing channel development. What are some key issues to consider during the recruiting process?
2. Define and describe the importance of the screening process in channel development.
3. Discuss the selection criteria used to SPEAR the best channel intermediary. Describe some of the basic administration and distribution functions of intermediaries sought by producers.
4. How can producers motivate marketing channel members to support their own interests?
5. What is the value to channel members of recognizing that channel relationships can be expected to pass through four life cycle stages?
6. Why is maturity the most dangerous stage of a channel relationship? How can this maturity stage be extended?
7. Discuss some of the ways that channel partners can strengthen their relationships by providing better services to one another.

Endnotes

1. Kovar, Joseph (2000), "EMC Opens Clariion Line to Channel," *Computer Reseller News,* 884, 22–24.
2. Brady, Anna (1995), "Partner Your Way to Providing Quality and Value at the Lowest Conceivable Price," *Journal of Business Strategy,* 16 (2), 52.
3. Garfield, Maynard M. (1992), "Reduce Customer Turnover for Long-Term Success," *Marketing News,* 24 (May 28), 20.
4. Anonymous (1999), "A Leader beyond Bricks-and-Mortar," *Chain Store Age,* December 15, 66–68; and Bliss, Jeff (1998), "IBM Software's Alliance with Sun Heats Up," *Computer Reseller News,* May 11, 3–6.
5. Templin, Neal, and Jeffrey Cole (1994), "Manufacturers Use Suppliers to Help Them Develop New Products," *The Wall Street Journal,* December 19, A1–A6.
6. Hagendorf, Jennifer (2000), "Everdream Solves IT Nightmares," *Computer Reseller News,* March 13, 77–78.
7. Anonymous (2000), "Specialty Stores Raising the Bar," *Dsn Retailing Today,* 39 (18), A18–19.
8. Bigness, John (1995), "In Today's Economy, There Is Big Money to Be Made in Logistics," *The Wall Street Journal,* September 6, A1–A9.
9. Anonymous (1990), "For Kodak, Agents Are Their Business Partners," *Agency Sales Magazine,* 20 (6), 4–7.

10. Hlavacek, James D., and Tommy J. McCuistion (1983), "Industrial Distributors—When, Who and How?" *Harvard Business Review,* March–April, 96–101.
11. Anonymous (1995), "Superior Industrial Supply: Service Cements Relationships," *Industrial Distribution,* 84 (12), 46.
12. Alexander, Antoinette (2000), "Macola Rebuilds Its Channel," 15 (7), 55–56.
13. Garfield, Maynard M. (1992), "Reduce Customer Turnover for Long-Term Success," *Marketing News,* 24 (May 28), 20.
14. McClenahen, John S. (1993), "Global Grasp," *Industry Week,* June 7, 51–53.
15. Shipley, David D. (1984), "Selection and Motivation of Distribution Intermediaries," *Industrial Marketing Management,* 13, 249–56.
16. Strutton, David, Lou E. Pelton, and James R. Lumpkin (1995), "The Influence between Psychological Climate and Franchisor–Franchisee Solidarity," *Journal of Business Research,* 34 (2), 81–91.
17. McKenna, Joseph F. (1992), "A Champion of Common Sense," *Industry Week,* April 6, 11–12.
18. De Santa, Richard (1998), "Unsaleable Merchandise: The Kindest Cut of All," *Supermarket Business,* 53 (6), 13–17.
19. Kelley, William (1991), "Making It Different," *Sales and Marketing Management,* 143 (5), 52–60.
20. Schiller, Zachary, and Wendy Zellner (1992), "Clout! More and More Retail Giants Rule the Marketplace," *Business Week,* December 21, 66–73.
21. Wanchek, Natasha (1998), "Apple's Last Resort: No Club Med," *MC Technology Marketing Intelligence,* 18 (4), 12–16.
22. Treacy, Michael (1995), "You Need a Value Discipline—But Which One?" *Fortune,* April 17, 185.
23. Cespedes, Frank V. (1992), "Once More: How Do You Improve Customer Service?" *Business Horizons,* March–April, 58–67.
24. Lusch, Robert F., Deborah Zizzo, and James M. Kenderdine (1994), "Strategic Renewal in Distribution," *Marketing Management,* 2 (2), 20–29.

part III

Cases

Case 3.1

SAP/Microsoft: Dancing with the Bear

To provide enterprise business solutions for sustained competitive advantage.

—Mission Statement

On an American Airline flight from Pittsburgh to Atlanta, in seat 4B, Stephen Rietzke (alliance director for Systems, Applications and Products in Data Processing, Inc. [SAP]) looked over the slides of a PowerPoint presentation. Stephen must present an hour-long overview at SAP's meeting in Atlanta. The presentation consists of the highlights of the recent performance and forecasts of SAP's alliance with software leader Microsoft. As Stephen sat planning his presentation, he thought back to the start of the alliance and how it all began.

In 1992, Stephen received a phone call from SAP corporate headquarters in Waldorf, Germany. The phone call instructed Stephen to analyze an expansive list of prospective alliance partners in order to instigate a change in direction for one of the largest business software application vendors in the world, SAP. Stephen hung up the phone and proceeded to compile a brief list of prospective alliance partners.

This call initiated a defining moment in the business software industry. The software market consists of numerous large and small business software companies. Many of these software vendors focused on niche markets or limited their markets to either mainframe or microcomputer formats. The crossover from mainframe to microcomputer had yet to be conquered. The phone call from Waldorf, Germany, was to change this.

Background

In Mannheim, Germany, in 1972, three engineers had an idea: to create a company that produces and markets standard software for integrated business solutions. The company they started, Systemanalyse and Programmentwicklung @, is now called Systems, Applications, and Products in Data Processing Inc. or SAP AG for short.

From the beginning, SAP approached application software from a business viewpoint. By collaborating with business and information technology (IT) executives and partners worldwide, SAP developed a unique understanding of the challenges faced in implementing technology solutions for business users. SAP developed software that could help

---

Source: This case was prepared by Rick Rasor, Robert Taylor, and Amy Ward under the direction of Lou Pelton (University of North Texas) for the purpose of class discussion and is not intended to illustrate effective or ineffective management practices.

companies link their business processes, tying together disparate functions and helping their whole enterprise run more smoothly. The versatile, modular software could be quickly and easily adapted to new business processes, too, so as business grew, so did its capabilities.

SAP's innovative thinking soon made it the top software vendor in Germany. Today, SAP is the largest supplier of business application software in the world and the world's fourth largest independent software supplier, overall. Led by the continued technological leadership of SAP's flagship R/3 System, sales in the last three months of 1996 were the best in the company's history.

The company's headquarters are located in Waldorf, Germany, with regional offices located in more than 40 countries worldwide. SAP currently employs 1,250 employees around the globe. And, so far, SAP has helped more than 7,500 companies in 85 countries receive better returns on information. A better return on information means meeting customers' needs faster. It means making the most of changes in the marketplace.

To make sure that customers get a better return on information, SAP has created the SAP Partner Program. The Partner Program helps SAP provide an end-to-end service for customers. The Partner Program combines leading resources, products, and services from companies worldwide. Partners provide expertise in hardware, complementary software, industry and business practices, information technology and implementation support. The Partner Program allows SAP to focus on what it does best by developing leading-edge business application software solutions.

Microsoft

Background

Microsoft was founded as a partnership on April 4, 1975, by William "Bill" H. Gates III and Paul G. Allen and was incorporated on June 25, 1981. Since its creation, Microsoft's mission has been "to create software for the personal computer that empowers and enriches people in the workplace, at school, and at home." Over the years, Microsoft, best known for the development of the Windows platform, has grown to become an international company with offices in more than 50 countries and with products in over 30 languages. As a global company, Microsoft strives to develop products that meet the needs of consumers worldwide. Microsoft pursues this challenge through its partnering strategy.

Partnering Programs

Microsoft currently has 12 partnering programs in which prospective partners may become involved. Each partnering program aims to utilize the unique strengths of each channel member. By analyzing a prospective business partner's business focus, primary business, customer base, and technology focus, Microsoft determines which program best suits the prospective partner. For example, a business that resells software and whose information and resources include Microsoft Intercom and Microsoft Direct Access would qualify for the Microsoft Certified Solution Provider partnering program. By categorizing prospective business partners, Microsoft can optimize the results of the partnership and ensure that its customers' needs continue to be met.

Microsoft's partnering mission statement is as follows: "Microsoft's core business model fosters growth and opportunity for the firms that partner with us to deliver compelling customer solutions based on Microsoft platform products and tools. To respond to the diverse needs of all of our channel partners, we offer many different partnering programs and resource offerings to you to help you succeed with Microsoft products."

Microsoft chooses to pursue a *keiretsu* partnering strategy. Microsoft organizes its enterprise *keiretsus,* such as the SAP project, around value-added products and service chains.

Microsoft enterprise *keiretsus* provide customers with:

- Better enterprise operating systems, optimized for multiple hardware platforms.
- Integrated enterprise management solutions for improved centralized administration of disparate systems, as well as reduced computing costs.
- Integrated line-of-business and packaged client–server applications, optimized for Microsoft's operating systems and server applications.
- Comprehensive partner services complement Microsoft's direct services and focusing on global, multivendor services and support.
- The opportunity to leverage the core competencies of providers at every level of the supply chain to receive the best services.

According to Deborah Willingham, vice president of Microsoft's Enterprise Customer Unit, "Collaborating with industry partners is not just practical; it is critical to meeting Microsoft's goals. By partnering, we can get closer to achieving [our] goals while maintaining our focus on core products and technology."

How Partners Benefit

Microsoft's investment in partners allows them to focus on their core competencies. Also, as demand for Microsoft products such as Windows NT and BackOffice expands worldwide, so too does the market for complementary services, solutions, and systems. As the market continues to grow, Microsoft's partners will be able to increase their business substantially. In addition to increased business, Microsoft's partners will also be able to collaborate with Microsoft on new technology, which will maintain their integration with Microsoft products. This integration of products and services will ensure the continued growth of the partnership and will ensure that the products remain compatible through upgrades.

R/3 Technology Overview

SAP's R/3 System presents a standard business software application for client–server computing. R/3 optimally supports all business activities by allowing easy adjustment and high flexibility to change and progress. At the core (see Exhibit 3.1.1) R/3 contains powerful programs for accounting and controlling, production and materials management, quality management and plant maintenance, sales and distribution, human resources management, and project management. R/3 also allows integration of banks and other business partners into intercompany communications.

Alliance Overview

With the R/3 System, SAP possesses a product with multi-tier management capability. SAP wants to obtain worldwide acceptance for R/3 by interfacing the product with current management information technology systems. Integrating R/3 with existing IT systems would not only create a competitive advantage for SAP; it would also reduce costs to the customer in both time and money.

In 1993 SAP entered into a technology-based alliance with the Microsoft Corporation which allowed SAP access to Microsoft's vast technology infrastructure. SAP and Microsoft jointly integrated R/3 with a variety of Microsoft's existing software and hardware applications. In return SAP offered Microsoft access to its industry-leading advances in the client-server arena. Together SAP and Microsoft now offer fully integrated R/3 System solutions. R/3 easily integrates with Windows NT, Windows 3.1, Windows 95, and Windows for Workgroups, Microsoft Excel, Access, Word, and Microsoft SQL Server platforms.

Another major factor of consideration for the alliance is the increasing business reliance on electronic commerce and the Internet. By integrating R/3 with the Microsoft Internet Information Server companies now have the capability of sending faxes, e-mail, and Internet e-mail directly from the Microsoft Exchange while working within the R/3 System.

Microsoft (as well as other alliance partners) allows SAP simplified system consultation and provision of installations and ongoing support worldwide. To assure this, both SAP and Microsoft have opened competency centers. Competency centers provide training and customer support for the R/3–Microsoft system. Alliances such as this allow SAP access to new technologies. This gives SAP the ability to keep R/3 compatible with the latest developments in the industry.

Several factors make the SAP–Microsoft alliance a good marriage. Both SAP and Microsoft have one common goal, the co-development of the R/3 business application system and Microsoft platforms into a worldwide industry standard. Microsoft sells platforms, personal productivity software products and tools for Windows- and Intel-based systems. SAP sells enterprise business solutions (R/3 system and other products). Microsoft can provide customers with the network operating system, database, Internet and programming development products and tools, while SAP can provide the business application software that sits on top of it.

Traditionally Microsoft focused mainly on distributing its products through channels, and SAP marketed its products through a direct sales force. Recently both companies have broken these traditions. SAP now focuses on "down market" initiatives and Microsoft is trying to sell "up enterprise." In other words, both companies want to meet in the middle.

Both SAP and Microsoft now focus their attention in all business software markets, regardless of customer size, with focus on both horizontal cross-industry solutions and vertical industry solutions. This brings a common goal of "enabling the total supply chain through business software automation." Both companies possess the products and the desire necessary, making this "extended supply chain" a reality.

Another interesting factor is that SAP practices an open door policy with its competitors. SAP works with numerous horizontal and vertical information technology companies, forming marketing partnerships. On the other hand, Microsoft does not traditionally work well with others, especially companies such as IBM, Oracle, and Computer Associates. By partnering with SAP, Microsoft maintains a "back door" to the other companies in the industry.

"When you dance with the bear, you let the bear lead," is a common phrase used among SAP employees. In this case the bear represents Microsoft. Microsoft is definitely the leader in this partnership (see Exhibit 3.1.2). More and more organizations turn to the Microsoft NT Server Platform today because of its strong, integrated security, scalable performance, and broad choice of hardware platforms. This makes Microsoft the perfect alliance partner for SAP, but Microsoft also needs SAP. Microsoft wants to provide mission critical platforms that rival mainframe and beyond

Exhibit 3.1.1

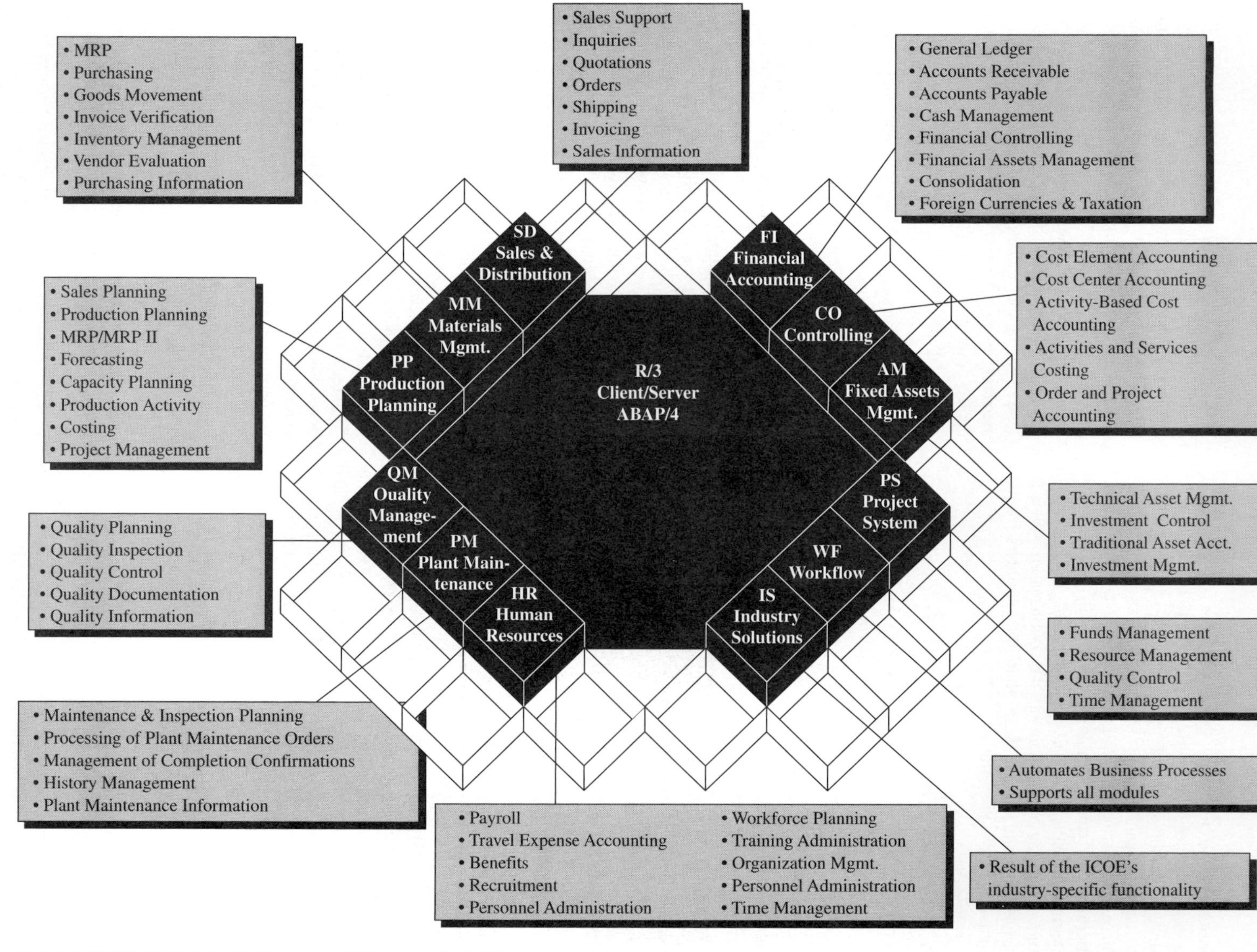

• MRP
• Purchasing
• Goods Movement
• Invoice Verification
• Inventory Management
• Vendor Evaluation
• Purchasing Information
• Sales Support
• Inquiries
• Quotations
• Orders
• Shipping
• Invoicing
• Sales Information
• General Ledger
• Accounts Receivable
• Accounts Payable
• Cash Management
• Financial Controlling
• Financial Assets Management
• Consolidation
• Foreign Currencies & Taxation
• Sales Planning
• Production Planning
• MRP/MRP II
• Forecasting
• Capacity Planning
• Production Activity
• Costing
• Project Management
SD Sales & Distribution
MM Materials Mgmt.
PP Production Planning
FI Financial Accounting
CO Controlling
AM Fixed Assets Mgmt.
R/3 Client/Server ABAP/4
QM Quality Management
PM Plant Maintenance
HR Human Resources
PS Project System
WF Workflow
IS Industry Solutions
• Cost Element Accounting
• Cost Center Accounting
• Activity-Based Cost Accounting
• Activities and Services Costing
• Order and Project Accounting
• Quality Planning
• Quality Inspection
• Quality Control
• Quality Documentation
• Quality Information
• Technical Asset Mgmt.
• Investment Control
• Traditional Asset Acct.
• Investment Mgmt.
• Funds Management
• Resource Management
• Quality Control
• Time Management
• Maintenance & Inspection Planning
• Processing of Plant Maintenance Orders
• Management of Completion Confirmations
• History Management
• Plant Maintenance Information
• Automates Business Processes
• Supports all modules
• Payroll
• Travel Expense Accounting
• Benefits
• Recruitment
• Personnel Administration
• Workforce Planning
• Training Administration
• Organization Mgmt.
• Personnel Administration
• Time Management
• Result of the ICOE's industry-specific functionality

Exhibit 3.1.2
SAP/Microsoft relationship history

Apr. 1993	Joint development agreement between SAP and Microsoft.
Apr. 1994	First release of R/3 on Windows NT server.
Oct. 1995	SAP availability of R/3 on Microsoft SQL Server.
Oct. 1995	First customer goes online.
Sept. 1996	More than 3,200 R/3 installations on Windows NT Server.
Mar. 1997	R/3 gains Microsoft BackOffice Logo certification.
Sept. 1997	More than 45% of all new R/3 installations are currently installed on Windows NT Server.

computing requirements; therefore Microsoft desires access to SAP's marketplace. At this point Microsoft and SAP do not compete with one another; this gives them a truly symbiotic alliance. Since R/3's integration into the Windows NT Server platform, more than 45 percent of all new R/3 installations have been on the Windows NT Server. Microsoft and SAP continue to expand their horizons and enjoy a successful business relationship.

Partner Contributions

SAP Contributions

For this alliance, SAP will contribute the business software applications (mainly the R/3 technology) for the technology infrastructure that Microsoft provides. The business software applications allow mid-market and small-enterprise customers to increase the productivity of their current systems while reducing the cost of maintaining their core systems. SAP also contributes name recognition to the alliance. In Germany, SAP's name recognition rivals Microsoft's name recognition in the United States. SAP currently ranks fourth worldwide in software providers and controls 30 percent of the business software applications market while its closest competitor controls only 10 percent of the business software applications market. Capital contributions from SAP will consist of capital for the introduction of current technology, user assistance programs, and future product development. SAP will also jointly fund and support competency centers. One of these centers will be located at SAP headquarters in Waldorf, Germany. At the competency centers, extensive joint product testing will take place to improve integration between R/3 and BackOffice and to ensure that the products remain symbiotic through future upgrades.

Microsoft Contributions

Microsoft, although the larger partner, does not contribute a disproportionate amount of resources. Each of the partners in this alliance contributes equally, ensuring that the foundation for a true alliance exists. For this alliance Microsoft will contribute the technological infrastructure, the operating system in which R/3 works. Microsoft's tremendous name recognition around the world will also be a significant contribution to the alliance. Microsoft's name recognition provides SAP the opportunity to increase its own name recognition and provides for immense growth opportunities for SAP. Capital contributions from Microsoft will consist of capital for the introduction of current technology, user assistance programs, and future product development. A jointly funded competency center will be located at Microsoft headquarters in Redmond, Washington, where joint product testing will take place to improve integration between R/3 and BackOffice and to ensure that the products remain symbiotic through upgrades.

Decision Environment

Alliance teams signify one hallmark of a true alliance. The SAP–Microsoft alliance has such a hallmark. Part of the formation of the alliance included the formation of an alliance team. Each partner contributes an alliance director and additional staff to make decisions regarding the alliance. With the health and survival of the alliance as their primary goals and concerns, the alliance team can ensure that the alliance remains on course. Problems that arise can be jointly resolved, which protects the interests of the alliance and of the partners. Given Microsoft's keiretsu philosophy of partnerships, the alliance team enables this to be a long-term alliance with no impending end. Without the alliance, team people would handle conflicts that arose at the corporate level of each company with their own company's agenda as their primary concern. This type of decision environment would impede the success of an alliance. The fact that SAP and Microsoft support an alliance team bodes well for the success of this alliance.

Future Concerns

Alliances are like marriages—for success, each partner must have an enormous amount of trust for the other. Currently SAP and Microsoft seem to possess this critical trust; perhaps this stems from the lack of direct competition with one another. The "traveling companion" relationship shared by SAP and Microsoft bodes well for the continued success of the alliance. History shows us, though, that many more alliances fail than succeed.

Recently, Microsoft has been under investigation by the U.S. Department of Justice. Charged with unfair practices such as bundling (making buyers purchase unnecessary products in order to receive the desired product by bundling the products together), the company has responded by fighting back with advertising and in court. Microsoft also agreed to unbundle its web browser in an effort to reduce Department of Justice concerns. This brings up a few questions:

- What threats exist to the relationship between SAP and Microsoft?
- Will the litigation against Microsoft affect the future of the relationship? If so, in what way?
- What would stop either partner from forming alliances with the other partner's competitor? And if this happened, how would it affect the current relationship?
- How should Rietzke evaluate the quality and success of the relationship? Be specific. What measures should be used?
- Finally, what possible problems could arise from the partners' exchange of technology? How should the alliance influence product development processes? Why?

Sources of information:
http://www.sap.com/partner
http://www.microsoft.com/germany/partner/sap/us
http://www.microsoft.com

Case 3.2

AmeriServe

Introduction

In October 1997, Jeffrey Raltz, logistics analyst for AmeriServe/PFS, was researching information on the possible partnership between AmeriServe, Miller Brewing Company, and J. B. Hunt. Miller had 500 carriers and numerous distributors in its network, but was considering J. B. Hunt for a role as its primary carrier. Raltz realized Miller needed to reorganize its distribution network for continuous growth and logistical value. He also realized that in order to increase economic value and density, J. B. Hunt needed to put in place a dedicated lanes transportation system to keep its trucks full to and from sites of distribution. (Load density simply means full truck-loads of products.) AmeriServe stood to gain revenue through more efficient shipping of its products, but was concerned about the role it would play in the partnership.

Raltz was preparing to make recommendations for the future. He had just completed a marker analysis of the beer industry including Anheuser-Busch, Coors, Stroh's, and numerous regional beers. Miller was strongest in the Midwest, southeast, and Texas, but weakest in New England, a region replete with microbreweries, and California, which was saturated with Mexican imports like Corona. Miller had networks effectively in place in the northeastern, southeastern, and southwestern United States, but their efficiency could be improved. The northwestern United States had to receive Miller products from Erwindale, California, or Milwaukee, Wisconsin. The great distance created extensive uncertainty among retailers attempting to provide time and place utility.

Raltz wondered if the question was not more complex than just re-engineering a distribution channel. Miller wanted control over its product. It also wanted to dissolve its relationships with approximately 420 regional carriers, which was in itself a complex issue. J. B. Hunt was willing to take

Source: This case was prepared by Lauren Daniels, Chris Jarrard, and Muniu Muiruri under the direction of Dr. Lou Pelton (University of North Texas) for the purposes of class discussion, and is not intended to illustrate effective or ineffective management practices.

on the enormous responsibility of being Miller's primary carrier as long as it got increased economic value and density out of the partnership. Raltz and AmeriServe/PFS were slowly evaluating how much involvement they should have with Miller and J. B. Hunt. To make the partnership work, Raltz knew he had to show his manager and executives from Miller and J. B. Hunt how AmeriServe/PFS would be able to add value to the supply chain. Raltz would present his recommendations and plan of action to executives of the three companies at the next executive meeting, in just 30 days.

The Players

AmeriServe/PFS

AmeriServe/PFS, which is a subsidiary of Holberg Industries Inc., procures and distributes food, supplies, and equipment to 14 major restaurant chains (including Wendy's, Burger King, Arby's, Dairy Queen, and nearly 800 KFC restaurants), and over 600 beverage distribution centers throughout North America. AmeriServe/PFS's mission is to provide custom-tailored distribution and related services that deliver a competitive advantage to the customer. As the largest food service and restaurant equipment supplier in the U.S., AmeriServe/PFS manages the distribution of over 4 billion pounds of goods annually.

AmeriServe/PFS's integrated Logistics Management Group manages over 12,000 beverage shipments for PepsiCo. At an annual transportation expense of over $30,000,000, this group delivers yearly savings in excess of $2,000,000 at a service level of 99 percent. The Logistics Management Group, formerly part of the PFS division of PepsiCo, was originally limited to the distribution of food, supplies, and equipment to the PepsiCo restaurants, but grew to incorporate the distribution of PepsiCo beverages. In July 1997, AmeriServe purchased PFS, creating opportunities to distribute goods to a variety of clients nationwide. Its scope now includes AmeriServe/PFS's incumbent business, and will soon incorporate inbound movements from their suppliers. The merging of PFS's customer service culture with AmeriServe's expertise in selling services to diverse groups of franchisees created a synergy that translated into the largest food and supply distributor in the nation.

J. B. Hunt

J. B. Hunt Transport Services Inc. is a diversified transportation services and logistics company. Through its subsidiaries, J. B. Hunt transports primarily full-load containerized freight throughout the continental U.S. and portions of Canada and Mexico. The company also provides logistics and transportation-related services that may use either J. B. Hunt equipment and employees, or equipment and services provided by unrelated third parties in the industry.

Miller Brewing Company

In June of 1969, Phillip Morris acquired 53 percent interest in Miller Brewing Company for $130,000,000. In 1970, Phillip Morris acquired the remaining outstanding shares, 47 percent, for $25,000,000 and $72,000,000 in notes due in 1982. Miller is the second largest brewing company in the U.S. It owns and operates Molson Breweries, the second largest beer importer in the United States. Internationally, Miller has formed a number of alliances with brewers from Japan, Brazil, China, and England. Miller owns eight breweries (see Exhibit 3.2.1 for continental U.S. locations and distribution areas), and majority interests in the Celis Brewery in Austin, Texas, and the Shipyard Brewery in Portland, Maine. It also owns a beer distributorship in Oklahoma and a hops processing facility in Wisconsin.

Miller Products

Miller has 15 different beers in all. The most popular brands come from the premium segment comprises of Miller Lite, Miller Lite Ice, Miller Genuine Draft, Miller Genuine Draft Lite, Miller Beer, and Icehouse. Containers (bottles, cans, and kegs) for beer products are purchased from various suppliers.

In 1996, shipment volume for Miller, including imports, exports, and nonalcohol brew, decreased 2.7 percent from the previous year, while the U.S. industry was up 1.8 percent. Intense competition, combined with softness in most of Miller's brands, resulted in the lower shipment volume. Despite higher shipments of Miller Lite in 1996, shipments of other premium-price brands decreased. Yet Miller depended on its premium brands, which accounted for nearly 83 percent of its total shipments. Miller's share of the U.S. industry (based on shipments) was 21.6 percent, down 1.0 share point from 1995.

Miller had spoken with many firms, including J. B. Hunt, AmeriServe/PFS, and other companies about a proposed partnership. After evaluating its needs, J. B. Hunt considered partnering with Miller. AmeriServe/PFS analyzed its needs and had also considered being the third link.

The Beer Industry

According to *IMPACT,* a publication that tracks the United States alcoholic beverage industry, consumers spent about

Exhibit 3.2.1

Miller brewing facilities, 1996 assigned ship plant areas (Headquarters: Milwaukee, WI.)

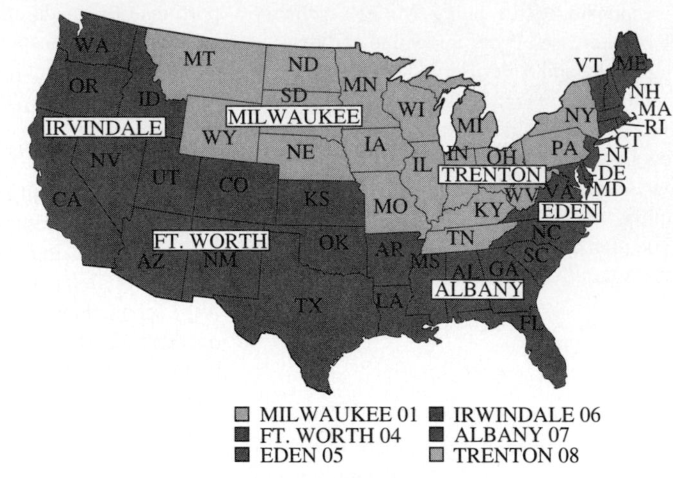

$90 million for 6.6 billion gallons of alcoholic beverages in 1995. Beer accounted for the largest portion of the industry dollar. Consumers spent approximately $50 billion on 5.8 billion gallons of beer in 1995, accounting for an 87 percent share of the industry, as measured by volume.

The U.S. alcoholic beverage industry underwent a consolidation prompted by the combined challenges of declining U.S. consumption trends in the highly developed marketplace and the steady rise in legal and regulatory actions. The increased scale needed to compete established numerous barriers to entry for smaller competitors.

Three producers dominated the U.S. beer industry (see Exhibits 3.2.2 and 3.2.3), commanding a combined 78 percent market share of the nation's beer products. Anheuser-Busch had a leading 45 percent share, Miller Brewing had a 23 percent share, and Adolph Coors had a 10 percent share.

Pricing in this industry moves in concert; the industry leader hikes prices and the rest follow. This price leadership helped boost industry profit margins to healthy levels. But a decline in real disposable income tends to put downward pressure on the prices of consumer products, because consumers move away from premium-priced, brand-name

Exhibit 3.2.2

Sales of leading U.S. brewers (in millions of barrels)

	Shipments			**Market Share**		
Company	*1990*	*1994*	*1995*	*1990*	*1994*	*1995*
Anheuser-Busch	84.6	85.9	84.8	43.5%	45.4%	45.2%
Miller Brewing	42.8	43.7	43.3	22.0	23.1	23.1
Adolph Coors	19.2	18.6	18.7	9.9	9.8	10.0
Stroh Brewery	26.2	19.1	17.1	13.5	10.1	9.1
S&P Co.	8.0	7.6	7.0	4.1	4.0	3.7
Total—leading brewers	180.8	174.9	170.9	92.9	92.4	91.1
Others	13.8	15.0	15.1	7.1	7.9	8.0
Total	194.6	189.3	187.6	100	100	100

Exhibit 3.2.3

Top 10 beer brands ranked by 1995 unit sales

	Sales (Mil. Barrels)			Market Share		
Company	*1990*	*1994*	*1995*	*1990*	*1994*	*1995*
1. Budwelser	47.9	39.1	37.2	24.8%	20.9%	20.0%
2. Bud Light	11.8	16.3	17.9	6.1	8.7	9.6
3. Miller Lite	19.9	15.5	15.8	10.3	8.3	8.5
4. Coors Light	11.6	12.5	12.9	6.0	6.7	7.0
5. Busch	9.4	8.5	8.1	4.9	4.5	4.4
6. Natural Light	3.0	7.1	7.1	1.6	3.8	3.8
7. Miller Genuine Draft	5.8	6.1	5.8	3.0	3.3	3.1
8. Milwaukee's Best	6.6	5.0	4.7	3.4	2.7	2.5
9. Miller High Life	6.0	4.4	4.4	3.1	2.4	2.4
10. Bush Light Draft	1.9	4.0	4.2	1.0	2.1	2.3
Total Top 10	123.9	118.5	118.1	64.2	63.3	63.6
All others	69.2	68.7	67.5	35.8	36.7	36.4
Total	193.1	187.2	185.6	100	100	100

products toward value-priced brands. The alcoholic beverage industry last experienced this scenario in the early 1990s, when value-priced brands such as Busch and Natural Light cut into the market shares of such premium-priced brands as Budweiser, Michelob, and Molson. One of the most distinguishing characteristics of the industry is how heavily it is regulated and taxed. In 1995, every barrel of beer was taxed $18 and every six-pack was taxed 32 cents. In 1995, the U.S. government collected $3.3 billion from the beer industry.

In addition to pricing, population also drives demand. With the U.S. population growing at an annual rate of only about 1%, the American market for all alcoholic beverages is quite mature. Demographic trends affect the industry as well. Studies show that the largest group of purchasers for these products is young adults, a post–baby-boom demographic group that is growing very slowly. The aging population does not favor brewers, and the baby boom generation, that group of 80 million consumers between the ages of 32 and 52, is demonstrating an increased interest in healthy living and has therefore cut back its beer consumption.

Miller's Distribution System

Distribution is one of the principal methods of competition in the beer industry. Miller was losing revenue and market share to its competition because of its distribution system.

Under that system, over 500 trucking companies delivered beer on a domestic scale, but Miller did not know when the carriers were coming to pick up beer for delivery. It had a general idea, but the trucks were never on time. Numerous independent distributors controlled the flow and distribution of the product in their own territories. If Distributor X controlled the North Texas region, it dictated what grocery stores, convenience stores, and restaurants would receive Miller products. Miller had no control over the distribution of its product. It did, however, have "deep pockets." Because Miller is owned by Philip Morris, it had never (until recently) considered reengineering its supply chain. But with regional breweries competing for market share, Miller had to create a competitive advantage in distribution to stay alive.

The Partnership*

In the proposed distribution system, AmeriServe/PFS would provide loads for Hunt to carry when not carrying Miller loads. AmeriServe and J. B. Hunt would develop an in-house

*It's important to note that the proposed partnership is still being considered. The partnership has not been approved yet and may never be approved, so the information is all speculative.

continuous-move software program that would inform Hunt's truckers where and when loads were ready to be shipped. If the software showed that a load from Miller leaving Dallas would arrive in Boston at the same time an AmeriServe/PFS load was leaving Boston for Fort Worth, then a continuous move could be accomplished. This creation of a just-in-time (JIT), point-to-point, "dense" distribution network would provide benefits for all companies involved. The dedicated lanes would allow continuous movement of Miller and AmeriServe/PFS products with minimum interruptions and downtime. Hunt would gain load density, thus creating economies of scale. Miller would achieve more control over its logistics, and distributors would concentrate on New England, the northwestern U.S., and California to work on an intensive system within these markets. AmeriServe/PFS would gain another cost-reducing channel of distribution. J. B. Hunt would charge Miller or AmeriServe/PFS for each load the companies ordered, and if Hunt's trucks remained full at all times, it would give both Miller and AmeriServe a discount on those loads. The proposed partnership could be a win-win situation.

Decision Options

The first option that Raltz considered was to not get involved with the partnership at all. AmeriServe/PFS wanted to manage as much freight as possible but Miller and J. B. Hunt were dominating the program. Raltz was uneasy about the minor role that AmeriServe/PFS might have to take if they did commit to the partnership.

The second option that Raltz wanted to present was a limited role by AmeriServe/PFS, in which they used the partnership as one cost-effective channel of distribution among others. AmeriServe/PFS could build density into the system by having J. B. Hunt, as the primary carrier, distribute all of their products on the same trucks as Miller's.

The third option that Raltz was considering was an equal partnering agreement in which all decisions would be split equally between Miller, J. B. Hunt, and AmeriServe/PFS. AmeriServe could team with J. B. Hunt and integrate continuous-move software programs that would benefit both companies in their strategic planning processes. AmeriServe/PFS could also set up a long-term alliance with Philip Morris to possibly work on other supply-chain issues in other strategic business units. AmeriServe/PFS would further benefit because it could control its freight when it was being moved with Miller products.

AmeriServe/PFS historically takes a slow, methodical approach to decision making when it involves a partnership. However, Raltz knew that Miller and J. B. Hunt would want a decision by their next executive meeting. Raltz and his team needed to spend the next couple of weeks evaluating all three options. As the team leader, he needed to present his ideas and options to his upper-level executives first, before the executive meeting in a few weeks. Raltz was confident that he would be prepared with the decision that most benefited AmeriServe/PFS at least a week before the meeting was scheduled to take place.

Conclusion

A successful partnership requires each partner to add value. Miller wanted to add value to its supply chain by decreasing its number of regional carriers and distributors. J. B. Hunt would be the primary carrier and, together with AmeriServe/PFS, would work on an integrated continuous-move software program that would create an effective transportation system of combined Miller and AmeriServe/PFS products. Raltz understood that Miller and J. B. Hunt had deep pockets. Philip Morris owns Miller and doesn't have to spend the time evaluating and analyzing all decision options like AmeriServe/PFS does. Time may be the biggest factor against this partnership because Miller and J. B. Hunt are ready to go, and AmeriServe/PFS is still methodically evaluating its position. Raltz knew that a partnership had the opportunity to be successful from a strategic standpoint, but he was being very careful as to how far AmeriServe/PFS committed itself before he knew where they stood. If Raltz finds out that AmeriServe/PFS has to take a minor position in the partnership, then he may pull the plug. If Raltz sees that it is going to be an equal partnership, he may go in front of AmeriServe/PFS's executives and speak favorably of the proposed partnership. From AmeriServe/PFS's standpoint, it all comes down to control.

Case 3.3

Indiana Wine Grape Council

Joyce A. Young
Indiana State University

Faye S. McIntyre
Rockhurst College

In March 1994, Marcia Brown, marketing specialist for the Indiana Wine Grape Council (IWGC), was examining the industry's annual sales report for the previous year. Sales for the Indiana wine grape industry increased approximately 30 percent in 1993, yet Brown was anything but exuberant. Indiana wine represented about 1 percent (53,000 gallons) of all wine sales in the state. Currently, 90 percent of the state-produced volume is sold primarily to tourists at the eleven wineries scattered across the state. Brown realizes the industry must expand its retail distribution for continued growth.

Brown has just completed an extensive market analysis of the industry and now is preparing to make recommendations for the future. One major issue is the lack of a state-wide channel of distribution for Indiana wine. There are many alcoholic beverage wholesalers, both large and small, in the state. Retailers appear enthusiastic about regional wines; however, Indiana wine is virtually nonexistent on retail shelves. Of the distribution that does exist, Brown noticed that more times than not, the Indiana product was on a bottom shelf.

Moreover, Brown wondered if the question was not more complex than just how to design a distribution channel and the support mechanisms that would ensure extensive retail shelf space throughout the state. The majority of the wineries approach the industry with tunnel vision. Wine-making is a way of life, not a business, and profit margins are not meant to be shared with distributors. As a result, the wineries are complacent with their environment. To capture the attention of the wineries, Brown is well aware that her approach to the channel design needs to balance progress with tradition. Brown must present her recommendations and a plan of action to the wineries' proprietors at their next executive meeting, two weeks away.

A Brief Course in Wine

"Wine has never been America's favorite beverage. In fact, 30 percent of all Americans don't drink alcoholic beverages of any kind, and another 30 percent do not drink wine. This leaves only 40 percent of Americans who drink wine at all—and in the final analysis, only 5 percent of the population drink 75 percent of all the wine."[1] In the United States, a "wine drinker" is classified as a person who drinks as little as one glass of wine a week. Compare that behavior to the French who consume wine at every meal, and one could conclude that wine is not ingrained in the American culture.

For those Americans that drink wine, what type of wine do they prefer? In the late 1970s, Americans began drinking more white wines than red wines. This trend continues into the 1990s, with white wine now accounting for seventy percent of the volume. Until recently, however, wineries continued to grow more red grapes than white grapes. Some of the most common varieties of grapes are listed in Exhibit 3.3.1. Since the maturing process takes between three to five years from planting of vines to the day wine can be produced from the grapes, wineries could not simply rip out red vines and replace them. The wineries have finally caught up with demand. Unfortunately, the consumer is "seeing red" again. Recent medical findings suggest that drinking five ounces (i.e., a single glass) of red wine each day reduces the occurrence of coronary heart disease.[2]

In addition to red and white wines, American consumers also may select a rosé—a wine, such as White Zinfandel, in

Note: All information contained in this case is based on data gathered during field and student research. Names have been disguised at the request of the Indiana Wine Grape Council.

[1]Kevin Zraly, *Windows of the World Complete Wine Course* (New York: Sterling Publishing, 1992), 47.

[2]Patricia Thomas, "A Toast to the Heart," *Harvard Health Letter* 19:5 (March 1994), 4–5.

Exhibit 3.3.1

Commonly grown grapes in the United States

Red Grapes	*White Grapes*
Cabernet Sauvignon	Chardonnay
Zinfandel	Sauvignon Blanc
Merlot	Johannesberg Riesling
Pinot Noir	Chenin Blanc

which the red grape skins are allowed to ferment with the juice only long enough to take on the rosé color. Within the red, white, and rosé categories, consumers may choose from varietal or jug wines. A varietal wine is a wine named after the predominant grape that constitutes at least seventy-five percent of the wine's volume such as a Chardonnay or a Cabernet Sauvignon. A jug wine is a simple drinking wine that contains a number of different grapes and is usually labeled with a generic name such as Chablis, Rosé, or Burgundy. Given that Gallo is the largest winery in the world and the major producer of jug wines, it is not surprising that jug wines account for the largest volume of wine sold in the United States.[3]

Industry Background for Indiana

Indiana has a rich but obscure history in grape growing and wine making. The industry was born in 1802 in Vevay, a city in southeastern Indiana on the Ohio River.[4] There, Swiss settler John James Dufour and his associates planted the first Indiana grape crop. With their initial harvest in 1806, Dufour and friends established the first successful commercial vineyard in the United States. Over the last century, the industry has experienced a gradual decline within the state.

Wine is considered an agricultural product in Indiana. Thus, the industry receives research and marketing support from the state. The IWGC, a state governmental agency, was established by the legislature in 1989 to develop a successful wine grape industry. The staff consists of three persons: Brown, an office assistant, and a university sponsored enologist. Marketing efforts are currently focused on tourism (i.e., getting people to visit the wineries) and wine tastings across the state. The IWGC represents the interests of eleven independent wineries; however, the wineries are under no obligation to incorporate the suggestions of the IWGC.

As shown in Exhibit 3.3.2, most of the wineries are located in central and southern Indiana. The industry is dominated by small, family-owned operations which produce over ninety different wines. In 1993, thirty of the wines were award winners in competitions across the United States. Some wineries have trouble in maintaining sufficient inventories from season to season. The most popular varieties often are sold out before the next season's harvest is ready for bottling. As a result, shortages at the retail level are common. Some wineries import grapes from California and Europe to provide a wider variety of grapes than the local growing season and climate allow. Indiana's climate is more conducive to French-American hybrids and Native American grapes than European varieties.

Products are available for purchase at the wineries and, in some cases, through mail order. In addition, three wineries, Pommard, Chandler, and St. Veran, maintain restaurants on the facility grounds. The Palmer Winery is the only facility that currently uses a wholesaler (Jefferson Distributing). Four wineries, Wilson, Semillion, Vessels, and Harmony, sell their products directly to retailers within local markets. Although the wineries do not perceive intrastate competition and often work together at wine tastings across the state, the camaraderie stops with the Palmer Winery which is less than receptive to a cooperative distribution effort with the other ten wineries.

The channel pricing structure for a typical 750 milliliter bottle of Indiana produced wine is presented in Exhibit 3.3.3. A tourist would pay approximately $5.60 if purchased at the winery. In order to compete with popular jug wines, such as Gallo, Almaden, and Taylor, the wineries feel that the retail price for Indiana produced wine must be kept low.

Promotional activity to stimulate demand at the retail level is not a priority for the wineries and is seldom undertaken. Though the Indiana Alcoholic Beverage Commission prohibits several forms of trade promotion (i.e., cooperative advertising between channel levels, rebates, and coupons), wine sampling within liquor stores and reseller support, such as promotional allowances, displays, point of purchase

---

[3]Zraly, *Windows of the World Complete Wine Course,* 52.

[4]Indiana Wine Grape Council, *Tourism Brochure* (1993).

EXHIBIT 3.3.2

Indiana and its wineries

1. Capital Winery
2. Wilson Winery
3. Semillion Winery
4. Palmer Winery
5. Vessels Winery
6. Harmony Winery
7. Pommard Winery
8. Chandler Winery
9. Talbot Winery
10. St. Veran Winery
11. Lakeland Winery

Gary
11
South Bend
Fort Wayne
Lafayette
Muncie
Indianapolis
1
Richmond
Terre Haute
2
3
4
5
10
Bloomington
9
8
7
Jeffersonville
Evansville
6

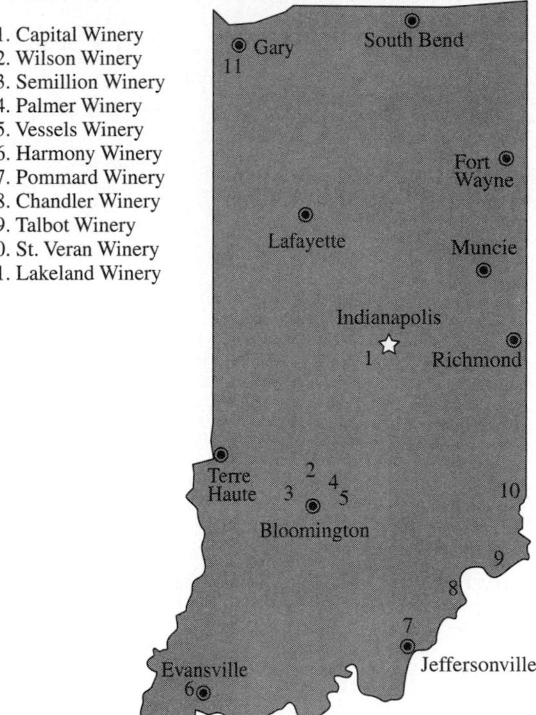

EXHIBIT 3.3.3

Channel pricing structure for a typical bottle of Indiana produced wine

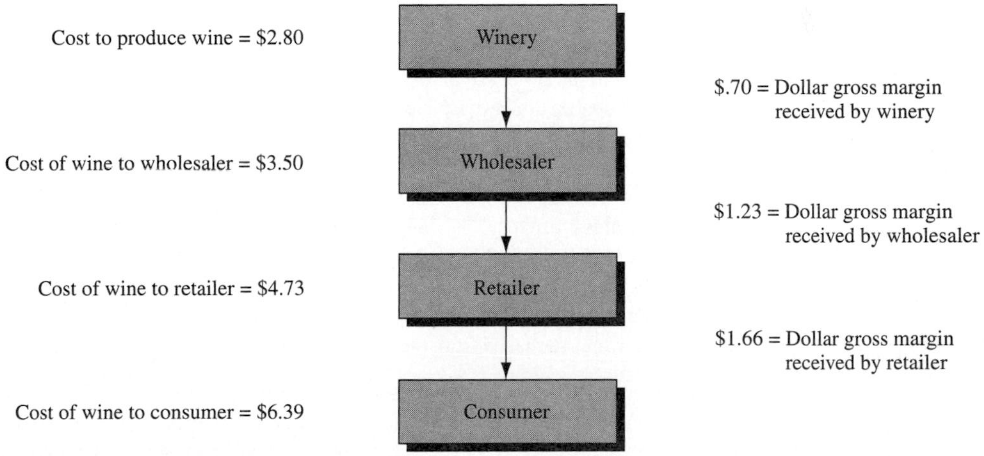

Cost to produce wine = $2.80
Winery
$.70 = Dollar gross margin received by winery
Cost of wine to wholesaler = $3.50
Wholesaler
$1.23 = Dollar gross margin received by wholesaler
Cost of wine to retailer = $4.73
Retailer
$1.66 = Dollar gross margin received by retailer
Cost of wine to consumer = $6.39
Consumer

Exhibit 3.3.4
Alcoholic beverage wholesalers

Wholesaler Name	*Beverage Type*	*Locations*	*Market Coverage*
Hoosier Wine	Wine	Indianapolis	Statewide
Lincoln Distributing	Liquor and Wine	Indianapolis*	Statewide
		Evansville	
		South Bend	
		Gary	
		Fort Wayne	
Sycamore Liquors	Liquor and Wine	Indianapolis*	Statewide
		Evansville	
		South Bend	
Irish Beverage	Liquor and Wine	South Bend	Northern Indiana
Jefferson Distributing	Liquor and Wine	Jeffersonville	Southern Indiana

*Indicates a central warehouse that supplies the other locations as needed.

material, contests and incentives, are permissible.[5] Most of the wine bottle labels are attractive and eye-catching; however, all labels focus solely on the individual winery and lack universal product codes (UPCs).

The Current Environment in Indiana

Brown is aware of the existing channel structure and the interorganizational behavior among producers, wholesalers, and retailers within the channel. As shown in Exhibit 3.3.4, there are five major alcoholic beverage wholesalers in Indiana, all of which ship via company-owned trucks. Each wholesaler has exclusive distribution of several national brands within the state. Though a contract may exist between a wholesaler and an alcoholic beverage producer, the relationship is conventional in nature. Each wholesaler maintains an outside sales force compensated by base plus commission. A sales representative visits each retail account at least weekly to take orders, build displays, maintain shelf space, convey product information, and cultivate close relationships with retail staff.

In addition, many small beer distributors exist throughout the state. Typically, they are aligned closely with a single brand and have an approximate sales territory of four counties. The service level provided to retailers by these local distributors is high. Drivers routinely stock shelves and rotate products. Few of the beer distributors possess permits to distribute wine. On average, a wine permit purchased from the state is $500 per year. Permits are available as long as a state-designated area has not reached its quota. If the quota has been reached, a distributor can buy an existing permit from another distributor, subject to the commission's approval.

In Indiana, alcoholic beverages are available at several types of retailers: liquor stores, food stores, and pharmacies. The locus for purchasing decisions ranges from the store level to more centralized authorization in larger retail chains such as Krogers. With the development of scanner technology, a buyer's initial decision to adopt a product may be influenced by the presence of a UPC symbol on the package.

More importantly, the alcoholic beverage industry in the United States is a mature market,[6] and the national brands typically compete on price.[7] Buyers frequently switch wholesale suppliers to save a few pennies per bottle. In-store displays and shelf space/location are vital to the marketing efforts of the national producers. As a result, retailers appear to hold the most power in the distribution channel.

Brown's Decision

Brown realizes that an individual winery cannot compete aggressively in the retail marketplace over the long-term. Given that most wine is purchased within forty-eight hours of consumption, she knows that Indiana produced wine must be present in local markets. After speaking extensively with a representative of the Indiana Alcoholic Beverage Commission concerning the legality of cooperative distribution, Brown concludes that a joint marketing effort holds the key to the puzzle.

[5] Indiana Alcoholic Beverage Commission, *Indiana Alcoholic Beverage Laws and Rules* (Charlottesville, VA: Michie Company Law Publishers, 1994).

[6] "A Mature Market," *Indiana Beverage Journal* (August 1993), 4.

[7] Laura Holson, "Why California Winemakers Are Crying in Their Chardonnay," *Business Week,* 3183 (October 15, 1990), 36.

Case 3.4

Factory Direct Selling by Cironi's Sewing Center

J. B. Wilkinson
Youngstown State University

Gary B. Frank
University of Akron

"To do, or not to do, another factory warehouse sale. That is the question!" quipped Tony Cironi to himself as he pondered whether it was advisable to run another factory-direct-to-consumer (FDC) warehouse sale. A year earlier Tony had enthusiastically committed to doing his first, and so far only, FDC warehouse sale with Viking-White Sewing (VWS), a sewing machine manufacturer headquartered in Cleveland, Ohio. However, Tony's postsale evaluation had left him with mixed feelings about that type of sales promotion. Profits had been disappointing, and although he had protected his turf, he had concerns about the ethics of FDCs and their long-term effects on independent sewing machine dealers. Consequently, he had not pushed to do another one. But now he would have to sort through the facts and resolve his ambivalent feelings about FDCs because the Singer sales representative had just called to ask if Tony would be interested in putting on an FDC for Singer Sewing Machine Company (SSMC).

Tony had agreed to meet with the rep to discuss terms and arrangements. But even as he reached for his files on the previous year's Viking-White FDC, Tony felt vaguely upset. "I'm damned if I do and damned if I don't," he muttered to himself.

> Looks to me like the manufacturer has all the advantages and none of the grief in doing these FDCs. But if I don't do it, someone else will, and my Singer sewing machine sales will be down for a year!

Factory Direct Selling

Factory direct selling can be implemented in a number of different formats and is prevalent in the household appliance industry. In the sewing machine industry, factory direct selling has taken the form of special promotions which are co-sponsored by manufacturers and dealers. It is typically presented to consumers as a factory-authorized inventory reduction sale or FDC warehouse sale. The typical format involves an off-premise warehouse or storefront location, extensive public-notice-type advertising, a short time period, and local dealer involvement for after-sale service.

In the sewing machine industry, Viking-White Sewing was the first sewing machine manufacturer to run FDCs. The idea had originated with Joe Fulmer, owner of a large sewing machine dealership in Dayton, Ohio, called The Stitching Post. Fulmer presented the idea to John Howitt, a VWS sales representative who convinced his firm to authorize such promotions. By 1988, Fulmer was running FDCs all over the country with cooperation from local dealers, and other sewing machine manufacturers were copying the VWS format.

Factory-direct-to-consumer warehouse sales have been and continue to be a heated and controversial issue in the sewing machine industry. Many dealers view the practice as predatory while others have profited greatly. Small dealers with nonexclusive franchises run the risk of outside dealers invading their areas and making the "easy" sales through FDCs, leaving the local shops to cope with after-sale problems. Medium-to-large sewing machine dealers see FDCs as a means of competing with off-price retailers, factory outlets or malls, and large supermarket-type appliance dealers.

Note: By J. B. Wilkinson, Youngstown State University, and Gary B. Frank, University of Akron, with thanks to Bob Barnes of Barnes Sewing Center in Akron, Ohio, for his cooperation in the field research for this case. Originally presented at a workshop of the Decision Sciences Institute, November 1990. This case was written solely for the purpose of stimulating student discussion. All individuals and incidents are real, but names have been disguised at the organization's request.

The Independent Sewing Machine Dealers Association (ISMDA) has taken a stand against the practice and has been seeking dealer support for a legal fund to pursue trial cases against dealers who run FDCs outside their own dealer territories. To this end, ISMDA has sponsored a number of full page advocacy ads in the industry's trade journal (*Round Bobbin*) stating the association's objections to FDCs and other types of off-premise sales by dealers outside their dealer territories (Exhibit 3.4.1). Typical of the FDCs that ISMDA objects to are the "motel sales" mounted by several large sewing machine dealers across the United States. Such sales are usually advertised in the local newspaper and held in a motel room for a day. Advertised products may or may not be immediately available to buyers depending on whether a truck with sufficient inventory is parked nearby.

ISMDA objects to off-premise sales done by dealers outside their dealer territories on two basic grounds: (1) they represent an unfair method of competition and (2) they often rely on practices that are deceptive to consumers. ISMDA contends that dealers who conduct FDC sales outside their own territories are invaders, "poaching" customers away from local dealers who cannot match the low prices which are advertised for selected brands and models. FDCs and motel sales can occur at any time and dealers have little if any warning that such a sale is about to occur in their territory. The first indication that a dealer may have of an upcoming FDC or motel sale is when the advertisement appears in the local newspaper. By then it is too late for any local dealer to retaliate.

Local dealers are faced with a number of frustrations. First, they are unable to offer loss leader prices on all brands and models on an everyday basis and unable to predict which brands and models might be the target of an FDC or motel sale. As a result, they are usually caught off-guard when such a sale occurs. Second, they are left with the after-sale service problems on the products which are sold to local customers at such sales. Their contracts with manufacturers require them to perform after-sale service on manufacturers' branded products for customers who reside in their market area. Products sold by FDCs or motel sales have a higher incidence of problems, since they are not checked or tested before delivery. Dealing with irate customers after such a sale creates a number of problems for local dealers, including loss of brand and dealer credibility if product problems cannot be resolved.

FDCs and motel sales also create opportunities for deceptive practices. For example, bait-and-switch is common. Sewing machine models which lack a feature that most sewers desire (e.g., "free arm") are advertised at a very low price. Because shoppers are not familiar with sewing machines by model number, they are drawn to the sale by the loss leader price on what looks to be a desirable machine model. At the sale, they are persuaded to buy a different model at a price which provides a healthy profit margin to the sponsor of the sale.

Another problem which often occurs is product unavailability. The products, purchased from a nonlocal source, may never be delivered, and buyers have no readily available recourse. Buyers also have no recourse if the products have been verbally misrepresented. Sale sponsor and salespeople are from "out of town" and are thus difficult to confront.

Despite these very serious objections, ISMDA has had little impact on off-premise sales done by dealers outside their territories. Large dealers and U.S. manufacturers have not been supportive. Some large dealers have even started to sell through toll-free 800 telephone numbers.

Cironi's Viking-White FDC

The initial proposal to sponsor a Viking-White factory warehouse sale was presented to Tony early in Spring 1988 by a VWS sales representative. Tony's immediate reaction was negative, but his subsequent investigation of other dealers' experiences caused him to decide in favor of the VWS proposal.

Tony's opportunity to observe a factory-direct-to-consumer warehouse sale firsthand was provided by Joe Fulmer, the dealer who had initiated FDCs in the sewing machine industry. Fulmer's FDC was conducted May 18–21, 1988, and Tony drove down to Dayton for the event. Based on observation of sales and his knowledge of dealer costs, Tony figured that Fulmer had to have cleared, *as a minimum,* \$30,000 profit on approximately \$120,000 in sales. As Tony observed to his wife afterward:

> That's pretty good for only several days' work! And the people who bought at that sale will be back to buy attachments, sewing accessories, cabinets and other stuff!

In the end, the factor that loomed largest in Tony's mind was the possibility of a local competitor running a Viking-White FDC in his area—Akron, Ohio. He had added the Viking and White brands of sewing machines 6 months earlier, but his sales of those brands were disappointing. His share of Viking-White area sales was only 15 percent despite the fact that Cironi's Sewing Center was the largest (44 percent share of Akron area sewing machine sales) and fastest-growing sewing machine dealer in the Akron area.

Tony's addition of the Viking and White brands was part of a major strategic shift in the positioning of Cironi's Sewing Center. In searching for ways to expand volume, Tony had rejected the route taken by other independent sewing dealers, who had diversified into new merchandise areas including small appliances, ceiling fans, electronics, and stereo equipment. Instead, Tony had decided to position the store as a "category killer." He had seen the success other specialty retailers, such as Toys "R" Us, had when they focused on providing the entire range of available merchandise in a category. Tony had decided that he would make Cironi's Sewing Center the area superstore for sewing machines.

Part of Tony's problem was that VWS followed an intensive distribution policy. As a result, most sewing machine dealers in the Akron area carried the Viking and White brands, advertised them extensively, and offered frequent price reductions. In fact, the Akron market was considered to be highly price-competitive and overstored for sewing machines, primarily because the Singer brand was carried by all eight independent sewing machine dealers in the area, by Jo Ann Fabrics (a chain of fabric stores with four stores in the Akron area), and by Sears, Montgomery Ward, Zayre, and Best Products.

However, positioned as a category killer, Tony carried many additional brands of sewing machines (Baby Lock, Bernina, Pfaff, Elna, Singer, and Necchi), and several of these brands (e.g., Bernina, Pfaff, and Elna) were distributed by him under exclusive territorial franchise agreements. Many local consumers were unfamiliar with these high-quality, high-priced European machines. However, shoppers who came into Cironi's Sewing Center to compare prices, model availability, and dealer assurances on well-known, inexpensive, lower-margin brands such as Viking-White or Singer often changed their minds and actually purchased a higher-priced Bernina, Pfaff, or Elna sewing machine. As a result, Tony consistently achieved a higher gross margin (40 percent) than other sewing machine dealers in the area, who struggled for gross margins of 30 to 35 percent.

Another factor contributing to Tony's impressive growth in sales—45 percent increase in dollar sales in 1988—was a heavy advertising and promotion campaign. This campaign had several components. Tony bought a quarter page color ad in the yellow pages, 100 percent larger than the nearest competitors' ads, which were black and white. He advertised frequently in the metropolitan newspaper and in several suburban papers. Over a period of several years he had developed a computerized database of sewing customers which was used for direct mailings of sales promotions. Finally, on a quarterly basis he included a discount coupon in a coupon book that was widely distributed by mail throughout the region.

In combination, the new sewing machine franchises and heavy promotion had spurred Cironi's unusual growth in a mature market. Tony's trading area expanded from local to regional. The added sewing machine lines had also opened up new markets. For example, Tony had been successful in winning major contracts for industrial sewing machines in two school districts—a success that was directly attributable to having exclusive territorial franchises for Bernina and Elna machines. The addition of these higher-priced brands had fueled Tony's spectacular sales growth and market share performance. Their high prices acted to boost sales revenue, and their quality attracted shoppers from all over Northeast Ohio.

Yet, regardless of his strength in the premier brands, Tony was well aware of the need to establish himself as a Viking-White full-service dealer. Viking-White Sewing had high brand loyalty in the Akron area, and failure to carry the Viking and White brands would weaken his reputation as a full-line, full-service sewing center. But if a competitor ran a factory-direct-to-consumer warehouse sale for VWS, Tony's sales of Viking and White machines would be a "big zero" for the year, and he might even lose his franchise.

In the end, and in Tony's words:

> What the heck! I'll run the VWS FDC. Even if I break even, at least I will have protected my territory. As it stands now, some dealer in California might agree to sponsor a FDC with VWS *in my territory*! I can't allow that to happen. Competition is tough enough as it is!

Planning the Viking-White FDC warehouse sale was surprisingly simple. The VWS sales representative provided directions for time, location, promotion, and managing the event. Tony followed the recommended format and came up with the following plan:

Time. October 20–23, 1988.

Location. A commercial warehouse located on the opposite side of town, 10 miles away from Tony's store. Rental was $1000 for 2400 square feet of warehouse space for the period from October 18 to October 25, 1988 (2 days prior to sale, 4 sale days, and 2 days after sale).

Product. Ninety percent of the White and Viking product lines (twenty models). VWS was to supply 1000 machines on consignment; all shipping costs paid by the manufacturer. Sixty sewing machine cabinets from a cabinet company; all shipping costs paid by the dealer.

Price. Price leaders at near dealer cost (5 percent markup on retail) for Viking ($198), Sergers ($278), and White ($78)

Exhibit 3.4.1
ISMDA advocacy advertisement: Round Bobbin, *July 1990, p. 33.*

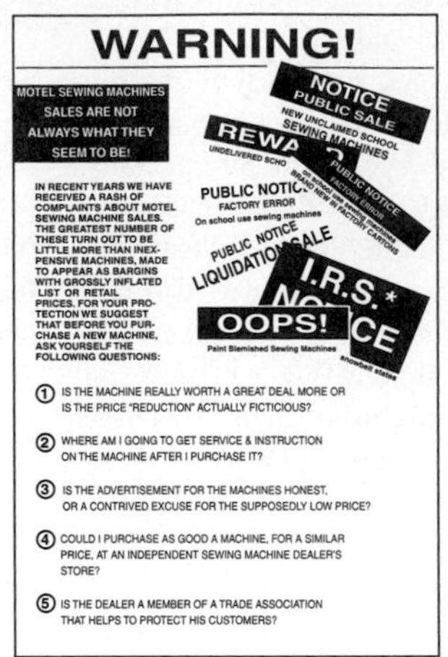

models prominently featured in advertisement. Average markup on retail of 40 percent on remainder (as opposed to 44 percent usual initial markup on retail). Markup of 20 percent on retail for cabinets (as opposed to 50 to 60 percent normal markup).

Advertising. Wednesday full-page, two-side, newspaper insert (Exhibits 3.4.2 and 3.4.3), Friday quarter-page ad, and Sunday quarter-page ad (Exhibit 3.4.4), for cost of $12,000, $2500, and $3500, respectively.

Sales. Five salespeople (area dealers) paid on commission (5 percent on sales) plus room and board ($40 per day each). VWS sales representative furnished by the manufacturer.

Evaluation of the Sale

Throughout the sale, Tony kept meticulous daily records of unit and dollar sales, shopper counts, and purchases (Exhibit 3.4.5). After the sale, he assessed the outcome as best he could (Exhibit 3.4.6), filed all the material related to the sale, and said to himself:

> This is crazy! I work myself into a frenzy over this sale, and what happens? I sell 278 machines and 22 cabinets for a grand total of $91,000. Cost of the merchandise alone was $56,550 for the machines and $3,200 for the cabinets—not to mention the shipping costs. I had to return most of the cabinets so my shipping cost for those suckers was $1,000! About the only reasonable cost in the whole mess was the telephone charges—only $150 for temporary phone installation and use during the sale.

Tony's problems didn't end when the sale was over. As he put it:

> I've had a steady stream of after-sale problems—people opening up cartons and finding the wrong machine inside, breaking machines in the setup process, or simply demanding service on a perfectly O.K. machine. And the lessons have been a real headache! More than 200 people so far have requested the free lessons that were part of the deal. At $5 to $6 an hour for two hours of instruction per class, with five to ten people in a class, I've spent at least $400 on those lessons.

The thing that really left a bad taste in Tony's mouth was the "repack" incident. (A "repack" is a product that has been returned to a manufacturer, repaired if necessary, and repackaged for sale as a new product.) When Tony examined a White overlock machine returned by a customer who had bought the machine on the first day of the sale, he found that the machine was filthy and definitely did not work properly. "Thank goodness," he said, "I was able to satisfy the customer with a new machine and identify the other repacks in the warehouse inventory. To think that White would do this to me. I can only hope that no other repacks were sold before I wised up to the situation!"

Singer's FDC Proposal

Shortly after the initial contact from Singer, a factory sales representative met with Tony to explain Singer's format for an FDC warehouse sale. As Tony suspected, Singer's format differed little from that used by VWS. Singer would supply and deliver (without charge) a large number of machines on consignment to the warehouse sale site. A Singer sales representative would be on hand to assist with the sale. However, Tony would have to make all the arrangements for renting the warehouse, advertising the sale, finding area

Exhibit 3.4.2

Newspaper insert for Viking-White warehouse sale (Front)

PUBLIC NOTICE

FACTORY DIRECT SEWING MACHINE

WAREHOUSE SALE

ALL RESIDENTS OF NORTHEAST OHIO HAVE A UNIQUE OPPORTUNITY TO GET THE SEWING MACHINE OF THEIR CHOICE AT A REMARKABLE SAVINGS, DURING THE MILLION DOLLAR FACTORY AUTHORIZED STOCK REDUCTION SALE. MANY PRICES ARE BELOW OUR REGULAR WHOLESALE COST!!!

FREE ARMS-FLAT BEDS-PORTABLES-ZIG-ZAGS
AUTOMATICS-COMPUTERS-OVERLOCKS-CABINETS

—4 DAYS ONLY!!!—

THURS., OCT. 20; FRI., OCT. 21; SAT., OCT. 22; SUN., OCT. 23

9 AM - 9 PM

ONE THOUSAND MACHINES TO CHOOSE FROM. ALL ARE MEW IN FACTORY CARTONS. SOME OPEN STOCK DISPLAY MODELS, AND BUSINESS SCHOOL MACHINES. ALL IN FIRST CLASS OPERATING CONDITION, WITH FULL FACTORY WARRANTY. THIS LOCATION ONLY. HURRY, SOME QUANTITIES LIMITED.

OUR GUARANTEE

We will provide our full line of FREE SERVICES with all machines sold, even at these incredibly low prices.

- **Up to 25-year factory parts warranty**
- **Up to 5 years free service**

Complete training done to assure each individual full satisfaction with their new sewing machine. (Lessons and Service given by **Barnes Sewing Center, State Rd. Shopping Center, Cuyahoga Falls, Ohio**).

SALE HELD AT
VIKING /WHITE WAREHOUSE
3200 GILCHRIST RD.
MOGADORE
(Across from O'Nell's Dist. Center)
EXIT 27 OFF I-76
PHONE 784-5673
LIMITED QUANTITIES

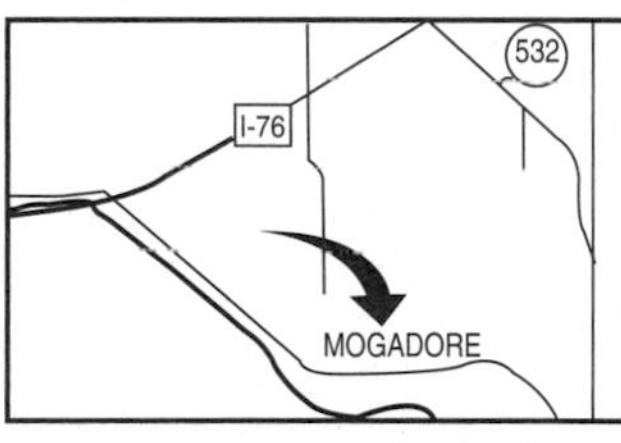

MASTERCARD, VISA, DISCOVER, PERSONAL CHECKS, INSTANT CREDIT & 90 DAYS SAME AS CASH

Exhibit 3.4.3
Newspaper insert for Viking-White warehouse sale (Back)

SAVE!!! SAVE!!! SAVE!!!
WAREHOUSE SALE

ONE THOUSAND SEWING MACHINES TO CHOOSE FROM:

VIKING

• 12 built in stitches including overcast, blind hem, and stretch stitches • Easy button holes (any size) • Automatic tension • 100% jam free • Never needs oiling • All metal construction • Reg. $599

WAREHOUSE PRICE $298

CUT YOUR SEWING TIME IN HALF
VIKING HUSKYLOCK & WHITE SUPERLOCK SERGERS FROM $278

WHITE

• Zig Zag • Two stretch stiches • Manual Buttonhole • Super portable free arm • Only 11 Lbs • Reg. $299

WAREHOUSE PRICE $98

VIKING

• 21 built in stitches • Easy button holes (any size) • Self-adjusting tension • 100% jam free • All metal construction • Never needs oiling • Reg. $899

WAREHOUSE PRICE $498

WHITE

• Sews denim to lingerie • Free arm • Basic stitches • Color coded stitch dials • Drop feed • Lighted sewing area • Reg. $349

WAREHOUSE PRICE $148

PARSONS ALL WOOD CABINETS
TO FIT ANY SEWING MACHINE
50% -70% OFF

One Example Reg. $399 4 Drawer Pecan Model 250

WAREHOUSE PRICE $148

14 Styles To Choose From

VIKING

• Computer regulates speed and provides stitch control • Computerized stitch selection & ability to mirror stiches • 10 stiches of which 8 are turn off on • Easy automatic buttonholes • Push button stitch selector & digital length width display • Self-adjusting tension • Never needs oiling • Jam-proof feeding shuttle • Two lights for maxium visiability • Advance Swedish construction • Every thing you need for easy enjoyale sewing • For hundreds of dollars less than any other sewing machine in this class • Reg. $1099

WAREHOUSE PRICE $698

WHITE

One dial stitch selection • Zig Zag • Overcast • Stretch stitches • Blind hem • Built-in buttonholer • Darns • Embroiders • Sews on buttons & much more • Reg. $479

WAREHOUSE PRICE $188

ALL MODELS SPECIALLY PRICED FOR THIS EVENT!

4 DAYS ONLY

ALL MODELS SPECIALLY PRICED FOR THIS EVENT!

THURS., OCT. 20; FRI., OCT. 21; SAT., OCT. 22; SUN. OCT. 23

9 AM – 9 PM

INSTANT CREDIT & 90 DAYS SAME AS CASH

EXHIBIT 3.4.4

Quarter-page advertisement for Viking-White warehouse sale

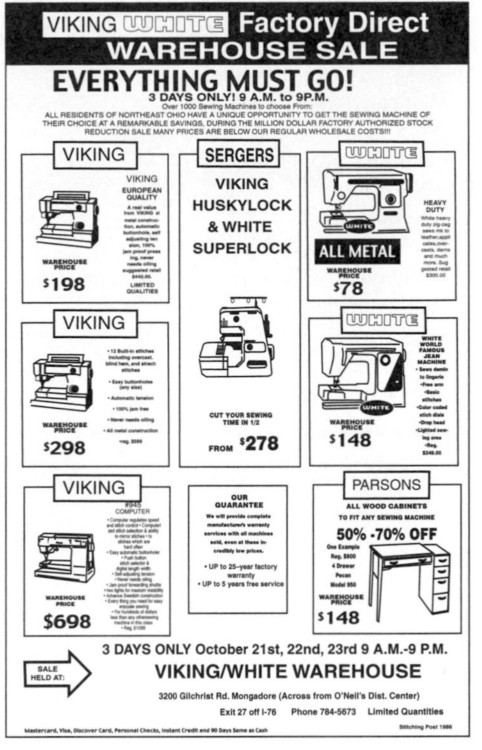

EXHIBIT 3.4.5

Per day sewing machine sales and traffic estimates for the Viking-White FDC

Day	*Dollar Sales*	*Unit Sales*	*Customer Traffic*
Thursday, Oct. 20	$39,150	165	420
Friday, Oct. 21	23,490	70	270
Saturday, Oct. 22	17,660	50	150
Sunday, Oct. 23	6,700	15	60
Total	$87,000	300	900

dealers who were willing to work the sale on commission, setting up and dismantling the sale, and so forth. Fixed costs for warehouse rent, advertising, telephone, and sales expense would be the same as for the VWS FDC. The FDC would be scheduled for September or October, 1989, depending on warehouse and dealer availability.

Once again, Tony faced a dilemma. If he did not agree to do the Singer FDC, someone else probably would. The Singer brand accounted for close to 45 percent of all sewing machine sales in the Akron area ($960,000 in 1988, excluding mass merchandisers' house brands). Singer was distributed by all local sewing machine dealers. Competition was fierce; dealer margins for Singer were the lowest in the industry (25 percent compared to 30 percent for Necchi, 37 percent for Viking-

Exhibit 3.4.6

Sales, expenses and profit, Viking-White FDC, October 20–23, 1988

	Sewing Machines		Cabinets	
Sales		$87,000	$4,000	
Cost of sales		56,550	3,200	
Gross margin		$30,450	$ 800	
Combined gross margin				$31,250
Expenses:				
Warehouse rent	$ 1,000			
Advertising	18,000			
Telephone	150			
Shipping (cabinets)	1,000			
Sales commission	4,550			
Sales expense	800			
Total				25,500
Profit				$ 5,750*

* Excludes after-sale service costs.

Exhibit 3.4.7

Dollar sales by brand, June 1988–May 1989

Month	Baby Lock	Bernina	Elna	Pfaff	Necchi	Singer	Viking White
1988							
June	$3,695	$ 8,180	$ 965	$ 8,758	$1,180	$ 299	$ 1,270
July	5,293	12,400	1,250	3,950	1,000	1,310	2,800
Aug	4,958	14,560	1,400	11,400	2,026	3,315	965
Sept	2,395	11,500	1,350	11,833	395	290	2,750
Oct	3,550	7,950	680	4,800	750	500	87,770*
Nov	5,620	11,855	1,100	14,459	580	1,650	7,848
Dec	2,605	31,500	1,850	15,980	600	2,680	4,900
1989							
Jan	6,391	14,800	1,680	9,850	650	420	1,700
Feb	9,706	10,880	575	3,800	648	800	4,500
Mar	10,283	17,295	2,950	8,850	1,005	1,775	5,260
Apr	5,882	12,980	1,100	13,640	720	1,920	1,800
May	4,867	16,268	2,350	5,950	817	650	4,700

Total store sales, June 1988–May 1989 = $431,176

* Includes factory warehouse sales

White or Elna, and 45 percent for Bernina or Pfaff). Moreover, Cironi's Sewing Center accounted for only 5 percent of all 1988 Singer sales in the Akron area.

Factors influencing whether or not to do a Singer FDC clearly differed from those that went into making the Viking-White decision. Cironi's Sewing Center had held nearly a 15 percent share of Viking-White's 12 percent share of Akron area sewing machine sales prior to the VWS warehouse sale. Even though the VWS warehouse sale had been disappointing, Tony still considered the Viking and White brands to be essential to the merchandise offering of a full-service sewing machine dealer. VWS actively supported full-service sewing machine dealers through innovative merchandise/promotion programs designed to improve dealer sales and profit performance. In return, sewing machine dealers felt a commitment to the Viking and White brands.

Conversely, Singer seemed to be following price and distribution policies which were detrimental to the survival of full-service dealers. For example, Singer's decision to distribute the Singer brand of sewing machines through Sears had seriously hurt independent dealer sales. Independent dealers viewed Singer buyers as notorious price shoppers, and Sears could sell the volume necessary to support low markups. But when a Singer machine needed repair or after-sale service, independent dealers were expected to provide the necessary service *regardless of who sold the machine*. Although Singer reimbursed dealers for services covered under warranty, many dealers viewed this arrangement as a nuisance.

Tony wondered if he should lend his good name and reputation to a Singer warehouse sale. If Singer could not get a reputable local dealer to act as a sponsor and provide after-sale service, potential buyers might be "turned off." It would be more profitable for Tony to sell any other brand of sewing machine to a potential buyer. A successful Singer FDC might cannibalize potential sales of his other brands—brands which had higher profit margins. Following this train of thought, Tony reached for his files, saying to himself:

> I never really examined the issue of cannibalism. Do these factory warehouse sales cannibalize sales of other brands? Did my sales of Viking-White actually increase or merely shift from future time periods to the sale? Did I sacrifice future profits for current sales when I ran that FDC? If so, I'm not going to bite the Singer bait—margins on Singer are bad enough as it is. I could wind up with less profit than I did on the Viking-White deal. If I can't do at least as well as I did on the Viking-White warehouse sale, I shouldn't touch the Singer FDC!

Tony reached for his sales journal. The answer to his concern about cannibalism might be there—in those month-to-month dollar sales by brand (Exhibit 3.4.7). If the Viking-White warehouse sale had adverse effects on overall sales and profits, chances are that a Singer FDC would be the same—*or worse!*

part

IV

Channel Mesosystem

chapter 11 Transaction Costs and Vertical Marketing Systems 356

chapter 12 Franchising in the Global Economy 384

chapter 13 Developing Long-Term Value 414

chapter 14 Strategic Partnering Agreements 438

chapter

11

Transaction Costs and Vertical Marketing Systems

Learning Objectives

After reading this chapter, you should be able to:

- Explain why transaction cost economics (TCE) provides a more realistic account of the economics of exchange than does a production orientation.
- Discuss how resource scarcity affects transaction flows.
- Understand how transaction costs impact channel members' *market* versus *hierarchy* decision.
- Discuss why channel structures are best designed one "building block" at a time.
- Describe the parameters associated with the vertical integration decision.
- Understand when a corporate, administered, or contractual vertical marketing system should be used.
- Describe when a business organization should or should not vertically integrate.

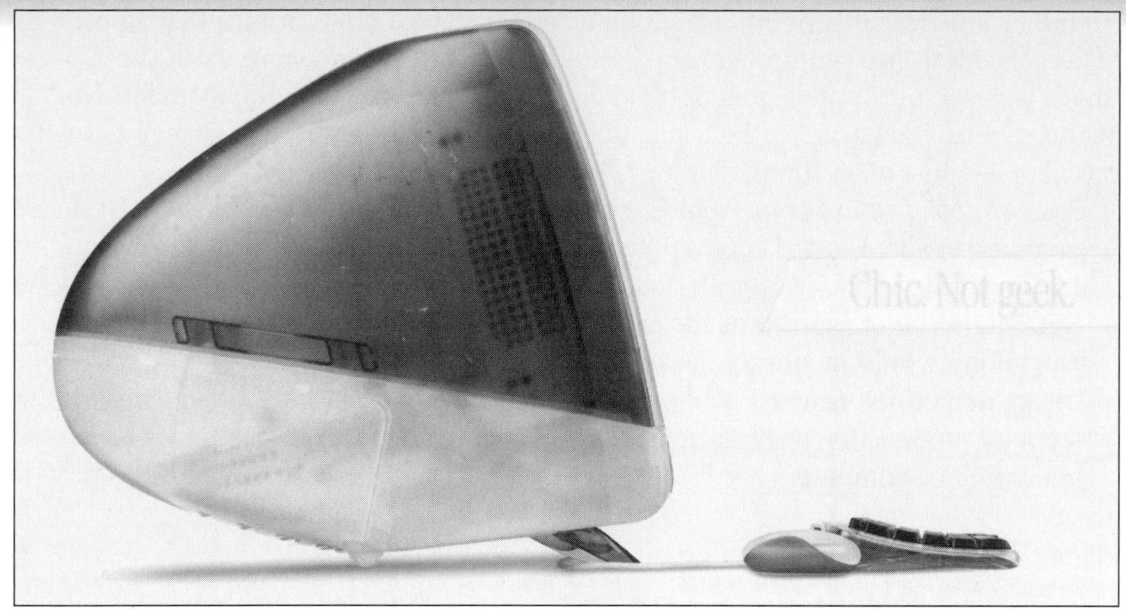

An exchange process is the mechanism that joins together channel members. This connection allows resources to be pooled and mutual risks to be jointly assessed as the channel members attempt to achieve mutually agreed-upon (collective) goals. Sometimes these exchange processes can be controlled. Desirable outcomes usually occur as a result of that control. The extremely successful performance of Dell Computers illustrates how control over exchange processes in the personal computer industry can yield fundamental competitive advantages. Dell's primary distribution strategy, which focuses on minimizing inventory and bringing products to market quickly, has enabled it to increase market share and achieve high returns on investment.[1]

At other times, exchange processes cannot be controlled and the results are usually less than what companies would hope for. Consider, for example, the 1997 experiences of R. J. Reynolds Tobacco Co. (RJR). The firm introduced an unconventional brand called Eclipse (e.g., a cigarette with less second-hand smoke, no lingering odors, no ashes) through conventional channels. The new brand basically got smoked. By that, we mean that very few smokers tried Eclipse, apparently because RJR was unable to exercise its traditional control over how the brand was distributed. RJR recently relaunched the brand, this time through channels (e.g., direct mail and internet sales in a limited number of states) over which it can exercise control.[2] In an uncertain environment (which describes the tobacco industry), the cornerstone for continuity in these exchange processes follows from the fact that all exchange results from the exchange partners' mutually- agreed-upon goal-seeking behaviors.[3]

To further illustrate this point, let's examine the exchange relationships that Apple Computer has developed with other firms (see Exhibit 11.1). The continuity of these exchanges is based on Apple's goal of building market share in the highly competitive personal computer industry. For exchange to occur in this market, each exchange partner–in this case Apple–must meet four conditions. They must:

1. **Possess goal preferences.** Apple's goal is to introduce the Power Mac G4 System to gain market share in the personal computer market. The Power Mac is jointly developed by Apple, Motorola, and IBM.[4]
2. **Anticipate the outcomes of the exchange.** Apple anticipated that its improved technology would increase sales of its PC Mac.
3. **Direct its actions toward goal preferences.** Apple entered into agreements with major software producers like Microsoft to develop software applications for its new generation of computers.

Exhibit 11.1

Conditions for exchange continuity

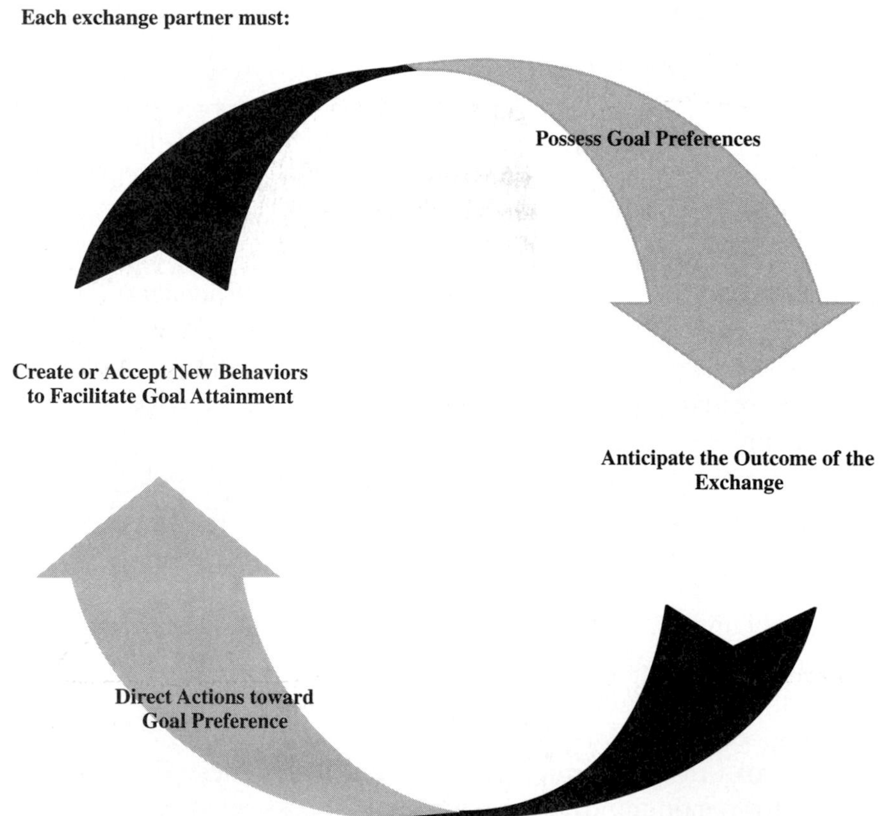

4. **Create or accept new behaviors to facilitate goal attainment.** Apple entered into an unprecedented alliance with its traditional rival, IBM, to advance its market position. IBM acted based on a similar premise.

* * * *

The ways in which these four conditions are met will, of course, differ across exchange partners. One may also assume that each channel member will receive different *value* from participating in the exchange. Exchange value represents a quantifiable assessment of the costs and benefits derived from the exchange *offering* (e.g., the product or service) and the exchange *process* itself.

The costs that channel members incur in their efforts to maximize exchange value are called **opportunity costs**. These are the resources that a firm must surrender to gain something else. All people must constantly deal with opportunity costs in their own lives. You are choosing, voluntarily, to read this sentence right now, when you have other activities you could be pursuing. And yet you have chosen to bear the costs in time, effort, and forgone opportunities to pursue more entertaining activities because you believe that the value you gain through reading this chapter will eventually compensate for the cost of what you are giving up. By the way, we appreciate your reasoning.

Firms go through essentially the same process. Like you, many firms consciously try to *avoid* opportunity costs. As cost avoiders, firms constantly strive to minimize the costs associated with any marketing exchange process. The possibility of avoiding some or all of the costs associated with performance of indispensable channel functions—by either farming them out to someone else or performing the function in-house—is the primary impetus underlying the formation of marketing channels. According to Ronald Coase, the purpose is to minimize the costs of engaging in exchanges with other firms or individuals.[5] You can read about cost avoidance in Channel Surfing 11.1.

Transaction Cost Analysis

Transaction costs are all the expenses resulting from negotiating, monitoring, and enforcing activities that are necessary for a firm to accomplish its distribution tasks through exchange. Transaction costs also involve the cost of arranging, monitoring, and enforcing contracts.[6] Transaction costs can be contrasted with production costs, which are the costs associated with executing a contract. Some transactions occur *outside* the firm channel, in the market setting. For example, Dallas-based Texas Instruments, Inc. (TI) distributes its electronic data interchange (EDI) technology *outside* the firm. The new technology, called EDI Gateway, allows computers to more efficiently transfer information between companies. TI elected to share this proprietary technology with Advantis, a technology partnership formed by IBM and Sears. By choosing an outside channel, TI linked itself with one of the major users of EDI—Sears. TI also capitalized on IBM's established EDI customer base. This decision made a lot of sense. TI chose to minimize its costs and engage in exchange with other parties to fulfill its goals.

Other transactions can occur *within* the firm (a hierarchy).[7] Traditional economic theory

Channel Surfing 11.1

Today's Successful e-Businesses Are Moving beyond Cost Avoidance

Successful e-businesses understand that staying competitive in rapidly changing markets requires innovative thinking and the ability to shift website distribution strategies in a purposeful, customer-oriented fashion. When it first began business, eBay took a lot of hits in terms of outages and questionable selling practices. But they responded quickly and revamped their focus, and have since become very successful. Many of eBay's e-business peers are learning that success usually smiles on those who make customer service a priority and how that generally requires having a distribution system that can transform in response to changing market demands. Today, eBay does.

Even during this early stage of e-evolution, certain facts of distribution life have become clear. To be competitive in the real world, e-businesses should offer multiple channels to their customers. The winning strategy—it seems—is usually a multichannel one. What's up with that? Wasn't the whole notion underlying the idea of being a dot-com trying to avoid such distribution costs? Yes it was, but time and experience have suggested that, ultimately, the hybrid model of "clicks and bricks" still seems to offer the winning hand. What you learned in Marketing (or Marketing Channels) 101 still applies.

By working more cooperatively with their distributors, astute dot-coms have moved beyond the simple notion of attempting to avoid distribution costs that someone, though hopefully not a customer, was going to have to bear anyway. By working hand-in-hand, Web-based supplying and distributing firms have moved into a realm similar to more traditional manufacturing-distributor cost-reduction practices. It is no longer strictly a case of adhering to an "I'll get mine, you get yours however you can" business philosophy. Quite the contrary is true, in fact. Today's more sophisticated e-managers are seeking distributor relationships that feature enhanced traditional manufacturing cost-reduction strategies such as value analysis and materials handling standardization. The long-term successes of these integrative cost avoidance strategies will rest primarily on the twin pillars of trust and communication.

Points to Ponder

- Why is trusted communication necessary for these new channels orientations to work effectively? What would likely happen if such trust were missing?

Source: Adapted from Porter, Anne Millen (1994), "Beyond Cost Avoidance," *Purchasing,* 117 (8), 11–12; and Richardson, Helen L. (198), "Customer Service Drives Warehouse Choices," *Transportation and Distribution,* 39 (12), 59–64.

suggests that firms should continue to expand (within the hierarchy) until the marginal cost of an extra transaction is greater than the cost of a market transaction.[8] Markets and hierarchies represent the extremes on a continuum of exchange. In between these extremes are hybrid exchange types that are neither wholly market nor wholly hierarchical. Examples of hybrid exchange types are franchise systems and buying groups. This continuum is illustrated in Exhibit 11.2.

Transaction costs occur whenever firms transfer title of economic assets and enforce their exclusive rights to those assets. In a general sense, transaction costs are simply opportunity costs with both fixed and variable components.[9] For example, TI's research and production facilities are fixed costs. Those costs will be incurred by TI regardless of EDI Gateway's success or failure in the market. The sales and marketing efforts associated with EDI Gateway, on the other hand, are variable costs.

Whether a given transaction can be completed at a lower cost through the market or within the firm is perhaps the most important economic decision channel members face. This

Exhibit 11.2

The continuum of exchange

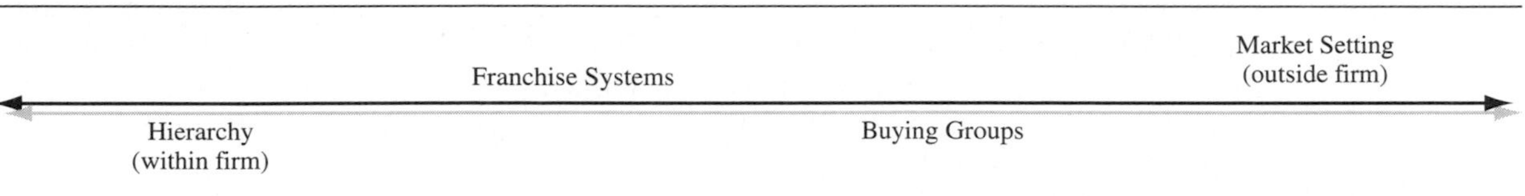

decision is made via **transaction cost analysis** (TCA), which states that firms should pursue the most efficient channel arrangements based on cost avoidance.[10] In channels management, this process is also known as a "make" (i.e., within the firm) or "buy" (i.e., through the market) decision. When the cost of exchange is higher through the market, firms gain economic advantage by internalizing transactions. Measurement costs influence the market versus hierarchy decision.

Internal versus External Transactions

How do transaction costs relate to channels structure or design?

Oliver Williamson, the father of transaction cost economies, suggests that three conditions must be present for firms to choose hierarchy over market:[11]

- A high level of environmental uncertainty should exist in the transaction cost assessment.
- The assets involved should be highly specialized and unique to the exchange process.
- The transaction should occur frequently.

Others, however, believe that the existence of a distribution pipeline is necessary for many large-scale organizations. Proprietary distribution channels are valued resources that have often proven attractive to potential exchange partners. Having a portfolio of inside and outside projects allows channel members to take full advantage of their distribution system.

Transaction cost analysis addresses the choice between hierarchy and market only in the most general sense of choosing a channel design where, say, a manufacturer performs all distribution tasks for itself through vertical integration as opposed to using one or more intermediaries to perform some or most distribution tasks. These extremes can be illustrated by reviewing the experiences of two well-known American firms, Sherwin-Williams Company and Curtis Mathes.

Sherwin Williams's Hierarchical Channel Structure. Sherwin Williams's current stature as the largest paint producer in the United States may be due to its ability to internalize transactions. The Ohio-based company built the nation's largest paint distribution channel *within* the firm (hierarchy), allowing it to function as both a producer and retailer of paint products.[12] In other words, Sherwin-Williams vertically integrated its operations.

The hierarchy channel structure allows Sherwin-Williams greater control over how its offerings are retailed. Its store personnel exclusively promote the Sherwin-Williams line and are given extensive product training to support their sales efforts. Sherwin-Williams thus ensures that its internal channel members highlight each product's principal selling points. Sherwin-Williams never directly faces lower-price, off-brand alternatives in its own stores. In addition, price-clipping practices that dominate at building supply mega-discounters such as Home Depot or Builders Square are avoided. Sherwin-Williams also maintains control over its product and pricing information rather than letting this information fall into the hands of potential competitors. Because of the hierarchy, the paint manufacturer is better able to monitor and enforce each retail unit's performance.[13]

When the opportunity for market expansion arises, Sherwin-Williams always rejects the idea of distributing through outside retail outlets. Instead, Sherwin-Williams acquires retail chains that already sell paint products. With this in mind, Sherwin-Williams recently bought Old Quaker Paint Company, a California-based chain of home improvement and building supply stores, converting the stores to the Sherwin-Williams brand.

By maintaining control of the entire channel, Sherwin-Williams has consistently outpaced the competition in an otherwise sluggish building supply sector. When housing starts drop, the demand for paint and painting supplies also dips. Despite the occasional drop in housing construction, Sherwin-Williams boasts 21 straight years of profitable operations.

Curtis Mathes's Market-Based Channel Structure. Curtis Mathes is a full-line producer of televisions, VCRs, stereos, and other consumer electronic components. Curtis Mathes had sold its products through a network of some 300 namesake retail outlets. Like Sherwin Williams, Curtis Mathes managed to build a sustainable competitive advantage by tightly controlling the company's retail distribution. Curtis Mathes has long been perceived as a high-quality producer that provided outstanding customer service and after-sales support.

But over time this differential advantage actually led to a problem for Curtis Mathes. Several years ago, Curtis Mathes realized that rapidly growing demand for its products could no longer be accommodated through company-owned outlets. In response, Curtis Mathes grew its channels of distribution by pursuing the market option. The company entered a distribution agreement with the Independent Distributor Association (IDA). Now, IDA retail members also sell Curtis Mathes brand-name products. In fact, Curtis Mathes is still adding several new dealers each month because of this association.[14] As a trade-off, by choosing the market option Curtis Mathes did have to surrender to any channel members control over how its products are merchandised at the retail level, a development which may eventually lead to other problems.

Information: The Core of Transaction Costs

One way or another, channel members' transaction costs always relate to information procurement. **Exchange information** is material knowledge that affects the behaviors, experiences, and/or outcomes associated with an exchange. This information can relate to a wide variety of exchange activities. One can tell a lot about these activities based on where the information originates. For instance, information concerned with production times, cycles, and product specifications usually originates from producers, whereas customer information usually arises from distributors or retailers. There are many types of information costs that channel members must consider. The types of information costs are summarized in Exhibit 11.3.

Exhibit 11.3

Types of information costs

Information Category	*Real World Application*
Commodity and labor inputs	Channel members require information relating to resource availability and price. Sherwin-Williams needs to know the costs of procuring chemical compounds and dyes for paint products.
Market behaviors	Curtis Mathes solicits relevant information about other channel members. Information concerned with new consumer electronics products introduced to the market also proves useful to Curtis Mathes' product planning and distribution decisions.
Pricing information	Pricing policy will have a significant impact on economic forces within any distribution channel. Since pricing directly affects a firm's profitability, information about price changes is essential to any effort to control transaction costs. For example, if Lasting Paint stores plan a major price reduction at the retail level, Sherwin-Williams may need to follow suit.
Monitoring and enforcing agreements	Curtis Mathes spent years establishing a unique brand identity. As a result, the company is particularly concerned about the way the terms of its new dealership agreement are monitored and enforced. By no means does Curtis Mathes want to see standards governing product quality or customer support compromised in its new channel arrangements.

When channel members don't freely exchange information with up- or downstream partners, the ensuing costs may destroy the exchange relationship. For example, French tire giant Groupe Michelin's failure to share exchange information with its dealers nearly crippled the tire producer. Members of Michelin's distribution network were disgruntled over the tire maker's failure to share product and delivery information. Because they were not receiving information, these dealers frequently failed to have products in stock when and where customers wanted them. Michelin's largest U.S. distributor, Sears, reacted by buying more tires from Bridgestone Inc., Goodyear Tire & Rubber Co., and Pirelli SpA—some of Michelin's biggest rivals. At that point, Michelin recognized that to preserve its market leadership it needed to provide more, better, and timelier information to its distributors. Groupe Michelin quickly overcame the problems associated with its poor dissemination of information simply by opening its doors to valued customers. For the first time, Michelin invited outsiders into its formerly closed headquarters. Michelin also installed information systems to link dealer and production facilities. Michelin is still striving to provide material knowledge to improve the exchange value for its customers.[15]

The way that information flows through a distribution channel also imparts exchange value. For instance, a brief spell of dry weather in Europe is likely of little concern to you. But several years back such information seriously impacted the world's commodity markets just because the conditions it implied did not bode well Europe's sugar crop. The same season, a tattered logistics system and lack of fertilizer contributed to a poor Cuban sugar crop. Although Cuba's crop provides only a relatively small portion of the sugar consumed worldwide, problems there still impact supply.

You would think these critical incidents would have a major effect on sugar markets, right? While these conditions did indeed alert commodities brokers to the possibility of a tighter supply, it was actually a rumor that sent prices soaring on commodity exchange markets. The rumor was that the Chinese—generally a resource market for sugar—had purchased 100,000 tons of sugar. A domino effect was unleashed, generating speculation that the Chinese sugar crop was in peril.[16]

The story doesn't end here. In the United States alone nearly 50,000 sugar contracts were transacted that day, more than doubling the average daily volume. Manufacturers of products with sugar as a key ingredient quickly increased their orders to skirt declining supply and higher prices. Wholesale price indices were adjusted to reflect anticipated sugar price hikes. Overnight, consumers began paying higher prices for many food products. See how information can influence transaction costs in the marketplace? And because exchange information is imperfect, transactions costs are often dealt with in less than the efficient manner.

Transaction Cost Analysis: Problems and Limitations

Recall that the focus of transaction cost analysis is the cost of conducting the transactions (exchanges) required for a firm to achieve its distribution tasks. Transaction costs are essentially the sacrifices associated with performing tasks such as gathering information, negotiating, monitoring activities, and a number of other functions. Some exchanges are relatively simple, while others are extraordinarily complicated. The complexity of an exchange might be related to the nature of the product, firm, and/or market involved in the transaction.[17]

The conventional exchange activities surrounding the purchase of a fast-food meal offer a useful illustration. Whataburger is a Texas-based fast-food franchise. When a consumer pulls into a Whataburger drive-thru, the ensuing transaction is fairly routine, right? The consumer makes a selection from the illuminated menu. A voice prompts her for the order and tells her the cost. The customer knows, from experience, to pull up to the window, pay for the food, and receive her order.

However, this transaction may not prove as simple as expected. First-time Whataburger patrons are often surprised to hear, "Cash, credit, or bank debit card?" from the voice at the drive-thru. But regular Whataburger customers know that this franchise system offers three payment options. In this case, the complexity of the exchange depends on the channel members involved. Still, for the typical consumer, a transaction involving a burger, fries, and a soft drink does not require extensive deliberation.

Consider how complex this same transaction is when it is evaluated from the seller's viewpoint. Transaction costs are expended to acquire, operate, and maintain the supplies and equipment needed to complete the customer's order. Labor, training, and food costs are additional resources expended in the exchange. Of course, capital expenditures related to the building and restaurant equipment are incurred. Making the "pay by credit" option available to consumers also introduces new costs into our fast-food transaction.

So there is more to this seemingly simple exchange than meets the eye. Even obtaining meat and potatoes from preapproved vendors has not proven all that simple for Whataburger, where executives have been the focus of a kickback scandal. Company executives allegedly demanded kickbacks from suppliers before they would be placed on a preferred franchisee vendor list. Now, Whataburger franchisees tend to not trust their franchise management. Trust has been violated and once-strong franchisor-franchisee relationships have been diminished.[18] Costs, costs and more costs!

As transactions become more complex, isolating the particular costs and benefits associated with the exchange process becomes more difficult. When transactions involve more than two parties, the difficulty of calculating exchange costs and benefits increases exponentially. The costs and benefits of economic exchange must then be allocated to different channel members at different times, as well.

A host of problems potentially underlie transactions between supplying firms and consuming markets. For this reason, transaction cost analysis is hardly a panacea, plagued as it is by certain limitations. As such, the successful use of TCA requires each channel member to negotiate, monitor, and enforce the aspects of exchange reflected in the acronym BOUNDS: **B**ounded rationality, **O**pportunism, **U**ncertainty, **N**umber of firms, **D**ata impact, and **S**pecificity of assets. Let's examine each of these factors in detail.

Bounded Rationality

Transaction cost analysis operates based on the assumption that individuals and organizations behave rationally. This implies that a spirit of bounded rationality prevails in marketing channels. **Bounded rationality** exists within the systematic decision process that guides each channel member's analysis of transaction costs. This decision process relates directly to the channel member's ability to process information. Bounded rationality presumes that exchange decisions are always governed by economic rationality. But channel members evaluate much more than short-term economics in their channel relationships.

Consider the example of Applied Microsystems, a small software firm that has managed to leap ahead of its much larger competitors for what would seem like a totally irrational reason. Applied Microsystems manufactures software applications that help programmers debug programs in computer microprocessors. Many other, much larger companies—Intel and Microsoft come to mind—market similar emulators at a substantially lower cost than Applied Microsystems. Yet this company has managed to grab a large share of the emulator market.

What gives? Evidently, Applied Microsystems has developed an enviable brand identity with their frog logos, "Rocket Frog" and "Rambo Frog," each of which is prominently positioned in print promotional campaigns. Rocket Frog symbolizes the emulator's fast performance. Rambo Frog epitomizes the emulator's "search and destroy" capabilities. The frogs have helped develop a positive association between Applied Microsystems and its market.

This *technobranding,* as one advertising executive calls it, has more than compensated for the higher discrete costs of Applied Microsystems' emulator. Without question, high tech buyers tend to use rational criteria in their decision making, but many such purchases are ultimately made based on chemistry and/or on having a relationship with the product. That's where the cute frogs jumped in. As we said earlier, quantifying the costs and benefits associated with the exchange process is difficult.

Bounded rationality presupposes that channel members, on both sides of the exchange equation, are constrained by reason. Bounded rationality is based on a concept known as **satisficing**. Satisficing suggests people continually revise their target or goal whenever it falls short of their original aspiration.[19] Channel managers always try to distribute or acquire products and services at the best possible price, delivery, and credit terms. The key phrase here, of course, is *best possible,* because optimal outcomes often lie beyond one's reach. To complicate matters further, individuals faced with the same constraints often make different decisions.

Opportunism

The possibility that one or both channel members will behave opportunistically is another obstacle blocking the accurate assessment of transactional costs. **Opportunism** refers to a situation where information has been disseminated with the intention of disguising one's true purpose or meaning or otherwise misleading one's exchange partner.[20] When intermediaries control most of the assets involved in a particular transaction, they presumably understand that they are relatively indispensable, at least in the short run. Such intermediaries sometimes behave in ways that are logically consistent with this understanding. For instance, they may demand exchange terms or practices that are heavily skewed toward their self-interests. Such opportunism increases their exchange partners' transaction costs, often to the point where the hierarchy emerges as the preferred distribution option because the hierarchy permits manufacturers or retailers to keep control over key transaction assets in-house.

Transaction cost analysis views opportunism as a likely consequence of exchange. This is one reason why TCA suggests that firms usually should use vertical integration rather than the market when developing channel systems; firms have greater control over opportunistic behavior when their channel functions are performed *inside* rather than *outside* of the organization. But opportunistic behaviors may also occur within firms. For instance, a decision to use employee sales representatives (hierarchy) rather than manufacturer's agents (market) offers no guarantee that opportunistic behaviors will be eliminated or even lessened. Internal salespeople have on occasion been known to act opportunistically.[21]

Opportunism costs are difficult to measure. Seagood Trading Corporation charged that Martin-Brower Company (a food distributor) and Long John Silver's (a fast-food seafood restaurant chain) conspired to keep Seagood from receiving storage and delivery terms similar to the favorable terms Silver's received. Sound fishy? Certainly, Seagood thought so. It claimed that Martin-Brower's agreement with Silver's forced Seagood to bear extraordinary transaction costs, which may have hampered Seagood's ability to compete. Was the distribution agreement between Martin-Brower and Silver's opportunistic? That is a tough question, because one cannot always be certain of the intent of the original distribution agreement.[22]

Other times, however, opportunism is blatant. For example, franchisees sometimes seek out openings in their franchise contract that permit them to procure lower-priced supplies outside the franchise system. By reducing supply costs, franchisees can improve their profitability. Distribution cost savings are often available in the form of merchandise credits. Franchisees may not always record these credits, a practice that results in the overstatement of true supply costs. By recording these transactions at higher costs, franchisee profits appear lower. Since some royalties are tied to profit performance, franchisees can reduce their royalty obligations by misleading their franchisors.

Uncertainty

As you now know, channel members operate in unpredictable environments. Furthermore, exchange costs are often highly speculative or based on imperfect information. As this uncertainty increases, transaction costs become more difficult to estimate.

Environmental uncertainty is especially problematic in high technology industries because of their high research and development costs. As new technologies develop, such as wireless communication devices, channel members vie anew for the most advantageous market positions. Some channel members will be left behind and will perish, others will be repositioned and emerge as new market leaders, and entirely new entrants will join the fray.

Channel members often adopt contingency plans to minimize the dangers of dynamic, uncertain environments. Since channel members can never be sure about the direction or magnitude of changes in their environment, estimating uncertainty costs is a demanding exercise. When environmental uncertainty is relatively high, channel member performance can generally be improved by entering long-term exchange agreements and routinizing transactions.[23] Exhibit 11.4 illustrates how transaction performance generally improves as transaction uncertainty is reduced.

Transaction cost analysis usually prescribes vertical integration (hierarchy) as the best way to deal with market uncertainty, but doing so offers no guarantee. Super communication carriers like AT&T, Qwest, and Teleglobe have consistently attempted to reinvent the business-to-business market by bundling Internet access and vertical integration practices, but have fallen far short of their own expectations.[24] Still, uncertainty remains present even *within* the firm. For instance, hiring people to perform internal channel functions exposes firms to uncertainty about health care costs, disability, and unemployment compensation, as well as the possibility of lawsuits. The costs and risks associated with hiring are higher than ever.[25]

Number of Firms

Some industries have fewer firms than others. Markets with only a few large competitors—known as *oligopolistic markets*—limit transaction costs because of the limited number of exchange alternatives. When the numbers of buyers and sellers are limited, a great deal of dependency develops between buyers and sellers. Conversely, the greater the number of buyers and sellers, the less dependent any one channel member is on another.

The U.S. tobacco industry is an example of an oligopoly. Why is this significant? Because legislative initiatives aimed at curbing domestic smoking do not bode well for the industry. The ranks of U.S. smokers continue to decline. Falling demand for an industry's offering normally leads to a customer-dominated environment (a buyer's market). Not here, though.

By eliminating the transaction costs associated with high levels of competition, the remaining tobacco companies are able to operate in less risky environs. American Tobacco

Exhibit 11.4

Transaction uncertainty and performance

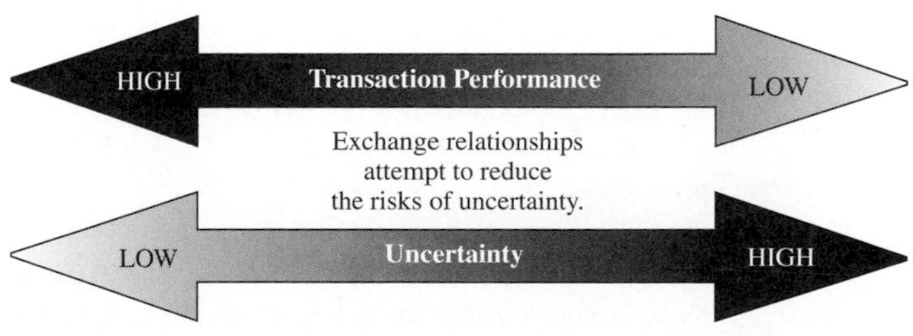

Company was recently acquired by B.A.T. Industries PLC. American Tobacco was among the least powerful U.S. cigarette companies. American Tobacco Company's declining brands—Pall Mall, Lucky Strike, and Tareyton—could no longer compete with Marlboro or Camel. By eliminating a competitor, B.A.T. Industries plans to increase its market position in the global tobacco industry.[26]

Oligopsonistic market structures allow costs and benefits to be dispersed across fewer organizations. As a result, top brands gain even more control over the market. As the number of potential exchange partners decreases within an industry, more control over transaction costs can be expected.

Data Impact

Information, or data, helps *push* products and services through distribution channels. The concept of *data impact* captures the opportunity channel members have to use information to mislead other firms in the market. The impact that information has on any transaction is compounded because one channel member is often more powerful than the others. As we discussed earlier in the chapter, contrary to traditional economic assumptions, channel members never operate under full and perfect information. Some channel members acquire power based solely on their knowledge.

Specificity of Assets

Transaction-specific assets are the tangible and intangible resources that are required to perform a particular distribution task. Several types of transaction-specific assets can come into play in an exchange.[27]

- **Specific site assets.** Specific site assets refer to the strategic positioning of inventory and transportation facilities to minimize logistics costs. For example, United Parcel Service (UPS) strategically locates its distribution centers to minimize transaction costs. Its site selection process is often customized to large customers' needs.
- **Specific human assets.** Specific human assets refer to special labor resources or skills that are tailored to the needs of transaction partners. P&G has customer teams dedicated exclusively to Wal-Mart and Kmart. These customer teams assist in merchandising and store planning. The teams are well trained in each retailer's culture and retailing objectives. In a sense, these teams become part of the retailing institution.
- **Brand capital.** Brand capital assets refer to an exchange partner's willingness to invest in the maintenance of brand or store identity. Nike has established a number of cooperative promotional strategies with its biggest customers. It is not uncommon to see Foot Locker, a major retailer of sport shoes and apparel, tag itself onto Nike advertisements. Both Nike and Foot Locker benefit from jointly promoting the product.
- **Time specificity.** Coordinated production and distribution schedules require hands-on control over inputs and outputs in the channel of distribution. Consider that Coca-Cola's major customers in Japan—Ito Yokado, Daiei supermarkets, and 7-Eleven

convenience stores—all demand predictable deliveries. As such, Coca-Cola had to arrange special distribution schedules to overcome a seemingly insurmountable obstacle: daytime Tokyo traffic.[28]

Each transaction-specific asset has varying levels of value to each channel member involved in the exchange. The value of a transaction-specific asset is known as its **asset specificity.** A distinguishing aspect of transaction-specific assets is that they hold little or no value outside of the explicit exchange between channel members. In other words, many of the resources tied up in the transaction only have asset specificity (value) to that particular channel member. At the same time, the value of the assets decreases once they are removed from the exchange relationship.

Just how important a particular transaction-specific asset is depends on the nature of the exchange. Although we have said that various channel members are likely to value a transaction-specific asset differently, definite patterns can be recognized. The presence of transaction-specific assets infers a commitment by each party to the economic exchange itself.[29] Transaction cost analysis argues that, under conditions of uncertainty, the costs of vertical integration are usually less than the losses from opportunism when a channel member has invested substantially in transaction-specific assets.

Investment in transaction-specific assets by channel members also tends to increase their commitment to the exchange. As a result of this increased interdependence, both parties want to preserve the relationship—meaning neither party wants to risk the relationship by engaging in disruptive or opportunistic behaviors. Sometimes, though, firms seek to avoid an excessive dependency on one transaction while simultaneously attempting to make their exchange partner more dependent on them. Channel members rarely make isolated decisions regarding their transaction options. In reality, they manage a portfolio of exchange relationships. Each exchange in their portfolio features different transaction-specific assets, frequencies of exchange, and environmental uncertainties.[30]

Economic Exchange Relationships

Without question, the trade-off between exchange costs and exchange utilities influences channel relationships. But by now it should also be evident that transaction cost analysis alone is insufficient to successfully manage channel member interactions. Transaction costs provide useful economic *signals,* but fail to fully capture the qualitative aspects of the informal interactions that develop in most channel exchange relationships. Moreover, TCA fails to make any real distinction between short-run and long-run channel concerns. For example, wholesalers have been known to decline the short-term opportunity to carry a hot-selling item when doing so might jeopardize a long-standing relationship with a valued customer.

We examine more about these and other related issues in the second part of this chapter. The first topic we consider is how transaction cost analysis can be used to determine how best to build marketing channels. To introduce this topic, we invite you to recall your childhood experiences with children's building blocks.

Most of you have, at some point in your past, played with Lego-type building blocks (or their equivalent). You likely recall how all those different size and color building blocks could fit together in such logical, creative, and sturdy ways. Whether or not you realized it at the time, you were learning valuable lessons about design and construction, and many of those lessons actually apply to today's reading.

What are those lessons? Well, partly that a lot of cool and unusual configurations can be constructed from some basic building blocks. But what is more important, your recollections should suggest that in the process of building channels, marketing and distribution pieces can (and should) be fitted together in similarly logical, creative, and sturdy ways.

Building Channels

Rather than going it alone in a distribution setting, almost all organizations benefit from properly attaching themselves to one or more partners. When the right channel pieces are selected and correctly aligned, the marketing results can exceed the sum of the parts (that's synergy!). Successful marketing channels are constructed and rebuilt by carefully positioning one relationship-building-block at a time—just like you assembled those Lego-type blocks as a child.

Perhaps now more than ever—given the rise and prominence of Internet-based technology in marketing channels—claims repeatedly arise stating that the intermediary portions of marketing channels are approaching obsolescence. According to these views, either the manufacturing, retailing, or e-business portions of the U.S. economy are poised to assert their dominance by assuming control of most intermediary channel functions. Hardly! Actually, in many industries wholesalers and other intermediaries have grown in strength. And there are few things more critical to today's e-sellers than safely, accurately, and efficiently traversing that last mile to the customer's front door. For that to happen, it is clear that some sort of intermediary must usually become involved.[31]

Because of the position they hold in distribution systems, resellers enjoy a unique opportunity to cluster offerings from many producers. This allows resellers to achieve economies of scale and transaction cost reductions on each sales call or marketing effort. Winning new customers in industrial or consumer markets usually requires multiple sales calls. When the expense of these calls is added to the fixed support costs associated with direct selling and/or distribution efforts, cost differentials between having producers perform the necessary functions and having intermediaries perform them can be compelling.

You may have heard the saying that goes something like this: "*You can eliminate wholesalers, but you cannot eliminate their functions.*" So true! Remember that intermediary functions include those activities necessary to create information, promotion, negotiation, ordering, risk taking, and possession utility. These functions facilitate forward, backward, or reciprocal marketing flows. Someone has to perform these tasks in all channels of distribution. On average, the most important distribution decision faced by a marketing organization is whether it can perform any or all of these functions more efficiently and effectively through the use of intermediaries or through vertical integration. From a producer's perspective, a **vertical integration** decision relates to whether the firm should establish its own sales branches and warehouse facilities or its own retailing units. Similar decisions are also faced by wholesalers and retailers. Here, though, the decision pertains to whether they can perform one or more channel functions more efficiently than other intermediaries and/or producers.

Firms elect to vertically integrate for two primary reasons: the opportunity to achieve cost reduction and the opportunity to attain more control over one's environment or channel.[32] Steel production channels illustrate how vertical integration can reduce costs while increasing environmental control. By integrating blast furnaces, converters, and primary reduction units, the need to reheat between stages is eliminated. Metal handling costs are dramatically reduced as a result. Vertical integration also ensures that the supply of raw materials necessary for production is available when needed. Access to end-user steel markets is also guaranteed. This environmental control offers the vertically integrated producer strategic advantages over competitors.

In most business settings, however, an organization's costs of marketing through intermediaries do not substantially differ from what the firm would spend to receive the same services through its own efforts.[33] Then why do so many firms perform selling and distribution functions themselves through vertical integration? Three considerations come into play. First, the firm must consider the question of *channel efficiency,* which centers on how well the channel design performs. Second, it needs to look at *channel effectiveness,* that is, how well the channel design meshes with the firm's marketing strategy. Finally, firms vertically integrate because they seek more control over their environments.

Vertical Marketing Systems

Recall that a conventional marketing channel involves some combination of independent producer, intermediary, and retailer organizations. In contrast, a **vertical marketing system (VMS)** consists of a producer(s), wholesaler(s), and retailer(s) acting together as a unified system. Vertical marketing systems are nearly as common today as are conventional channels. The features/advantages of vertical marketing systems are listed in Exhibit 11.5 and are discussed below.

In conventional systems, each channel member is a separate business attempting to maximize its own profits. Because individual members act independently, profits for the channel as a whole are frequently lessened. Manufacturers, wholesalers, and retailers generally deal with one another at "arm's length," negotiating aggressively over transaction terms.[34] In VMSs, on the other hand, one channel member either owns the others, franchises the others, or has so much legitimate or contractual power that the other firms cooperate. VMSs are managed channel systems, purposefully designed to achieve operating economies and maximum market impact.

EXHIBIT 11.5

Conventional marketing channels versus vertical marketing systems

Conventional Marketing Channels	*Vertical Marketing Systems*
Independent	Unified
Separate, autonomous members	Linked as a single competitive unit
Aggressive intrachannel negotiations	One clear leader with legitimate or contractual power
Conflict not controlled	Conflict controlled; stable structure and membership
Sometimes fail to see big picture	Channelwide perspective

VMSs originally emerged as a way to control channel member behavior and reduce the conflict that arises when channel members independently pursue their own objectives. Ideally, VMS units operate at near-optimal levels and have stable structures and memberships. Channel member coordination is achieved through the use of plans and comprehensive programs. Members are, in effect, preprogrammed or reprogrammed to achieve certain channel economies. A firm's entry into a VMS is controlled by the system requirements and market demands. Member loyalty is through contractual agreements or ownership.

In vertical marketing systems, entire channel systems are linked together as a single competitive unit, with at least one firm that possesses enough strength relative to other members to organize channel resources. This firm is the channel leader. It maintains channelwide perspective and prompts other channel members to perform the functions that they do best. This

Channel Surfing 11.2

Logical Extensions: Three Types of Vertical Marketing Systems

Administered VMSs are similar to conventional channels in that the participating firms are independently owned and operated. They differ, however, in that the system features highly effective interorganizational management—usually emanating from one dominant firm. One reason that Frito-Lay remains in the chips is that its 10,000+ member store-door delivery system is built to allow its agents to visit each retail outlet, trade out unsold items, and restock shelves with fresh items as often as 55 times per year. You can see how significant transaction cost advantages should accrue to both Frito-Lay, as producer, and its thousands of distributors as a result of their mutual participation in such a system. Regardless of which side of the exchange relationship you occupy, it is nice to know what's happening when!

Contractual VMSs consist of independent firms operating at different channel levels that integrate their distribution agendas on a contractual basis. The type of channel system discussed in the next chapter—franchising—is an enormously popular form of contractual VMS.

A *corporate VMS* exists whenever a firm owns and manages organizations operating at other channel levels. Corporate VMSs also exist whenever a primary marketing function is performed by a single organization across two or more channel levels. Examples of corporate VMSs include Sears, which secures more than 40 percent of the goods it sells from companies it partly or completely owns; Sherwin-Williams, which owns more than 2,000 paint stores; and Giant Foods, a major regional grocery store chain, which operates bottling and bakery facilities to stock stores. Corporate VMSs should lower transaction costs and provide major channel players more control over their value-added streams.

Corporate VMSs can be forward or backward integrated. When a manufacturer owns and operates wholesaling and/or retailing units, it is said to be *forward integrated.* When a retailer or wholesaler owns and operates production facilities, it is said to be *backward integrated.* Hart, Shaffner, and Marx, the well-known men's suit manufacturer is forward integrated. The Limited, which owns its own warehouses, is backward integrated.

Points to Ponder

- What sorts of transaction cost advantages can be wrangled from each type of VMS?
- In your view, which consideration is more important when managing a corporate VMS: control over the way a channel function was performed or control over its cost?

Source: Adapted from Tatge, Mark (2000), "The Harder Side of Sears," *Forbes,* November 13, 282–87; and Wellman, David (2000), "Extreme Indulgence," *Supermarket Business,* 55 (3), 55–58.

directly contrasts with conventional systems, where independent members often assume that their competitive advantages arise strictly from autonomous actions taken at their channel levels. In conventional channels there is often a failure to see the big picture. This is a big mistake. In the face of rising global competition (e.g., Microsoft versus Ashisuto K.K.), intraindustry competition (e.g., Snapple versus Coke), intrachannel competition (e.g., Goodyear selling tires direct to franchisees and to independent garages through tire wholesalers), and channel system competition (e.g., Sears versus Wal-Mart), there is a compelling need to overcome inconsistencies in the actions of channel intermediaries.

Finally, VMSs often provide effective strategic options for organizations struggling in competitive markets. For example, some years back Kodak concluded that it needed to control its own marketing channel to successfully distribute in Japan. On top of the problems following naturally from Japan's multilayered, tightly knit distribution system, Kodak knew that Fuji Photo, its major in-country competitor, already held a 65 percent market share. So the U.S. firm developed its own distribution system by establishing a VMS. Through this system, called Kodak Japan, Ltd., Kodak quickly managed to gain access to some 300,000+ Japanese outlets that sell photographic products.[35]

Henri Poincare said, "Science is built up with facts, as a house is with stones. But a collection of facts is no more a science than a heap of stones is a house."[36] Similarly, each stone (organization) that goes into building a house (VMS) has a different shape and density (configuration and strength). A lasting structure can be constructed only if these disparate parts are effectively fit and mortared together. Once in place, the stones that make up a house have great resilience against threatening environmental forces such as the weather (competition). The resulting edifice reflects the strength of a complete system rather than the limitations of a single stone. Three broad categories of vertical marketing systems exist: administered, contractual, and corporate. Some additional details about each of these three broad systems are provided in Channel Surfing 11.2

When Should Organizations Vertically Integrate?

The decision of whether to develop or continue to use a vertical marketing system usually depends on whether it is more appropriate for the firm to make or buy the performance of one or more of its channel functions.

According to most broadly accepted economic definitions, a vertically integrated firm has common ownership of two or more enterprises, one of which uses as input the output of the other. The purchase of a dairy farm by an ice cream manufacturer, for example, would be vertical integration, because the dairy's output, milk, is used as an input for the production of ice cream. The milk is an intermediate output, and the ice cream is the final product of this production sequence. In this example, apparently, an ice cream producer decided to *make* its own milk rather than *buy* it through other channel arrangements that would be available.

Vertical integration is often pursued in hopes that a firm can increase its profits, but this goal can only be achieved if the vertical integration yields greater efficiency within the channel. Transaction costs, you will recall, are those costs incurred when undertaking any kind of attempt to obtain inputs or distribute outputs within the channel. Transaction costs include the costs of monitoring, information exchange, managerial time, and negotiation that occur,

Channel Surfing 11.3

When Should Firms Vertically Integrate?

A critical question facing many firms is whether and when they should pursue a vertically integrated channel system. Channels experts have identified several conditions that should be in place before pursuing a vertical integration strategy. It appears more appropriate to pursue a vertical integration strategy when:

- Few organizations that perform specific channel functions efficiently are available in a market or when the environment in which a firm operates is highly uncertain.
- Changing to new channel partners would prove extremely costly should existing partners fail to perform as expected.
- The buying decision is complex and/or involves high involvement, or when required customer service levels are high.
- Channel members can potentially free-ride on the efforts of others, or when it is difficult to monitor the activities of outsiders.
- An opportunity exists to gain substantial economies of scale of channel functions or flows.
- The product in question is closely tied to the firm's core business.

But managers should understand that it is not necessary for all these conditions to be satisfied before a vertically integrated channel system represents the best strategic option.

Primarily based on its analysis of these criteria, Anne Klein, an upscale women's apparel manufacturer, has long managed its own separate retail outlets and boutiques within selected department stores. The firm also sends employees to work on the sales floors of larger stores. Anne Klein has found it can extract larger profit margins by controlling distribution and markdown activities. Many other women's clothing makers are now producing and placing their own print advertising, usually because they were unhappy about having to share costs with retailers' store advertising. In each setting, such forward vertical integration provides for more continuity of performance and more control over the promotion and sales functions.

Points to Ponder

- What other conditions should be in place before firms like Anne Klein should opt to "make" rather than "buy" the performance of a particular channel function?

Source: Adapted from Stucky, John, and David White (1993), "When and When Not to Vertically Integrate," *Sloan Management Review,* 34 (Spring), 71–83; and Anonymous (1990), "Can Ms Fashion Bounce Back," *Business Week,* January 16, 64–70.

whether these take place in the channel or inside the firm. Vertical integration will lead to efficiency gains and thus higher profits for an organization only when it costs less to "make" an intermediate output (e.g., the milk in the previous example) than it does to "buy" it on the open market.

There are many occasions in which the pursuit of a vertical integration strategy makes sense. What should be understood, though, is that situations also arise when such a strategy may prove detrimental, as discussed below.

Benefits of Vertical Integration

As noted, a basic reason why organizations seek control over their channels is to ensure suitable levels of profits. Still, a vertically integrated system is unlikely to prove profitable unless the fixed costs of retaining one's own channel can be allocated over a sufficiently large volume of business.[37] As the volume of business flowing through a channel increases, organizations are better able to specialize in the performance of particular functions. Such organizations are able to reap the benefits of economies of scale. Assuming that the firm has adequate power and size, vertical integration has historically been the likely response in channels facing intense competition, resource scarcity, and variable demand.[38] But the make-or-buy decision in channels is complicated and potentially hazardous, and it does not offer any assurance of greater efficiency.

Obviously, shifting the responsibility for channel functions from the market (buying your own) to the firm (making your own) offers no assurance of greater efficiency. Consider Sony, the Japanese electronics manufacturer. Sony purchased Columbia Studios several years ago. The opportunity to achieve significant production and distribution synergies appeared clear. But as the size and complexity of a firm increases, so does the size and complexity of its problems. Such was the case with Sony. This particular exercise in vertical integration is now widely viewed as a failure.

Costs of Vertical Integration

Because vertically integrated systems have a captive source of supply or demand, normal incentives to perform efficiently can be dulled. Managers of newly vertically integrated channel units sometimes pursue goals that are incompatible with corporate goals. Investment in unnecessary overhead is also a common problem.[39] Administered and contractual VMSs result from the combined efforts of independent channel members to limit or bypass the market that exists between them. However, the positive forces associated with open market competition that sharpen channel members' performances no longer exist. Other structural and administrative problems can result from vertical integration. The formation of corporate VMSs often leads to a need for more employees to service the various distribution levels. In turn, this brings higher payrolls, more benefits and, possibly, more union involvement. Certain critics have blamed much of the U.S. auto industry's woes during the 1970s and 1980s on their excessive vertical integration. When deciding to integrate because of apparent short-term rewards, organizations often limit their future ability to strike out in innovative directions.[40] Rather than emerging as synergistic success stories, the payoffs of many vertically integrated channels have proven elusive.[41] Some additional reasons underlying these failures are detailed in Exhibit 11.6.

In the process of emphasizing their distinctive competencies, many companies exploit one competitive advantage. But in a corporate VMS, such focus can actually be a liability. Manufacturers that emphasize low cost, for example, may run their factories efficiently, but find it difficult to be innovative with respect to research and development, design, or marketing functions. Furthermore, manufacturing cultures that support longer, lower-cost production runs may prove incompatible with a marketing emphasis on a wider product line or customized products. Marketers seek these things to better satisfy customer desires. Finally, as firms vertically integrate, they grow larger. Size typically promotes inertia. Inertia, in turn, inhibits communication, innovation, and flexibility. After all, battleships are harder to turn about than are patrol boats.

These arguments suggest vertical integration should be pursued only as an option of last resort. Organizations should make rather than buy only after they have convinced themselves, through rigorous analysis, that channel ownership is necessary. Following this rule of thumb

Exhibit 11.6

Functional areas where synergies in vertically integrated channels have proven hard to obtain

Functional Area	*Watch Out For:*
Channels of distribution	While products and markets may appear similar, distribution channels can differ radically. Even when channels are similar, the end-user markets may differ.
Organizational integration	Highly centralized and highly decentralized organizations do not mix easily within VMSs.
Inventory control	Across the units that comprise a corporate VMS, agreement on the levels, deployment, and ownership of inventory often prove elusive.
Allocation of costs	Cost allocation techniques are a continual source of strife across unit levels.

will discourage unnecessary investment in the distribution function. It is unlikely that all or even the majority of the 10 market conditions that should logically lead to vertical integration will be in place. But this rule hardly precludes pursuit of vertical integration when the proposed system's strengths allow it to exploit the opportunities available in the internal and external environment facing the firm.

Improving Relationships through Traditional Vertical Channel Design

Another new view of the vertical relationship among manufacturers, resellers, and customers also is emerging.[42] This view takes the administration of marketing channels a step beyond simple considerations of "total quality," "customer need satisfaction," or even "exceeding customer expectations." This new view requires that organizations first think of every product as a service. In other words, each organization should look at what the product in question *does,* rather than what it *is*. Once that perspective is adopted, the task of marketing the product to the next channel level becomes only one of the organization's opportunities to do something extra for its customers. The process that results is known as *bundling,* which, as we have discussed in previous chapters, means that a desirable collection of benefits is spliced together to pursue or sustain a preferred customer relationship. Toyota practices bundling with its Lexus automobile. Dealers track every Lexus sold in the United States on a national computer, making each car's maintenance history available to every North American dealer. Toyota goes to this extraordinary length because Lexus is committed to doing everything possible to ensure that its relationship with customers does not end at the showroom door.

Once an organization views a product as a service, there may be a willingness to contract out channel functions that it previously performed. This is known as **unbundling.** IBM, long famous for the intensity of its vertical integration, no longer handles its own warehousing. In the early 1990s, 21 parts warehouses were eliminated in favor of six outside vendors. Commodore business machines went even further. While IBM was divesting its warehouses, Commodore unbundled virtually all of its postsale services for consumer products. Commodore's new channel partner is an innovative division of FedEx called Business Logistics Systems (BLS). FedEx employees staff a 24-hour consumer help line for Commodore. If a customer's computer crashes, FedEx picks it up the morning after you call, and drops off a replacement. Often, FedEx even does the repairs at its Memphis hub. Unless they ask, customers never even know they are dealing with FedEx employees, with the obvious exception of the delivery/pickup person.[43] This sort of collaboration is slowly replacing competition in relationships between many manufacturers and suppliers/resellers. *Integrated relationships* are emerging in some channels, where outsourcing processes are elevated from a simple cost-cutting measure to the level of strategic planning.

In the long run the market will surely not take kindly to channel members that try to take advantage of suppliers or resellers. A far more preferable option is the pursuit of win-win channels, wherein suppliers or resellers receive the benefits of long-term channel relationships. Moreover, end users gain more say over integration processes. In integrated relationships, rather than pitting suppliers (resellers) against one another to achieve the lowest cost, purchasing (distribution) managers work closely with a few select suppliers (resellers) to reduce total cost. More and more companies, including market leaders such as Proctor & Gamble, are electing to pursue this particular approach to managing their channel relationships.

Bundling and integrated relationships require companies to analyze more than the manufacturing or distribution costs they usually focus on. Companies that pursue integrated relationships must instead identify transaction costs—that is, everything above the marginal costs associated with making a product or delivering a service. Transaction costs include inventory costs, technical support costs, managerial and labor overhead costs, and just plain waste. They also include the costs of reaching agreements, ensuring that conditions of exchange are fulfilled (i.e., monitoring costs), and of being vulnerable to opportunistic behavior. Transaction costs occur in every exchange. But excessive transaction costs are most likely to result from the wrong kind of channel design—namely, excessive vertical integration.

Companies that think of the products they make, buy, or sell as services can gain economies along the entire chain of transactions. New products can be conceived when manufacturers think not just about what is being produced but also about how customers use it. Xerox discovered this when it redefined its business as document processing. At General Electric, a continuing series of "town meetings," where employees look for ways to improve processes, expanded to include joint sessions with customers such as Sears. Issues such as whether to share a single system with customers to track purchase orders have been discussed at GE. This has resulted in a new slogan: "GE and its customers—one system, not systems." The slogan captures a key to success in vertical marketing systems. In fact, the credo suggests that GE aspires to a future where GE attaches itself to its customers in ways that are logical and creative—just the same way those Lego® blocks fit together.

Key Terms

asset specificity
bounded rationality
exchange information
exchange process
opportunism
opportunity costs
satisficing
transaction cost analysis

transaction costs
transaction-specific assets
unbundling
vertical integration
vertical marketing system (VMS)

Chapter Summary

Exchange processes can persist indefinitely or until some specified condition is met. The natural course of an exchange is affected by the environmental conditions in which it occurs. Each exchange transaction thus differs from all other transactions. For exchange to occur in marketing channels, each party must possess goal preferences, anticipate the outcomes of the exchange, direct its actions toward goal preferences, and be willing to create or accept new behaviors to facilitate attainment of those goals.

Value is a quantifiable assessment of the costs and benefits jointly derived from the offering and the exchange process itself. Various types of value can be derived from channel exchange. Exchange value and value relationships change over time. This is why exchange inputs are valued relative to how, when, and where they are obtained. Scarcity also affects the costs of goods and services. The demand for products strongly influences the valuation of outputs. The success of channel members depends in no small measure on their ability to prepare for exchange and adapt to unanticipated changes in supply and demand. Channel members can estimate value based on primacy of the exchange, vicarious roletaking, transaction regularity, and subjective probability.

Firms cannot exist without markets, nor can markets exist without firms. Firms and markets thus share a common purpose. The sense of cooperation deriving from this shared purpose implies that each channel member's willingness to assist the other should produce an outcome that neither can attain individually. But channel members also incur opportunity costs—embodied by resources which must be surrendered to gain something else—in their efforts to maximize exchange value. Opportunity costs provide the backbone of a concept known as *transaction cost analysis (TCA)*. TCA suggests that firms should pursue the most cost efficient channel arrangements based on cost avoidance. As avoiders, firms constantly try to minimize the costs of market exchanges.

Transaction costs involve all expenses resulting from the negotiating, monitoring, and enforcing activities that are necessary for firms to accomplish their distribution tasks through exchange. Transaction costs also involve the cost of arranging, monitoring, and enforcing contracts. Transaction costs occur whenever firms transfer title of economic assets and enforce their exclusive rights to those assets. In a general sense, transaction costs are simply opportunity costs that feature both fixed and variable components.

Firms can seek to build relationships and channel transactions outside the firm, that is, in the market setting. Transactions can also occur within the firm, that is, within the hierarchy. According to traditional economic theory, firms should expand internally until the marginal cost of an extra transaction outweighs the cost of market exchange. TCA relates to channel design decisions in those circumstances where, for example, a manufacturer performs all distribution tasks for itself through vertical integration as opposed to using one or more intermediaries to perform some or most distribution tasks.

Three conditions must be present for firms to choose hierarchy over market: (1) a high level of environmental uncertainty must exist in the transaction cost assessment; (2) the assets involved must be highly specialized and unique to the exchange process; and (3) the transaction must occur frequently.

Either directly or indirectly, channel members' transaction costs always relate to information procurement. Exchange information is material knowledge that affects the behaviors, experiences, and outcomes associated with an exchange. The types of information costs that channel members must account for include commodity and labor inputs, market behavior costs, pricing data, monitoring and enforcement agreements, and costs relating to efforts aimed at protecting property rights.

Transaction cost analysis hardly offers channel members a panacea, plagued as it is by certain limitations. These limitations frequently relate to the complexity of exchange, which in turn can relate to the nature of the product, firm, or market involved in the transaction. The complexity of an exchange makes isolating the particular costs and benefits associated with it difficult to assess. At other times, one or both exchange partners fail to act rationally or pursue opportunistic outcomes. Each behavior poses another obstacle undermining the accurate assessment of transaction costs. Opportunism involves a situation where information is disseminated with the intention of disguising one's true purpose or otherwise misleading one's exchange partner. TCA assumes that opportunism is likely to arise in channel settings. This is a primary reason why TCA theorists suggest firms should use vertical integration rather than the market when developing channel systems. Channel members also operate in unpredictable environments. For this reason, transaction costs are often speculative or based on imperfect information. Another potential problem area is the number of firms in the industry. Oligopolies tend to limit transaction costs because of the limited number of exchange alternatives. Also, the impact that data have on a transaction complicates the situation.

Rather than trying to go it alone in a distribution setting, almost all marketing organizations are better off affixing themselves to one or more partners. These partners can be independently operated or managed as a single corporate system. Probably the most important distribution decision faced by manufacturers or retailers is whether they can perform any or all of these channel functions more efficiently and effectively through the use of intermediaries or through vertical integration. From the manufacturer's perspective, a vertical integration decision relates to whether the firm should establish its own sales branches and warehouse facilities, or, in some instances, its own retailing units. The two primary reasons why firms vertically integrate are cost reduction and environmental control.

Vertical marketing systems (VMSs) have emerged in recent years to challenge the dominance of conventional marketing channels. VMSs consist of a producer(s), wholesaler(s), and retailer(s) acting together as a unified system. In a VMS, one channel member either owns the others, franchises the others, or has so much legitimate or contractual power that the other firms cooperate.

The three types of VMSs are administered, contractual, and corporate. An administered VMS is a conventional marketing channel characterized by highly effective interorganizational management. Contractual VMSs consist of independent firms operating at different channel levels that integrate their distribution agendas on a *contractual* basis. These formal contracts are intended to secure greater economies of scale and market impact than any member could achieve alone.

Within a VMS, an entire channel is linked together as a single unit of competition. This directly contrasts with conventional channels, where independent members often assume that their competitive advantages result strictly from actions taken at their channel level. The development of VMSs often provides an effective strategic option for organizations that are struggling in competitive markets.

When a manufacturer owns and operates wholesaling and/or retailing units, the VMS is forward integrated. When retailers or wholesalers operate manufacturing facilities, a backward-integrated VMS exists. No firm operates a complete corporate VMS—from raw material to the final user's doorstep—across all distribution functions. A completely vertically integrated firm is inevitably afflicted with diseconomies because each channel activity cannot achieve minimum average cost levels.

The make-or-buy issue lies at the heart of the vertical integration decision. Assuming that the firm in question has adequate power and size, vertical integration has historically been shown to be the likely response in marketing channels facing intense competition, resource scarcity, and variable demand. But the make-or-buy decision in marketing channels remains complicated and potentially hazardous. For one thing, because the vertically integrated unit has a captive source of supply or demand, normal incentives to perform efficiently within the channel can be dulled. The cumulative result of these inefficiencies is called control loss—or those losses resulting from employee behaviors within vertically integrated systems that are not consistent with the firm's overall profit-maximization objectives.

Another new view of the vertical relationship among manufacturers, resellers, and customers is emerging. This new view requires that organizations think of every product as a service. Each organization should look at what the product in question does, rather than what it is. Once that perspective is adopted, the task of marketing the product to the next channel level becomes only one of the organization's opportunities to do something extra for its customers. This leads to a sense of bundling, where a desirable collection of benefits is spliced together to pursue or sustain a preferred customer relationship. Moreover, once an organization views a product as a service, a willingness to contract out channel functions emerges. This process is known as *unbundling,* and can lead to natural efficiencies within marketing channels.

Channel Challenges

1. One economist at the London School of Economics has suggested that "Economic order is cumulatively developmental. Structural change occurs as an evolving, necessarily fragmentary, transformation of ordering arrangements. An economic process cannot be explained as a succession of episodic shifts." After reading this chapter do you agree or disagree? Why?
2. American educator and author William Lyon Phelps asserted, "The value of anything is not what you get paid for it, nor what it costs to produce, but what you can get for it at an auction." How does Phelps's assertion support or refute the input-combiner orientation in deriving exchange value?
3. Sometime during your college experience you will likely work in a project group or team. Select an experience of working with your classmates on a project. Which economic exchange relationship best describes your experience? What was the consequence of the exchange? Do you think your perception of the exchange relationship affected the consequences of the exchange? If so, how?
4. KFC Holdings is the listed Malaysian franchisor of Colonel Sanders' famous chicken recipes. With 105 outlets it has become one of Southeast Asia's most dynamic food companies and the sixth largest KFC operation in the world. Furthermore, KFC Holdings holds about 60 percent of Malaysia's fast-food market share. Vertical integration is a cornerstone of KFC Holdings's success. The company owns feedmills, poultry farms, and bakeries in Malaysia and China. Is this forward or backward integration? What are the dis/advantages of KFC Holdings's vertical integration?
5. Vertical integration offers no universal recipe for market success. Consider the U.S. automobile industry. U.S. automakers are returning to older patterns of supplier relations, contracting out most manufacturing processes to a few, select suppliers. Why might vertical integration be declining in the U.S. auto industry? What other industries might shy away from vertical integration?
6. Corona Extra has become a worldwide beer brand, and it has catapulted Mexico to the 10th largest beer brewing nation in the world. Much of the success of Grupo Modelo—the maker of Corona Extra beer—is attributed to the producer's formation of "beer clusters." These clusters group together resource market suppliers with agro-industrial, glass, aluminum, and cardboard manufacturers. The members of the beer cluster work together to attain economies of scales in inputs and to ensure quality control. Grupo Modelo has ventured into more than 50 countries using these beer clusters. Based on your understanding of vertical marketing systems, how do these beer clusters forge channel relationships?
7. Former President Richard M. Nixon once noted an apparent paradox in the Chinese word for "crisis." When the Chinese write the word for "crisis," they use two brush strokes. One brush stroke designates danger, and the other one stands for opportunity. How might these brush strokes relate to a channel member's decision to vertically integrate?

Review Questions

1. What is meant by the *continuity of exchange*?
2. How does goal-seeking behavior relate to the continuity of exchange?
3. What is economic cooperation? Describe the economic basis and three conditions required for cooperation to occur.
4. Define and describe the concept of transaction cost analysis.
5. Define the BOUNDS of exchange, according to transaction cost analysis, that must be managed by each channel member.
6. Define and describe relationship value according to the concept of transaction cost economics.
7. Why do marketing organizations function best as systems assembled from the building blocks of individual members? Why are wholesalers important in marketing channels?
8. Define *vertical integration.* What are two primary reasons for vertical integration?
9. Define *vertical marketing system.* Describe the three types of vertical marketing systems.

10. Describe some of the advantages of vertical marketing systems over conventional marketing channels.
11. When should a firm pursue a vertical integration strategy?
12. What are some of the drawbacks of vertical marketing systems?
13. What principle in a traditional vertical channel design is used to improve relationships between marketing channel members?

Endnotes

1. Kramer, Kenneth L., and Jason Dedrick (2000), "Refining and Extending the Business Model with Information Technology: Dell Computer Corporation," *Information Society,* 16 (1), 5–21.
2. Beardi, Cara (2000), "Eclipse Tries Again via Web, Direct Sales," *Advertising Age,* 71 (23), 48–51.
3. Houston, Franklin, and Jule Gassenheimer (1987), "Marketing and Exchange," *Journal of Marketing,* 51 (October), 3–18.
4. Beale, Stephen (2000), "Motorola and IBM Reveal Power PC Plans," *Macworld,* 17 (1), 25–26.
5. Conner, Kathleen (1991), "A Historical Comparison of Resource-Based Theory and Five-Schools of Thought within Industrial Organization Economics: Do We Have a New Theory of Economic Thought," *Journal of Management,* 17(1), 121–54.
6. Matthews, R. C. O. (1986), "The Economics of Institutions and the Sources of Growth," *Economic Journal,* 96 (December), 903–10.
7. Industrial Marketing and Purchasing Group (1982), "An Interaction Approach," *International Marketing and Purchasing of Industrial Goods,* Chichester, England: Academic Press Limited, 10–27.
8. Conner, "A Historical Comparison of Resource-Based Theory," 121–54.
9. Dahlman, Carl J. (1979), "The Problem of Externality," *Journal of Legal Studies,* 22 (1), 141–62.
10. For a comprehensive understanding of transaction cost analysis (TCA), the reader should consult Williamson, Oliver E. (1979), "Transaction Cost-Economics: The Governance of Contractual Relations," *Journal of Law and Economics,* 22 (October), 3–61.
11. Williamson, Oliver E. (1975), *Markets and Hierarchies: Analysis and Antitrust Implications,* New York, NY: Free Press.
12. Hume, Claudia (2000), "Who Is Making the Numbers," *Chemical Week,* 162 (49), 32–36.
13. For a complete discussion of the Sherwin-Williams EIS information tracking system, see Booker, Ellis (1993), "Pushing Decision Support beyond Executive Suite," *Computerworld,* 27 (December 20), 65.
14. Amato-McCoy, Deena (2000), "Web Bank Plans to Enable TV Access," *Bank Systems and Technology,* 35(1), 25–29.
15. Browning, E. S. (1994), "Michelin Is Setting Out on the Road to Transformation; Tire Maker Tears Down Strict Systems, Reduces Secrecy in Bid to Modernize," *The Wall Street Journal,* September 2, B4.
16. McGee, Suzanne (1994), "Commodities: Sugar Prices Move Higher on Rumors of Buying by Chinese, Concern about World-Wide Crops," *The Wall Street Journal,* September 8, C15.
17. Cunningham, M.T., and E. Homse (1986), "Controlling the Marketing-Purchasing Interface: Resource Development and Organizational Implications," *Industrial Marketing and Purchasing,* 1 (2), 3–27; and Williamson, Oliver, E. (1985), *The Economic Institutions of Capitalism,* New York, NY: Free Press.
18. Van Warner, Rick (1994), "Kickbacks Can Trip Up a Company: Set Honesty as the Only Policy," *Nation's Restaurant News,* 28 (January 24), 19.
19. de Lisser, Elena (1994), "Marketing," *The Wall Street Journal,* April 13, B1.
20. Williamson, *The Economic Institutions of Capitalism,* 47.
21. Anderson, Erin (1985), "The Salesperson as Outside Agent or Employee: A Transaction Cost Analysis," *Marketing Science,* 4 (Summer), 234–54.
22. Casper, Carol (1993), "Rough Waters," *Restaurant Business,* 92 (15), 121–40.
23. Noordeweir, Thomas G, George John, and John R. Nevin (1990), "Performance Outcomes of Purchasing Agreements in Industrial Buyer–Vendor Relationships," *Journal of Marketing,* 54 (October), 80–93.
24. Murray, John (2000), "From Start to Finish," *Satellite Communications,* 24 (5), 22–27.

25. Gupta, Udayan (1993), "William Sahlman, a Teacher, Critic and Businessman, Talks about What It Takes to Start a Small Business These Days," *The Wall Street Journal,* October 15, R21.
26. re. American Tobacco/B.A.T.
27. Lohtia, Ritu, Charles M. Brooks, and Robert E. Krapfel (1994), "What Constitutes a Transaction-Specific Asset? An Examination of the Dimensions and Types," *Journal of Business Research,* 30 (July), 261–70.
28. Nooteboom, Bart (1993), "Research Note: An Analysis of Specificity in Transaction Cost Economics," *Organization Studies,* 14 (3), 443–51.
29. Krapfel, Robert E. Jr., Deborah Salmond, and Robert Spekman (1991), "A Strategic Approach to Managing Buyer–Seller Relationships," *European Journal of Marketing,* 25 (9), 22–37.
30. Fuller, Joseph B., James O'Conor, and Richard Rawlinson (1993), "Tailored Logistics: The Next Advantage," *Harvard Business Review,* May/June, 87–98.
31. St. Onge, Art (2000), "The Challenge of the Final Mile," *Modern Materials Handling,* 55 (2), 43–44.
32. Scherer F. M. (1980), *Industrial Market Structure and Economic Performance,* Second Edition, Chicago: Rand McNally, 78.
33. Alderson, Wroe (1958), "The Analytical Framework for Marketing," *Proceedings—Conference of Marketing Teachers from Far Western States,* Berkeley: University of California Press.
34. Davidson, William R. (1970), "Changes in Distributive Institutions," *Journal of Marketing,* 34 (January), 7.
35. Yates, Ronald E. (1991), "Japan's Markets Still Monopolistic Maze for Foreign Firms," *Chicago Tribune,* January 14, A1.
36. Poincare, Henri (1952), *Science and Method,* Dover, England: Dover Publications, 244.
37. Stigler, George J. (1951), "The Division of Labor Is Limited by the Extent of the Market," *Journal of Political Economy,* 59 (June), 63–72.
38. Dwyer, F. Robert, and M. Ann Welsh (1985), "Environmental Relationships of the Internal Polity Economy of Marketing Channels," *Journal of Marketing Research,* 22 (November), 409–17.
39. Phillips, Lynn W. (1982), "Explaining Control Losses in Corporate Marketing Systems: An Organization Analysis," *Journal of Marketing Research,* 19 (November), 525–49.
40. Hayes, Robert H., and William J. Abernathy (1980), "Managing Our Way to Economic Decline," *Harvard Business Review,* July–August, 67–77.
41. Best, William J., and Ron E. Seger (1989), "Distribution Synergies: Easy to See, Harder to Get," *Mergers & Acquisitions,* September–October, 48–53; Harrigan, Kathyrn Rudie (1983), "A Framework for Looking at Vertical Integration," *Journal of Business Strategy,* (February), 30–37.
42. FedEx/Commodore and IBM examples.
43. Fortune (1991), "There Are No Products—Only Services," *Fortune,* January 14, 32; Sheombar, Haydee S. (1992), "EDI-Induced Redesign of Co-ordination in Logistics," *International Journal of Physical Distribution and Logistics,* 22 (8), 4–14.

chapter

12

Franchising in the Global Economy

Learning Objectives

After reading this chapter, you should be able to:

- Define *franchising, franchising relationships, franchisors,* and *franchisees* in vertical marketing systems.
- Discuss the benefits franchisors and franchisees receive from the franchising channel.
- Discuss the primary concerns of franchisors and franchisees.
- Describe the current domestic and global trends in franchising channels.
- Explain the processes in deciding whether to join a franchising system.
- List and describe the potential sources of conflict in franchising channels.
- Provide an overview of the current legal and ethical standards in franchising channels.
- Understand the methods used to resolve franchising channel conflicts.
- Discuss the future direction of franchising.

Tony Stone Images

The days of the 15-cent hamburger are long gone, but McDonald's still leads the franchising pack. The chain anticipates the number of its locations will roughly double within the next 12 years. Not bad for a business founded 45 years ago by a middle-aged milkshake machine salesperson.

The franchise community itself has a lot to celebrate—growing numbers of healthy franchise systems, revenues that will soon exceed the trillion dollar mark, and numerous channel relationships that have withstood the tests of time. But franchising's strengths are hardly limited to just its numbers; they also follow from the channel structure's flexibility. Some of its most hardy pioneers have remained strong precisely because they adapted to their changing environments during the course of their evolution.

In 1924, Howard Johnson opened a soda fountain in a Massachusetts drugstore. He had $500, three flavors, and one big dream. He soon expanded the menu with burgers and hot dogs and established a series of roadside stands. When the stock market crash and ensuing depression threatened Mr. Johnson's dream of providing travelers good food at reasonable prices, he pursued a different strategy. Howard persuaded a fellow entrepreneur to use the Howard Johnson name (e.g., brand) on a Cape Cod restaurant in exchange for a fee and an agreement to buy his company's food and supplies. The franchise concept worked. The Howard Johnson name quickly became familiar from coast to coast.

HoJo has come a long way, but the path to success has often proved bumpy. When fast-food franchises took to the highways during the 1950s, many family restaurants were run off the road. But inns and hotels were also soon wearing the Howard Johnson label, and their numbers proliferated. The Howard Johnson name remains near the top of the mind of midmarket travelers at home and abroad. Newly repositioned, Howard Johnson International Inc. is some 500 strong with more than 50 properties located outside the United States.

"Franchising brands will have to be more global in the future," says Mary Mahoney, HoJo's current CEO. "Travelers want to stay at places they know and trust . . . what's more, technology and improved transplantation are making it more attractive for hotels to be part of wider distribution networks." The challenge, she maintains, is to use technology effectively as a tool.

Another franchising system that has grown stronger by changing with the times is One Hour Martinizing Dry Cleaning. The franchise was established in 1949 when Henry Martin amended his name to describe a kinder, gentler, dry-cleaning process that he had developed. At first his franchise sold equipment to dry-cleaning stores. Once that market became saturated, Martin's strategy turned toward marketing the martinizing cleaning process to existing and prospective franchisees. Since the late 1980s, One Hour Martinizing retooled its locations in keeping with more stringent environmental regulations. The franchising system now boasts 600 national and 200 international sites.[1]

One Hour Martinizing franchisees use everything from automated point-of-purchase systems that track the whereabouts of each clothing item, to direct-mail campaigns designed to secure customers who fit into a particular demographic or lifestyle profile. The company has a stand-alone research department that tracks relevant environmental trends. As a result, the company now offers an increasing amount of laundry services in relation to dry-cleaning services. Today's hard-working two-income families apparently don't want to squander leisure time washing clothes.

* * * *

In this chapter, we will look closely at the contractual vertical marketing system known as *franchising*. We have singled this type of vertical marketing system out for extra attention because franchises are an increasingly important part of the U.S. economy. Franchising is also growing on a global scale. First we will discuss the franchising relationship as a whole, and the various types and benefits of franchising. We will then consider relevant franchising and environmental trends, sources of franchising conflict, and current legal standards in franchising. The chapter closes with a discussion of how to make franchise relationships work and some predictions about the future of franchising.

Franchising Systems

Franchising is, among other things, a system of marketing and distribution wherein an independent, often small, businessperson (the **franchisee**) is granted the right to market the goods and services of another (the **franchisor**) in accordance with established standards and practices. In its ideal state, the franchisor obtains new sources of expansion capital, self-motivated vendors for its products, and the opportunity to enter new markets. Franchisees, on the other hand, acquire the sort of products, expertise, and stability usually reserved for larger enterprises. By buying a franchise, as opposed to starting a new business, franchisees can substantially lessen the risk incurred in building a business from the ground up, while gaining significant experience in their marketplace through the assistance provided to them by their franchisor. Finally, franchisees generally gain better name and product recognition.

However you define it, it is clear that franchising is one of the most successful marketing concepts ever created. Franchising channels are unique. The primary reason why franchising relationships differ from the channel relationships we have considered previously is that they consist of three relationships:

- **Legal relationship.** The backbone of the legal relationship is the contract that exists between the franchisor and franchisee. This legal relationship prescribes that each party must adhere to certain responsibilities and obligations.
- **Business relationship.** The business relationship ties the franchise partners together in the day-to-day activities necessary to provide acceptable products and services to customers. The franchisee operates the business substantially under the franchisor's trade name and/or marketing plan. While the legal relationship is essentially static, the business relationship is dynamic; it is prone to change in response to varying market circumstances. These changes, in turn, often lead to conflict between franchisors and franchisees. However, as long as both parties share a commitment to satisfy the market's needs and rely on one another to provide the best products and/or services, these conflicts can be worked out. We learned earlier that firms should pursue channel designs that minimize conflict by building mutually beneficial relationships. Successful franchises should operate on the same premise.
- **Nonbusiness relationship.** The nonbusiness relationship is the strong, forward-looking, cooperative association that exists between two independent channel members—a franchisor and a franchisee—each acting individually for its own best interests. If the legal and business dimensions of a franchising relationship are executed properly, each channel member will realize that its success is tied directly to the success of the other. Franchisors and franchisees are intrinsically related to one another.

The 1980s saw a 94 percent increase in franchised sales. By the 1990s, franchising activities accounted for about one-third of all retail sales in America. In the century ahead, franchising is expected to capture an increasing share of domestic and international business. More than 500,000 franchises operate in the United States, and they now account for about $1 trillion in sales. Some 4,000 companies currently operate in more than 70 franchised industries.[2]

Franchising systems consist of networks of franchisors and franchisees. Within this system, franchisees receive the training, guidance, and preparation necessary to use trade secrets, operational procedures, and the systemwide promotions required to develop and maintain a profitable business. Franchisors, in turn, receive the expansion of a proven concept and method of operation to multiple locations and to multiple product or service offerings.

In this arrangement, the franchisor is akin to the symphony conductor and the franchisee can be compared to musicians who occupy first chairs: strong, capable players in their own right who perform most effectively when operating under the carefully measured directives of a conductor/franchisor. Franchisees generally have a desire to go into business for themselves and exhibit an entrepreneurial spirit. When properly developed, the franchising approach helps both the franchisor and franchisee realize the profit potential of the business. Century 21, Holiday Inn, Midas, Singer Sewing Machine, and Wendy's are all examples of successful franchised businesses.

Benefits of Franchising

Franchising obviously benefits both franchisors and franchisees; if it did not, this channel design would not exist. First, franchising offers franchisors an alternative to developing a company-owned outlet and provides them with an opportunity for rapid market penetration at a relatively low cost using independent entrepreneurs. Market expansion is largely financed through franchisee funds. While more control is available in corporate vertical marketing systems, franchisors can still exercise a good deal of control through the legal relationship. Furthermore, franchisors do not have to motivate franchisees as much as they would corporate employees. This is because franchisees are generally self-motivated; they have a financial investment at stake and can benefit directly from the business's success. Also, cooperative advertising—which is available through the franchising system—usually achieves better results than individual advertising. Other advantages for franchisors include increased cash flows (from franchising fees), economies of scale in system administration, and the fact that little borrowing is needed to expand. Finally, franchisees, as local entrepreneurs, are likely to gain community acceptance more quickly than a corporate entity and can provide franchisors with an insightful view of local business conditions.

Perhaps the biggest benefit received by franchisees is the extensive assistance provided by franchisors. In exchange for start-up fees, established franchise systems offer proven products or concepts, recognizable brands and/or images that create credibility, and established business procedures. Many franchise packages include standardized methods for operations, promotion, site location analysis, accounting and finance, and personnel training. In short, franchising offers franchisees a turnkey way of starting a business. Franchises have historically demonstrated five-year survival rates of more than 85 percent, whereas independent business ventures have less than a 25 percent 5-year survival rate.[3] Another view of the benefits that can be gained by franchisees is offered in Channel Surfing 12.1.

Channel Surfing 12.1

Everybody Is a Winner

Use the term *franchising* around DuPont Flooring Systems these days and you could get an earful about how franchisees can benefit from entering a franchise system that is run the right way. Phrases like "mutual capabilities," "dedicated channels of distribution," and "delivering value to both the franchisee and customer" are used in the DuPont franchise system. And what's more, DuPont is actually walking its talk. The values reflected in such phrases capture the letter and spirit of the approach that DuPont management took when it entered the franchising marketplace.

Add to that the opportunity to acquire one of the nation's prototype flooring operations and to be part of a time-tested operating system and management process, and you can easily see why potential franchisees are clamoring to get on board the DuPont franchising train—uh, we mean chain. Mutual benefit, long the foundation of any successful franchising relationship, should stand behind the reasons why any company such as DuPont would offer franchise opportunities to qualified prospects. Like DuPont representative Craig Corey says, "You have to be in a position to deliver value—value to the consumer and value to the people you want as your franchisees. Otherwise, why bother." We couldn't have said it better ourselves.

Points to Ponder

- What other conditions would need to be in place before a franchising opportunity would provide the "right" answer for persons looking to go into business for themselves?

Types of Franchising

There are three broad types of franchises. The first generation of franchises, called **tied-house franchising systems,** sprang up among German brewers in the 18th century. These brewers contracted with taverns to sell their brand of beer exclusively. The second generation appeared during the 19th century, when the Singer Sewing Machine company elected to sell its products to its salespeople, who, in turn, were expected to find markets for the products. This arrangement, known as **product/tradename franchising,** involves the use of franchisees to distribute a product under a franchisor's trademark. This type of franchising dominates automobile, retail gasoline, and soft drink distribution.

The third generation of franchising, known as **business format franchising,** was introduced in the 20th century by the A&W Restaurant Company. This franchise form seeks to have franchisees replicate a complete business concept—including product or service, trademark, and methods of operation—in their own communities. More than 2,000 types of franchisors operating primarily in the service sector currently use business formats. Business format franchising has accounted for most of the unit growth of franchising in the United States and abroad since 1950. In recent decades, this type of franchising has become much more significant in its share of all-franchised units, currently operating in about 70 distinct business segments and representing 19 broader business categories.[4] These are summarized in Exhibit 12.1.

To adapt to the changing demands of the marketplace, franchisors have continuously altered the specific prototypes of these broad formats. According to Arthur Anderson & Co., about 90 percent of current franchising prototypes have been developed during the past 10

Exhibit 12.1

Current FGC categories and segments in which business format franchising operates

Business Categories	*Examples*
Automotive products and services	Muffler and transmission repairs
Business aids and services	Accounting/tax services; advertising/direct mail; business aids and services; business brokers; check cashing; financial service centers; insurance; packaging, shipping and mail services; publications; shopping services; telecommunication services
Construction and home improvement	Materials, service, and remodeling; water conditioning; home appliance sales, rental, and repair; home furnishings, retail, and services; home inspection/radon detection; security systems; lawn, garden, and agricultural supplies and services
Convenience stores	Convenience stores; quicky marts; ice cream stores
Eucational products and services	Speed reading; beauty and cosmetology schools; computer and technical skills enhancement seminars; motivational programs
Employment services	Office personnel; health care workers; assembly line workers
Health and beauty aids	Cosmetics; hair salons and services; dental centers; health aids and services; optical aids and services; vitamin and mineral stores; weight control
Laundry and dry cleaning	Laundrymats; dry cleaning stores
Lodging	Hotels and motels; campgrounds
Maintenance and cleaning services	Maid and personal services; janitorial services; maintenance; chemicals and related products
Miscellaneous services	Children's services; dating services
Printing/copying and signs	Printing/photocopying; photography and supplies; signs
Real estate services	Real estate agencies
Recreation, entertainment, and travel	Equipment and supplies; exercise; sports, entertainment, and services; travel agencies, transportation services
Rental services: auto and truck	Automotive and truck rental services
Rental services: equipment and retail	Rental equipment and supplies; formal wear rental; uniform rental systems; video/audio sales and rental
Restaurants (all types)	Fast food; donut shops; coffee shops; pancake and waffle houses
Retailing: food (nonconvenience)	Baked goods; candy; snacks; ice cream; yogurt, specialty foods; beverages
Retailing: nonfood	Specialty retail; craft and variety; bookstores; clothing; shoes; computers; electronics; florist shops; drugstores jewelry; tools and hardware; pet sales; supplies, and services

Source: Arthur Anderson & Co. (1993), *Franchising in the Economy, 1989–1992,* Washington, DC: International Franchise Association Educational Foundation, Inc.

years.[5] The reasons for these innovations in franchising formats include the desire to segment older, female, and minority markets and reactions to emerging socioeconomic trends.

An example of market-sensitive adaptation can be found in the maturing restaurant franchising sector, where Pizza Hut and KFC have developed kiosks featuring tiny, closet-like physical facilities and food cart formats to complement their full-sized restaurants. Each franchisor is trying to penetrate malls, subways, and airports. Why? Because that is where the customers are. Responding to the existence of more working couples, many franchises also are developing new specialty prototypes that emphasize superconvenient service.

Concerns of Franchisees

In and of itself, franchising hardly guarantees a profit. However, some franchisees feel that franchisors have guaranteed them a profit and are thus offended when profits fail to materialize. Indeed, unless the franchise is run by entrepreneurs who are allowed to manage their business under acceptable guidelines with a keen eye for profit, franchisees may not be successful at all.

A second concern of franchisees is the fact that their business can revert to the franchisor or be transferred to another franchisee when their contract expires. Similarly, **encroachment** occurs when the franchisor opens another franchise too near an existing franchisee. Franchisors are sometimes guilty of wanting to sell more units rather than investing the money or effort necessary to improve the profitability of existing franchises. Understandably, existing franchisees find this troubling. But no easy solution is available. Encroachment concerns cannot be resolved by guaranteeing franchisees a protected radius because local markets and demand conditions constantly change.

When people choose franchising as a vehicle for market entry, they de facto give up some independence. This is cause for considerable concern. Franchised outlets generally must look alike, follow certain procedures, and fill out prescribed forms. Their franchisor is authorized to audit the books and has the right to terminate the relationship as per their contract. Franchisees are also sometimes required by contract to buy supplies from their franchisor or franchisor-sanctioned suppliers. Many franchisees chafe under the conditions imposed by the franchising agreement.

Most franchisors collect promotional monies from franchisees and pool it to launch promotional campaigns. Issues of when and how to spend promotional dollars and the effectiveness of various creative approaches frequently lead to differences of opinion in franchising channels. When Burger King, for example, promotes and sells 99-cent Whoppers, out of whose profits do you think those value prices came? That's right, franchisees'. Technically, Burger King Corp. cannot price Whoppers—doing so would involve illegal resale price maintenance. But they skirt this problem by promoting special prices available at "participating stores." Franchisees are pressured to follow through.

In many franchising channels franchisors make products available to franchisees for sale. In such situations, the pricing of that product affects the profitability of both parties. In those situations where franchisees must purchase goods or supplies from their franchisor, pricing structures can boost the franchisor's profitability at the franchisees' expense.

Concerns of Franchisors

Franchisors have the same concern about profits as do franchisees. Franchisees who decide to buy supplies or equipment from independent sources, for instance, adversely affect the franchisor's profitability. Furthermore, franchisees occasionally "sit on a market." This occurs when individual franchisees recognize that their market could support additional franchises, yet they resist expansion and are unwilling to share the market with anyone else. Should the franchisor impose an expansion upon them, conflicts will likely arise.

Most franchising agreements specify payment of royalty fees to franchisors. A major concern of franchisors is whether their franchisees are reporting their gross sales honestly, or whether they are purposely understating sales to avoid royalties.[6] Trade secrets, marketing strategies, strategic plans, and the like are frequently revealed to franchisees. If these were circulated to competitors, a franchising program would be injured. For these reasons, franchisors are concerned about having their own franchisees competing against them under another name.[7]

You might get the impression from this discussion of franchisee and franchisor concerns that there are insurmountable obstacles to the establishment of good relationships in a franchising system. To the contrary, there are common interests between the franchisor and franchisee. With a long-term view on each side, these shared interests should result in the resolution of differences. At their best, franchising systems illustrate how synergy can emerge in marketing channels. Each participant brings its particular strengths to the arrangement.

Relevant Trends in the Franchising Environment

The key to spotting a future franchising success and not being seduced by a fad like gourmet popcorn lies in identifying the right environmental trends. Any channel's external environment is always highly uncertain. It is always changing. Scanning the environment—appraising, predicting, and monitoring external factors is extremely important when considering the franchising channel. Here we will discuss the social, cultural, demographic, economic, international, and industry trends that all point to a healthy picture for franchising.

Social, Cultural, and Demographic Trends

Consumer interest in sociocultural issues such as education and employment security or the increasing expectation of convenience and value are driving current franchise development. For example, even the casual observer knows that public education is currently struggling with budget cuts and sinking student test scores. FUTUREKIDS, a Los Angeles–based computer education franchisor, definitely noticed these trends. In a little over four years, the firm has sold over 150 successful franchises, which offer computer-based learning for kids ages 3 to 12.[8] Changing workplace customs are another relevant trend to which franchise offerings are responding. Not so many years ago, the norm in many offices was the three-martini business lunch. Now busy managers often dine in their offices while they work. In response, We-Bag-It offers the first upscale—priced at $7.00 to $10.00—lunch aimed at this market, featuring a soup of the day, an entree, fresh vegetables, rolls or croissants, fresh-baked cookies, and a beverage made with natural juices.[9]

Another cultural trend you may have noticed is that, year by year, Americans are getting heavier. Whether their actions are the cause or the effect of this weighty matter is subject to debate, but it is clear that having it your way at fast-food franchisees these days increasingly means with bacon. The fast-food industry has long used bacon to spice up their menus, but until recently did little to promote adding pork to customers' burgers. No longer.

From in-store displays at McDonald's that pronounce "Make it Bacon," to Culver's Franchising Systems pushing "Shakes and Bacon," fast-feeders are dipping into the pork barrel. Even Subway, known for promoting healthy fare, is banking on bacon's appeal. "Even though we have seven sandwiches with less than six grams of fat, the customer has a choice to go beyond that," said company representative Nick Hautfield.[10] And often customers do. Better taste, higher profits, and franchises' commonsensical reactions to changing environmental standards are driving the bacon binge.

Current demographic trends are having a significant effect on the formation of new franchise prototypes. They also support the growth of existing franchises. For instance, business ownership by women is growing at a faster rate than is business ownership by men, having increased fivefold during the past decade alone.[11] Minorities, currently accounting for 22 percent of the labor force, will constitute an increasingly larger percentage during the balance of the decade. And the U.S. population as a whole is rapidly aging. Franchisors that specialize in providing convenient door-to-door products, as well as health care, decorating, and cleaning services, should do well in the comparatively affluent—and growing—55 and older market.

Corporate belt-tightening is another cultural trend that has influenced franchising. Successful and industrious managers who have had their fill of corporate life and displaced corporate executives are common profiles of the latest wave of prospects entering franchising.[12] The enticements are straightforward: you can finally be your own boss, make a decent income, perhaps bring the kids into the business, and, eventually, build it into something significant.

Economic Trends

Economic trends play a role in the formation and success of franchises and franchise forms. Americans have already witnessed a shift from a manufacturing-oriented economy to one dominated by service providers. During the same period, the franchising concept has continued to mature with the development and success of the business format franchise type. The concurrent growth of the service economy and franchising is hardly a coincidence. Rather, this growth represents the consummation of a practical business marriage. In automotive services alone franchise applications range from A (AAMCO Transmissions) to Z (Ziebart Rustproofing). Franchise channels are particularly prominent in equipment rentals, beauty salons, bookkeeping, accounting, tax preparation, education, real estate sales, printing, lodging, lawn care, and employment services.

Special challenges are associated with the successful distribution of a service. This is primarily because services vary in quality, are intangible, and cannot be inventoried. Franchising's primary attributes—the ease of capital formation, the presence of motivated entrepreneurs who provide good service along with standardized systems and procedures to control operations—nicely address the problems inherently faced by service firms.[13] The availability of multiple franchised locations offering uniform service also appeals to mobile consumers. Finally, because promotional efforts in franchising are centralized and delivered systemwide, the tangible aspects of services are increased.

As you probably noticed, during the last decade the U.S. economy did quite well. For the franchise community, this boom period represented both an opportunity and a threat. The

In English, 7-Eleven's motto is "Always Open!" In Bahasa Malaysia, it translates into, "Buka jam." Even on the "jammed" streets of Hong Kong, the message in Chinese is the same: create time and convenience utility for consumers!

Neal Herndon

boom proved an opportunity in that consumers' confidence was high, and their spending patterns reflected that confidence. But the boom proved a threat in that high employment drained the pool of potential franchisees. Formerly downsized corporate managers, once the prime prospects for franchise ownership, increasingly kept their jobs. In response, most franchise systems, like Dunkin' Donuts and BaskinRobbins, became more selective and sophisticated in their recruitment and selection processes.[14] They have increasingly armed themselves with an arsenal of marketing tools—including niche marketing, strategic alliances, and outsourcing opportunities—aimed at penetrating the minds of prospective franchisees.

International Trends

Many developing countries are experiencing trends similar to those that have made franchising so successful in the United States. Governments around the world are becoming aware of the benefits that franchising can bring to their economies. In many parts of the world, banks have set up lending divisions to market loans to franchisees. Improvements in transportation and communication have made the job of controlling foreign franchisees easier, and the assimilation of Western innovations has created greater global standardization and consumer acceptance. Business format franchisors have benefited most from these trends. The McDonald's format, for instance, provides franchisees with a globally known brand name; a proven menu; specialized equipment; standardized store locations, design, and operating procedures; world-class promotions; and continuous training through its Hamburger University.

From a strictly business perspective, international franchising involves less risk than many other forms of international marketing, such as direct investment. It also provides industries whose offerings cannot be exported (such as services) an opportunity for market expansion. In addition, international franchising is typically regulated less in the host country since the domestic capital outflows are small compared to other forms of foreign investment.[15]

The most common foreign entry modes used by franchisors involve the transferral of domestic rights to a master franchisor. A *master franchisor* is a local entrepreneur who assumes the rights and responsibilities of establishing or selling franchises throughout a country or large territory within a country. Potential frictions between the franchisor and the customs and values of the host country can be reduced in this way. While there is some loss of control and a danger of relaxed standards, this entry mode is generally used when host government regulations are relatively restrictive, when political or economic risk is high, or when the franchisor's foreign investment resources are limited.[16] Master franchisors operate domestically, as well. Elby's and Shoney's Big Boy restaurants are run in this fashion.

Industry Trends

The growth in the number, diversity, and sophistication of franchisees has placed increased demands on those charged with managing the franchisor-franchisee relationship. Just as franchisors and franchising itself have grown, so too have the power and size of many franchisees. Today over 20 percent of franchisees own multiple units.[17] Given their greater investment, these franchisees want more say about how they operate their businesses. Franchisees are more willing to press their causes and concerns. Such trends often lead to more power sharing within franchising systems.[18]

Bigger, stronger, and more aggressive franchisees are increasingly banding together to assert their rights vis-à-vis the obligations of powerful franchisors. For example, Adventureland Video, Inc., franchisees organized a cooperative for greater purchasing power, while Computerland's European franchisees united to secure reduced royalty payments and more control over pricing and promotion decisions.

Franchisee associations can benefit franchisors just as much as franchisees. Such associations have helped Arby's, Burger King, and Dunkin' Donuts to either ward off corporate takeovers or reduce the adverse effects of such takeovers. Indeed, franchisors have begun to encourage associations and have established mentoring programs among their franchisees. Typical of these is the "Big Brothers" program of Maids International, a cleaning and maintenance franchise. In this program, rookie franchisees are paired with veterans who provide advice on running the businesses. Mentoring programs and associations shift some managerial responsibility from franchisors onto the franchise system itself. Power is thereby redistributed among all levels of the system. Of course, these efforts should be combined with an ongoing training program by the franchisor.[19]

Technological Trends

We cannot ignore the impact that technological trends are having on franchising. Consider this: Surfing—Web surfing, that is—is a great sport. It is popular both at home and in the workplace—maybe a little too popular according to many employers. Still, this simple technological pastime occupies literally millions of people each day. Web surfing reflects an application of technology that real people use in the real world. But by itself, Web technology is not all that fascinating to most people anymore. It is the way that the technology is applied in the "real world" that ultimately leads to its successful utilization. Nowhere is this premise more obvious than with channels applications that successfully utilize the technology we call the *Internet.*

Internet technology has literally changed the world and how we do business in it. In particular, the ways that products are marketed and that business organizations communicate with one another have been changed. Such applications reflect common uses of the technology that is available to all companies, including, of course, franchise companies. But franchise companies, unlike more traditional business channels, have to consider the real world of independent franchise owners. Many independent franchise owners literally gasp at the hint of anything having to do with a computer, let alone the Internet. As such, franchise companies should consider the practical, political, legal, and marketing issues associated with the franchisor-franchisee relationship before they arbitrarily implement any new technologies.

Most franchise companies are turning to the latest Internet technologies in an attempt to increase the success potential for their franchisees. Clearly, the Internet offers franchisors an enticing opportunity to implement applications that are simultaneously tangible, viable, and valuable to franchisees operating in the real world. An example of how Internet technology is being used in franchising channels is discussed in Channel Surfing 12.2.

Channel Surfing 12.2

Using the Internet to Recruit Franchisees

Today the overwhelming majority of franchise companies have commercial websites. However, just a few years ago, only a small percentage did. The big push for websites over the last few years followed primarily from a website's ability to promote the franchisor's program to potential franchisees surfing the Web. These "franchisee solicitation websites" reduce postage and printing costs by eliminating the need to send a full marketing kit to a prospective franchisee upon first contact. Franchise companies can now direct prospects to their websites to view detailed information about their offerings, and qualify the prospect in the process.

Rick Swalwell, vice president of marketing for Medicap Pharmacies, Inc. (www.medicaprx.com), vouches for the Web's franchise marketing effectiveness. "At first," he says, "we felt that we could use the Web as a cost-effective lead generator, designed to attract pharmacists surfing the Web looking for investments." It worked, and as Swalwell puts it "the cost to develop and maintain our website was justified with the sale of a single franchise." Since then, Medicap has upgraded its website to include the promotion of individual franchised locations to potential customers in addition to its original offering to potential franchisees.

Just a few years ago many websites heavily emphasized animation to attract prospects. Today, however, modern franchiser websites tend to be clean, simple, and straight to the point. Depth of content and the speed with which information is delivered are now paramount considerations for franchising websites. Most franchise companies, such as Western Sizzlin' (www.Western-sizzlin.com) and MaxCARE (www.maxcarecleaning.com) target both franchisee prospects and potential customers on their site.

Points to Ponder

- Can you think of some other ways that Internet technology could be usefully applied in franchise channel settings? If so, describe them.

Source: Adapted from Scott, Nancy Rathbun (2000), "Franchises Boldly Go into the Web Universe: All Things Internet Being Explored by Franchise Systems," *Franchising World,* 32 (5), 8–12.

Exhibit 12.2

Four steps potential franchisees should follow to improve the odds of franchising success

Franchisees should:

- *Nail the Numbers.* Franchisors should give franchisees a detailed statement of financial conditions and expectations no later than two weeks before any money is scheduled to change hands.
- *Measure Management.* Franchisees should seek and scrutinize disclosure forms that describe at least the last 10 years of the work history of each of the franchisor's officers and key managers.
- *Cross-Examine Current Franchisees.* Prospective franchisees should obtain a list of all current franchisees, including those who have recently left. Randomly calling and then visiting several names will keep prospects from being steered toward franchisor favorites. Serving a few days' apprenticeship in one or two will also yield tremendous insights.
- *Comb the Contract.* Franchise agreements establish control over most aspects of the business. Attorneys with franchising experience should look for inequities in the agreements and help franchisees secure a better deal.

Internal Environmental Factors

If today's white-collar job market continues to shrink, the prospects of franchising relationships will continue to have a lot of appeal for many people. Although the trends we have just discussed certainly point to a positive environment for franchising, the external environment is only half the story. Persons considering whether to become franchisees often fail to scan the internal environment—local market conditions, the legitimacy of the franchisor, their own personal situation, and all other factors associated with the business opportunity are equally important variables in the decision-making process. Anyone considering a franchising relationship should follow the four essential steps shown in Exhibit 12.2 to improve the odds of their success. You can further protect yourself by:[20]

- Self-evaluation.
- Investigating the franchise.
- Studying the disclosure document.
- Checking out the disclosures.
- Questioning earnings claims.
- Obtaining professional advice.
- Knowing your legal rights.

Conflicts in Franchising

Getting along in franchise channels seems simple. Yet headlines such as "Franchising Hell," "Franchising Fracas," or "Fed-Up Franchisees" appear regularly in the business press.[21] Just how does the typical franchising channel relationship work out? Current estimates are that only about 33 percent of all franchisees do really well, another 33 percent essentially break even, and the final third lose money. Meanwhile, legal disputes between franchisors and franchisees have more than tripled since 1990.[22] We'll look more closely at the legal standards for each of these areas of conflict in the next section.

More often than not the factors most critical to success are rooted in the franchisor-franchisee relationship. Ideally, the interests of franchisors and franchisees are one and the same—the better franchisees do, the more revenue the franchisor makes. But channel life often fails to follow the ideal, and franchisors and franchisees can become adversarial. Remember that a franchisor is not just operating one business; it also influences other channel members (franchisees) as they run their business as part of a closely integrated channel system. The converse is true, as well: A single franchisee's actions not only influence the franchisor, but all of its fellow franchisees. The major sources of conflict in franchise channels are summarized in Exhibit 12.3. Let's examine a few of the most egregious.

Up-front Fees

The up-front fee is a big revenue and profit generator for franchisors. To close a deal, commission franchise salespeople have been known to exaggerate the franchise potential. Dallas-based employment agency Snelling Personnel Services was once accused of promoting inflated revenue and profit projections to its prospective franchisees.

Tying Agreements

Tying agreements force franchisees to agree to purchase much of their supplies and raw materials from the franchisor or from franchisor-endorsed suppliers. At Little Caesars Enterprises, Inc., franchisees say they have been forced to buy pizza ingredients and paper products from a company-owned distributor. In so doing, these franchisees claim they have paid up to 15 percent more than for identical items available elsewhere. Franchisees in other systems report that when they complain or refuse to go along with these tying agreements, they

Exhibit 12.3

Major source of conflict

Major sources of conflict generated by franchisors as perceived by franchisees	*Major sources of conflict generated by franchisees as perceived by franchisors*
• Dual distribution implications • Redirection/termination of franchise • Full-line requirements to purchase standardized products from franchisor • Questionable use of advertising and promotional revenues • Asymmetrical nature of franchise agreement (power inequities)	• Release of proprietary information to outside parties • Nonpayment or "short" payment of royalties • Refusal of franchisees to adhere to standardized conditions in franchise agreements

Source: Adapted from Storholm, Gordon, and Eberhard E. Schueing (1994) "Ethical Implications of Business Format Franchising," *Journal of Business Ethics*, 13, 181–88.

are terminated or sued.[23] However, franchisors can legally require franchisees to purchase materials or products from them when doing so is necessary to ensure that quality or consistency standards are met.

Capricious Termination

Franchisees are frequently alarmed about their lack of security, since franchisors can terminate agreements or fail to renew them at the end of a prespecified period. Terminations usually result from one of three causes: (1) expiration of the term of the contract, (2) franchisee bankruptcy, or (3) some default in the franchisee's performance. Problems arise when franchisees perceive that their contracts are being terminated on arbitrary grounds. This practice, known as **capricious termination,** has been called the "Achilles heel" of the franchising industry.[24]

Encroachment

As we discussed earlier in the chapter, encroachment is the franchisor's placement of a new company-owned or franchised unit too close to an existing one. Encroachment represents probably the most basic conflict between franchisors and franchisees. As franchising has matured as a way of doing business, competition between established franchisors and franchisees has intensified, while the availability of prime sites for new growth has decreased.[25]

In theory, franchisors cut their own throats if they overpopulate a market with outlets. In fact, however, it is sometimes difficult to resist the money to be made by selling new franchisees and expanding the flow of royalty income, even when the average outlet's revenues are endangered by such actions.

Franchised product encroachment in the 1990s is also occurring through catalog and telemarketing sales channels. A third form of encroachment results from the extension of trademark awareness into fields other than those featured in the original franchise. Consider the retail shoemaker who subsequently establishes a franchised chain of shoe repair facilities under the same mark. While the two concepts may not directly compete, poor service by one unit can adversely affect the good will of the other.

Lack of Cooperation

Franchisees can be a source of conflict, too. According to Tricon, owner of KFC, Pizza Hut, and Taco Bell, too many franchisees resist changes that are needed to keep their systems competitive. As for Little Caesars, it says franchisees have no reason to gripe because they are free to purchase pizza ingredients—except for two trade-secret items—from sources the company approves. Many franchisors say franchisees don't do their homework and expect too much, too easy. Franchisors also claim that franchisees demand more because they are more powerful. Not that many years ago, most franchisees were indeed Mom and Pop shops with single units. Now many franchisees own multiple units and, with more economic clout, are organizing. They might hire lawyers or lobbyists to press their causes. Each side in any franchising system will benefit from a better feel and appreciation for the others' concerns.

Anything these days can be franchised, from steel bungee-jumping towers (Air Boingo) to gun shops (Strictly Shooting). For small-business owners, franchising provides an alternative way of raising capital for growth. From laid-off managers to early retirees, more and more people see franchising as an easy way to realize the American dream of owning a business. Yet, bad management or poor locations have "done in" any number of franchisees in past years. Slow economic growth in many regions, oversaturation in other markets, or debt loads from leveraged buyouts are putting new pressures on franchisors to squeeze franchisees. As franchisors expand into new markets, they're increasingly vying for the existing franchisees' customers. These new pressures are in addition to an already unequal power structure in an industry that has traditionally featured inconsistent laws and enforcement.

Current Legal Standards in Franchising

Being unpopular with franchisees can cause unexpected troubles for franchisors. In the late 1980s, Burger King Corporation franchisees blocked Burger King's attempt to spin off its fast-food chain as a defense against a takeover bid by Grand Metropolitan PLC. Already put out by what they saw as mismanagement by Burger King's owner Pillsbury, Burger King franchisees feared they would become a part of an undercapitalized, debt-burdened spinoff. The franchisees threatened an injunction. The rebellion helped seal Pillsbury's fate, easing Grand Met's acquisition.[26] Franchisees have grown wary of spinoffs, mergers, and other restructuring moves by franchisors. On the other hand, as Dunkin' Donuts discovered, franchisees can be powerful allies. Dunkin' Donuts' franchisees pledged their support and bought advertisements backing the chain in its bid to fend off a hostile takeover from a Canadian group.

After several years of no hearings on federal fair-franchising legislation, in 2000 franchisors and franchisees began to gear up to do battle again on Washington's Capitol Hill. A bill, introduced during the 106th Congress, took many members of the franchising community by surprise. Among other things, the bill seeks to promote equitable franchisee agreements, to establish uniform standards of conduct in franchise relationships, and to give franchisees adequate recourse against abusive practices by unprincipled franchisors.[27] A final resolution may take years. Most legal contests between franchisors and franchisees entail disputes regarding information disclosure (misrepresenting facts), tying agreements, or capricious termination. Market expansion and encroachment problems are usually regarded as ethical rather than legal concerns.

Disclosure

Many investors have lost fortunes to deceitful franchise operators. Faced with excessive fraud and failure, the FTC established FTC Rule 436. According to the rule, comprehensive disclosure must occur at the first personal meeting between the players or, failing that, at least 10 business days prior to the franchise agreement execution. The basic aim of the rule is to provide relevant facts and, more importantly, to prevent fraud and misrepresentation.[28]

To comply with Rule 436, franchisors are free to either follow the **FTC disclosure format** or use the **Uniform Franchise Offering Circular (UFOC).** The categories of information included in the FTC and UFOC formats include but are not limited to information about the franchisor and any predecessors; litigation and bankruptcy history; description of the franchise; recurring fees payable to the franchisor; supervision expectations; trademarks, patents, and copyrights; termination and renewal specifications; statistical information concerning the number of participation obligations; public figure involvement; financial information concerning the franchisor; business experience of officers and directors; financing arrangements; territory and sales restrictions; personal participation obligations; and the franchisor contractual documents themselves.

Mandatory Purchases from the Franchisor

In addition to the added complexities posed by **dual distribution,** where the franchisor distributes through both franchisee outlets and company-owned outlets, many cases of tri-distribution also exist. There, the franchisor is not only an independent marketer and franchisee, but also a supplier. Courts continue to grapple with this reality. In such situations, concerns also surface with respect to product mix offerings and the subsequent impact on inventory investment. Buying goods that might be bought less expensively through other sources has been discussed above.

Distribution conflicts in franchising systems can form in a variety of ways. In *Rosenberg v. Pillsbury Co.,* the court ruled that Häagen-Dazs did not breach its duty of good faith to its franchisees by distributing prepackaged pints of ice cream to supermarkets. The judgment was based on the "unambiguous terms of the franchise agreement." The franchise agreement explicitly reserved to Haagen-Dazs the right to distribute products through any other distribution method which may be established.[29]

Termination and Renewal

Perhaps no portion of the franchising relationship has proven more perplexing to the courts or to franchisees than the renewal/termination clause. Most contracts carry terms of 5, 10, or 15 years with a 5-year renewal option. Consider the franchisee who builds a successful business and has come to the end of the contract period, at which point the franchisor (who has the right of first refusal) decides not to renew and to operate the unit itself. This happens and obviously raises some ethical issues, but it is legal.[30]

Advertising and Promotions

The most important asset that franchisees buy is a customer base. Customers readily walk through the door because the franchisor has already established its concept. Along with royalties, advertising moneys are also paid to promote the franchising system as a whole.

Promotional decisions by the franchisor may not always be in the best interests of all franchisees within a franchise system. In *Gregory v. Popeye's Famous Fried Chicken and Biscuits, Inc.,* a number of franchisees complained that Popeye's failed to provide adequate advertising in the Detroit, Michigan, area. The court decreed against the franchisees, contending that their franchising agreement did not impose a duty for franchisors to please individuals by selecting advertising that specifically benefited a particular market or store. The ruling gave franchisors sole discretion over the timing, selection, and placement of advertising.[31] Clearly, promotions are of primary concern to franchisees as market exposure through advertising literally can be the lifeblood of their success; however, franchisors retain the legal right to make promotional decisions autonomously.

Expansion (Encroachment)

Encroachment is always one of the major concerns of franchisees. On the one hand, the franchisor must continually expand its system in order to grow its market share and maintain its

Channel Surfing 12.3

Fairness Should Prevail in All Relationships

Conflict is inevitable in all types of marketing channels. The franchise channel system managed by Mail Boxes Etc. (MBE) is no different, particularly given that franchisee concerns about encroachment are present constantly. Such concerns represent a dilemma for virtually all successful franchise systems. Here's the issue that is on the table: While MBE recognizes how important it is to maintain strong franchisee relationships, like all franchises, MBE also faces the pressure to constantly expand its market presence. Otherwise, MBE has little hope of remaining competitive in an ever changing marketplace.

Being a smart company, MBE understands this issue. In response, MBE's new president announced a set of core values for the firm. These values—caring, honesty, fairness, respect, commitment, and accountability—now exist as guideposts by which all MBE relationships will be managed. At the same time, a leadership team was established within the franchise. Its first task was to develop an encroachment policy that would not inhibit MBE's international and domestic market expansion, but at the same time protect its franchisees' interests. After soliciting comments and suggestions from franchisees themselves, the task force developed five issues that needed to be addressed before a productive policy could be developed:

- The first issue addressed basic terminology. The term *encroachment* clearly has negative connotations. The team determined that *center placement* more effectively described the policy's objectives, and did so without any negative connotations.

The other four issues were embodied in the objectives that this policy ultimately must address:

- To ensure that MBE franchisees were given advance notice of any proposed center being located near or contiguous to their territory.
- To ensure that franchisees receive opportunity to raise concerns about the proposed locations.
- To ensure that franchisees are provided a forum for the fair resolution of any dispute resulting from the center's proposed placement.
- To ensure that the new policy is published and used by MBE.

MBE has developed a clearly defined policy that it believes will address the issue of encroachment in a productive manner that will allow the continued expansion of the MBE franchise. The policy is not perfect (what policy could be?), but it represents a fruitful start.

Points to Ponder

- What proposals can you make for improving MBE's encroachment policy?

Source: Adapted from Bloom, Bruce V. (1998), "Eye on Encroachment," *Franchising World,* 30 (5), 32–33.

competitiveness. On the other, a franchisee who has a large investment in money and effort sunk in its franchise wants to enhance its stability and minimize negative impacts. As business owners, franchisees should easily recognize that competition from other channel systems can prove threatening to their economic well-being. That's just the way a free-market system works. But the same franchisees could understandably become quite upset when their business is negatively impacted by the expansion of their own franchise system.

Intuitively, any franchisee should realize that selling franchises or adding new concepts is part of the franchisor's business. It is also assumed that when one buys a franchised business, some protection for that business is provided. Franchisors constantly weigh the choice of whether to sell more franchises in a market that is already being served or nurturing the existing franchises. How these questions are resolved may raise some quasilegal questions since the issue of encroachment often serves as an impetus to lawsuits.[32] But this issue often involves ethicality and moral rights rather than legal concerns. Channel Surfing 12.3 describes how one franchise system is attempting to resolve encroachment problems before they actually arise.

Successful, nonlitigious solutions to these problems (particularly the issues of expansion/encroachment and termination/renewal) have included franchisors giving franchisees the right of first refusal on new concepts or territorial expansions. In pursuit of mutually agreeable outcomes, franchisors have begun to voluntarily offer more advantageous contractual provisions in the areas of renewal, royalty, or promotional payments as quid pro quo for reductions in exclusive territories.[33] Still, drafting a perfect solution to encroachment is impossible. Such a solution should provide franchisors with the necessary flexibility in the face of market changes and provide franchisees sufficient investment protection.

Irrespective of the strength of their legal positions, franchisors must develop plans for expansion that (1) take into account their and their franchisees' objectives, (2) accurately and objectively identify the benefits of expansion to the system, and (3) give each party a fair, inexpensive, and quick means of resolving disputes.

Making Franchise Relationships Work

Let's say you just opened a franchise two weeks ago. Business is booming. Then, out of nowhere, a snag pops up: a software glitch that is not explained in the franchisor's manual. You call franchise headquarters for assistance and are put on hold for 20 minutes. In the meantime, your waiting customers begin to complain and walk out. Headquarters finally advises that the tech person just went on vacation and no one else can help you. A voice on the other end of the phone says to you: "You'll just have to wing it until the end-of-the-month inspection."

Sounds like a formula for failure, doesn't it? Probably. It also sounds like this franchisor doesn't care enough about its franchisees. As you well know by now, the franchisor-franchisee relationship can be a tenuous one. The Channels Relationship Model advocates interaction that fosters cooperative, long-term interaction between these channel partners. In this section, we will discuss three methods of fostering such a relationship: CARE, intelligent contracts, and strategic franchising partnerships.

CARE

First and foremost, to make the franchising relationship work, franchisors must take CARE of their franchisees: Communication, Awareness, Rapport, and Expertise.[34]

First, franchisors must ensure that their franchisees are able to *communicate* with them and feel as though they belong to the franchising system. Most successful franchising organizations create newsletters that enhance communication. Effective franchisors often ask their franchisees to form committees to participate in advertising, new product and development, or grievance and operations decisions. Franchisors can also provide seminars, supplemental training programs, and field representatives to enhance communications.

Awareness is also a key to a successful franchising system. Franchisors should make their franchisees aware that they are appreciated and viewed as a vital component of the channel. Many franchisors provide performance awards. Some offer performance incentives, such as cash or trips, to particularly productive franchisees.

Next, franchisors need to develop strong personal *rapport* with their franchisees. Some franchisors do this by providing birthday gifts, flowers on special days, or remembrances for services performed or goals reached. Others confer public recognition at annual meetings or through newsletters for the promotional, publicity, or community service of franchisees. At its core, rapport implies sympathetic understanding. As such, the development of rapport also requires open two-way communication, empathy and, at times, just plain listening.

Lastly, franchisors must provide *expertise* to franchisees. Most initial meetings between franchisor and franchisee are concerned with the nuts and bolts of the franchising operation. However, as the relationship matures, meetings should concentrate on specific areas such as finance, management, and marketing. Toll-free hotlines to allow franchisees immediate access to the expertise available from the franchisor are becoming commonplace. Franchisors typically provide computer and special promotions expertise, as well as product/service research and development.

Intelligent Contracts

Even with CARE, problems may still arise. The contract remains at the heart of the franchise, providing the basis for a discrete or relational relationship. Unfortunately, many contracts greatly favor the franchisor. Typically, such contracts are specific in detailing the franchisees' obligations, but are ambiguous regarding the obligations of the franchisor or the rights of the franchisee. Power is concentrated in the hands of franchisors and can be used with little regard to the hardships that may be imposed within the system.

Franchising is unique among other channel alternatives in that it features a mechanism to reduce the potential for serious channel conflict—*intelligent contracts.* An intelligent contract is one that explicitly addresses how all the concerns of franchisors and franchisees will be addressed, when and if they arise. The types of inequities and ambiguities that often lead to franchisor-franchisee conflict can be removed by designing intelligent contracts that specify:[35]

- The unique roles of each contracting party.
- Franchisor and franchisee operating procedures as precisely as possible within the antitrust-based obligations of both parties.

- How the performance standards of the franchisee and franchisor will be established and revised.
- The criteria that must be met before market or product expansion can occur.
- All reasonable causes that can lead to the franchisor's termination of the franchising agreement.

Other examples of franchising problems and possible solutions are shown in Exhibit 12.4.

Strategic Franchising Partnerships

Franchisors and franchisees who share common goals from the beginning will be more likely to develop strategic relationships. Common goals can be developed through strategic franchising partnerships.

Changes already unfolding in the relationships between franchisors and franchisees indicate the growing interest in strategic franchising partnerships. These changes are largely a result of transformations in individual leadership styles, both of the franchisor and franchisee.

Exhibit 12.4

Franchisor-franchisee problems and their resolutions

Problems	*Resolution*
Poor advertising and promotional materials	Invite franchisees to participate on advertising and promotional committees; solicit franchisees' advice and recommendations regarding local promotional and advertising efforts.
Incomplete operating manuals	Ask franchisees to help update and revise manuals; emphasize training manuals as part of the franchising system.
Poor training	Revamp training program, using suggestions of franchisees for how to improve training; emphasize training as a means of ensuring standardization, quality, and committment to the goals and policies of the franchise system.
Lack of proper disclosure of information	Improve newsletters, memos, and communication materials; bring all franchisees online with the franchising system itself.
Inadequate availability for advice	Set up hotlines; increase number of field representatives; schedule regular meetings with franchisees on an individual and group basis.
Inadequate marketing research	Establish franchisee-led marketing research committees; improve headquarters marketing research programs.
Insufficient follow-up training and information	Offer refresher courses; publish bulletins and updates on operating procedures.
Inadequate equipment package	Form franchisee advisory council to evaluate and improve equipment and procedures.
Inappropriate or poor site selections	Evaluate and improve site selection criteria for both franchisor and franchisees.

Source: Adapted from Justis, Robert, and Richard Judd (1989), *Franchising,* Cincinnati, OH: South-Western Publishing Co.

Industry experts also believe these changes are being prompted by the pressure of increased scrutiny at the state and federal legislative levels.[36]

The pursuit of partnerships through franchising embraces many of the management concepts discussed earlier in this chapter, including open lines of communication, organized franchise forums such as franchising associations or committees, ongoing training, and an attitude of working together responsibly. Information exchange in franchise channels is particularly important because system performance is based on franchisees serving as field operatives to relay customer information to the franchisor. In general, franchisors can become less of a parent and more of a partner to their franchisees by addressing the following issues:[37]

- **Mutual responsibility.** Charles Cocotas, president of TCBY Systems, Inc., considers himself the champion of his franchisees. He refers to TCBY franchisees as his customers and describes them as the engine that powers the income of the franchise system. Cocotas suggests that franchisors and franchisees have a built-in responsibility to work together closely, cooperatively, and harmoniously. The cornerstone of this approach is strikingly simple: Franchisors should never lose sight of how it feels to be a franchisee.
- **Communicating up and down.** The communication process must be improved from the perspective of how well and how much information flows from the franchisors to the franchisees. Communication must also flow backward to the franchisor. Advisory councils should provide input pertaining to such issues as marketing, promotion and advertising, new product lines, supplier relations, and long-run strategic planning. Advisory councils are typically organized as an elected body intended to represent all the franchisees in the franchising system. The membership includes franchisees from different regions, and the terms of office are normally staggered. The sizes of the councils vary widely, depending on the size of the franchising system.

  Because of their lesser strength, an argument can be made that franchisees have the right and a need to be organized. The franchisor has a responsibility to promote and nurture such councils. Communications remains the primary tool to foster a sense of partnership and, thus, avoid conflict with their franchisees.
- **Franchisees as customers.** Are franchisees the customers of franchisors? Yes, but too many franchisees probably feel like they work for their franchisors. TCBY's Cocotas suggests that his customers are not the consumers who buy the yogurt. His customers are the people who *sell* the yogurt—the franchisees. If Cocotas' customers are not supported, he loses. Successful relationships take a team effort.
- **Leadership and attitude.** Creating a climate where there are open lines of communication, a commitment to mutual goals, and a sense of responsibility to achieve those goals requires leadership. An attitude of open franchisor support for franchisees can be reflected in ongoing training, on-site visits, and other little things, such as a consistently positive response to those telephone calls that franchisees will inevitably make for help in the business.[38]

What is franchise system partnering really about? It's about trying to move a franchising relationship in a more positive direction. In the meantime, Channel Surfing 12.4 offers a discussion of commonly held myths about franchising conflicts and the facts that should dispel those myths.

Channel Surfing 12.4

Franchising Conflict: Fiction and Fact

Here is our Top Ten list of the myths and facts of conflict management within franchising channels. Strictly speaking, sticking with the facts and avoiding the errors embedded in the myths should go a long way toward helping franchisors and franchisees have a productive, long-term relationship. Enjoy them.

Myth #1: Conflict in franchising channels can be avoided through effective communication and competent management.
Fact: There will always be conflict in franchising channels, regardless of the kind of management and communication you have. It is far better to expect conflict than to be unprepared when it occurs.

Myth #2: Because the franchise arrangement is based on a legal contract, problems should be addressed by immediately quoting that contract and proposing legal action.
Fact: The franchise contract should be pulled out only as a clarifier of the legal responsibilities of both parties, and only as a last resort. Threats of legal action usually exacerbate the problem, not help it. Discussing the problem and searching for a solution are always better alternatives.

Myth #3: Good franchisees are those that follow the system. Bad franchisees are those who constantly call the corporate office, questioning the franchisor's policies and practices.
Fact: Communication is always a plus in any relationship, franchising or otherwise. Often, the franchisee is trying to bring a problem to the attention of the franchisor that is prohibiting him/her from running the business more effectively.

Myth #4: Franchisees tend to be too emotional. Let them cool off, then focus more logically on the issues.
Fact: The role of emotions in conflict cannot, and should not, be avoided in franchising relationships. Instead, they should be acknowledged and heard. Then each party should make an effort to develop an understanding of the other person's viewpoint. Easier said than done, to be sure, but the effort should be made.

Myth #5: If franchisees don't like the franchisor's solutions, then it is clear that they don't fully understand the problem.
Fact: Franchisees should also be involved in problem identification and the development of a solution, in so far as those problems and the resulting solutions relate to them.

Myth #6: Franchisors must take a position and stick with it so as not to appear weak and lose control.
Fact: Let's face it, ego trips often prevent franchisees from approaching franchisors with problems, or vice versa. It is far better for both parties to remain flexible—especially when faced with new information.

Myth #7: If the franchisor gives in on one issue, the franchisee will expect the same in the future.
Fact: Not so. Marketing relationships are almost never a zero-sum game. The mentality of win-lose situations should be avoided in franchising channels. Cooperation in developing mutually acceptable solutions will generally result in win-win outcomes.

Myth #8: Franchisors should never give up something without getting something in return.
Fact: Again, negotiation is the key. Serious, earnest, genuine negotiation.

Myth #9: Use the element of surprise to maintain the upper hand
Fact: Are you kidding? Forcing franchisees to accept new programs or procedures, especially those in which they were not involved in developing, will fail to evoke a positive response. Change is always feared and thus should be instituted progressively.

Myth #10: A win-win solution to all conflicts is not realistic
Fact: Yes, it is. The success of both parties can only be ensured if they work together. Coercion and manipulation will only hurt the chances of success. Win-win solutions are possible if both parties are willing to work toward them.

Points to Ponder

- Of the 10 myths listed, which do you think is the most meaningful when considered against the broader context of channel relationships? Why?

Source: Adapted from Trocchio, Carole (1993), "Ten Myths of Conflict Resolution," *Franchising World,* July/August, 33–34; Bernstein, Charles (1994), "Franchising: Explosive Issues Fuel Debate," *Restaurants & Institutions,* October 15, 61–67; and Luciano, Lani (1994), "How to Fight Your Franchisor and Win," *Money (Money Guide Supplement),* 28–32.

What's in Franchising's Future?

Pulling out our trusty crystal ball, we see four predominant trends in the future of franchising: diversity, flexibility, conversion franchising, and multiple unit franchising.

Diversity

We believe franchisees will become increasingly diverse in terms of their cultural, economic, educational, and ethnic backgrounds. They are likely to be even more vocal, harder to manage, less easily satisfied, more disgruntled, and more anxious than earlier franchisees.

Furthermore, American consumers are also increasingly skeptical and more difficult to please. Niche marketing, improved customer service, innovative managerial techniques, and the pursuit of far-ranging markets will be demanded. Julia and Eric Henderson sell Baskin-Robbins ice cream to the 4,500 residents of Wasilla, Alaska, where winter is the predominant season. Believe it or not, their sales were 72 percent over original projections! Why have Alaskans fallen so hard for ice cream? The Hendersons don't really know. They did, however, understand that the demographics looked good, pointing toward a growing, youth-dominated market featuring little competition. The Hendersons persuaded Baskin-Robbins to give them a shot and they are apparently serving the needs of their market.[39] But in other, more saturated markets, the days of just throwing up another franchise and watching customers run through the doors are gone.

Flexibility

Flexibility will emerge as the centerpiece of effective franchise development. Tough economies and competitive markets demand flexible approaches. Even franchises with well-established concepts are adapting their operations to meet the changing economy and customer base. Notable changes have occurred in the fast-food industries, where even industry leader McDonald's acknowledges that it must adapt. It has begun to develop satellite or fill-in stores in downtown areas.[40]

Conversion Franchising

Conversion franchising, in which small-business owners trade in their autonomy to become part of franchise systems, is gaining speed. The format is especially popular in the international arena, where it accounts for some 20 percent of international franchise units. The practice is becoming more a matter of necessity than choice in maturing foreign markets such as Mexico and in much of Southeast Asia, where prime real-estate prices are skyrocketing. Ex-independent businesses can be up and running quickly and can more easily capitalize on existing customer bases. This translates into near instant revenue streams for U.S.-based franchises. General Nutrition Corporation cuts store opening time to 45 days for conversions, down from 120 or more days for new stores.[41]

Before expanding a franchising concept to an overseas market, a franchisor must be certain that the company is ready for transplanting. Many of the best markets in foreign countries have already been developed. Still, at a time when thinking globally while acting locally is no longer an alternative but an imperative, the vast majority of U.S. franchisors are still confined to the domestic market. This is surprising, and likely to change, given that U.S. franchising systems have always been the leaders in exporting this kind of business. Moreover, U.S. franchisors and businesses in general will continue to face increasing competition at home from their European and Japanese counterparts.[42]

Only about 20 percent of all U.S. franchise systems now have foreign operations; however, a substantial percentage of U.S. franchises currently without foreign operations are planning to increase their overseas operation.[43] For those U.S. franchisers ready to expand, there are three ways to set up an overseas franchise system: (1) selling individual franchises overseas, (2) appointing a master franchisor, or (3) setting up a joint venture with foreign investors.

Multiple Unit Franchising

For the 28 MotoPhoto franchisees operating in the Washington, DC, area, Dick Schulman is the person to call when problems crop up. As the franchisor's area representative, Schulman not only owns MotoPhoto units himself, he also recruits and supports his local franchisees. Schulman is only one of an expanding number of franchisees who own, manage, or support the needs of more than one franchising unit. The opportunity to engage in **multiple unit franchising (MUF)** has attracted more participants each year since Century 21 pioneered the concept in the early 1970s. Multiple unit franchisors may function as area representatives, like Schulman, or they may serve as area developers or master franchisees.[44]

As Schulman does for MotoPhoto, *area representatives* provide support and deal with the day-to-day obligations of the franchisor on the local level. Area representatives may also recruit franchisees on behalf of their franchisor. In many ways, area representatives perform like middle managers in a large corporation. *Area developers* are franchisees who are given the right to open and operate branch outlets within a specific geographic territory. While they have no right to sell franchises themselves, area developers may be responsible for opening a certain number of locations in a given area over a given time frame. *Master franchisees* function as independent selling organizations that recruit and support franchise prospects within a specific geographic area, frequently an entire state or country. Within these regions, master franchisees have the right to sell franchises. In return, they receive a portion of the franchise fee, along with part of the ongoing royalties paid by the new franchisee.

The use of MUFs, in its various forms, is likely to expand in the future because:

- Franchisors will have a larger pool of talented, management-oriented professionals from which to recruit, thanks to corporate downsizing and the widely shared perception that other business opportunities are shrinking.
- It is unlikely that franchisors who expand internationally will be able to service their overseas franchisees efficiently or effectively without the presence of someone in each country.
- The option provides ways for franchisees to grow and prosper financially, while remaining within their original franchising system.

As franchisors face sophisticated investor/franchisees who own multiple franchises and who themselves oversee the franchising of a geographic region, state, or country, the task of managing the networks of relationships will grow complex.

Key Terms

business format franchising
capricious termination
conversion franchising
dual distribution
encroachment
franchisee
franchising
franchising systems
franchisor
FTC disclosure format
multiple unit franchising (MUF)
product/tradename franchising
tied-house franchising systems
Uniform Franchise Offering Circular (UFOC)

Chapter Summary

Franchising involves a contractually based, continuing channel relationship in which a franchisor provides a licensed privilege to do business in a specified area plus assistance in organizing, training, merchandising, and management in return for a consideration from the franchisee. This consideration usually takes the form of start-up fees, continuing royalty fees, and the franchisee's agreement to abide by the constraints of the franchising contract. Franchising relationships actually consist of three relationships: legal, business, and a relationally oriented association between the franchisor and franchisee.

Franchising provides opportunities for all parties involved in the channel relationship. For the franchisor, franchising offers an alternative to developing a company-owned chain, a vertical market expansion financed essentially through externally sourced franchisee funds, and a highly motivated channel management team. For the franchisee, franchising provides an alternative to independent operation, proven products/services/concepts and operating procedures, and an established brand/image that creates instant credibility and attractiveness in the market.

Two forms of franchising arrangements predominate. In one form, known as product/trademark franchising, franchisees distribute a product under a franchisor's trademark. Automotive dealerships are a good example. In the other, known as the business format franchise, franchisees replicate a complete business concept, including product or service, trademark, and methods of operation, in their own communities. The fast-food industry provides numerous examples. The specific prototypes of these broad formats are being altered to adapt to the changing demands of today's marketplace.

Franchisees are deeply concerned with profits. They are likewise concerned with the possibility of losing their business at the end of the contractual period, franchisor expansion in their territories, and getting requisite returns for the royalty fees and promotional payments made to their franchisor. Franchisors are also deeply concerned with profits. They are also concerned with whether franchisees honor their contractual agreements in the areas of purchasing, operating procedures, and income reporting.

Life in the United States is filled with change. Franchising is affected by these changes, which present both challenges and opportunities to the industry. One of the strengths of the franchising channel form is that it can change to rapidly accommodate the changing consumer and industry needs that emerge as a consequence of social/cultural/demographic, economic, international, and industry changes.

Franchisees tend to be entrepreneurs. Such an orientation contributes to the probability of an individual franchisee's success. Beyond this, prospective franchisees can improve their chances for success if they nail the numbers (in their franchising contract), measure (franchisors) management, cross-examine current franchisees, and carefully comb the franchising contract.

Ideally, the interests of franchisors and franchisees are one and the same: The better franchisees do, the better franchisors do. But life in channels often fails to follow the ideal; franchising systems are rife with potential and actual conflicts of interest. Conflicts frequently arise over the issues of tying agreements, expansion/encroachment, whether termination/renewal clauses are executed capriciously, and/or whether less than full or accurate disclosure of facts and conditions pertaining to the franchising arrangement has been provided. After years of relative inaction, legislators at both the state and federal level are again introducing measures to address the concerns of both franchisors and franchisees.

To make franchise relationships work, franchisors should ensure that their franchisees are always able to communicate with them and feel a part of the franchising system. Franchisors should make sure their franchisees are aware that they are appreciated, particularly when their performance merits such consideration. Franchisors should also strive to develop a sense of rapport with their franchisees and must provide the necessary expertise to them. Beyond these considerations, franchising is unique among other marketing channel alternatives in that it features a mechanism to substantially reduce the potential for serious channel conflict—the intelligent contract design. An intelligent contract specifies the unique roles of each contracting party; franchisor and franchisee operating procedures as precisely as possible within the antitrust-based obligations of both parties; how the performance standards of the franchisee and franchisor will be established and revised; the criteria that must be met before market or product expansion can occur; and all reasonable causes that can lead to the franchisor's termination of the franchising agreement. Finally, franchisors should, in most instances, strive to develop a strategic partnership with their franchisees. This end can be achieved by successfully addressing the following issues: mutual responsibility, communicating up and down the channel, treating franchisees as customers, and providing leadership and a positive attitude.

Looking toward the future, it is apparent that the franchising industry will continue to become more diverse. Flexibility will emerge as perhaps the major factor contributing to or inhibiting the success of future franchising channels. Conversion franchising will gain speed, particularly within international markets, and U.S.-based franchises will increasingly look overseas for their future expansion and growth in profitability. Finally, multiple unit franchising will continue to gain popularity and strength within the U.S. and international franchising systems.

Channel Challenges

1. Abe Gustin, Jr., CEO of Applebee's International, Inc., states, "Our franchisees have a say in everything we do—whether it's a change in the look of a building, adding or taking out a menu item, or what advertising will look like. It's really a partnership of 61 people, us and 60 franchisees. We have the use of 61 brains instead of one." How does Gustin's statement relate to the view of franchising as an orchestrated network?
2. Princeton, New Jersey–based Berlitz International, Inc., dates back to the 1870s, but it only recently began to franchise its language instruction products and services. Frank Garton, vice president of worldwide franchising, suggests that "properly utilized, franchisees can operate like an ongoing focus group on the products and services." Why might franchisees be good sources for new product development? How might the solicitation of feedback enhance franchisees' satisfaction with a franchise system?
3. A 1995 research study by Georgia Tech's DuPree Center for Entrepreneurship and New Venture Development indicates that nearly 75 percent of all franchisers will fail within 10 years. Yet the number of franchise stores in the United States alone grew over 13 percent in the first half of the 1990s. Do you think franchising will continue to grow in the new millennium despite the high failure rates? Why or why not?
4. Discovery Zone, Inc., a chain of indoor playgrounds for children, has few franchised operations. In fact, franchisees own less than a dozen of the nearly 300 Discovery Zone units. Currently, Discovery Zone faces a lawsuit from its few franchisees. The franchisees allege that Discovery Zone stopped supporting franchisees after a few months and that it competes against them. One franchisee charges that Discovery Zone failed to develop marketing programs to retain customers. How would you resolve this franchisor-franchisee conflict? What implications regarding franchise relationships can be gleaned from this example (i.e., a chain with just a few franchisees)?
5. Many franchisors are adding kiosks and carts—essentially "express" versions of their franchises—in hospitals, airports, and other retail sites. Many franchisees complain that these franchisor-owned kiosks represent franchisor encroachment. One KFC spokesperson counters: "We see the concept of nontraditional distribution points as a win-win for both the KFC and franchisees." Are company-owned kiosks encroaching on franchisees' territories? Why or why not? What alternative methods may be used to extend into nontraditional distribution points and keep franchisees happy?

Review Questions

1. What is a franchise system? What benefits are received by franchisees and franchisors under this system?
2. Discuss the differences between product/trade name franchises and business format franchises.
3. What are some of the common concerns or problems of franchisees and franchisors?
4. How do current economic trends impact franchise systems?
5. What essential steps should prospective franchisees take to improve their opportunities for success?
6. What are potential sources of conflict in franchise relationships?
7. What are some of the current legal and ethical standards in franchising?
8. What are some of the methods used to resolve conflicts in franchise relationships?
9. What future directions exist for improving franchise relationships?

Endnotes

1. Sheridan, Margaret (1999), "Two Way Street," *Restaurants & Institutions,* 109 (34), 57–62.
2. Emerson, Robert W. (1998), "Franchise Termination: Legal Rights and Practical Effects When Franchisees Claim That the Franchisor Discriminates," *American Business Law Journal,* 35 (4), 559–645.
3. Adapted from Hoffman, Richard C., and John F. Preble (1993), "Franchising into the Twenty-First Century," *Business Horizons,* September–October, 35–43; and Cross, James C., and Bruce J. Walker (1987), "Service Marketing and Franchising: A Practical Business Marriage," *Business Horizons,* November–December, 50–58.
4. Hoffman, Richard C. and John F. Preble (1991), "Franchising: Selecting a Strategy for Rapid Growth," *Long Range Planning,* 24 (4), 74–85.
5. Arthur Anderson & Co. (1993), *Franchising in the Economy, 1989–1992,* Washington, DC: International Franchise Association Educational Foundation, Inc.
6. Selz, David D. (1982), "Legal Considerations," *Complete Handbook of Franchising,* Reading, MA: Addison-Wesley.
7. Justis, Robert, and Richard Judd (1989), *Franchising,* Cincinnati, OH: Southwestern Publishing.
8. Moore, Lisa (1991), "The Flight to Franchising," *U.S. News & World Report,* June 10, 68–71.
9. Adapted from Whittemore, Meg (1991), "How Changes Are Affecting Franchising," *Nation's Business,* November, 65–67; and Whittemore, Meg (1991), "Franchising," *Nation's Business,* January, 68–69.
10. MacAuthur, Kate (2000), "Fast-Feeders Find Sizzle by Bringing on the Bacon," *Advertising Age,* 71 (13), 12–13.
11. *State of Small Business: A Report of the President* (1993), Washington, DC: U.S. Small Business Administration, Government Printing Office.
12. Whittemore, Meg (1991), "How Changes Are Affecting Franchising," *Nation's Business,* November, 65–67.
13. Cross, James C., and Bruce J. Walker (1987), "Service Marketing and Franchising: A Practical Business Marriage," *Business Horizons,* November–December, 50–58.
14. Smith, Gloria (1999), "Marketing in the New Millennium," *Franchising World,* 31 (6), 31–44.
15. Eroglu, Sevgin (1992), "The Internationalization Process of Franchising: A Conceptual Model," *International Marketing Review,* 9 (5), 19–30.
16. Welch, L. S. (1989), "Diffusion of Franchise System Use in International Operations," *International Marketing Review,* 6 (5), 7–19.
17. Walker, B. J. (1989), *A Comparison of International vs. Domestic Expansion by U.S. Franchise Systems,* Washington, DC: International Franchise Association, 124.
18. Nathewson, Frank, and Ralph Winter (1994), "Territorial Restrictions in Franchise Contracts," *Economic Inquiry,* 32 (April), 181–92.
19. Hoffman and Preble, "Franchising into the Twenty-First Century," 35–43.
20. *Franchising Opportunities Handbook* (1994)

Washington, DC: U.S. Department of Commerce, Government Printing Office, 12.

21. Bongiorno, Lori (1993), "Franchising Fracas," *Business Week,* March 22, 68–71; Stern, Richard L., and Reed Abelson (1991), "Franchise Hell," *Forbes,* September 2, 152–53; and DeGeorge, Gail (1989), "Fed-Up Franchisees: They're Mad as Hell and . . . " *Business Week,* 83–84.
22. Emerson, Robert W. (1998), "Franchise Termination: Legal Rights and Practical Efforts When Franchisees Claim the Franchisor Discriminates," *American Business Law Journal,* 35 (4), 559–645.
23. Bongiorno, "Franchising Fracas," 68–71.
24. Hunt, Shelby D. (1977), "Franchising: Promises, Problems, Prospects," *Journal of Retailing,* 53 (3), 71–84.
25. Mehegan, Sean (1995), "Fast Food Nation," *Restaurant News,* 94 (11), 30–35.
26. Martin, Richard (1995), "PepsiCo Profit Dip Could Lift Chain Franchising," *Nation's Restaurant News,* 29 (16), 3, 75.
27. Laird, Betsy (2000), "Congress Nibbling at Legislative Plate Full of Key Franchise Issues," *Franchise World,* 32 (4), 43–45.
28. Mohammed, Kenneth D. (1989), "Franchising Currents," *Franchise Law Journal,* 33.
29. Stadfield, L. Seth (1990), "Franchising Currents," *Franchise Law Journal,* 9.
30. Storholm, Gordon, and Eberhard E. Scheuing (1994), "Ethical Implications of Business Format Franchising," *Journal of Business Ethics,* 13, 181–88.
31. Borden, Neil D., Andrew A. Caffey, and Sharon C. Casey (1989), "Franchise Advertising Funds: Structural, Tax, Operational and Liability Issues," *Franchise Law Journal,* 10 (2), 38.
32. Storholm and Scheuing, "Ethical Implications of Business Format Franchising," 181–88.
33. Barkoff, Rupert M., and W. Michael (1994), "Encroachment: Franchising Enigma," *Franchising Update,* Second Quarter, 7–11.
34. Justis, Robert, and Richard Judd (1989), *Franchising,* Cincinnati, OH: Southwestern Publishing.
35. Stephenson, P. Ronald, and Robert G. House (1971), "A Perspective on Franchising: The Design of an Effective Relationship," *Business Horizons,* August, 35–42.
36. Strutton, David, Lou E. Pelton, and James R. Lumpkin (1993), "The Influence of Psychological Climate on Conflict Resolution Strategies in Franchising Relationships," *Journal of the Academy of Marketing Science,* 21 (3), 207–16.
37. Snow, Charles C., Raymond E. Miles, and Henry J. Coleman, Jr. (1992), "Managing 21st Century Organizations," *Organizational Dynamics,* Winter, 5–19.
38. Whittemore, Meg (1994), "Less a Partner, More a Parent," *Nation's Business,* March, 49–57.
39. Whittemore, Meg (1989), "Franchising's Appeal to Women," *Nation's Business,* November, 63–64.
40. Carlsson, Carl (1993), "Tough Times Require Flexibility," *Franchising World,* 25 (6), 42.
41. Steinberg, Carol (1993), "International Franchising: Shock of the New," *World Trade,* 6 (3), 130–34.
42. Eroglu, Sevgin (1992), "The Internationalization Process of Franchising Systems: A Conceptual Model," *International Marketing Review,* 9 (5), 19–30.
43. Gilman, Alan J. (1992), "Franchising: An International Frontier," *Chain Store Age Executive,* 68 (6), 70.
44. Whittemore, Meg, and Robert Perry (1993), "Multiple-Unit Franchising," *Nation's Business,* July, 53–57.

chapter

13

Developing Long-Term Value

Learning Objectives

After reading this chapter, you should be able to:

- Define the three types of exchange relationships.
- Discuss the four elements that are associated with all exchange episodes.
- Explain differences between discrete and relational exchange.
- Demonstrate how the presence of trust affects behavioral contracts.
- Discuss the role that reciprocity plays in social exchange.
- Explain the four stages of channel relationships.
- Identify the exchange governance norms that exist in all behavioral contracts.
- Apply the basic principles of relational exchange to buyer-seller dyads.

Courtesy Romp.com

This is a far cry from Mickey Mouse. There's no family friendly entertainment in this virtual theme park. Instead, Romp.com features "Girl of the Week" pictorials, Booty Calls, and Animal House humor, promising "a piece of ass in every adventure." Yet Michael Eisner, chairman and CEO of the The Walt Disney Company, checks it out regularly. You see, the cofounder of this freewheeling, raucous entertainment site targeted to male adolescents is Michael Eisner's son, Eric.

Eric Eisner clearly is a "chip off the old block" when it comes to developing marketing relationships. Romp.com registered over 200,000 users during its first six weeks. Eric and his partner Bruce Forman plan to build on the somewhat elusive 16- to 25-year-old loyal male fan base. What's next for these "Rompers"? Eisner and Forman plan to expand beyond broadband into the wireless market. As these young entrepreneurs duly note, the number of teens armed with wireless devices is skyrocketing. The ambitious, interactive visionaries are exploring partnership opportunities to syndicate the Romp.com content on wireless and other emerging media.[1]

Eric may be leveraging a couple of lessons learned from his lifetime mentor, his father. His dad helped make The Walt Disney Company the third largest media conglomerate in the world. Michael Eisner has a proven track record for developing long-term channel relationships in television, film, theme parks, and the Internet. Today, Disney owns the ABC network and has stakes in cable channels like ESPN and A&E Television Networks. Touchstone, Hollywood Pictures, and Miramax are all Disney film imprints. Will there be a future relationship between Romp.com and Disney? Maybe not. But there likely will be an enduring relationship between the father and son duo in the entertainment media industry.

* * * *

Whether you favor a relationship with Mickey Mouse or Romp.com's Bill Bilkman, you can appreciate how developing lifelong "connections" extends beyond filial relationships. Eric Eisner, Bruce Forman, and their team of thirty-something visionaries are finding ways to work together and apart over time. After all, the Romp.com founding fathers include an investment executive and former management consultant, a communications industry strategy manager, a public services fund-raiser, and a university professor. How did these markedly different types of individuals come together? A shared vision: Romp.com.

In this final part of the book, we address how shared values, purposes, and goals can serve as a mechanism for developing and sustaining long-term channel relationships. In this chapter, we will look at exchange relationships—what they are, what they are comprised of, the stages of channel relationships, and the norms that govern them. In Chapter 14, we explore the emerging role of strategic partnering agreements.

Exchange Relationships: Bridging Transactions

Exchange processes lie at the heart of the CRM model, and, as discussed in Chapter 11, *transaction costs* provide the economic cornerstone on which channel member exchanges are based. But the interaction processes that connect channel members extend beyond simple economic considerations. A human component of exchange also exists. This human element arises in all relationships, as shown in the CRM.

If channel members only paid attention to the economic side of exchange transactions, much of the "heart of marketing" would be ignored.[2] But the task of separating individual economic exchanges from the complex networks of interpersonal relationships that evolve in dynamic markets is difficult, thus the term *exchange relationships.* This is particularly true in modern marketing channels.[3]

Why are exchange relationships so complex? There are two reasons. First, all people are different. Second, human interactions provide the only means through which exchange relationships can develop. Microeconomic theories traditionally assume that each participant in any exchange always behaves in rational, self-supporting, and profit-maximizing—in other words, economic—ways. While useful, this explanation fails to completely capture the entire range of human behaviors, which, of course, includes irrational emotional behaviors, as well. Thus, the exchange economics theory we discussed in Chapter 11 can never fully capture the complexity of human interaction in channel settings. Three basic types of human interaction can arise in business domains.[4] These are discussed below and are illustrated in Exhibit 13.1.

Calculative Exchange Relationships

Calculative exchange relationships are entirely based on the economic returns (profits) derived from a transaction. In situations where each party to a transaction knows little about the other party, calculative exchange relationships usually predominate. This type of relationship generally does not last long. In calculative exchange relationships, behaviors must conform to precise transaction terms.

To illustrate, consider that being a giant drugmaker in the 2000s is not easy. Development costs are soaring, generic products are nipping at sales volumes, and prices are under

Exhibit 13.1

A continuum of exchange relationships

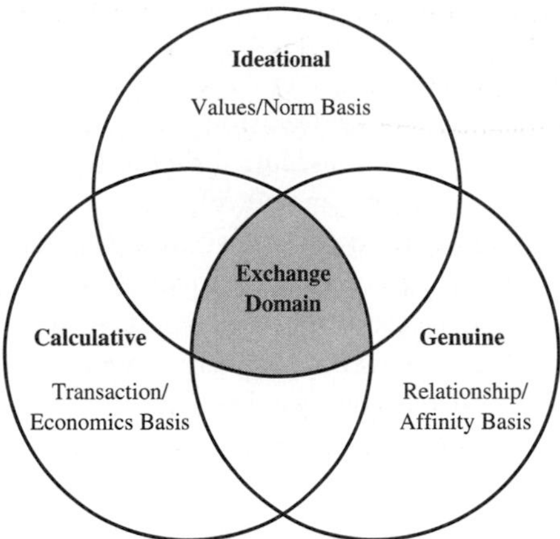

assault from a variety of public sources. In response to these pressures, companies such as SmithKline-Beckman Corporation and Bristol-Meyers Company are seeking new long-term partners. Not so with Merck & Company. "Merck wants to be alone—but with lots of friends."[5] The company is purposefully entering a series of short-term, precisely delineated relationships with channel partners that perform specific research, sales, or distribution functions. Given the uncertainty that predominates in the drug industry, Merck strategists feel that, for now, calculative exchange relationships are the way to go.

Ideational Exchange Relationships

The next category of human interaction is **ideational relationships.** Here, each exchange partner is viewed by the other as a conveyor of ideas, ideals, and opinions. In ideational relationships, the values of each party underlie the transaction process. These values provide a basis for the development of norms, which then guide behaviors in any future interactions shared by the current exchange partners. In business settings the keys to successful ideational relationships are always the same: compatible partners who are willing to subvert organizational egos to give a new relationship time to succeed.

In The Net Economy, ideational relationships are becoming a reality: for example, the channel interactions between Atlanta-based NetBank and AmeriTrade. NetBank is a virtual bank with over 100,000 customers that has developed a long-term relationship with Ameritrade. NetBank will offer full-line banking services to Ameritrade's one million brokerage customers. Together, these dot-com titans keep pace with E*Trade Bank. E*Trade Bank (formerly Telebank) has become the largest dot-com player. But the ideational relationship extends beyond growing its customer base: "We needed to create deeper and more meaningful relationships with the households we serve," according to Mike Fitzgerald. As Fitzgerald notes, a traditional bank manages between $2.5 and $3 million per employee while NetBank manages about $16 million per employee. NetBank passes the $1.6 billion cost savings back to their customers. Together, they hope to work with Ameritrade and customers to continue this win-win relationship.[6]

Genuine Relationships

Genuine relationships are highly evolved interactions in which *partners* are willing to share personal information. Decisions and behaviors in genuine relationships are no longer based on purely rational transaction criteria. Instead, they are best illustrated as friendships or economic kinships. In genuine relationships, exchange parties share behaviorial norms (as in ideational relationships) as well as a personal affinity for one another. Genuine relationships are characterized by a high frequency of exchange. A broad variety of elements—including products, services, ideas, or viewpoints—are subject to exchange. Emotional ties, along with their accompanying baggage, are present in this sort of exchange relationship.

To illustrate how genuine relationships work in marketing channels, consider the long and winding road traveled by Ford Motor Company in its efforts to penetrate the Japanese automotive market. In 1925, a small waterfront warehouse in Yokohama was sufficiently large to house Ford's entry into Japan. To be successful, Ford's assembly subsidiary needed to develop ongoing supplier relationships with Japanese manufacturers. But Ford did not realize this at the time. So for four decades, Ford's performance in Japan was, at best, tepid. Ford failed because it did not develop the proper market relationships.

Then, in 1965, Ford began buying parts for the automobiles it sold in Asia from a fledgling Japanese automaker called Mazda. Soon after, Mazda introduced the rotary engine to the United States market. Unfortunately, the energy crunch of the 1970s proved disastrous for rotary engines because they were widely viewed as inefficient gas-guzzlers. Not surprisingly, Mazda's sales plummeted. Yet the relationship between Ford and Mazda continued. By 1979, this relationship was so strong that Ford actually took financial measures to rescue the struggling Japanese firm.

Ford and Mazda's relationship eventually matured into the most successful marriage in the industry's history. As you might imagine, their recent good fortune didn't arise by accident. Former Ford President Phillip E. Benton once remarked, "There has been a lot of hard work put into making it work."[7] How do marketing relationships sometimes develop to the point where the importance of the relationship transcends the importance of any individual transaction, as did Ford and Mazda's? More important, why is such a state desirable? We consider these questions in the next section.

Exchange Episodes

Each party in a transaction must give and receive utility for exchange to occur. Exchange utility, as you may recall from Chapter 1, is the combination of benefits and costs traded back and forth between channel members as a result of their participation in an exchange or a relationship. In the Ford/Mazda relationship, for instance, Ford provided international marketing and financial expertise, while Mazda supplied manufacturing and product development capability. As a result, Ford and Mazda achieved more together than either could have alone. The Mazda MX-6 and Ford Probe became the first "domestic" cars built by a Japanese firm in the United States. Ford's Escort was engineered by Mazda and built by Ford, and Mazda sold the Ford-built Navajo utility vehicle.[8] Ford's sales in Japan increased by over 72,000 units, and Mazda's United States sales topped 350,000 units. Over the course of their ongoing relationship, Ford and Mazda have played different channel roles at different times with respect to one another.

Exhibit 13.2

Components of a marketing exchange episode

Products and Services
- Primary object of any exchange episode
- May be more or less important, depending on the importance of other factors

Information Exchange
- Technical, institutional, or market
- Evaluate for accuracy/reliability, breadth/depth, formality, and control

Financial Exchange
- Mutual assignment of value
- Ultimate economic measure of exchange

Social Exchange
- Must be purposeful and adaptive
- Trust and commitment are key to long-term relationship

When studying channel relationships, we need to differentiate between exchange episodes and the longer-term aspects of a relationship. An **exchange episode** is a separate and distinct transaction, such as Ford's acquiring parts from Mazda. In marketing channels, exchange episodes are completed based on prespecified terms of exchange. Exchange episodes can be consummated even when the channel participants have little allegiance toward one another or as part of an ongoing relationship. Either way, four elements *must* be associated with any marketing exchange episode.[9] These elements are discussed below and are summarized in Exhibit 13.2: products and services, information exchange, financial exchange, and social exchange.

Products and Services

Products and/or services are usually the primary object of interest in any marketing exchange episodes. Whether you are purchasing fruit from a roadside stand or a personal computer from a retail store, the product's characteristics will likely influence the nature of the exchange relationship. In the case of purchasing fruit from a roadside stand—probably a one-time transaction—the product's quality probably outweighs the importance of any interaction occurring between the buyer and seller. By contrast, purchasing a computer may require substantial buyer-seller dialogue to properly identify the buyer's computing needs. Follow-up visits may be required. The buyer's perception of the seller is often an important factor in such an exchange setting.

Information Exchange

Information is technical, institutional, or market intelligence conveyed from one channel member to another through personal or impersonal means.[10] As the tenor of this book reflects the unprecedented role of information technology or marketing channels, you are now acutely aware of the role of **information exchange.** Any of these three types of information can be a source of power or dependence among channel participants.[11] *Technical information* informs exchange partners about product or service specifications, performance data, or exchange terms. The product or service's complexity influences how often and how much technical information will be exchanged within a single episode.

Institutional information relates to the attributes of those organizations that are party to an exchange episode. The amount of institutional information shared between exchange partners generally differs based on their expectations for the channel's performance: the higher their expectations, the greater their need for institutional information. Institutional information can be dispersed or withheld in ways that promote or dampen confidence in one's exchange partner. *Market information* relates to the economic, technological, sociopolitical, or regulatory circumstances associated with the exchange episode. Market information is valuable because it offers a more complete picture of the channel environment in which the transaction develops.[12]

In an information exchange, the information received is evaluated for certain characteristics. From the time each party agrees to the transaction's terms and initiates the exchange, the accuracy of the information is scrutinized. But because they involve only isolated transactions, individual exchange episodes can offer only limited insight into the accuracy and reliability of the information.

Information received by either channel partner is also evaluated with respect to its breadth and depth. *Information breadth* specifies the list of topics or issues addressed in the information transfer. Imagine that you are shopping for a home entertainment system. Some sales representatives you encounter may have a limited knowledge of many of the components that comprise an entertainment system, such as televisions, stereo receivers, speakers, cassette recorders, or compact disk players. Such salespeople provide only a shallow overview of a breadth of topics. Other salespeople may have extensive knowledge of particular components and are thus capable of providing extensive information about them. This is what is meant by *information depth.*

The degree of formality with which information is transferred between the parties involved in exchange episodes also should be evaluated. *Formality* addresses how closely participants comply with standard channel practices when they exchange information. Because there is no guarantee of continuity when most marketing relationships begin, information is transferred through formal means. This information exchange can become less formal over time. For example, when you enter a full-service restaurant for the first time, you expect to be seated, handed a menu, and served by a waitperson. The waitperson has to ask for your order. In turn, you may ask about a particular menu offering, and he or she will respond accordingly. This information exchange is formal and consistent with accepted practice. But with successive visits to the restaurant, the information exchange may become less formal. Finally, if you become a regular customer, informal communication is likely because the waitperson will be familiar with your desires.

Finally, flows of information between channel members are often tightly controlled by one or both parties. Here, the notion of control refers to each party's (un)willingness to provide flexible procedures for obtaining or conveying information. Parties in exchange episodes usually exercise tight control over how information is received or sent.

Financial Exchange

Some form of financial exchange must be present within exchange episodes in market settings. All exchange requires a mutual acknowledgment of value between each participant.

Money is the economic indicator of exchange value in most societies; however, the objects of financial exchange vary across market settings. The ultimate economic measure for products or services is the value assigned to them by potential exchange partners. Take PepsiCo's trade deal with Russia.[13] The $3.5 billion, 10-year agreement included a barter of Pepsi syrup and bottling equipment for Russian vodka. Similarly, Peru obtained Argentinean wheat by exchanging iron ore.[14]

Generating the hard currency necessary to acquire goods is difficult, especially in international trade. A process known as *compensatory trade* prevails in such cases. **Compensatory trade** refers to the mutually agreed upon obligation to quid pro quo compensate any party for the goods or services it renders. This payment can take whatever form the parties can agree upon.

Social Exchange

Social exchange is the final element that must be present in any exchange episode. The act of exchange requires a social process.[15] **Social exchange** involves any set of observable behaviors on the part of at least two individuals. For social exchange to occur, at least some portion of these behaviors must be made in response to one's exchange counterpart.

Two conditions are necessary for social exchange to occur in an exchange episode. First, the exchange must be purposeful. This implies that each participant has a conscious objective and believes that this objective can be reached through taking part in the exchange. In essence, each party assesses the expected utility associated with entering a transaction. Then, this expected utility is compared to the utility available without the exchange association. When the expected utility arising from the exchange is greater than the utility existing without it, social exchange is likely.

The second condition involves a willingness among the partners to adapt their behaviors or expectations to achieve outcomes sought through the exchange. To illustrate the concept of adaptation and its relationship to assessing expected utility, consider your role as a student in this class. You presumably expect to achieve the utility of learning the course material. However, your ability to achieve this outcome depends partially on your interactions with your instructor and peers. Note-taking procedures may need to be adapted to the instructor's teaching method, or scheduled activities may have to be compromised to meet with peers outside of class. At the same time, the instructor is surely adapting his or her teaching style to the class's aptitude.

Adaptation. If you are the only party in the exchange who is adapting, then a *unilateral adaptation*—a one-sided adaptation—is said to be taking place. One party is willing to adjust its behaviors to satisfy the other's expectations. Conversely, a *symbiotic adaptation* signals a willingness shared among channel members to mutually adapt their behaviors to gain desired outcomes. Although symbiotic adaptation assumes a common *end* (outcome sought) between the exchange partners, each party may adapt *means* differently to any given situation. Regardless of the direction or cause of the adaption, however, each party benefits. The Ford/Mazda relationship shows how symbiotic adaptation works.[16] In 1987, Mazda did not have a sport-utility vehicle. So it decided to buy a modified version of the Ford Explorer. Ford accommodated the request with the objective of earning the right to build Mazda's pickup trucks. Mazda's Takuma Marukawa remarked of this exchange episode: "For the first time, we were the purchaser, making requests to the manufacturer in terms of quality and so on."[17]

Expected behaviors in exchange episodes are generally bound by precisely defined transaction terms. For this reason, there is little opportunity for symbiotic adaptation in exchange episodes. By contrast, unilateral adaptation is not likely to support the continuity of exchange episodes, although simply having social exchange is sometimes enough to overcome short-term problems as they arise. According to social exchange theory, adaptation evolves over time between exchange partners. Social exchange thus plays a pivotal role in sustaining successive exchange episodes by fostering symbiotic adaptation. Exhibit 13.3 illustrates how Ford and Mazda managed to build a strong relationship based on shared purpose and values and a mutual willingness to adapt over time.

Trust and Commitment. Social exchange provides a necessary baseline from which relationships can develop. But what fosters the initial exchange? The answer is that exchange relationships can only be established based on mutual **trust**—the belief that the candor, hu-

Exhibit 13.3

Ford and Mazda: partnering for success

Partnering Principle	*How Ford-Mazda Make It Work*
Exchange partners must constructively analyze the relationship.	Frequent meetings at all levels should include an opportunity for socializing.
Relationships change over time, so ongoing attention is necessary.	Trust cannot be developed exclusively at a boardroom table.
Relationships must have shared purpose.	Appoint an observer who takes responsibility for identifying any challenges that confront the alliance.
Successful relationships are those that serve the function for which they were originally formed.	Allow no sacrifice deals. Exchange episodes should be viable for all partners. It is up to top management to ensure that a general balance is maintained.
Relationships evolve from core values.	Exchange partners need to maintain their independence, as well. They should concentrate on sustaining their strengths since that made them desirable partners in the first place.
The set of norms which govern good relationships must be adaptable.	Anticipate cultural differences. Exchange partners should be flexible enough to accommodate each other's differences.
Top management must continually demonstrate its commitment to preserving the relationship.	

Source: Adapted from Treece and Miller (1992), "The Partners: Surprise! Ford and Mazda Have Built a Strong Team. Here's How," *Business Week,* February 10, 102–7; and Wilmot, William W. (1975), *Dyadic Communication: A Transactional Perspective,* Reading, MA: Addison-Wesley.

manity, and truthfulness of others is reliable.[18] The presence of trust implies that each party within an exchange believes its counterpart's commitment is credible and will be honored. Trust is reflected in the presence of a system of norms establishing each party's expectations about the other's performance. To illustrate, let's return to your role as a student. If you perform well on an assignment, you presumably trust that your instructor will give you a good grade. But if your initial performance was not consistent with the instructor's expectations, you should be able to clarify those expectations and improve your performance, as long as you trust the instructor's commitment.

Trust encourages constructive dialogue and cooperative problem solving between exchange partners. The absence of trust often leads to the termination of exchange relationships. Even if termination does not occur, an absence of trust forces channel members to waste time and resources on activities aimed at defending themselves from one another. In marketing channels, trust is the product of a social process that unfolds over time. For trust to be maintained in marketing channels, each party's performance must continually conform to the expectations of its channel counterpart.

Once it exists, trust can lead to the commitment of both channel participants to their exchange relationship. At that point, the exchange partners are likely to work diligently at preserving their relationship investment by cooperating with one another. Each is then more likely to resist short-term channel alternatives in favor of the expected long-term benefits of staying with its existing partner. A shared belief emerges that neither partner will act opportunistically toward the other. This dramatically increases the likelihood that the exchange partners will pursue high-risk, high-return channel strategies.

Trust and commitment lead to the sort of cooperative behaviors that facilitate relational exchange. When trust and commitment are each present, they yield outcomes that foster greater efficiency, productivity, and effectiveness within the channel. Both Kodak's Office Imaging Unit and Malcolm Baldrige Award winner Motorola Corporation clearly recognize the value of trust and commitment. Each firm conducts periodic surveys of major suppliers to measure their own performance at meeting obligations to their exchange partners.

The Discrete/Relational Exchange Continuum

As suggested earlier in the chapter, business transactions sometimes involve a one-shot, impersonal sort of exchange,[19] while others are based on long-term relationships. Suppose you are driving on Interstate 95 from Miami to Philadelphia for the first time. You exit near Baltimore and make a cash purchase of gas at an independent gasoline station. You have no expectation of ever stopping there again. Yet you willingly engage in product and financial exchange, you and the station attendant precisely understand the norms and conditions governing behavior within the transaction, and you pay the posted rate for the amount of gasoline put in your car. Although we don't often think about it, an economic contract exists that guides behaviors within this type of transaction. The scope of the Channel Relationship Model (CRM) obviously extends beyond "stop and go" fill-ups at out-of-state gas stations. The CRM portrays the interaction process as a range extending from one-time transactions to long-term, ongoing exchange.

The above example involves a discrete exchange. A **discrete exchange** is a transaction that has little social or information exchange and no significant past or likelihood of a future

This Citibank advertisement exemplifies the shift from a transactional, one-time to a long-term, relationship-building approach to servicing customer needs in the banking industry.

Courtesy Citibank

relationship with the other participant. A highly discrete, or *transactional,* exchange can be identified by the following conditions:

- There is little interpersonal involvement between the exchange parties.
- Communication is functional and used only to complete the transaction.
- The product or service exchange essentially involves a trade-off of money and an easily monetized asset.
- There is no past or implied future social exchange.[20]

At the opposite end of the exchange scale lies relational exchange. A **relational exchange,** also called *relationalism,* involves a long-term, continuous, and complex interrelationship. In such a relationship, any single transaction is viewed as relatively unimportant by participating channel members. Moreover, individual exchange episodes or transactions often become routinized within the context of the larger relationship. In relational exchange there is an implicit obligation to preserve the channel relationship itself.[21] The behaviors expected from the parties engaged in relational exchange have been compared to the behaviors expected by a man and woman bound by a marital contract: "[T]he sale merely consummates the courtship. Then the marriage begins. How good the marriage is depends on how well the relationship is managed."[22] In a similar vein, an overriding goal in most marketing relationships should be to sustain the relationship after the first sale when situational changes arise. Sony has entered into a number of relational exchanges in the United States. Channel Surfing 13.1 discusses some of its surprising successes.

Ongoing channel relationships are increasingly commonplace among suppliers and their customers. Nearly 46 percent of transcontinental relationships observed in one study were at least 10 years old; only 12 percent were less than five years old.[23] Fortune 100 companies like General Motors and General Electric are cultivating long-term relationships with selected vendors in the pursuit of quality control and cost-containment. On the other side, the Pentagon's failure to engage in long-term vendor relationships is often blamed for defense contract cost overruns.[24]

Highly discrete exchanges reside at one end of a continuum; highly relational exchanges at the other. As Exhibit 13.4 illustrates, exchanges can be identified as either discrete or

Channel Surfing 13.1

Global Exchange: Sony's Interaction with American Society

When many Americans turn on their television sets, play back messages on their answering machines, or record programs on their VCRs, they are enjoying the fruits of a relationship dating back to development of the transistor. As the world's leading manufacturer and marketer of consumer electronics, Sony Corporation's success has depended on American technology and financing. Akio Morita, the late chairman and cofounder of Sony, acknowledged that, "Our company was catapulted to its early commercial success as a result of licensing and then commercializing the brilliant work done by American scientists at Bell Labs to create the transistor." When Sony needed to raise capital for expansion in the 1960s, it turned to American investors. In fact, Sony was the first Japanese company listed on the New York Stock Exchange. Sony has long had a vested interest in the United States.

Over the last four decades, Sony's interaction with American society has become even more intricate. Today, Sony has 11 U.S. manufacturing facilities employing over 10,000 Americans. Over the years, Sony has engaged in an array of research and development activities—from semiconductor and software design to the development of high-definition television—in the United States. In return, many U.S. companies have benefited from Sony's technology transfer arrangements. Sony brought its latest technology to Advanced Micro Devices (AMD) to initiate a state-of-the-art integrated circuit manufacturing operation in an idle part of AMD's San Antonio, Texas, location.

Perhaps Akio Morita himself best summed up the nature of the reciprocal relations between companies that are often necessary to successfully compete in the global marketplace when he said, "A partnership is by definition a two-way street, and being part of the solution to each other's problems is what partnerships are all about."

Points to Ponder

- Where do you think Sony would be in today's marketplace if it only considered American firms as competitors rather than as opportunities for alliances and relationships?

Source: Adapted from Hokrein, Dale (1994), "It's All about Relationships, Not Profits," *The Augusta Chronicle,* January 2, 16a, 221; and Morita, Akio (1994), "Changing Trade Winds: A New Look on U.S. Japan Trade Relations," *Executive Speeches,* 8(6), 33–35.

EXHIBIT 13.4

Discrete/relational exchange continuum

Discrete Exchange	*Exchange Characteristics*	*Relational Exchange*
Situational		
Transaction has a distinct beginning and end. The duration of exchange is extremely short, and performance indicates completion.	Exchange timing	Ongoing, continuous exchange in which each exchange episode is linked to previous experiences. The duration of exchange is longer.
Tied to explicit terms of the transaction. Each party to the transaction has well-defined obligations solely for the purpose of completing the transaction at hand. The obligations are standardized.	Responsibilities	The obligation to sustain the relationship transcends the precise terms of any particular exchange episode. Responsibilities are customized to the exchanged partners.
Expectation of each party is limited to the transaction completion. Cash payment in return for monetized commodity. Conflicts are expected to be resolved at ingression point.	Expectations	Exchange partners have shared interest in preserving the alliance. The expectations of each party are on future exchange rather than a specific exchange episode.
Process		
Very little personal interaction. Any personal interaction follows protocol for the exchange episode. Generally formal.	Personal relations	High frequency of interpersonal relations. Personal relationships evolve and adapt over time. While some interaction is formal, the exchange relationship is predominated by informal relations.
Little to no joint effort demonstrated in exchange. Transaction cooperation is limited to consummating the immediate transaction at hand.	Cooperation	High interdependence between exchange partners. Joint efforts are related to both performance and planning.
Total transferability probable because there is little reliance on the other party to complete the transaction.	Transferability	Very limited transferability because the exchange episodes are tailored to the exchange partners.
Outcomes		
Costs are determined on a transaction-by-transaction basis with little consideration of opportunity costs.	Costs	Costs are shared by exchange partners over time. There is a tacit agreement that the burdens will be distributed equitably during the relationship.
There is a clear and predetermined allocation of benefits from the transaction that extends from the transaction terms. There is an exclusive apportionment between parties.	Benefits	Judicious allocation of exchange utility is based on contentment of all exchange partners.

relational by evaluating them relative to three dimensions: situational contexts, process characteristics, and outcomes. As to situational contexts, discrete exchanges have a known beginning, middle, and end. They are usually of short duration and feature standardized terms of exchange. Neither party has any intention of using the exchange episode as a stepping-stone to future relations.

Relational exchanges, on the other hand, involve ongoing relationships. These relationships are frequently customized out of deference to the other exchange partner's needs. Efforts to sustain the relationship in the face of problems that arise in the channel system are shared among the exchange partners.

In terms of process characteristics, discrete exchange is predicated on a competitive marketplace in which channel participants are easily replaced; neither party has a sense of dependence on the other. Relational exchanges can evolve to a point where each participant becomes dependent on their counterpart. As to outcomes, in discrete exchanges, the parties explicitly divide transaction costs and benefits. This division is based on the terms of the exchange. Conversely, the costs and benefits associated with the relationship are shared over time in relational exchange.

Stages of Channel Relationships

Channel relationships result from an interaction process in which connections have been developed between two organizational parties. If they are sustained over a long enough period of time, most relationships eventually pass through four stages of development: awareness, exploration, expansion, and commitment.[25] Over time, a relationship can produce a mutual orientation that leads to mutual commitment. On the other hand, a relationship may be dissolved during any one of these stages.

Awareness

In this first stage in relationship building, sometimes called the prerelationship stage, there is an awareness of the potential partners, but little more. Initial selection of an exchange partner is often based on the geographical distance between the two parties. Just as a family is more likely to become friends with next-door neighbors than those down the street, buyers are apt to be more aware of local vendors. Social distance also influences awareness. *Social distance* refers to the degree of familiarity each party has with the other's way of doing business.

There are several reasons for seeking out new exchange partners. Among them are the possibility that:

- Vendor analysis indicates inadequate performance from existing suppliers.
- Change in the channel environment requires a reassessment of existing suppliers. (Legal restrictions that prevent current suppliers from providing customary lot sizes would illustrate such an environmental change.)
- One is exposed to aggressive promotional efforts by nonsupplying companies that are currently vying for consideration.

During the awareness stage, evaluation of a prospective channel partner is usually based on a sample delivery. Performance expectations are highly uncertain and subject to change at this early stage. Essentially, each channel member views the other as a prospect, and feels it is testing the waters with no obligation for future interaction. Commitment to the other party is at or near zero, but if things work out the two channel members may move toward the exploration stage.

Exploration

The next stage in the process of building a channel relationship is exploration. This stage refers to the trying-out period that exists between a buyer and seller. During exploration, one or more trial transactions will likely occur. These trials allow the fit between the two parties to be evaluated. As mutual experience is gained, uncertainty about the other party is reduced. Mutual commitment to the relationship remains relatively low, but at least the parties have made initial steps.

Several evaluative criteria may be used during a relationship's exploratory period. Time-distance is one yardstick used for speculating on future relations among the parties. Time-distance addresses the amount of time that lapses between the point of social exchange and actual delivery on a promise. Technological-distance is also used. This refers to the compatibility between the organization's product and process technologies. Differences in, say, the organization's process technologies are sometimes attractive. These differences afford the opportunity for the other party to improve its technology. Cultural-differences are also used as evaluative criteria. This dimension relates to each party's normative value systems. Because it is often difficult to reconcile differences in norms and operational standards, discrepancies in channel members' cultures can represent a serious impediment to their continued exchange relations.

The historical successes of Corning illustrate the importance of the exploration stage. Corning has been involved in over 48 alliances since 1924, including partnerships with companies such as Dow Chemical and Owens-Illinois. Corning's standing policy is to regard each company in any related industry as a potential partner. Corning is constantly conducting background checks on the qualities of potential exchange partners. For example, its 1973 alliance with Germany-based Siemens to produce and market optical fiber for the telecommunications industry was the culmination of such exploration.[26]

During the exploratory stage, channel relationships are fragile. Minimal levels of investment and interdependence make termination relatively simple. But channel members are often willing to adapt during the exploration stage to achieve greater exchange coordination with a prospect. The exploration stage also provides the first opportunity for trust-building between the exchange partners.

Expansion

The expansion stage is when exchange partners confront and close any variations in time, technological, or cultural distance. When the expansion stage is managed successfully, each exchange partner receives more utility. Each party's investment in the relationship is then raised, and several large agreements are likely to be established between the channel members. During expansion, exchange partners become more willing to expose themselves to risks to achieve greater coordination. But in reality, channel members' exposure to risk often *lessens* because of the developing trust. The exchange partners will each exhibit high adaptation and flexibility. Expansion is based on each party's satisfaction with the other's role performance. In fact, performance expectations within the channel become institutionalized. Relationships should continue to expand as long as each channel member continues to be satisfied.

Commitment

Some relationships move beyond expansion to a final stage in which each partner commits to the relationship. In the commitment stage, an implicit behavioral contract emerges encouraging the continuity of the relationship. Each participant comes to view the value of its channel

Exhibit 13.5

The four stages of a channel relationship

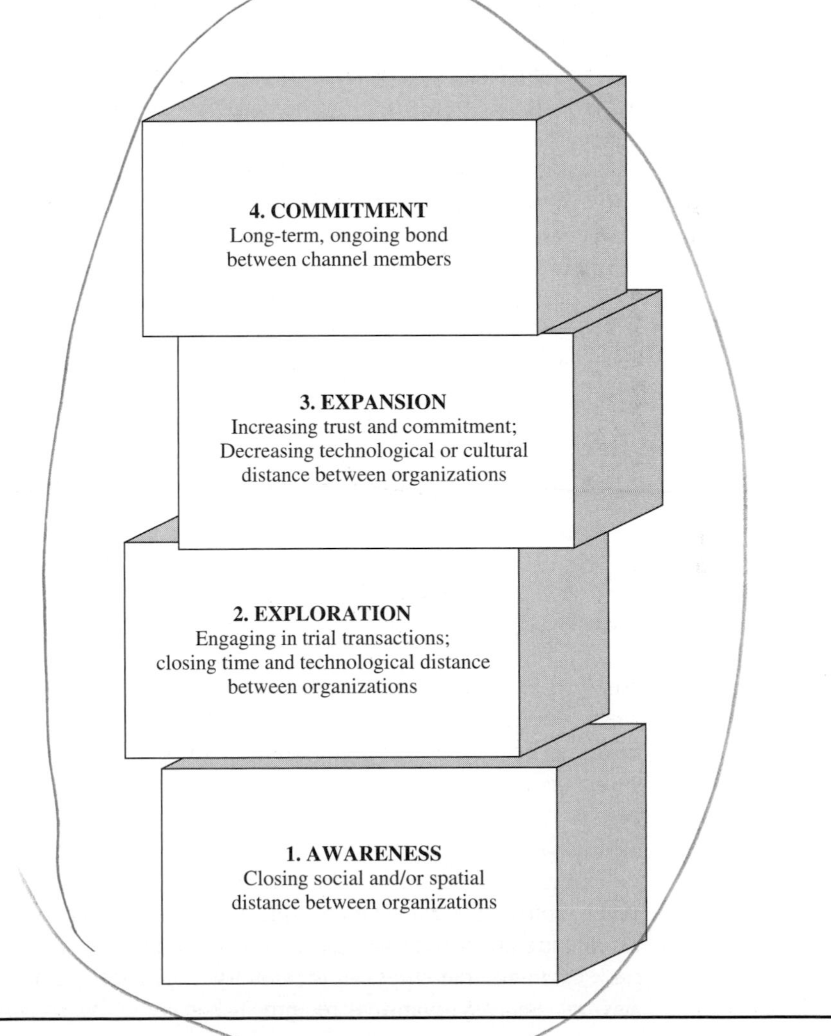

relationship as greater than the value associated with any specific transaction or set of transactions. The exchange partners must have experienced trust, achieved satisfaction, and expanded their association for this to occur. Theirs is now a relationship characterized by complete adaptation and flexibility based on a mutual desire to sustain the relationship. Consequently, they will then be committed to advancing the channel relationship further.[27]

Three conditions must be satisfied to achieve commitment within a channel relationship: investment, tenacity, and consistency. *Investment* suggests that each partner has contributed resources to the relationship in pursuit of some future goal. Each party must believe it is the beneficiary of a roughly equitable contribution from the other. However, there is no need for an exact matching of contributions since the partners often have different types of resources to bring to the relationship. *Tenacity* refers to the strength of each participant's sense of obligation to the relationship's future. When exchange partners are each willing to adjust in response to changes in the channel climate, tenacity is in evidence.

Finally, there must be an expectation that each party's investment and tenacity will be stable or *consistent* over time. The primary basis for such stability in a marketing relationship is reciprocity. **Reciprocity** suggests that each party's behavior within the context of the channel relationship is contingent on the perceived behavior of the other party. When a relationship enters the commitment stage, the investment, tenacity, and consistency associated with the exchange can be described as *reciprocal.* The next section offers a detailed discussion of reciprocity and other norms that govern exchange relationships. But first, look at Exhibit 13.5 on the previous page, which summarizes the four stages of a channel relationship, along with the primary characteristics of each stage.

Exchange Governance Norms

By now it should be clear that exchange can range from simple, focused episodes to long-term, complex relationships. In this way, the exchange process can be viewed as a behavioral contract—an agreement between parties to either do or not do something in return for some compensation. All behavioral contracts are governed by norms. In this section we discuss five key **exchange governance norms:** reciprocity, relational communication, solidarity, role integrity, and mutuality.

Reciprocity

Reciprocity is the most basic norm governing social exchange. When someone says hello to you, you probably feel compelled to reply. In doing so, you are reciprocating. In marketing relationships, reciprocity does not imply that each party's reaction to the other's behavior will be identical. However, it does hold that each exchange partner's behavior affects the other. Reciprocity suggests people should help those who have helped them and not injure those who have helped them.[28] In everyday social interactions, we are generally grateful to others when they grant us a favor. In marketing interactions, relationships prosper when all partners receive utility from their involvement in the exchange. As relationships progress from awareness to commitment, the expectations for reciprocity increase.

There are three types of reciprocity: nonreciprocal behaviors, symmetrical reciprocal behaviors, and asymmetrical reciprocal behaviors. *Nonreciprocal behaviors* suggest that one party's verbal or nonverbal behaviors are ignored by the other party. Have you ever talked to someone who is not listening? If so, you have experienced nonreciprocal behavior. No relationship can exist for long if nonreciprocal behavior occurs regularly. Nonreciprocal behaviors are unilateral rather than contingent on another's behaviors. As such, the conditions necessary for moving beyond awareness will not be met, and no exchange relationship will be initiated.

Symmetrical reciprocity suggests that a bilateral awareness of the other party's behaviors exists. Before it acts or reacts, each party seeks cues from the other. Channel members who engage in symmetrical reciprocity are usually roughly equivalent in power and/or size.

In *asymmetrical reciprocity,* one exchange partner is more powerful than the other. The subordinate partner reciprocates to cues initiated by the more powerful party. While exchange relationships can be sustained under conditions reflecting asymmetrical reciprocity, the highest stage of relationship building—commitment—requires symmetrical reciprocity among the channel partners.

The development of reciprocity is contingent on the perceptions that each participant holds toward their exchange partner's behaviors. These perceptions derive from communication that occurs within the channel. Communication provides the means through which each exchange partner can affect and be affected by the other. Communication allows people to assign meanings to verbal and nonverbal cues. But this meaning may vary based on differences in channel climate.

Communication plays a pivotal role in exchange relationships. Once a relationship has achieved commitment, each party's behavior is simultaneously a response to the other party's past behavior and a stimulus to the other party's future behavior. Our discussion now turns to the principles of relational communication.

Relational Communication

Recall from Chapter 4 that channel communications occur in an open system. In an open system, communication is *activated* when each party acknowledges the other. So, just as the awareness stage designates the beginning of relationship building, it likewise represents the point at which relational communication can begin. Relational communication usually begins with each party's recognition that the other party is aware of them. If and when a relationship is formed, it will be maintained through a set of communicative transactions. Communicative transactions are characterized by three properties: wholeness, synergy, and equifinality.[29]

Wholeness is based on the assumption that an interactive system exists in which a change in one party influences all others in the relationship. In a channel system, the property of wholeness implies that the interpretation of an exchange partner's behaviors will vary in response to changes in those behaviors. Wholeness also suggests that relational communication has circularity and feedback and will invoke a response.

Synergy is the second property of relational communication. Synergism holds that the value of the outcomes resulting from two or more parties working together will exceed the total value of their individual efforts. The property prescribes that relationships formed by two or more parties generate another set of behaviors to which meanings can be assigned. Party *A* may assign meaning to its perceptions of *B*'s behaviors, and vice versa. However, synergism generates another set of behaviors distinct from the behaviors identified with *A* and *B* individually. *A* and *B* will each assign meaning to those independent behaviors. This is where equifinality comes into play. The *equifinality* property suggests there are multiple paths to the same destination. The patterns of relationship between exchange partners are due, in part, to the communicative properties of the relationship. They are, thus, likely to formulate strategies for managing relational communication.

Communication strategies can be autonomous or collaborative.[30] *Autonomous communication strategies* generally involve infrequent, standardized messages and one-way information flows issuing from the more powerful channel member. These strategies are more likely to be used in discrete transactions, since communication requirements are limited to that which is necessary to immediately complete the transaction. Because there is minimal feedback in discrete exchange, there is little opportunity or need for the give and take associated with collaborative communication. For example, when you stop at an out-of-town self-service gas station, you are likely to direct the information flow. You may hand the clerk $10.00 (nonverbal cue) and specify the pump (verbal cue) at the same time. Little feedback is necessary. There is virtually no equifinality or synergy.

As relationships develop, more *collaborative communication strategies* are used. A relationship will not develop without there first being a two-way exchange of information concerned with the parties' respective goals, wants, issues, inputs, and priorities.[31] Information is exchanged more frequently in collaborative communication, and information exchange flows in both directions. Since relational exchanges are characterized by higher levels of interdependence, exchange partners need to interact more. Collaborative communication promotes coordination between exchange members.[32] This last point is critical because relational exchanges generally involve conditions of resource uncertainty, and therefore informal and flexible communication is often needed.

Highly relational exchanges are characterized by wholeness, implying that efforts at information exchange are modified in a collaborative fashion in response to the perceived best interests of the relationship. At high levels of relationalism the best interests of the relationship are also generally consistent with the channel partners' interests. Collaborative communication strategies also introduce the properties of synergy and equifinality in the communication process. For instance, Compaq, the personal computer marketer, flourished by competing only against IBM and using collaborative strategies to develop cooperation among all other potential competitors. This cooperation helped Compaq become a billion-dollar company in a saturated computer industry. This ability to develop cooperation with others flows from the company's core values and corporate culture.[33] Compaq's collaborative strategy demonstrates the importance of the linkages among channel members rendered in the CRM.

Other Exchange Governance Norms

Other norms that regulate all exchange relationships are solidarity, role integrity, and mutuality. When considered together, these exchange governance norms capture the complete set of values reflected in each party's channel objectives and intentions toward the exchange in question.[34] Furthermore, as shown in Exhibit 13.6, the relative presence or absence of these governance norms in a relationship between two channel members affects the extent to which their relationship is discrete or relational.

Exhibit 13.6

Influence of governance norms on a channel exchange relationship

Type of Exchange Relationship		
Discrete		*Relational*
Presence of Norm	***Exchange Governance Norms***	*Presence of Norm*
Low	Solidarity	High
Low	Mutuality	High
Low	Role Integrity	High
High	Reciprocity	High

In their positive form, these norms act as agents encouraging the partners to continue participating in the exchange relationship. When present, they also foster reciprocity in the relationship and ensure that each party's role behaviors are consistent with how they are supposed to act in the relationship. As channel relationships move from the transactional to the relational context, channel member behaviors become more flexible. This is necessary so that the channel members can engage in mutual planning and coordination efforts. But each partner's actions must remain compatible with its counterpart's expectations.

Contractual solidarity is the glue that binds exchange partners together. *Solidarity* permits exchange partners to create and sustain a relationship from the stage of awareness on through to commitment. In discrete transactions, solidarity focuses solely on the consummation of the individual transaction. This consummation process is primarily governed by the terms of the contract. In relational exchanges, on the other hand, solidarity is concerned with preserving the relationship itself. There, the norm is internalized by each party to the exchange. By this point, these individuals have jointly arrived at the view that preserving the relationship is more important than any specific transaction. The relational norm of solidarity is predicated on flexibility, reciprocity, and a willingness to adapt to exchange partners' needs to sustain the relationship.

Role integrity assesses the degree to which each party to an exchange fulfills its promises and satisfies the expectations of its partners. Discrete transactions have narrow role expectations, which are usually limited to the specific terms of the individual transaction agreement. Relational roles are complex and multidimensional. Here, behavioral expectations extend well beyond individual exchange episodes. Over time, the presence of role integrity promotes the stability of an exchange by aligning the role expectations of each channel member.

The *mutuality* norm addresses the returns each party receives from doing or refraining from doing something. Exchange partners create outcomes. These benefits (and costs) must be distributed between them. Mutuality suggests each partner is entitled to an equitable distribution of exchange outcomes. This sense of entitlement (or obligation) often leads to conflict within exchange relationships. In discrete transactions, the parties operate from a short-term perspective, dividing outcomes as agreed upon in advance. Because everything is settled upon before the completion of each transaction, the parties have little concern for future surplus. In a relational exchange, however, the mutuality norm indicates that the allocation of exchange outcomes is administered on a long-term basis. In the presence of mutuality, a channel member may be willing to give up a bit now for special considerations in the future.

Relationship Selling

Exchange governance norms can be easily related to the buyer-seller context. This is useful, particularly since boundary-spanning salespeople are often the party most responsible for establishing and maintaining relationship-oriented exchanges. Buyers and sellers both benefit when ongoing relationships are developed. Five levels of relationships may develop as marketers move from the discrete transaction to relational exchange.[35] Each stage builds upon the one preceding it.

The first stage of buyer-seller relationships is highly discrete. Exchanges are initially characterized by discrete solidarity. Salespeople should understand the effect that these early behaviors will have on the relationship. Indeed, the future course of buyer-seller interactions is often defined soon after they meet. Perhaps the salesperson merely shakes a customer's hand and thanks her or him for the order. Hopefully, however, there is more. The second stage is *reactive marketing.* In the reactive marketing phase, salespeople invite customer feedback after the sale. For instance, a salesperson might tape a quarter to the back of a business card featuring the following message, "Here's a quarter. Give me a call." This tactic is intended to drive home the notion that the salesperson is available to handle any problems arising from the transaction.

By the third stage, known as *accountability,* sellers make conscious efforts to expand their customers' role sets. Sales firms follow up after the sale to monitor buyers' satisfaction and explore avenues for improving components of exchange episodes. Invitations for customers to become involved in the design of either products or services and/or the transaction process might be tendered. The fourth stage is demonstrating *continuing interest* in customers. This interest should be proactive. By now, sellers have assumed the challenge of ensuring that customers obtain the maximum benefit possible from the offering.

The final stage of buyer-seller relationships is a *real partnership.* Here, sellers form alliances with customers. The exchange partners might codesign the offering or investigate how each can benefit further from their association. Procter & Gamble and Wal-Mart have formed an alliance based on relationship selling. Procter & Gamble supplies a crew of trained professionals who work at Wal-Mart stores to reengineer systems that will improve the marketing of Procter & Gamble products. This alliance evolved to the point where a long-term commitment now exists between the two giants.

Key Terms

calculative exchange relationships
compensatory trade
discrete exchange
exchange episode
exchange governance norms
genuine relationships
ideational relationships
information
information exchange
reciprocity
relational exchange
social exchange
trust

Chapter Summary

While individual transactions are the economic cornerstone of exchange, they do not always describe the complex relationships that often emerge between channel members. Individual transactions may be referred to as exchange episodes. Four elements are invariably associated with marketing exchange episodes: products and services, and information, financial, and social exchange. The sum of all the costs and benefits associated with these exchange episodes is called *exchange utility*. Each party to a transaction both gives and receives utility. It is important to differentiate between exchange episodes and longer-term aspects of exchange.

All transactions range from discrete (or transactional) to relational exchange. Discrete exchange describes highly impersonal, one-time transactions. In discrete exchange, there is only minor social exchange with little concern for the possibility of future interactions. Conversely, relational exchange may be compared to the behavioral actions and reactions that occur in a successful marriage. It addresses the long-term, ongoing relationships that develop between exchange partners. More and more companies are engaging in relational exchange with each other. These companies are more concerned with sustaining exchange relationships and less concerned with enforcing the precise terms of an exchange episode. Ongoing relationships are customized over time to the particular needs associated with each exchange partner.

On their path to the preferred state of relationalism, relationships move through four stages: awareness, exploration, expansion, and commitment. The norm of reciprocity, reflective of the *give* and *take* that sometimes develops between exchange partners, provides the impetus necessary to move from awareness through to the commitment stage. Reciprocity can be facilitated or inhibited within an exchange relationship by the type of communication processes that evolve between channel members. In autonomous communication strategies, exchange between channel members is infrequent. This strategy is typically associated with discrete exchange. By contrast, collaborative communication strategies generally prevail within highly relational exchange. Collaborative strategies are associated with more frequent communication and more information sharing. Collaborative strategies are consistent with the cooperative character of relational exchange.

The importance of developing and preserving exchange relationships can be demonstrated in buyer-seller interactions. The relational orientation has become known as *relationship selling.* In relationship selling, sellers actively engage customers as partners. For instance, buyers and sellers might codesign product offerings so they can each benefit directly from the exchange association.

Channel Challenges

1. An African proverb states, "A market is not held for the sake of one person." How does this proverb relate to the role of adaptation in social exchange?
2. W. F. Whyte has suggested that, "The waitress who bears up under pressure does not simply respond to her customers. She acts with some skill to control their behavior." What components of an exchange episode are transacted between customers and a waiter or waitress in full-service restaurants? How would your answer differ if you were interacting with an order-taker at a fast-food restaurant?
3. Jordan Lewis, author of *Partnerships for Profit,* suggests that, "Competition has become a team sport." What does Lewis's contention suggest about relational exchange in the marketplace? Think about your favorite sports team. Describe how that team's successes or failures have been fostered or inhibited by the relative presence or absence of solidarity, role integrity, and mutuality.
4. Joseph T. Brophy, president of the Travelers Insurance Company, states that, "In the past, we were in a transaction processing business. . . . It was pretty simple, we paid claims and we were measured on our accuracy, timeliness and friendliness on the phone." As the cost of health care has soared in recent years, Travelers Insurance has had to develop partnerships with its customers. Do you think relationship building is important to Travelers Insurance? Why or why not?

5. Because many men have to be coaxed into shopping for clothes, *GQ* magazine has started an incentive program with several retailers of men's clothing. The "Return on Investment" program rewards the most active male shoppers with credits that can be redeemed for clothing and accessories, vacations, and other merchandise donated by *GQ* and participating vendors. How does this *GQ* program attempt to engage consumers in relationship marketing? Try to relate how awareness, exploration, expansion, and commitment are manifested within *GQ*'s program.

Review Questions

1. Why are human interactions important in exchange relationships? Define and describe the principal lines of human interaction.
2. What is a marketing exchange episode? What four elements are associated with every marketing exchange episode?
3. How is trust involved in exchange relationships?
4. Define and describe the difference between discrete and relational exchanges.
5. Describe the four stages involved in relationship development.
6. How is reciprocity important in the development of marketing exchange relationships?
7. Define communicative transactions. Describe three key aspects of communicative transactions with respect to the development of marketing channel relationships.
8. Define relational communications. Describe three properties used to characterize relational communications.
9. Differentiate between autonomous and collaborative communication strategies.
10. How can the buyer-seller dyad be used to describe the five levels of relational exchange in marketing channels?

Endnotes

1. Gruenwedel, Eric (2000), "Romp 'n Roll," *Adweek* (Southwest Edition), 41(27, July 3), IQ14.
2. Houston, Franklin S., and Jule B. Gassenheimer (1987), "Marketing and Exchange," *Journal of Marketing,* 51 (October), 10.
3. Strutton, David, and Lou E. Pelton (1994), "Toward a Triadic Network of Behavioral Channels: The Role of Structure, Power and Climate in Dyadic Exchange," *Journal of Marketing Theory and Practice,* 2 (4), 39–51.
4. Adapted from Sjostrand, Sven-Erik (1989), "Institutional Economics—An Overview," in *Perspectives on the Economics of Organization,* Crafoord Lectures 1, Oliver E. Williamson, Sven-Erik Sjostrand, and Jan Johanson, eds., Lund, Sweden: Lund University Press, 49–64.
5. Weer, Joseph, and Emily T. Smith (1995), "Merck Wants to Be Alone—But with Lots of Friends," *Business Week,* October 2, 62.
6. Marlin, Steven (2000), "NetBank and Ameritrade Ally to Catch Rival E*Trade," *Bank Systems & Technology,* 37 (October 10), 14, 22.
7. Treece, James B., and Karen Lowry Miler (1992), "The Partners: Surprise! Ford and Mazda Have Built a Strong Team. Here's How," *Business Week,* February 10, 102–7.
8. Radosevich, Lynda (1993), "Ford, Mazda Put Car Quality On-Line," *Computerworld,* 27 (March 1), 51–52.
9. IMP Group (1982), "An Interaction Approach," *International Marketing and Purchasing of Industrial Goods,* Chichester: Wiley, 10–27.
10. Fulk, Janet, and Sirish Mai (1986), "Distortion of Communication in Hierarchical Relationships," in *Communication Yearbook,* Volume 9, I. L. McLaughlin, ed., Beverly Hills, CA: Sage.
11. Ford, David (1990), *Understanding Business Markets: Interaction, Relationships and Networks,* London: Academic Press.
12. Huber, George, and Richard Draft (1987), "The

Information Environment of Organizations," in *Handbook of Organizational Communication: An Interdisciplinary Perspective,* Frederick Jablin et al., eds., Newbury Park, CA: Sage.

13. Harrison, Michael (1990), "Back to Barter," *Maclean's,* 103(April 23), 32–34.
14. Daniels, John D., and Lee H. Radebaugh (1992), *International Business: Environments and Operations,* Sixth Edition, Reading, MA: Addison-Wesley.
15. Blau, Peter (1967), *Exchange and Power in Social Life,* Second Edition, London: John Wiley & Sons.
16. Hallén, Lars, Jan Johanson, and Nazeem Seyed-Mohamed (1991), "Interfirm Adaptation in Business Relationships," *Journal of Marketing,* 55(April), 31.
17. Treece and Miler, "The Partners: Surprise! Ford and Mazda Have Built a Strong Team," 104.
18. Gurtman, Michael (1992), "Trust, Distrust and Interpersonal Problems: A Circumplex Analysis," *Journal of Personality and Social Psychology,* 62 (June), 989–1002.
19. Miles, Morgan P., Danny R. Arnold, and Henry W. Nash (1990), "Adaptive Communications: The Adaptations of the Seller's Interpersonal Style to the Stage of the Dyad's Relationship and the Buyer's Communication Style," *Journal of Personal Selling & Sales Management,* 10 (Winter), 21–27.
20. Macneil, Ian R. (1978), "Contracts: Adjustment of Long-Term Relations under Classical, Neoclassical and Relational Contract Law," *Northwestern University Law Review,* 72 (6), 855–905.
21. Kaufmann, Patrick J., and Louis W. Stern (1988), "Relational Exchange Norms, Perceptions of Unfairness and Retained Hostility in Commercial Litigation," *Journal of Conflict Resolution,* 32 (Summer), 534–52.
22. Levitt, Theodore (1983), *The Marketing Imagination,* New York, NY: Free Press.
23. Campbell, N. C. G. (1984), "Structure and Stability of Industrial Market Networks: Developing a Research Methodology," in *Proceedings of the Conference on Research Developments in International Marketing,* P. Turnbull and S. J. Paliwoda, eds., Manchester: UMIST, 208–27.
24. Wilson, D. T., and V. Mummalaneni (1986), "Bonding and Commitment in Buyer-Seller Relationships: A Preliminary Conceptualization," *Industrial Marketing and Purchasing,* 1 (3), 44–58.
25. Adapted from Dwyer, F. Robert, Paul H. Schurr, and Sejo Oh (1987), "Developing Buyer-Seller Relationships," *Journal of Marketing,* 51 (April), 11–27; and Ford, David (1980),"The Development of Buyer-Seller Relationships in Industrial Markets," *European Journal of Marketing,* 14 (5/6), 339–54.
26. Wrubel, Robert (1992), "Joint Ventures and Alliances: Corning," *Financial World,* 161 (September 29), 44.
27. Houston, Franklin S., and Jule B. Gassenheimer (1987), "Marketing and Exchange," *Journal of Marketing,* 51 (October), 3–18.
28. Gouldner, Alvin (1960), "The Norm of Reciprocity: A Preliminary Statement," *American Sociological Review,* 25 (April), 161–78; and Komorita, S. S., J. A. Hilty, and C. D. Parks (1991), "Reciprocity and Cooperation in Social Dilemmas," *Journal of Conflict Resolution,* 35 (September), 494–518.
29. Wilmot, William W. (1975), *Dyadic Communication: A Transactional Perspective,* Reading, MA: Addison-Wesley, 81–113.
30. Mohr, Jakki, and John R. Nevin (1990), "Communication Strategies in Marketing Channels: A Theoretical Perspective," *Journal of Marketing,* October, 36–51.
31. Dwyer, Schurr, and Oh, "Developing Buyer-Seller Relationships," 11–27; and Ford, "The Development of Buyer-Seller Relationships in Industrial Markets," 339–54.
32. Guiltinan, Joseph, Ismail Rejab, and William Rodgers (1980), "Factors Influencing Coordination in a Franchise Channel," *Journal of Retailing,* 56 (Fall), 41–58.
33. Jarillo, J. Carlos, and Howard H. Stevenson (1991), "Co-operative Strategies—The Payoffs and the Pitfalls," *Long Range Planning,* 24 (February), 64–70.
34. Macneil, "Contracts: Adjustments of Long-Term Economic Relations," 854–905; and Kaufmann and Stern, "Relational Exchange Norms, Perceptions of Unfairness, and Retained Hostility," 534–52.
35. Caruso, Thomas E. (1992), "The Five Levels of Relationship," *Marketing News,* 26 (June 8), 21–22.

chapter

14

Strategic Partnering Agreements

Learning Objectives

After reading this chapter, you should be able to:

- Define strategic alliances and discuss their impact on the U.S. economy.
- List and discuss reasons why channel members form strategic alliances.
- Describe the three global alliance strategies, and assess their costs and benefits.
- Explain the process by which most alliances are developed.
- Discuss why many strategic alliances fail despite their intuitive appeal.

Wide World Photo

In 1936, it was the centerpiece of Japan's fanaticism for an American pastime. The Korakuen Company was responsible for the construction and operation of its namesake Korakuen Stadium, the first stadium built for Japanese professional baseball. But the aging stadium was demolished in 1988 to make way for a state-of-the-art, all-weather sports stadium: the Tokyo Dome. The Tokyo Dome, affectionately labeled the "Big Egg" by baseball enthusiasts worldwide, is home field to the Yomiuri Giants and the Nippon Ham Fighters. It is also home to the Tokyo Baseball Hall of Fame.

Japan's first domed-stadium, the futuristic Tokyo Dome borrows more than a pastime from American culture. Encompassing more than 1,240,000 cubic meters of enclosed space, and accommodating 55,000 baseball fans, the Tokyo Dome's architectural design owes much to American architect-philosopher R. Buckminster Fuller. After all, Bucky Fuller is the inventor of the geodesic dome, an efficient architectural design that uses less material and spans great distances. Air pressure (higher inside than outside of the dome) inflates a membrane sheltering the stadium.

The air-conditioned structure provides year-round comfort for a variety of sporting events, concerts, and trade fairs. Today, the renamed Tokyo Dome Corporation leverages this geodesic edifice as a multipurpose recreation and entertainment center that includes a bowling center, ice rink, and sauna. Amidst Japanese umpires' proclamations of "Daida!" to fallen batters, cheers for an American-born marvel abound: Bucky![1]

****

Geodesic domes, a 1960s-era architectural design constructed of networks of intersecting triangles, are making a comeback. The structure's popularity derives primarily from its strength and economy. Geodesic domes illustrate how diverse elements can be strategically fit together to reinforce a structure's strength. Triangles are the strongest geometric shape and triangular network designs provide freestanding, self-supporting forms that require no internal supports. Geodesic domes feature favorable *strength-to-weight* ratios. The U.S. military exploits this strength-to-weight ratio by using geodesic domes as radar stations in the Arctic. Geodesic domes also offer outstanding *efficiency and economy*. Furthermore, the interiors of geodesic domes are open, offering maximum space and light. Because the dome's design requires fewer materials to enclose a space, less resources are needed to complete the structure. Spherical structures also have about 40 percent less exterior surface than traditional buildings, so they cost less to heat or cool.[2]

From San Francisco's Exploratorium to the 400,000-square-foot roof of Atlanta's Georgia Dome, geodesic domes are illustrating how individual parts can be fit together just so to increase a structure's overall strength. The geodesic dome's innovative design offers many implications for the construction and performance of the long-term channel relationships known as *strategic alliances*.

Strategic Alliances: Definition and Characteristics

We have discussed the importance of forging long-term relationships through the interaction process. Now we will look at a specific and increasingly important type of long-term relationship: the strategic alliance. First, we will take a good look at just what a strategic alliance is—the definition and characteristics of a strategic alliance, why companies form strategic alliances, and the types of strategic alliances that currently exist. Next, we will walk through the steps of developing a strategic alliance—the questions companies must grapple with; choosing long-term, committed partners; developing a strategic plan; and assessing the success of the relationship. Finally, strategic alliances are no more the perfect answer for every organization than any other type of relationship we have discussed; thus, we close with a look at the reasons strategic alliances fail.

The architectural merits of geodesic designs can be related to channel interaction processes in the following ways:

- **Strength-to-weight ratio.** Geodesic domes are lightweight but exceedingly strong. Channel members are increasingly collaborating as partners to achieve the same result. Strategic alliances allow organizations to reduce the duplication of resources and efforts (i.e., becoming more lightweight), while bolstering their collective market strength. Market competition often involves teams of firms rather than individual organizations.

A recent strategic alliance between Olympus Hospitality Group and Carlson Hotels Worldwide illustrates how the strength-to-weight ratio concept applies to marketing channels. The strategic partnering agreement creates a joint venture, "Park Hospitality," that will allow each company to benefit from each other's expertise. Together, these companies will expand the Park Plaza, Park Inns, Radisson Hotels & Resorts, and Regent International Hotels brands. Collectively, Park Hospitality will fortify its market position. As one PriceWaterhouseCoopers analyst notes "Olympus is a savvy real-estate investor, but it doesn't have the hotel organization. Radisson has a substantial infrastructure of development staff, reservations technology, cross-company integration with [food & beverage] and travel agencies that can drive more business to Olympus' properties and also establish a platform to grow the brands and investments."[3]

- **Load distribution.** Just as each strut bears part of the weight put on a geodesic dome, each channel member bears some of the weight of market forces that impact overall channel performance. Channel firms can likewise lessen the uncertainty of the channel environment by spreading risks across members. This is particularly true in industries where massive outlays of capital are needed to introduce new products. For example, General Electric and France's SNECMA pooled capital, research competencies, and manufacturing capabilities to compete in the costly and risky jet design industry.[4] Likewise, new product introductions in the biotechnology industry may take upwards of $200 million and 10 years of development. In response, biotechnology firms like Matrix Pharmaceuticals and Medeva of London are cooperating to bring new biotech products to the market.
- **Economy and efficiency**. Geodesic domes vary greatly in size, materials, and architectural configuration. However, each geodesic dome shares a common principle: *economy and efficiency*. Along much the same vein, Coca-Cola and Schweppes now jointly operate a soft drink bottling plant. Doing so allows them to capitalize on the economy of a single bottling facility and to infuse total quality management principles into the joint production. In this way, each company can economically and efficiently quench the market's thirst for soft drinks.[5]

These advantages are fostering a collaborative mind-set among many channel members. In many channel settings, traditional individualistic perspectives are fading away. The geodesic dome's popularity largely results from its *do more with less* capacity. Future market environments will similarly be characterized by a need to share resources and risk—allowing each firm to do more with less. Lorenzo Necci, president of Italy's EniChem, asserts that "companies that cling to a 'go-it-alone mentality' are in danger of going the way of the dinosaur."[6]

One way companies can avoid extinction is by forming and maintaining channel relationships called *strategic alliances*. A **strategic alliance** is a type of long-term alliance which offers a natural linkage between the internal environment and the interaction process because it emphasizes how collaboration is a function of long-term, win-win interaction. The term *strategic alliance* also can be used to describe a number of organizational structures in which two or more channel members cooperate and form a partnership based on mutual goals. But a strategic alliance is not just a cooperative relationship. It is a **symbiotic relationship**, as well—an interdependent, mutually beneficial channel relationship between two or more parties. As the CRM illustrates, strategic alliances are formed within the channel mesosystem that exists between channel members operating at different channel levels or at the same level. The premise for strategic alliances is this: Once an alliance is formed, strategic partners will presumably be able to operate with greater efficiency and more effectiveness in channel exosystem change, that is, in the marketplace, than they could alone. David Lei offers the following definition of strategic alliances: "Coalignments between two or more firms in which the partners hope to learn and acquire from each other technologies, products, skills and knowledge that are not available to other competitors."[7] The components of Lei's definition are examined below.

Coalignment

The term **coalignment** implies that a channel member joins or links its organization with other channel members in pursuit of a common objective. While the timeline for achieving these objectives may vary across partners (more about that later), a sense of shared purpose should exist among the strategic partners.[8]

Perhaps the best example of coalignment can be found between the golden arches. When asked about Coca-Cola Company, McDonald's CEO Mike Quinlan states, "They are our partner." One of Coca-Cola's top executives (and incidentally a McDonald's board member), Don Keough, agrees that Coke's relationship with McDonald's is "an enormously important strategic alliance." This alliance is important not just because McDonald's is Coca-Cola's largest fountain-sales customer. The coalignment is based on a common purpose: to combat Tricon. PepsiCo is a competitive soft-drink threat to Coca-Cola *and* it is loosely affiliated with Tricon's Pizza Hut, Taco Bell, and KFC operations, which rival McDonald's.[9]

The basis for any strategic alliance clearly should follow from a common purpose shared among the alliance partners. The importance of a common business objective cannot be taken lightly. As one expert notes, "Without a shared objective, partners have not agreed on what new value they will create together. Then, when tough choices have to be made, there is no basis for deciding and conflict often follows."[10]

Exchanging Technologies, Products, Skills, and Knowledge

In today's turbulent global marketplace, channel collaboration is no longer confined to traditional two-party alliances. Strategic alliances often involve relationships among several channel members, each of whom features different core competencies. Companies are coaligning to pool resources and exploit market opportunities. Accordingly, the sense that markets can be shared among firms is emerging in many channel settings. The communications software consortium known as General Magic, Inc., provides an example of how markets can be shared. General Magic links firms such as IBM, Intel, Nuance, and Speechworks to offer speech recognition and telephony applications. In turn, this network of companies loosely aligned to meet market needs serves a diverse portfolio of customers like American Airlines,

Charles Schwab, Home Shopping Network, and United Parcel Service. As you probably know, these partners compete fiercely on many fronts. But in this special venue, they work together to develop and share new information technologies.

Competitive Edge

Like other strategic alliances, the General Magic consortium involves an exchange of technologies, products, skills, and knowledge among its partners. As a result, alliance partners garner a collective competitive advantage in the marketplace. Some suggest that strategic alliances are best suited for allowing channel members to develop more favorable competitive positions and should not be used for any other purpose.[11] To gain these competitive advantages, each channel member must contribute some value to the strategic alliance.

The value of these contributions cannot necessarily be measured by size, however. Jose A. Collazo, chairman and CEO of Infonet Services, has been involved with more than 100 alliances in 46 countries. Collazo asserts, "The assets you are willing to put into play [in

Exhibit 14.1

Myriad strategic alliance forms

Form of Alliance	*Alliance Partners*	*Description*
Collaborative advertising	American Express and Toys "R" Us	Cooperative effort for television advertising and other promotional activities.
Cooperative bidding	Boeing, General Dynamics, and Lockheed	Cooperated together in winning advanced tactical fighter contract.
Cross-licensing	Hoffman-LaRoche (HL) and Glaxo	HL and Glaxo agreed for HL to sell Zantac, an anti-ulcer drug, in the United States.
Cross-manufacturing	Ford and Mazda	Design and build similar cars on same manufacturing/assembly line.
Internal spin-offs	Cummins Engine and Toshiba Corp.	Created new company to develop and market silicon nitride products.
Lease service agreement	CIGNA and United Motor Works	Arrangement to provide financing services for non-U.S. firms and governments.
Research and development partnership	Cytel and Sumitomo Chemicals	Alliance to develop the next generation of biotechnology drugs.
Resource venturing	Swift Chemical, Texasgulf, RTZ, and US Borax	Canadian-based mining natural resource venture.
Shared distribution	Nissan and Volkswagen	Nissan sells Volkswagen's cars and Volkswagen distributes Nissan's cars in Europe.
Technology transfer	IBM and Apple Computer	Arrangement to develop next generation of operating software systems.

Source: Lei, David, and John W. Slocum, Jr. (1991), "Global Strategic Alliances: Payoffs and Pitfalls," *Organizational Dynamics,* 19 (3), 48.

Channel Surfing 14.1

Zen and the Art of a Strategic Alliance

For over 30 years Jordan Lewis, author of *Partnerships for Profit: Structuring and Managing Strategic Alliances,* has been actively involved in helping, building, and repairs. The author is widely known for his "touchy-feely" approach to management, but Lewis's views are surprisingly consistent with established relationship management principles. For instance, Lewis suggests that strategic alliances are increasingly necessary for businesses of all sizes and in every industry worldwide. In his book, strategic alliances are referred to as relationships between companies that create more value than market transactions. Lewis feels strategic alliances are essential not only because competition is more intense today than ever before, but because its nature has also changed. To succeed in today's rugged markets, companies have to excel. That's a given. But, according to Lewis, American firms are finding that they can no longer excel by going alone.

Lewis believes the key to keeping an alliance together lies in having a shared objective that both firms regard as important enough to make needed adjustments to reach it. Lewis suggests strategic alliances often run aground because of bad habits ingrained from years of experience with traditional channel relationships. Too often partners see the alliance as a win-lose proposition, whereby each firm benefits only at the other's expense. Lewis is doing his best to change these views.

Points to Ponder

- What is the most important organizational value underlying the success or failure of strategic alliances? Is it critical that each strategic partner share this value? Why or why not?

Source: Adapted from Anonymous (1994), "Nelson, B&Y Alliance Promises Technology Solutions," *National Real Estate Investor,* 36 (12), 6; and Capowski, Genevieve (1994), "Zen and the Art of an Alliance," *Management Review,* 83 (12), 17–19.

alliances] define the structure. Some assets are apparent; some are hidden."[12] The apparent assets may include a firm's established distribution network, capital and physical resources, manufacturing capabilities, and/or buying power. But many alliances thrive on less visible assets like research and development proficiency, marketplace acceptance, or management prowess.

Increased global competition is a major factor contributing to the increase in strategic alliances. Robert Rodgers, vice president of technology and strategic business development at McDonnell Douglas Corporation, notes that a state of "increased competition between companies has led, and will continue to lead, to increased cooperation among companies. Everywhere you look, companies are forming strategic alliances."[13] Strategic alliances come in many shapes, sizes, and forms. Exhibit 14.1 illustrates how companies as diverse as American Express and Toys "R" Us, Cummins Engine and Toshiba Corporation, and CIGNA and United Motor Works have teamed up to achieve specific objectives aimed at fostering competitive marketplace advantages. Channel Surfing 14.1 discusses some other values that are created by strategic alliances.

The Nature and Scope of Strategic Alliances

Shopping for a new car? Consider how strategic alliances might impact your decision. General Motors alone:

- Builds Corollas in California with Toyota of Japan.
- Produces vans in England with Toyota-rival Isuzu Motors.
- Manufactures Pontiacs and other GM cars in South Korea in partnership with the Daewoo Group.

In fact, each American automaker has a stake in a Japanese auto manufacturer, including DaimlerChrysler's ongoing relationship with Mitsubishi. Moreover, each U.S. car company is engaged in a wide range of alliance activities with other, nonautomotive Japanese companies.

Despite the heated competition between the American and Japanese car industries, these rivals have feverishly pursued collaborative agreements. America's automobile parts suppliers alone have over 200 collaborative arrangements with Japanese partners. And strategic alliances are hardly limited to U.S.-Japanese partnerships. Did you know Ford also has a strategic alliance with Germany's Volkswagen to produce cars in South America? Identifying automotive alliances from the brand designation on the automobile is proving increasingly difficult. Nissan has a strategic alliance with Volkswagen, and Volvo and Renault have another.

The most dramatic example of global alliances may be The Alliance of Automobile Manufacturers, a new trade organization that includes BMW, DaimlerChrysler AG, Ford Motor Company, General Motors Corporation, Mazda Corporation, Nissan Motor, Toyota Motor, Volkswagen AG, and Volvo AB. A fundamental goal of this alliance is to address public policy issues of common interest, such as safety and environmental responsibility. Ultimately, the alliance seeks to maintain consistent global regulatory standards.

The road to strategic alliance success travels far beyond the automotive sector. IBM, Apple, and Motorola; Texas Instruments and Hitachi; and Whirlpool and Philips Electronics represent just a few examples of strategic alliances in the global marketplace.[14] Many U.S. corporations have formed long-standing technology-sharing and production relationships with Asian and European firms. Industry giants Eastman Kodak and General Electric (GE) exemplify this type of global strategic alliance strategy. If you have ever bought an electronics product bearing an Eastman Kodak or GE brand, you have actually purchased a foreign-made good. One hundred percent of the electronic items produced by Eastman Kodak and GE are manufactured by foreign alliance partners.[15]

IBM claims it has engaged in over 4,000 alliances. Exhibit 14.2 illustrates how IBM's alliances with a diversified portfolio of channel partners have helped the computer giant strengthen specific elements of its overall business. Note how each element relates to a specific objective, and how IBM's selection of an alliance partner rests on whether the partner can help it achieve a predetermined business objective.

Impact of Strategic Alliances

As a concept, strategic alliances are not *new*. Yet, alliances have clearly emerged in the recent past as one of the most popular business development options available in the global

Exhibit 14.2

IBM: Partnering helps achieve goals

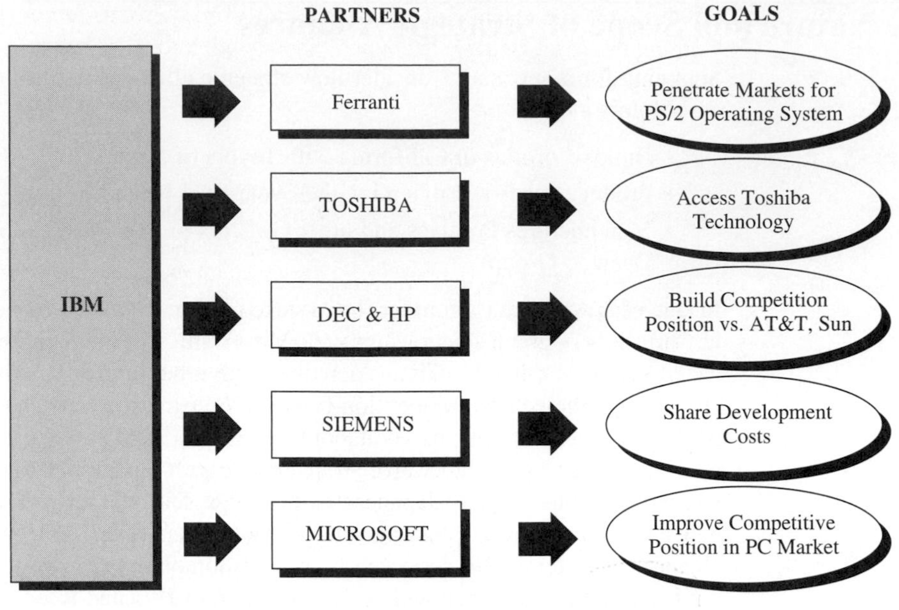

Source: Krubasik, Edward, and Hartmut Lautenschlager (1993), "Forming Successful Strategic Alliances in High Tech Businesses," in *Collaborating to Compete: Using Strategic Alliances and Acquisitions in the Global Marketplace,* Joel Bleeke and David Ernst, eds., New York: John Wiley & Sons, 61.

marketplace. An unprecedented escalation in the formation and scope of strategic alliances occurred during the past decade. More than 45,000 alliances were formed in the United States between 1988 and 2001, and the rate of domestic strategic alliance formation continues to grow by nearly 30 percent annually. Historically, strategic alliances have posted higher returns-on-investment (ROI) than other U.S. companies.[16] While on average alliances outperform more conventional business development approaches like mergers or acquisitions, they are inevitably expensive propositions. Enormous investments in time, capital, and human resources are required. But strategic alliances are not newfangled modes of collaborative channel relationships. Channel relationships have always existed along a temporal continuum, ranging from short-term to long-term interaction.

The undisputed pioneer and world heavyweight champion of strategic alliances—dating back to the 1920s—is Corning, Inc. The name Corning may conjure up images of casserole dishes, but Corning is an extremely diversified company. For example, in 1938 Corning entered an alliance with Owens-Illinois to create Owens-Corning Fiberglass. While Owens-Illinois brought established manufacturing and distribution competencies to the alliance, Corning brought investment capital and research and development skills. Corning's initial $10 million investment in Owens-Illinois eventually grew to $300 million. This alliance has lasted almost 50 years. Today, more than half of Corning's profits come from 23 strategic alliances with companies in countries as diverse as South Korea, Mexico, and India. Corning's alliance partners are equally diverse, including Siemens of West Germany, CIBA-Geigy of

Switzerland, and Asahi Chemical of South Korea. From food enzymes to fiber optic cable, Corning has exercised the strategic alliance option to seize market opportunities and confront market challenges.[17]

Rationale for Strategic Alliance Formation

What lies behind this fundamental market shift toward strategic alliances as a way to achieve long-term, collaborative channel relationships? The fiercely competitive marketplace itself is perhaps the primary contributing factor. Channel members are entering strategic alliances to attain market and profitability objectives they could never dream of reaching alone. After all, each channel member has finite resources and competencies.

A strategic alliance affords new market opportunities for channel members. Consider a recent *Electronic Business* survey of 455 electronics CEOs. Over 85 percent of the CEOs reported that their firms were involved in strategic alliances. Almost 67 percent of the respondents noted that these alliances played a prominent role in their competitive positioning. Nearly 80 percent said their alliances were driven by a need to access new markets and enhance marketing, distribution, or sales operations.[18] Couched within this notion of developing a stronger competitive position, strategic alliances offer a host of advantages to its partners. For your convenience, note how the first letter of each advantage listed below fits together to form the acronym **MERGE.**

- **M**arket entry. Strategic alliances can open new markets to channel members. This is especially true when firms are attempting to market across international borders. Individual channel members often lack the resources, expertise, or experience needed to successfully penetrate a foreign market. Strategic alliances provide channels members with a way to overcome such limitations and extend their operation's range by capitalizing on a partner's expertise in the host country. German pharmaceutical giant Hoechst, for instance, entered a strategic alliance with Copley Pharmaceuticals to gain entry into the rapidly growing managed U.S. health care market.[19]
- **E**conomy. Strategic alliances can facilitate reductions in wasteful, redundant activities. At the same time, alliance partners can pool limited resources. In this way, strategic alliances can lead to economies of scale in the procurement and allocation of resources. Philips Electronics and DuPont integrated their optical media businesses, entering a $400 million joint venture. As Michael Hartnagel, a member of the joint venture's policy committee, sagely notes, "We were smart enough to realize that we could not do everything ourselves."[20]
- **R**isk reduction. Strategic alliances can reduce the risks involved in market and product development and accelerate the time-to-market for new products. For example, new partnerships can also yield technological advantages. New pharmaceutical products can cost about $200 million by the time they get to market. By forming a partnership, pharmaceutical giant Merck & Co, Inc., can assist DuPont in developing and distributing DuPont's experimental compounds.[21] Together these two companies reduce the risk of pharmaceutical product launches. Merck capitalizes on the already developed experimental compounds, and Dupont benefits from Merck's extensive distribution network.

- **G**ain market share. The past is often assumed to be a prologue to the future. But a high market share today comes with no guarantee of an equally strong position tomorrow. Many competitors fail to anticipate imminent competitive threats. In the 1980s most European construction equipment companies viewed Caterpillar as their key competitor. They failed to foresee the global impact of Komatsu, Hitachi, and Sumitomo. These Asian heavy equipment manufacturers substantially eroded European-based companies' market share in the 1990s.[22]
- **E**xpansion. Strategic alliances can expedite channel members' expansion into related and unrelated industries. Strategic alliances frequently allow firms with little experience in a particular industry or market to move quickly up the learning curve and successfully capitalize on fleeting opportunities. When Blockbuster Entertainment Corp. wanted to expand beyond the video business, it used a number of strategic alliances. Blockbuster first established a strong presence in the retail music industry by forging an alliance with Virgin Retail Group. Blockbuster then reorganized to accommodate a new ventures division that actively seeks out profitable alliances.[23]

While the MERGE acronym makes it easy to identify the reasons for developing strategic alliances, you should be careful not to confuse the strategic alliance business form with a merger or acquisition strategy. As a point of clarification, a **merger** is a statutory combination of two or more companies that occurs when all properties are transferred to a single organizational entity. An **acquisition** likewise involves a takeover of an organization's possessions. For our purposes, the acronym MERGE simply reinforces the notion of a consolidation or blending of two or more alliance partners.

The overriding rationale for strategic alliances lies in the opportunity to create exchange value and gain positioning advantages by combining channel members' complementary strengths.[24] The alliance's exchange value may not always result in an equal payoff, but a *win-win* situation must be *possible* for each alliance partner. Exhibit 14.3 demonstrates how complementary relationships can result in successful strategic alliances. Note how each partner brings a singular market strength to the alliance. Channel Surfing 14.2 then tells a tale of how two partners brought extraordinary strengths to their alliance.

Exhibit 14.3

Complementary partners make for successful alliances

Partner Strength	*Partner Strength*	*Alliance Objective*
PepsiCo: Marketing clout in beverage market	Lipton: Recognized tea brand and customer franchise	To sell canned iced tea beverages jointly
KFC: Established brand and store format, operation skills	Mitsubishi: Real estate and site selection in Japan	To establish a KFC chain in Japan
Siemens: Presence in worldwide telecommunications markets and cable manufacturing technology	Corning: Technological strength in optical fibers and glass	To create a fiber optic cable business
Ericsson: Technological strength in public telecommunications networks	Hewlett-Packard: Computers, software, and access to electronics channel	To create and market network management systems

Channel Surfing 14.2

Where *Shao Mai* Meets *Spaetzel Dumplings*: On Fashionable Fare

Tim Ng, executive director of Hong Kong clothing giant Giordano, may prefer traditional *shao mai*: the small, meat-filled dumplings among the small treats at *dim sum*. Alternatively, Otto Beishem, retail giant Metro AG founder, likely prefers traditional German *spaetzel dumplings*. But these channel managers' tastes converge when it comes to fashion. Together, they hope to feast on Europeans' growing demand for fashionable, affordable clothing.

Metro AG, the huge European conglomerate that owns and operates more than 2,000 wholesale stores, supermarkets, hypermarkets, department stores, and specialty stores, is entering into a strategic alliance with the popular Hong Kong retailer. Giordano International is partnering with SB Warenhaus (Real), a wholly owned subsidiary of Metro AG, to bring casual attire to Germany and other European markets. As Ng notes, "Now that we have a prominent and experienced partner in Metro AG, we will develop as fast as the local management can cope in terms of experience and know-how."

Ng notes that the strategic alliance helps two strong retail partners capitalize on their own strengths. Giordano brings product development, training, marketing, and merchandising skills to the table. Real serves up a platter of 240 hypermarkets, where Giordano's *Bluestar Exchange* low-priced fashion label will be merchandised to adults and children.

But Giordano is no stranger to strategic alliances. It has entered into an alliance with China Enterprise resources to initially develop retail shops and counters in Beijing, Shanghai, and Guangzhou. Giordano hopes to expand with over 350 retail shops throughout the Chinese mainland. A joint venture with a Japanese firm is also in the pipeline.

Strategic alliances are the backbone of Giordano's global expansion. It already operates over 800 outlets in Asia, Australia, and the Middle East. Tim Ng understands the power of partnering, acknowledging that strategic alliances will be the key to Giordano's aspirations for growth: "It has always been our long-term plan to be a global company."

Points to Ponder

- How will Giordano maintain its brand equity as it expands globally?

Source: Adapted from Anonymous (2001), "Popular Retailer Expands into Europe," *Hong Kong Trader*, February, 5.

Types of Strategic Alliances

Before potential alliance partners can properly structure an alliance, they must consider the channel exosystems and channel microsystems depicted in the Channel Relationship Model. In the channel exosystem, potential partners must ask themselves what macroenvironmental forces would favor one type of strategic alliance over another. Often, these forces relate to competitive threats present in the marketplace. Alliance partners should pursue strategic options that provide sustainable competitive advantages. Recall from Chapter 5 that many other environmental factors can also affect channel strategy. These factors range from market entry barriers to cultural differences. The channel microsystem is especially critical to the choice of strategic alliance options. You will recall from Chapter 6 that exchange partners attempt to coordinate channel activities to avert channel conflict. While this is not always possible, the decision to pursue a strategic alliance reinforces the importance of a positive channel setting.

Looking back at Exhibit 14.1, you can see that many strategic options are available for developing and maintaining alliances. However, three major categories of strategic alliance options predominate in today's global marketplace. These are licensing arrangements, joint ventures, and consortia.[25] Our attention now turns to these strategic alliance categories.

Licensing Arrangements

A **licensing arrangement** revolves around a contractual agreement in which one alliance partner makes intangible assets such as technology, skills, and knowledge available to another partner in exchange for some remuneration such as royalties. This is the least sophisticated strategic alliance option. Alliance partners engaging in licensing agreements do not take an equity stake in one another, and the scope of the alliance is generally limited to the agreement's highly prespecified terms. Although less flexible than joint ventures and consortia, a licensing arrangement offers an attractive strategic alliance alternative because little to no capital investment is needed to enter new markets. Moreover, licensing agreements may be the only strategic option available in some markets because local governments prohibit foreign ownership. Licensing agreements can be categorized into manufacturing and service agreements.

Manufacturing Agreements. Manufacturing agreements are on the rise in international markets. The principal reason behind their global appeal is the limited cooperation required between organizational cultures involved in the manufacturing licensing agreement. Also, the exchange value that results from an international manufacturing licensing agreement is usually straightforward: a swap of technology for market entry into a new country or region.

A decision to manufacture in another country often leads to cost savings. But the impetus for true strategic alliances should extend beyond the labor or resource cost savings achieved. In manufacturing licensing agreements, for example, the licensing channel member may seek an alliance partner that can help it capitalize on its technology advantage. The alliance partners can then collectively establish global standards to preempt competitive threats. Licensee firms presumably know the host country and/or regional market well. Together the alliance partners can establish a pioneering advantage at the early strategies of the technology's life cycle. This makes manufacturing agreement-type strategic alliances especially attractive in technology-driven markets. Toshiba Corporation, for instance, licensed its technology to Singapore's mega-manufacturer Chartered Semiconductor Manufacturing Ltd. The manufacturing licensing agreement will facilitate Toshiba's dissemination of semiconductor-related technology in Southeast Asian and Pacific markets.[26]

Have you tried Oreo cookies in countries like Singapore or Malaysia? They are exactly the same cookies available at your local grocery store. U.S. food manufacturers sell over $80 billion worth of foods produced by licensed foreign manufacturers. In fact, nearly half of all publicly held U.S. food manufacturers are involved in some form of manufacturing licensing agreements. Many U.S. food manufacturers use **outbound licensing**—granting other manufacturers contractual permission to use their brand names. Rather than butting heads with high market entry barriers, U.S. food producers increasingly opt to generate a market presence through foreign manufacturers.[27]

The impact of manufacturing license arrangements can be remarkable. Have you ever heard of J.G. Hook, a popular clothing line boasting more than $200 million in wholesale sales in 1993? Today, the one-time manufacturer of soft goods doesn't make anything! All of its manufacturing output is licensed. According to founder and president Max Raab, manufacturing licensing alliances will help J.G. Hook build a global presence by the year 2000.[28] Nor are licensing arrangements limited to U.S. firms contracting manufacturing activities abroad. Davis Furniture Industries of High Point, North Carolina, has acquired several European manufacturing licenses to build contemporary European office furniture for U.S. markets.[29]

Service Agreements. Service-oriented licensing arrangements can also be enacted. Franchising is the most common form of international licensing. Anheuser-Busch and Coca-Cola regularly license through franchise agreements. Franchise licensing agreements afford several advantages including:

- The opportunity for quick market entry with a minimal investment because franchisees essentially fund the firm's expansion into new markets.
- Standardized business models that allow the lead firm to maintain a standard global image of its brand name or product.
- Managerial control over operations and marketing programs in the newly developed markets.

Many international markets are ripe for franchise licensing agreements. China is the world's most under-retailed country. While China's ambiguous franchise laws pose an initial barrier to entry, savvy alliance partners view China as a fertile market opportunity for franchise licensing arrangements in the future.[30]

Joint Ventures

Joint ventures involve the creation of a new organizational entity by two or more existing firms. The previously existing firms then assume active roles in developing and implementing a marketing strategy for the joint venture. Joint ventures are among the most popular strategic alliance options in the global marketplace. However, joint ventures also require a greater assumption of risk by each alliance partner.

Unlike licensing agreements, joint ventures require that organizational cultures be intermingled. In joint ventures, alliance partners engage in a dynamic exchange of resources. This sharing of resources—and thus risks, as well—gives joint ventures a relative advantage over licensing agreements: Each alliance partner in a joint venture has a stake in the new entity's success. A greater exchange of skills, systems, and market knowledge usually unfolds between alliance partners that are involved in a joint venture.

For example, an alliance among apparel industry giants JC Penney Co., Milliken & Company, and Robinson Manufacturing, along with chemical giant DuPont, was formed to allow a special consumer group—women who walk for exercise—to pull a line of products through the distribution pipeline. The idea was for the companies to pool resources, exchange information, and go beyond their traditional roles to create a *virtual company*. The virtual company successfully created a seamless pipeline for manufacturing, distributing, and retailing an apparel line targeted toward health-conscious women. The product was tested in 50 JC Penney stores and eventually dropped due to weak sales. But the strategic partnership was not a failure. Each company felt joint venture was a great learning experience that enriched the firm. As a result of this experience, the companies are willing to have another go at a joint venture.[31]

The three primary reasons for participating in joint ventures are to gain (1) channel access, (2) management expertise, and (3) sustainable competitive advantages via pooled resources. When contrasted with licensing arrangements, joint ventures also serve up other advantages. Joint ventures provide the opportunity to:

- Learn through participating in an alliance. The extensive exchange of value that occurs between the exchange partners fosters greater collaboration.
- Take advantage of pooled resources controlled by complementary partners. These pooled resources facilitate fast upgrading of managerial and technological processes within each organization.
- Achieve economies of scale in resource procurement and manufacturing processes.
- Develop an almost immediate market presence because of the critical mass resulting from the consolidation of two or more alliance partners.

In the past, conventional joint ventures usually functioned as operational structures. These operational structures sought to allocate specific resources toward a predetermined market objective. Not much flexibility was available. The type of joint venture emerging today, on the other hand, is typically less structured and offers more opportunity to adapt to changes in internal and external channel environments. Such flexibility allows joint ventures to seize market opportunities extending beyond those specified in the venture's original goals. Exhibit 14.4 illustrates how these emerging types of joint ventures take shape in Japan. Rather than simply exchanging organizational know-how, venture partners are sharing products, distribution channels, manufacturing systems, and a host of less conspicuous assets. This new type of joint venture requires substantial openness among the alliance partners.[32]

An amazing variety of joint ventures are up and running around the world. For instance, all of Europe's smart card manufacturers have established a U.S. presence via joint venture in anticipation of America's adoption of the combination "credit-bank" cards. What U.S. smart card business there is so far is already going to European-based manufacturers, where the cards have been used longer and production costs have already been lowered. American manufacturers are discussing joint ventures with European smart card makers as a way to lower their risk while positioning themselves to serve future U.S. demand. The biggest international success so far is in Germany, where smart cards have been distributed to 80 million citizens in conjunction with the national health card program.[33]

Consortia

Consortia have long been a Japanese trademark, existing in the form of ***keiretsus***. The *keiretsu* is a family of companies, centered around a large trading company or financial institution. Companies are joined together through interlocking boards of directors, bank holdings, and close personal relationships between senior management. These families of companies usually consist of 20 to 50 industrial firms. Family companies are extremely committed to the *keiretsu* as a whole, more so than to any single company. Family companies generally agree to not sell any holdings outside the *keiretsu*. Sumitomo and Mitsubishi are prominent *keiretsus*.[34]

Exhibit 14.4

Strategic partnership matrix

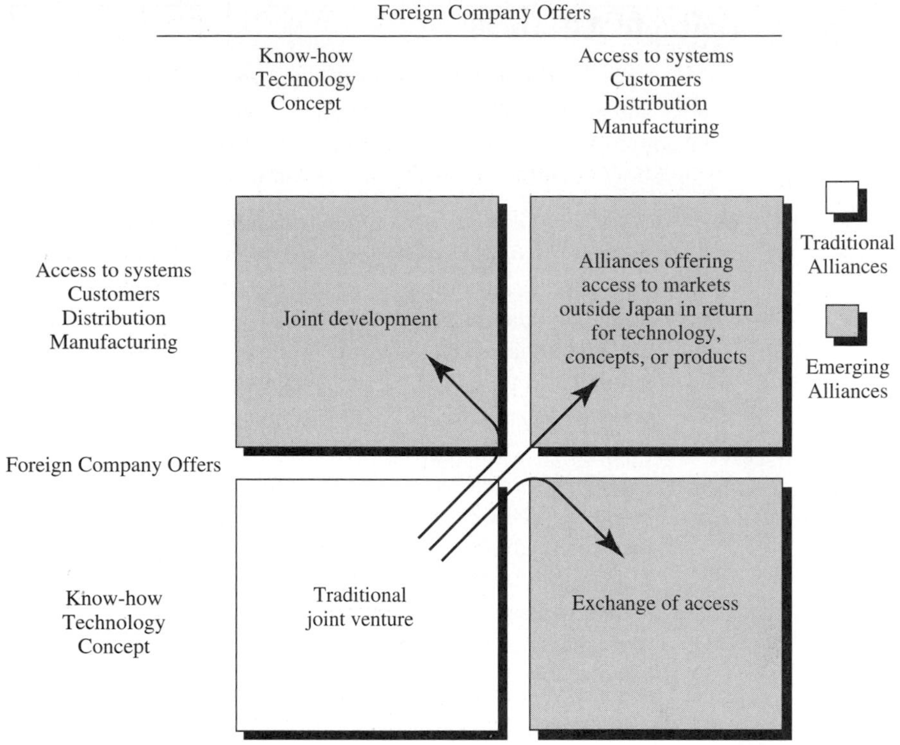

Foreign Company Offers

Foreign Company Offers	Know-how Technology Concept	Access to systems Customers Distribution Manufacturing
Access to systems Customers Distribution Manufacturing	Joint development	Alliances offering access to markets outside Japan in return for technology, concepts, or products
Know-how Technology Concept	Traditional joint venture	Exchange of access

Traditional Alliances

Emerging Alliances

More recently, South Korea has effectively used *keiretsu*-like consortia to catapult itself into a position of international information technology leadership. In South Korea, these groups are known as ***chaebol***—large conglomerates of major companies. *Chaebols* are managed by family members who have been selected and trained for the position. Rather than having a bank or holding company at its core, as *keiretsus* do, however, *chaebols* center around the Korean national government as their primary source of capital. Samsung and Daewoo are each successful *chaebols.*

Consistent with the spirit of Asia's *keiretsu* and *chaebol,* consortia are the most sophisticated strategic alliance forms currently operating in the West. **Consortia** are highly integrated, industrywide, coordinated alliance structures, generally consisting of 10 to 50 firms. Consortia are less integrated than traditional *keiretsus*; however, they share the risks and benefits associated with the outcomes of their coordinated activities. Usually, consortia operations are highly specific to a particular industry or technology market.

In the United States and Europe, consortia are just coming of age. When U.S. Memories, a semiconductor consortium, attempted to jump-start the domestic semiconductor industry, it proved a failure. In Europe, sparked by diplomatic efforts to bury ancient national enmities, consortia such as ESPRIT (European Strategic Program for Information Technologies) are emerging. ESPRIT is attempting to revitalize Europe's competitiveness in the information and communications high technology industries.[35]

Developing Strategic Alliances

As strategic alliances have grown in importance and popularity, so too has the number of books and articles offering managerial prescriptions for developing successful alliances. Several suggestions are consistently mentioned. For starters, when an alliance is first considered, firms should carefully evaluate the answer to the following questions:[36]

- *What are the relative advantages of pursuing a stated business objective with and without the alliance?* Strategic alliances are usually born out of a firm's recognition that it lacks the competency or resources to compete alone in a particular market. But not all companies pursue strategic alliances as a means of fulfilling their organizational vision. Consider Gillette, a technology leader in razor blade manufacturing. Gillette avoids strategic alliances in its core businesses. Gillette believes strategic alliances would dilute the strong control it now exercises over production technology.[37]
- *Does true, meaningful exchange value exist that can be realized through this alliance?* There is no assurance that a firm will benefit from a strategic alliance. In fact, many alliances turn out to be the first step toward an acquisition. Acquisitions often occur when a weak firm enters into an alliance with a strong firm, but the weaker partner fails to realize any exchange value other than a capital infusion. In such cases, no mutuality exists between the alliance partners.[38]

Once a firm determines it is likely to benefit from a strategic alliance, a four-step process is usually necessary to successfully bring off the alliance. The steps in alliance formation are: (1) achieving strategic harmony, (2) selecting partners, (3) developing action plans to achieve alliance objectives, and (4) assessing the extent to which the alliance reaches stated goals. Although we will present the four steps in a linear fashion for purposes of explanation, bear in mind that dangers are invariably associated with following a cookie-cutter, recipelike approach to alliance formation. Strategic alliances are symbiotic, with each relationship depending on the unique characteristics of each alliance partner. Accordingly, the specific actions taken during each stage should be tailored to accommodate the alliance's special exchange characteristics.

Achieving Strategic Harmony

Many alliances encounter problems before they get started. A well-designed alliance begins with a single, clear strategic vision. You may think this an obvious first step, but hundreds of strategic alliances have failed because the partners lacked a shared purpose; strategic harmony was missing.

Practical reasons usually lie behind the formation of channel alliances. Channel alliances potentially allow channel partners to improve inventory management, increase order processing efficiency, and/or achieve better coordination of marketing strategies and tactics. But strategic harmony must exist between the channel partners for such outcomes to be achieved—and it often proves elusive. For instance, Montedison and Hercules formed an alliance to create Adria Labs to market an anticancer drug. Montedison viewed Adria Labs as a sales and marketing branch created to serve its existing pharmaceutical division. Hercules, on the other hand, saw Adria Labs as a stand-alone, self-sufficient entity capable of marketing its own line of products. Hercules felt Adria Labs offered a pathway to global expansion, while Montedison's strategy was to fortify existing plans to introduce Italian-made drugs into the U.S. market. The differing visions of Adria Labs was a source of extraordinary conflict, and the alliance was swiftly terminated.[39]

On the surface, the development of strategic harmony would appear to involve simply negotiating an agreement regarding the expected outcomes of the alliance. However, strategic harmony is unlikely to be realized if a sense of imbalance exists between the alliance partners. One-sided alliances tend to fail.[40] Difficulties often result from efforts to meld two or more organizational cultures into one. This problem is particularly acute in global strategic alliances where cultural differences can be pronounced. Flexibility is the key to the successful negotiation of an alliance strategy. But some organizations' cultures are far less prone to flexibility in the negotiating process.

Another dilemma confronting alliance partners in their pursuit of strategic harmony relates to the transfer of technology, products, skills, and knowledge. The role that organizational culture plays in strategic alliance formation is summarized by the following four categories:

- **The quarterback.** Quarterbacks can transfer their skills to others, but do not receive skills well. Management in these organizations is usually hierarchical and features strong, nontransferable skills, systems, and cultures. Unfortunately, this type of alliance partner tends to be inflexible at the strategy development stage.
- **The wide receiver.** Wide receivers easily accept skills from other organizations, but fail to do a good job of transferring their own skills to other partners. These partners learn a great deal through alliance formation, but have difficulty actively managing the exchange of technologies, products, skills, or knowledge. An opportunity to achieve strategic harmony with such a partner exists, but wide receivers must recognize their own shortcomings.
- **The spectator.** Spectators are not particularly good at receiving or transferring exchange value. They are prone to an "us versus them" mind-set which hardly serves the ends of strategic development or strategic harmony well. The cultures of spectator firms are generally so distinctive that they block the development of successful strategic alliances.
- **The utility player.** Utility players can perform any position; they are highly flexible. Utility players can transfer and receive skills from other organizations and willingly adapt to accommodate other partners' systems. Such organizations have open management cultures. They feature the easiest cultures from which to pursue strategic harmony in an alliance. Utility players excel at channel collaboration.[41]

While strategic alliances usually feature long-term orientations, the perception of exactly what constitutes the *long term* is likely to vary across alliance partners. U.S. companies are generally perceived to have a relatively short time orientation with respect to planning horizons and performance outcomes. This differs markedly from Asian companies, which frequently plan and measure performance outcomes in intervals of decades rather than years. Alliance participants should make sure they share compatible timeline expectations early on in the strategy development process.

Selecting Alliance Partners

The selection of appropriate alliance partners is critical to the formation of successful strategic alliances. In alliances, as in any other channel relationship, the channel microsystem influences the interaction process. The partners' individual characteristics should mesh together in a logical, complementary, and mutually beneficial fashion. Generally speaking, strategic alliance partners should supplement one another with respect to products, market presence, or functional skills. Alliance partners must each contribute to and benefit from the alliance. Channel members with nothing to contribute will likely diminish their partners' market strengths, rather than augment them. Often, weaker partners seeking capital infusions through joint ventures or other strategic alliance types lack the core competencies needed to nurture collaborative relationships.

History tells us that most combinations of alliance partners do not enjoy enduring relationships. The chemistry that exists between strategic partners influences the alliance's life expectancy. For strategic alliances to evolve into enduring and collaborative interfirm arrangements, firms must first seek partners who themselves possess a long-term orientation. The combination of alliance partners can take many forms, but are best considered along two dimensions, as illustrated in Exhibit 14.5. One dimension is the partner's *relative market strength*. The other is the partner's *relative contribution to the alliance's competitive position*. We classify these combinations into five groups:[42]

The Racer. A Racer is an alliance between two or more strong, direct competitors vying for overall leadership in a given market. Both partners want to get to the finish line first, but each is willing to concede a lap in exchange for some other, longer-term benefit. In an organizational context, Racer alliance partners want to create short-term synergies for specific products and/or markets. Racer alliance relationships are typically characterized by prespecified agreements regarding the extent of the collaborative activities.

An agreement (and spirit) of shared control thus arises between the partners, but is confined to a relatively small domain of collaboration. This is because each alliance partner continues to compete against each other on the larger track. For this reason, racer alliances often succumb to competitive tensions. Racer alliances are prone to either dissolution or to one alliance partner acquiring the other.

The shotgun marriage between Fujitsu and British computer maker ICL falls into the Racer category. As one MIT researcher notes, "Fujitsu 'quite deliberately' worked its British computer-making ally into a corner where it had no choice but to sell."[43] Racer alliances' impermanent nature is widely recognized. Consider EniChem SpA and Norsk Hydro—two global giants in the chemical industry. Their attempts to forge a fertilizer joint venture collapsed because each alliance partner was more concerned about its own, rather than the alliance's, competitive positioning effort.

The Uninsured. Uninsured drivers should not be on the road. So it is with uninsured alliances, which represent partnerships forged between the weak. Two firms band together in the hope that one plus one will equal three. But in reality, the result is often less than two. Rather than attain market power, each alliance partner tends to bring the other down because the alliance features more *pooled problems* than *pooled resources*. The collective deficiencies are too great for the weak partners to overcome.

Exhibit 14.5

Selecting alliance partners: potentially bumpy roads

Nonenduring Relationships			
Alliance Type	*Description*	*Aspiration Level*	*Probable Outcome*
The racer	Two strong, direct competitors partner to create some short-term synergies in product and/or market development.	Each alliance member is willing to concede one battle, but each company is determined to win the market war.	The alliance is prone toward dissolution or acquisition by one party because there is inherent *competitive tension* between the alliance members.
The uninsured	Two or more weak companies join forces to increase market power by pooling capital, human, and operational resources.	The immediacy of goal fulfillment is tantamount to each member's market survival. Each member feels the other(s) can fill the gap in its present business operation.	Each of the alliance members tends to bring the other down. They tend to "fall" together because the alliance represents more *pooled problems* than *pooled competencies*.
The road hog	One weak company links with a strong, direct competitor to avoid acquisition.	The weak company has essentially surrendered to its stronger partner, but it hopes to muster some autonomy in its operations. The stronger partner sees the alliance as an inroad toward acquisition.	The weaker company remains weak, and its stronger partner is likely to dissolve the alliance through acquisition or divestiture. The weaker firm is viewed as *property* rather than a collaborative partner.
The back-seat driver	One weak company collaborates with a much stronger company that can provide *complementary resources* to enhance its current offerings in the marketplace. It essentially "rides the coat tails" of the stronger, complementary company.	The weaker partner hopes to increase its power, while the stonger party hopes to reinforce its market position through partnering. Both parties in the alliance are fully aware of the asymmetric power at the onset.	At some point, the weaker party garners enough power to become an effective equal to its partner. When this happens, there is no incentive to preserve the alliance.
Enduring Relationships			
Alliance Type	*Description*	*Aspiration Level*	*Probable Outcome*
Traveling companion	The alliance members are essentially *complementary equals*. They each contribute different functional strengths while maintaining a sense of shared purpose.	Each member of the alliance is committed to truly collaborative, long-term, and joint success. Each partner views the other as an equal contributor to the alliance's mission.	The alliance is likely to endure because there is a greater incentive to preserve the relationship than to dissolve it.

Source: Adapted from Bleeke, Joel, and David Ernst, "Is Your Strategic Alliance a Sale?" *Harvard Business Review,* 73 (January/February 1995), 97–105.

Such alliances are generally doomed from the start. Consider the Alcazar alliance among Austrian, SAS, and Swissair. The success of this European alliance rested on KLM's insistence on staying connected with U.S. carrier Northwest. Northwest brought its own set of financial woes and the alliance was viewed as a confederation of 98-pound weaklings.

The Road Hog. Road Hogs have little concern for other drivers on the road. Representing a partnership fashioned between a weaker and much stronger firm, Road Hog alliances typically promise mixed outcomes for their participants. The Road Hog is going to take up both lanes in its drive to grab market control. The weak firm's only recourse is to surrender in the hope of marshaling some degree of autonomy in its own operations. However, the stronger alliance partner has little concern for its weaker partner. That's what makes a Road Hog a Road Hog. Sega Enterprises has invested over $90 million in struggling Atari in exchange for access to some key video game technologies. Most industry experts expect that Sega will either acquire Atari or dissolve its relationship after garnering the research and development information it wants.

In Road Hog alliances, the stronger firm is likely to eye acquisition of its weaker partner from the outset of the relationship. These firms often compete against each other in the marketplace. Ultimately, the relationship becomes the weak versus the strong, and the stronger party views the weaker partner as a capital investment. This type of alliance rarely lasts more than five years. The relationship is generally dissolved through acquisition or divestiture.

The Back-Seat Driver. Here, an alliance is again formed between a weak firm and a strong firm. However, in the back-seat driver alliance the weaker partner gains strength from the alliance. Eventually, the alliance partners become equals. At that point, the alliance usually dissolves since the weaker party can now survive on its own. The weaker partner has essentially accepted a back-seat status until it can move into the driver's seat on its own. The stronger party is always expected to be in the driver's seat, strengthening its position by capitalizing on the weaker party.

Traveling Companion. Traveling companion alliances are relationships between complementary equals. Such partnerships are based on a genuine sense of collaboration. Both alliance partners have the willingness and flexibility to build on each other's core competencies. Usually, each partner contributes different product, geographic, or functional strengths to the alliance. Traveling companion alliances last longer than strategic alliance's median life span of seven years since neither party has a desire to end the partnership. Electronic Data Systems (EDS) and Moore Corporation enjoy a traveling companion alliance. The partners entered a 10-year commitment whereby EDS provides computer services for Moore. In return, Moore's U.S. subsidiary supplies printing services for EDS.

Developing Action Plans

Once a strategic alliance is formed, the partners will generally form what is known as an **alliance team,** which consists of managerial employees from each firm engaged in the strategic alliance. While, in part, these designates represent the interests of their firm, team members' highest priority should be the maintenance and success of the alliance itself. This is a difficult responsibility because the team member has to be more highly committed to the alliance than to her or his own organization. At times, alliance team members must compromise an individual firm's objectives so as to preserve an alliance's shared vision. Why is this a difficult task? Loyalty is an important credo in most organizations. But alliance team members must remember that a successful alliance is the ultimate goal of the organization they represent.

Alliance team members have three major functions. The principal function of team members is to chart a path for the strategic alliance. This course should reflect the common vision of the alliance and should include specific action plans that are jointly developed to realize the common vision.

The second function is to identify key links in the value chain. Remember from Chapter 9 that the value chain represents the true, incremental exchange value that can be recognized by each partner at various stages of the alliance. Alliance team members should avoid overly ambitious expectations. Consider the Philips and DuPont optical venture. Each company invested over $150 million in the alliance, but along the way they forgot to establish common objectives. The partners had high expectations for the alliance's competitive position in the $400 billion optical market. However, both partners ended up disenchanted with the alliance's lack of collective market strength, and the relationship was dissolved.[44]

An alliance team's final function is to ensure evenhanded returns to each partner. Each alliance partner must benefit from the collaboration. If not, there is little incentive for the partnership to continue. Each team member must be committed to the long-term welfare of other exchange partners.

Assessing Alliance Performance

The final stage in developing a strategic alliance relates to the periodic assessment or monitoring of alliance performance. This monitoring process should not be mistaken for continuous interference in individual firm activities or systems. Here, performance is evaluated as part of the alliance partners' joint, collaborative activities. The purpose is to assess whether the alliance is staying the strategic course originally charted. Three questions should be considered:

- Has the alliance met the benchmarks agreed upon at the outset of the alliance?
- How might alliance objectives be modified to accommodate changes in an alliance partner's position?
- What changes in the channels environment should make the strategic partners reassess their strategic course of action?

The Downside of Strategic Alliances

Given the widespread popularity of the various strategic alliance options we have discussed, one might assume that strategic alliances offer a cure for whatever ails your company in continuously changing marketplaces. Not quite. About 70 percent of joint ventures fail and over 80 percent of current strategic alliance options are likely to vanish by century's end. Strategic alliances that operate across international borders have even lower chances of survival. Whereas the life span for strategic alliances in general is seven years, international joint ventures are not likely to enjoy even a four-year life span, and less than 10 percent last an entire decade. Moreover, less than a third of international joint ventures meet or exceed the alliance partners' expectations.[45]

Why do strategic alliances fail? Exhibit 14.6 summarizes, on a percentage basis, the common causes of strategic alliance failures. A lack of strategy development is apparently the chief culprit. This suggests that the strategic alliance form itself is not at fault. Managers will have to spend more time formulating workable, realistic strategies to succeed in strategic alliances. More effort should also be allocated toward choosing the right alliance partners. Other factors contributing to the failure of strategic alliances include:

- The absence of a compelling reason for forming a strategic alliance in the first place, that is, some alliances are a bad idea and don't deserve to see the light of day.
- One or both partners are burdened by unrealistic expectations regarding the synergies that would result from the alliance.
- The strategic partners' corporate cultures clash with one another.
- One (or both) of the parties was insufficiently interested in the strategic alliance. When this circumstance arises, windows of opportunity to improve performance in functional areas are likely to slam shut before the companies can leap through.[46]

So how are companies likely to build successful, long-term collaborative coalignments? Choosing the right partner has a great deal of impact on alliance performance. Alliance partners who produce complementary products or operate in similar markets are apt to forge a more successful business marriage. Relatively simple measures, such as learning about the

Exhibit 14.6

Reasons underlying strategic alliance failure: percentage breakout

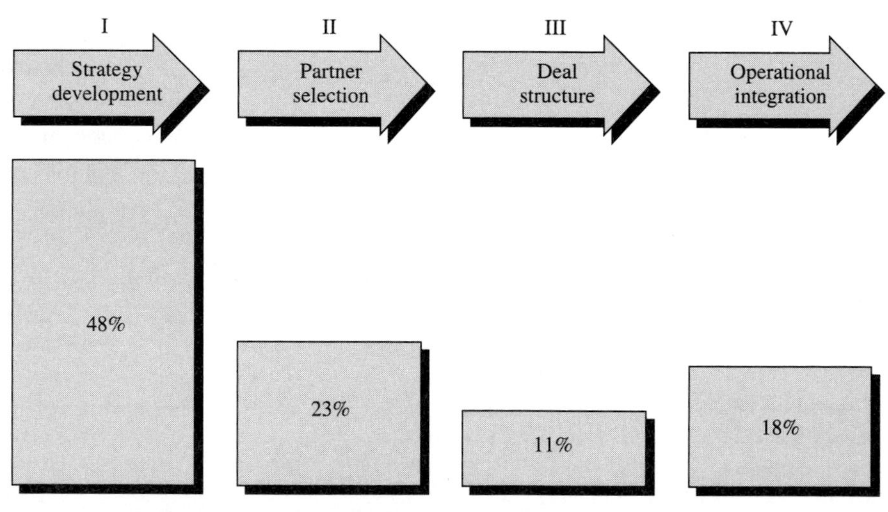

Source: Stratford, Sherman (1992), "Are Strategic Alliance Working?" *Fortune,* September 21, 77–78.

partners' technology, operating systems, and culture will go a long way toward facilitating successful strategic alliances, as well. Other factors are also known to improve the chances of a strategic alliance meeting or exceeding its alliance partners' expectations. Patience is one prescription frequently recommended by strategic alliance experts.

Channel members should not rush into deals or expect immediate results from the strategic alliance. After all, a strategic alliance itself represents a long-term commitment to collective channel performance. Finally, alliance partners should remember that strategic alliances are like geodesic domes: Alliance success is best achieved by strategically arranging the right elements to reinforce a structure's strength.

Key Terms

acquisition
alliance team
chaebol
coalignment
consortia
joint ventures
keiretsu
licensing arrangement
merger
outbound licensing
strategic alliances
symbiotic relationship

Chapter Summary

Channel members are increasingly collaborating as partners. Properly managed collaboration allows channel members to reduce the duplication of resources and efforts, while bolstering their collective market strengths. Channel members are also able to lessen the uncertainty posed by their channel environments by spreading risks. Collaboration likewise offers channel members the opportunity to achieve greater efficiency.

The term *strategic alliance* describes a number of organizational structures in which two or more channel members cooperate and form a partnership based on mutual goals. Strategic alliances are also symbiotic relationships—interdependent, mutually beneficial exchanges between two or more parties. Strategic alliances often involve an overarching relationship between a series of channel members, each of which features different core competencies. Regardless of the strategic alliance's shape or size, it is critically important that the strategic partners share common goals. Strategic alliances often allow cooperating channel members to achieve favorable competitive positions.

Paradoxically, a state of increased competition among companies has led to a state of increased cooperation—in the form of strategic alliances—among companies. Strategic alliances are profoundly influencing conduct and consumption in global marketing channels. The rate of domestic alliance formation has been growing by over 25 percent annually.

Strategic alliances offer several advantages for their participants, including the opportunity to open new market channels, reduce wasteful or redundant activities, lower the risks involved in market and product development, gain market share, and expand into related and unrelated industries. But the overriding rationale for strategic alliances lies in their ability to create exchange value and positioning advantages by combining the complementary strengths of channel members.

Three categories of strategic alliance options predominate. Licensing arrangements revolve around a contractual agreement where one alliance partner makes intangible assets such as technology, skills, and knowledge available to another partner in exchange for some remunerative consideration. Joint ventures involve the creation of a new organizational entity by two or more existing firms. These firms then assume active roles in developing and implementing a marketing strategy for the joint venture. Consortia are highly integrated, industrywide coordinated alliance structures, generally consisting of 10 to 50 firms. Consortia share the risks and benefits associated with the outcomes of their coordinated activities. Consortia operations are usually highly specific to a particular industry or technology market.

Prior to entering a strategic alliance, channel members should evaluate the answers to two questions: What are the relative advantages of pursuing a stated business objective with and without the alliance? and Does meaningful exchange value exist that can be realized through this alliance? Once a firm determines it is likely to benefit from a strategic alliance, a four-step process is necessary to bring off the alliance. These steps are: achieving strategic harmony, selecting partners, developing action plans to achieve strategic objectives, and assessing the extent to which the alliance reaches stated goals.

Many alliances experience problems almost before they begin. Well-designed alliances begin with clear strategic visions—a sense of strategic harmony exists among the partners. Strategic harmony is unlikely to be achieved if the alliance is one-sided. Strategic partners should also share a common orientation toward the future. The partners' individual characteristics should mesh together in a logical, complementary, and mutually beneficial fashion. Generally speaking, strategic alliance partners should select partners that complement one another with respect to products, market presence, or functional skills.

Once a strategic alliance is formed, the partners will generally form an alliance team. This team consists of employees from each firm engaged in the strategic alliance. While these designates, in part, represent their firm's interests, team members' highest priority should be the maintenance and success of the alliance itself. The alliance's performance should be evaluated as part of the partners' collaborative efforts. This evaluation should determine whether alliance benchmarks have been achieved, whether objectives need to be modified, and whether environmental changes have occurred that should make the partners reassess their strategic course of action.

Many strategic alliances fail. Shortfalls in partner selection or alliance strategy development are the primary culprits. Channel members should not rush into deals or expect immediate results from a strategic alliance. Patience is usually a virtue, particularly since strategic alliances themselves represent a long-term commitment to collective channel performance.

Channel Challenges

1. It is not uncommon to see drivers talking on cellular telephones as they cruise down the highway. Nokia Mobile Phones has experienced phenomenal market growth since 1994. Nokia's market surge may be attributable to a strategic alliance formed with AT&T Corporation. AT&T will resell the Nokia cellular telephones that are manufactured in the United States, South Korea, and Hong Kong. However, Nokia faces a global challenge: Many of its suppliers are also its competitors. How might the Nokia-AT&T alliance help defray the supplier-competitor conundrum?
2. Rick Dowden, president and CEO of Volvo North America, once commented on the Volvo-Renault alliance: "There are no provisions in our agreement for dissolving this relationship. It is intended to be a marriage." However, the Volvo-Renault relationship ended in a bitter divorce. How might provisions for alliance dissolution foster better partnering relationships? How might they hinder partner relationships?
3. The development of the European Union might suggest a great deal of promise for cross-border alliance formation among European firms. However, alliances between European firms have not had a particularly good record of success. Some have cited differences in management characteristics as a common cause for the European alliance failures. Consider the following table:

Table to accompany Channel Challenge 3

	Western Europe, i.e., United Kingdom	*Northern Europe, i.e., France*	*Eastern Europe, i.e., Germany*
Corporate approach	Commercial	Administrative	Industrial
Social philosophy	Pragmatic	Rational	Holistic
Managerial attributes	Experimental	Professional	Developmental

How might corporate approach, social philosophy, and managerial attributes contribute to alliance failures among European partners? How does this table illuminate the challenges of combining organizational cultures in the global marketplace?

4. Perry Ellis International, a popular designer clothing label, boasts over $800 million in retail sales worldwide. Yet the company manufactures nothing; it only licenses its designs. Its licensing partners assume the manufacturing and distribution risks. Why would strategic partners be willing to shoulder the risks in a licensing agreement? Why must Perry Ellis International be careful in choosing licensing venture partners?

5. Sun Tzu, the renowned fourth century B.C. war strategist, once wrote:

   Know the other and know yourself;
   One hundred challenges without danger;
   Know not the other and yet know yourself;
   One triumph for one defeat;
   Know not the other and know not yourself;
   Every challenge is certain peril.

What does Sun Tzu's writings suggest about knowing alliance partners? Why is it important to know oneself before entering into a strategic alliance?

Review Questions

1. What are strategic alliances?
2. What does the term *coalignment* imply?
3. Why do channel members employ strategic alliances? What does the acronym MERGE suggest?
4. What steps are necessary in forging a strategic alliance?
5. What are three global alliance strategies?
6. How have strategic alliances impacted the U.S. economy?
7. In selecting alliance partners, what "type" of channel member is the most attractive for long-term success?
8. Why do many strategic alliances fail despite their intuitive appeal?

Endnotes

1. http://www.tokyo-dome.co.jp.
2. Knauer, Gene (1992), "The Return of the Geodesic Dome," *The Futurist,* 26 (January/February), 29–32; and Frankel, Elena (1993), "Still Standing," *Home,* 39 (September), 30.
3. Frabotta, David (2000), "Carlson to Grow Park Brands," *Hotel & Motel Management,* 215 (July 3), 1,54.
4. From Revesz, Therese R., and Mimi Cauley De La Sierra (1987), "Competitive Alliances: Forging Ties Abroad," *Management Review* (March), 57.
5. In an interview with Jordan Lewis (1994) printed in

"Zen and the Art of an Alliance," *Management Review,* December, 17–19.
6. Revesz and De La Sierra, "Competitive Alliances," 57.
7. Lei, David (1993), "Offensive and Defensive Uses of Alliances," *Long Range Planning,* 26 (August), 32.
8. Murray, Edwin A. Jr., and John F. Mahon (1993), "Strategic Alliances: Gateway to the New Europe?" *Long Range Planning,* 26 (August), 102–11.
9. "Things Go Better with Coke—Just Ask McDonald's" (1994), *Fortune,* October, 116.
10. Lewis interview in "Zen and the Art of an Alliance," 17–19.
11. Young, Joyce A., Lou E. Pelton, and Faye Gilbert (1995), "Speculation on Strategic Alliance Failures: Gender and Family Orientation in Strategic Bridging," *Seventh Bi-Annual World Marketing Congress, Melbourne,* Australia: Academy of Marketing Science; Sheth, Jagdish N., and Atul Parvatiyar (1992), "Toward a Theory of Business Alliance Formation," *Scandinavian International Business Review,* 1 (3), 71–87.
12. Interview with Jose A. Collazo (1993) in "Strategic Alliances Keep Customers Plugged In," *Management Review,* March, 25.
13. Roberts, Dr. Roger F. (1992), "Competition and Cooperation: The Role of Strategic Alliances," *Executive Speeches,* October/November, 13; "When Multinationals Marry," *Economist,* September 19, 19.
14. Young, Pelton, and Gilbert, "Speculation on Strategic Alliance Failures."
15. Lei, David, and John W. Slocum Jr. (1992), "Global Strategy, Competence-Building and Strategic Alliances," *California Management Review,* 35 (Fall), 81–97.
16. Pekar, Peter, and Robert Allio (1994), "Making Alliances Work—Guidelines for Success," *Long Range Planning,* 27 (August), 54–65.
17. Rigby, Darrell K., and Robin W. T. Buchanen (1994), "Putting More Strategy into Strategic Alliances," *Directors & Boards,* 18 (Winter), 14–19.
18. Almassy, Stephen E., and E. B. Baatz (1992), "455 Electronics Execs Say Rugged Individualism Is Fading," *Electronic Business,* 18 (March 30), 38–46.
19. Plishner, Emily S. (1993), "Hoechst Repositions in U.S. Pharmaceutical Market," *Chemical Week,* 153 (October 20), 12.
20. Revesz and De La Sierra, "Competitive Alliances," 57.
21. Anfuso, Dawn (1994), "Helping Two Companies Form a Third," *Personnel Journal,* 73 (January), 63.
22. Abravanel, Roger, and David Ernst (1993), "Alliance versus Acquisition: Strategic Choices for 'National Champions,'" in *Collaborating to Compete: Using Strategic Alliances and Acquisitions in the Global Marketplace,* Joel Bleeke and David Ernst, eds., New York: John Wiley & Sons, 232.
23. Zbar, Jeffery (1993), "Blockbuster Stars as Global Brand," *Advertising Age,* 64 (March 15), 1, 54.
24. Bleeke, Joel and David Ernst (1995), "Is Your Strategic Alliance Really a Sale?" *Harvard Business Review,* 73 (January/February), 97–105.
25. Lei, David, and John W. Slocum Jr. (1991), "Global Strategic Alliances: Payoffs and Pitfalls," *Organizational Dynamics,* 19 (Winter), 44–62.
26. "Technology Transfer Agreement Reached" (1995), *Japan 21st,* 40 (January), 75–76.
27. Henderson, Dennis R., Ian M. Sheldon, and Kathleen N. Thomas (1994), "International Licensing of Foods and Beverages Makes Markets Truly Global," *FoodReview,* 17 (September–December), 7–12.
28. Underwood, Elaine (1994), "Designers Forget the Fuss of Factory and Warehouse," *Brandweek,* 35 (June 13), 40.
29. McMorrow, Eileen (1994), "Davis Furniture Looks to Europe, 50 Years On," *Facilities Design & Management,* 13 (June), 24–25.
30. From "Franchising in China" (1994), *East Asian Executive Reports,* 16 (April 15), 6, 10.
31. Thornton, Meg (1995), "Tomorrow's Blueprint," *Apparel Industry Magazine,* 56 (March), QR10–14.
32. Jones, Kevin K., and Walter E. Shill (1993), "Japan: Allying for Advantage," in *Collaborating to Compete: Using Strategic Alliances and Acquisitions in the Global Marketplace,* 115–44.
33. Allen, Catherine (1995), "Get Smart," *Bank Management,* 71 (2), 58–63.
34. Lei, David, and John W. Slocum Jr. (1991), "Global Strategic Alliances: Payoffs and Pitfalls," *Organizational Dynamics,* 19 (Winter), 44–62.
35. Lei and Slocum Jr., "Global Strategic Alliances: Payoffs and Pitfalls," 44–62.
36. Bluestein, Abraham (1994), "A Four-Step Process for Creating Alliances," *Directors & Boards,* 18 (Winter), 25–27.
37. Rigby and Buchanen, "Putting More Strategy into Strategic Alliances," 14–19.
38. Bleeke and Ernst, eds., *Collaborating to Compete: Using Strategic Alliances and Acquisitions in the Global Marketplace.*

39. Rigby and Buchanen, "Putting More Strategy into Strategic Alliances," 14–19.
40. Krubasik, Edward, and Hartmut Lautenschlager (1993), "Forming Successful Strategic Alliances in High-Tech Businesses," in *Collaborating to Compete: Using Strategic Alliances and Acquisitions in the Global Marketplace,* 55–65.
41. Adapted from Bleeke, Joel, and David Ernst (1993), "Manager's Choice," in *Collaborating to Compete: Using Strategic Alliances and Acquisitions in the Global Marketplace,* 12.
42. The following is based on the seminal research funded by McKinsey & Company, Inc., and reported in Bleeke and Ernst, "Is Your Strategic Alliance Really a Sale?" 97–105. The typology presented here is an adaptation of Bleeke and Ernst's article, and it was previously conceptualized in Young, Joyce A., and Lou E. Pelton (1995), "Strategic Alliances: Perils and Promise in the Rose Garden," in *1995 Proceedings of the Southern Marketing Association,* Orlando, Florida: Southern Marketing Association.
43. Main, Jeremy (1990), "Making Global Alliances Work," *Fortune,* December 17, 124.
44. Rigby and Buchanen, "Putting More Strategy into Strategic Alliances," 16–18.
45. Savona, David (1992), "When Companies Divorce," *International Business,* 5 (November), 48–51; and Doorley, Thomas L. III (1993), "Teaming Up for Success," *Business Quarterly,* 57 (Summer), 99–103.
46. Sherman, Stratford (1992), "Are Strategic Alliances Working?" *Fortune,* September 21, 77–78.

part IV

Cases

Case 4.1

The Country's Best Yogurt

Lisa Hill
Ouachita Baptist University

Carl Stark
Henderson State University

Anita Williams
Henderson State University

S. Darren Hollingsworth
Southwest Arkansas Planning and Development District, Inc.

The Country's Best Yogurt (TCBY) was founded in 1981 by Frank Hickingbotham of Little Rock, Arkansas. The first TCBY store opened in October of that same year in west Little Rock. The company's purposes include franchising and retail sales of frozen yogurt as a premium alternative to ice cream. TCBY grew very rapidly in its first decade. In 1984 TCBY became a publicly traded corporation. TCBY operated 102 stores in 1984 with total sales of $11.5 million. Net income that year was $1,011,000 ($.06 per share). Sales and franchising revenues totaled $7.7 million. By fiscal year 1989, TCBY operated 1,582 stores in fifty states and five foreign countries, with system-wide sales of $303 million. Net income for fiscal 1989 was $29,493,000 ($1.10 per share), and sales and franchising revenues totaled $144.6 million. By 1990 the company had 675 franchise groups and over 1,800 stores across the United States, Canada, the Caribbean, and several other foreign countries. Its international headquarters is in the 40-story TCBY Tower in Little Rock.

TCBY became the international leader in the growing market for frozen yogurt franchising. Total annual retail sales of frozen yogurt by all companies was estimated at $190 million in 1985. Estimated sales for 1989 were $1 billion, with growth rates of more than 20 percent per year forecast for the next few years. Total retail sales of frozen yogurt are expected to surpass $2.5 billion by the mid-1990s.

Source: This case was written from public sources by Lisa Hill, Carl Stark, Anita Williams, and S. Darren Hollingsworth as a basis for class discussion rather than to illustrate either effective or ineffective handling of an administrative situation.

TCBY's company objective is to appeal to today's health-conscious consumers with a product that is more nutritionally acceptable than ice cream and does not have the unpleasant aftertaste associated with traditional yogurt. Emphasis is placed on three goals: great tasting products, friendly people, and an environment that is immaculately clean. TCBY tries to make its product distinctive and to emphasize its lower calorie, fat, and cholesterol content compared to ice cream. TCBY seeks to make its franchisee team effective by providing a great deal of support. Responsibilities for planning TCBY's management and marketing efforts rest with Herren C. Hickingbotham, President, and the company's marketing executives.

Strengths

One of TCBY's strengths is its brand awareness. TCBY is known for its quality products and has a 34 percent market share in the frozen yogurt franchising and retail business. When many people think of frozen yogurt, they think first of TCBY. Analysts believe that the key to TCBY's capturing market share is for the company to establish itself as the national brand of yogurt. TCBY is well known internationally and is expanding further into the international market. As of December 1990, international stores included fifty-two in Canada, six in Taiwan, six in Malaysia, four in Singapore, four in the Bahamas, and two in Japan. TCBY increased market awareness through coordinated national and local advertising. The first national television advertising for TCBY was by Johnny Carson on the *Tonight Show* and Willard Scott on the *Today Show.* Most of the company's television advertising is in the daytime, with selected advertising during prime time. Other advertising is done through newspaper inserts and through product partnerships with well-known companies such as M & M Mars, which makes the candy toppings used with TCBY yogurt. TCBY also has national promotions throughout the year: at Christmas, featuring gift certificates; Valentine's Day, promoting Sweetheart pies; and other promotions on Washington's Birthday, Easter, Mother's Day, Father's Day, Independence Day, and Halloween.

A second strength is the fact that TCBY's products lend themselves well to the current health and fitness emphasis in the United States. TCBY's slogan is "All the Pleasure. None of the Guilt." The slogan is registered for the company's exclusive use. TCBY sells several types of frozen yogurt: (1) Regular, which is 96 percent fat free and has about one-half the calories of premium ice cream; (2) Nonfat, which contains no cholesterol; (3) No Sugar Added, which is nonfat and is made with Nutrasweet; and (4) Frozen Tofu, which is cholesterol free and lactose free for persons who are lactose intolerant. The company introduced an Ultra Slim-Fast shake made with Ultra Slim-Fast powder and TCBY frozen yogurt. It provides an appealing variation for people who are on the popular Ultra Slim-Fast diet plan. TCBY promotes its products as "good for you."

Another strength is the franchisee support program. The company selects its franchisees carefully. The training program begins with ten days at "Yogurt U" in Little Rock, where franchisees learn about store operations. A "mini" TCBY unit is used in the program. The company provides operating manuals and marketing materials to its franchisees. In 1990, the initial capital investment for a franchise ranged from $98,000 to $241,200 for an existing structure.

The costs follow:

Leasing of Existing Space	*Range*
Initial Franchise Fee	$10,000–$20,000
Leasehold Improvements/ Construction	$20,000–$90,000
Equipment, Furniture, Signs	$42,000–$48,000
Inventory & Supplies	$8,500–$12,500
Prepaid Expenses & Deposits	$5,000–$7,500
Grand Opening & Promotional Expense	$2,500–$7,200
Working Capital	$10,000–$20,000
Total Est. Initial Investment	$98,000–$241,000

(Source: TCBY: Franchise Disclosure Statement, 1990.)

In 1990, the initial investment for a franchise if a TCBY freestanding building was constructed ranged from $153,000 to $375,000, with costs as follows:

TCBY Freestanding Building	*Range*
Initial Franchise Fee	$10,000–$20,000
Leasehold Improvements/ Construction	$65,000–$185,000
Equipment, Furniture, Signs	$52,000–$121,000
Inventory & Supplies	$8,500–$12,500
Prepaid Expenses & Deposits	$5,000–$10,000
Grand Opening & Promotional Expense	$2,500–$7,200
Working Capital	$10,000–$20,000
Total Est. Initial Investment	$153,000–$375,700

(Source: TCBY: Franchise Disclosure Statement, 1990.)

A new franchisee for TCBY has easy access to many items needed for start-up and for day-to-day business through the wholly owned subsidiaries of TCBY Enterprises, Inc. One of these subsidiaries is Americana Foods, Inc., the manufacturing company that makes the food products for TCBY. Using its own food manufacturing company provides TCBY with products that are consistently high quality nationwide, and provides a dependable supply of necessary food items. Franchisees may choose from more than 30 yogurt flavors and a number of frozen yogurt specialty items. The equipment package needed for start-up may be purchased through Riverport Equipment Company, another subsidiary of TCBY Enterprises. Franchisees are not required to purchase their equipment from Riverport, but they may. A limited financing program is made available to franchisees to cover part of their equipment and leasehold cost. This financing is available through a TCBY subsidiary, American Acceptance Corporation. The first two stores purchased by a franchisee are not eligible for financing because of TCBY's strong emphasis on operational experience and performance.

A team of 65 field managers works as liaison between franchisees and officers of the corporation. Field managers make regular visits to the stores in their territories. Part of the field managers' job is to help franchisees with marketing ideas and cost control analysis. In addition, regular franchisee meetings are held to provide opportunities for discussion of franchisee concerns with the company's management. In March 1990, an organization was formed by angry franchisees in an effort to voice their concerns.

Weaknesses

One weakness faced by TCBY is that many consumers think its products are too expensive. People who were relatively free with their money in the 1980s are now more conservative and price conscious. They still want quality products but look for products they can purchase at lower prices. Consumers are interested in getting more value for their money.

Another weakness with which Hickingbotham must deal is the decline in same-store sales. "Same-store sales" is defined as the comparison of individual store sales for a particular year with its sales during the same period of the previous year. Same-store sales decreased 13 percent from fiscal year 1989 to fiscal year 1990. Many franchisees who have experienced declines in sales attribute a large portion of the declines to competition from new stores in the same vicinity. However, the company carefully selects locations for new stores in order to prevent competition with existing stores. Management believes the primary reason for the decline in same-store sales is the competition TCBY now faces from other companies entering the market. As of 1990, the firm had 17,000 competitive units outside of the TCBY system.

Opportunities

TCBY has an opportunity to increase its market share through advertising, both to attract consumers from the competition and to bring in new customers. According to a recent marketing study done by M/A/R/C of Dallas, Texas, 30 percent of the United States' population has not tried frozen yogurt. This means there is a huge potential for TCBY to increase its market share.

Another opportunity for TCBY is expansion into nontraditional sales outlets. In 1989, TCBY began a joint venture with Marriott Corporation to put stores and carts in major airports and toll road plazas. By the end of fiscal year 1990, this venture comprised 34 stores and 93 carts. A new subsidiary, TCBY National Sales Company, coordinates the new outlets. Two new programs implemented by the company in 1991 are the following: (1) Market Area Partnership (MAP), which was set up to market TCBY products through retail channels such as large grocery store chains; and (2) the placement of TCBY units in Sears and other retail chains and in large sports arenas.

Expanding its product line is a third opportunity for TCBY. In 1989 and 1990, the company introduced several new product items, including a new line of gourmet cakes and pies, the Yog-a-bar, the Ultra Slim-Fast shake, the Shiver, nonfat no-cholesterol yogurt, and several others. TCBY's research and development department tests new yogurt flavors and makes them available to franchisees. To respond to changes in the market, TCBY introduced two new value items, the Waffle Cone and the Sundette (a small sundae), that sell for $.99. The lower-priced items boosted sales at many TCBY locations, and franchisees hope that revenues will continue to rise from sales of these items.

Threats

A major threat facing TCBY is competition. In 1991, TCBY had 34 percent of the market for frozen yogurt, while its closest competitor had only a 9.7 percent share. However, more companies, many of them nationally recognized, are getting into the market. McDonald's Corporation replaced its soft serve ice cream with frozen yogurt. International Dairy Queen also entered the market. Baskin-Robbins added frozen yogurt to its line of ice cream products, and Haagen-Dazs added a new frozen yogurt to its product line in supermarkets. Convenience stores and grocery store chains, such as the Kroger Company, have frozen yogurt machines in their facilities.

Some analysts say that TCBY's success created its competition, because other companies, observing the fast-growing market for frozen yogurt, wanted a portion of the market for themselves. Others say that the competition always existed but became more visible because well-known companies entered the market. A spokesperson for TCBY said that competition will prove beneficial to the company in the long run because competitors will introduce more customers to frozen yogurt; and TCBY, as the market leader, will end up gaining many of these new customers. However, in the short run, TCBY feels the effects of increased competition. For example, in February 1991, the second largest TCBY franchisee in Illinois filed for Chapter 11 (bankruptcy reorganization). The reasons cited in the petition were "competition and declining sales." Other franchisees went bankrupt, and competitors bought some stores. In March 1991, Royalty Yogurt of Fort Lauderdale, Florida, purchased 34 TCBY locations in Florida with plans to convert them into Royalty shops.

A second threat facing TCBY is that of disenchanted franchisees. Many franchisees began to complain after experiencing a significant decline in sales. They blamed the decline on both increased competition and cannibalization from new TCBY stores. Part of the complaint was that the company was not shouldering its share of the problem and that it was making profits at their expense. Management attributed the decline to increased competition, pointing to its location selection process designed to avoid cannibalization of sales.

Some franchisees accuse TCBY of charging its stores more than competing chains charge theirs for yogurt. A franchisee association, formed to head off dissident franchisees, is requesting that TCBY reduce the wholesale price it charges for yogurt by 15–20 percent. The company says that prices have not increased since 1983. Additionally, some franchisees complain that the national advertising campaign is ineffective. These franchisees are asking the company to waive advertising payments and royalties (though the majority of franchisees request that additional funds be spent on advertising) and to restructure their loans. TCBY charges a continuing service fee and a royalty of 4 percent of gross sales, exclusive of sales tax. Franchisees must contribute 3 percent of gross sales, excluding sales tax, to TCBY's national advertising fund. The advertising fund has three purposes: (1) to produce all of the company's advertising materials; (2) to promote brand awareness through media advertising; and (3) to provide for national research to evaluate the impact of the company's marketing expenditures. TCBY wants each of its stores to join a local market co-op advertising association. Once a co-op association is formed, franchisees are required to participate in it.

Another threat is the downturn in the economy. As a result of both heightened competition and reduced consumer spending, TCBY's profits fell 32 percent from 1989 to 1990 and were down 22 percent in the first quarter of 1991 from the same period in 1990. Stockholders were unhappy because the adverse circumstances caused a sharp drop in TCBY stock prices from a high of almost $25.00 in the first quarter to below $5.00 per share in the last quarter of 1990. Some shareholders sued, alleging deception and misrepresentation.

Herren Hickingbotham and TCBY's marketing team were facing some uncertainties after a difficult year in 1990 and the large reduction in profits for the first quarter of 1991. Several adverse events in 1990, both internal and external, caused the decline in company performance. The company needs to examine several issues to decide what actions it should take to increase performance during the next few years.

Case 4.2

Tom, Dick, and Harry Consider a Pretzel Franchise

Wilke D. English
University of Mary Hardin—Baylor

Dick and Harry were just finishing lunch in the university cafeteria when Tom arrived on the scene, out-of-breath and quite animated.

"Hey, dudes!" Tom called excitedly. "I have been looking all over for you guys. Listen, I found this really cool way to make 'big money' for us!"

"Yeah, right," said Dick, sarcastically. "Really 'big money,' just like on the *Wheel of Fortune.* Do we get a date with Vanna, too?" (Tom was always coming up with bizarre ways to make money . . . last time he was going to buy all of the Texas Lotto tickets for a guaranteed win.

"No, I am serious," Tom insisted. "I was at the County

Fair this last weekend with Amy and there was this really cool pretzel stand. The guy working the stand was selling pretzels from a little cart as fast as he could make them. I asked him where he got that cart and he said that he was a 'Philly's Famous' franchisee. I tried to talk with him some more, but he was too busy to talk, so he gave me these brochures."

Tom handed the two brochures to Dick and Harry who spread them out on the table. (The brochures are reproduced as Exhibits 4.2.1–4.2.4).

Wholesale Distributor Brochure

The brochures were somewhat confusing in that they appeared to be offering substantially different approaches to the market. One brochure (Exhibits 4.2.1, 4.2.2) seemed to be offering a business opportunity to be a wholesale distributor for the pretzels and sell them to retailers such as grocery stores and retail food vendors. The other brochure (Exhibits 4.2.3, 4.2.4) was offering a push cart from which the pretzels could be prepared and sold.

"This isn't a franchise," said Dick looking at the first brochure.

"It's not?" asked Tom. "The guy working the stand said he was the franchisee."

"Well I don't know what he said, all I know is that it doesn't look like a franchisee to me," said Dick. "They want you to be a wholesale distributor and get their pretzels placed in grocery stores. I know from lectures in my marketing classes that the battle for shelf space in supermarkets is ferocious and to get something placed into the freezer department is next to impossible."

"Next to impossible unless you want to pay megabuck slotting allowances," Harry chimed in.

"What's a 'slotting allowance'?" asked Tom.

"Slotting allowances are fees that manufacturers and distributors have to pay to the grocery store in order to buy shelf space," explained Harry. "The grocery store executives have realized that their shelves represent a valuable commodity which is in short supply. There are too many products vying for too little shelf space. So the grocers simply 'auction' their shelves to the highest bidder."

"Yeah, and the freezers are the toughest spot to place a product," added Dick. "Freezers are bulky and expensive so adding freezer space is difficult. In addition, that is where many, if not most, of the new food products have been targeted . . . frozen microwaveable pizzas, microwaveable burritos, Lean Cuisine, Healthy Choice, frozen m**a**cro-waveable pitas . . ."

"I presume you meant m**i**crowaveable, not m**a**crowaveable . . .?" chided Harry.

"Yeah, m**i**crowaveable . . . I guess I was still thinking about the macroeconomics test I bombed this morning," said Dick sheepishly. "But m**i**crowaveable . . . m**a**crowaveable . . . m**u**crowaveable . . . it really doesn't matter. We don't have any money to pay slotting allowances. And without paying the slotting allowances I don't see any way that we are going to get our one little product into the grocers' freezer cases."

"That's another good point," added Harry. "Most wholesalers carry a variety of products, they are well-known and trusted by the retailer. The retailers don't know us or our brand of pretzels from the man in the moon."

"Right," agreed Dick. "Not only is there the recognition factor, but by carrying multiple lines, distributors can sometimes reduce the shelf space devoted to their other products to give a new item a try. But pretzels would be our only item . . . I don't see how we could ever be successful as a one-item grocery wholesaler."

Cart Vendor Brochure

"But what about the cart?" countered Tom. "We could get a cart like the guy I talked to . . . he seemed to be making a lot of money. He was obviously a retailer, not a wholesale distributor. That cart was really cool."

"Oh, joy!" said Dick sarcastically. "Won't Mom and Dad be proud? Here I graduate from college next semester, and what am I doing? . . . vending pretzels from some stupid push-cart!"

"It's *not* stupid," said Tom in a huff. "It was a nice-looking cart and he was selling lots of pretzels. And if you are selling lots, you are making lots. I don't think that there is anything stupid about making lots of money!"

A Pallet of Pretzels

"OK, it's not a stupid cart, although I would feel awfully stupid pushing it around. And look at this, they send you a *pallet* of pretzels," said Dick.

"Yeah, I saw that on the other brochure as well," said Harry. " 'A pallet of pretzels,' like we move them with a forklift? Do we bake them? Do we freeze them?"

"I get the impression from the distributor brochure that they ship them to you frozen," offered Dick. "Boy is your Mom going to be mad when she finds that you have crammed a *pallet-load* of pretzels in her freezer! Look, here's a 1-800 number let's give them a call."

Later: From the call they learned that the pretzels are baked in Dallas and shipped frozen. If you do not have freezer

Comparison of Pretzel Franchises

	Cart	Full Kitchen		
	Philly's Famous	*Auntie Anne's*	*Pretzel Time*	*Pretzel Twister*
History				
Established in	1991	1988	1991	1992
1st Franchised in	1993	1989	1992	1993
Franchised Units (8/31/93)	0	130	60	1
Company Units (8/31/93)	0	6	12	1
Total Units (8/31/93)	0	136	72	2
Projected New for 1994	50	150	120	20
Distribution	US = 0	US = 136	US = 72	US = 2
North America	0	16 states	23 states	
Concentration	NA	65PA, 13NJ	13NY, 7TX	
Registered	FL, OR	16 states	23 states	
Store Type	RM, cart	RM, 500SF	RM, 500SF	RM, 600SF
Financial				
Earnings Claim	No	Yes	No	No
Cash Investment	$14,900	$50–$70K	$80–$120K	$86–$115K
Total Investment	$23,000	$130–$194K*	$80–$120K	$86–$115K
Fees				
Franchise	$14,900	$21,000	$10,000	$10,000
Royalty	0%	5%	7%	4%
Advertising	3%	1%	1%	1%
Contract Years	10/10	5/5	20/5	10/5
Area Dev. Agreement	No	No	Yes/5	No
Sub-Franchise Contract	No	No	No	No
Expand in Territory		Yes	Yes	Yes
Passive Ownership	Discouraged	Discouraged	Allowed	Discouraged
Avg # Employees	2FT	3FT, 10PT	3FT, 9PT	2FT, 4PT
Franchisor Training/Support				
Financial Assistance	NA	No	No	
Site Selection Assistance	NA	Yes	Yes	Yes
Lease Negotiation	NA	Yes	Yes	Yes
Co-op Advertising	NA	Yes	Yes	Yes
Training (days)	2HQ	9HQ, 7OS	5HQ, 5OS	5HQ, 5OS
On-Going Support (YES = provided, yes = pay extra)				
a. Central Data Processing				
b. Central Purchasing		YES	YES	
c. Field Oper. Eval	yes	YES	YES	YES
d. Field Training	yes	YES	YES	
e. Initial Store Opening		YES	YES	YES
f. Inventory Control			YES	YES
g. Newsletter	YES	YES	YES	
h. Regional Meetings		YES	YES	
i. Telephone Hotline	YES		YES	
# Employees Franchisor	4	46	9	3

Sources: *The Source Book of Franchise Opportunities: 1994 Edition,* Bond and Bond, *corp. brochure

space, the Philly's Famous company will try to help you find space at public storage freezer facilities. You would pay a storage fee to the public storage operator.

"See, no problem," said Tom happily. "As we sell them, we get them from the freezer facility . . . Mom's freezer remains undefiled."

"Well, that's one relief," admitted Dick.

"Then, let's do it!" said Tom enthusiastically. "The fee is $15,000, so that would be only $5,000 apiece. Surely we can come up with $5,000 each. It is really not that much."

"Not so fast," cautioned Harry. "Aside from the fact that $5,000 just happens to be $4,900 more dollars than I seem to have in my bank account at the moment, I think that we should check out some other franchises . . . you know, to compare."

"That's right," agreed Dick. "Even if we agree with their brochure which touts pretzels as the greatest thing since canned beer, we need to check out several franchises. Who knows, maybe these guys are really overpriced and some other company will sell you a cart and supplies for $10,000."

"Or maybe loan you the cart and give you the supplies on consignment so our costs would be almost zero!" volunteered Harry. "But regardless, we need to check out some other companies. It is never smart to just go with the first one you come to."

"Fair enough," said Tom. "Listen, the guy with the cart said that there was going to be a franchise trade show next weekend . . . but I don't know what we would trade them . . ."

"No, a trade show is not a place where you barter and trade," explained Dick. "It is a convention where suppliers in one particular industry, that is, in one particular 'trade,' all come together and show what they have to offer. They usually have a big exhibition hall and dozens of suppliers manning the various booths and showing their wares."

At the Trade Show

The business opportunities trade show was held at the convention center in a neighboring city. The exhibition hall was huge, almost as big as a football field and it was filled with literally dozens of promoters hawking their wares. There seemed to be franchises for virtually everything, from paper shredding to cemetery tending, from bagels to pretzels.

Tom was dumfounded at the size of the exhibition hall and the incredible variety of business opportunities that were being presented, although he was surprised that neither McDonald's nor Burger King were there. Tom, being the impetuous enthusiast that he is, wanted to talk with every exhibitor. In fact, Tom wanted to sign up for every business opportunity

Exhibit 4.2.1

"When Ordinary Just Won't Do"

ALL NATURAL, FAT FREE,
NO CHOLESTEROL
WITH NO PRESERVATIVES
PHILADELPHIA
SOFT PRETZELS
IN GOURMET FLAVORS

Dear Entrepreneur:

Every now and then a product comes to the marketplace and creates immediate recognition. The vitality and enthusiasm for *PHILLY'S FAMOUS™ SOFT PRETZELS* are based on quality and uniqueness. Our recipes exceed all others and once you sample our *PHILLY'S FAMOUS SOFT PRETZEL* in any of our distinctive flavors or our Original Philly Twist Flavor ... you, too, will be convinced.

Want to increase your profit line? At this point in time, the market is wide open for a gourmet flavored soft pretzel to be distributed as a frozen product. Our product lines, including pretzel nuggets and retail pre-packaged for take-home sales, provide additional sales impact and will position you, the distributor, with a very marketable sales line. The product has proven itself over time with other brands of lesser quality. Now is the ideal time for a healthy, tasty market contender to anticipate and respond to the consumers' tastes. As part of a huge national snack food industry, the market has relatively few soft pretzel companies competing for snack food consumer dollars, while the demand for the product remains great.

JUST HEAT 'EM AND EAT 'EM! Made of the finest, natural ingredients, *PHILLY'S FAMOUS™ SOFT PRETZELS* are highly salable, especially given the consumer demand for flavorful, nutritious and healthy snack foods. We can supply product sample packages and arrange to provide you with additional program information.

Most sincerely,

Hank Lotman, President and Founder
PHILLY'S FAMOUS SOFT PRETZELS

Exhibit 4.2.2

GOURMET SOFT PRETZELS • ONION RYE • CAJUN

Philly's Famous™ is ready to set you up in business if you are ready to earn the profits!

SOFT PRETZEL CART INVESTMENT

$15,000

(small additional rental charge for secured locations)

To Include

★ 1 Cart (includes propane gas tank and hooded grill or electric oven) ★ 1 Menu Display ★ 1 Training Manual ★ 2 Spray Bottles ★ 2 Salt / Cinnamon Sugar Shakers ★ 1 Philly's Famous Parka Jacket ★ 2 Philly's Famous Sweatshirts ★ 2 Philly's Famous Golf Shirts ★ 2 Philly's Famous Long Sleeve Oxford Shirts ★ 1 Philly's Famous hat ★ 1 Philly's Famous Apron ★ 2700 Pretzels (1 Pallet) Retail Value of Over $3,300.!

Product Overview

Suggested Average Cost	Per Pretzel	Per Case
Retail Price	1.25	62.50
Franchisee Avg. Cost	.30	15.00

Distributor's wholesale product cost of 30¢ per soft pretzel is marked up to a consumer retail price of $1.25. This computes to a mark up of 316% or 95¢ gross profit per soft pretzel or $47.50 per case gross profit. This amazing profit potential is why cart franchisees will eagerly want to be part of the Philly's Famous™ program.

Note: Profit figures per pretzel have been prepared to provide a representation of potential profits, however, no warranty is expressed or implied herein by Philly's Famous™ or its representatives.

- DISCOUNT STORES
- CLUB STORES
- SUPERMARKETS
- FESTIVALS
- SPORTING EVENTS
- FUND RAISERS
- CORPORATE PICNICS
- FAIRS
- CHARITIES
- STREET CORNERS
- CARNIVALS

Opportunity Highlights

★ *Instant Cash Returns*
★ *No Cold calls*
★ *Be Your Own Boss*
★ *Have Lots Of Fun*
★ *Unlimited Locations*
★ *Perfect For Full Or Part Time Income*

Training Manual

Includes:

- product/company background
- product preparation
- handling large crowds
- storage of product
- how to create contacts
- how to get permits
- how to book events
- target locations
- transporting the cart
- and much, much more...

Specifications

★ 32" X 72" X 37"
★ Heavy Duty Fiberglass Sandwich Construction
★ Lightweight (approximately 150 lbs.)
★ 1 Fibrecore Recessed Molded Sink
★ Fresh Water Storage Tank With Hand Pump
★ Permanent Lettered Easy Maintenance Gel Coat Finished Panels
★ Heavy Duty Casters (2 swivel, 2 stationary)
★ Huge Lettered Umbrella
★ Push Rail
★ Easy To Transport
★ Easy Interior Storage Of Product
★ Refrigeration/Freezer Storage Available at Additional Charge

ORIGINAL PHILLY TWIST • CINNAMON RAISIN

with every company. After talking to only three exhibitors in nearly two hours, Dick and Harry pulled Tom aside.

"Look," they said. "We can't spend a lifetime talking to every single exhibitor that is at this show. We said we were interested in pretzels so let's limit our search to pretzel companies only."

"Fair enough," agreed Tom.

Report on the Pretzel Franchises

There were three other pretzel franchises at the convention in addition to the Philly's Famous cart franchise mentioned earlier. The other three franchises were quite different from the cart franchise (see Exhibits 4.2.5–4.2.8 for corporate brochures). In each of the other three the pretzels would have to be made from scratch. This would include mixing the ingredients to make the dough, rolling the dough, hand-twisting them into the distinctive pretzel shape, and baking. Because an entire kitchen with mixing equipment and ovens would have to be provided, these other franchises were considerably more expensive, ranging from a little under \$100,000 to nearly \$200,000. After seeing some of these prices, that \$15,000 cart did not look so expensive after all.

But the biggest problem to Tom was that every franchise claimed to have *the best* product offering. Consider these quotes from the various brochures:

> "Better than the best you've ever tasted!" Auntie Anne's
> "Our secret ingredients and exclusive recipe creates a taste and flavor unrivaled by others!" The Pretzel Twister
> "The finest pretzel that anyone has ever sampled, challenging all market competitors!" Philly's Famous Soft Pretzel Company
> "These pretzels are second to none!" Pretzel Time

By the time the lads left the frenetic noise of the exhibition hall their heads were absolutely swimming. What they needed was a common format to compare the various offerings. Harry found that common format in *The Source Book of Franchise Opportunities,* an encyclopedic collection of data on nearly 2500 franchising opportunities. Using the data contained in *The Source Book,* Harry was able to develop the table on p. 471.

Now What?

Both Tom and Dick agreed that Harry had worked very hard to put together the comparison chart, but they were much less certain as to what they could do with it.

Exhibit 4.2.3

Store Location Guide

Hand-Rolled Soft Pretzels

"Better than the best you've ever tasted"®

WINTER 1993 / SPRING 1994

Auntie Anne's, Inc., 1994

EXHIBIT 4.2.4

Hand-Rolled
Soft Pretzels

Initial Investment Range

	LOW		HIGH
FRANCHISE FEE	$28,000	-	$28,000
LEASE & UTILITY[1] SECURITY DEPOSITS	4,000	-	7,000
LEASEHOLD IMPROVEMENTS,[2] FURNITURE & FIXTURES	75,000	-	110,000
EQUIPMENT	17,000	-	20,000
INITIAL INVENTORY	3,300	-	4,000
INSURANCE	400	-	2,500
TRAINING	500	-	2,000
GRAND OPENING ADVERTISING	500	-	2,500
SIGNAGE	4,000	-	8,000
OFFICE EQUIPMENT & SUPPLIES	500	-	1,000
WORKING CAPITAL	2,000	-	6,000
PROFESSIONAL FEES	2,000	-	3,000
TOTAL INITIAL INVESTMENT	$137,200	-	$194,000

[1] Assumes security deposit and first month rent.

[2] Includes architect fees.

All costs are estimated as of June 1, 1994, and will vary depending upon location, size of store, architectural requirements and store configuration.

P.O. Box 529, Gap, Pennsylvania 17527
(717) 442-4766

EXHIBIT 4.2.5

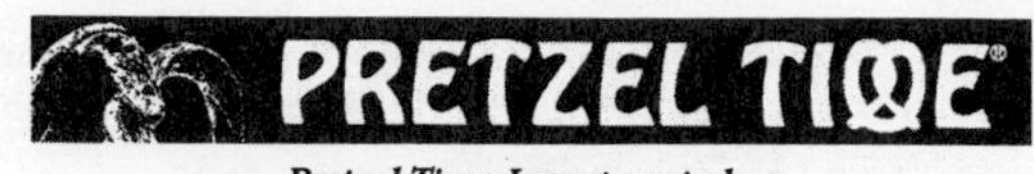

Pretzel Time Incorporated

Contact: Ellen Saikia
Public Relations Specialist
Work: (717) 540-8163
Home: (717) 764-0158

PRETZEL TIME, INC.
COMPANY HISTORY

Pretzel Time, Inc. is a franchisor and operator of hand-rolled soft pretzel outlets located primarily in regional and super-regional malls throughout the United States. The company specializes in the sale of hot, fresh pretzels; specialty toppings; and drinks. At Pretzel Time, pretzel making becomes an art, as demonstrated by the professional pretzel rollers and twisters who entertain customers at the storefronts. The company offers pretzels in a variety of flavors, salted or unsalted, and without butter on request. The product is low-fat (only four grams of fat in one regular pretzel), high in carbohydrates, and above all, simply delicious.

Pretzel Time was founded by Martin Lisiewski and began operation in April 1991 from its home office in Harrisburg, Pennsylvania. The first company-owned store opened in October 1991 at the Trumbull Shopping Park, a super-regional mall in Trumbull, Connecticut. Sales at the Trumbull location increased 117 percent in the third month of operation, and the company recouped its initial investment by the fourth month.

The first franchise location began operation in Great Falls, Montana, in February 1992. Franchise growth has been rapid, with 8 franchises open at the end of 1992, 118 by end 1993, and approximately 185 open in the United States, Canada, and Mexico as of August 1994. Pretzel Time has experienced a phenomenal growth rate of nearly 5000 percent over the past 2 1/2 years.

Pretzel Time is a branded partner with Host-Marriott Corporation, and with the development of a cart and countertop merchandising system, has recently expanded into airports, travel plazas, amusement parks, and university campuses across the nation. The company has developing rights in all 50 states, Canada, Mexico, and Puerto Rico, and is the first hand-rolled soft pretzel franchisor to move into foreign markets. Pretzel Time conservatively estimates at least 210 locations across the United States, Canada, and Mexico by end 1994.

The 15th Annual Franchise 500 January edition of *Entrepreneur Magazine* recognized Pretzel Time as 9th among the top 30 new franchises and 157th among the 500 best franchise opportunities, a testament to the Pretzel Time's concept and a forecast of the company's continued success.

# # #

4800 Linglestown Road, Suite 202 ▪ Harrisburg, PA 17112
Phone: 717-671-5610 ▪ Fax: 717-671-5628

Exhibit 4.2.6

FLYING FRUIT FANTASY FRUITSHAKES™

2706 South Horseshoe Drive Suite 112 , Naples, Florida 33942 813.643.2075 813.643.5639 (Fax)

Dear Prospective Franchisee:

Thanks for your interest in becoming a Pretzel Time franchisee. We appreciate your inquiry and hope you'll take a few moments to get to know our company.

Pretzel Time, Inc. presents one of the most reasonable franchise opportunities today. As you begin to research our rapidly expanding company, we think you'll become increasingly excited about the prospect of becoming part of our team. The professionals at Pretzel Time have over 50 combined years of restaurant experience, and have used their expertise to put together a franchising program that offers affordability as well as tremendous growth potential to entrepreneurs.

Pretzel Time's concept provides an opportunity for business people to expand at their own pace, without much concern about the competitors. Consider these categories: seafood, hamburgers, pizza, subs, tacos, doughnuts, and chicken. Doubtlessly, dozens of brand names come to mind when you think about them. Pretzel Time's homemade, hand-rolled fresh pretzels are a hot new concept in a market saturated with hundreds of mediocre options in the same old categories. Consumers love the idea of an alternative to the tired fast foods that have always been available to them.

Pretzel Time franchisees serve a superior product in a clean, attractive environment to people who can't get enough of what we have to offer Our franchise fee is extremely low compared to other programs in the market. Our decor package, adapts easily to a number of existing structures. The product line is easy to manage and the investment in equipment and smallwares is kept to a minimum. The majority of your cash investment won't be used for non-recoverable fixed assets, so you can acquire multiple units quickly, if you wish. Pretzel Time is now offering a reduced franchise fee of only $1,000 for each new location to franchisees in full compliance with Pretzel Time standards.

Our leasing program makes it easier than you might imagine to get started. At Pretzel Time, we hold the lease on most locations, and simply sublet to you. Developers like the idea of dealing directly with a major corporation with an established success rate, and we're happy to support you in this way.

We suggest you carefully review the materials in this portfolio, so that you can make a well-informed decision whether to become a Pretzel Time franchisee. We're confident that after you learn more about us, you'll want to join our organization.

Exhibit 4.2.7

FLYING FRUIT FANTASY FRUITSHAKES™

2706 South Horseshoe Drive Suite 112, Naples, Florida 33942 813.643.2075 813.643.5639 (Fax)

July 11, 1994

Dr. W.D. English
Marketing Department
UMHB
Belton, TX 76513

Dear Dr. English:

Hand twisted soft pretzel stores are opening in malls across the country to rave reviews. Once you have tasted our soft gourmet pretzels in one of their many varieties, you'll know why. Accompanied by our all new Flying Fruit Fantasy Fruitshakes, Pretzel Twister is on the leading edge. **TWO GREAT CONCEPTS, ONE GREAT FRANCHISE!**

Thank you for your recent inquiry. The Pretzel Twister has taken a winning idea and improved upon it. Our secret recipe and unique taste are unsurpassed. We have simplified the baking process with our pioneering use of the conveyor oven, much like the most successful pizza franchisors have. Our streamlined operation means more consistent quality and lower operating costs. We provide our store owners with the best management tools including training on computerized payroll and bookkeeping. The new store design, by the award winning International Design Group is contemporary, bright, and appealing.

If you'd like to know more, please complete the enclosed Evaluation Form. Doing so will not obligate either of us in any way. Once we receive your form, we will send you a **FREE VIDEO** which explains The Pretzel Twister franchise system.

I encourage you to carefully study the differences between our opportunity with others. If you call, I will be more than happy to discuss the main benefits to operating under our system. To anyone interested in owning their own hand twisted soft pretzel bakery I firmly believe that The Pretzel Twister has the most to offer. Of course if you have any questions, please feel free to call me at **813-643-2075**. Again I thank you for your interest, and look forward to receiving the Evaluation Form soon.

Sincerely,

Keith Johnson
President

EXHIBIT 4.2.8

FREQUENTLY ASKED QUESTIONS ABOUT OUR FRANCHISE PROGRAM

How do The Pretzel Twister™ pretzels compare to others in taste?

- Our customers say they are addictive and often ask, "What did you put in these to make them so good?" Our secret ingredients and exclusive recipe creates a taste and flavor unrivaled by others!

What is the average size of The Pretzel Twister™ bakery and where is the best location?

- Our stores can range in size from 450 to 900 square feet and are best suited for enclosed shopping malls or very busy areas with heavy foot traffic.

What is the total investment required to open a store?

- This will depend on the condition of the space where the store will be built. It will depend on whether the space was previously used as a food service or was previously unoccupied and is completely void of utilities. See the chart below.

	Low	High
Franchise Fee	$12,500	$12,500
Equipment, Fixtures, & Leasehold Improvements, Signage, etc...	$72,000	$105,000
Initial Supplies & Inventory	$700	$1,500
Security Deposits and Working Capital	$6,300	$21,500
Total	$91,500	$140,500

What other fees are required?

- There is a continuing service and royalty fee of 4% of gross sales. Currently 1% must be allocated for local advertising although the total advertising contribution may be increased to 2%. There are no additional royalties or fees associated with the Flying Fruit Fantasy Fruitshakes® products.

What is the term of my franchise agreement?

- The term of the agreement is for 10 years with two additional renewals at your option.

What do I receive for my franchise and service fees?

PRE-OPENING ASSISTANCE:

- Site selection and store design assistance.
- Complete turnkey packages are available
- Business start up manual—This invaluable manual covers everything you need to know about forming a business in your state.
- Complete operations manual and training program, including training in Naples, FL , as well as on-site training in payroll, accounting, daily operations, equipment, maintenance and more.
- Simplified and proven concepts and use of our exclusive recipes and trademarks.

CONTINUING SUPPORT:

- Access to ongoing research and development in the areas of new products, equipment, packaging. We will work with food service distributors to negotiate the best possible prices. Savings are passed directly to the franchise owners.
- Ongoing advertising, promotion and publicity material.
- Periodic visits to your area by our management to consult with you on aspects of your business.
- Complete dedication of our staff to assist franchisees in realizing their goals.
- Continuous updates of the operations manual.

"Nice chart, Harry," said Tom, "But what do we do with it? About all I can see is that if we can barely afford the 'stupid' push-cart, we sure can't afford $150,000 for an RM location. Which reminds me, what does RM stand for anyway?"

"RM stands for Regional Mall," answered Harry.

"Oh, that's cool, I like malls," said Tom. "But if we have to come up with $150,000 I don't think that is going to be a very viable option. I don't have that kind of money, do you?"

"No, but my Grandad does," said Harry. "Grandad said that he had been thinking about setting me up with a franchise upon my graduation . . . in fact it was Grandad who had the franchise *Source Book.* He had already underlined a dozen or more offerings in the $100,000 to $350,000 range. He had not highlighted any pretzel franchises, but the cost seems to be within his range."

"Well, in that case, let me have another look at that chart," said Tom. "You know, all of the offerings are kinda similar, but kinda different."

"I guess you pretty well covered both ends with that statement," retorted Harry.

"But look," continued Tom. "They all want a franchise fee, but the fees are not all the same. I mean, what's a franchise fee, anyway? Is it like a federal license?"

"A franchise fee is a one-time fee that you have to pay to the franchisor for the privilege of doing business in the name of the franchise," explained Harry. "It's like a cover charge at a dance hall . . . you know, where you pay a $3.00 cover charge for the 'privilege' of paying $2.50 for a beer. The franchise fee is the admission fee so that they can then charge you for more stuff . . . like the royalties you have to pay and overcharging for the supplies that you have to buy from them."

"You don't sound too pleased with the idea of paying a franchise fee," questioned Tom.

"No, I'm not," said Harry. "Of course buying into a franchise usually gets you more name recognition than you would have if you were an independent. But Philly's Famous with no listed units, and Pretzel Twister with 2 listed units . . . I can't see much name recognition there. Seems to me I could be $10,000 further down the road if I opened up something on my own. And I'm not sure that I want some franchisor telling me everything to do. But Grandad says that what really counts is the proven business package and support that the franchise system provides. I just don't know . . ."

Case 4.3

MEMC: The Silicon Wafer Industry

In 1995, MEMC was the second largest producer of silicon wafers in the world with control of about 20% of the global market. MEMC was incorporated in 1989 when Monsanto Company's spun off Dynamit Nobel Silicon Holding's, Inc. to German-owned VEBA AG. The story of MEMC is the story of the silicon wafer industry in the U.S. In order to understand the development of the silicon wafer market, it is necessary to look at how MEMC has created a marketing channel for silicon wafers.

Monsanto created MEMC St. Peters in 1959 when they built a plant in St. Peters, Missouri. The technology for developing silicon wafer chips was new and the market was just beginning to develop. As it is said "First come, first served"—the first to market with a product in demand is usually the one to reap the benefits. Also, since the cost of developing the silicon manufacturing technology is high, the cost of entry represents a barrier to possible competitors.

Being the first to reach the market was not the only factor in MEMC's success. The ability to produce a high quality product at a price that the market can bear was essential in MEMC's vault to the second largest silicon wafer producer in the world. The high cost of producing a quality wafer is a primary reason for chipmakers not to manufacture their own silicon wafers. Chipmakers such as IBM were quick to realize that silicon wafer manufacturing costs should be outsourced. This was one of the catalysts for the IBM/MEMC joint venture in the early 1980s. Through this joint venture, MEMC was responsible for innovations such as the first 200-millimeter wafer.

The 200mm wafer was a breakthrough in semi-conductor technology and this meant that MEMC was the only silicon

Source: Prepared by Lance Lin, James Swank and Ellen Vong, under the supervision of Dr. Lou E. Pelton, University of North Texas.

wafer manufacturer able to provide this technology. What a strategic advantage! The expectations of the IBM alliance were based on IBM's leadership role in the development of semi-conductor technology and MEMC's ability to produce high quality silicon wafers efficiently.

Another reason for companies involved in the development of semi-conductor technology to form alliances is the short product-to-market cycle time requirement. This means that companies such as IBM need to create new products faster. Since MEMC's core competency is silicon wafer manufacturing, IBM can utilize their expertise in making new semi-conductor products. Without the MEMC alliance, IBM would have to make wafers and the lack of wafer-manufacturing expertise would mean slower product-to-market cycle times.

Instead of using a traditional commodity-based approach to marketing, MEMC's management has built marketing channels based on customer needs. This is due to the fact that silicon wafers are an event-based product. They are manufactured to meet the needs of a chip manufacturer, and the design is dynamic in nature. This creates an environment that is conducive to alliances predicated on MEMC's ability to create wafers for a customer's needs.

The alliance approach is based on the concept of MEMC's core competency of producing silicon wafers and chip manufacturers that can create new products for the technology market. The IBM joint venture was a good one because MEMC knew that IBM had a history of being able to develop semi-conductor technology and this gave MEMC a competitive advantage because new semi-conductors define new applications of the silicon wafer. The expectations of the IBM alliance were based on IBM's leadership role in the development of semi-conductor technology and MEMC's ability to produce high quality silicon wafers efficiently.

Prior to going public, MEMC needed to form a strategic business plan that would solidify their position in the silicon wafer industry. The company raised about 370 million from its 45 percent offering when it went public. They had to decide how to structure the offering and how to utilize the funds. The selection of specific projects for these funds would be crucial for MEMC's continuing success as a supplier of silicon wafers.

The choice of projects must be based on the continuing development of marketing channels through profitable customer relationships with companies such as IBM. The expectations of future projects would be based on the success of ventures such as the IBM alliance. Looking for new ventures in 1995, Texas Instruments (TI) was considered for a possible alliance.

TI has been a leader in the development of semi-conductor products. It was May 1954 when Gordon Teal, a scientist at Texas Instruments Inc., set the electronics world on its ear with a record player and a transistor made of sand. Since then, TI has been successful in maintaining a leadership position in the chip manufacturing business.

TI made some smart decisions in the mid 80s while facing increasing competition from Japanese manufacturers. Texas Instruments' decision to stay in the DRAM memory chip business while its competitors were getting out fast proved to be a smart move. The dropout of the competition left TI with virtually no competition in the market for DRAM chips.

In addition to smart business moves, TI has developed new applications for chips such as improved graphic chips and improved megabit chips. TI has also been involved in several successful alliances such as the one with Sun Microsystems, Inc. They worked together to produce the UltraSparc 64-bit microprocessor in 1994.

The history of TI is not all rosy. In the mid 80s, TI suffered from a glut of chips on the market along with the rest of the top chipmakers. The glut forced lay-offs in TI's manufacturing force and led some industry analysts to believe that TI may not survive the downturn. Also, TI was involved in many different ventures such as oil exploration and defense contract fulfillment. These ventures diverted TI's strained resources away from chip making.

TI was able to survive by cutting labor and beginning a cost-cutting program led by CEO Jerry R. Junkins. The success of TI will be predicated on the ability to stay lean in the face of stiff Japanese competition from firms such as Hitachi and develop new technology that will satisfy customers.

Time Line

- 1959—Monsanto constructs MEMC St. Peters.
- 1960s—Development of granular polysilicon
- 1980s—Joint venture with IBM to develop 200 mm wafer
- 1989—VEBA AG buys MEMC St. Peters from Monsanto
- May 95—MEMC Electronic Materials goes public and announces joint venture with Texas Instruments

Industry Background

Silicon sand is perhaps one of the most abundant elements on earth. However, after a series of chemical treatments and physical manipulations, silicon sand can be made into a cylinder-shaped solid. By slicing this cylinder into thin disks, it becomes the very basic building element of semiconductors. These silicon disks, or wafers, vary in diameter from 100 millimeter (4 inches) to 300 millimeter (12 inches), and hundreds of semiconductor chips can be made from one single wafer. Although there has been an increasing demand for semiconductors ever since their invention in late 1950s, there are only a handful of firms manufacturing silicon wafers. Top ten firms supply 60% of the wafers needed by the semiconductor industry, and most of them are Japanese companies. These firms include, but are not limited to, Canon, Hitachi, Formosa Plastics, Applied Materials, and MEMC. Being the second largest wafer manufacturer in the world, MEMC is the leading worldwide supplier of silicon wafers outside of Japan. Because of the relative scarcity of suppliers, all silicon wafer manufacturers have to maintain close relationships with their customers, the semiconductor producers.

Four classes of semiconductors are currently being made and used in many different ways: optoelectronics (1% of the total output), discrete devices (13%), analog chips (12%), and integrated circuits, or IC (74%). Although semiconductors can be used in many different product categories, such as consumer electronics and automobiles, their major applications are in computers, which consume about 50% of all semiconductors being produced. Because of the booming growth of the computer market, all semiconductor manufacturers are facing throat-cutting price wars. For example, the price for dynamic random-access memory (DRAM) chips has dropped 75% in 1996. In order to keep the profitability, semiconductor manufacturers are changing their focuses to two directions: to be more efficient in current manufacturing processes to cut costs or to come up with new products with higher profit margins. Due to the fast-changing nature of the computer market, semiconductor manufacturers have to keep developing newer processing chips and more efficient ways to use silicon wafers. Traditionally, semiconductor manufacturers use smaller silicon wafers such as 100, 150, and 200 millimeter wafers. However, because of the fierce competition in the marketplace, prices for the semiconductors made out of these traditional wafers have dropped drastically. To keep the profitability and develop new products, semiconductor manufacturers' focuses have changed to improving process technology—that is, how to use those silicon wafers more efficiently. Because all semiconductor chips are made from a particular wafer and processed simultaneously at each stage in the manufacturing process, the larger sized wafers allow for a greater yield from the same manufacturing process and allow chip makers to spread their fixed costs over a larger volume of finished products. For example, a 200-millimeter (8 inches) wafer has a surface area of approximately 48.7 square inches, while a 300-millimeter (12 inches) wafer has a surface area of almost 109.6 square inches. That is a 125% increase in usable wafer surface area. At the same time, the actual size of the elements that make up the chip is shrinking from 0.35 microns to 0.25 microns. Not only will components take up less space, but they also will be faster and need less energy. Nevertheless, no matter whether the focus is on cost cutting or on innovation, semiconductor makers have to work closely with a handful of silicon wafer suppliers to secure the supply of this key element.

From wafer makers' perspective, although the demand for their products has been soaring through the roof, they are somehow cautious in adding capacity. Two reasons behind this hesitation: historic experiences and financial concerns. In 1984, demand for computer chips was also on a joyride like now, and all wafer producers invested daringly to catch the train. However, the sudden chip sales bust in 1985 immediately sent these wafer makers into a downward whirl and created a surplus of wafers. That resulted in a dramatic decrease in profit margin, which didn't recover until several years later. This painful lesson has made wafer makers slow down their pace this time as they face a new booming demand. Another issue that stands in the way is the financial and time requirements for building a new fabrication facility, or fab. A new wafer fab costs at least 1.25 billion dollars, which doubles every three years, six months of design, twelve months of construction, three months for equipment installation, and thousands of square feet for space. Unless a wafer maker can be sure that there is, or will be, an outlet for its wafers, building a new fab can be a risky investment. Furthermore, once a fab is built, it is not easy to convert its manufacturing process from making one kind of wafer, say, the 150 millimeter ones, to another kind. Hence, instead of investing all those capitals in building a relatively strict facility, almost all semiconductor manufacturers ally with some silicon wafer producers. For example, MEMC ally with AMD (USA), Mitsubishi (Japan), Samsung (South Korea), and Texas Instruments. By allying with these semiconductor manufacturers, MEMC can diversify its manufacturing locations, extend its worldwide market reach, lessen its dependence on any one region's economy of customer base, and most importantly, customize its wafers according to customer requirements.

After examining all issues from both the buyers' (semiconductor manufacturers) and the suppliers' (wafer suppliers) side, it is understandable why almost every firm in these two industries is allying with some partners. By using strategic alliances, both parties can share crucial market information in a timely way and ease the financial burden for investments. More importantly, both parties can be sure that there will be a steady supply/outlet for necessary resources in difficult times.

A New Partner in Sherman, Texas?

Texas Instruments had a problem. It was repositioning itself in the industry from a large company with many businesses to a semi-conductor/digital signal processing company. Due to this factor and growing market conditions, their need for silicon wafers drastically increased. How could they keep up with this increased need?

MEMC has traditionally sought to form joint ventures to remain ahead in the industry. At the time of TI's restructuring, MEMC had just gone public and had an influx of capital. They were a leading producer of silicon wafers in the industry. A joint venture between MEMC and TI began to sound pretty good.

When Texas Instruments and MEMC decided to form this joint venture and build a new state-of-art silicon wafer factory, they had to decide where they would locate this new site. While several areas in North Texas were considered initially, Sherman seemed to be ideal for several reasons. Incentives, logistics, the workforce, community, and its close proximity to the Sherman TI plant were all considered before the final decision was made.

Incentives are probably at the top of the list for companies choosing to relocate or those building new plants. MEMC Southwest had federal, state, and local incentives that made Sherman appealing. The Job Training Partnership Act of 1982, which is funded through the Department of Labor provides job training services to economically disadvantaged workers who face significant employment barriers. The state of Texas has $250 million available under this act for job training. Texas is also attractive because it is a right-to-work state, there is no state income tax, and union activity is very low. TI negotiated with city leaders to obtain financial incentives from Sherman. They received tax abatements, grants for job creation and investment. Because Sherman is an *Enterprise Zone,* new companies are entitled to additional grants and financial incentives through the Secretary of Housing and Urban Development.

MEMC Southwest wanted this new plant to provide products not only for TI, but for all of its North American customers. Sherman is located at the top of what industry analysts have dubbed the *silicon corridor.* This area is located just north of Dallas along U.S. 75 and stretches to the Oklahoma border. High technology companies have clustered along this area. Sherman purchased over 850 acres of undeveloped land adjacent to U.S. 75 and opened three industrial parks. U.S. 75 runs through Sherman and would give MEMC Southwest easy access to I-45, I-30, I-35, and I-20. Grayson County Airport, formerly Perrin Air Force Base, provides local accessibility to air transportation and DFW Airport, Dallas Love Field, and the Alliance Airport are all within 75 miles. Access to all these modes gives TI and MEMC the ability to move product in a cost-effective manner. Sherman provides the logistic capabilities MEMC Southwest needed.

Could a small town like Sherman support the labor requirements of this joint venture? Not only would MEMC Southwest create as many as 1,500 jobs in the area, but they would also require a highly skilled workforce. Sherman has a labor pool reaching over 300,000 potential employees within a 50-mile radius that spans seven counties, some of which are in southern Oklahoma. In addition, under the Job Training Partnership Act program, Texas has more than $250 million in federal funds available annually for training services to disadvantaged, unskilled, and dislocated Texans. Sherman has a stable workforce available at a cost that ranks lower than comparable U.S. markets.

MEMC Southwest had to look at the local community as well if they wanted to attract employees to Sherman. The Sherman Independent School District has enrollment of over 6000. There are approximately 16 students to each teacher. SAT and ACT test scores are above state and national averages. Both Austin College and Grayson County College are located in Sherman with Southeastern State, the University of North Texas, and Texas A&M at Commerce all within 70 miles. Property taxes are low at $2.67703 per $100 valuation. The churches and synagogues represent fifty-six denominations. It has 12 public parks, 2 golf courses, 3 libraries, and 3 theaters. Sherman has been able to maintain the quality of life a small town offers.

Finally, choosing a location close to TI made sense. The close proximity of TI and MEMC facilitated the ease of sharing pooled resources such as employees, technology, and information. It would minimize any distribution barriers. It would also make any collaboration on the new state-of-the-art facility flow more smoothly if the two companies were located near each other. In addition, MEMC's decision to locate close to TI would prove its commitment to the success of this joint venture. All of these benefits proved Sherman was the clear choice.

Case 4.4

Divorce on the Alliance Highway

Introduction

In December of 1993, Pehr Gyllenhammar, the flamboyant and super-articulate head of Volvo since 1971, faced a difficult challenge that lay ahead. This sophisticated and charismatic leader, fondly known as "the emperor" among his colleagues, attempted to convince his company's shareholders to agree upon a merger with France's long-established, premier car company, Renault on December 7, 1993.

On September 10, 1993, Volvo and Renault unveiled a complex merger plan in Paris to join their car, truck and certain other operations to form the world's sixth biggest auto group and one of Europe's top 20 corporations. This new company, known as Renault-Volvo RVA would begin operations on January 1, 1994, pending certain regulatory clarifications.

Much to Volvo's dismay, the announcement caused a serious plunge in Volvo's benchmark B-stock, the class of equity most traded internationally. However, Gyllenhammar, who was accustomed to the abrupt swings in Volvo's price, added that he desired for a more positive reaction to the merger and explained that he fully understood the dimensions and consequences of this gigantic merger.

The terms of this merger lay in the issues of the French "golden share" and Renault's privatization. When Renault became privatized, Volvo would emerge as Renault-Volvo's biggest single shareholder with a combined direct and indirect holdings of 35% with the French's 65%. The timing of the company's privatization was not set. This agreement would also prohibit Volvo from selling any of its current stakes in both Renault and Volvo or the new company. In addition, the French had sought to draw a "golden share" which would curb hostile takeover attempts. But, it would also prevent Volvo from possibly obtaining majority control of Renault-Volvo except on friendly terms. Furthermore, in the case of any unwanted occurrences, the "golden share" would allow the French government to reduce Volvo's stake in the new company from 35% to 20%.

One can certainly derive French authority from these terms as they had induced opposition from Volvo's shareholders. Pehr Gyllenhammar was so sure that his company's investors would easily come to terms with the merger plan in November. Unfortunately, the growing opposition towards the deal among Volvo's holders forced Gyllenhammar to postpone the meeting for a month to give him more time to persuade the company's shareholders. Soren Gyll, Volvo's chief executive officer, said that this delay would allow the French and Volvo management to clarify certain controversial parts of the merger. Somehow, there were problems in allaying the details in a smooth fashion.

Gyllenhammar knew the deal would propel him to the center of the European auto industry, as he would be the acting chairperson of the new company. The greed of power blinded him and he did not bother clarifying the outstanding conditions of the merger, Renault's privatization and the French "golden share," with his company's shareholders. On the contrary, most of them were well aware of these imminent terms and caused many of its investors, such as Skandia Insurance Co. and Wasa Group, to openly oppose the deal. Aktiespararna, Sweden's federation of small investors (10% of Volvo's stakes), launched a proxy battle in an attempt to force annulment or major renegotiations of the corporate marriage. Nevertheless, there was support behind the embattled Volvo management from Sweden's Fourth National Pension Insurance Fund and Folksam Sak och Liv, a Stockholm mutual insurer. Many investors had expected a written pledge from the French Industry Minister Gerard Longuet regarding the nonapplication of the "golden share" but the French wrested easily. Despite assurances from the French premier Louis Schweitzer, Volvo's shareholders knew that the French government seemed more interested in advancing its national policy rather than maximizing equal shareholder value in the merged company.

The tactical blunders of promoting the merger had resulted in extreme criticism of Pehr Gyllenhammar's position in the company. Thomas Halvorsen, the president of the Fourth Fund, had decided to push for a new slate of Volvo directors.

While shouldering these critical issues, Pehr Gyllenhammar had only hope to secure this deal and his shaky reputation.

History of Volvo

The 1920s were the decade when the car made a real breakthrough, both in the USA and in Europe. The Volvo was one of the cars that changed our way of life. Volvo was born on April 14, 1927. The first car was nicknamed "Jakob"; however, the dream began some years earlier. Assar

Gabrielsson and Gustak Larson were the two men behind the Volvo.

Gabrielsson and Larson joined forces in 1924. They had the same idea: to build a Swedish car for Swedish roads. Assar Gabrielsson had a Bachelor of Science in Economics and was a businessman. He began his career at SKF in Goteborg. Later he became head of SKF's subsidiary in France. After a few years in this position, he returned to Sweden to be sales manager of SKF.

Gustaf Larson was an engineer and designer. He received his degree from the University of Technology in Stockholm. His career also began at SKF, which gave the two the opportunity to meet. Most believe this is where they developed the idea of a Swedish car manufacturer.

In 1924, Gabrielsson and Larson began serious plans for producing cars and entered a verbal agreement on this idea. They both developed the car alongside their careers at SKF. Once there was something concrete to be seen, SKF became interested. SKF provided financial backing, the factory premises, and the name, AB Volvo. In 1927, the first series-manufactured car made its appearance. This was the year Volvo operations were officially recognized.

Over the years, Volvo has become a giant. They began exporting cars to Belgium, Italy, Great Britain, Netherlands, and many other countries. In 1961, Volvo made plans to become established in the European Economic Community (EEC) market. This helped increase production in the Ghent plant to 5,550 cars compared with 2,650 in the start-up year.

Volvo began having problems with outer tariff walls and other obstacles associated with exporting. This created uncertainty with respect to long-range planning of export activities within Volvo. Volvo began entering agreements with Peugeot and Renault to help solve some of the trading and manufacturing problems. These agreements were to combine knowledge and technology to design and produce passenger car engines in a new company. This was finalized in 1979.

Volvo has changed in many ways over the years. They have entered new markets and increased production. The founders, Gabrielsson and Larson, founded the expression "building cars the Volvo way." Quality has always been the firm ground on which Volvo was built and is also one of the guiding principles the company's high-tech operations maintains today.

History of Renault

A strange vehicle named "Voiturette" had come to life on December 24, 1898. The company had known only one master. Its founder and creator was Louis Renault. Renault's passion in life was his factory in Billancourt and his life's work.

Louis Renault had two essential advantages to his business. They were the financial support of his brothers, well-off tradesmen, and his remarkable knowledge of mechanical things. Renault patented the direct drive system; this was the transmission mechanism that enabled his first vehicle. Manufacturers all over the world adopted this system.

The company had begun to grow and change. They began filling vast orders for taxis in 1914. There was a shift in production from a craft-oriented operation to a full-scale industrial manufacturer. The company introduced "Taylorism" to France. This was a form of division of labor. By the eve of the First World War, Louis Renault had become a man of substance and influence.

During World War I the company turned into a veritable arsenal. It manufactured everything such as shells, stretchers, tanks, aircraft engines, and later planes. Renault was the leading private industrial firm in France by 1919. After the war, Renault focused its attention on manufacturing trucks, commercial vehicles, tractors, railcars, and aircraft.

By the outbreak of World War II, the company had expanded greatly. It had several manufacturing locations in Belgium, England, and France. Louis Renault kept his plants busy during the Occupation of France by filling orders requested by the German forces. After the Liberation of France, Renault was imprisoned for this behavior. He died on October 24, 1944. A decree issued by General de Gaulle led to the confiscation of his assets and the nationalization of the company. The company became property of the French government and became Regie Nationale des Usines Renault in 1945. The Renault story had entered a new era.

Through the years, numerous individuals ran the company. It was as competitive and successful as any privately owned company. The Regie became a bastion of unionism and an example for industrial relations; however, it also had a few crisis points along the way. The American market was a failure for Renault in the beginning of the 60s and again later in the century. Their focus was primarily on the European market.

Renault rapidly expanded and their ambitious product policy led to runaway costs that caused the company great losses. Through the 80s, Renault was trying to recover some profits. They closed the historic Billancourt site, but most importantly, they implemented the Total Quality Management philosophy. This philosophy is what kept Renault in existence.

Renault had also entered many partnerships. They believed they stood to gain most of their strength through these joint ventures. Renault entered partnerships with Peugeot, Volvo, and others. Some provided benefit to the company while others failed. Regardless of the failed ventures, Renault focuses on being the most competitive manufacturer in Europe by the year 2000.

Firm Focus

Organizational Philosophy

Volvo devotes so much attention to safety that the name Volvo is synonymous with safe cars. Safety means that you can relax and enjoy your journey when you drive. And, it demands design features that also make it fun to drive.

Principal Decision-Makers

The decision-makers of Volvo hold very similar positions to important decision-makers of other firms in this industry. They have a board of directors, secretary to the board, and a group executive committee. An annual general meeting elects the board of directors. There are ten members with one board of directors. The board also has two deputy members, plus one secretary residing.

The other part of the organization consists of a group executive committee. They deal with engineering, operating sectors, and a legal counsel. The committee has twelve members, a president, and a vice president. The members are elected every year.

Organizational Design

Volvo is one of the best examples of integration among leading Swedish industrial firms and Swedish banks where there is serious commitment and enthusiam from both sides. In this case, such close interlock between financial and industrial institutions is similar to a Japanese *KEIRETSU,* which is why Sweden is often stereotyped as the "Japan of Europe." Banks not only provide a great deal of financial security and protection for these companies from possible acquisitions by outsiders, but also they are building stronger bounding relationships among these companies. There are three main **bank-blocks** in Sweden with leading banks as follows: Handelsbanken, Skandinaviska Enskilda Bank, and Sparbanken. These types of alliances mean sharing control. Volvo holds a prominent position in the relationship with Handelsbanken, while SAAB, for example, another large Swedish auto manufacturing firm, has a prominent relationship with Skandinaviska Enskilda Bank. When looking at this type of consortia, many similarities can be found in the Japanese KEIRETSUS. One of the most famous Japanese KEIRETSUs is Mitsubishi Corporation. Mitsubishi's *three-diamond* logo is a perfect example of the way a Japanese KEIRETSU is set up. A bank at the center, the Matsushita Bank of Tokyo, supports three main industries. Then each industry has three other subindustries, where each subindustry overlooks five other industrial firms. Such a design of infrastructure has proven to be successful in Japan, but now is going through a series of changes due to the changing global environment.

Market Position

Over fifty percent of Volvo's sales are to customers outside of Sweden. Volvo has steadily increased this percentage, annually, as part of their objective with respect to foreign

Comparison of Mitsubishi's and Volvo's industrial design

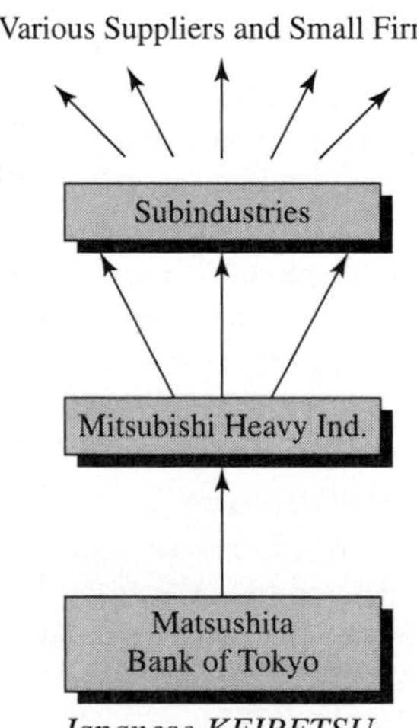

Japanese KEIRETSU

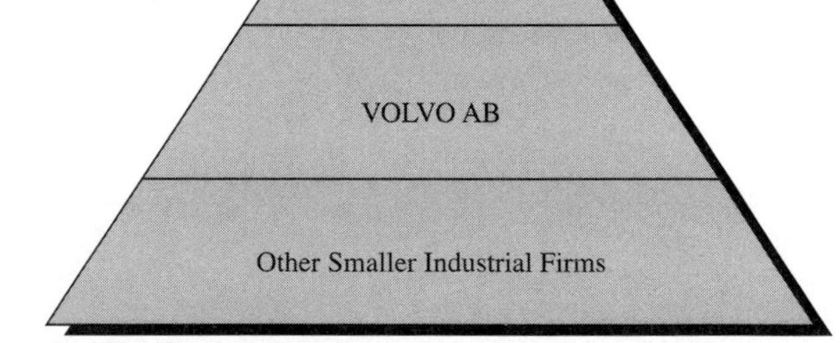

Swedish Consortia

ownership. The natural development of equity acquired internationally is largely tied to the high number of sales outside of Sweden.

Nature and Scope

Volvo researches, develops, manufactures, and produces many models of cars, buses, and trucks (lorries). Trucks are produced for light duty (efficient local distribution), robust work (demanding construction operation), and heavy duty (efficient long haul transport).

A subsidiary, Volvo Buses, produces complete buses from the development stage. Volvo Buses is the global leader in their arena, and works mainly out of Europe. There are bus subsidiaries, however, in Canada (Prévost Car, Inc. and Nova Bus Corporation), China, and Israel (Merkavim), to name a few. They also provide a commitment for product support in many areas, including public transportation systems solutions.

Another subsidiary is Volvo Aero, which is in the aircraft engine industry. They conduct operations in seven areas, including military engines, space propulsion, and vehicle components.

Volvo also has operations in other areas; however, these are the most significant segments of the organization.

In all areas of the Volvo organization, the emphasis is placed on safety, the quality of their customers' driving experience, and the environment. This is the reason Volvo devotes a large part of their company to research and development in all areas.

Motivation of the Firm

Volvo's motivation for developing a strategic alliance with Renault was associated around a few areas. These areas included financial strength, a larger share of the market, and combining their efforts on research and development. Volvo hoped to improve themselves in all of these areas through the alliance.

Volvo and Renault gained financial strength with the partnership. The two companies were able to reduce expenses by preventing duplication of processes and combining cash flow to make them more effective. Volvo and Renault captured a larger portion of the market through the alliance. With the partnership, the companies would become the fourth largest carmaker in Europe and the second largest truck manufacturer in the world.

Research and development was another area that was a motivation for the partnership. Volvo had brand equity for safety that Renault acquired after the alliance. Together they developed, produced, analyzed, and tested safety applications. They were also able to concentrate on producing environmentally safe cars.

Organizational Culture

According to Lawrence and Spybey, one of the main aspects that define environment in which Scandinavian organization exists is "what one might call *low differentiation:* that is to say, people, groups, classes, and sexes are less apart, or less marked off from each other than in many other western societies." Volvo is a perfect example of the way Swedish companies are structured in terms of control and direction.

First of all, it has a single board of directors which, is a typical case for many Swedish Companies. Volvo's board of directors consists of one Managing Director/Verkstallande Director, VDI, Pehr Gyllenhammar, eight employee representatives, and five other non-executive directors with directorships and assignments in other companies. Trade union representatives are positively welcomed to participation, as well as the union committee that represents more than 5,200 employees. Such participation is encouraged by law, which was set up by Swedish government in 1972, and is a perfect example of the Scandinavian style of management.

Another very distinctly Scandinavian trait, that our group identified at Volvo, is participative decision making, which tends to be a very slow process while "searching for a perfect compromise". In order for managers not to set themselves above their colleagues, "it is normal for a Swedish manager to consult his subordinates, and not just consult them cosmetically." However, this participatory approach is one basis that could add to the bureaucratic process; when more people will be added to the organizational functioning, the slower it will go.

Swedish economic life is both internationalist and insular with no foreign banks present and relatively few foreign companies, according to Lawrence and Spybey. There is a high level of interlock among the major Swedish companies, and especially among those in the same *bank-blocks.* Two of Volvo's major shareholders are the Fourth pension fund, with 7.5 percent of the voting rights, and the insurance company Folksam, with 3.5 percent of voting rights. The third largest shareholder is the Fifth AP-Fond, which historically, has always voted against proposed alliances with their 1.3 percent of Volvo's shares.

There are many other significant shareholders. They include Aktiesparana (Sweden's federation of small investors), SPP pension fund, and the Skandia Group Insurance Company. For example, Volvo is associated with Handelsbank where it has a more eminent and influential position. Moreover, on the board of directors at Volvo, Pehr Gyllenhammar also had a directorship position at Nordbanken, therefore, such close interaction between a company and a bank from the same block gives an unusual degree of financial security by eliminating the possibility of take-over from the outside.

Decision Environment

[SIC 3711: Motor Vehicles and Passenger Car Bodies]
In the early 1990s, the sales of automobiles approached 50 million units globally. Japan, North America, and Western Europe "accounted for 75% of global production and sales of motor vehicles" (Encyclopedia of Global Industries). There was a large concentration of the market. Six companies in the automobile industry controlled more than 50% of worldwide sales in 1992. There was intense global competition among these companies. The top automobile companies included: General Motors, Ford, Toyota, Volkswagen AG, Nissan, and Fiat SpA. Intense competition promoted global production for lower costs in labor, regulations, etc.

Strategic Partnership

In 1969, Peugeot and Renault joined forces to become Peugeot Renault SA. Two years later, in 1971, Volvo also joined forces with Peugeot and Renault. The new combined name was Peugeot Renault Volvo SA, organized for the development of a new engine, which was to be manufactured by Française de Mécanique. During the creation of this engine, there was a fuel crisis, which caused a truncation of the engine from eight cylinders to a V6. The engine was ready in 1974, and the next year it was available in four car models (two were Peugeot, one was Renault, and one was Volvo). Many other cars used the engine in the following years (it was used by various car companies).

As part of the cooperation between Renault and Volvo, in 1981 Volvo took over the Renault agency in Sweden, Denmark, and Norway. In addition, as part of the same deal, Volvo ceased importing Renault (except for the R5, Traffic and Master) due to the threat against Volvo's own models.

In April 1990, Renault developed the document called "General Logistics Policy." (It was updated in 1991 to take into account its implementation time of over one year, and the experiences gained from the implementation.) The agreement between Volvo and Renault, for cooperation on the car, truck, and bus, was signed in late 1990.

Volvo began importing all Renault models with the cooperation, except for the larger "Safrane" model (a competitive threat), until 1998. In 1992, as the Volvo-Renault alliance developed, two joint organizations were developed. One organization was created to improve quality, and the other, for improving purchasing. Another joint organization was in early development stages for strategic product planning.

These organizations were successful with many new policies including a procedure to evaluate the logistics of their suppliers. Both Renault and Volvo judge their suppliers in two areas:

1) their ability to produce the most economical, high quality parts, and
2) their ability to deliver these parts on time and packaged to the manufacturer needs.

Renault and Volvo chose to reaffirm and define the basic principles of the policy for achieving an extremely fast and reliable exchange of information between suppliers and manufacturers. Both car companies tested ten of their suppliers in these areas.

In September of 1993, the presentation, to Volvo shareholders and employees, of the main principles for a merger took place. They planned to create a company with 100,000 workers and to produce two million cars annually. The combination of Renault and Volvo would be the fourth largest carmaker in Europe and the second largest truck maker in the world. Both Renault and Volvo believed they would be getting some savings through "synergy," along with more standard financial gains in areas such as procurement, sharing more components, and jointly developing more models. These savings were estimated at FFr42 billion (approximately US$7 billion). P. G. Gyllenhammar said that the new company would be open to other partners after the initial structure was solidfied. The Volvo stockholders and employees already had increasing doubts, through, and the alliance negotiations became quite drawn out.

On November 22, 1993, Edouard Balladur, the French prime minister, promised the Swedish government, as soon as the automobile and financial markets allowed it (approx., late 1994), France would privatize its sixty-five percent hold in Renault-Volvo. Another point was made by the Prime Minister about the "golden share," France's additional stake in the new company. The French government would not use this additional share to reduce Volvo's hold, as long as Volvo didn't remove their stake in the alliance.

The French government would hold forty-seven percent of Renault-Volvo, while Volvo would only hold eighteen percent. An additional thirty-five percent would be held by

RVC, which is a holding group. RVC would be fifty-one percent owned by the French government and forty-nine percent owned by Volvo. The management was not strictly defined. It would be an intermingling of Renault or Volvo appointed persons. A supervisory board would be German-style with "extended powers," with Pehr Gyllenhammar as the chair to head it. There would also be a management board, chaired by Renault's Louis Schweitzer, with responsibility for running the new group.

The merger also allowed for swifter responses and shorter lines of command as a streamlined or "lean" organization.

Both Renault and Volvo have extensive bus and "lorry" (truck) operations, which, together, would become the second largest company in size, behind Mercedes Benz. Volvo made 43,000 heavy trucks, while Renault only made 31,600 in 1992.

Volvo stockholders questioned the French government's commitment to the plan of Renault's privatization and the fact that the French would own a majority of Renault-Volvo. The merger was subsequently called off, and P. G. Gyllenhammar, along with the entire Volvo Board of Directors, resigned. A new board was elected in January of 1994.

Critical Issues

In considering the alliance, "business issues have been mixed with *political* and *social* ones," said Mr. Gyllenhammar.

One of the critical issues we discussed about the Volvo Renault strategic alliance is the rise of corporate nationalism throughout Europe. The spread of nationalism into the affairs of corporations is an extension of the nationalistic sentiments. These sentiments have played a prominent role in stalling the European Community's attempts to widen and deepen the single market concept through mechanisms like a single currency. Professor Markides of Uppsala University confirms that these nationalistic problems become more of an issue during times of economic difficulty. In this case, there was a general feeling throughout many Swedish industrial organizations which influenced decision-making, that Volvo, a symbol of Sweden's industrial prowess, was being bargained away too cheaply to a foreign partner that could not be entrusted with the fate of Swedish jobs.

The second critical issue lies in cultural conflict. During the interview with Mr. Greg Bantel, a retail operation manager of the Central Regional Office for North America, he also mentioned a cultural critical issue that stresses the significant differences in behavior of these ethnic groups. Since it is typical for Scandinavian managers to always [*sic*] search for a perfect compromise and try to find the ultimate balance in the proposed relationship the decision making process tends to be very slow. Learning from previous experience of Volvo's attempted alliances with other [*sic*] directly controlled by the French government will be sold to private investors under a broadly based public offering. Then, Renault-Volvo will become a publicly traded company.

The trusted hard core of French institutional shareholders will control 51% of RVC; Volvo 49%. RVC's stake in Renault-Volvo will guarantee unassailable control through various anti-takeover provisions and other terms of shareholders' pact between Volvo and the French government. The timing of Renault's privatization was uncertain but it was tentatively set for the second half of 1994, or before June, 1995.

The Process

Louis Schweitzer, Renault's chairman and chief executive officer, was trying to convince and guarantee the Swedish critics that the merger would be a prerequisite to privatization. According to Mr. Schweitzer, a clear decision had to be made for the actual date but in an unpredictable market, shares would only be sold when the market was willing to buy. Since Volvo shareholders receive payments from a new company, they were anxiously waiting for the new, merged company to be privatized and make its stock market introduction soon. However, some Swedish investors were worried that a change in government could derail and delay the privatization program.

Bibliography

"AB Volvo: Big Swedish Merger Insurer to Vote against the Renault Merger." *The Wall Street Journal.* December 1, 1993. Section A; Page 17. Copyright 1993 Dow Jones & Company, Incorporated.

"Back to the Way We Were." *Economist.* November 6, 1993. Edition 329: Pages 83–84.

"Backing for Volvo Merger." *The New York Times,* Late Edition. November 26, 1993. Section D; Financial Desk; Page 12. Copyright 1993 The New York Times Company.

Ball, Matthew. "Seducing the Swedes." *Economist.* November 27, 1993. Edition 329: Page 73.

Business World. Home Final Ed. Business section. August

30, 1993. Page 4d. Copyright 1993 Dow Jones & Company Incorporated.

Encyclopedia of Global Industries. Scott Heil, ed. Detroit, MI: Gale, 1999.

"Insurers Join Protest of Planned Merger by Volvo, Renault." *The Wall Street Journal.* November 11, 1993. Section A; Page 10. Copyright 1993 Dow Jones & Company, Incorporated.

http://www.renault.com

http://www.volvo.se/corpinfo/

Moore, Stephen D. "Marriage of Renault. Volvo Isn't All Bliss; Officers Begin 'Road Show' Amid Drop in Swedish Concern's Stock." *The Wall Street Journal.* September 10, 1993. Section B; Page 2A. Copyright 1993 Dow Jones & Company Incorporated.

Moore, Stephen D., and Timothy Aeppel. "Renault, Volvo Unveil Proposal on Their Merger: French-Swedish Company to Be Among Largest of World's Car Makers."

Moore, Stephen D. "Volvo-Renault Merger Plan Gets Boost as Two Big Investors Indicate Support." *The Wall Street Journal.* November 26, 1993. Section A; Page 6

Riding, Alan. "Renault-Volvo Marriage Is On." *The New York Times,* Late Edition. September 7, 1993. Section D; Foreign Desk; Page 1. Copyright 1993 The New York Times Company.

Stevenson, Richard W. "The Nationalist Roadblock in Europe." *The New York Times,* Late Edition. December 19, 1993. Section 3; Financial Desk; Page 9. Copyright 1993 The New York Times Company.

Taylor, Alex III. "Why Breaking Up with Renault Is Volvo's Gain." *Fortune.* December 27, 1993. Edition 128: Page 13; Asian 11.

Tierney, Christine. "Is It Too Late for Renault and Volvo Grand Alliance?" *The Financial Express.* May 4, 1997. Copyright 1997; Indian Express Newspapers (Bombay) Ltd.

Troy, Leo, PhD. *Almanac of Business and Industrial Financial Ratios.* 1997 Edition (28th Annual Edition). Englewood Cliffs, NJ: Prentice-Hall.

Case 4.5

EQUILON: A Texaco/Shell Strategic Partnership

On June 6, 1944, the battle to liberate Europe began. Allied troops stormed the beaches of France and began the slow process of finishing off the German Reich. Many factors contributed to the eventual success of the allied forces. One of the most important factors, was the vast amount of U.S. soldiers that were sent to fight. Another major factor was the abundance of natural and man-made resources that the allies possessed. Toward the end of the war, the German military machine was running low on many crucial supplies. The allied forces on the other hand were well-stocked. Both Shell and Texaco supplied the allies with aviation fuel, gasoline, and chemicals used to make rubber. Needless to say, these products were absolutely essential to the war effort. Shell and Texaco actually took part in the greatest strategic alliance of this century. Fifty-four years later, these two companies are venturing into another alliance. The future of nations is not at stake, but the goal is somewhat the same. By combining forces, the companies hope to achieve synergy. With this alliance called Equilon, Shell and Texaco plan to bring about lower costs, margin improvements of at least $800 million, and greater returns on assets. These goals will be accomplished by the integration and overlapping of functions, assets, and ideas of the two companies. Equilon will develop and facilitate these actions. This alliance has the potential to be very successful. Much like the allied forces of World War II, no one will know just how successful it will be until they actually engage in the action.

Source: Prepared by Greg Gelmer, Jason Brazell, Rick Foerster, Cindy Boris, and Rachael Doering under the supervision of Dr. Lou E. Pelton, University of North Texas.

Texaco

Joseph Cullinan, an oilman from southeast Texas, founded The Texas Company in 1902 during a major oil rush at

Spindletop Oil Field near present day Beaumont, Texas: Just as the company got off the ground, Spindletop's oil production dwindled. The lack of crude oil put The Texas Company's future in question, but in early 1903, the company made a major oil discovery in Sour Lake, Texas. With its crude oil supply secured, The Texas Company built a refinery in Port Arthur, Texas and a pipeline to Oklahoma. In 1903, the company adopted its first logo: a five-point star based on the lone star of the Texas flag, and in 1906, the company registered the name Texaco as a trademark. In 1959, The Texas Company decided to officially change its name to Texaco, Inc. Texaco's first filling station opened in Brooklyn, NY in 1911, and by 1928, the company's U.S. market grew to cover the continental United States. Since then, Texaco has continued to grow and has become one of the top oil companies in the world. Based on 1997 figures, Texaco has $29.6 billion in assets and approximately 29,000 employees.

Mission

Texaco has always emphasized certain qualities, including the desire to be one of the leading worldwide oil and petrochemical companies with a high rate of return to its stockholders. Texaco focuses on customer satisfaction as well as producing exceptional products and services. "For generations, Texaco has been a quintessential brand, synonymous with exceptional products and services in America and around the world," says John Darnel, vice president of sales for Equilon Enterprises, who was formerly vice president, sales and marketing, for Texaco Lubricants Company.

Organizational Structure and Culture

Texaco is led by CEO and chairman of the board, Peter Bijur. He and the board of directors, which is made up of various subcommittees, are the key decision makers for Texaco. Texaco has decided to form global management teams rather than having a geographic organization structure. These teams are each made of a president, vice president and numerous managers. Texaco has a small, but effective, executive management team located in White Plains, NY, that is involved in all of the alliance decisions. Although Texaco's workforce is getting smaller, the company has strong visions and values focused on diversity, trust and a respect for the individual.

Market Position

Texaco's primary focus is on worldwide exploration and production of natural gas. Texaco is ranked as one of the top 5 oil companies in the world and controls 7.1 percent of total U.S. gasoline and automotive lubricant sales, as well as about 6.6 percent of total U.S. refining capacity. Although Texaco's asset and workforce size is decreasing, the Equilon alliance adds financial strength. With this alliance, Texaco will gain market share and generate $45 billion in annual revenues.

Motivation for an Alliance

In the highly competitive, capital intensive U.S. downstream oil and lubricants business, Texaco was challenged to find innovative ways to convert their business into valuable assets. Since returns on investments and capital employed for downstream U.S. operations were well below acceptable levels in previous years, Texaco needed some help. Faced with the possibility of continuing single-digit returns from these downstream operations, Texaco decided to apply a strategy of asset management to propel its downstream business into a platform for growth.

The Decision Environment

U.S. lubricant's base oil production is controlled by five, vertically integrated, multinational companies. Exxon, Chevron, Mobil, Shell, and Texaco account for sixty percent of U.S. lubricant base oil. This high concentration of seller power indicates a strong oligopolistic industrial structure. Competition among the few, as oligopoly is often called, is highly personalized. Each firm tends to be aware of product developments or price moves made by the other firms, and because of this, competition in the industry is ineffective as a whole. Another characteristic of an oligopoly is that it is extremely difficult for new competitors to enter. Economies of scale are often the most pervasive barrier to entry, as well as complex technologies, extensive distribution networks, and elaborate sales and marketing activities.

Unlike many industries in the world, the lubricant industry's top five companies can focus on each other without having to worry about new competition entering the industry. Competition between these companies has become more specialized and this allows them to compete on other levels. Lubricant companies have become more competitive in areas like oil and gas exploration and production, and in the production of cost-effective and efficient oil and gas. Some other principal methods of competition include geological, geophysical, engineering, research and technology, experience and expertise, and economic analysis in connection with property acquisitions.

Along with the direct competition between companies, some other externalities that have an impact on the lubricant industry are the various laws and regulations now in force, in standby status, or under construction. These laws and regulations deal with such matters as

- Production restrictions
- Import and export controls
- Price controls
- Crude oil and refined product allocations
- Refined product specifications
- Environmental, health and safety regulations
- Retroactive and prospective tax increases
- Cancellation of contract rights
- Expropriation of property
- Divestiture of certain operations
- Foreign exchange rate changes and restrictions as to convertibility of currencies
- Tariffs and other international trade restrictions
- Employee strikes and other industrial disputes

Along with these various laws and regulations, lubricant companies have to consider the steady decline in oil prices. On Monday, November 30, the price of oil sank to a twelve-year low and this caused a sharp fall in the value of most U.S. oil companies' stocks. Because of the low prices, oil companies now realize they must become as efficient as possible in order to remain profitable and capable of generating the capital needed to compete and supply energy products in the future. The idea of oil companies partnering together to cut costs is one of self-preservation rather than domination in the oil industry. Companies like Texaco and Shell, and Mobil and Exxon have decided to work together because they will not be able to survive in the future unless they cut costs and gain capital.

U.S. lubricant companies have had to adapt to many things over the past several years. Given the oligopolistic nature of the oil industry, the many laws and regulations oil companies must follow, and the decline of oil prices, companies have no choice but to merge if they want to survive. This is the major reason why Texaco and Shell have formed the two new lubricant companies Equilon and Motiva. They want to lower costs and increase profits by combining each of the companies' competitive advantages. These two new alliances between Texaco and Shell have also put pressure on other lubricant companies, and they are responding in the same manner. Companies like Mobil and Exxon have decided to merge together, and many other companies are in the process of doing the same thing.

Nature and Scope of the Strategic Partnership

In response to fierce competition in the downstream market driving down profit margins, Texaco Inc. and Shell Oil Company joined to create two alliances with the purpose of generating greater efficiencies, higher margins, and growth opportunities. On March 18, 1997, Texaco and Shell signed a memorandum of understanding to combine the major elements of their midwestern and western U.S. refining and marketing activities and their total U.S. transportation, trading, and lubricants businesses. In January 1998, the newly formed limited liability company, Equilon Enterprises, began operations. Equilon aligns the biggest (Shell) and the ninth largest (Texaco) U.S. refining companies to form the sixth largest refining company in the United States. The venture includes all of Texaco and Shell's lubricant business and Texaco's U.S. coolant business; however, the exploration, production, and chemical businesses of the two companies are not included in the new company. The alliance will continue to market petroleum products separately under the Shell and Texaco brand names.

Terms of the Agreement

Under the terms of the agreement, Shell owns a 56 percent interest and Texaco owns a 44 percent interest in Equilon Enterprises. Due to antitrust legislation, Shell and Texaco are required to divest certain assets in order to obtain Federal Trade Commission and state approval of the joint venture. In accordance with this agreement, the following assets required divestiture:

1. Shell will divest its Anacortes, WA refinery, which has a rated capacity of 108,000 barrels per day.
2. Texaco and Shell must divest their interests in either the Colonial or Plantation pipelines. Texaco has a 14.27 percent interest in the Colonial pipeline and Shell has a 24.04 percent interest in the Plantation pipeline. These pipelines transport refined products from the Gulf Coast to the East Coast.
3. Texaco and Shell must sell a limited number of retail stores in San Diego.
4. In Hawaii, either Shell's terminal and stations or Texaco's terminal and stations on the island of Oahu must be sold.
5. Texaco and Shell must release jobbers and open dealers from their contracts in Hawaii.
6. Shell must release jobbers and open dealers from their contracts in Oregon and Washington, with the option to rebrand if they choose.

Terminals	*Terminals*	*Terminals*
19 crude oil and products terminals (own or have partial interest)	57 crude oil and products terminals (own or have partial interest)	67 crude oil and products terminals (own or have partial interest)
Pipeline	*Pipeline*	*Pipeline*
Ownership interest in approximately 30,000 miles of pipeline throughout the United States.	Ownership interest in approximately 15,600 miles of pipeline throughout the United States.	Ownership interest in approximately 45,600 miles of pipeline in the United States.
Retail Marketing	*Retail Marketing*	*Retail Marketing*
Approximately 4,400 Texaco-branded outlets in 24 states.	Approximately 4,477 Shell-branded outlets in 19 states.	Approximately 9,000 branded outlets in all or parts of 32 states.
Texaco percent of Market Share in joint venture area: 6%	Shell percent of Market Share in joint venture area: 8%	Equilon percent of Market Share in joint venture area: 14.3%
Lubricants Plants (5)	*Lubricants Plants (5)*	*Lubricants Plants*
River Rouge, MI Capacity: 7,300 bpd		River Rouge, MI Capacity: 7,300 bpd
	Deer Park, TX Capacity: 9,500 bpd (2 trains)	Deer Park, TX Capacity: 9,500 bpd (2 trains)
Charleston, SC Capacity: 8,250 bpd		Charleston, SC Capacity: 8,250 bpd
	Martinez, CA Capacity: 5,000 bpd	Martinez, CA Capacity: 5,000 bpd
Galena Park, TX Capacity: 8,600		Galena Park, TX Capacity: 8,600
	Wood River, IL Capacity: 8,300 bpd (2 units)	Wood River, IL Capacity: 8,300 bpd (2 units)
Los Angeles, CA Capacity: 5,500 bpd		Los Angeles, CA Capacity: 5,500 bpd
	Carson, CA Capacity: 2,300 bpd	Carson, CA Capacity: 2,300 bpd
Norfolk, VA Capacity: 4,100 bpd		Norfolk, VA Capacity: 4,100 bpd
	Metairie, LA Capacity: 3,300 bpd	Metairie, LA Capacity: 3,300 bpd

(*continued*)

Equilon is comprised of a number of Texaco's and Shell's western and midwestern assets. Equilon currently owns seven refineries, with a total capacity of 846,270 barrels per day, and 9,000 retail stores in 32 states. A fully stand-alone organization within Equilon Enterprises is Equilon Lubricants. Equilon Lubricants is comprised of 10 Texaco and Shell lubricant plants, with assets worth $750 million. The above table shows the breakdown of contributions made by Texaco and Shell to the Equilon venture.

Texaco Assets	*Shell Assets*	*Equilon Assets*
Texaco Refineries (4)	**Shell Refineries (3)**	**Equilon Refineries**
Anacortes, WA Capacity: 140,125 bpd		Anacortes, WA Capacity: 140,125 bpd
	Martinez, CA Capacity: 155,300 bpd	Martinez, CA Capacity: 155,300 bpd
El Dorado, KS Capacity: 99,750 bpd		El Dorado, KS Capacity: 99,750 bpd
	Wood River, IL Capacity: 274,500 bpd	Wood River, IL Capacity: 274,500 bpd
Los Angeles, CA Capacity: 90,250 bpd		Los Angeles, CA Capacity: 90,250 bpd
Bakersfield, CA Capacity: 58,045 bpd		Bakersfield, CA Capacity: 58,045 bpd
	Odessa, TX Capacity: 28,300 bpd	Odessa, TX Capacity: 28,300 bpd
Total Texaco Capacity: 388,170 bpd	**Total Shell Capacity:** 458,100 bpd	**Equilon Refinery Capacity:** 846,270 bpd
Texaco Percent of U.S. Capacity: 2.5%	**Shell Percent of U.S. Capacity:** 3.6%	**Equilon Percent of U.S. Capacity:** 5.3%

Strengthening Ties

Texaco and Shell have a relationship that continues beyond Equilon. Texaco and Shell have added another joint venture in the U.S. market, Motiva Enterprises. Motiva Enterprises is a partnership between Texaco, Shell, and Saudi Refining, Inc. that combines the refining and marketing operations in the eastern United States. Motiva markets gasoline and other petroleum products under the Texaco and Shell brand names in all or parts of 27 states. In addition to Motiva Enterprises, Texaco and Shell also jointly own two organizations that support the operations of both Motiva and Equilon. Equiva Services LLC provides administrative support services to the joint venture companies, and Equiva Trading Company functions as the companies' trading unit. The chart on the next page illustrates the interelatedness of the Texaco and Shell alliances.

Texaco has a history of maintaining long-term alliances. The largest and most enduring is Caltex. Formed in 1936, Caltex is a 50 percent downstream joint venture with Chevron. Caltex is a leading marketer in many of the nearly 60 countries in which it operates. From 1994 to 1997, Caltex's cost-containment efforts have resulted in a 15 percent cost reduction. Just as Caltex has consistently added shareholder value, Equilon and Motiva are expected to achieve strong results in the competitive U.S. downstream market. The long-term success Texaco has experienced in alliances such as Caltex, gives Texaco the blueprints needed to ensure that its new alliances with Shell are a success.

Outcomes of the Strategic Partnership

By adopting the best practices of both companies, and sharing management systems, business processes, and support functions, Texaco and Shell expected to achieve substantial cost efficiencies in the Equilon venture. The emphasis of Equilon was to improve performance and growth opportunities in the United States. To compete effectively, Equilon Enterprises needed to be quick, lean, and aggressive, and it needed strong financial capabilities and appropriate policies and procedures to supports its business. One of the immediate priorities of the joint venture was to integrate Texaco and Shell's financial reporting systems. Consequently, financial controls were required to protect Equilon's assets and to guarantee the integrity of the financial data. To ensure that Equilon met the objectives of Texaco and Shell, support functions such as a fiscal leadership council were formed among the companies to help guide the financial functions of

Equilon/Motiva operating structure

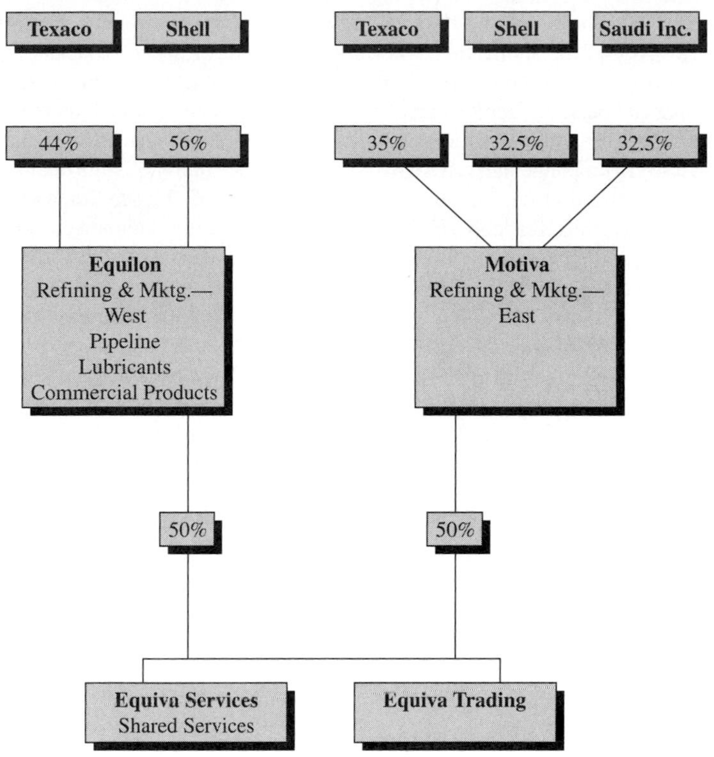

the alliance and to ensure that they are coordinated and aligned closely. These teams have helped to capture and track synergies and restructure Equilon's asset base. As a result, Equilon is well positioned financially for future growth, with a debt to total capital ratio of 25 percent.

Equilon Enterprises LLC is estimated to be in a near tie with Motiva Enterprises as the largest retail gasoline marketer in the United States and is the sixth largest refiner. Annual gross revenue is estimated at $24 billion. On a national basis, Equilon Enterprises, with both the Texaco and Shell brands, has an estimated 14.3 percent market share in its geographic area. According to the most recent Lundberg Survey, Equilon Enterprises is number one in market share in Arkansas, Oregon, California, Kentucky, Missouri, New Mexico and Washington; and number two in market share in Alaska, Arizona, Colorado, Hawaii, Illinois, Nebraska, Nevada, and Utah.

Equilon and Motiva are changing the way Texaco and Shell operate their downstream businesses by improving performance and creating an environment to grow. The two companies are enjoying the benefits associated with shared history, research, technical expertise, marketing systems, and a diverse, talented and well-qualified work force. Equilon and Motiva comprise a potent force in the U.S. downstream business. They have almost 15 percent of total U.S. gasoline and automotive lubricant sales, as well as about 12 percent of total U.S. refining capacity. Their combined assets make the ventures number one in U.S. market share for refining capacity, branded gasoline sales and lubricant sales. Equilon has completed almost one full year of operations and the company is exceeding expectations.

The Texaco/Shell Combination

There is a need for a radical change in the way that petroleum and marketing companies operate in the United States. For several years, the industry has faced difficult business conditions requiring increased efficiencies. Equilon is a step toward a much needed change for Texaco and Shell. Equilon is creating substantial efficiencies by integrating overlapping functions and assets of Texaco and Shell. Although Shell is very large, size was not Texaco's prime motivation when choosing alliance partners. Texaco chose to collaborate with Shell because of its strong financial position, market share in the U.S., and brand recognition. The critical factor was in finding companies who possessed complementary strengths. For example, Shell's Rotella brand diesel engine oil has a strong position in the truck market, while Texaco's Havoline Formula brand motor oil is a top seller in the passenger vehicle market. Texaco CEO, Peter Bijur, believes that by uniting the complementary strengths of Texaco and Shell, Equilon and Motiva will possess economic potential far greater than the companies could obtain independently, resulting in a more competitive company with the ability to create greater value for both brands.

Critical Issues

Equilon is creating cost efficiencies for Texaco and Shell by combining the companies' western U.S. marketing activities. However, with this joining there is the possibility for major conflicts to arise because products will continue to be sold under each brand name separately. Therefore, Texaco and Shell will still be competing against one another in the U.S. market. This presents a potential conflict of interest for Equilon marketing employees, many of whom originally worked for and most likely continue to hold strong allegiances with Shell or Texaco. Can Equilon successfully meet marketing objectives for Texaco and Shell if the two companies continue to compete with one another?

Recent trends in oil prices are expected to hurt oil companies' income significantly next year. Two major competitors of Texaco and Shell, Exxon Mobil and BP Amoco, recently announced plans to merge. Ever since Texaco Inc. and Shell Oil Co. combined the assets of their western and midwestern U.S. refining and marketing businesses along with their nationwide trading, transportation, and lubricants businesses to form Equilon Enterprises, there have been rumors of Texaco and Shell discussing a possible merger. However, on December 2, both companies failed to create a joint venture in Europe due to a disagreement on the percentage share. Shell wanted an 88-12 split which would not have given Texaco maximized shareholder value. Some believed that this venture was a precursor to a full merger. At this present time, Texaco CEO Peter Bijur has dismissed any speculation of the two companies merging together, but has not ruled out any deals for the future. In light of the current industry environment, can Texaco and Shell remain competitive in an alliance environment or will a merger be necessary in order to survive?

Bibliography

Most of the information included in this case study was taken from Texaco and Equilon Enterprises internal documents and an interview with John Doering, C & I National Account Sales Manager, Equilon Enterprises.

American Petroleum Institute Homepage. http://www.api.org/news. (Accessed 12/3/98).

Anonymous. "Common Financial Strategies Among Top 10 Oil and Gas Firms." *Oil and Gas Journal.* 96(16): 27-33. 1998 Apr 20.

Anonymous. "FTC Okays Texaco/Shell/Armco Refining Merger." *Oil and Gas Journal.* 95(52): 24. 1997 Dec 29.

Callum, Janice L. "Industrial Uses of Soy Oil. Industrial Agricultural Products Center." http://www.ianr.unl.edu. (Accessed 11/24/98).

Chance, David. "Texaco Chief Coy on Merger Prospects." *Reuters.* http://biz.yahoo.com/rf/981202/bfk.html. (Accessed 12/3/98).

Emond, Mark. "FTC Okays Biggest R&M Merger." *National Petroleum News.* 90(2): 13. 1998 Feb.

McAuley, Tony. "Big Oil Merging to Survive, not Dominate." *Reuters.* 1998 Dec. 1. (Accessed 12/3/98)

"Texaco CEO Says Shell Talks Failed over Split." *Reuters* http://biz.yahoo.com/rf/981202/xp.html. (Accessed 12/3/98).

Texaco Homepage. http://www.texaco.com. (Accessed 12/3/98).

"U.S. Oil Shares Sink as Crude Hits 12 Year Low." *Reuters.* 1998 Nov. 30. http://biz.yahoo.com. (Accessed 12/3/98).

Case 4.6

Ryder Case Study

It is January 15, 1998. Admiral Edward Straw, the President of Ryder Integrated Logistics, is sitting at his desk amid a generous amount of paperwork and research done by the Ryder/Andersen/IBM Alliance Team. The sun is bright outside in Miami, Florida, but Edward knows he will not be able to step outside until it is dark. Admiral Straw will have spent the whole week going over the material in front of him—trying to resolve a dilemma. He has to make a recommendation at Monday morning's Board of Directors meeting which will affect the future of Ryder Integrated Logistics and its alliance partners Andersen Consulting and IBM Global Services.

Over the last year, Edward has been a driving force behind the strategic alliance formation of Ryder Integrated Logistics, Andersen Consulting, and IBM Global Services. He knows what an impact this alliance could have on Ryder's domestic and international market share. However, to continue building international momentum, Ryder and the Alliance must address the industry trend toward integrated software systems. For several months, the Admiral has worked with the Alliance Team to gather information about possible alliance partners in the software industry to add to the current alliance. After intense investigation into the industry and various companies' offerings, the team has narrowed the selection down to two options. By Monday morning, Admiral Edward Straw must make his recommendation to the Board of Directors.

Background of Ryder Integrated Logistics

Ryder is the world's largest provider of integrated logistics and transportation solutions. Ryder's transportation solutions are custom-designed to help businesses improve customer service, reduce inventory, and speed products to market. With annual revenue of more than $5.5 billion and assets in excess of $6 billion, Ryder is one of the 275 largest companies in the United States. Ryder's common stock is one of the twenty stocks that comprise the Dow Jones Transportation Average, and is also a component of the Standard & Poor's Transportation Index. Ryder is an international, market-driven company focused on three core competencies—integrated

Source: Prepared by Angela Butterfield, Eran Har-Evan and Ellie Tiemann under the supervision of Dr. Lou E. Pelton, University of North Texas.

Exhibit 4.6.1

Ryder System, Inc. timeline

- 1933—Company founded by James A. Ryder in Miami, FL.
- 1939—Company involved in two businesses: leasing and over the road hauling.
- 1947—Sales approached $700,000 for the year.
- 1952—Acquired Great Southern Trucking, which was renamed Ryder Truck Lines. Marked Ryder's move into national spotlight.
- 1955—Ryder System Inc. incorporated. Issued 160,000 shares of common stock over the counter at $10 per share.
- 1957—Expanded Truck Leasing and Rental into Canada.
- 1965—Sold Ryder Truck Lines.
- 1968—Launched One Way consumer truck rental.
- 1971—Truck Leasing and rental expanded to the United Kingdom.
- 1978—Revenue surpassed the $1 billion mark.
- 1979—M. Anthony Burns elected President and Chief Operating Officer.
- 1982—Entered aviation business, and acquired Commercial Carriers, and auto transport company.
- 1983—M. Anthony Burns becomes Chief Executive Officer. Acquired Interstate Contract Carrier Corporation, an irregular route common carrier.
- 1988—Began to streamline organization.
- 1990—Trimmed assets and costs to improve performance in recessionary environment.
- 1991—Reorganized Vehicle Leasing & Services Division, separating consumer truck rental from commercial services.
- 1992—Formally established international division.
- 1993—Began operations in Poland.
- 1994—Acquired LogiCorp, a logistics management company. Began operations in Mexico.
- 1995—Began operations in Argentina and Brazil.
- 1996—Sold One Way consumer truck rental.

logistics, truck leasing and rental, and public transportation services.

Ryder Integrated Logistics, a division of Ryder System, Inc., is the company's fastest growing business, and is the largest third party logistics company in the United States. It is the Ryder Integrated Logistics division that is involved in the alliance with Andersen Consulting and IBM Global Services. Ryder Integrated Logistics (RIL) provides its clients with integrated logistics solutions ranging from inbound movement of raw materials to manufacturing facilities, through the delivery of finished good to their final destinations. RIL's management of the client's supply chain targets customer's objectives such as faster order-cycle times, reduced inventory expense, fewer facilities, greater flexibility, and improved customer service. Outside of the United States, Ryder offers logistics and freight management services in Canada, the United Kingdom, Germany, Poland, Mexico, Argentina, Brazil, and the Netherlands.

Decisions within Ryder System, Inc., that pertain to the Ryder Integrated Logistics division follow the organizational chart in Exhibit 4.6.2.

The three men listed in the chart are the strategic decision-makers that impact any decisions made regarding the Alliance, and any projects relating to the Alliance. However, they are only responsible for Ryder's involvement in the partnership. The Alliance Team is formed of professionals from RIL, Andersen Consulting, and IBM Global Services. This team makes daily decisions about the inner-workings of the Alliance. The next section on the internal decision environment will explain the role of the Alliance Team in more detail.

Internal Decision Environment

Admiral Edward Straw should consider different factors that may impact the Alliance. These factors create the overall decision environment of the Alliance and may be divided into internal and external factors. The internal decision environment of the Alliance consists of the Alliance Team. The size of the Alliance Team varies, depending on project it is handling. It includes managers from the three partners and consists of about twenty people in total. However, there are

Exhibit 4.6.2

Ryder Integrated Logistics division decisions

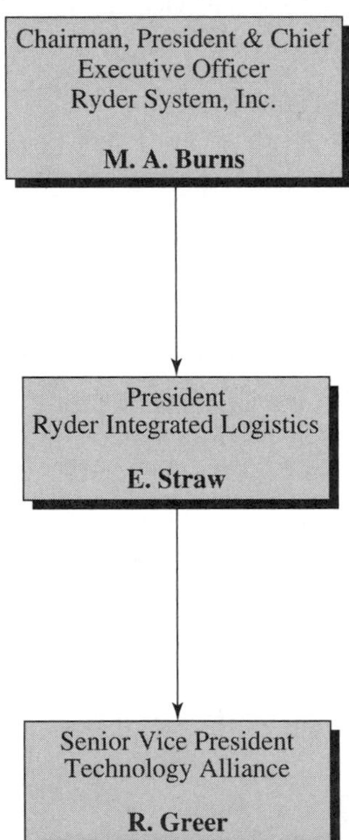

two permanent executives in the alliance team, both from Ryder.

The alliance team is positioned within Ryder directly under Ray Greer, the Senior Vice-President of the Technology Alliance. Thus, the team gets support from and direct access to the top management. Support and access are essential in maintaining long-term relationships. The function of the alliance team is to manage the Alliance. The team approaches employees of the three partners, at any level, and even on sight, in order to create projects that improve activities or that make them more efficient. The team is also responsible for solving any problems that may arise within the Alliance.

Alliance Organizational Impacts

The formation of the Alliance has created an organizational impact within Ryder. In terms of communication with employees, daily questions and answers are posted in databases on Lotus Notes. In addition, meetings with all employees are held every six weeks. In terms of the organizational design, Ryder is trying to retain logistics expertise within the firm, and to serve as a benchmark for other organizations in the logistics industry. Most of Ryder's five hundred and seventy Management Information Systems employees are being reviewed by, and will most likely be placed in equivalent positions within, Andersen Consulting and IBM Global Services. In terms of retaining the organization, there is emphasis on maintaining leadership, and on strongly complying with the Information Technology contract.

External Decision Environment

The external decision environment of the Alliance is facing progressive changes with respect to the importance of logistics, customer demand, and the nature of solutions. The next discussion addresses more specifically the general industry trends.

From the business industry's viewpoint, efficient logistics is becoming a competitive advantage. American companies spend more than five hundred billion dollars a year owning and holding inventory. This figure is about ten to twenty percent of their total costs and is evidence of how substantial logistics costs are. In addition, logistics is now a boardroom function, not a loading dock function. Logistics is being incorporated as a key strategic area in many firms' strategic plans. Also, product delivery and availability are becoming as important as product quality. In short, logistics is gaining more importance in the business management process.

From the customers' perspective, there is demand for more aggressive service commitments at minimum costs. Ryder is addressing this situation by integrating logistics and information technology for the customer through its alliance, thus quickly delivering high capacity, high technology solutions for developing businesses.

From a general business perspective, consolidations and alliances are becoming common in business, including the logistics industry. Today, firms that want to perform according to the highest standards must focus on their own expertise. By bringing in partners and forming an alliance, each partner can focus on its own expertise, while integrating core competencies. For example, Ryder focuses on logistics in this alliance—its core expertise.

By bringing in partners, the next trend evolves. Companies are moving from a transactional approach to a holistic approach, which means that companies are looking at the sum of the whole, rather than at the sum of individual parts. Better coordination and a long-term perspective may translate into higher efficiency, and better customer service.

The previously mentioned trend can specifically be traced in logistics. Integrated logistics solutions are expanding across the entire supply chain. To align processes, eliminate duplication and waste and to increase efficiency, companies are creating a seamless flow of information across the entire supply chain.

The next trend lies in the nature of those solutions. Solutions are more commonly based on information technology. Information technology is becoming a competitive advantage in its own right. Savings from information technology may exceed the costs incurred by it, especially in logistics.

From implementation of information technology solutions, the next trend evolves. There is a growing need for integrated software systems in supply chain management. Such software specifically addresses the integration of different specialized activities into one streamlined process.

The Alliance Mission Statement

> Ryder is committed to maintain and improve its position as the market leader in logistics and transportation solutions.
>
> To strengthen this position, the Alliance partners are evaluating options for partnerships that will expand and enhance the Alliance's information technology capabilities.

Possible New Alliance Partners

After considering many possible companies, Edward has narrowed his choices to two allied groups of companies. One of these groups will enable the Ryder, Andersen and IBM alliance to improve their ability to provide fully integrated logistics solutions. InterTrans Logistics, i2 Technologies, Roadshow International and BDM International is one of the groups of companies that he is considering.

InterTrans Logistics is a market-leading provider of enterprise-wide, fully integrated, supply chain management software. Their products furnish the information and decision support capabilities necessary to increase the management efficiency of many supply chain processes. The design of the software applications that they offer helps manage the daily operations and the planning aspects of transportation and logistics activities across the supply chain. InterTrans is a member of the IBM Solution Developer Program. As a member of this program, InterTrans combines its client/server applications with IBM's.

Another company in this group of allied companies is i2 Technologies. It is a leading provider of planning and scheduling software for global supply chain management. Its family of products provides comprehensive, intelligent support for planning and scheduling functions across the supply chain. InterTrans and i2 are alliance partners. They have integrated their technologies in order to provide users with enhanced supply chain planning solutions.

Roadshow International is the world's leader in map-based route management software for vehicle fleets. They develop, market and support wireless applications that allow real-time control of pickup, delivery and field service operations. Their products use technology that allows speedy manipulation of full-color commercial maps and routes on a dispatcher's computer screen. The solutions calculate routes based on actual costs, providing efficient operations support and valuable strategic planning capabilities. Roadshow and InterTrans Logistics are cross-marketing their product lines through a partnership. Roadshow is also part of an alliance of companies called the Microsoft Value Chain (MVC). The member companies of the MVC are committed to developing integrated Windows NT operating system-based solutions.

BDM International, Inc., is a multinational information technology company that furnishes systems, solutions and services to both public sector and commercial customers. The Integrated Supply Chain Solutions business at BDM helps customers solve problems in the areas of Enterprise Resource Planning, Manufacturing Execution Systems and Warehouse Management Systems. BDM has allied with InterTrans to cross-market their product lines.

These companies are globally established and are innovators of leading edge technology. Products and services that help clients efficiently manage various supply chain processes are the focus of these companies. Full integration with strategic partners compliments these companies with leading client/server solutions.

Another Option

The alternative to the group of companies mentioned above is an allied group of companies comprised of Manugistics, Incorporated, Cass Logistics Software and EXE Technologies. These companies offer a slightly different selection of technologies.

Manugistics, Inc., is the leading provider and a pioneer of software and services for integrated supply chain management. Manugistics software and services integrate planning activities for product demand, distribution, manufacturing and transportation across the entire supply chain. Manugistics is currently partnered with IBM and Andersen Consulting.

Cass Logistics Software supplies services and systems such as rate management and shipping planning. They offer software applications that automate business processes that require rate information from anywhere in the world. Cass is an official business partner of IBM and Manugistics.

EXE Technologies is the world's largest Warehouse Management Systems software company. They provide comprehensive products and services to meet the needs of companies around the world that are involved in managing the supply chain. EXE has allied with Manugistics to couple their technology and functionality.

These companies are globally established and are market leaders in their areas of expertise. The design of their software applications meets the needs of companies around the world that are involved in logistics and transportation services.

The Dilemma

The characteristics of these two groups of companies have presented Edward with a very difficult decision. Both groups of companies are market leaders. Both groups are technological innovators. To aid him in making his decision, Edward has made a list of criteria that he will use to help him select a new alliance partner. These criteria are:

- The company must act as a system integrator.
- The company must have global resources.
- The company must possess skill in multiple technologies.
- The company must be able to grow with a business that is growing by 40% annually.

He will also be considering environmental factors such as time, money and corporate culture. He hopes that by using these criteria, he can make the right choice between two extremely suitable groups. The Admiral knows that the key to making the current alliance successful is dynamic, efficient and timely information. By choosing a software partner who is able to add to these variables, Edward will enhance the current alliance's ability to provide more comprehensive supply chain logistics solutions to their clients. He also knows that by taking on an information technology partner, the Alliance will propel itself ahead of the competition and strengthen its foothold as a market leader.

Edward knew the critical importance of his decision. He was expected to make a recommendation to the Board on Monday, so he began his deliberation. As he sat at his desk, he wondered to himself, "Should I be concerned with Roadshow's membership in the Microsoft Value Chain?" He also wondered what additional selection criteria he should use to help him with his decision. As he looked at the research in front of him, he hoped that he would make the right choice.

Bibliography

All information included in this case study was taken from internal documents provided by the Alliance Team and Ryder Integrated Logistics, except:

Alliances of InterTrans Logistics Solutions; "Roadshow International Inc." http://www.itls.com/busall.htm#i2 (Accessed 11/16/97)

BDM Homepage; "ISC Solutions" http://www.bdm.com/bdm/iscs/default.html (Accessed 11/16/97)

Cass Logistics; "API/data Mart Capabilities" http://www.casssoftware.com/cprel.htm (Accessed 11/16/97)

EXE Technologies Homepage; http://www.exe.com/ (Accessed 11/11/97)

i2innovations; "i2 technologies" http://www.i2.com/html/i2innovations.html (Accessed 11/16/97)

InterTrans Logistics Homepage; "i2 Technologies Reaches Agreement With InterTrans Logistics" http://www.itls.com (Accessed 11/16/97)

Manugistics–Who We Are; "About Manugistics" http://www.manu.com/html/manugistics.html (Accessed 11/11/97)